Dedicated to
the Deaf of the Past
and the
Deaf Children of the Present
and the Future

AN ILLUSTRATED HISTORY OF

THE CALIFORNIA SCHOOL FOR THE DEAF

SAN FRANCISCO • BERKELEY • FREMONT

THE EAGLE SOARS TO ENLIGHTENMENT

This book is produced into reality
by the proceeds from the
Donald N. Parodi Memorial Charitable Trust.

KENNETH W. NORTON

INTRODUCTION BY HENRY KLOPPING

CALIFORNIA SCHOOL FOR THE DEAF
FREMONT

The Eagle Soars to Enlightenment

Author: Kenneth Norton
Project Editor: Dr. Henry Klopping
Book Designer: Robert Pawlak

Published by
The Donald Parodi Memorial Charitable Trust
P.O. Box 1641
Fremont, CA 94538

The text font for this book is Bembo with Bellevue display.

California School for the Deaf.

The Illustrated History of the California School for the Deaf-San Francisco-Berkeley-Fremont / California School for the Deaf.

Library of Congress cataloging-in-publication data:
Library of Congress card number: 00-110197
ISBN 0-9705856-0-8

Includes biographicial references and index.

1. California School for the Deaf-History.
2. Schools-California-San Francisco-Berkeley-Fremont-History-19th Century.

Manufactured by *Global Interprint, Inc.*
Printed in Hong Kong.

Photo credit:
Front endsheet and Chapter 10 opener: *Mike Peterson*

Cover: At the front of the entrance of the California School for the Deaf, Dan Peknik (left), Jenny Contreras, and Benjamin Jarashow, walking by the statue of The Bear Hunt. *Front endsheets: Highreaching viewpoint of* The Bear Hunt, *one of Douglas Tilden's magnificent sculptures. Berkeley school in 1874 (right), taken from Garber Street near College Avenue .*

CALIFORNIA
SCHOOL
for the DEAF
Established 1860

Contents

We Came, We Saw
We Conquered!

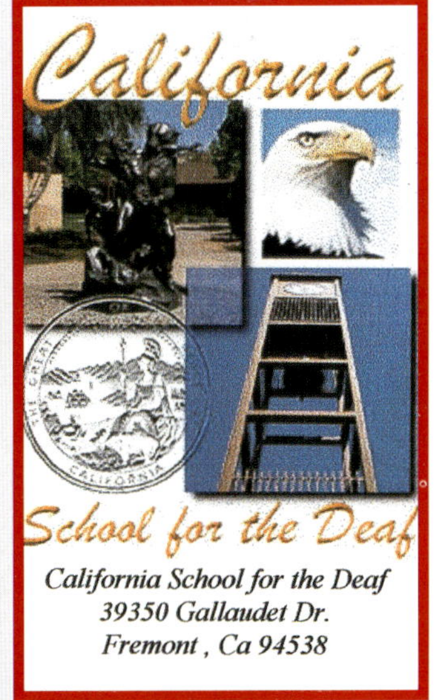

California
School for the Deaf
California School for the Deaf
39350 Gallaudet Dr.
Fremont , Ca 94538

Introduction

The Eagle Soars to Enlightenment

A school for the deaf plays a much greater role in the lives of the children it serves, and when they become alumni the school remains a significant part of their adult life. It is not uncommon for alumni to frequently visit the school after they graduate and for many a great part of their social life is in some way connected to the school. Homecoming brings out hundreds of graduates, some who are in their eighties and nineties. When I think of my own school back in Flagstaff, Arizona, which I thoroughly enjoyed attending, I know that it could never have the significance to me that the California School for the Deaf has for its alumni. In fact, I have not been back to my high school since a year or two after graduating and have never attended an alumni reunion.

It is the importance of the California School for the Deaf to the community it serves that makes *The Eagle Soars to Enlightenment* such an important historical document, and I am pleased that our beloved alumnus Kenneth W. Norton was willing to take on the difficult task of writing the history of CSD. A better person to write the history of the school could not be found. Ken is a walking encyclopedia of the history of the school, and it is especially fitting that Ken experienced the school as a youth, graduating from CSD and eventually returning to fill out his professional life. Since his retirement, he has continued to be closely associated with the school. The well being of the students enrolled has been his main concern in life outside his family. He did not hesitate when asked to take on the challenge of writing *The Eagle Soars to Enlightenment* and he has spent more than four years meticulously culling thousands of documents and pictures for the information that is found in his book. Ken knows that it is important that future generations of deaf people and others interested in the history of CSD have the opportunity to read about events, activities, personalities, and a myriad of things connected to the school.

Ken Norton has written a wonderful book that will forever document the history of CSD. It is a book that will bring enjoyment to every person who picks it up and peruses the content and pictures that he has so eloquently put together. Our thanks to this dedicated alumnus who has made sure that no stone was left unturned in putting together this monument.

Henry Klopping,
Superintendent

Prologue

California School for the Deaf

A Fanfare of a Rich and Remarkable History

This book is a mission to celebrate *The California School for the Deaf's* history and bring this literary piece to the public as well as Deaf people, who have distinguished themselves in this history. It is the writer's hope in compiling the data, anecdotes, and photographs in the History of CSD that a balance be achieved by including the different eras, the various age groups of the students, the chronology of the staff by years, and the departments and their accomplishments and activities.

Although this book mainly focuses on the years from 1960 to 2000, it includes part of *A History of the California School for the Deaf - 1860 to 1960*, written by Caroline Burnes and Catherine Ramger. After 100 years, the new era became energized during the years of 1960 to 2000. Simple life pre-1960 was vanishing rapidly.

In late 1996, Dr. Henry Klopping, Superintendent of the California School for the Deaf-Fremont, conjectured that a history book was needed to document the history of CSD from 1960 to 2000. In addition, he suggested that it would be opportune to have the history book published in the dawn of the 21st Century. Consequentially, he asked this writer to do the job. With love for the alma mater in his blood, he accepted. As time passes by, although retired, he finds writing this book to be as time-consuming as any full-time job.

Nobody, much less the writer, can possibly read every printed source and monograph on CSD history from 1860 to 2000. The writer was educated at CSD-Berkeley and returned there as a teacher and a coach from 1961 to 1975, and then dean of students until 1990. Hence, he is comfortably-thick with the history but still depends for information on particular subjects in *The California News* and many other publications, and on the information and advice of experts, of colleagues, former students, and many friends. It has been gratifying to find people so generous with their special knowledge. The writer has sought out, talked with and profited by conversations with many friends.

This *History* is primarily written for readers to enjoy, and to gain insight into the school's achievements with footnote references, bibliographies, and other "scholarly apparatus" suppressed. Also, this book intends to tell the stories to render the character and soul of some CSD people and productive workers that reflect the past 40 years.

For the record, the term of Gallaudet College mentioned in this book is pre-1986. Gallaudet changed status from college to university in October, 1986.

- Kenneth Walters Norton

This book of
The Illustrated History of the California School for the Deaf-San Francisco, Berkeley, Fremont
is published by the proceeds from the
Donald N. Parodi Memorial Charitable Trust.

Donald N. Parodi
Memorial Charitable Trust

The Donald N. Parodi Memorial Charitable Trust was established in 1991 by Donald N. Parodi, 1960 CSD graduate. The purposes of the Charitable Trust are: ***to enrich and enhance the programs of CSD, especially its services to deaf children; to improve and expand the facilities and equipment of the school; to expand and improve the services of the school to the community of deaf persons in California; to encourage more wide-spread charitable contributions from the general public for the use and benefit of the school.***

The principal of the Charitable Trust is to be invested and reinvested in perpetuity.

Only interest earned from the principal is distributed to support school activities and functions within the Trustees' absolute discretion. According to the Will, only two causes have been supported financially by the principal of the Trust: part of the expenses of the construction of the Bell Tower, and the improvement of the physical facilities of the CSD historical museum.

Five members compose the Trustees of the Charitable Trust.

One Trustee is the Superintendent of the California School for the Deaf, Fremont, serving ex officio, with full powers and responsibilities of any other Trustee. *(Superintendent Henry Klopping)*

Second Trustee is appointed by the Alumni Association of CSD. *(Kenneth W. Norton)*

Third Trustee is appointed by the Association of Parents, Teachers and Counselors of CSD. *(Celia May Baldwin)*

Fourth Trustee is appointed by the California Association of the Deaf. *(Julian Singleton)*

Fifth Trustee is a designatee of the Settlor. *(Gerald N. Lindberg)*

Each Trustee serves a term of five years with their appointments staggered.

Since the founding of the Charitable Trust, the proceeds have served a wide range of needs of CSD children and staff such as children's participation in camps, conferences, and workshops; computers for children's use, short term school projects, educational equipment, special annual awards to seniors, and in many other areas to meet students' needs.

DONALD N. PARODI
1939 - 1989

DONALD PARODI was especially proud to be a member of the 1960 graduating class as it was an historic period in time, the 100th anniversary of the founding of the *California School for the Deaf* in 1860. He, perhaps more than any other member of the class, appreciated the significance of the school's long existence and the impact it had on the lives of deaf children.

Parodi came to the Berkeley School in 1946 at the age of seven from a broken family, with no speech and no education. At CSD he embraced teachers who provided skills for communication and learning, counselors who accepted and guided him in a residential setting, and classmates with similar problems and attributes. The school was a dream come true and like home for Parodi.

Miss Robinson, supervising teacher of the intermediate department, saw a troubled and lonesome boy. She gave him his first job, straightening books on shelves and cleaning the library. His eyes widened as Miss Robinson handed him his first wages of ten cents for a job well done. She continued to teach him how to manage and save his earnings. Parodi gained a reputation as a good worker.

Soon Principal and Mrs. Myron Leenhouts, who lived in the elegant Victorian house on the campus, hired him as a house cleaner. Each day of work made him more aware of the beauty of rare wood, glass, and china. He began a lifelong hobby of collecting china in the blue Lorne pattern; dishes identical to those collected and used by Dr. Warring Wilkinson, head of the school from 1864 to 1909.

By graduation time in 1960, the foundation for Parodi's vocation had been well established. Sign language was his prime mode of expression. His only published written work in *The California News* appeared in the last issue of his last year in school, the very last article on the last page.

He wrote: *"Since I came to CSD in 1946, I have watched our school change from the old-fashioned, red brick buildings to the new, modern structures which are in Spanish style architecture. Dr. Stevenson had planned for many years to improve this campus. All the old buildings are gone except the principal's house.*

I want to express my appreciation to Dr. Stevenson, Mr. Birck, former dean, the teachers and the counselors for the advice and help given to me through these years that I have been at CSD."

After graduation Parodi became the house cleaner for the famous Sally Sanford, noted for her Victorian homes in San Francisco and Sausalito. In the 1960s San Francisco had a building boom and interest in Victorian houses diminished. Many houses were demolished and the rest took a drop in value.

Over the next few years Parodi bought three Victorian flats containing ten apartments. As landlord he did most of the repairs and remodeling himself. Some years later he bought a ranch near Stockton, California.

In the 1970s Parodi returned to the Berkeley campus and found Ralph Neesam and Mildred Albronda exploring a basement room in the high school building. It contained CSD treasures of the past hundred years. The three of them created a school historical committee with the goal of establishing a museum. The goal was setback when it was announced that the school was moving! Of necessity the focus shifted to locating and saving as many objects as possible. A schoolwide committee was formed to identify and earmark historic items for a museum planned for the new school. Parodi volunteered a great deal of his time to this project.

In 1980 the school moved to Fremont and Parodi frequented the new museum for the next nine years stocking it with objects he had collected and repaired broken items. He often said the museum was his real home. As a result of this strong attachment, he established the *Donald N. Parodi Memorial Charitable Trust* just before he died of a serious illness at the age of 49.

Chronology

Important dates and events in the History of the California School for the Deaf 1860 - 2000

1860
On May 1, a rented home on Tehama Street in San Francisco becomes the first school with Theophilus DeRutte, the first of three deaf students, and a graduate of the New York School for the Deaf, Henry B. Crandall, himself deaf, as the first teacher.

1869
School opens in a beautiful new stone building of Gothic style architecture, costing over $150,000, at a site in the foothills of the new town of Berkeley, with "a view of surpassing loveliness over varied and extensive landscape and San Francisco Bay."

1875
During a windstorm on January 17 the new school, only six years old, is destroyed by fire. A group of nearly forty men donate a thousand dollars each toward a temporary wooden structure and school is able to reopen on April 17 for the seventy-five students.

1885
Principal Warring Wilkinson publishes *The Daily News*, the school's first newspaper. (It has continued under various names, now known as *The California News*.)

1890
The Educational Building is expanded with the addition of a second floor, a 160-foot tower and an assembly hall. The Strauss clock is purchased for $1,375 from the Strauss donation of $5,000. The Assembly Hall, newly built, stocked with 616 folding opera style seats and stained glass windows.

1892
Douglas Tilden displays his sculpture, "The Bear Hunt", in Paris (now erected at the Fremont school).

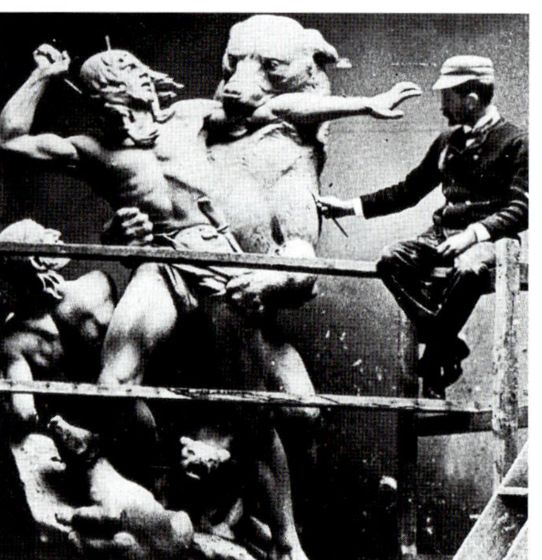

1894
Granville S. Redmond's (CSD 1890) first painting, "Winter on the Seine," is admitted to the Paris Salon (Now installed in the CSD museum). In 1918, Charlie Chaplin, world famous comedian, sets up a painting studio for Redmond in his movie complex. Redmond teaches Chaplin sign language.

1900
Principal Caldwell has driven an automobile ever since 1891. It was reported that he may be the first teacher of the deaf in this country who learned how to drive a car. Also, it is said he is the first one who taught the deaf how to do it.

1906
At 5:13 A.M. on April 18, students are awakened by a strong earthquake that causes damage to chimneys, towers, peaks and slate roofs, but with two days of out-of-doors classes, school goes on as usual.

1929
For the first time pupils are able to "hear" a presidential inaugural word. Herbert Hoover's induction into the office of President was interpreted from the radio by enterprising interpreter Elwood Stevenson and Sally Blaker. The radio is loaned to the school by Sherman Clay and Company at Telegraph Avenue and Channing Way, Berkeley.

1932
The first phase of the building program is completed with the completion of the primary girl's dormitory, a primary boy's dormitory, a kitchen-dining room, a primary school building, an auditorium, and a dedication ceremony with the laying of a cornerstone at the entrance of the auditorium on February 29, 1932. Governor James Rolph attends, speaks and uses sign language to say, "I love you all."

1942
CSD is prepared for blackouts which occur quite often during World War II. The student's study hall windows are blacked out with paint, and wire netting is tacked over them, so the students can continue with study hour work during blackouts. The students of the cabinet shop are busy building warplane models of the Allies, the United States, England and Russia, and the Axis (enemy) Germany and Japan in response to the U.S. government,s need of 500,000 models. They are needed for military practice to identify the types of warplanes.

1951
CSD is honored by a visit from Dr. Richard Brill in February. Dr. Brill is the newly appointed superintendent of the new CSD-Riverside. He returned to Berkeley as an old friend of many on the old school staff, having been a teacher at CSD shortly before the war.

1966
Sheldon McArtor, vocational instructor, is honored by the State Department of Education upon his retirement for serving deaf students for thirty years without missing a day.

1980
The Berkeley school's final Open House and "Opening of the Cornerstone" Ceremony are held on Monday, May 26. At the ceremony, the cornerstone, which was laid at the entrance of the auditorium on February 29, 1932, is opened. The items from the cornerstone are viewed by the audience. To name a few, the articles are the eyeglasses of Theophilus d,Estrella, a pamphlet of the building program, the model of a hand of Douglas Tilden, the document of early history of the school, and the letters from previous superintendents.

1984
The kickoff for the Deaf Awareness Month on May 1 is held on the steps of the Capitol in Sacramento. Students sign "American the Beautiful," speeches are made, 1,000 balloons are released, and the legislators attend a reception after the ceremonies.

1993
On December 3, the Bell Tower is erected, adding a new landmark to the school campus.

1994
On May 3 Scott O,Donnell, a 1987 graduate of CSD, runs out of Palm Drive at Stanford University, carrying the Olympic flame which was lit in Greece months before. Scott, among 5,000 community heroes is selected among Torchbearers for the 1996 Olympic Torch Relay.

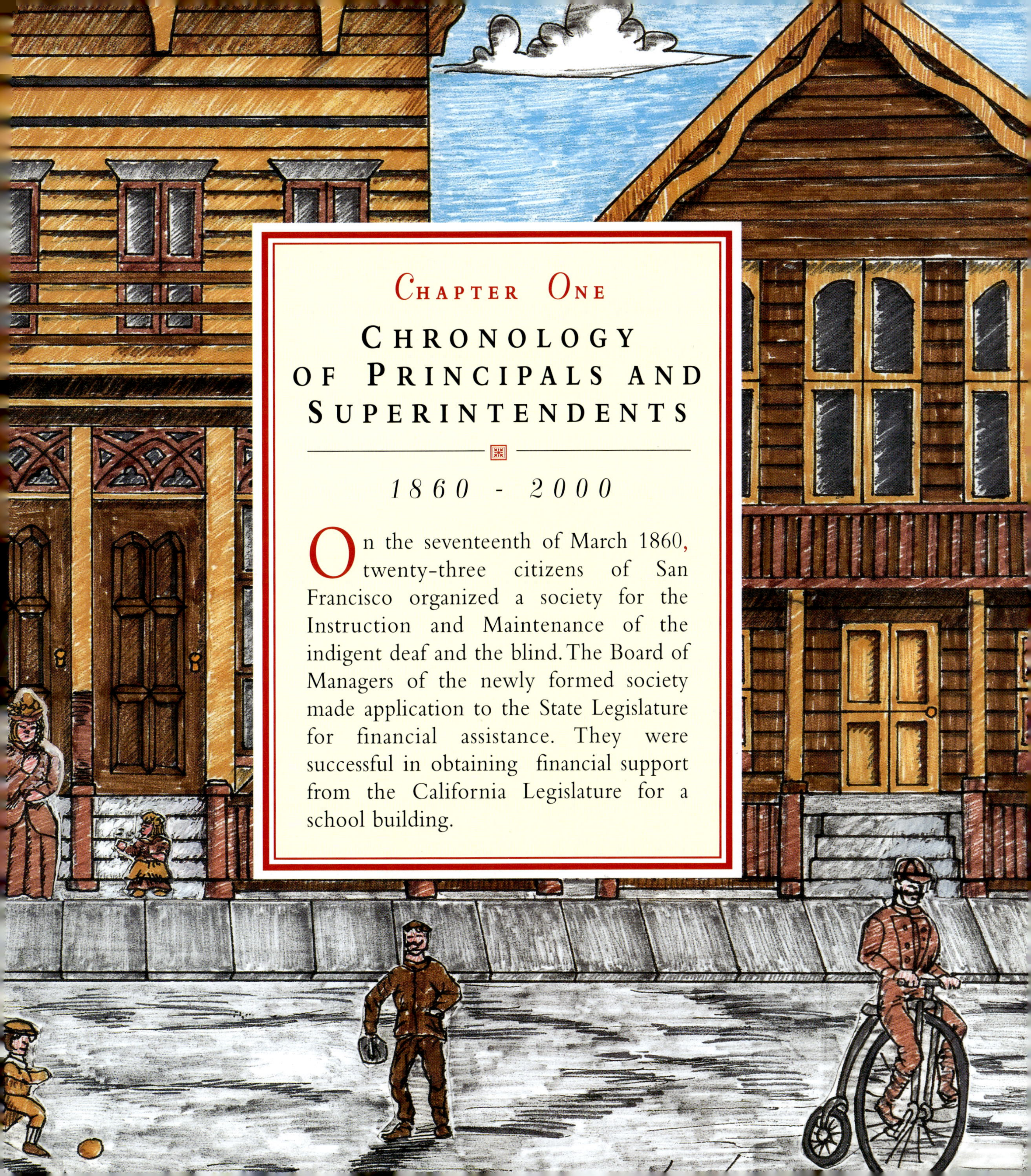

Chapter One

Chronology of Principals and Superintendents

1860 - 2000

On the seventeenth of March 1860, twenty-three citizens of San Francisco organized a society for the Instruction and Maintenance of the indigent deaf and the blind. The Board of Managers of the newly formed society made application to the State Legislature for financial assistance. They were successful in obtaining financial support from the California Legislature for a school building.

This rented building, second from the left, housed the first class for deaf children in the State of California.

Rather than waiting a year until a building could be completed, the Board rented a house at No.15 Tehama Street in San Francisco. They hired a first teacher, H. B. Crandall, himself deaf, from the New York Institution (Fanwood). The first school (rented) began May 1,1860 with three local deaf pupils. In 1861, the school moved to the newly completed building at Mission and Sparks (16th) Streets in San Francisco.

1861-1865 Mrs. Pomeroy (Fannie) B. Clark

Pomeroy B. Clark, who was one of the twenty-three ladies and president of the Board of Managers, was elected principal February 7, 1861. She announced her resignation October 10, 1864 due to ill health but continued as principal until February 1865.

Pomeroy B. Clark — First Principal of the California School for the Deaf.

Preceding Spread: The middle building where the school first started on Tehama Street in San Francisco in May, 1860. This sketch was drawn by Long Lo, CSD '91.

IN 1857, Mrs. Giles H. De Voe, a younger sister of Mrs. Pomeroy B. Clark, was said to have initiated the movement to found a school for deaf children in San Francisco. Since De Voe had founded a school for the deaf children in New York City, according to the Rev. Thomas Gallaudet, before she moved to San Francisco, naturally she became interested in starting a similar school in San Francisco.

In 1858, when Mrs. De Voe left California, Mrs. Clark took over the project of establishing a school for the deaf. Presumably, both De Voe and Clark became interested in the deaf because one of their sisters, Libbie, was deaf. Probably, it is proper to say that the credit for founding the first school for the deaf in California goes to both sisters, Clark and De Voe.

1865 John M. Francis

John M. Francis from the Ohio Institution took charge of the Institution on February 6, 1865. Not being a very robust man, the work soon proved too severe for his health as he had to teach all the time as well as to supervise the entire school. He resigned on account of poor health in the summer of 1865 but he consented to remain until a new principal was appointed in November. The principal was being paid $2,500 a year.

John M. Francis — Second Principal, for only nine months.

Dr. Warring Wilkinson — Third Principal, for forty-four illustrious years!

1865-1909 Dr. Warring Wilkinson

At the age of 30 years, Warring Wilkinson from the New York Institute (Fanwood) became principal in the latter part of November, 1865. The young principal at once took steps to have the school made a state institution. Eventually, in February 1867, the Board of Directors selected 130 acres of land across the Bay in Berkeley for the site of a large building to house and educate not only deaf children in California but also those from Oregon and Nevada. Once the site was selected, it was decided to use stone that could be quarried nearby. Ground was broken July 29, 1887, and the cornerstone was laid September 26, 1867. The ceremony included an original ode written for the occasion by Bret Harte, who was a friend of Wilkinson. It was estimated that the school would cost $150,000, which Wilkinson said would be the cheapest building in the State, though yet the best built. The school moved from San Francisco to Berkeley in 1869.

One thousand eucalyptus trees from Australia were planted on the slopes back of the new school building. Now grown tall, these trees seem native to the spot.

Despite several setbacks like a big fire that destroyed the building in 1875, epidemics that killed several students, and the big 1906 earthquake that lightly damaged some of the buildings, Wilkinson continued keeping the school in excellent condition. Authorities in various fields of education, individuals like a principal of a public school and a professor of English Literature and History at the University of California, were invited to come to examine the pupils in order to testify as to the competency of the instruction. Their reports were highly complimentary.

After a 44-year tenure, Dr. Wilkinson retired in 1909.

> ***"The period just preceding his resignation is signalized by the largest actual attendance of pupils and the largest list of new admissions ever recorded. Besides it is conceded that in last July's Convention of the California Association of the Deaf (tenth Convention), Dr. Wilkinson surpassed himself in the exhibition of his mastery of the sign language while addressing the Association."***
>
> Theophilus d'Estrella

1909-1911 Douglas Keith

Douglas Keith, secretary to Dr. Wilkinson, was elected principal by the Board October 1, 1909. He was a clerk in the Institution for twenty years, and was unanimously appointed. *The California News* states that in May of 1911 some former students of the school sent a petition to Governor Johnson that listed some charges against Keith. One of the charges was that Keith's

The faculty of the school in 1887. (Left to right) Charles S. Perry, Martha S. Day (teacher of the Blind), Theophilus d'Estrella, Charles T. Wilkinson (teacher of the Blind), Henry Frank, E.R. Carroll, N.F. Whipple, George B. Goodall, Dr. Warring Wilkinson, and Douglas Tilden.

Douglas Keith — Fourth Principal, for only two years.

Laurance Edwards Milligan — Fifth Principal, for eight years.

appointment as Principal was illegal, since he had not the experience in teaching the deaf and the blind which the law required.

After an investigation conducted by Governor Johnson, Keith resigned in December 1911.

William A. Caldwell was chosen to act as principal for a seven-month period before a new principal was appointed in 1912.

1912-1920 LAURANCE EDWARDS MILLIGAN

Laurance Milligan, with experience as teacher at the Georgia school and as principal at the Montana school, became principal in 1912. He saw action in the Spanish American War, 1898-1899, with Company I, 5th Illinois Volunteer Infantry. His father was superintendent of the Wisconsin Institution. It was natural that Milligan followed his father's steps so after his service in the war, he became a Normal Fellow (graduate school for hearing students) at Gallaudet College. He received his M.A. degree in 1900. Milligan sought separation of the Deaf and the Blind Departments into two distinct schools.

There were two hundred fifteen deaf pupils enrolled June 30, 1914. At this time the California Association of the Deaf began a custom of presenting medals—a gold medal to the best student in the Advanced Department, a silver medal to the best pupil in the Intermediate Department and a bronze medal to the best Primary pupil.

At the age of forty-four Milligan died of tuberculosis on March 28, 1920. His untimely death was a serious loss to CSD.

1920-1927 William Andrew Caldwell

William A. Caldwell, well-known teacher at the Indiana school and administrator of the Florida school, led the California school two different times. First, he was acting principal for a short time after Keith left. Secondly, after Milligan died, Caldwell became principal. F. H. O'Donnell was appointed Vice Principal.

Caldwell started to teach at a school in Indiana and this experience was very unpleasant because the pupils were antagonistic and difficult to control, causing Caldwell to feel that he was incompetent, not considering himself a disciplinarian. He determined never to attempt to teach again. Later working in a railroad company, Caldwell was lured by a friend to teach at the Indiana School for the Deaf for a year. This was a momentous step and "a year" turned out to be fifty years of devoted labor for the Deaf.

In 1927, Caldwell retired from CSD and passed away in Berkeley, March 22, 1933.

William Andrew Caldwell — Sixth Principal, for seven years.

1927-1928 George W. Berry

George W. Berry, teacher at the California School for the Deaf and earlier at the Missouri school, was appointed acting principal from September 1927 to June 1928.

George W. Berry — Acting Principal, for a year.

1928-1960 Dr. Elwood A. Stevenson

Elwood A. Stevenson, from Brooklyn, New York, had been a teacher at the Fanwood school, superintendent at the Kansas school, administrator at the Kentucky school, and superintendent at the Minnesota school. After a year of persuasion, he finally accepted the superintendency of the California school and began July 1, 1928. During his administration, the ancient Romanesque buildings were razed and new California Spanish-style buildings were erected.

During Stevenson's last two years in high school, he was honored for his outstanding performance on the baseball team, mostly as second baseman, by being chosen on the Greater New York City All-Star High School baseball team. Stevenson made a momentous decision, not to choose a baseball player career, nor one as a civil engineer, but to become a teacher of the deaf, a career that was illustrious for fifty years

Three thousand one hundred fifty-three children had attended CSD by the year of 1960; of this total, more than half were under the jurisdiction of Stevenson. He left a long record of accomplishment in the education of the deaf. His career had brought him many honors. He received the degree of Doctor of Letters from Gallaudet College in 1943. He was a member of Rotary, a thirty-two degree Mason, and he had held numerous civic offices. He served as president and again as Secretary of the Convention of American Instructors of the Deaf.

After 32 years of devoted service at CSD, Stevenson retired in 1960.

Dr. Elwood A. Stevenson — Seventh Superintendent, for thirty-two years as distingushed administrator.

Dr. Hugo F. Schunhoff — Eighth Superintendent, for fifteen years.

1960-1975 Dr. Hugo F. Schunhoff

Dr. Hugo F. Schunhoff, from Illinois, had taught at schools for the deaf in Minnesota, Illinois, Texas, Missouri and Kendall in Washington, D. C. He was superintendent of the West Virginia school for seven years. In 1960, he became superintendent of the California School for the Deaf–Berkeley. It was during his term that the state of California made a decision to abandon the Berkeley school for a site in Fremont. Another state decision, mandating retirement at age 67, forced him to retire in 1975. (A further account of Dr. Schunhoff is featured in this chapter.)

1975-present Dr. Henry Klopping

Dr. Henry Klopping, from Arizona, was Associate Dean of Students and Adjunct Professor of Administration at Gallaudet University in Washington, D. C. He had been a counselor and teacher at the Arizona school as well as a teacher trainer at Arizona and California State University–Northridge. He was appointed superintendent of the California School for the Deaf–Berkeley in 1975. In the summer of 1980, the school was moved from Berkeley to Fremont, where the state had built a California Rustic-style school. It was designed to be a one floor earthquake-proof school building and included eighteen residential cottages. On June 1, 2000, Dr. Klopping begins his 26th year as superintendent of the school that started 140 years ago. (A lengthy account of Dr. Klopping is in this chapter.)

Dr. Henry Klopping — Ninth Superintendent. In charge of the move of the school.

As Time Goes, the Titles Change

Prior to the 1930-31 school year, (since the school was founded in 1860) the principal (now superintendent) had been head of the school responsible for all education departments, classifying the students and supervising the teachers. The new position of supervising teacher was implemented in 1930. Miss Mary W. Robinson, who had a strong background in the education of the deaf through her experience at the New York School for the Deaf on Lexington Avenue, New York City, took the position of supervising teacher to coordinate the education programs of all classes. This eased the burden from the office of Dr. Elwood Stevenson, principal.

In 1934, the title of Stevenson's position was changed to superintendent. As the enrollment steadily grew in the fall of 1935, two new supervising teachers were appended to the educational staff: Edna L. Wolf for the Primary Department, and Marshall S. Hester for the Advanced Department. Robinson focused only on the Intermediate Department until she retired in 1958. In 1971, the titles of the supervising teachers of all the departments were changed to the working title of Principals.

In the book, *A History of the California School for the Deaf* from 1860 to 1960, Caroline Burnes and Catherine Ramger gave detailed accounts of the Principals/Superintendents from 1860 to 1960. Since 1960 two Superintendents have served the California School for the Deaf — Dr. Hugo Schunhoff and Dr. Henry Klopping.

The accounts of their superintendency follow.

June 1, 1977, was one of the most memorable days in CSD history. A number of state officials, the school staff, the entire student body, Fremont city officials, interested citizens, and the deaf community witnessed the groundbreaking ceremonies in Fremont. (Previous page, lower right.)

The 1960's graphic look at the entrance of the Berkeley School. (Note the letters-CSD-on the hill at the upper right.)

Dr. Hugo Schunhoff
Superintendent
1960 - 1975

Dr. Hugo F. Schunhoff — Came to Berkeley with broad experience in the field of education of the Deaf.

The California School for the Deaf at Berkeley opened its new year on September 8, 1960, with a new superintendent, Dr. Hugo F. Schunhoff. He was born in Fort Gage, Illinois, December 21, 1907, grew up on a farm, attended rural schools and graduated from Sparta High School in 1925.

Dr. Schunhoff came to Berkeley with broad experience in the field of education of the deaf. He was a graduate of Illinois College in Jacksonville, and he subsequently received his Master of Education degree from the University of Missouri and Doctorate of Education degree from the University of Maryland. He took his training to teach the deaf in the Graduate Education Department at Gallaudet College, receiving a Master of Arts degree in Education of the Deaf in 1933.

Upon completing his training course, Dr. Schunhoff took a position as a teacher in the Minnesota School for the Deaf and later in the Illinois School, leaving to become principal at the Texas School for the Deaf. While in Texas he was a member of the faculty of the University of Texas, working on the program of training teachers of the deaf. Following this, he became principal of the Missouri School for the Deaf, and before going to West Virginia, was director of the Teacher Education Department, both graduate and undergraduate, and Principal of the Kendall School at Gallaudet College. During World War II, he was with the Aural Rehabilitation Clinic of Deshon General Hospital, Butler, Pennsylvania, working with deafened army personnel.

Mrs. Schunhoff was the former Mary Jane Moore, of Jacksonville, Illinois, a graduate of Illinois College. When Dr. and Mrs. Schunhoff moved to Berkeley, they had two children, John, 13, and Janet, 10. After driving to Berkeley from West Virginia, they settled in the superintendent's residence near the Dwight Way entrance to the campus on the north side.

Dr. Schunhoff, Mary Jane, John and Janet.

Dr. Schunhoff made his first official appearance as superintendent at the faculty meeting on the opening of school. He was introduced by Dr. Elwood A. Stevenson, his predecessor, and he gave a short address that was enthusiastically applauded. The school family wished him a most successful administration and a pleasant life on the campus.

Dr. and Mrs. Schunhoff first met Dr. and Mrs. Stevenson while attending the Convention of American Instructors of the Deaf in West Hartford, Connecticut, in 1955. Later they spent a week as neighbors in a new dormitory at the Tennessee convention of the A.I.D. in 1957. This was the beginning of a wonderful friendship which grew and continued during their years together in Berkeley.

On November 16, 1960, Dr. Schunhoff delivered an address, "Road Signs in the Education of the Deaf" at a combined meeting of the Teachers' Association and Association of Parents, Teachers, and Counselors. He pointed out that road sign No.1 implied the percentage of congenitally deaf children in schools for the deaf was steadily increasing. A second road sign showed that more and more multiply handicapped deaf children had knocked at school doors for admission. One of the last road signs, he emphasized in his address, said, "You and I have a part in a very serious job of teacher recruitment."

His reign at the Berkeley school was steady and efficient, even during the 1972 crisis that preceded the third relocation.

Several of his accomplishments were:

- Dr. Schunhoff became president of the Conference of Executives of American Schools for the Deaf at its 35th meeting in Washington, D.C.
- Changes in department designations were made: Advanced Department to High School Department; Intermediate to Junior High Department; Upper Primary to Elementary; Lower Primary to Lower School.
- On June 8, 1965, he attended the bill-signing ceremony at the rose garden of the White House establishing the National Technical Institute for the Deaf in Rochester, New York, and received a pen from President Lyndon B. Johnson.
- He was involved in the support of publishing the book *The Deaf at Work* in 1967.
- He was an honorary chairperson of the first tryouts, Berkeley Classic, in preparation for the World Games for the Deaf in Belgrade, Yugoslavia, in 1969.
- He hired a good number of deaf teachers whose alma mater was the Berkeley school.

Dr. and Mrs. Schunhoff were staunch supporters of the CSD sports program. They rarely missed watching CSD teams playing football games from 1961 to 1974. They drove far away in rain or sunshine to watch the games. Whenever they could not make trips, they would write notes to coaches to bolster the team. In 1975, the Foothills Athletic Association presented Dr. and Mrs. Schunhoff a framed C letter with the words, "No.1 FANS" in appreciation of their dedicated support for many years.

> ***"Not only will I miss him, I know that his dedication to this school and the people connected with it will make his passing felt by many. He was a true believer in Deaf people and was one of the leaders of his time in promoting Deaf people into positions of responsibility."***
>
> Dr. Henry Klopping

> ***"He was a mentor to young people in the profession. I was certainly on of them. He played a significant role in my career."***
>
> Jacob Arcanin

The foundation pond between the superintendent's office and the dining room was built in 1932. Children sauntered daily past the courtyard toward the dining room.

Nearly five hundred friends of Dr. and Mrs. Schunhoff gathered to host a retirement banquet Friday, February 21, 1975, at Goodman's in Jack London Square, Oakland. Dr. Schunhoff had retired as of December 31, 1974, as a result of California Public Employees' Retirement Law, which made retirement compulsory at the age of 67. The State Department of Education had arranged to keep Dr. Schunhoff on duty for three additional months for which he had volunteered his services until June, 1975. At the banquet, he received a number of certificates and citations of appreciation. The highlight of the evening was the presentation of two platform rockers to Hugo and Mary Jane from over five hundred friends.

After spending several years in retirement at their home in Concord, California, the Schunhoffs moved to Sun City, Arizona, to enjoy their retirement in the environment of the senior citizens village. They continued being loyal to CSDF by donating one thousand dollars to the Bell Tower project fund. Hugo appeared at the dedication of the Bell Tower in 1995 and it was his last visit to CSDF.

On December 23, 1997, at the age of 90, Dr. Schunhoff passed away in Phoenix, Arizona after a lengthy illness. He was buried next to Mary Jane in Jacksonville, Illinois.

On this page is an excerpt from the article, "Slow. Road Slippery When Wet," was Dr. Hugo Schunhoff's last write-up, two years before he passed away. It is considered a "follow-up paper on his first write-up, "Road Signs in the Education of the Deaf" shortly after he became superintendent of CSD in 1960.

"The deaf child must become BILINGUAL. I accept the premise that ASL is the deaf child's native language. I am happy in the fact that some of our deaf leaders are to improve ASL. I am in agreement in your using ASL with the young deaf child. I do not understand all of the various "directions" in progress. I do remind any who might forget — "The deaf person must be bilingual." He must write the language of his community. He must read the language of his community. Unless you are educating the deaf child to read and write straight English, better than we did, you will have failed. We did not do very well. As you evaluate results, use better written language as your goal. Good ASL will come easy."

Dr. Hugo Schunhoff

Dr. Henry Klopping
Superintendent
1975 - Present

Dr. Henry Klopping — This uneasy atmosphere was finally eased when Dr. Klopping was appointed superintendent of the California School.

Spirit of Fire

In the spring of 1975, CSD–Berkeley faced an uneasy situation at the school. The superintendent's position became vacant that summer. The plans for relocation and design of the new school were not clear, and a decline in enrollment was noted due to the closing of two elementary dormitories, Norton and Runde Halls, and part of the Auditorium.

This uneasy atmosphere was finally eased when Dr. Henry Klopping at the age of 33 was appointed superintendent of the California School for the Deaf–Berkeley, effective June 1, 1975. The announcement was made on May 21, 1975, by Dr. Barry L. Griffing, Associate State Superintendent of Public Instruction for Special Education of Sacramento, California, at a gathering of the entire student body and campus staff members. Dr. Klopping, addressing an audience at the outdoor quadrangle, expressed his excitement in running CSD, praised Dr. Schunhoff for his past achievements, and stated he looked forward to working with each of the students and staff members.

After several months of the Klopping administration, feelings of uneasiness among the students and staff members quickly evaporated. They became excited and enthusiastic about Klopping's dynamic leadership. Hence, CSD has enjoyed being in excellent and strong hands. He readily absorbed the mammoth mission of relocation; the burden of dealing with the architectural work of the new school and the task of moving the entire school to Fremont.

From a childhood dream and the potential of a promising career in law, he rose instead to become a teacher of the deaf and to the position of Associate Dean of Student Life at Gallaudet College in Washington, D.C. before becoming superintendent of California School for the Deaf–Berkeley.

Higher Education

In 1966, Dr. Klopping received his Master's degree in Special Education, Area of the Deaf, and his Doctorate in Education in 1971 from the University of Arizona. His Master of Arts in Supervision and Administration, Area of the Deaf, was received in 1969 from California State University–Northridge.

"How on earth do you put into writing the deepest feelings, you as a parent of children who have had to be advocated for so fiercely? Deafness was never a handicap to my Deaf children, ignorance in the field of deafness was. Dr. Klopping stands out among his peers in his conviction and practice of supporting parents. In a recent study to identify the problems associated with involving parents and families in education, it was noted that there were eight consistent problems. They are as follows: "time"; "feeling intimidated by principals, counselors, and teachers"; "not understanding the system"; "transportation"; "childcare"; "language and cultural differences"; "parents feeling they were not welcome at the school", and "professionals making the parents feel uncomfortable". I reflected on how Dr. Klopping has worked to set a completely different picture for parent involvement at CSDF."

Marilyn Cassidy
Mother of three deaf children

Childhood to College Life

Dr. Klopping was born of deaf parents in Omaha, Nebraska, just before his family moved to Flagstaff, Arizona. One of ten children, he attended public schools in Flagstaff. His father, Albert, was a construction contractor and his mother, Nina, busily raised ten children. Klopping obtained his Bachelor of Arts degree in Political Science from Arizona State University in 1963. When he commenced his studies at the University of Arizona for a degree in law, he worked as a counselor at the Arizona School for the Deaf to support himself. At that time, despite the fact he dreamed of becoming a lawyer, he diverted his interest to the problems of the deaf that his parents did not experience; decided to change his major and proceed into the field of the education of the deaf. After receiving his Master of Arts degree in the education of the deaf, he became a teacher at the Arizona School for the Deaf for three years before participating in the Leadership Training Program. In 1969, he married his university sweetheart, Sandra Lee "Bunny" Baldridge, who was also born of deaf parents. Both of her parents, Paul and Peggy, were staff members at the Indiana School for the Deaf, respectively vocational principal and teacher assistant.

Constructive Accomplishments

A few years of positive accomplishments in developing new programs and his enthusiastic involvement in the design of the new school have proved Klopping to be the most fitting person for taking over the reins of CSD.

Here is a list of the new programs established, follow-ups on the construction of the new school, and other achievements during the Klopping Administration.

- Community education centers for educational, recreational, cultural, and other related community activities and services in accordance with needs, interests, and concerns of the deaf community.
- The Student Advisory Council and the Employees' Council that meet with the superintendent periodically.
- Opening the Primary dormitories for the Special Unit Department.
- First Western States Basketball Tournament held at CSD.
- Frequent trips to Palo Alto to check with the design work of the new school to make sure everything was on the right track.
- Independent Living Skills conducted during the summer work program.

- Heavy involvement in foreseeing the progress of the new school construction.
- Promotion of the involvement in the Kellogg/Gallaudet project known as "Special School of the Future."
- Drastic increase of the enrollment and expansion of the school staff.
- Implementation of the Community Advisory Council.

Involvement in the Deaf Community

Throughout his career, Klopping has been the key in removing the barriers of employment for the deaf at the school. He hired a number of deaf people to work at CSD, perhaps the largest number of deaf employees among the national schools for the deaf. He encourages deaf citizens to participate in civic affairs and politics in Fremont, Sacramento and Washington, D.C. He and his wife Bunny have faithfully attended many local, state and national organizations of the deaf, events and celebrations including weddings, plays and funerals presented by the deaf. From his involvement, the deaf people develop trust in his credibility. Klopping was a man for the entire deaf community. Interestingly, because of their fluent usage of sign language, both he and his wife Bunny have often been taken for deaf persons when among the deaf community.

Dedication to Education and Welfare

Dr. Klopping is a man with genuine empathy for deaf children and adults. The new school in Fremont has made not only remarkable physical progress, but has also become recognized by its academic and athletic achievements as one of the outstanding schools for the deaf in the world. Klopping was elected president of the Conference of Educational Administrators Serving the Deaf in 1984. This was the highest honor in the area of school administrators and programs for the deaf.

In 1986, President Ronald Reagan appointed Dr. Klopping to a national 12-member commission on deaf education. A strong advocate for residential programs for the deaf, he emphasized, "Congress and the president need to come to an understanding that the least restrictive environment is not the same thing for all kids."

The California Association of Teachers of the Hearing Impaired (CATHI) at its state convention honored Dr. Klopping by presenting him with the award for "Outstanding Contributor to Deaf Education in the State of California." He was recognized by CATHI for his years of service—in fighting for improvement in the education of the deaf and being a tremendous leader in the field of deaf education in the nation.

Dr. Henry Klopping

- also known as "Hank"

Dr. Klopping is frequently involved in the exciting athletic events–home or away. Yet, he finds time to communicate with students, staff, parents and friends in the midst of games. The underlying principle of his thinking is to involve people. Hank has strongly emphasized to all new parents that he has an "open door policy." Considerable attention is given to the school's focus on enhancing parental involvement and hospitality.

> ***"One of the exceptional facts about Dr. Klopping is his accessibility. In my experience, he is the only superintendent who has made his home phone number available to staff and parents. I have had to phone him at home on numerous occasions to inform him of unexpected problems. He has always responded in a pleasant and helpful manner, even in the middle of the night. His sense of responsibility and his deep commitment to the students of this school have always been very clear."***
>
> pointed out by
> Bobbie Alexander
> Assistant to Dean of Students

Klopping is completing his 25th year as Superintendent of CSD. He finds the challenge of his job in a world of constant change, in a rapid pace and with unlimited expectations.

Busy Home Life

Currently, he resides in Fremont with his gorgeous wife Bunny and their beautiful children, including two daughters, Margaret and Kimi, three sons, Chris and the twins Cort and Paul. Bunny is in her 19th year of teaching at Ohlone College as a full time professor.

Not only do the Kloppings lead a busy life, raising five children but they enjoy entertaining their friends frequently at their spacious home on special occasions. Annually, their children join their parents to welcome the entire CSD student body to an Open House for a Christmas celebration. The students get big thrills seeing the fully decorated house with Christmas trimmings. Also, the Kloppings annually honor seniors by inviting them to a BBQ feast and a party on an evening a week before their graduation. Participants in the Family Orientation weekend and members of the Association of parents, Teachers, and Counselors, also, have annual gatherings at the Kloppings' home. Many other gatherings find cheerful times with the Kloppings.

The Klopping family— Front row: Paul, Bunny, Chris and Cort. Back row: Margaret, Hank and Kimi. This photo was taken at the United States Air Force Academy on Christopher Klopping's graduation day.

CSD Staff Members Who Became Superintendents
at the California School for the Deaf — *Berkeley*

Douglas Keith
William Caldwell
George Berry (Acting)

CSD Staff Members Who Became Superintendents
at other schools

Truman Ingle	Missouri School for the Deaf
Marshall Hester	New Mexico School for the Deaf
Edward Tillinghast	Arizona School for the Deaf
Roy Parks	Arkansas School for the Deaf
Richard Brill	California School for the Deaf–Riverside
Lloyd Harrison	Missouri School for the Deaf
Joseph Youngs	Governor Baxter School for the Deaf–Maine
Francis Dunning	Hawaii School for the Deaf
Barry Griffing	Arizona School for the Deaf
F. Eugene Thomure	Delaware School for the Deaf
Gilbert Delgado	New Mexico School for the Deaf
Michael Finneran	Mississippi School for the Deaf
Ronald Stern	New Mexico School for the Deaf

CSD Products Who Became Superintendents / Vice Presidents

Tim Jaech	Wisconsin School for the Deaf
Robert Davila	National Technical Institute for the Deaf New York School for the Deaf–Fanwood Model Secondary School for the Deaf Kendall Demonstration Elementary School

ADELINE ST.
RUSSELL ST.
SHATTUCK AVE.
OREGON
STEWART
WARD
DERBY
CARLTON
EDDY
COLLEGE AVE.
AETNA ST.
MARK ST.
WARRING ST.
FOWLER ST.
DWIGHT WAY
CHANNING WAY
DURANT ST.
PROSPECT ST.

CHAPTER TWO

HISTORY OF CSD

1860 - 1960

Pertinent Excerpts of A History of CSD 1860 - 1960

Notwithstanding, a book, entitled *A History of the California School for the Deaf, 1860 to 1960,* was printed in 1960 to coincide with the celebration of CSD's Centennial. The author's wish is to include pertinent excerpts of the book written by Caroline Burnes and Catherine Marshall Ramger, in this chapter. So the history extends from 1860 to 2000.

The author has added new factual information, amusing anecdotes, comments and photographs to the original history of the California School for the Deaf.

Caroline Hyman-Burnes.

Catherine Marshall-Ramger.

Caroline Burnes, a librarian, and Catherine Ramger, a high school teacher, prepared a thesis in partial fulfillment of the requirements for a degree. It was developed into their book.

The author recalled a conversation with Caroline Burnes at CSD–Berkeley in 1963 about her book. She said, "Dr. Byron Burnes and I are not alumni of CSD, but since we have worked at and loved the school for many years, we feel we are part of you, alumni."

Beginnings in California 1860 - 1865

In California, education of the deaf traces its inception to a group of twenty-three ladies meeting on the seventeenth of March, 1860, to organize a Society for the Instruction and Maintenance of the Indigent Deaf and Dumb, and the Blind. The reports give credit to Mrs. Pomeroy B. Clark as the leader of this movement. Subsequently she was president of the Board of Managers and Principal of the School until ill-health forced her to relinquish the task in 1865.

The Board of Managers of the newly formed society immediately made application to the State Legislature for financial assistance. The Legislature responded by the passage of an Act appropriating $10,000 for the erection of a suitable building. Rather than wait until the completion of this building, the Lady Managers rented a house on Tehama Street in San Francisco and opened it to pupils on May 1, 1860. The first pupils numbered three, a boy, Theophilus De Rutte (d'Estrella), and two girls. At the end of six months, however, there were already sixteen pupils enrolled

H. B. Crandall, himself deaf and a graduate of the New York Institute (Fanwood), was the first teacher appointed to CSD in San Francisco in 1860. In 1862, he married Kate Mead, the seventh pupil to enter the school, and they had four children. Crandall retired in 1874.

Preceding pages:
Bird eye's view of Berkeley in 1900. Note CSD campus at left lower corner of the architect's sketch.

Mrs. Metcalf, the oldest daughter of Crandall, was head of the Portland Day School for the Deaf. Then her oldest daughter took her place as head of that school, and her youngest daughter was a teacher at the Washington School for the Deaf. Metcalf and her two sisters taught the deaf. Her two daughters followed her footsteps profession. Three generations of teachers of the deaf. What a remarkable record!

H.B. Crandall — First CSD teacher.

In the beginning the institution was supported, aside from the $10,000 appropriation of public funds for construction purposes, mostly through charitable donations from interested people and through fund-raising activities of the Board of Managers. The Board obtained funds to purchase the lots on which the new building was erected. They presented this land to the State. There were those who thought the school might well be supported by the parents of the pupils and by charity. It was immediately apparent that few of the pupils would be from families with means and that such a precarious existence would never support the type of school envisioned by the founders, who vowed to pattern them on successful eastern institutions. Moreover, at a later period, when a movement to require tuition was again instigated, Dr. Warring Wilkinson pointed out how undemocratic it would be and vowed that it would engender a difficult situation if some of the pupils felt they should be more privileged than others. He knew that charging tuition had been attempted elsewhere and had always failed.

Kate Mead— Seventh CSD student, eventually the wife of Crandall.

The upkeep for the school came to about $6,000 in 1861, and this sum was obtained from donations and collections. Many necessary materials and supplies were also donated.

In 1861, it became evident that there was need for more room than the edifice originally planned would afford, so an additional $10,000 was obtained from the State. The City of San Francisco appropriated $7,000 for purchase and improvement of the grounds whereon the Institution was to be located. Together with an additional $2,000 from donations, the school, situated at the corner of Mission and 16th Streets, cost $29,000 as the land value was continually increasing.

By 1862 there were twenty deaf pupils. Charitable affairs were organized in order to raise money. The quarters were already crowded.

Mrs. Clark's report in 1863 estimated, from what she termed the best information available, that there were between 150 and 180 deaf and dumb, and blind children of school age in the state, whereas there were but thirty-one pupils enrolled in the school that year.

The managers reported in 1864 that they had raised $11,000 in all (since the establishment of the school) and there were thirty-three deaf pupils then. At this time the difficulty encountered in securing capable teachers of the deaf was mentioned.

Ill-health forced Mrs. Clark to resign as principal in 1864 and Mr. J. M. Francis arrived in February, 1865, and took over her duties but his health was not equal to the task and he subsequently resigned in the summer of 1865. In November, Professor Warring Wilkinson, formerly of the New York Institution (Fanwood), came out as Principal.

Thereupon began a long period of continual growth and change for the Institution with Mr. Wilkinson proving a most capable helmsman.

The Institutions Under Warring Wilkinson 1865 - 1909

From his initial report in 1865 until the final one in 1909, Mr. Wilkinson's reports were always vigorous and constructive; the writings of a cultured man. His whole heart was obviously in his chosen field, and he had had good training for his position. It was said that originally he intended to stay but a few years. In the end, his incumbency covered forty-four years.

Wilkinson in his very first report, after a scant month at the helm, petitioned for change of the name of the Institution to eliminate the term "indigent," pointing out that it was by no means a pauper establishment, but one set up in

Left to right:

Theophilus d'Estrella — First student at the San Francisco school.

Mary Wright — Fourth student, graduated in 1871.

Caroline Douglass — Tenth student, from Los Angeles.

accordance with the belief that every child had a right to an education with the added provision that the deaf and dumb, and the blind children required special methods of instruction and therefore special accommodation. He also remarked on the evils of giving alms to the deaf beggars; advocating that all the deaf be taught a means of earning a living. He advised the desirability of teaching trades to the pupils, the ultimate aim being to make a good, useful citizen of every pupil. It was then his contention that the children should enter school at the age of eight and remain about twelve years although at the time the legal length of stay was only five years.

The advisability of educating the deaf and the blind separately is mentioned this early. It is noted that whereas the blind can obtain education along with normal children, this is not true of the deaf. Wilkinson thought that the two classes could be administered under the same management, however.

In 1866, the State Legislature passed an Act approving the reorganization of the Institution. The directors, appointed by the Legislature, met April 9, 1866. The faculty and staff were reappointed just as they had been previous to the reorganization. The new law changed the status of the Institution, making it a legitimate rather than natural child of the State. The directors received a compensation and a $25,000 per annum appropriation was assured the Institution. The children were no longer limited to a stay of five years, but were to be admitted between the years of six and twenty-five. Any deaf child resident of California might attend the Institution.

The report submitted by Wilkinson September 30, 1867, was the biennial report as required by the above Act. He stated that there were forty-eight deaf pupils at that time.

Left to right:

James C. Harlan — Twenty-eighth student in 1862, from Missouri.

Charles T. Smith — Admitted in 1863, from Shasta, California.

John L. Krantz — Admitted in 1865, from Germany.

When the California School for the Deaf was established in San Francisco in 1860, its population was only 56, 800.

Second Relocation of CSD

The Board of Directors had been instructed to attend to the removal of the Institution from its San Francisco location to a larger, more suitable site. They began preparations to do so, advertising for six months in most papers published within seventy-five miles of San Francisco for proposals. Eventually, in February, 1867, they selected a site of 130 acres situated four miles north of Oakland adjoining the tract belonging to the College of California (today the University of California) for which they paid $12,000. Wilkinson waxed poetic in describing the marvelous view the site afforded:

> *. . . and an outlook over a varied and extensive landscape and water view of surpassing loveliness. It lies directly in front of the Golden Gate, through which we look upon the heaving, restless ocean, with all its solemn mysteries and suggestions, and see the long lines of smoke which herald the coming steamers and the white-winged fleets of commerce, long before they are visible to the Queen City of the Pacific. It seems appropriate thus to grace the very threshold of the State with an imposing structure devoted to benevolent uses. It is like the "salve" on the old Roman doorstep—indicative of the generous disposition of our people, and cannot fail to impress all newcomers to our shores with the worth of civilization whose first care is the relief of the unfortunate.*

When the California School for the Deaf and Blind moved from San Francisco to Berkeley in 1869, the population in the area was only 200.

Even today, no school in the United State has a more magnificent panorama daily spread before it than has the California School for the Deaf in Berkeley, situated on the foothills, and looking westward to the inspiring silhouette of San Francisco and the Golden Gate with its graceful bridge.

Once a site was selected, architects were immediately appointed to draw up plans. It was decided to use stone that could be quarried nearby. Ground was broken July 29, 1867, and the cornerstone was laid September 26, 1867. Wilkinson intended the new establishment to serve not only the deaf children of California, but those of Oregon, Nevada, and other neighboring states as well, charging $300 per pupil per year.

The work on the new edifice went apace up to October 21, 1868, when a rather severe earthquake caused some damage and necessitated repairs to the not-yet-completed structure. Beside this, Wilkinson mentions the rains, the new eight-hour day and a shortage of funds as hindrances. To that date $158,000 had been spent.

It was in 1871 that Mrs. Harriet B. Willard took up duties as housekeeper; her connection with the school covered sixteen years and Willard Hall was so named in her honor.

A building costing $5,000, large enough to accommodate four shops, had been erected, and Wilkinson was most enthusiastic about the shoe and cabinet shops already established. For the ensuing biennial he asked for $72,000, making the upkeep about $36,000 per year.

It is of human interest to remark that one thousand eucalyptus trees were planted on the slopes back of the school building. Now grown tall, these trees seem native to the spot.

Authorities in various fields of education, men like William G. Dodge, principal of a public school, and William Swinton, professor of English Literature and History at the University of California, were invited to come to examine the pupils in order to testify as to the competency of the instruction. Their reports were highly complimentary.

The first building erected on the Berkeley site. Considered a fine example of the institutional architecture of its day, this building was destroyed by fire on January 17, 1875.

Bret Harte's Poem

"Dr. Wilkinson entered upon his work in the San Francisco school in December 1865 — coming to California by the Panama route. Among his fellow-passengers was Bret Harte, with whom there began then a lifelong friendship. (Bret Harte was a famed author, writing the lawless, burly life of early California mining camps and poems.) *One of the early fruits of that friendship was one of Bret Harte's poems, which was written for the services at the time of the laying the cornerstone of the first building, which was erected in Berkeley two years later. When the cornerstone of this building was laid in September, 1867, the poem by Bret Harte was read."*

This quotation above was taken from *The Story of the Evolution of a Hamlet into a City of Culture and Commerce* by William Warren Ferrier, Berkeley, California.

The title of the poem was *Our Bethsaida*. Only the last two stanzas are mentioned here.

Ah, Bethsaida's pool no more
Sees the miracle of yore!
Faith no more to blinded eyes
Brings the light that skill denies;
Not again shall part on earth
Lips that nature sealed from birth
Though his face the Master hides
Love eternal still abides
Underneath the arching sky;
And His hand through Science guides
Speechless lip and sightless eye.

This is our Bethsaida's pool,
This our Thaumaturgic school;
We, O Lord, more dumb than these—
Knowing but of bended knees
And the sign of clasped hands—
Here upon our western sands,
By these broad Pacific seas
Through these stones are eloquent,
And our feeble, faltering speech,
Gains what once the pebbles lent
On the legendary beach
Unto Old Demosthenes.

During the next biennium a Robert W. Durham of Butte County bequeathed the school a portion of his estate from which about $55,000 was realized. This was the first such bequest in the history of the school. The income from this capital was thereafter used in various ways and proved helpful at numerous times.

The curriculum at this time included Dr. Harvey Peet's Elementary Lessons, Scripture Lessons, Life of Christ, Acts of Apostles, Geography, Select Stories, Written Arithmetic, Mental Arithmetic, Chemistry, Natural Philosophy, Algebra, Paley's Natural Theology, Latin and Writing.

Grave Setback

During a strong windstorm on the afternoon of January 17, 1875, the new building was totally destroyed by fire. It was ironical that precautions taken to prevent recurrence of the type of damage caused by the earthquake previously mentioned were now factors contributing to such rapid spread of the fire that nothing was saved. There was, however, no loss of life, for which everyone gave thanks. Vacation time was announced at once. A week of flood and storm complicated matters. The harassed directors set about trying to rent temporary quarters, but decided finally that a wooden structure for use during reconstruction would cost no more than renting and would afterwards still belong to the State. A group of nearly forty men subscribed a thousand dollars each, the total sum to go toward this temporary structure.

During a strong windstorm in the afternoon of January 17, 1875, the new building was totally demolished by fire. There was no loss of life.

After the fire of 1875, this building was erected and used as temporary quarters. Forty men contributed $1,000 each to construct this building. Later it became the shop building. It was destroyed by fire on October 30, 1910.

The school was able to reopen April 17, 1875. The misfortune the school had suffered had the effect of publicizing the institution and brought an influx of applications. Statistics of the day foreshadowed the phenomenal growth the State would experience so the directors and the principal, calling attention to the probable increase in population, urged the expediency of a school of adequate facilities. The deaf population of the school was then seventy-five pupils.

First CSD Students at University of California

In the fall of 1873, Theophilus d'Estrella, the first pupil of the school, and Charles T. Smith were the first deaf students at the University of California, when they entered the Freshman Class. Smith took only two years of chemistry and physics, intending to become a metallurgist, but Wilkinson lured him to teach at CSD. Smith was considered one of the finest teachers and well liked by his students. A big loss was felt when Smith died of necrosis of the skull at the age of 21.

D'Estrella, congenitally deaf, had a difficult time and in his junior year abandoned his studies, which he stated was for financial reasons. Wilkinson at this time expressed the hope of obtaining the services of a regular professor versed in sign language who would accompany students to classes and interpret the lectures. Eventually, d'Estrella took Smith's position as a teacher.

It was Wilkinson's firm conviction that a person could be highly intelligent even though unable to speak. It was held by some at that time, and still is, that in order to acquire an education, a child must be able to speak.

The fire ruins (1875) of the first CSD building were used for stone walls around the school campus. The walls still exist in Berkeley.

Theophilus d'Estrella –
A student of the University of Cal –
an inmate of the D D & B Inst.

Immediately after dinner (usually at 4½ P.M.) Sunday afternoon Jan 10th, I went into Frank's room in front near to the boy's Sitting Room. About 5 minutes passed while I was writing a letter. Messrs Frank & Fowler were present. We heard a great noise and thought that the boys were playing. But I saw the door open and Frank & Fowler running out – I still sat writing – saw some boys gathering together in front and the smoke rolling. I went out and saw a small flame breaking out from the western roof of the rear – thought it was such small matter to be easily stopped out.

I went up to the second story in the rear and saw the smoke coming down – went in the Chapel and saw the flame breaking out between the boards of its ceiling. Then I went to the closet, where clothes were kept and got all my clothing – Saw Wilkinson coming from the third story in front after boys. He told me to get out as fast as possible. But as I was not scary I went down into Frank's room and put my clothings in my valise. I took with me my valise & writing box & got out. [illegible] out, I saw the flame catching at the tower very fast. The whole roof of the rear and of the chapel was in fire.

asked to get in for my books, but Prof. Wilkinson did not let me in – So I obeyed him and helped him looking after boys. About 20 minutes after I first saw the fire, roof of the front gave way to fire – Soon the whole building was in flames ——

Theop. d'Estrella –

ORIGINAL NOTES – *handwriting by Theophilus d'Estrella, explaining how the first school building was destroyed by fire in Berkeley.*

Rebuilt in Berkeley

The school gardens were supplying vegetables in 1875 and the orchards were expected to help supply fruits in a year or so. A plank walk extended three-quarters of a mile down from the school to the horsecars.

During the summer of 1876 Wilkinson traveled east to observe first hand as many schools for the deaf as possible and so determine how the new California School should be built. Upon his return he announced his confirmed advocacy of the so-called cottage or segregated system as being decidedly safer, more economical and easier to manage.

In September 1876, the school experienced a diphtheria epidemic–at the same time a similar epidemic in San Francisco caused the death of a thousand children. Three of the school children died.

When the contract for the new school was awarded to W. E. Boone, at a cost of $84,000, Wilkinson emphasized that the plan provided for indefinite expansion. Ground was broken April 30, 1877, the 17th anniversary of the opening of the school.

During this period of reconstruction there were no provisions for vocational training which Wilkinson had, from the first, strongly favored. He had set up cabinet and shoe repair shops, but the overcrowding of facilities had made it necessary to use the shop quarters as additional dormitory space for boys. Due to the fire hazard of these quarters only emergency cases were admitted.

In the late 1870s a drought caused the failure of the spring which had, until then, supplied the school with water. A water source was always a critical problem for the school and quite large sums of money were spent seeking a supply on the grounds or nearby.

View of the school in about 1881. At this time the Educational Building (middle) had but one story. At the left, Durham Hall, a dormitory for girls. At the right, Moss Hall, a dormitory for boys. Behind Moss Hall, Bartlett Hall, a dormitory for boys.

It should be noted that even at this early date Wilkinson was remarking again and again that this was a school for mentally normally deaf children and that subnormal dumb (without speech) children ought to have a school of their own.

William A. Caldwell began his long association with the institution in 1884, coming from the Indiana School. Douglas Tilden also joined the faculty, while d'Estrella resigned his teaching duties to pursue his art studies at the School of Design in San Francisco. D'Estrella continued to teach art at the school, however.

Between May fourth and June twenty-third, 1883, Wilkinson traveled about visiting and inspecting vocational training setups in thirty-one eastern schools and similar institutions.

With a $2,500 appropriation from the Legislature, a printing "office" and a woodworking shop had been set up. A small monthly magazine, *Pacific Monthly*, was published by the printing shop pupils for over a year at subscription rates of a dollar a year and ten cents a copy. A daily paper was put out also. This finally became the monthly school paper, *The California News*, which has continued to this day. Wilkinson termed printing a remunerative, respectable craft, peculiarly fitting as a means of livelihood for the deaf man. The new bakery and cooking school were being erected at this time. With $3,000 the library was equipped with cases ($750) and books (1,000 volumes costing $1,000).

It was in 1886 that Wilkinson drew attention to the outstanding talents of Tilden and d'Estrella, suggesting to the Board that they be sent abroad to study with the view of making them heads of art departments at the school—departments of sculpture, drawing and painting.

The Board of Directors had decided to loan Douglas Tilden $600 a year for three years to further his art studies in New York and Paris. From September 1887 to May 1888, he was at the National Academy of Design in New York City. He then sailed for Paris. It is noted that ten deaf-mutes were exhibiting in the Paris salon in 1888 and one took a third class medal. Tilden was to exhibit two works in the Salon himself and one *The Tired Boxer*, would receive an "Honorable Mention," the highest honor an American sculptor had ever received.

Although the Legislature had made an appropriation of $30,000 for the completion of the second story of the Educational Building, growth of the State had brought about a greatly increased demand for labor so that costs had risen sharply. It was necessary to ask $15,000 more and at the same time be so bold as to seek $50,000 for a girls' dormitory.

In December 1887, the Reverend Fred H. Wines, editor of the *International Record of Charities and Correction*, and for twenty years the Secretary of the Illinois Board of Charities visited among many other institutions the California School and his complimentary report was reproduced in the Report of the Principal for 1888:

The Tired Boxer, *a 29 1/4 inch high bronze statue, was dedicated at the Olympic Club in San Franicsco on January 2, 1893. It was destroyed in the earthquake and fire in April, 1906.*

"The California School for the Deaf is fortunately situated in a very favorable part of the commonwealth. It will not be possible to enumerate all the places that have access. To do so would require a book. To the west is a matchless panoramic view of San Francisco Bay, the Golden Gate and Mt. Tamalpais. On a clear day the city of San Francisco, with its skyscrapers and seven hills, stands out like an enchanted city. The bridge that spans the Golden Gate can be seen from the classrooms that face the west."

Dr. Winfield Runde
The California News
April 1944

Today has been given to a visit to the deaf and dumb at Berkeley. . . . The school is in its way a gem, probably the most perfect in respect of its general arrangement and the admirable balance of all its parts, that I have ever seen. . . . This Institution is organized on the cottage plan. The number of pupils is one hundred and sixty and they are divided into ten classes, not including the class in articulation. In the highest class I found the pupils studying Latin, and I learned that six have entered the University. I met a Mr. Thedore Grady here, a deaf mute, who spent one year at the Johns Hopkins University in Baltimore. These instances illustrate the fact that the deaf and dumb are capable of pursuing their studies, if encouraged to do so, in company of those who can both hear and speak—a fact not generally recognized.

. . . . The dining room presents an elegant appearance; is finished in white cedar, and has an elevated, ornamental roof; the windows are round-headed and have stained glass. The kitchen is lofty and handsome, with a tiled floor and a tiled dado. There is no necessity for a scullery, since dishes can be washed the year round on a porch outside, and no need for a refrigerator, because, in this climate, meats can be kept without ice. I was shown the room devoted to a cooking school, where a beautiful pictorial effect has been obtained by the selection of handsome colored china and its aesthetic arrangement on the dresser. Beneath the dining room is a gymnasium, with $500 worth of Sargent's apparatus. All of the buildings are ratproof. There are no sewer connections and no inside water closet pipes; these are all outside the buildings. From the front windows and from the portico of the school building one looks over the bay through the Golden Gate, upon the broad Pacific Ocean. It is one of the finest views in California.

Continuation of the Building Process

By 1890, the Educational Building was completed as originally planned, with a dignified 160 foot tower and an Assembly Hall that was 112 feet by 125 feet. The Strauss Clock was placed in the tower. This clock was purchased for $1,375 with money from the Strauss fund, hence the name. The clock itself was a product of the Seth Thomas Clock Co.; it had four dials, ran eight days without winding. It carried a five-year guarantee that it would not vary fifteen seconds in a month. The Assembly Hall had 616 folding opera seats and stained glass windows. The needed Girls' Dormitory was also under construction. Now Dr. Wilkinson began asking for a hospital, and for a Boys' Dormitory.

During this period the feasibility of electric light had been investigated on a small scale and Wilkinson was most enthusiastic about it both from the standpoint of economy and because it promised better lighting with greater safety than gas. Dr. Wilkinson noted that he felt the electric light had come to stay (!).

With the idea of rectifying any ill effects isolation might be having on the California School, once again Dr. Wilkinson went traveling, spending the academic year 1891-1892 abroad on the Continent, visiting schools in France, Italy, Switzerland, Austria, Germany and England. He decried the attitude that education of the deaf was to be considered miraculous. To emphasize the attitude he found and was criticizing, he quoted the head of a Vienna Institution who, when informed that six deaf-mutes had matriculated at the University of California, exclaimed, "That is impossible."

With the addition of the school second story in 1890, from the front windows of the Educational Building one could see over the San Francisco Bay through the Golden Gate, and upon the broad Pacific Ocean.

Note the fine architecture inside the Educational Building and a group of girls studying in one of the classrooms.

Now, at last, nineteen years after the drafting of the first plans, the Institution was considered actually completed and it was determined to name the various residential halls, honoring persons whose services to the institution made such action appropriate. The following designations were made:

House No.1, erected in 1878, was to be called Moss Hall. J. Mora Moss had been President of the Board for ten years and had died during his third term of office. By his devotion and unselfish zeal in behalf of the Institution, it was deemed eminently proper to commemorate his name in connection with the work he loved so well.

House No. 2, erected in 1878, was to be called Strauss Hall. Louis Strauss, of San Francisco, left by bequest to the Institution $5,000, the interest from which was to be expended for such purposes as the Directors might determine.

House No. 3, erected in 1881, was to be called Willard Hall. Mrs. Harriet B. Willard had been Chief Matron of the Institution for sixteen years and by her high Christian character and loving tenderness not only endeared herself to the officers and pupils, but left the impress of her life and devotion to duty upon all who had come after her.

House No. 4, erected in 1890, was to be called Durham Hall. Mr. Robert Durham bequeathed an estate which netted the Institution after all expenses of litigation were paid, $33,673, the income of which has since been of inestimable benefit to the Institution and its pupils.

Moss Hall, a dormitory for boys. Starting in 1878, the boys appreciated living in the "ward" bedroom on the three floors. The wardrobe lockers and the "gang" shower room were in the basement. In 1949, Moss Hall was demolished to make room for two new girls's dormitories.

House No. 5, erected in 1894, was to be called Bartlett House. Dr. W.C. Bartlett had been a member of the Board for nearly eight years and for most of that time he had been President. During that long period he had never missed a meeting of the Directors, while his courtesy, sturdy honesty of purpose, and impartiality had led his fellow members to feel that the naming of the last hall erected in their administration was only a just tribute to his merit as an officer and his worth as a man.

Noting that the streets to the west and north of the Institution were as unkempt now, twenty-five years after, as they had been in 1869, Dr. Wilkinson chided the Legislature for failing his repeated request for funds to remedy the shameful conditions. At the same time he advised erection of a brick or stone wall around the grounds.

Each time a dormitory had been built, no provision had been made to furnish them. Wilkinson had usually gone ahead and had the halls built, then asked for money to furnish them. One can sense that the continued "begging" for funds may have wearied him. At this time he was asking for $26,590 altogether for the work mentioned above.

Granville Redmond's first picture, "A Winter Morning on the Seine," was admitted to the French Saloon in 1895 and subsequently to the School. James W. Howson graduated from the University of California in 1897, the second deaf student to do so. He went on to take a graduate course in chemistry and metallurgy, earning his Master's degree. In 1901, he joined the School faculty. Winfield Runde, Frances Norton and Anne Lindstrom were at Gallaudet-the first from California to go there.

"A memorable feature about Moss Hall, built in 1878, was the old -fashioned drinking water fountain outside on the dormitory's north side. One of the consistently favorable comments was of the water's exquisite taste and it was always at just the right temperature — neither too warm nor too cold. The fountain was a thin pipe, with a cloverleaf design handle that rose up through a metal grill set in a square of granite. The pipe was rather long and curved slightly upward so that one could drink the water. It could be the drinkers were reminded of the story of the 'old oaken bucket that gathered water from the bottom of a cool well.' Oh, delicious and thirst slaking! The perfect place to drink after a hike up the east Berkeley hills."

Ken Shaffer,'46

Durham Hall covered with the purple wisteria at the fence by the dormitory for girls.

The girls peeking through the famous wisteria for pictures taken annually between 1890 and 1920 at Durham Hall.

The first of the CSD alumni to graduate from Gallaudet College. Left to right, Anne Lindstrom (Cowley), Frances Norton (Mrs. W.S. Runde), and Winfield Scott Runde. Dr. Runde was the first Californian to enter college. Dr. Caldwell prepared the young ladies for the freshman class and when they entered college, they became Dr. Runde's classmates, all graduating in 1901. Dr. and Mrs. Runde returned to CSD to teach for many years.

In October of 1898 the Institution began a siege with scarlet fever. When the Berkeley City health Officer quarantined the school, it caused a veritable panic and many pupils went home. School had to be recessed for a while. This served to emphasize the need for the hospital for which Wilkinson had been asking in each of his reports over the years. In May 1901, a dreaded small pox epidemic broke out and the Institution was again under quarantine. This misfortune led the Board of Directors to borrow money from the trust funds and build a hospital, hoping to force the Legislature to make good the loan with an appropriation.

It was 1902 that Dr. Wilkinson first advised the segregation of the deaf and the blind although he believed the two departments could be administrated by one Principal and a good Vice-Principal. He was anticipating the need for the separation, asking that plans be drawn at this time with the intention of presenting them to the Legislature in January, 1905.

The "famous" earthquake of April 18, 1906, termed the most important event of the two years under review, and indeed in the history of the Institution and of California, did not do so much damage to the school as knowledge of the catastrophic effect it had in San Francisco would indicate. There was no accompanying fire, for one thing. The first sharp jolt at 5:13 a.m. awakened and frightened everyone. The second, more severe shock, which lasted twenty seconds, caused quite some damage. Chimneys were thrown down, others cracked. The towers, peaks, and slate roofs apparently suffered most. Interior cracks appeared. The main walls held firm and some departments showed no effects at all, so school went on as usual except that for the two days following the first shocks classes were held out-of-doors. Dr. Wilkinson had to send out an official notice assuring the parents that no one, especially no child, had been even slightly injured. Even so, a few children were removed from school to flee the state with their terrified families.

For the first time, in 1906, the School Physican made out his own report, thus relieving the principal of that burden.

Dr. Wilkinson's report for the biennium ending June 30, 1908, was his last as he submitted his resignation July 28, 1909, to take effect October 1, 1909. From the foregoing history of his forty-four years as principal, it is clear that his departure marked the end of an era, as it were. In an interview with a reporter of the San Francisco Call, he said, "My eyesight has been failing me and I feel that I need and have earned a rest. There are a few preliminaries yet to be gone over before my resignation will be placed in the hands of the Directors, but I shall sever my connections with the Institution this year."

Dr. Warring Wilkinson — retired in 1909 after 44 years of serving CSD as principal. Dr Wilkinson took great pride in the efficient operation of the school. He was especially proud of the fresh spring water (flowing up to 10,000 gallons daily) that ran through the site and he utilized the water in the most modern plumbing and sanitation devices. He operated a dairy at the school and gleaned vegetables and fruits from gardens and orchards on the grounds.

Interim
1909 - 1928

The new Industrial Building was erected in 1915. Vocations taught that year were art, barbering, basket-making, bookbinding, cabinet making, carpentry, domestic science, dressmaking, gardening, painting, photography, printing, sewing, shoemaking, and typewriting. In 1916, dairying, rug weaving, silk weaving and rope splicing were added.

When Dr. Wilkinson resigned July 28, 1909, Douglas Keith was appointed his successor. Keith had first come to the Institution as a clerk in 1888. He had no training or experience in the field of education of the deaf or of the blind. Therefore, when agitation led to an investigation by the Governor, it immediately became apparent that he lacked proper qualification for the position of principal. This investigation and its conclusions led to his resignation whereupon Caldwell became Acting Principal until August 1, 1912, when the Board of Directors selected Mr. Laurance Edwards Milligan as Principal. Mr. Milligan had been the president of the State Schools for the Deaf, Blind and Backward children at Boulder, Montana.

Milligan at once asked for the revision of the laws governing the Institution. Formulated in 1872, they were outmoded and sometimes inoperative. He also recommended appointing a Head Matron and centralizing responsibility in the domestic department. Milligan felt that complete separation of the deaf and blind schools should be effected at once and any revisions made should bear that separation in mind. Finally he drew attention to the need for a pension system. Meanwhile he "created" positions for teachers who had earned retirement by reason of length of service. He appointed this one bookkeeper, that one librarian, and so on.

The new industrial building was nearing completion-a three-story, 50x100 foot structure of cement and brick, costing $29,999 plus extra for sewerage connections and partitions. Twenty thousand dollars were set aside for equipment. It was planned to have printing and carpentry, shoe and harness making, barbering and a physical and psychological laboratory.

The water supply was still a problem. New electric wiring and plumbing improvements were needed. Milligan had to ask for larger appropriations, citing the increased cost of living; however, a teacher at that time might be earning only seventy-five dollars a month.

School hours from 8:00 to 12:50 for academic work and from 2:00 to 4:00 for industrial shop work were resumed. There were now an oral department of seven classes, a manual department of four classes, and three upper classes with combined instruction. The course of study had been revised and systematized.

Elimination of the objectionable term "asylum" from all codes referring to the school was now sought. The Board felt that the chief executive officer should be designated as principal or superintendent rather than "principal teacher," and also that the laws of 1872 limiting his salary to $3,000 per annum should be repealed.

At this time it was suggested that some provision be made for aid to deaf students seeking higher education at the National College for the Deaf at Washington, D.C., since the cost of transportation from California to D.C. was a stumbling block for them. The sum of $300 per year per student was suggested.

By 1914 pensions had not yet been obtained. There were two hundred fifteen deaf pupils enrolled June 30, 1914.

Separation of Schools

The official name of the school was changed by the Legislature from the California Institution for the Deaf and the Blind to the California School of the Deaf and the Blind. The valuation of the school land and buildings was placed at $1,231,500.

This building behind the Educational Building housed the assembly hall, often called "the chapel" which the deaf and blind students shared until 1929 when both schools were separated.

The laws governing the school were revised and brought up to date by the Legislature of 1915. Separation of the school for the deaf and the school for the blind was prepared for by this revision.

Letters were sent out to the cities in the State having a population of 1,000 or over inquiring about desirable sites for removal of either one or the other school. A school for the blind would need fifteen to fifty acres, while a school for the deaf would require 160-320 acres.

Miss Lizzie Moffat passed away April 14, 1915, after twenty-five years of teaching articulation. The executrix of her estate donated five hundred volumes to the school. Mr. Henry Frank, too, died after having served forty-five years. He was deaf and a graduate of Fanwood in New York.

Because of the difficulty in securing trained teachers, Milligan instituted a Normal Course patterned after those of Northampton and Gallaudet College.

At this time the California Association of the Deaf began a custom of presenting medals- a gold medal to the best student in the Advanced Department, a silver medal to the best pupil in the Intermediate Department and a bronze medal to the best Primary pupil.

The gymnasium had been completed and equipped. This building had a 55x50 foot main floor with a stage at one end. There was a 22x77 foot swimming pool of from two to eight foot depth. There was also a new 44-stall dairy barn with facilities for separating and pasteurizing the milk. The School had purchased two Ford "machines," a five-passenger sedan and a light truck.

In his report for 1918, Mr. Milligan mentioned that the graduates of the School were employed at both the Ford Motor Company in Detroit and the Goodrich Tire Company of Akron. The war made it easy for the deaf workmen to find employment.

The "Chapel", usually a busy place during the weekends. The students attended ethics meetings Saturday morning, enjoyed the silent movies Saturday evening, listened to moral lectures Sunday morning and delighted in storytelling Sunday evening.

Dr. Wilkinson's death occurred on April 7, 1918. From the time of his resignation until his passing he had been listed on the School roster as Principal Emeritus.

Milligan continued to seek separation of the Deaf and the Blind Departments into two distinct schools. He also asked that his Assistant principal be relieved of classroom duties in order to do justice to his supervisory tasks. He inaugurated a system of Teachers' Reports.

Central heating had been introduced and the wiring renewed. An outdoor street-lighting system was still needed. No underground water supply had been located.

Laurance E. Milligan died March 28, 1920. Caldwell once again became acting principal and prepared the Thirty-forth Biennial Report on June 20, 1920. Caldwell continued the drive for segregation of the deaf and the blind, preparing statistics to show that there were several hundred deaf or blind children in the State who should be at school, but could not presently be admitted because of the inadequate facilities. He mentioned holding classes in a cloakroom for lack of proper classrooms.

In addition to the death of the principal, some nine teachers left the school for various reasons while a like number of replacement were hired.

Speaking of difficulties the deaf child has in trying to understand and use English, Caldwell quoted Peter Roberts, in his *Teachers' Manual: A Rational System for Teaching English to Foreigners,* where he says, "Trust the ear, the receptive organ of the language. The eye can aid and so can the hand but it is contrary to nature to learn a language by those senses." Caldwell felt that this pointed up precisely the difficulty the deaf child faces, "It is contrary to nature." He went on to say "and when we come to the eccentricities of mode and tense, it is no wonder that he sometimes loses heart in the verbal jungle. Philologists are agreed, I believe, that English is one of the most difficult languages in the world. Teachers of the deaf are not disposed to dispute this."

Dr. William Caldwell, Principal 1920-1927, was the owner of the first automobile seen at CSD-Berkeley in 1901. The vehicle was known as the "Toledo" steam locomobile, "horseless-carriage". On one occasion, he was warned by a policeman in Golden Gate Park in San Francisco for speeding over ten miles per hour. Caldwell was one of the outstanding teachers of the Deaf, a continuous service of exactly fifty years in the work of the education of the Deaf.

The July 27, 1921 regular monthly meeting of the Board of Directors was adjourned sine die as an act of the Legislature providing for reorganization of the schools of the state had placed the School under the control of the Director of Education. This was a very important milestone in the history of the school.

A subsequent act provided for the creation of an Institution to be known as the California School for the Blind, setting aside a portion of the site belonging to the California School for the Deaf and the Blind for the use of the newly created school.

These two acts made revision of the laws governing the School for the Deaf necessary and Caldwell suggested this should be done.

Another act of the legislature in 1921 provided for division of the land and separation of the School for the Blind from the School for the Deaf but unfortunately did not appropriate any funds for construction of school facilities for the School of the Blind. It was a mandatory provision of the act that this division be accomplished within six months of the enactment, so on January 30, 1922, the Principal officially announced the separation and the appointment of H.C. Harter as acting principal of the "new" School of the Blind. On July 1, 1922, Dr. Richard S. French became the principal of the School for the Blind. The two schools had to continue sharing facilities during a building program for the Blind begun in 1923 but final separation of the two schools was achieved in July, 1929.

It is noted that interested groups from the University of California and elsewhere were paying visits to the California School for the Deaf or requesting demonstrations or information.

The Boy Scouts of the School formed Troop 11 and three became Eagle Scouts, the first, together with one more in Los Angeles, in the United States to attain this rank.

Whereas barbering was discontinued because the boys did not like it, Caldwell thought auto repair looked like a promising vocational field. He wondered if the school could fit the boys to be assistants in a garage where they could then actually learn the work. The trades and occupations taught at this time are given as follows:

> **Art, barbering, bookkeeping, cabinet work, dairying, domestic science, dressmaking, gardening, laundry work, photography, printing, sewing and fancy work, shoemaking, silk reeling, and sloyd.**

Taken ill with influenza in April 1927, Caldwell found himself unable to carry out the tasks of his office and felt obliged to tender his resignation, effective September 15, 1927. George W. Berry, a member of the faculty at the time, was appointed Acting Principal in order to give the director of education time and opportunity to select a suitable successor to Mr. Caldwell. Mr. Berry

The eleventh Special Convention of the National Association of the Deaf was held in San Francisco, July 19-24, 1915, and Milligan remarked in his report that ***"The educated deaf of the nation were a fine body of men and women and a credit to the state schools that had educated them."***

Laurance Milligan
Principal

Before (1890 to 1927). The clock tower was built to add to the Educational Building in 1890.

After (1927 to 1949). Since the clock tower was considered unsafe because of earthquake hazards, it was removed in 1927. The Strauss bell was stored until 1950, when a new adminstration building with a tower was erected.

served from September 15, 1927 to June 30, 1928. Under the circumstances no important changes took place during his tenure. However, it was at this time that the clock tower and the Strauss Clock, were removed, since the tower was considered unsafe.

Rounding Out a Century
1928 - 1960

That the Deaf in the United States enjoyed fuller, happier lives than the deaf in any other country in the world was undoubtedly due to the educational facilities open to them and that education of the deaf in this country had achieved such a high level was due to those able men and women who had dedicated their lives to the education and welfare of the deaf. The School for the Deaf at Berkeley had been fortunate in having had such a man at the helm since July, 1928. This man, Dr. Elwood A. Stevenson, had consistently held to the high goals for the education of the deaf that were formulated by the pioneering Gallaudet and by Dr. Harvey Peet and Dr. Wilkinson.

Dr. Stevenson was a man with genuine sympathy and empathy for deaf children and deaf adults. This quality in a hearing person was of immeasurable value to the welfare of the deaf.

Dr. Stevenson became superintendent of the California School on July 1, 1928, coming from Minnesota, where he had been superintendent of the State School for the Deaf at Faribault. He accepted the position at Berkeley only after receiving assurance of cooperation in carrying out a vigorous program of modernization and educational improvement. W.S. Ferrier, in a history of the city of Berkeley, said:

> **For some time before the appointment of Dr. Stevenson it had become evident that the work of the School needed a general reorganization and also that a new type of work was needed. It was thought at one time that the difficulties arising from having the two institutions on the historic site were too great to be overcome and the State Director of Education recommended such separation as seemed likely to relocate both elsewhere on new and separate grounds. When State Director William J. Cooper was in 1927 scanning the country for a successor to Dr. Caldwell, the name of Dr. Stevenson, who was superintendent of an up-to-date school at Faribault, Minnesota, was presented for his consideration. The change**

from Minnesota to California, which was not long thereafter suggested, did not appeal to him. Persuaded, however, to come and make some investigation of the California field, the opportunity for service here, if a proper course of procedure should be entered upon, became commanding. Among the things considered then and agreed to was a uniformity of work for the deaf throughout the state and such common course of study as would render more effective that which was being done by city boards of education in several of the leading cities, a coordination of their work at Berkeley thus making it possible for the parent pioneer institution to meet the present-day demands for the education of the deaf.

The new Principal, Elwood A. Stevenson, took office July 1, 1928.

Dr. Stevenson had a clearly articulated program for himself, the school, and the state, which he believed should be followed through and it was only upon the recognition and endorsement of this program that he felt he could accept the position offered him. He outlined his program as follows:

- Supervision of all special education pertaining to the deaf and the hard of hearing throughout the state.
- Direct charge and supervision of courses of training of teachers for the deaf and the hard of hearing at San Francisco State Teachers College.
- Responsibility of the approval and issuance of credentials to teachers seeking certificates to teach the deaf and the hard of hearing in the state.
- Study and planning of a unified course of study to be followed by all California schools for the deaf, including proper grading, classification, entrance age, and use of materials and text books.
- Setting up of specific educational requirements and special training of all teachers of the deaf and of the hard of hearing in the state.
- Same system of records and transcripts for transfer and check up.

Having been assured of cooperation in achieving these goals, Dr. Stevenson was finally persuaded to accept the challenge the new position thus offered. Immediately upon becoming superintendent of the school at Berkeley, which was as yet the sole residential school for the deaf in the State of California, Dr. Stevenson was also made the chief of a new State Bureau for the Deaf, a part of the State Department of Special Education. In this capacity it was to be Dr. Stevenson's task to arrange that the work of all day schools for the deaf and the hard of hearing in the state be properly coordinated.

"A son of deaf parents himself, Dr. Stevenson has served the California School for the Deaf with unusually sympathetic understanding and with noteworthy achievement. During his regime the school has made not only remarkable physical progress, but has also become recognized by its academic achievements as one of the outstanding schools for the deaf in the world."

Myron Leenhouts
Principal 1953

"With the opening in 1932 of the new, large dining room that was part of the Primary Unit, Louis Byouk, older boys' counselor, was responsible for arranging the monthly rotation of the Moss Hall boys by their names in alphabetical order to serve as waiters in the dining room. The waiters wore white coats and aprons. Many of the boys enjoyed this chore especially because Mrs. Bertha Griffin, supervising dietitian, treated them to special meals, such as pancakes, hashed brown potatoes, certain meat cuts, pies, extra milk, etc. Many of them looked forward to their turn to be waiters.

There was a rigorous separation of the sexes, except in class. Here, again, it paid off to be a waiter because they could flirt outrageously with the girls and no one could tell if this was service with a smile or a smile mostly directly at one lovely person."

KEN SHAFFER, '46

Modernization of the School Needed

At the school in Berkeley, the old buildings were not only obsolete, but were also quite unsafe, as was to be seen later when the time came for razing them. Mr. Alfred Eichler, State Supervising Architect, wrote that the ancient brick and mortar walls were in such dangerously weakened condition that clam shell buckets could simply bite out sections of the walls and deposit them in waiting trucks—this in a region where earthquakes are of fairly frequent occurrence. There was also, of course, the danger of fire. In addition to all this structural weakness, the buildings were entirely inadequate in capacity for it was estimated that there must be about nine hundred deaf children in the state and of these only a few more than two hundred could be accommodated by the crowded school and therefore the other children were being deprived of their educational rights. In view of this palpable evidence of the need for it, Dr. Stevenson set to work at once to plan and execute a far-sighted building program.

Fortunately the Berkeley site was large and it was decided to begin the modernization by erecting a complete Primary School which could be begun and almost completed without disturbing the existing buildings, thus enabling the school program to continue uninterrupted. Mr. Eichler stated that throughout the building process not a single school day was lost.

In January 1929 *The California News* reported that the Legislature had approved a plan calling for an expenditure of $1,790,000 of which $1,200,000 would be apportioned over ten-year period, the additional $590,000 to be appropriated after this period but within fifteen years.The first appropriation was $300,000 with subsequent ones to be $200,000 to $250,000 each biennium.

With the first $300,000 a Primary Girls Dormitory, a Primary Boys Dormitory, and a kitchen-dining room unit were built February 29, 1932 was a happy day for it marked the dedication and the laying of the cornerstone of the new Primary School Building.

Superintendent Stevenson declared a half-holiday for the school and Governor James Rolph came down from Sacramento for the ceremonies. The kind governor even made the touching gesture of learning to say, "I love you all," in the sign language.The new structures were in California Spanish style with beige stucco walls and red tile roofs. The interiors were handsome and appropriate to the age of youngsters who would live in them. Understandably everyone could be and was very proud of them.

In his report for 1934, Dr. Stevenson noted that the other states were watching with interest the plans and organization being developed in California. Thus, in this field as in many others, the State of California was proving its leadership.

"One noon before Christmas in 1947, a big bowl of mashed potatoes was served to each table with eight boys sitting in the dining room. Donald Bullock, a table monitor, let the boys help themselves with the potatoes. What a surprise! No mashed potatoes left for Don. Stunned, he ordered a waiter to bring some more potatoes. Don continued talking with his girl friend across several tables. The boys again helped themselves with the second bowl of potatoes. What a shock! No potatoes were saved for Don. Infuriated he ordered a third bowl. When the potatoes were brought to him, Don told the boys that he staked an imaginative sign saying "For Don Only" into the new bowl of potatoes. Two of the boys smiled and started to scoop more. Don fumed at the boys but he paused for a moment for the boys were Don, too. The boys were Don Ingraham and Don McCune."

Don Ingraham, '50

Dr. Stevenson felt that only teachers with the special training needed to fit them for teaching the deaf and the hard of hearing could maintain the proper educational standards. It was and always had been difficult to obtain such personnel so, in 1934, Dr Stevenson established a Normal Training Course in conjunction with San Francisco State College. Unfortunately, due to monetary and jurisdictional conflict, this course was continued for only four years. Twenty-three young men and women were trained during the four-year period and all of them subsequently taught in various schools for the deaf in the United States.

Bedrooms with wardrobe closets like this in Primary Hall from the 1930s to 1970s.

War and Depression

The depression first hampered and then suspended the building program. The war further postponed it. Once normal activities could be resumed, the program was immediately continued. Costs had skyrocketed, but with the great increase in population in the state, the need of a larger school was more urgent than ever. The new plant with a capacity of four hundred ninety-two pupils is valued at $9,000,000.

The School was composed of five departments, four of them academic and one vocational. Each department has its own supervising teacher. The academic divisions were designed: Lower Primary, Upper Primary, Intermediate, and Advanced. The vocational department was housed in a most up-to-date shop building where each trade taught has first-class modern tools and equipment with which to work.

The school staff included the following personnel: a superintendent, a principal, a business manager, a psychologist - audiologist, five supervising teachers, a typist-clerk, forty-nine academic teachers, three adjustment teachers, a librarian, a speech correctionist, twelve vocational teachers, a boys' athletic director, a girls' physical education instructor, a dean of students, two senior counselors, forty counselors, nine administrative office workers, a dietician, a physician, a dentist, an ear-nose-throat specialist, an opthalmologist on call, five nurses at the hospital, and fifty-eight workers needed for maintenance and other services.

The academic curriculum took the pupils from nursery school or primary school through twelve or more years of instruction. Pupils who qualified could then take the entrance examination for admittance to Gallaudet College. The minimum entrance age was 5 1/2 years, and a pupil could continue in school until the age of twenty-one if necessary. A number of pupils entered at the intermediate level, transferring from any one of the numerous day schools in the state, or from another state school if the family has just moved to California.

The vocational department included eleven trades: shoe repair, cabinet making and upholstery, printing, baking and cake decorating, sloyd, primary sewing, advanced dressmaking, home economics, business techniques, homemaking, art and industrial design, and general machine and auto mechanics. Many deaf men followed the trades of printing or baking. Some entered into the shoe repair business, others took up carpentry. Metal work was another useful trade, deaf women were frequently trained and employed to operate modern business machines.

Over the entrance to the Educational Building, built in 1949, was a stone plaque bearing the carved form of a human hand with the first two fingers in an upright position. It was transferred from the old Educational Building (razed in 1948) to the new building. This stone hand stands for "ephphatha" meaning "be opened".

In line with the recognized importance of the automobile in the life of modern man, driver-training was offered the older boys and girls.

The physical plant consisted of six dormitories, one building with both dormitory and classroom facilities for the nursery children, a primary school building, an intermediate-advanced school building, a regular gymnasium, an auditorium, a hospital, a kitchen, a bakery, three dining rooms, a practice cottage, and a power plant. Most of the buildings were connected by covered arcades and all were of the same architectural style. There was a fine athletic field with a regulation size football gridiron and running track. There were appropriate playgrounds for each dormitory. The school had two libraries, one for the primary unit and the other in the advanced school building. The facilities of these libraries were frequently used by students from nearby colleges and universities who needed information regarding the deaf or the hard of hearing child. The audiologist-psychologist with his up-to-date facilities and equipment served both the school and the community.

Newly built for the high school and intermediate departments in 1949.

Vocational Training Building, built in 1953 was the newest building of its kind in the state. The vocational department imncluded eleven trades: Shoe repair, cabinet making, upholstery, printing, baking and cake decorating, sloyd, primary sewing, advanced dressmaking, home economics, business techniques, homemaking, art and industrial design, general machine and auto mechanics.

Student Activities in the 1950s

Student organizations and extra-curricular activities were encouraged as every effort was bent toward enriching the lives of the children. The deaf child, like any other child, needed to learn to get along with others. The various organizations included the Boy Scouts , the Camp Fire Girls, a Literary Society, a Student Body and its council, the Foothills Athletic Association and the Girls Athletic Association.

The Boy Scouts undertook the regular scouting program and some attained Explorer rank. They made public appearances to help raise funds for worthy causes such as the Polio Fund, the Community Chest, and, during the war, to sell War Bonds. Each winter they spent a few days in snow camp near Sonora.

Divided into several groups with picturesque "Indian" names, the Camp Fire Girls also carried on the regular activities of that organization. They took part in the Grand Council Fire each year. Several of the girls reached the Torch Bearer rank.

Under the direction of the boys' physical education instructor, who was also the coach, the boys took part in an athletic program appropriate to their age and physical ability. Football, basketball, baseball, and track teams competed with teams from other public and private schools. The competing teams belonged to the Bay Counties Athletic League and the school hosted two of the league basketball tournaments. The older boys who were no longer eligible to compete in these games made up a team called the Silent Five and play teams of boys like

The Girls Athletic Association (1950). Front row, left to right: Beverly Gamache, Joyce Ross, Verona Chavez, Betty Weaver, Jeanette Davis, Beverly Katz, Corrine Lee, LaRue Rohn, Carol Rush, Second row: Nazelie Elmassian, P.E. Director, Patty Jones, Connie Black, Marie Arellanes, Darlene Becher, Virginia Villar, Lou Braden, Rosie Ikeda, Bernice Hoare, Grace Gomes, manager. Third row: Julie Kern, Beatrice Dickerson, Draga Lewis, Denise Elder, Ann Robinson, Charlotte Douglas, Jacklyn Lee, and Tsuru Miyashiro.

themselves from the surrounding communities. Annually the Foothills Athletic Association sponsored a big formal dinner dance which was a very important social event for the pupils. The girls wore lovely formals (frequently the product of their own nimble fingers in sewing classes) and the boys transformed the auditorium into a veritable fairyland with unique decorations which were never quite the same as those of previous years. The Girls Athletic Association sponsored a similar dance, but it was less formal. It took place just before the Christmas holidays with the auditorium decorated appropriately. The students enjoyed dancing. Music for their dances was furnished by a record-player.

The d'Estrella Literary Society, which was so named in honor of Theophilus d'Estrella who helped to establish it, met once a month. While a faculty committee oversaw procedure in general, the meetings and the programs were in charge of the student officers and of committees of students. The basic aims of the society were to acquaint the pupils with the various forms of literature and to give them poise in appearing before an audience. The programs were made up of debates, readings, story-telling, skits, poetry declamation,

Panaoramic view from the swimming pool, lower, across the campus to the San Francisco Bay with two of the world's most famous bridges.

monologues, and so forth. Each year there was a contest for which the members may volunteer and prizes are distributed to the winners. Each year the society sponsored the Junior Class Play which was a full-length production, well-costumed, with appropriate settings. These plays invariably drew a large audience of both deaf and hearing adults. For the benefit of those in the auditorium who may not understand the signed dialogues, an interpreter read the parts orally offstage. Productions included, "Little Women," "The Cat and the Canary," "Comedy of Errors," "Hamlet," "Charley's Aunt," and "Around the World in Eighty Days."

Of the pupils who graduated from this school, most hold respectable jobs and are good, worthy citizens contributing to the common welfare of their communities to a creditable degree. To date 3,153 pupils received instruction at CSD. One hundred forty-nine have gone to Gallaudet College, fifteen prior to 1928 and 134 from that date to 1960. Of this number sixty-six graduated from the College. Many of these graduates have gone on to take further work at other colleges and universities. Many of them are now teaching in schools for the deaf.

Thus the California School for the Deaf looks back over a hundred years of existence with pardonable pride. As stated previously the overall goal of the school is to rescue the deaf child from a possible state of illiteracy and ignorance since deafness is the handicap which places the greatest difficulty in the way of education. With proper techniques, learned from experience and improved over the years, this handicap has been overcome for most deaf children. Those children at CSD lead full, happy lives both in the classroom and outside it. Visitors are always welcome to come and see this for themselves. Many visitors do come each year to the school. It is hoped that they leave with a better understanding of the problems met with in the education of the deaf, and with a better understanding of the deaf themselves.

"It is interesting to note here that Wilkinson and Stevenson together served CSD for a total of three quarters of a century; that both came from the NewYork Institution now known as Fanwood; and that both were born in the month of May."

Caroline Burnes
&
Catherine Ramger
History of CSD, 1860-1960

RONALD RANSOM & FLORENCE WYCKOFF

Ronald Ransom, '69, has his reminiscent experiences with Florence Wyckoff, granddaughter of Dr. Warring Wilkinson, Superintendent of CSD from 1869 to 1909, when Ransom and Wyckoff lived in Watsonville, California. Briefly after Florence Wyckoff married Hubert Wyckoff, a lawyer, they rented Ransom's grandparents' ranch house during the 1950s. Soon Florence became cognizant of the communication between Ransom and the grandparents through lipreading. That was how Florence's fondness for Ransom blossomed when he was a little boy. Possibly, the reason that Florence became deeply interested in Ransom was because of his deafness.

Because of Ron's fascination with machinery as well as loud noises, occasionally, Florence took Ron to the sites of the water drilling works. One day on the way back home, riding in Florence's fine car, Ron decided to help handle the stick shift with both hands. Much to Ron's surprise, suddenly the car rattled and halted. Immediately, Ron sensed he was in trouble for pulling the reverse gear which caused major damage in the gear box. Florence did not display any anger and bought Ron an ice cream cone to comfort his remorsefulness. After the transmission was back in service, Florence and Ron continued their happy drives.

From the experiences of associating with Florence, Ron was impressed with Florence's generosity and compassion. Ron called her "Aunt Bobo." They have kept contact with each other to this day. Who is Florence Wyckoff? What makes her a special person in Ron's life. To answer these questions, it is necessary to turn to her background.

FLORENCE'S BACKGROUND

During his superintendency at CSD–Berkeley, Dr. Warring Wilkinson and his wife, Florence, lived on the school grounds with their daughter, Maud, who became deaf at the age of eight and was educated at her father's school. Maud later married Dr. Leon Richardson, a classic professor at the University, and had two daughters who were born on the CSD site and lived there during their early childhood years. One daughter, Mrs. Hubert (Florence) Wyckoff was a 1926 University of California–Berkeley graduate with a long list of accomplishments including 20 years service on the California Governor's Advisory Committee on Children and Youth, and membership on the State Board of Public Health where she worked for the passage of the Federal Migrant Health Act.

In 1999, Florence reached 95 years of age, still living in Watsonville. Florence has an oak desk that her Grandfather Warring sat behind in his CSD office for 44 years. The desk is to be donated to the CSD museum.

CSD

ONE of the CSD students' proudest feats during the 1940s was the construction of the huge CSD letters on the hill above the school campus. After a long struggle, Frank Sladek, '41, a student leader, finally secured the green light from superintendents of both the deaf and blind schools to construct the CSD letters. Earl Ruffa, '42, with his "crew" (older HS boys) laid the foundation on the steep slope of the famous hill.

In September 1940, the boys of the Foothills Athletic Association and Moss Hall began construction of a huge block-letter sign, "C S D," 26 feet high, 16 feet wide, 31/2 feet thick, behind the campus, high in the Berkeley hills.

The head groundskeeper offered tips on purchasing material such as cement, lumber, reinforced steel rods and let the students operate a cement mixer. A chain of young boys passed one-gallon cans of wet cement up the hill from the mixer on the bottom to the new letters being constructed. The CSD letters were completed in the spring of 1941.

In 1945, as the supply of paint was available just before the end of World War II, the leaders of the Foothills Athletic Association painted the CSD letters bright orange. The CSD letters could be seen five miles away.

The CSD project has brought fond memories of those who were involved in this gigantic venture. These letters are 60 years old now. Sadly, the letters could not be taken to a Fremont hill in 1980.

---

*(This account above was summarized from the article in the Alumni Eagle, February, 1985, written by Frank Sladek. –*Author*)*

Sentences
Journal
Problem

Chapter Three

ENLIGHTENMENT

Ideal Establishment for Education

Since the California School for the Deaf opened its doors in San Francisco in 1860, it has enjoyed national and international recognition for the quality of its programs and the innovativeness of its faculty and staff. CSD has always fostered a genuine belief in the capabilities of deaf people - from the fact that its first teacher was deaf to the present day when half of the teachers and more than half of the residence staff are deaf.

CSD is the FIFTH Oldest School in the State of California!

1851
San Jose
Bellarmine High School

1855
San Francisco
St. Ignatius High School

1856
San Francisco
Lowell High School

1856
Sacramento High School

1860
California School for the Deaf

1863
San Jose High School Berkeley
St.Mary's High School

1865
Los Angeles
Loyola High School

1867
Petaluma High School

1869
Oakland High School

Cal-Hi Sports Record Book

Preceding pages:
Typical 1900 classroom scene in the presence of Dr. Warring Wilkinson, taken by Theophilus d'Estrella.

The educational spirit of CSD is reflected in a commitment and belief in deaf people and the programs described in this chapter have as their foundation this belief in the equality of deaf persons.

The last quarter of a century has seen many changes in the overall delivery of services to the deaf at CSD. Beginning in the fall of 1975, and at the direction of the new Superintendent Henry Klopping, the school espoused a philosophy of Total Education. The school began to look at the whole deaf person and the program reflected that not only the academic, but extracurricular programming, should be nurtured. The importance of after school programming and its impact on the overall development of the deaf child garnered support among staff, and student development programming in the residence program supported the academic efforts in the instructional program. From the introduction of Total Education to the present time a number of innovative undertakings by the school have resulted in a much changed program at CSD. The following is a sampling of the changes that have occurred in the overall program.

Technology - From the tie-in with Stanford University and then the University of California main frame computer, computers have become a big part of the life of staff and students at the school. In 1982, the school authored and sold "Blocks 82" throughout the nation which was used on the Apple IIe. Today, thanks to the efforts of the community, through Net Days instituted throughout the state by State Superintendent, Delaine Eastin, each classroom is wired so that the Internet is accessible in each classroom, office, and cottage and teachers use the computer in their daily instruction of students

Total Communication to ASL - From the days of "If You Say It Sign It" to the present day when ASL is used throughout the campus, there has been a major change in the thinking and practice of staff members. Accessibility to communication is key for all deaf people on campus and there is an expectation that ASL be used on the campus at all times. To make sure that all is accessible to the deaf, interpreters are now employed or hired on contract versus the time when some staff members voluntarily interpreted for deaf people, but there was no expectation that deaf people have the same access as hearing people on campus. Equal access to everything is key to the health of the school.

Superintendent's 1998-99 Cabinet weekly meeting to oversee and implement school programs. Left to right: Aronica Jones, Business Manager; David West, Director of Outreach; Vikki King, Director of Personnel; Dr. Debra Guthmann, Director of Pupil Personnel Services; Dr. Henry Klopping, Superintendent; Jacob Arcanin, Assistant Superintendent; Michael Finneran, Dean of Student Life; Ronald Stern, Director of Instruction.

❋ *Bilingual/Bicultural Movement* - As explained elsewhere in this book, the bilingual/bicultural movement has a positive impact on the thinking and acting of staff, students and parents. The legitimacy of ASL as a true language and its use in assisting the deaf person to understand and use English gained complete acceptance by the school community. The CSD Mission and Values Statement is reflective of the bilingual/bicultural movement.

❋ *Vocational Programming* - While many schools downplayed and eliminated vocational programming for deaf students, CSD has made such programming equal in importance to the academic programming for students. Changes have impacted the types of vocational offerings students have, but in addition the establishment of the Career Center and its emphasis on the Transition Partnership Program of students working on and off campus with the intent of students entering the labor force full time upon graduation has made a big difference in the lives of many graduates of the school. The school quickly discovered that students failed on the job, not because of a lack of training to do a job, but rather because they did not have the proper work ethic that made them successful employees. The addition of a School to Career (STC) component to the school has further strengthened the need to tie academic learning with the vocational preparation of the large number of CSD graduates who will not enter and complete a four year college program.

❋ *Academic Programming* - Throughout the United States, deaf students have not performed to the level of their hearing peers. Expectations for deaf students have not been as high as they are for hearing students when, in fact, many deaf students are capable of performing at the same academic level as their hearing peers. CSD recognized the need to become a part of the educational reform movement that was sweeping the country and became, in 1995, one of the Challenge Schools of the California Department of Education. In 1975, the

Director of Instruction Ron Stern's 1999-2000 team: Laura Peterson, High School Academic Principal, left; Brenda LaCosse, Early Childhood Education Principal; Debbie Ayers, Physical Education Supervisor; Ethan Bernstein, High School Administrative Principal; Pat Moore, Vocational Principal; Ron Stern, Director of Instruction; Eugene LaCosse, Elementary Principal; Robin Zane, Middle School Principal, Susan Loggins, Career Education Center Supervisor.

school developed a Curriculum for the Deaf, which was widely marketed throughout the nation. With the educational reform movement, the school recognized that deaf students do not need a curriculum, designed for the deaf, but rather a challenging rigorous curriculum such as those experienced by high performing students in local school districts. CSD no longer has its own curriculum for the deaf, and in the case of English has adopted the Fremont Unified School District Curriculum for use with students. For those students who have the ability to undertake the rigors of an academic program that prepares them for college and beyond, CSD is working hard to assure that those students have an academic program equal to those offered hearing students.

❋ *Outreach* - The expertise of staff at CSD, the comprehensiveness of program, and the creative innovative staff have led to many requests from local school districts and the community at large, for technical assistance. CSD responded by establishing the Outreach Division to implement the "Special Schools of the Future" project funded initially by Gallaudet University through the Kellogg Foundation and some state general funding. Currently the outreach program is totally state funded, and although inadequate in staffing to meet all of the requests for services, does provide some services to local school districts and the greater community. Since its inception, the outreach program has provided sign language classes for government agencies, including police and fire, parent education classes, seminars for educational professionals in a number of academic and vocational areas, and many other offerings to meet the needs of requesting parties. Probably one of the most successful programs promoted by Outreach were the Hispanic Family and Black Family Weekend parent education programs for families in California. It is anticipated that this part of the school program will grow dramatically in the years to come.

Twenty-eight faculty staff members and one hundred ninety-two students of 1915 under the reign of Principal Laurance E. Milligan.

❋ Volunteer Program - CSD has gone from having no volunteer program to the present when a half-time volunteer coordinator is responsible for handling well in excess of one hundred volunteers who give the equivalent of about 7 full time positions of work to the school annually. Volunteers are especially interested in assisting in the instructional program, but also assist in all other parts of the school as well.

❋ *Infant/Early Childhood Education* - Because it is now well documented that the acquisition of language requires early intervention, CSD began to enroll children at an earlier age in the 1980s. First the school established pre-

Names of the California School Over the Years

1860
California Institution for the Education of the Deaf and Dumb, and the Blind

1869
California Institution for the Deaf and the Blind

1914
California School for the Deaf and the Blind

1922
California School for the Deaf

1953
California School for the Deaf-Berkeley

1980
California School for the Deaf-Fremont

school classes to serve children three and up and in 1986 added an infant component to the school. Currently, CSD has more than 50 youngsters enrolled in the Early Childhood Education Department. The infant program has been so successful, that it has been recognized by the State as one of the exemplary programs that others can be modeled after. The results of this program have proven that deaf children, if given access to language at an early age, will show better results in academic achievement. Deaf children of deaf parents have had access to language at an early age, with results showing that they were academically superior to deaf children of hearing parents. With the introduction of the early childhood education program at CSD, deaf children of hearing parents are now finding language accessible to them at the critical early age, and their academic achievement is showing much improvement.

New Position: Director of Instruction - Since 1961, as Assistant Superintendent for Instruction, the role had included responsibility for the academic programs and supervision of all the principals. In 1982, at the new Fremont school, Dr. Henry Klopping created a new position, Director of Instruction, to take over the responsibilities of Assistant Superintendent for Instruction. Jacob S. Arcanin not only assumed the position of Assistant Superintendent, but also new assignments working closely with Superintendent Klopping. Marianne DeLuca was the first person to become Director of Instruction and continued that role until she retired in 1990. Ronald Stern was appointed to fill that position and continued until resigning in the summer of 2000 to become the superintendent of the New Mexico School for the Deaf.

These youngsters learn the traffic rules. The results of this Early Childhood Program prove that deaf children, if given access to language at an early age, show better results in academic achievement.

Although these are just a few of the changes and new challenge undertaken by CSD in the past quarter of a century, they are representative of the ever changing activities that propel the school forward. The following sections of this chapter present the various departments at CSD as they are today. Undoubtedly, these departments will undergo additional change in the years ahead as CSD continues to be on the cutting edge of education of the deaf.

INFANT PROGRAM- *TODDLING INTO FINEST CARE*

In January, 1986, following the establishment of the pre-school program, the Parent/Infant Program was added, enabling CSD to serve deaf students from birth to 21. The program was established to serve deaf children, from birth to three years, and their families who lived in Fremont, Union City and Newark. The program, later renamed The Department of Early Childhood Education (ECE), now serves children and their families from birth to six years old. The three major components are the Parent/Infant Program covering both home-based and school-based services, the Preschool/Pre-kindergarten Program, and the Kindergarten Program. The ECE Department is committed to early, consistent, and meaningful communication between the deaf child and the significant others in his/her environment. Exposure to a complete language system, American Sign Language (ASL), is seen as the means to develop fluency in both ASL and English. Literacy is highly valued, as evidenced by the frequent storytelling opportunities and copious availability of reading material. Partnership with parents is viewed as essential for the academic and social-emotional success of CSD students.

The Department of Early Childhood Education of CSD is committed to early, consistent, and meaningful communication between the deaf children and the teachers in his/her environment. Exposure to a complete language system, American Sign Language, is seen as the means to develop fluency in both ASL and English. The ECE students learning about the life of fish by teacher David Eberwein, 92 graduate.

ECE Playground lot for ECE children. ECE youngsters witnessing the "dedication" of a playhouse before they swarmed and admired a new plaything added to the lot. (The photo of the playhouse is shown elsewhere in this book.)

Learn Best Through Play and Active Exploration

The ECE Department supports the view that children learn best through play and active exploration. Each child develops at his or her own pace and in his or her own time. ECE programs are based on developmentally appropriate practices in a play environment. Staff are keenly aware of, and respond to, each child's unique needs and style of learning. CSD views each family and child from a deaf perspective, respecting individual family cultures and diversity, focusing on the strengths of each family and child. The program provides a stimulating language-rich environment that provides easy access to language models from a variety of age levels, a variety of skill levels, and a variety of styles.

- **Home-based program** for infants 0-18 months of age
- **School-based programs** based on the following:
  - *Toddlers* (18-36 months), 3 half-days per week
  - *Preschoolers* (3-4 years), 4 half-days per week
  - *Pre-kindergartners* (4-5 years), 5 half-days per week
  - *Kindergartners* (5-6 years), 5 days per week (approximately 5 hours perday)
- **Playgroup** (parent participation required) for infants, toddlers, and preschoolers

- **Home visits** for infants, toddlers, and preschoolers, 2-4 times per month
- **ASL classes and individual consultation or tutoring**
- **Audiological services:** routine testing, assistance with hearing aids, instruction, etc
- **Speech instruction**
- **Family potluck dinners**
- **Family sign language classes**
- **Parent/Family workshops**
- **Parent support groups**

ECE Scene of family sign language class tutoring by Sylvia Malzkuhn.

The ECE children presenting the hand sign of "I LOVE YOU."

ECE: One of the State's Sixteen Model Sites

CSD's ECE program is chosen as a visitation site by a program called the Supporting Early Education Delivery Systems (SEEDS) Project. This involves having many different preschool sites coming to visit CSD's program. CSD was selected from a large number of applicants for this program, and ECE is considered a model program. CSD is very proud of this achievement and ready to offer assistance relating to this program to other schools.

A Feather in CSD's Hat

CSD was honored when State Superintendent of Public Instruction, Delaine Eastin, chose ECE Principal, Brenda LaCosse, to serve on her statewide preschool task force on October 14, 1997. LaCosse brings with her a sensitivity to language and culture, and over 20 years of working with children in the area of deaf education. The task force is working on the possibility of a free public education to all 3-and 4-year-old children in the State of California. LaCosse hopes that if the State of California decides to offer universal preschools, CSD would be able to extend its preschool to include hearing children of deaf parents.

Enjoying the relaxing period between classes.

The Elementary students and the staff attending one of the assembly meetings in the Elementary Activity Center.

Elementary School-
Trekking Toward the World of Basics

The Elementary School Department provides a comprehensive developmentally and academically based educational program which serves Elementary and Special Needs elementary-aged deaf children, from the first through the fifth grades. The department focuses upon the "whole child."

The teachers, principal, and adjustment teacher in the Elementary Department promote maximum progress for students in relation to their development, social and emotional maturation, academics, critical thinking, and reasoning skills, given their functioning levels when they enter the Elementary Department.

Changes in the Different Academic Departments

In 1935, the Primary Department was set up, separate from one department that had been used to contain all classes. Also, the junior high school and high school formed their departments that year. In short, the concept of one department for all classes became obsolete in the California school system. However, in 1954, the Primary Department was divided into two divisions, the Lower Primary Department and the Upper Primary Department. Christine Stricklin, who was one of the primary teachers, became supervising teacher of the Lower Department.

In October 1961, as agreed upon at a conference in Sacramento, the Lower Primary Department became officially known as the Lower School. The Upper

Circa 1898 an elementary class at the Berkeley school. Every pupil spelling "C" according to the teacher pointing to the first letter of COW on the board.

School was under the rein of Principal, Gerald Pollard, who left for the University of Illinois to work on his doctorate. As that year there were fewer students in both departments, they were combined under the direction of Evelyn Shellgrain. Since then this combined department has been called the Elementary School.

ELEMENTARY SPECIAL NEEDS

The Elementary School Department provides two types of programs: Elementary and Elementary Special Needs. These programs concentrate on the students, learning styles, pace of acquiring new learning, memory skills, ability to pay attention in class, and to the work presented to them. Their ability to apply knowledge in new, unique situations and settings is emphasized. The Elementary Special Needs Program makes provisions for students who benefit from individual pacing, repetition, practice and review, and offers smaller groups for optimal success.

Teacher Rosemary Merchant illustrating the life cycle of silkworms to the first grade class.

ENRICHMENT OF LEARNING PATHS

Paths is an exciting curriculum that was written to help children develop better thinking skills, more responsible ways of behaving, and improving academic performance. PATHS stands for **P**roviding **A**lternative **Th**inking **S**trategies. The elementary cottage counselors, teachers and guidance counselors are teamed to work closely with each other to help develop five major goals of the PATHS curriculum.

Teacher Diane Caughrean preparing the Special Needs students to develop abilities in thinking and solving problems for themselves.

"It could be said that we are products of our elementary education, for it is at this level that the foundations for future success in school are established. In the Elementary Department, highly skilled teachers open the doors for our young students to become fluent communicators in both ASL and English, effective readers, responsible conscientious citizens, and proud Deaf role models."

Eugene LaCosse
Elementary Principal

1. *To increase children's abilities to think and solve problems for themselves.*
2. *To increase children's abilities to use their thinking skills to act responsibly and maturely.*
3. *To improve children's understanding of themselves and teachers.*
4. *To improve children's feeling about themselves (self-esteem).*
5. *To increase children's abilities to learn effectively in school.*

One of the PATHS methods is called *Doing Turtle*, which is considered the most effective way for children to develop self-control skills. Through the lovely tale of a little turtle who learns to go into his shell when his friends upset him, children learn to calm down by crossing their hands over their chests and taking three deep breaths.

When asked how certain children felt the PATHS ideas helped them, they had positive responses:

Paloma McClelland- "Doing Turtle *helps me calm down when someone cuts into my line after recess."*

Svenna Pedersen- *"Sometimes when I get mad at my sister I go into my bedroom to calm down."*
Brendan Stern- *"PATHS is cool! If you don't show self-control, you have few friends!."*

Aaron Brock- *"Yesterday when my mom bawled me out, I did* Turtle *and then I felt better."*

Elementary teacher Ed Copra dividing his teaching language and reading plans to two groups of the fourth grade class. One group doing book reports with the teacher, while the other group edits their book reports on a computer.

K.I.T.V. PRODUCTIONS

The 5th grade students produce a weekly news show called the Elementary Report. They learn to prepare pre-production, tape, and edit the weekly show. Requirements for the job of KITV News Reporter include having a pleasant personality and good attitude, good work habits, excellent signing skills, a sense of responsibility, and lots of enthusiasm. Shows may cover many topics, such as new students, noted people like Christopher Columbus, field trips, and Halloween safety tips. However, the KITV program does not occur every year, depending on circumstance of class schedule.

SCIENCE FAIR

Eggs popping into bottles through holes smaller than the egg, rocket corks bouncing off the ceiling and rainbows created before your eyes! The Elementary Department Science Fair was part of magic show and part circus but most of all, the fair has been a great success every year. Each class works hard, plans with great care and comes through with flying colors. Rosemary Merchant's class once presented a banner stating "The World is a Rainbow of Color." The students were able to twirl rainbow disks to see how colors blend together to form white light.

Every year the Science Fair is an unfailingly exciting event for everybody. All elementary students receive a certificate to remember the worthy course.

At the Berkeley school on the blackboard, asking "Where is your home?" This lass answering "Irvington" which was one of five towns, merging into Fremont. The picture was taken circa 1900, long before CSD moved to Fremont.

With social studies fifth graders, teacher Terry Viall discussing Japanese culture using emperor and empress dolls and relating dolls to a Japanese folktale.

Joanne Serna, speech teacher, and Julio Amador, 7th grader from San Rafael, work on saying words correctly using a phonics rule.

"Speak Out" Speech Class

A number of students go to speech class on a regular basis, individually or in groups. They work on skills to help them improve their speech. The students want to try to talk to hearing people and be able to understand what hearing people say. They claim using the computer and playing speech games are fun activities. Some of them were asked,"Why do you like Speech/Listening Skills?" Here are what they emphasized:

Jeni Jackerson - age 10
"I like speech because it is fun. Sometimes I go to a fast food restaurant and I need to tell them what I want."

Charles Herbold - age 9
"... because I can communicate with hearing people."

Sal Guido - age 7
"Singing, playing, learning words, that's why I'm happy!"

Promotion and Awards Ceremony

A Promotion and Awards Ceremony takes place annually in June to honor fifth graders who move on to Middle School in the following school year.

Below are the names of *Supervising Teacher and Principal* from 1935 to present:

Edna L. Wolf, *Supervising Teacher* - 1935 to 1965
Evelyn Shellgrain, *Supervising Teacher/Principal* - 1965 to 1977
Patricia Dorrance, *Principal* - 1977 to 1985
Leslie Ladd, *Principal* - 1985 to 1992
Sharon Vickers, *Principal* - 1992 to 1998
Eugene LaCosse, *Principal* - 1998 to present

A Letter of Appreciation to CSD-Fremont

We enjoyed reading the letter in the November 22, 1996, issue of *The California News* from Mr. Richard Mendugno, a new parent who recently moved here from Canada. He was describing the positive attributes of the school that led to his decision to relocate to Fremont to provide better opportunities for his deaf daughter. Like him and many other parents, we moved to this area so that our children could benefit from the finest school in the country. For this reason, we care deeply about the quality of education our children are receiving and want very much to be a partner in this process. We value the opportunity to work closely with the teachers, administration and parents who share our commitment to make CSD the best it can be.

In the process of working to make CSD an even better school, it is easy for all of us to concentrate on problems and forget to take the time to appreciate the positive aspects that are already in place. This is why we enjoyed Mr. Mendugno's letter as it reinforces our feelings that Fremont is the place to be.

More specifically, we have found the physical environment of the many classrooms and surrounding areas to be bright and colorful with creative presentation of the work of students and teachers. We like the fact that the ratio of deaf and hearing staff is equal throughout the school. We find the signing abilities of many staff and parents to be commendable. We appreciate the commitment among the staff to create a "deaf friendly" environment at the school by signing all the time. We value the diversity in the school population, both among the students and staff. We are often thrilled when our children are challenged appropriately. We are positively overwhelmed with the wealth of after-school activities that are available for our children. We admire the dedication of many staff members. We take delight in the interest exhibited by many hearing parents and staff in learning more about deaf culture. We love the open invitation by the school to visit and maintain close contact with the staff.

With children in three different departments (middle school, elementary school, and pre-school), we look forward to many more years of collaboration to provide our children with the kind of education they deserve. We thank you for making this possible.

Tom and Kathy Holcomb
Parents of *Leala, Tara and Gary*

Middle School Department-
Faring into the World of Innovations

Starting in 1932, the Middle School was named the Intermediate Department when the new primary school building opened for both intermediate and elementary departments. Prior to the fall of 1932, all classes from first to senior grades were combined under a supervising teacher in a red brick educational building. The name was again changed to Junior High in the 1950s. Since 1992, it has been called the Middle School.

Twenty-four hour communication access to Principal Celia May Baldwin. At this writing, Baldwin is promoted to the position of Dean of Student Life. Robin Zane takes her place.

The Middle School Department is comprised of 6th, 7th, and 8th grades adhering to a curriculum based upon the state curriculum framework. Each student is required to take two periods of English, a period each of science, social studies, and mathematics. The English department, covering both reading and writing, is a high proponent of literature. Each student is taught to read and discuss classic literature identified by grade levels on the list.

In addition to this special needs program, there is a curriculum designed for multi-handicapped students. Normally, there are two or three classes with lower teacher-student ratio, focusing on functional academic and living skills. The daily schedule is complemented by a period of physical education in addition to the following pre-planned enrichment courses such as: arts and crafts, deaf studies, family life education, creative drama, study skills, board games, journalism, leadership training, or critical thinking skills. As for eighth graders, the vocational department's exploration program is planned to sample different vocational classes.

Exciting Innovations Involved

A Theme for Each Class

A number of innovations have been developed under the leadership of Celia May Baldwin, who in 1989 was appointed as the first deaf female principal. These changes have evidently motivated the Middle School students educationally. One of the most exciting innovations is each class has its own name in lieu of regular grades such as 6A, 7b, or 8C. "New" names for classes have a specific theme every year. For instance, during the school year of 1997-98, the theme is "the sky is the limit." The names for 6th grades are "ceaseless," "limitless," "unfathomable" and "cosmic." For 7th grades they are "everlasting," "eternal," "macrocosmic" and "immeasurable." For 8th grades, "infinite," "universal," "amaranthine" and "boundless."

Rope Courses

Mental and physical challenges at the Challenge Sonoma Adventure Ropes Course in Sonoma, California, has been one of the high points of activities of the Middle School. The event has occurred from time to time whenever a fund is available. Taking Rope Courses, students and teachers test their agility, coordination, and nerves while climbing. As for the education aspect, lessons in team building, safety training, and development of self-confidence are highly beneficial.

Middle School students undertaking mental and physical challenges at the Challenge Sonoma Adventure Ropes Course in Sonoma to test their agility, coordination, and nerves while climbing ladders and balancing on high tension rope bridges.

Space Camp

For several years, the Sertoma Space Camp for the Hearing Impaired in Huntsville, Alabama, has invited some students of the Middle School to participate in the space camp program. The students are selected based on their academic accomplishments. The exciting events are to obtain experience learning about science and space in a hands-on type of environment, to pursue science and space related careers, and to have an opportunity to interact while exploring the different aspects of the United States Space program. The former participants stated that they were so fortunate to obtain this kind of special experience and better understanding of what the U. S. space program is all about. CSDF covers the tuition of the space camp which costs about $500. The parents of participants are asked to take care of the travel expenses.

Teacher Ethan Bernstein enlightening the eighth grade students on American history by using the multimedia technology to review the final trimester examinations. At this writing, Bernstein is promoted to high school principal.

Other Educational Events

- Annually, all teachers are disguised in full Halloween costume to "spook" all students to work harder on that day.
- Students learn how to raise money and donate it to a needy family at the Deaf Community Center.
- Seventeen weeks of the D.A.R.E. program for 6th graders keep students from drugs.
- An annual traditional storytelling contest is a popular learning experience for everyone.
- Every Monday morning the principal holds an assembly with the students to kick off the week and provide information on the week's events.
- Biennially students set up their science projects at the science fair.
- Visits from and to Horner Junior High are one of the highlights. Students make new friends and hearing students find a joy in learning ASL.
- Every year famous authors and illustrators pay a visit to CSDF and inspire many students to publish books for the contest.

Annually, the Middle School concludes its school year with a special 8th grade promotional ceremony. It is at that point that students officially transfer from Middle School to High School. With this department's emphasis of comprehensive education nurturing each student's academic, social and leadership potential, the 8th grade students are generally primed for a highly successful transition to High School.

Below is a list of the supervising teachers and principals:

Supervising Teacher / Principals

Mary W. Robinson, *Supervising Teacher* - 1935 to 1958

Erwin Marshall, *Supervising Teacher / Principal* - 1958 to 1979

Emory Marsh, *Principal* - 1979 to 1984

Ronald Stern, *Principal* - 1984 to 1989

Celia May Baldwin, *Principal* - 1989 to 1999

Robin Zane, *Principal* - 1999 to present

At the Middle School's January 4, 1999 assembly, Astronaut Steve Smith inspired the students with his talk about a space walk and a space suit he wore while he was fixing the Hubble Space Telescope. He explained that there were eight layers of fabric to protect him against micro meteorites. At the end of the assembly, Smith presented the school a plaque with an American flag that traveled with him on the shuttle Discovery for four million miles into outer space. Art Jimenez, left, Art's son James Jimenez, Celia Baldwin, Astronaut Steve Smith. (The Jimenez family has known Steve Smith for many years.)

SPECIAL UNIT DEPARTMENT- *TRANSITIONAL STEPS*

During the 1960s and early 1970s, the increase in the number of deaf youngsters with additional handicapping conditions became apparent to the staff of the California School for the Deaf-Berkeley. These children did not respond to the regular classroom setting or dormitory environment, demonstrating severe behavior problems and learning difficulties. Hence, in 1975 with funding provided by a Title VI-B grant, the school established a special unit with emphasis on smaller class size and lower student/house parent ratios.

Principal Les Rudy, 1975 to 1979.

Les Rudy was appointed first principal of the Special Unit. He transferred from the California School for the Deaf-Riverside, where he was principal of the Special Unit for six years. He received intensive training in the area of behavior and classroom management from Dr. Frank Hewitt, Professor at University of California-Los Angeles and author of *The Engineered Classroom, an Approach to Education of Emotional Disturbed Children.*

In the fall of 1976, the unit was expanded from 28 children to 52 children. The month of September was set aside for the arrival of the students for intensive training for instructional staff and residence counselors in the areas of behavior management, classroom and dormitory settings, and curriculum.

Renovation took place in Birck Hall for classrooms and the first floors of Runde and Norton Halls for dormitories which had been closed for four years due to earthquake hazards. Walt Thompson (Kip Phillips) assumed the role of Supervising Instructional Counselor, supervising sixteen residential staff.

All classes were self-contained. A staff psychologist was included in dealing primarily with student behavior. The Special Unit program successfully continued in the new school in Fremont. A separate academic building and two cottages were designed only for Special Unit children. The programs grew to become more meaningful with both an educational as well as functional curriculum. Expectations were raised.

The awards for their achievements instilled pride, motivation, and self-esteem in the Special Needs students. At right, Principal Eugene LaCosse.

- In 1992, the first pre-school class was started.
- Pre-vocational skills and community/ job awareness were expanded.
- Students learned to travel independently to and from their work sites in Fremont.
- Students participated in the annual Winter Play and Special Olympic Games.
- Students participated in campusˆ celebrations of traditional cultural events.
- Students contributed significantly to relief events which benefit the homeless, elderly and victims of natural disasters.

In 1996, the Special Unit Department was dissolved by merging with the regular academic departments. Students continue to receive appropriate instruction and curriculum along with greater opportunities for socialization with other students and development of a wider variety of work choices. The two residential cottages maintain special living programming for certain youngsters.

Below is the list of the Special Unit principals:

Special Unit Principals

Les Rudy - 1975 to 1979
Eugene LaCosse - 1979 to 1992
Dr. Ted Michaud - 1992 to 1996

High School Department-
Striding into Maturity

Typical 1904 classroom setting with teacher William Caldwell, later principal, 1920-27.

The largest academic department on campus, the High School, serves over 225 students annually in both required and elective courses. As part of the California Challenge School Initiative to raise learning standards and expectations, the high school prepares young adults for productive employment and citizenship while helping them gain an appreciation of the intrinsic value of a disciplined, liberal education. To that end, approximately thirty faculty members provide classes in the standard disciplines: the English language arts, the natural sciences,

Modern classroom for physics under the guidance of teacher Bill Baim. The students doing an experiment on free fall by using a gravity drop electronic timer. Microsoft Excel being used to make graph of two areas: length of free fall and time of travel.

To prepare for higher education, algebra teacher Clark Brooke giving individual attention to the students.

social sciences, and mathematics; and through electives as diverse as art, public speaking, broadcast journalism, photography, deaf studies, family life education, service learning, traffic safety education, leadership, computer programming and literacy. The high school department seeks to provide high quality, meaningful learning experiences to a diverse group of students whose enthusiasm, talent, and capacity for academic challenges make CSDF a unique place to learn.

Student learning experiences are supported through a comprehensive curriculum founded upon the State of California Frameworks in each of the disciplines; integration of the English Language Arts to support learning across that curriculum; and preparation for student examination against State Proficiency Standards.

Special Programs within the high school provide additional support to learners who may face particular challenges concerning what they learn and/or how they learn. The Practical Language in Applied Settings Program (PLAS) and the Special Needs Program are two such supports, representing integral elements of the high school program. The School^to^Career Program and Ohlone Work Program assist the secondary department in better preparing students for productive employment and applied learning upon graduation. Advance study at Ohlone Community College and Mission San Jose High School are additional academic options for qualified CSDF students.

Beyond the core academic program and special programs, the high school learning experience is enriched through a variety of special learning events as described below.

Annual Spring Play

The Annual Spring Play is an important event in the lives of high school students. Every year a large number of students has a chance to audition. In the past, the staff members directed the plays. For the last ten years, CSD has hired a professional director to prepare an entertaining play. More information about this topic is featured in "Portrayal of CSD Spring Plays" in this book.

Driver Education

Driver Education has been an integral part of each student's program since the middle of the 1960s. Prior to 1969, the program was offered part-time to a few students. In 1969, the program was offered to all students. Currently it is open only to juniors and seniors. Classroom driver education is taught daily during the fall trimester. During the first part of November, a representative from the Department of Motor Vehicles visits the school and gives the DMV written test to the students. A video cassette tape in ASL and manually coded in English is available for students who have difficulty reading the written test.

Practicum is offered to students during the winter and spring trimesters. The instructor maintains contact with parents during this time and recommends the kind of practice students need to be given at home to prepare them for their driver license. Stanley Bringer has been an instructor from 1969 to present. During his 30 years of experience teaching in the driver education at CSD-Berkeley and CSDˆFremont, he proudly reports there have been no accidents!

Whenever students need some help with their school life adjustment, adjustment teacher Edward Leighton is available in offering advice. Leighton with student Lidia Lindahl, '02. The other adjustment teachers are: Juddie Lamberton with the Elementary School, Laura Keen with the Middle School and Ann MacIntre with the Special Needs.

BIENNIAL SCIENCE FAIR

The High School Department exhibits the school wide science fair biennially. At one time, a huge banner with a flying saucer proclaiming the theme, TO BOLDLY GO, which meant that the students were not afraid to try new things. The purpose of the Science Fair is to give the students first hand experiences in developing their own experiments. The students have to follow the scientific method, where they have to identify a problem, form a hypothesis, observe the results and/or gather data, then form a conclusion based upon the interpretation of their data and/or observations.

With the information form their own conceived experiment the students stimulate other students' interest in science.

STORYTELLING COMPETITION AND AUTHOR / ILLUSTRATOR WORKSHOP

Annually in the spring, CSDF presents the Author/ Illustrator Workshop for all academic departments. Several well-known authors/ illustrators are usually invited to share their experiences in writing and illustrating with students. A number of students are inspired to develop their writing and storytelling skills. Also, they are involved in contests for best storytelling, illustrating and writing.

Graduation ceremony taking place in the quadrangle at the Berkeley school. Note the eagle on the roof overseeing annual event.

CLOSE-UP PROGRAM

For the first time in 1975, CSDB along with 87 high schools in the San Francisco Bay Area, was invited to participate in the Close-Up Program in Washington, D. C. Close-Up is a week long government studies program for high school students and teachers. Washington is a classroom where participants meet and discuss government with Congress people and witness the "living" system. It also creates a more realistic opportunity for involvement in and better understanding of our democratic process. Every year CSD tries to raise fellowship funds to send several students with a teacher to this enriching experience.

High School students in Gina Wood's English class evaluated CSD's new literary program. *Has CSD's literary program affected you? If so, how?*

"They helped me analyze the books and their meanings better. I have a better understanding of literature."
Julie Dolezal, '98

"I felt that program was trying to encourage me to read more! It affected me to want to read more!"
Jenny Contreras, '99

"Yes, by teaching. Teachers give us a lot of information that I never knew."
Grant Grahmann, '99

"I've learned to be open and to read different books, not just one kind."
Pauline Gonzales, '99

Other students stated::

"YES, It teaches me and shows me how to write essays and how to analyze poetry."

"NO, because I've always loved reading and I challenge myself; in another way the literary program has broadened my mind."

Student's Organizations

Academic life is imbued with the social and political scene through such student organizations as Junior National Association of the Deaf (Jr. NAD); Student Body Government (SBG); Student Council (SC); and freshman, sophomore, junior, and senior class organizations which focus upon student governance and finance with occasional service to the community.

CSD's Student Body has been in existence since 1936 with its focus on developing students, leadership skills in both the academic and residence areas. Officers are elected annually and they are responsible for such events as the Prom, winter fun activities, welcome and farewell parties among other events and activities. These have become traditions for some years now.

The principal obligation of the high school is to provide a happy, healthy, and challenging academic environment for students. The principal obligation of students is to contribute productively to that environment, thus creating an interesting, motivating, and amicable place to grow.

Below is a list of High School Principals and Assistant High School Principals from 1935 to 2000.

High School Supervising Teacher / Principals

Marshall S. Hester, *Supervising Teacher* - 1935 to 1944
Myron A. Leenhouts, *Principal and Supervising Teacher* - 1944 to 1958
Gilbert Delgado, *Supervising Teacher* - 1958 to 1964
F. Eugene Thomure, *Supervising Teacher* - 1964 to 1965
Ralph Neesam, *Supervising Teacher* - 1966 to 1970
Ralph Neesam, *Principal* - 1971 to 1972
Dean Swaim, *Principal* - 1972 to 1978
Ted Michaud, *Principal* - 1978 to 1992
Ellen Gorman Winters, *Principal* - 1992 to 1996
Dawn Riley, *Instructional Principal* - 1996 to 1997
Susan Loggins, *Instructional Principal* - 1997 to 1998
Gary W. Olsen, *Administrative Principal* - 1996 to 1999
Laura Peterson, *Academic Principal* - 1999 to Present
Ethan Bernstein, *Administrative Principal* - 1999 to Present

Assistant High School Principals

Ellen Gorman Winters - 1988 to 1992
Eugene LaCosse - 1992 to 1996

CAREER EDUCATIONAL / VOCATIONAL DERPARTMENT- *STEPPING TOWARD EMPLOYMENT*

The goal of the Career Education/Vocational Department is to prepare students for transition from school to work by assisting them in developing appropriate work habits, attitudes, and employability skills which enable them to successfully engage in employment or post-secondary training. The department offers pre-vocational and vocational training, career awareness activities, career counseling, work experience, transition activities, and conducts an annual graduate follow-up study. A community-based instruction program is offered for special needs students.

BRIEF HISTORY

In 1869, when CSD moved to Berkeley from San Francisco, the first two trades for vocational training, shoemaking and cabinetmaking, were established. A short account of the advent of the vocational department can be found in the excerpt of the 100-year history of CSD by Caroline Burnes and Catherine Ramger. During the 1870s, carpentry, gardening, and woodcarving were added to the vocational program. Printing, which was started in 1884, and woodworking are the only early trades that still exist in the present vocational program. Shoe repair and leather work were discontinued in 1966.

In 1913, many new trades were developed with a total of 15 trades taught that year. The new trades were: art, barbering, basket making, bookbinding,

Cabinet making was one of the first vocational training programs established in 1869.

Printing was started in 1884 and always been a popular trade at CSD.

Sewing and power machine operation was part of the vocation training from 1928 to 1975.

"Since the beginning of the Job Placement in 1985, the business community in Fremont and the Bay Area has been very supportive in providing many meaningful employment opportunities for junior and seniors. Enthusiastic employers have hired and trained students in a variety of positions."

Pat Moore
Vocational Principal

domestic science, dressmaking, painting, sewing and typewriting. Trades such as dairying, rug weaving, silk weaving, rope slicing and whipping, were taught but only for a brief period between 1917-1921. Baking, sloyd, horticulture and power machine operation were added to the vocational training program during the years of 1928 to 1936 but sloyd and power machine operation were eliminated in 1975. In 1964, upholstery was added and discontinued in 1988. A survey of the Vocational Training Program in 1965 indicated the need for an expansion of vocational areas in relation to labor market demands. The following year a major change was the separation of offset printing from the letterpress shop and the addition of equipment to enable complete training in the offset printing field. In 1968 a new auto body shop opened in a free standing building near the gymnasium, equipped with two work areas, a paint booth and equipment for auto body repairs.

MOST SUCCESSFUL TRADES, PRE-TECHNOLOGY ERA

Baking was one of the most successful trades taught at the Berkeley school between 1932 and 1972. A large number of students received intensive training in baking and became excellent employees in the bread and pastry business. One of them, Michael Skropeta, is the owner of a successful baking business, The Cake Box in Lafayette, California.

Graphic Arts, known as printing, was the other triumphant story as numerous former students became employed in the printing industries, from newspaper to small shops all over the country. A number of alumni own/owned printing businesses.

The CSD baking shop used to prepare breads, sweet rolls and cakes to feed the students at Berkeley and turned a number of students to be professional bakers.

CAREER PREPARATION

Vocational teachers provide students the opportunity to master the competencies in the California Vocational Statewide Curriculum frameworks which address standards required for competitive employment in the current job market. The eight vocational programs (Auto Body, Business Office Technology, Construction Technology. FEAST- Food Education, Art and Service Training, Graphic Arts, Horticulture Science, Mechanical Drawing, and Woodworking) and the Career Exploration Class have Vocational Advisory Committees (VAC) to provide advice on: instructional content, facilities, safety standards, equipment/technology needs, and industry standards. VAC membership is composed of representatives from business/industry, students, parents, community colleges, Regional Occupational Programs, and Department of Rehabilitation counselors. In addition to receiving advice from VAC members, each vocational teacher has a representative from the California Department of Education who provides updated information on curriculum standards.

A noteworthy accomplishment of seven vocational teachers has been their efforts to obtain Program Certification from the California Department of Education (CED). From 1995 to 1999, the programs listed are designated in the statewide Program of Excellence Career-Vocational Education Program Improvement and Certification System. The programs met the criteria and were certified as *Programs of Excellence*. The teachers' names were placed on a statewide honor roll and they received plaques from the CED.

Eighth and ninth grade students participate in a vocational exploration program where they sample the vocational classes. Students then select a vocational major and take courses throughout their high school career. The Career Exploration Class was added in 1987 and became a graduation requirement for all students in 1988. The course teaches students how to prepare for employment, and students create a portfolio which they use during job interviews and appointments with Department of Rehabilitation (DR) counselors.

Art is often one of hidden talents the CSD students discover in art class. Lanetra Williams expressing herself with acrylics.

The 1999 Yearbook Supplementary prepared by the seniors.

Yearbook / Web Page Team

Responsibility for creating the CSD Yearbook moved to the Vocational Department in 1992. The Class of 1994 voted to change the name of the ***Eagle*** yearbook to the ***Bell Tower*** yearbook. The Bell Tower is proudly displayed on their yearbook cover. The *CSD Bell Tower* is a student produced publication, and it remains a highly coveted honor to be selected for the yearbook staff.

Another exciting event was the Business Office Technology class which made its debut on-line in December, 1997. The following students created CSD's first homepage and sent CSD into cyberspace: Jay Baldridge, Aaron Bate, Chamroeum Dee and Jason Lamberton. The Web Page Organization was then established.

Students in both organizations take great pride in their work and strive to do better than the classes before them!

School-to-Career

The first School-to-Career direction was FEAST. A STC coordinator, a career counselor and a team of three teachers work together as a team to provide students with the skills they need to do relevant projects based on an integrated curriculum across four disciplines — English, mathematics, career exploration, and FEAST. Project FEAST was started at CSD-Berkeley in 1972. It was planned so that instruction in areas other than food service and preparation reinforced the occupational training. STC is nowadays part of a

Bryan Stanfield cutting shallots to prepare a business-like lunch for four guests, part of the competition.

The students, left, Michael McAdams, Alesia Jepson, Bernie Rada under the guidance of teacher Jeanne Loustalot, preparing hand shaped cookies so called "shaking hands" for a retirement tea reception.

national movement to reform education in the United States. It provides rigorous, relevant curriculum based on academic and industry standards. Academic and vocational/technical teachers work collaboratively to provide an integrated curriculum to students. The curriculum is organized around the student's vocational major or career pathway. FEAST was the pioneer career pathway in 1997.

Wall clock made by Manuelito Vallente won first place in the vocational competition in 1993.

Vocational Competition

The annual Vocational competition began in 1990 and has become an important and exciting aspect of the vocational program. The competition is held at CSD and VAC members and other representatives from businesses judge the students' vocational/technical projects, the Career Exploration Class job interviewing contest, and the Art students' creative endeavors. This event is a public relations coup for the school, and it provides the students with the opportunity to showcase their talents. With a focus on pride in producing quality work, cash prizes are awarded to first, second, and third place winners. Judges come from prestigious companies such as Safeway, Costco, Raley's, Microage, LSI Logic, Sun Microsystems, Hilton Hotel, and Lawrence Livermore Lab.

Ben Lewis, Mickey Mouse table and four chairs won second place in the woodworking competition in 1998.

Career Center

Career counselors assist students with developing realistic high school and post-secondary plans, and monitor their transition progress. Utilizing career awareness activities at school and in the community, they help students become more aware of their interests and aptitudes and the labor market. They work with community agencies, and conduct college preparation activities and parent workshops.

"It is always such an uplifting experience for me to visit with so many dedicated teachers and gifted students. I thoroughly enjoyed visiting all the classrooms and talking about your School-to-Career program. Observing what the students are doing is absolutely fascinating."

Delaine Eastin
State Superintendent of Public Instruction

The conception of the Career Center originated when Dean Swaim was Vocational Principal. Marcia Downie, Work Experience Coordinator, Debi Wilkinson, Hire Learning Coordinator, and Jill Cohen, Hire Learning Job Placement Specialist worked to solicit donations of funds and labor to refurbish a portable building for the "Career Center." It opened in 1986. Actually, it was Marcia Downie, who started career education by writing several grants that enabled the school to hire a staff to run career counseling and job placement in 1978.

Students participate in work experience opportunities in developmental stages (on-campus work, community volunteer work, and off-campus work placements). Job placement specialists, assisted by sign language interpreters and support staff, help students succeed in off-campus jobs. They conduct a job search class for working students' support group, interpret for job interviews, train students on the job, educate employers about Deaf students, and monitor students' progress at work.

Most juniors and seniors receive additional assistance from an on-campus DR Counselor of the Deaf. A full array of DR services, continuing beyond graduation, help these students implement their post-secondary plans.

Career Counseling/Transition Planning: Steve Orman working with Phaivanh Xayavong, a senior at CSD, on his after graduation transition plans. Xayavong is working on his application for a Cal Trans Service Assistant Position near Bakersfield.

Awards

A number of the vocational teachers received awards for their excellence in teaching work and other endeavors. Marcia Downie of Career Education received the *Sustained Superior Accomplishment* award for service to California State Department of Education in 1989. She had a vision to provide quality employment preparation services to students, set goals, and achieved them.

The Career Center received an award as the *Job Training Program of the Year* from the Alameda County Training and Employment Board and the Alameda Private Industry Council for the 1988-89 school year.

Mary Danko, the Job Placement Teacher, was selected as *Job Training Professional of the Year* by Alameda County Training and Employment Board for the 1989-1990 school year.

Pat Moore, Career Education/Vocational principal, received the California Department of Education's *Sustained Superior Accomplishment Award* in 1994. She is instrumental in making the Vocational Department and Career Center what they are today. Educational and career preparation standards have been upgraded under Pat Moore's enthusiastic, dedicated, and astute leadership.

Jeanne Loustalot, the FEAST teacher, was the recipient of the California Department of Education (CDE) *Sustained Superior Accomplishment Award* in 1993. Committed to preparing students for employment and a model of excellence, Loustalot's students experienced a high degree of success in the work world.

Bill Ash, the Graphic Arts teacher, and Robert Morrison, the woodworking teacher, Ron Rhodes, the Building Maintenance teacher (changed to Construction Technology in 1998), Gail Wright, the Mechanical Drawing teacher, Charles Farr, the Business Office Technology teacher, Rick Herbold, the Horticulture Science teacher, and Jeanne Loustalot received Program Certification from the California Department of Education.

The University of Arkansas Research and Training Program performed a site review of the Career Education/Vocational Program in the spring of 1999 and determined it to be a model transition program which will be recognized in a national publication.

Here is a list of supervising teachers and principals of the Vocational Department:

SUPERVISING TEACHER'S

Rudolf Wartenberg - 1944 to 1963
Lang Russel - 1963 to 1971

CAREER CENTER / TRANSITION SUPERVISOR

Marcia Downie - 1996 to 1998
Susan Loggins - 1998 to present

PRINCIPAL

Merle Whittom - 1972 to 1984
Dean Swaim - 1984 to 1988
Michael Finneran - 1988 to 1989
Pat Moore - 1989 to present

Brice Pruyn, operating a small offset printing press, pulls off an envelope to check its printing quality.

Volunteer Freddie Stocksick, left, Brice Pruyn, Vina Cornish, Graphic Arts teacher Bill Ash, inspecting together the quality of printing matter before running the Heidelberg GTO press.

Under the guidance of horticulture teacher Rick Herbold, the students learning to tender the landscape and the greenhouse plants, one of the finest vocational training programs offered at CSD.

Dr. Roy Holcomb, known as "Father of Total Communication" and one of the Founders of the International Association of Parents of the Deaf.

Bilingual - Bicultural Equation
ASL and English Together

Through the decades American Sign Language (ASL) was utilized and taken for granted among the schools for the Deaf, clubs for the Deaf, conventions of the National Association of the Deaf, the athletic competition for Deaf adults and many other events. ASL was appreciated by Deaf people while it was not fully accepted by hearing people.

Total Communication

As the 1960s emerged, researchers began to discover that early use of sign language did not really retard a Deaf child's development of speech or writing English as was thought for decades. The philosophy of ASL was more understood when Roy Holcomb, one of the founders of the International Association of Parents of the Deaf and the author of *Hazards of Deafness*, initiated the term, "Total Communication." It was defined as the right of every deaf child to learn to use all forms of communication so that he/she may have the opportunity to develop language competence at the earliest age.

Natural Language

In the 1970s, the interest in American Sign Language, identified as the natural language of the Deaf American people, grew rapidly. Sign language classes spread all over the nation. In the 1980s, the CSD's communication policy had been a prime subject presenting struggle among the committees to reach an agreement on a policy statement. In 1989, Dr. Carol Erting's presentation stirred interest and excitement among the CSD staff members to digest the concepts of the paper, "Unlocking the Curriculum."

Birth of CSD's BI/BI

A Bilingual-Bicultural program was introduced at the staff meeting on March 30, 1990. Dr. Klopping kicked off BI/BI by stating that "We have two cultures and two languages, and these should be celebrated." An explanation of the medical and cultural views of deafness is followed as:

A Change in the Way Deaf People View Themselves — *Pathological View vs. Cultural View*

- ***from disability to ability***
- ***from handicap to culture***
- ***from silent individuals to a vibrant community***
- ***from primitive gestures to a full-fledged language***

In 1991, Marlon Kuntze and Edward Bosso became Bilingual-Bicultural coordinators. They commenced to focus on providing information and raising awareness about bi-bi issues as they pertained to the education of Deaf children. After Bosso left CSD, Kuntze continued being coordinator and newsletter editor until he started his doctorate studies at Stanford University in 1995. However, he conducted numerous meetings with committees to ratify the statement of mission and values.

Statement of Mission and Values

- **Deaf people should be respected and empowered as culturally and linguistically distinct.**
- **American Sign Language (ASL) is the naturally evolving, fullfledged language of the American Deaf community. ASL structure is distinct from English; however, ASL has variations which allow inclusion of English-like vocabulary, phrases, and word order.**
- **Early, consistent and meaningful communication between family and child in whatever form is critical to language development.**
- **Language acquisition of ASL and English should begin as early as possible. Competency in ASL will enhance the ongoing development of English skills.**
- **Fluency in both ASL and written English is necessary and must be emphasized.**
- **Students have the right to an educational environment where they are able to understand and be understood by others.**
- **The ability of students to participate in an increasingly complex world is directly related to how well they are prepared to contribute to and benefit from our democratic society.**
- **Staff members should be competent in ASL and have an understanding of and an appreciation of Deaf culture.**
- **For educational progress to be effective, parents and the Deaf community must be given opportunities for involvement in various facets of school programming and operations.**
- **Relationship with the community at large contributes to the success of the school's mission.**

"If deaf people are to get ahead in our time, they must have a better image of themselves and their capabilities. They need concrete examples of what deaf people have already done so they can project for themselves a brighter future. If we can have Black studies, Jewish studies, why not Deaf studies?"

Frederick Schreiber
Executive Director of
National Association of the Deaf
1971

> ***"Reading may be more important for deaf children than hearing children because that is the only way deaf students can learn English."***
>
> MARLON KUNTZE
> Former CSD teacher and storyteller, currently doctorate student at Stanford University.

Deaf Studies

A new curriculum, an offshoot from the bi-bi objectives is the K-12 Deaf Studies introduced in 1996. The ASL/Deaf Studies Resource Teacher, Dee Kennedy, coordinates the schoolwide Deaf Studies curriculum. Teachers incorporate it into their classes throughout the school. The Resource Center tenders a wealth of Deaf Studies books, magazines, newspapers, posters and videotapes. Also, in the Center are files on notable people in Deaf history as well as files on Deaf agencies, organizations, schools for the deaf, literary works by Deaf people and issues related to Deaf people. Students and teachers take advantage of the vast information available in the Center for class assignments and projects. For instance, Kennedy developed booklets on William "Dummy" Hoy, the legendary first deaf major-leaguer, and Douglas Tilden, the Michelangelo of the West, for class assignments or projects. Also, she provides consultation for schoolwide endeavors such as the d'Estrella Storytelling contest and along with an English Curriculum Specialist, provides in-service workshops for the Author/Illustrator Contest, focusing on Deaf experiences and /or stories with Deaf characters in them.

The Deaf Studies Resource Center offers a wealth of Deaf Studies books, magazines, newspapers, posters and videotapes. Students and teachers take advantage of the vast information available in the Center for class assignments and projects. Deaf Studies Resource teacher Dee Kennedy, left, explaining the potentials of the Deaf Studies material to new teacher Joni Shouse.

PHYSICAL AND CHARACTER BUILDERS

The California School for the Deaf offers quality physical education instruction to classes from the first grade through high school. The department's major purpose is to help develop each child's total potential. From the standpoint of physical education, the goals for each student are to:

- *Develop and maintain a healthy fitness level (Note: Health-related physical fitness involves cardiovascular and muscular endurance, strength and flexibility).*
- *Develop an understanding of why being fit is important and how it is influenced by exercise.*
- *Develop gross motor skills, beginning with fundamental motor skills leading to specific skills in sports, with emphasis on lifetime sports.*
- *Develop understanding of fundamentals and rules of different sports.*
- *Develop abilities in teamwork, self-discipline, and sportsmanship.*

For students who have special medical or motor needs, the school also offers Adapted Physical Education programs.

The department has a grading policy that is based on three primary areas: student participation and attitude; student knowledge and understanding of rules, strategies and terms; student compliance with P.E. attire requirements.

Physical education activities are held outdoors on the school's athletic fields. However, depending on the weather and the type of activity, the gyms are available for student use.

In 1868, the first sport, baseball, was started at CSD in San Francisco a long time before physical education was implemented. In circa 1910, the course of gymnastics was initiated. In 1920, physical education was introduced to the curriculum. Only one instructor for each of the boys and girls class was available until 1973. After the school moved to Fremont, the P.E. staff was expanded to cover all classes from first grade through the twelfth grade.

INTERSCHOLASTIC COMPETITION

CSDF is a full-fledged member of the North Coast Section of California Interscholastic Federation (CIF) and abides by its regulations. Athletics are considered an important component of the comprehensive education program offered by the school. CSDF fields thirteen interscholastic teams during the school year as follows: Fall - boys and girls cross country; girls volleyball; football. Winter - boys and girls basketball; wrestling. Spring - boys and girls track; swimming; girls softball; baseball.

1915-1950 gymnasium in Berkeley.
1950-1980 gymnasium in Berkeley.
1980 to present gymnasium in Fremont..

Fencing and drill team in 1904 in front of Willard Hall.

The students using Reisit-A-Balls to perform abdominal crunches. This exercise improves the students' abdominal strength. The students featured are: back row, Lisa Jarashow, Middle row: Ian Guzman, Omar Guzman, Shanna Grossinger, Ashley Griffith; front: Tenaya Herbold.

The students using Hula-Hoops in an aerobic routine to improve cardiovascular fitness. Cherlynn Welsh, left, Dontae Ramirez, Ashley Griffith, Mac Sabate, Jory Pedersen, Zuelika Prader, Tenaya Herbold, and instructor Deb Ayres.

The physical education staff: Debbie Ayers, Supervisor, front, Ken Pedersen, Bob Ellis, Jodee Dike, Keith Adams, Chris Hamilton.

With the exception of football and wrestling, the school is a member of what many consider to be the State's biggest and finest small schools league, the Bay Counties League (BCL), which is made up of mostly private schools from different parts of the San Francisco Bay Area. Because most schools in the BCL do not field football or wrestling teams, the school is a member of different leagues for football and wrestling.

The highlight of the football, volleyball and spring season sports is usually competition against our sister school, the California School for the Deaf-Riverside. Hosting these exciting games alternates on a yearly basis between the schools. Additionally, there is an annual basketball and cheerleading tournament (The Western Schools Basketball Classic) involving seven other schools for the deaf. Each of the eight schools rotates hosting this tournament. Participating in this tournament is invariably highly exciting and memorable for student athletes and coaches, as well as fans.

More tidings on the feats of CSD interscholastic athletics are in the sports section of this book.

Below are the names of Physical Education Coordinator and Athletic Directors.

Physical Education Director

David Fraley - 1964 to 1975
Debbie Ayers - 1999 to present

Athletic Director

David Fraley - 1975 to 1984
Emory Marsh - 1984 to 1993
Robert Ellis - 1993 to 1996
Dennis Catron - 1996 to 1999
Leonard Gonazles - 1999 to present

Three students jumping rope to improve cardiovascular fitness and quickness. The students featured in this photo are Blair Rasmus, left, Jory Pedersen, Zuelika Prader.

The boys dipping in the new CSD pool in 1916.

The middle school students taking a break from their class and dipping in the Junior Olympic-size pool in Fremont in 1998.

STUDENT LIFE-
24- HOUR LEARNING ON CAMPUS

Supervising Instructional Counselors of the 1970s and 1980s: front left, Mary Thompson, Beverly Stevenson, Doris Morrison, Roberta Alexander. Back left, Ray Rasmus, Walter Thompson, Steve Orman.

SIC group of the 1980s and 1990s: Beverly Stevenson, left, Doris Morrison, Roberta Alexander, Kathy Schroenberg, LeeAnn Dreffs.

When a student steps outside the classroom, he or she finds no lack of things to do. CSDF believes that living on campus is a part-not apart from-the educational experience. Students as well as staff find plenty of opportunities to become involved at CSDF. This leads to a high quality student life program.

Small groups allow students to meet, get to know and study with other students, thus creating a vibrant learning environment. Students, both day and residential, are assigned to certain cottage counselors, who assist them in developing personal, educational and career goals. The cottage counselor staff is therefore a key element in the development process of the deaf child living in the residential setting. Almost every counselor has a special responsibility, like being a sponsor of an organization or being involved in athletics.

Cottages are offered to students who live as far away as Eureka to the north, San Luis Obispo to the south, and as near as San Jose. Each cottage is staffed by residential counselors with an Instructional Counselor leading the program. During the night, night attendants supervise the students in the cottages. Each department has its own supervisor, called a Supervising Instructional Counselor. Placement in cottages is based on age and academic level. Each cottage has at least two living rooms, study areas, a kitchenette and at least five pods. Each pod has two bedrooms (two students to each bedroom) and one bathroom.

Student Life Division handles all the residence departments: Elementary, Middle School, High School, and Special Unit. Student Life offers programs to guide and support personal growth, particularly in the areas of hygiene and self-esteem. Students are strongly encouraged to develop independently-from brushing teeth to driving cars. Life at CSDF is an exciting learning environment, with activities both inside and outside the classroom being equally educationally enriching.

INDEPENDENT LIVING SKILLS FOR SENIORS

The seniors reside in on-campus apartment settings, with one cottage for boys and another for girls. These cottages are part of the independent living skills education program under the guidance of two counselors for each cottage. The curriculum for independent living skills includes budgeting, purchasing and preparing meals, cleaning, studying and using leisure time.

In addition, decorating rooms, preparing dinner and entertainment for invited friends, attending to repairs around the apartment, caring for indoor plants and numerous other details are part of the development of skills.

The Middle school students doing their homework in the relaxing cottage atmosphere.

Playing various games is a pleasant way to spend their leisure in the cottage and the activity centers.

Assistance for New Students

As for new students, the Student Life Department realizes that the transition from home to school can be a difficult experience, but CSDF staff are always on hand to help. From assessment to enrollment, staff see their role as educational as well as practical. They work with new students and parents to meet their needs. Before the start of each school year, new students and parents have an opportunity to familiarize themselves with CSD's environment, scheduling, and staff members by staying on campus during an orientation weekend.

Student Activities

Student Activities provide techniques to develop leadership skills as well as to be part of the group. Informal or casual training, such as help with self-discipline, time-management, self-esteem, and interpersonal communication skills is provided on an ongoing basis throughout the year. A good ratio of students to staff allows students to develop these skills.

More than fifty student groups cover the wide spectrum of students' interests. High School and Middle School snack bars are run by the students themselves with adult supervision when needed. Several of the organizations are as follows: Girl Scouts & Boy Scouts, Brownies, Student Body Government

The students appreciate the opportunity of socializing with friends after their homework in the activity centers or cottages.

(SBG), Foothills Athletic Association (FAA), Student Councils (SC), Jr. Eagles, Amigos, Deaf African American Leadership Council, Junior National Association of the Deaf (Jr. NAD), Special Olympics, intramural program, and Judicial Board. Students participating in organizations learn how to run a meeting, work with diverse groups of people on various issues, communicate effectively with others, and plan a variety of activities.

As for facilities at CSD, regardless of a student's athletic ability, there are readily available athletic or intramural programs in which he or she may participate. The gymnasium has facilities for basketball, wrestling, gymnastics, general exercise, weight room, volleyball and many more sports. An Olympic-size outdoor swimming pool is attached to the gymnasium. Over twenty acres of playing fields are located on the edge of the campus. They are used by all the departments. More information on the sports programs is cited in the sports section of this book.

Proponents of the public residential school have long pointed to the extra-curricular and athletics programs as a pillar of strength of the public residential school.

Special Methods of Training

- The Scouting programs have their own camping trips each year which give scouts enriching and educational experiences.
- The Junior National Association of the Deaf (Jr. NAD) is an organization which holds a biennial convention at a different location throughout the nation, most times at one of the schools for the deaf. Participants gain a rich experience-both educationally and socially, in which they bring their experiences and share ideas with others at CSD. Incidentally, CSD hosted a successful convention in August, 1998.
- The Deaf African American Leadership Council and Amigos provide strong support of their own culture and instill pride in them.
- The focus of the Foothills Athletic Association (FAA) is on athletes as well as non-athletes who contribute to the school with their involvement in interscholastic competition. Each year they have their traditional athletic banquet, awarding "C" letters to athletes and managers.
- Jr. Eagles is a Middle School organization that focuses on student leadership skills. Through this organization, students are able to develop skills through participating in, or presiding over, meetings and by planning an array of events.

Students Aid Others

The Peer Advisor program was re-initiated during the second trimester of the 1997-1998 school year. The program is run by the Student Life office along with the Pupil Personnel office. That first year the staff members, Steve Orman, Cheryl Boyd, and Lin Grossinger led the program. The first peer advisors were

These students getting together for some years at CSD to share tidbits and laughter, and looking toward to a new millennium with zeal.

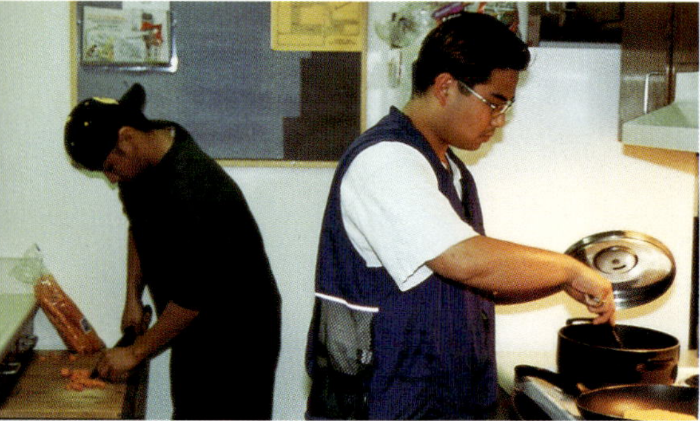

Participating in the independent living skills education program, seniors, Chan Saesee, left, and Stephen Peralta are preparing and cooking dinner for the roomates and themselves.

Danny Peknik, Valerie Hottle, Debbie Xiong, Julio Martinez, Jay Baldridge, and Jena Marie Daviton-Sciandra. The program offers an opportunity for students to work with peers who encounter typical everyday issues. A student who has a relationship problem with another student is a common example of the kinds of assistance a peer advisor would provide.

Students interested in applying for this position must have good academic standing, a strong aptitude, and a desire to work with people. An intensive week-end training retreat along with weekly ongoing training sessions are a requirement. Coping skills, verbal versus nonverbal communication, empathy, communication etiquette and barriers, and understanding resources available for students are a few of many fun filled activities that are learned in the process of becoming a peer advisor.

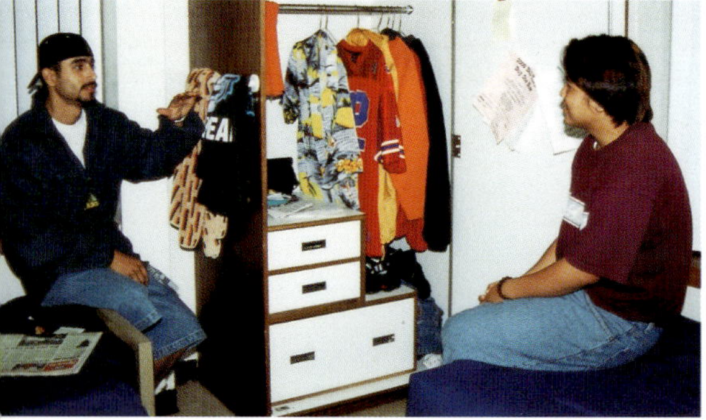

In their bedroom, seniors Ambrocio Valasco, left, and Jan Epitacio discussing their coming graduation.

The 1940s girls challenging in the marble game.

Below is a list of Deans of Students.

Girls and Boys

Ruth K. Birck, *Dean of Girls* - 1928 to 1957
Vernon S. Birck, *Dean of Boys* - 1931 to 1957

Dean of Students

Joseph P. Youngs - 1957 to 1961
Lang Russell - 1961 to 1963
Barry Griffing - 1963 to 1965
Jacob Arcanin - 1965 to 1967
Hubert Summers - January to June, 1968
Paul Small - 1968 to 1975
Kenneth Norton - 1975 to 1990
Michael Finneran - 1990 to 1999
Celia May Baldwin - 1999 to present

A bevy of the Berkeley school girls in 1888.

In early 2000, the news about the new hierarchy of the counseling staff was announced. The Student Life Division underwent some changes in the classifications of personnel in the spring of 2000. SICs (Supervising Instructional Counselors) and ICs (Instructional Counselors) were phased out. Instead, we currently have four SRPs (Supervisors of Residence Programs) who will be responsible for three subdivisions of the whole Student Life Program. Each SRP is assigned three SCs (supervising counselors) and each SC is responsible for two cottages. Special Unit cottages will have one SC each. With this new structure, CSD anticipate that the quality of each program will be enhanced. SRPs will channel time and energy to them. Night attendants will remain to supervise students during the night and early morning.

On a whole, the programs are the same except that both the Residence Department and the Academic Department are working toward the concept of "school and cottage partnership."

A storytelling illustration by the Dean of Girls Ruth Birck, from the 1930s to 1950s.

Weekend Homegoing

In 1977, Senate Bill 871 (Garamendi) was signed by Governor Edmund Brown providing appropriations to the Department of Education's six special schools: two California Schools for the Deaf (Berkeley and Riverside), the California School for the Blind, and the three Diagnostic Schools for Neurologically Handicapped Children. These appropriations are for the purpose of providing transportation to and from the homes of residential students on weekends and for school holiday periods. Passage of this bill was due to the impressive efforts of dedicated parents and friends who were the driving force in lobbying for the state to pay the costs of residential student transportation. Parents want their children at home on weekends so they can maintain their family relationships.

Weekend homegoing makes it possible for parents to maintain their family relationships on weekends. Buses and vans take some residential students home on Friday afternoons and bring them back to school on Sunday evenings.

Activities on the Weekends

Prior to the 1950s' most of the CSD students usually went home on trains as far as San Diego and the Oregon border but only for Christmas and summer vacations. On weekends during the school year, they stayed at school, due to the distance from their homes. In those days roads were two-way highways and some dirt roads in remote farm lands. Most parents could not afford travel expenses for their children to go home weekly. Hence, CSD had various planned activities for students on and off the campus. The activities included organized meetings of the Foothills Athletic Association (FAA), the Girls Athletic Association (GAA), the Literary Society (LS), vocational ethics sessions, morning chapel talks, evening storytelling, silent movies, holiday parties, FAA and GAA banquet and dances, and the Junior Class Play. The off campus activities included field trips, Scout camping, hiking, San Francisco treats, and watching the University of California football games. Also, students had abundant free time to play indoor games, softball games with staff members, sports practice, decorating for dances, and numerous other creative activities.

Since all residential students started going home for weekend in 1978, most of the activities mentioned above have to be held during weekdays, usually on Thursday evenings. Often students are permitted to stay on the campus during weekends for special occasions such as the annual "Big Game" with the Riverside school, basketball, volleyball, wrestling tournaments, football games on Saturday, and Scout campouts.

Ten school buses and 15 minibuses are scheduled to haul some students home every weekend.

Transportation Services

Prior to 1978, parents were responsible for the costs of transporting their children to and from CSD. Students who went home but were not picked up by family cars were escorted to and from Bay Area Rapid Transit and Greyhound stations in Oakland and San Francisco by CSD staff members of the residence department. Parents paid for their children's tickets.

In 1975, an enterprising group of parents in the San Joaquin County area were determined to organize and manage their own bus system. They held rummage sales, cake sales, and garage sales to raise funds and purchase their own 33 passenger bus. One of the parents drove the bus and other parents functioned as bus monitors. After SB 871 took effect on January 1, 1978, the parent group disbanded but the bus stops and routes that they arranged are still in operation with the Elk Grove Charter bus.

Expansion of the Transportation System

When CSD moved to Fremont in 1980, a greatly expanded Homegoing System was developed. More than eight charter buses and four CSD's school buses have handled the growing and complex needs of student travel to diverse locations. Since there is an adequate freeway system in the state, it has made

The students often invite their school friends to visit with family during weekends.

Safety is the top priority in the transportation. Every year CSD students perform a school bus emergency evacuation drill as required by law. David Huck, left, Jan Epitacio, and Tommy Nelson-Higgins learning new skills in evacuation techniques.

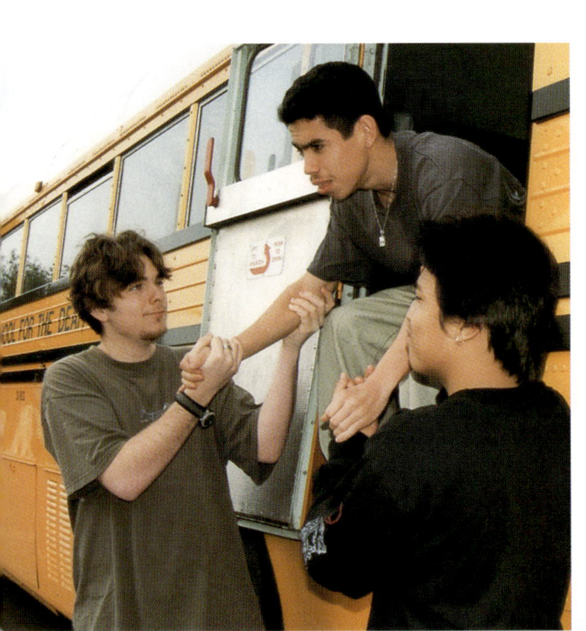

rapid travel possible. Between 1980 and 1984, two instructional counselors, John Standsfield and Dot Brown, set up the basic structure of the present system of charter buses, Rapid Transit, and airlines. During this period, day student home-to-school transportation, and all field trips including athletics became the responsibility of the transportation office.

The enlarging of the transportation system resulted in a new job classification at CSD, one which required a school bus driver certificate. The Transportation Coordinator position was created in 1984 and functions under the direction of the Dean of Students and assistant, Roberta Alexander. The first person to hold the position was Marlene Vance, 1984-86. The subsequent coordinators were Eric Marin, 1986-87, Dot Brown, 1987-89, and Laurolyn Bennett, 1989-present. In addition to its charter contractors and public transportation modes, CSD operates four of its own school buses and thirteen vans, which are in constant use for homegoing, educational, and recreational trips. As for weekend homegoing, students usually leave the campus on buses at two P.M. on Fridays. They return to school on Sundays after 7:00 P.M.

THE CLASSIC STORY

(This article was written by Sostenes E. Alvarez who was transferred from a mainstreamed school to CSDF in 1990. This gives the genuine feeling of how a number of transferees express the comparison between schools. Factually, 49 out of 50 transfers recount similar classic stories. Here is Alvarez's version.)

"I became a member of the residential students the last week of September, 1990. I was transferred from Skyline High School, a mainstream school in Oakland, because my family moved to Lodi and that school district enrolled me here at the California School for the Deaf in Fremont.

I began to have lots of friends compared to my mainstream school.

At first I lived in Cottage 9, which is one of the senior apartments. I really enjoyed myself there because it's independent living skills apartment, where I learned to cook and do my duties. Also, the same day I joined Cottage 9, I was selected to become the Independent Living Skills treasurer. I was shocked because the seniors hardly knew me. I also participated in the yearbook for one trimester. I really enjoyed learning about the yearbook's activities in a variety of ways.

When my career education teacher, Debi Wilkinson, told me how many units I had left to graduate, we decided to put me into the 11th grade, so I am now in the class of 1992. I understand and accept this transfer because of my need to have more experiences on campus.

Later this year I moved to Cottage 11, which seemed OK to me. I have no reason to complain. In fact, I became the most outstanding student in Cottage 11. I think the students were impressed.

This year I participated in the school play called the "The Wild Minds." I was the interpreter in the 'Dream' and played Greenfeet in 'The Bear Hunt' with Bob Hiltermann as the director of the show. My friends Phillip Tooch, Tom Olguin, Jennifer Castillo, Theron Parker, Jessica Miller, and I were picked to go to the California State University Northridge to perform 'The Bear Hunt.' We traveled around Los Angeles for a short time at night after we watched the show called the 'Gin Game.' It was so good and I met some of the deaf stars and got their autographs.

I also made the baseball team this year where I played left field. My batting average was .357.

Throughout this year I have learned and gotten experience about the deaf world, which I didn't get being raised in mainstream schools. I had a hard time getting involved in activities with hearing students, but after I joined CSD, things are different. I really enjoy being social with deaf students. I've developed many friendships and it's easy to communicate with them and with the staff too!"

Sostenes E. Alvarez
Class of 1992

CHAPTER FOUR

AUXILIARY SERVICES

Component Elements of Education

One of the major facets of the CSD's education program is the supporting services which sprawl throughout every corner of the campus. Without these services, the progress of the education program would be totally hampered.

The business office provides fiscal and personnel service for the school and provides the management of the plant operation. The plant operation encompasses building maintenance, janitorial service, kitchen service, watchmen, heat, and grounds care.

These auxiliary services are as important as pupil personnel, outreach, media program, library, and the Computer-assisted *Learning Lab.*

Pupil Personnel Services

Pupil Personnel Services (PPS) provide a variety of support services to the California School for the Deaf, Fremont community, as well as to other programs for deaf and hard of hearing students in Northern California. Direct services available to CSDF students include work with social workers, guidance counseling, psychological and educational evaluations. Indirect services to students are provided through consultation with parents, teachers, student life counselors, and administrators in regard to students' social, emotional and educational needs. In 1979 the Northern California Assessment Center for the Deaf was added to provide in-depth evaluations for deaf and hard of hearing students not enrolled at CSD.

In the paragraphs that follow PPS describes in more depth the nature of these services.

Counseling Department

Guidance counselors provide confidential individual, group and family counseling, with the goal of maximizing students' abilities to benefit from their educational programs. Counseling services are provided to meet students' needs as identified in the Individual Education Plan (IEP). In addition, the Counseling Department provides short term counseling, crisis intervention, support groups, prevention, mental health education, and consultation to staff.

Linda Grossinger, Supervisor, Counseling Center (left); Ann Moxley, Supervisor, Assessment Services; (middle) and Deborah Guthmann, Director, Division of Pupil Personnel Services.

Preceding spread: Students of the California School for the Deaf-Fremont.

Counseling Department: Fred Morrison, one of the guidance counselors discussing the personal potentials with a student. The other guidance counselors: Marilyn May, Audrey Webb, Carol Cambone, Frank Lester, Debbie Green, Roberta Mineo; Lindsay Gimble, Social Worker; Natasha Kordus, Behavior specialist; Patty Albee, Psychologist.

Social Work

The Social worker is the primary liaison between CSD and community agencies including Department of Social Services, Child Protective Services, foster care programs and mental health agencies. The Social Worker collaborates with psychologists, social workers, attorneys, probation officers and the police. The social Worker also provides case management services.

Positive Behavioral Intervention (PBI)

A behavioral specialist conducts functional analysis assessments, writes behavior plans,and provides consultation services for students who exhibit serious behavior problems that interfere with their ability to access their educational program. The behavior specialist also offers consultation and training to school and residence staff on a variety of behavioral issues.

Assessment Services

Assessment Services provide enrollment, three-year, and in-depth learning style assessment to all CSDF students through a multi-disciplinary approach.

EXCERPTS

from the letters written by parents to Dr. Ann Moxley and Penny Gaucheff, Northern California Assessment Center (NCAC).

We are writing to thank you for your diagnostic evaluation of our son. . . .

We were amazed by the comprehensiveness of the evaluation and the thoroughness of your approach. We learned a great deal more about our son, including a few things that surprised us. . . .

I want to express our thanks for the highest level of professional assistance and excellent service which we received at NCAC. . . .

The school cafeteria serves good nutrition daily but at times also students' favorite pizzas at lunch or supper time. The salad bars are also available in the dining rooms. Four separate dining rooms for elementary, middle, high school students and staff members are available.

Student Health Unit

The function of the Student Health Unit is to maintain medical screening and monitoring of medical conditions, dispense medications, treat minor medical problems and injuries, provide temporary care for ill students, and preserve school medical records. The medical staff maintains professional and open communication with students, all school staff, and parents. The staff consists of five registered nurses, one nurse practitioner, and one part-time physician. The Student Health Unit is open twenty-four hours a day, five days a week.

Neat Family

The CSDF Neat Family is a group of students who support each other to stay sober and drug-free. The group meetings consist of activities and lively discussions, designed to help students discover who they are and what they want in life—to take charge of their lives instead of just following others into trouble. The group is strictly confidential, and is led by two energetic group leaders who do not work at CSD, so that students may feel free to talk openly without later seeing their leader around campus.

Northern California Assessment Center for the Deaf and Hard-of-Hearing

The Northern California Assessment Center for the Deaf and Hard-of-Hearing (NCAC) provides free, comprehensive diagnostic and prescriptive evaluations of Deaf and Hard-of-Hearing students from birth through age 21 years who reside in Northern California. Referrals are made through the Local Education Agency (LEA) for such reasons as program placement concerns, lack of student progress, behavioral problems, determination of most appropriate mode of communication, specific education/learning problems or requests for educational recommendations.

The Assessment Center has a file of letters expressing appreciation felt by school districts and families for the services provided by the Center. Following are some excerpts from their letters.

> **.....We are writing to thank you for your recent diagnostic evaluation of our son. We were amazed by the comprehensiveness of the evaluation and the thoroughness of your approach. We learned a great deal more about our child, including a few things that surprised us, and much that confirmed what we had suspected or**

what previous testing had indicated. We understand better his learning needs and maybe most importantly, have some good ideas about how to help him more effectively. Thank you also for your sensitivity in working with us and especially for your sensitivity in testing our child. He tires easily in these kinds of situations, and you were infinitely patient and kind to him.

.....We are deeply grateful to you for your time and expertise. We are also appreciative that this is a service made available to us through the auspices of the CSDF. Your report was written so carefully and thoroughly, with so many varied recommendations, that it has given us much to think about. We are fortunate indeed to be the beneficiaries of your good work.

.....Thanks again, it was very informative and very pleasurable working with you.....

.....Thank you so much for all your wonderful work and insight into our dear daughter. Your skill and your warmth made the assessment process completely painless - even fun- so that the week we had unconsciously been dreading turned out to be quite enjoyable.......
There have been professionals in her life from its beginning, but none have made as lasting a contribution as yours. So many of the mysteries about her style and learning process make sense now, and we are beginning to understand how to help her in the years to come......

Happy cooking time for the kitchen staff. Most of them are able to communicate adequately with students in American Sign Language. Several deaf are permanent crew members.

Meal breaks bring students together for friendly conversation which reflects the development of social skills. Frequently, students as well as staff members flick lights to get attention for special announcements during meal time.

Pupil Personnel Services Division

In 1953 a new department of counseling and child guidance was formed. The department changed its title to Pupil Personnel Services in 1963. Following is the list of supervisors and directors.

DR. STEVEN B. GETZ,
Supervisor, Counseling & Child Guidance 1953 to 1957

DR. IRVING FUSFELD,
Supervisor, Counseling & Child Guidance 1957 to 1963

DR. RICHARD KRETSCHNER
Supervisor Pupil Personnel Services 1963 to 1965

In the coming years, I envision a significant growth in the Outreach Division, not only in the area of staff and programs, but in the quantity and quality of services. I expect to be significantly impacting school districts with support and technical assistance for Deaf children who are enrolled in their programs as well as to their families. Our technology component will continue to grow with additional support and the development of a professional technology training lab that will enable our staff to become more efficient and knowledgeable in this continually growing area.

David West
Director of Outreach Division

HARTLEY R. KOCH,
Supervisor, Pupil Personnel Services 1965 to 1969

ELOISE BRADLEY,
Supervisor, Pupil Personnel Services 1970 to 1971

DR. ELOISE McTIGUE,
Director, Pupil Personnel Services 1971 to 1995

DR. DEBRA GUTHMANN,
Director, Pupil Personnel Services 1995 to present

OUTREACH DIVISION

The Outreach Division at CSD is in charge of a variety of areas that provide support to families of deaf children, the deaf community, the education program of the deaf, and to other public school education programs of the deaf in Northern California. The major areas within this division encompass a weekly publication of The California News, community education, family education, and the volunteer program. The others are technical assistance to school districts, campus tours, scheduling of school facilities, and press/media relations.

Additional information on the first four areas and the list of directors and coordinators is given below.

DIRECTOR OF OUTREACH & TRAINING

RALPH NEESAM	1979 - 1983
DIANE MORTON	1983 - 1994
DAVID WEST	1994 - present

David West, Director, Outreach Division (left), outlines the proposed projects with Sandy Corey, Secretary.

EVOLUTION OF CSD NEWS PUBLICATIONS

The Daily News - 1885 to 1886

The first CSD news publication was initiated on October 12,1885, by Dr. Warring Wilkinson, Principal. The manuscript was written in longhand. Copies were passed around daily to readers, staff and older students.

This excerpt below from *The Daily News*, October17, 1885, explained how the News was printed:

> **This paper is printed by a hand copying press called the Cyclostyle. It is an ingenious instrument and an indefinite number of copies can be struck off from the original. It consists of a zinc plate over which is stretched a sheet of prepared paper similar to parchment. On this paper is written whatever is to be copied. The writing is done with a small steel wheel on the end of a stick like a pencil. As you write, the wheel revolves and marks the paper. When the writing is done, it leaves the paper like a stencil. The paper on which the impression is to be taken is placed between the stencil paper and the zinc plate, an ink roller, the same as is used in a printing office, is then passed over the stencil and the ink is forced through onto the paper, giving an exact copy of what is written on the stencil.**

In November, 1885, printing of *The Daily News* was started in the printing shop by the students. At that time, this paper had the largest circulation of any daily paper in Berkeley.

The Evening News - 1886 to 1887

The number of the issue was #198 when the name of the publication was changed to *The Evening News* on December16, 1886.

The Weekly News - 1887 to 1895

Again the publication changed its name to *The Weekly News* on September 10, 1887. The first photograph printed in this publication was of the Educational Building with the Strauss Clock Tower on December 31, 1892.

The name of The Evening News *was changed to the* Weekly News *in 1887.*

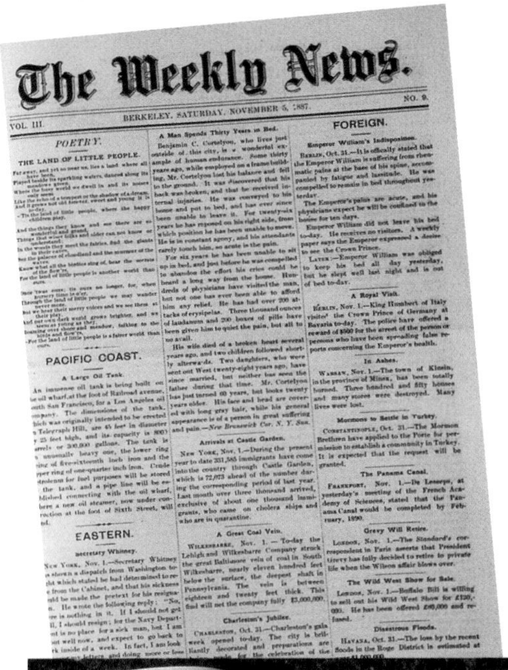
The Weekly News.

VOL. III — BERKELEY, SATURDAY, NOVEMBER 5, 1887. — NO. 9.

POETRY. — FOREIGN. — PACIFIC COAST. — EASTERN.

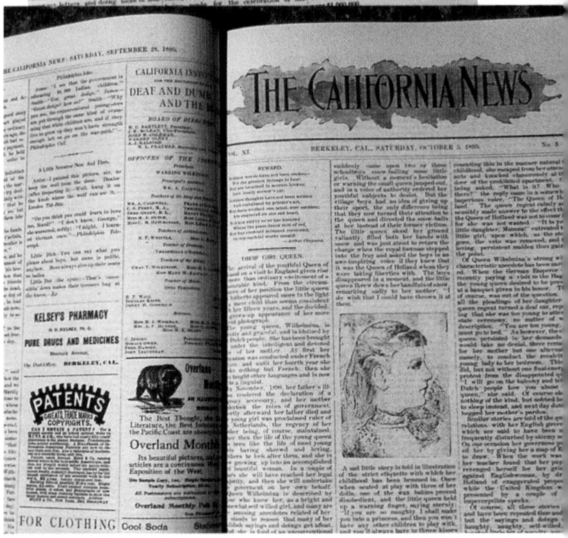
THE CALIFORNIA NEWS

In 1895, the name of The Weekly News *was converted to* The California News

The Daily News

Vol. 1 Berkeley October 12 '85 No 1

The "Daily News" begins with this number. It will appear every afternoon, and will contain the latest news from all parts of the world. In politics it will be neutral. A limited space will be given to Institution items.

No advertisements will be received because we have no room for them.

Papers will be delivered by carriers for five cents a week.

A chromo given to every club of ten subscribers.

All letters should be addressed to "The Daily News" Publishing Co. Inst. for the Deaf and Dumb and the Blind, Berkeley, Cal.

Cardinal McCloskey died at his residence in New York, Saturday, Oct. 10th. He was about seventy-five years old, and was the first American Cardinal

The California News - 1895 to present

Traditionally, school publications have been exchanged among the state schools for the deaf throughout the country, updating the deaf community with the news of its culture, starting in 1885. Since the eastern exchanges almost invariably spoke of the News as the "California News," CSD decided to adopt the name on January 5, 1895. After a decade since the conversion of the name of the school publication, *The California News* has existed.

The first CSD news publication was written in longhand in 1885 (previous page).

Special Unit Honors Students

The California News

June...August

Now That You've Asked

CALIFORNIA NEWS WINS LITTLE PAPER FAMILY AWARD

CSDF Is Off and Running

In 1991, The California News *won "Little Paper Family Award" for excellence in the Newsletter category .*

September 1973

The California News (CN) was awarded a Distinguished Achievement Award for Best Editorials from the Little Paper Family

September 1980

The California News was suspended due to moving the printing equipment from Berkeley to Fremont so it was not ready for operation. Instead, the Outreach Office sent out a two page weekly *Messages* in order to maintain school communication.

September 1982

The California News resumed publication but was distributed as a weekly newsletter.

June 1991

The most coveted school-for-the-deaf newsletter honor, the Little Paper Family Award, was bestowed upon *The California News* on June 28, 1991, by the Gallaudet University Alumni Association for excellence in the special category: *Newsletter.*

Present

The California News continues to be a weekly newsletter published through a collaboration effort between the Vocational Department and the Outreach Division. Students in the printing class take training in printing, assembling and distributing each issue. Also, some volunteers assist with the printing process and contribute in the areas of photography and writing. A copy of the newsletter is sent home each weekend with students and is distributed to the schools for the deaf throughout the nation.

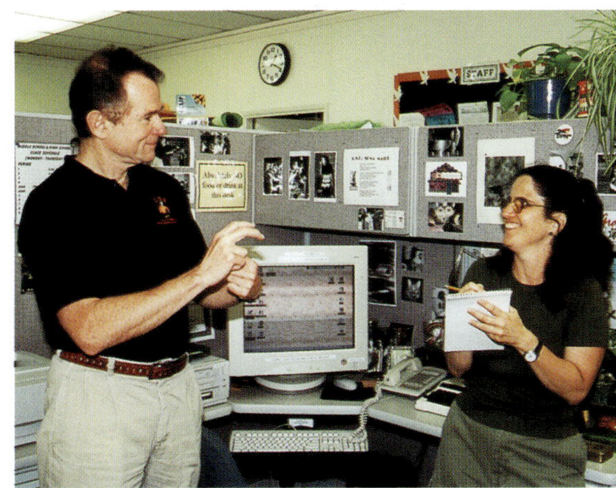

Meta Metal, the California News Editor, interviews Jack Lamberton, Coach of the 1999 CSD Championship Academic Bowl Team.

Harry Hauschildt,'73, with his science class, visiting the enormous NASA Ames Research Center at Sunnyvale, California, posed by a space suit, perhaps with a dream of being the first Deaf astronaut.

Every year seniors form a committee for the year book publication. Throughout the school year, they busily take pictures, write articles, layout and publish book with several faculty members for guidance.

EDITORS

WARRING WILKINSON,
Principal 1885 to 1894

WILLIAM A. CALDWELL,
Assistant Principal 1895 to 1927

GEORGE W. BERRY,
Acting Principal 1927 to 1928

ELWOOD A. STEVENSON,
Superintendent 1928 to 1931

WINFIELD S. RUNDE,
Teacher 1931 to 1938

MICHAEL LAPIDES,
Teacher 1938 to 1942

BYRON B. BURNES,
Teacher 1942 to 1969

RALPH NEESAM,
Principal, Outreach Director 1969 to 1979

LES RUDY,
Staff Development 1979 to 1982

SUZANNE SHACKLEFORD
1982 to 1987

CAROLE WELSH
1987 to 1992

CHARLES and HEIDI HOLMES,
Cottage Counselors
1992 to 1994

MARY DANKO
1994 to 1995

META METAL
1995 to present

Community Education Program

One of the justifications for bringing about the existence of "Martha's Vineyard" in Fremont is the efforts of the Community Education Program. A variety of lectures, workshops, and seminars on the culture of the Deaf, and the Deaf's language and life are conducted on and off campus through the Community Education Program. Hospitals, fire departments, police departments, schools, civic groups and other important organizations have been beneficiaries of increasing awareness and understanding of deaf people by the Outreach Division through its Community Education Program. Also, it has established a link between CSD, the deaf community, and the general community in Northern California.

In 1975 Dr. Henry Klopping, after a few months as a new superintendent, implemented a new concept of the Community Education Program at CSD, Berkeley, and appointed Leo Jacobs as the first coordinator. At that time, he focused on providing opportunities for deaf people to continue their education after graduation from high schools. There were limited choices for deaf people to participate in post-secondary education programs other than at Gallaudet University.

Dr. Roy Holcomb took over after Jacobs retired in 1979. They were both instrumental in implementing the Deaf Awareness programs in the Bay Area and in the state of California.

In 1985, Hedy Udkovich Stern filled this position after Dr. Holcomb retired. Soon afterwards, the continuing education program was eliminated since there were more and more opportunities for deaf people to choose their post-secondary education programs all over the country, including regional centers and community colleges. Stern was instrumental in starting the first American Sign Language (ASL) Storytelling Contest Feast for the Eyes that is now an annual tradition for Deaf Awareness Month on the first Friday night of May. She also established the first training class on Deaf Awareness for the cadets at the California Highway Patrol Academy in Sacramento to better prepare them on how to deal with deaf people they may meet on the job in daily life or in an emergency so that they may become more comfortable and knowledgeable on how to handle emergency and non-emergency situations appropriately and respectfully, by having some method of communication with deaf people, as well as how to find and use an interpreter.

What's next
in the future of CSD news?
You'll find the answer
in tomorrow's
The California News

Leslie Kramer, Volunteer Coordinator (left); Hedy Udkovich-Stern, Family Education Coordinator (middle); and Bridgetta Bourne-Firl, Community Education Program Coordinator, discussing the goals of the family, community and volunteer programs.

"There are three general tendencies of deaf employees. First, they work hard. Second, they are not easily distracted by noise, and focus intently on their work. Third, once they are hired, they often remain with the company for an extended period of time."

Malcolm Grossinger
1995
Community Education Coordinator

In the fall of 1990, Malcolm Grossinger from Washington, D. C. took over the position of community education coordinator. He continued the ongoing assignments that the previous coordinators started.The highlight of his stint with the Outreach Division was the implementation of the annual Job Fair for the Deaf at CSD. A number of employers and community agencies have been invited to set up booths in the gymnasium and meet deaf people.This workshop plays an important role in helping employers familiarize themselves with some aspects of Deaf Culture and give them an insight into how to communicate well with a deaf employee on the job site. In the Job Fair and workshop a great opportunity is offered interested deaf participants to make contact with different kinds of businesses with interpreters on hand. Every year at the Fair, a number of employers accept resumes from deaf participants for the possibility of future job opportunities.

Generally, the coordinator works closely with Gallaudet Regional Center at Ohlone College, Deaf Counseling and Referral Agency, and other organizations to provide workshops for the deaf community.The workshops cover such areas as financial opportunities, bilingualism/biculturalism (ASL/English and Culture of Deaf community), use of TTYs, employment opportunities for deaf people, leadership empowerment, and others.

It also established the annual, most observed special day in the history of the American Deaf culture—March 13th Deaf PAH. It was the memorial celebration of the event at Gallaudet University in 1988 which created a stark upheaval and proper restoration of the inalienable rights to the Deaf. Office of Community Education co-sponsored the event and activities that day with three other organizations, DCARA, Gallaudet University Alumni Association and Gallaudet University Regional Center, Ohlone College.

Family Education

When new young deaf children are admitted to CSD, the first few days are a critical time for school administrators, teachers and cottage counselors to introduce them to the school environment. The process of introduction includes children's parents and siblings.

To ease the separation and anxiety in family hearts, in 1976 the New Family Orientation headed by the family education coordinator offered an excellent weekend agenda. Traditionally, every year at the start of a new school year, the staff at CSD get acquainted with the new families of enrolling deaf children. The weekend is usually divided into *"parts"* —

Friday afternoon is devoted to the instructional department, which includes meeting the principals and teachers, and the opportunity to get a feel of what the students' school day would be like.

Friday evening the families pack into the Little Theater to meet members of the deaf community in a participatory game of "Deafywood Squares" (a remake of TV's popular Hollywood Squares). Questions posed are on the topics of CSD history, Deaf Culture and Deaf history. Saturday morning, the families hear a relevant keynote speech from a psychologist explaining about sending a child away to school. Research has proved that students learn better in a group where the child feels accepted and identifies with other members. The speech assures the family that the school is a place to spark confidence for the families and their deaf children to overcome separation anxiety.

Saturday afternoon finds the families in a meeting with Student Life staff members. The families have an opportunity to stay over for the weekend in the same cottages their children would be living in during the year. Also, they have the privilege of meeting counselors and getting first-hand experience of living in a cottage.

Saturday evening Dr. and Mrs. Klopping host a reception for parents and staff at their home.

Sunday morning offers various activities: introductions to the Deaf Studies program, the Communication Arts program; meetings with a panel of deaf adults, a panel of high school students, and a nurse from the Student Health Unit. CSD hopes the families are able to return home knowing their children are in the best of hands at CSD.

Hedy Udkovich Stern forwarded a thank you letter to the parents for participating on the parent panel during the orientation weekend in 1997. In the letter, she stated:

"The program and staff made me comfortable about leaving my child on Sunday and I know CSD will help my child have a good life."

Señora Lopez
Mother of Arturo Lopez

Every year our volunteers come from greatly diverse backgrounds and from various foreign countries. During the 1998-1999 school year, the volunteer program utilized the services of over 150 volunteers. Each volunteer is unique but all bring a myriad of talent and skill to CSD. Some provide is contributions by working in groups such as our volunteers who developed and operate our CSD museum, while others contribute individually. One very exciting example of an individual contribution is depicted by a professional software developer who volunteers in the elementary department working with teachers and students developing software, which is currently in use, to help improve the reading skills of deaf children. The CSD volunteers truly represent the best of the spirit of volunteerism.

Leslie Kramer
Volunteer Coordinator

As one parent remarked Saturday evening, "It is a relief to know that in a year's time, I will be on the other side of the table. The parents on the panel brought up a lot of issues and feelings that I needed to look at."

The idea of an orientation and training program for parents of preschool age deaf children was initiated in 1968 at the Berkeley School with the blessings of the California State Department of Education. The purpose of this program was to provide parents of preschool age deaf children appropriate information and techniques to the end that they accept and carry out the role of their parenthood in such a way that their deaf children may adjust and develop physically, mentally, and emotionally to the full extent of their abilities. Parents and child were invited to live in a fully furnished cottage on the campus of CSD-B for two one-week periods during the regular school year.

As the years passed, the name of this program was changed to Parent Orientation Program and then Parent Education Program. The program was divided into the Family Education and the Infant Education. The staff members of the Family Education continue providing American Sign Language and Deaf Culture classes for both parents and siblings on the CSD campus. Special informational and educational tours are arranged for families and visitors who are new to CSD and seek information about deaf education and family education.

Parent Education Director

MICHAELE POWELL	1968 to 1972
JOANNE McCAULLEY	1972 to 1983
ANN MacINTYRE	1983 to 1984
LINDA TWILLING	1984 to 1988
DEBBI SILBERG	1988 to 1992
HEDY UDKOVICH-STERN	1992 to present

Volunteer Program

National Volunteer Appreciation Week means a great deal to CSD as it celebrates and honors more than one hundred volunteers annually in the spring. Official Volunteer Certificates of Appreciation are distributed and snacks, flowers, cards, posters and other creative means are also amongst the show of appreciation.

Volunteers come to the school through a multitude of ways. Outreach office recruits many students from the Bay Area ASL classes, Deaf Studies classes, and interpreting training classes. Also, there are many members of the community who seek to give of their service. They are volunteers from both the deaf and hearing community, as young as 9 years old, through retirement age.

In January 1981, the Outreach Division established a Volunteer Program. The need for it was great to help students with homework, tutor a variety of subjects, interpret on field trips, help with scouts and after-school activities. Twelve volunteers were recruited. By the year of 1998, more than one hundred volunteers are in a wide range of departments including: Parent/Infant/Pre-School/Kindergarten Program, Elementary School, Middle School, High School, Athletics, Historical Museum, Student Life, Communication Arts, Graphic Arts, Career Center, Vocational–FEAST. Volunteers are involved in special events such as the Spring Play, NetDay96, Family Workshops, In-Service Days, and the annual Elementary Cottage Carnival.

A long-time dedicated volunteer, Clare Godfrey, did everything from fundraising to being a volunteer coordinator for eight years. Godfrey was really the heart of the CSD volunteer circle for many years. In 1995, she was awarded a plaque for her dedicated years as a volunteer when she retired.

A person taking over the volunteer program in 1995 was Leslie Kramer who has masterly carried it on and even expanded it considerably.

The following are the names of the official volunteer coordinators.

CLARE GODFREY 1987 to 1994
LESLIE KRAMER 1994 to present

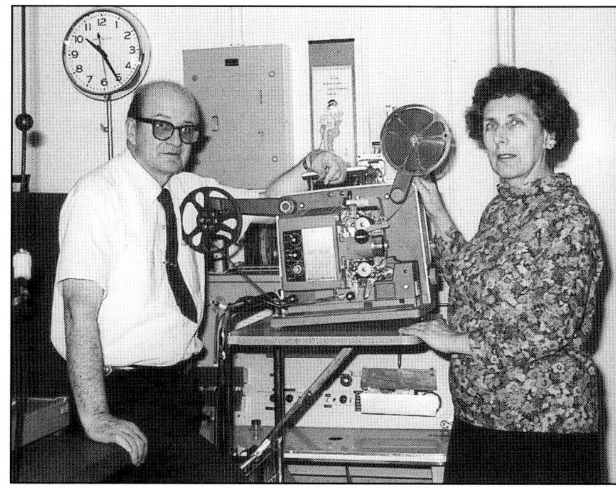

Arthur Willis (left), Supervisor of Educational Media and Lillian Boyd, secretary to the Supervisor. During the years of 1960s and 1970s, movie projectors were well used in classes or assemblies. A movie projector was in almost every home of deaf people to enable them to enjoy captioned films.

Curriculum and Media Services Department

The Curriculum and Media Services Department (CAMS) primarily supports the Instructional Division, with non-academic departments served as needed. CAMS includes the Media Center, the Library, the Instructional Television, the Computer-Assisted Learning Lab (CALL), the English Resources Center, the Deaf Studies Resources Center, the Historical Museum and Archives, a National Association of the Deaf Captioned Media Program Depository, and the services of a Reading Recovery/Elementary Reading Resources Teacher. Media Center services encompasses the use of slides, filmstrips, captioned videos, kraft rolls, construction paper, poster board, drymount tissue, overheads and transparencies, cameras and film, easels and pads, lettering sets, projection lamps, a drymount press, a chart printer, an Ellision lettering machine, a laminating machine.

The Education Visual Aids Media Center was established in 1966 in the Berkeley school. Note heavily demanded captioned films in stock during the pre-video tape days.

This library served the elementary and junior high departments in Crandall Elementary School Building during the years of 1932 to 1950. The library for high school students was in the Educational Building, which was demolished in 1949.

Teacher Helen Myers (right) and librarian Elsa Kleinman promoted interest in reading among the high school students in the Stevenson Educational Building library, which served from 1950 to 1980

A Visual Aid Center Dream
-some background-

March 1, 1966 was an illustrious day for CSD–B for it received official approval from the State Department of Education to establish an Educational Visual Aids Media Center. The dream for this exciting innovation finally became a reality after long hours of administrative discussion and planning regarding the proper procedure to follow in applying for grants. Hence, CSD–B qualified for financial aid through Title I of the Federal Elementary, Secondary Education Act of 1965.One of the teaching staff, Arthur Willis, was appointed coordinator of visual aids.The storage room in the basement of the high school building was converted into a well-equipped Media Center. By November, 1966, for every two classrooms, an overhead projector, a filmstrip projector, and a screen were supplied by the Captioned Films for the Deaf. At several teacher workshops, teachers were trained to manipulate "modern devices," such as a drymount press, a Thermofax machine, tape recorder, a filmstrip projector, a Kodak carousel slide projector.

From "Broom Closet" to a New Module

In 1972, a new portable module was set up between the Stevenson Building and the west wing which was built in 1960. The new air conditioned building was 60 feet long and 32 feet wide. (It was the only air conditioned building on the Berkeley campus at that time.) School staff members were elated with the long overdue move from the small room known as the "broom closet" to a larger and more suitable building. When CSD moved to Fremont, the Media Center module was relocated near the Middle School cottages and has been utilized since then as the Middle School Activity Center.

Library Services

Staffed by a full-time librarian and a part-time assistant, the CSD library serves class groups and individual students from preschool through 12th grade. The library houses a collection of hard cover books, paperbacks, reference books/materials, magazines, maps, and charts. Research tools/technology resources are also available.

Library Staff Members

- **Help teachers and students understand the learning resources and technology tools available and how to access them for educational, informational, or entertainment purposes.**

- Work hard to make the library a positive, stimulating environment where people want to spend time reading.
- Provide high quality library services that support classroom instruction and learning.
- Help students acquire the ability to intelligently select, evaluate, and interpret materials to improve literacy skills.
- Work with teachers to prepare in advance the resources their students will need to learn.
- Assist students with individual and whole class projects.
- Lead regular ASL storytelling sessions (pre-school through fifth grade).
- Set up attractive displays and special project exhibits.

This modern library, part of the Education Center in the Fremont school, serves all the departments. Attractive displays and special project exhibits are perpetually shown in the library.

Attractive and massive Neo-Gothic mahogany bookcase built by the deaf students in 1891 was placed in the library in the third floor of the Educational Building.

Frequently, pre-school through fifth grade students gather in a cozy corner of the library, enjoying ASL storytelling sessions presented by librarian Joyanne Burdett (right).

To cultivate creativity and reading skills, Linda Cox-Kuntze, an early childhood teacher, listens to a student signing the dialogues of the characters in the book.

FIRST LIBRARY AT THE BERKELEY SCHOOL

The first library was set up in the newly built Gothic stone building on the Berkeley campus in 1869. It was the exclusive property of Dr. Warring Wilkinson. In 1875, the building was demolished by fire. In 1878, the CSD's own first library was established in the new educational building. From approximately 1914 to 1923, Mr. Charles S. Perry and Mrs. Charles S. Perry were part–time librarians and curators of the museum at different times. Between 1923 and 1955, the libraries in the Educational Building, then Stevenson Secondary School Building and Caldwell Elementary School Building were monitored by classroom teachers and principals. In 1955, a full-time librarian was acquired.

LIBRARIANS

CAROLINE BURNES
1955 to 1969

ELSA KLEINMAN
1969 to 1991

JOYANNE BURDETT
1991 to present

Instructional Television Services

In the area of instructional television (ITV), the broadcast journalism teacher and students produce a daily news program plus high-interest programs for in-house viewing. Additionally, the television specialist creates special project videos with teachers as a supplement to classroom learning and instruction.

ITV arrived on the Berkeley campus in 1970 when the school's federally supported media program was expanded to include equipment for establishing a small closed circuit television system. The center of ITV activity was located in room 106 of the Caldwell Elementary School Building. Robert Schmitt came to the Berkeley School as a demonstration teacher and media specialist in 1968, later becaming an instructional television specialist. ITV was an important addition to CSDB's overall media program because it permitted students to produce their own learner-centered experience tapes. The program was well received by staff and students. One group who especially appreciated the new ITV services was the Athletic Department.The athletic staff used portable TV camera's extensively to film football and basketball games as well as wrestling matches. These were reviewed weekly by the coaches and teams in an effort to eliminate performance errors and weaknesses.

The scope of instruction television services expanded tremendously in 1980 when CSD moved to Fremont. ITV was now housed in a new facility six times its former size. Peter Rivest became the Instructional Television teacher in 1976 teaching studio production and editing to broadcast journalism classes. Gordon Craig, a new Television Production specialist, began in 1978 expanding production, technical, and creative services for classroom projects schoolwide including the cottage areas. In 1979, Marya Viducich was added to the team. She worked with ITV students to coordinate and produce successful interviews of distinguished people: *Barbara Bush*, wife of President George Bush; *Gloria Deukmejian*, wife of California Governor George Deukmejian; *Delain Eastin,* Superintendent of Public Instruction; *I King Jordan,* President of Gallaudet University and other celebrities.

Resource Centers

The English resource Teacher works with teachers on reading and writing strategies for classroom instruction while maintaining an up-to-date materials bank in the English Resource Center. Staff development, inservice training, and curriculum efforts include the collaborative drafting and implementation of content and performance English standards for the California Challenge School Initiative effort, implementation of the school's English curricula, the continual updating of literature lists, and ongoing investigation of authentic assessment approaches, including the use of portfolios.

Karl Blanco, junior, videtapes Gian Marcucci, senior, and Jonathan Kramer, junior, for student news program, "Your Daily News." (top) Antonia Nunez, junior, controls the switches by selecting which camera to tape as well as adding title and credits to the school program. (middle) Antonia Nunez is the technical director while the announcers co-host for "Your Daily News" under the guidance of instructor Peter Rivest. (bottom)

Elementary Reading Resource teacher Nancy Brill (right) poses as a "literacy coach", facilitating the Reading Recovery Early intervention Program with a first grade student. This kind of program, one teacher to one student reading tutoring basis, proves successful with a large percentage of the students assigned to the program.

With elementary teacher David Keim looking on, a student reads the story aloud in a one-to-one basis reading situation.

The Deaf Studies Resource Center houses a rich collection of ASL and Deaf Culture materials. The Deaf Studies Resource Teacher provides inservice training to teachers, develops Deaf Studies and ASL curricula, works with the English Resource Teacher on bilingual/bicultural schoolwide endeavors, and serves as a school consultant on Deaf studies/ASL issues.

The Reading Recovery/Elementary Reading Resource Teacher facilitates the Reading Recovery Early Intervention Program with first grade students, acts as a "literacy coach" in the Elementary Department, is the contact person for the "Best Practices" literacy training program giving assistance to the Elementary and Early Childhood Education (ECE), teaches in implementing lessons and techniques, and functions as a schoolwide consultant and committee member on literacy committees connected to CSD standards work/school reform efforts.

RESOURCE TEACHERS

English Resource Teacher

BONNIE LOEFFLER 1992 to 1994

LAURA PETERSON 1994 to 1999

Deaf Studies Resource Teacher

DEE KENNEDY 1992 to present

Reading Recovery/Elementary Reading Resource Teacher

NANCY BRILL 1997 to present

Computer-Assisted Learning Lab Services

CALL is where students may do lessons or projects with their teachers.

Open to all students through their regular classes, the Computer-Assisted Learning Lab (CALL) provides centeralized computer resources in support of classroom teaching and learning. In CALL, students can access online information/communication to increase their reading, writing and thinking skills. They can use online research and word processing to draft compositions and reports as well as analyze and share their findings using a wide array of technology tools including, but not limited to, spreadsheet software such as Microsoft Excel and presentation software such as HyperStudio, and PowerPoint. As a result, students grow in their ability to use technology to communicate in order to ultimately function independently in their acquisition of the learning and technological resources needed for becoming confident life-long learners in the 21st century. Teachers determine when to bring their classes to the CALL and decide what programs and/or lessons to use. A full-time CALL Coordinator creates new lab schedules every two weeks, assists teachers and students daily in the lab, provides inservice training as needed and maintains the software library. Additionally, an Educational Technology Resource Teacher spearheads the school's computer literacy development efforts, provides inservice training and functions as a consultant on integrating educational technology with curriculum objectives/outcomes and instructional needs.

Brief History of CALL

CALL coordinator Craig Salonen offers Jenny Contreras some technical tips on browsing the Internet.

In 1970, before the personal computer was marketed, CSD–Berkeley began use of the large mini computer (not a main frame, but still bigger than a refrigerator) at Stanford University. Twelve teletypes at CSD were connected by phone to the Stanford computer, where math was the only subject offered.

In 1973, CSD's Assistant Superintendent Jacob Arcanin met with the Assistant Director of the Lawrence Hall of Science (LHS), University of California, Berkeley. This meeting led directly to Title 1 funding proposal for computer use which was the beginning of a seven-year relationship of time-shared computer use.

At first, brave CSD teachers learned PILOT programming language, so they could program lessons for their students. The TTY's were connected by phone to a Nova Decision Minicomputer at LHS on the top of the hill just north of the CSD campus. Not only were the telephone charges much less to the Hall than they had been to Stanford, but the service was better! Thanks to Title 1 funding, CSD became part of the LHS time-sharing network, using all the programs written for their public access project. Treacy Hickok served as lab proctor at CSD.

Supervisor Bonnie Loeffler and her Media staff members. Left to right, back row: Gordon Craig, Linda Jarashow, Dee Kennedy, Bonnie Loeffler, Gloria Mann, Nancy Brill. Front row: Joyanne Burdett, Suzie Jacobs, Peter Rivest, Laura Pederson, Dee Bringer, Craig Salonen, and Jack Lamerton.

A student strides by the Learning Center of Media Center, Library, Instructional Television, Computer-Assisted Learning Lab and Museum.

Lab programmers worked with CSD staff members in the design and creation of nearly a dozen single-mode authoring programs for use by faculty and students. Each program allowed the writing of lessons using one specific question type (multiple choice, fill in the blank, etc). Computer-using teachers at that time included Margaret Coleman, Vic Hutchins, Gail Potwin (Wright), Mike Finneran, Stan Bringer, Ellen Winters, and Joyanne Burdett.

By 1977, Goeff Zawolkow was functioning as CSD's Computer Coordinator while teaching high school science full time. Margaret Irwin was hired by LHS, replacing Alice Obray as proctor of the time-sharing computer lab.

In 1981, IBM announced its first personal computer, the IBM-PC. In 1984, IBM selected 15 high schools in the nation which were demonstrating "exemplary computer use" and donated fifteen PC's and software to each of them. CSD–Fremont was ONE of the 15 high schools in the nation!

Jack Lamberton of IBM came to CSD for the 1992-93 school year as part of IBM's Faculty Loan Program. The following year, he was hired as the school's Educational Technology Resource Teacher. Under the guidance of the Educational Technology Committee, nine multimedia computers on roll-around carts were purchased for classroom use. In 1993, ten new Mac LC III's were purchased for the Elementary Department and in 1994, 24 new Macintosh LC 575 computers, each equipped with CD-ROM drive, were purchased for the CALL. They were networked with new Laser printers.

In 1998, the CALL was relocated from the Vocational Building to the Library Building making it more central and accessible to staff and students across departments. The current CALL contains 28 Macintosh LC 575 and PowerMacs, 15 Pentium I and II computers, 2 laptop computers and one portable LCD projector. The current CALL Coordinator is Craig Salonen.

Up to the Wire. NetDay *volunteers install the fiber optic network into the space above the ceiling. An estimated 100 miles of network have been installed in the buildings on campus. Higher to the Wire. With more* NetDay *volunteers, the more opportunity is for the students to be high on the technology level.*

Educational Media Department Supervisor

ARTHUR WILLIS	**1966 to 1976**
ROBERT SCHMITT	**1976 to 1991**

Curriculum and Media Services Department Supervisors

ROBERT SCHMITT	**1991 to 1992**
LESLIE LADD	**1992 to 1994**
BONNIE LOEFFLER	**1994 to 1999**

Wiring CSD is a Big Step Toward Advancing Education

NetDay, the internet project of State Superintendent Delaine Edstin, produced the CSD-related volunteer effort to string wires for the Internet into the school, garnered enthusiastic support from high-tech companies, Deaf Media, staff, parents, and politicians. Wiring CSD for the Internet was not only the first step toward upgrading education and computer technology, it was also the cheapest and easiest.

On a chilly, rainy day there was still cheer in the air when volunteers arrived and set up tables where bagels and oranges were sliced. More food was unloaded from vehicles. More volunteers came. Some were big; some were small; some carried flashlights and goggles; some carried food that had been prepared the night before. All carried the spirit of volunteerism.

Technicians and a large number of volunteers gathered on four separate NetDay dates: March 9, 1996, January 11, 1997, January 25, 1997 and March 28 1998. NetDay started as a statewide effort to bring the Internet into classrooms. The idea struck home with the mother/son team of Dr. Susan Rutherford, and

> ***"With computers and Internet access, we are giving our students a powerful learning tool and our teachers a powerful teaching tool as well."***
>
> Jack Lamberton
> Educational Technology Resource Teacher
>
> 

Jay Byron, and Jacob Arcanin, during the CalEd convention in Fremont in February, 1996. Realizing that among the three of them, they had the organizational and technical capabilities to pull together a volunteer effort, NetDay at CSD was conceived. Dr. Rutherford is the Executive Director of D.E.A.F. Media, Inc., which is a non-profit organization dedicated to serving the deaf community through a number of programs and services involving Deaf artists. Because of her long-standing ties with the Deaf community, especially the California School for the Deaf, and her work with her son, an expert in building computer networks, the project came together.The computers are connected to one another through building hubs. Hubs in each building are attached to a central switching hub that directs information between one building and another through fiber optic cables.It is also connected to a router which provides access to the off-campus Internet.

NetDay Heroes

The NetDay heroes, made up of Telephone Pioneers, CSD staff, parents, students, community volunteers, and wiring experts, clambered up through attics well-shielded with goggles, masks, and protective clothing.Deaf volunteers kept working together in coordination while hearing workers kept yelling down rooms and through walls to carry messages across.

As a whole, the project was a smashing success. Jack Lamberton, Educational Technology Resource teacher, stated that there were some 140 drops made in classrooms, which are ready to be hooked up to computers.

It definitely takes serious commitment on the part of teachers at this point to be really productive with computers. Eventually, all teachers will become comfortable with the Internet. They have to go through the process of experiencing, digesting, and developing programs to provide information available for deaf children so they can explore a great world beyond the campus. How do they convert this to instruction for schoolchildren? That is the challenging part.

The most important change of all has been an understanding that self-reliance and "how-to" are worthwhile and above all, acceptable. Accomplishing the NetDay task, whether it is as simple as stringing wires or as complicated as surfing the Internet, has given the volunteers involved a feeling of self-worth, satisfaction, and reward.

All classrooms are wired and by 1999 all classrooms have computers.

Individualized Educational Plan

The Individualized Education Plan (I.E.P.) was implemented in 1978, as a result of the passage of Public Law 94-142. The I.E.P. involved parents of deaf children in cooperation with educators in planning for an appropriate

individualized education program for their children. In other words, the I.E.P. spells out the program and services that the school is to provide to meet the children's needs.

Adequate information about a child's present level of functioning is needed to make appropriate plans either in school or at home. Each year CSD sets aside a formal I.E.P. week, usually in the last week of May. A number of meetings are scheduled each day by trained coordinators made up of supervisors and various support staff members. Jacob Arcanin, Assistant Superintendent, usually holds pre-meetings with parents to familiarize them with Public Law 94-142 and various aspects of the I.E.P. process. Each two-three hour I.E.P. process takes a great deal of effort and dedication on the part of the team of parents, their child, teachers, residential counselors, coordinator and related service staff.

These team members review assessment findings, prioritize individual's needs, and identify appropriate programs and services designed to meet such needs. As the student progresses, the program and services are modified according to the student's needs.

The I.E.P. process involves a review of a student's performance; identification of needs, goals, and objectives; a determination of program and services required; and then a decision as to where placement is to occur to implement the goals.

At the end of an I.E.P. meeting, it is hoped that each participant feels that the "whole" child is considered, that his/her priority needs are identified, a program developed, and that each participant has had an opportunity to participate at his/her desired level.

At an IEP meeting with parents in the library, Jacob Arcanin explained the purpose of IEP and pointed out the importance of parents' role in their child's IEP.

At the New Family Orientation meeting, the concerned parents, Jimmie and Yolanda Soto of Madera, inquired seriously of the school's academics, residential life and extra curricula activities before CSD enrolled their son Joey, 12.

CSD was honored to have this photograph of the junior high students taken and included in an Addison-Wesley textbook in late 1991. The students were (left to right) Gamil Campos, Stacie Young, Karina Pedersen and Jerry Pua.

BOOSTER FOR THE CSD EDUCATION PROGRAMS

The Instructional Television Program (ITV) became one of the most favorable segments of the education program in the 1980s. It was the Title 1 program that made ITV possible. What is Title 1?

In 1965, the Congress of the United States passed a landmark legislation entitled The Elementary and Secondary Education Act. Its purpose was to supplement the regular instructional program in the areas of reading, language, mathematics, parent education, health and auxiliary services and staff development. Since 1966, CSD Berkeley/Fremont has received funds appropriated through this legislation. Several components identified by both Title 1 staff and the Community Advisory Council (CAC) have been implemented as supplements to the school program. They included Computer Assisted Instruction (CAI), parent education, and curriculum development.

In 1993, within the broad areas of language, reading and mathematics, there were three basic thrusts supported by the Title 1 program funds: Media Services, listening skill development, and student aide assistance in the classroom. Complementing the significant services the Media Department provides to the staff and students, Title 1 funding provided the services of a Television Assistant who assisted in the video taping of student activities and commercial programming. These services have proved extremely valuable over the years.

Another broad component of the Title 1 program was that of Health/Auxiliary services. The funds provide the services of a half-time diagnostic teacher who assists in identifying students who have learning problems.

For the past several years, the direction of the Title 1 program has focused on the use of student assistants in the classrooms. To date, Title 1 has been an important aspect of the education program.

One of the first members of APTC, Mary E. Robinson. She was the first supervising teacher to coordinate the education program for all classes in 1930 to ease the burden from Principal Dr. Stevenson. After her retirement in 1958, she continued contributing money to send CSD athletes to the World Deaf Games.

Association of Parents, Teachers, and Counselers

"P.T.A."

In January, 1950, a group of concerned parents met with Dr. Elwood Stevenson, Superintendent, to discuss forming a Parent-Teacher Association (PTA) which was greatly needed at CSD–Berkeley. Dr. Stevenson became whole-heartedly enthusiastic, so the nucleus of PTA was formed with temporary elected officers and a set of goals.

On February 5, 1950, a large number of interested parents and teachers was involved in a discussion on the advantages of the new organization to the school and to pupils. They agreed that a worthwhile organization should represent all parents of the school and provide active and constructive support of the educational and social services of the school. The organizing committee was formed to draw up the framework of the PTA and to compile a Constitution and By-Laws to govern the body.

Rectification from PTA to APTC

On "The Association of Parents, Teachers, Counselors," the minutes of the very first meeting on June 8, 1950 in the Primary Auditorium was written as a birthright in longhand in the secretarial notebook:

> **"Upon being informed that it is inadvisable to call ourselves a Parent–Teacher Association, it was moved by Mrs. Sterling, seconded, was carried unanimously that the name of the association be amended to "The Association of Parents, Teachers, and Counselors of the California School for the Deaf."**

One of the first APTC committee members to focus on legislative issues and a strong advocate for deaf rights, Philip Lynch was father of Daniel Lynch,'53.

At this meeting, the first APTC officers were elected. The result of the voting was: President – *William Whitlock*, Vice-president – *Glen McCune*, Secretary – *Mrs. H. Marshburn*, Treasurer – *John Tingley*, Standing Committees: Legislative – *Philip Lynch*, Hospitality – *Mrs. Mildred Miller*, Membership – *Ms. Mary Robinson*, Program – *Harry Cook*, Publicity – *Clyde Herring*, Ways and Means – *Russell Lowell*. (Philip Lynch was father of Dan Lynch, '53, who is CSD

> ***"I wish all parents would be as supportive as the parents at this school."***
>
> A legislative aide
> Dec. 14, 1984

The watchful eagle above the snack bar at the gymnasium where APTC members sell goodies for fund raising projects on annual Open House Day.

teacher retiree. Philip Lynch was an advocate for deaf rights and helped to kill a bill that prohibited deaf people from possessing driver's licenses. He was district attorney in Solano County and was appointed judge by Governor Pat Brown. H. Marshburn was mother of Patricia Suzie Jacobs, '67, who is presently coordinator of the CSD Museum and Archives. Glen McCune was father of Donald McCune, '52, who lives in Soda Springs, California, and frequently visits the Bay Area. Clyde Herring was father of Robert Clyde Herring, '57.)

The membership fee per year was 50 cents in 1950 ($10 for a single or family in 1998). The first APTC project was selling tickets to a baseball game in Oakland. The Association was to receive 25 percent of the price of the tickets sold and the proceeds to go into a fund for the establishment and maintenance of a summer camp for deaf children. At a festival to benefit the summer camp fund, the first prizes APTC ever presented were a tablecloth and a radio-phonograph.

Highlights of APTC Activities

During the 50s, the activities included an annual steak barbecue in the fall, annual dinner in February, annual variety show and a sign language class. The total number of members was reported to be 350. The Campfire Girls and the Boy Scouts were the APTC's favorite recipients of the contributions.

In the 60s, APTC became more active in sponsoring the Open House at the school. It started its annual dinner in honor of the Senior Class and presented pin awards to the senior athletes.

In 1973, APTC and CSD Junior National Association of the Deaf jointly sponsored the Fund Raising Exhibition Basketball game between CSD staff members and the Oakland Raiders team, called Big Ben's Burlies, at the Merritt College gym. The purpose of raising money was to send two CSD wrestlers to the XII Games for the Deaf in Malmo, Sweden, that summer.

In the late 70s, APTC contributed one thousand dollars to the girls volleyball team, the boys football team and the cheerleaders for the flight expenses to the Big Game at CSD–Riverside. The Jog-a-Thons, directed by Bernice Singleton, Kathy Ash, Esther and Mel Pedersen, Margie and Henry Bell, and others were a financial boon to APTC. APTC started a tradition of presenting contributions toward decorations for Christmas trees in the dormitories.

On April 28, 1979, APTC held a 30-year Reunion banquet to honor the 150 former members who established and developed APTC.

The Cutie Cagers (female APTC members) beat the Aristocrats (local politicians including Assemblyman Alister McAlister) in the Donkey Basketball

Game on March 19, 1982 in the CSD gym. This fund raising event, sponsored by APTC, netted $900 and was organized by Claire Godfrey.

Every year APTC raises around $10,000, mainly from the sale of raffle tickets and the Fremont Police Association Annual Open Golf Tournament. APTC donates money to the school for various school activities such as field trips, students' trip to Close-Up in Washington, D. C., Black and Hispanic Parents' Weekend, Cub Scouts, Girl Scouts , Student Leadership Conference, and numerous others. To list all the contributions APTC has made would require many more pages, which implies how magnificent the continuity of the APTC's support has been to CSD. CSD is most grateful for APTC's efforts for making the lives of CSD students more exciting, interesting, educational and fun.

Esther and Mel Pedersen, parents of two students and active members of APTC, worked up a sweat in their effort to install 1995 APTC's Jog-A-Thon. *These two authentic 49er helmets were given away to the CSD families who sold the most tickets for the APTC raffle.*

Following is a list of APTC Presidents from 1950 to 2000

WILLIAM WHITLOCK	1950-52	CLAIRE GODFREY	1978-80
MRS. JOHN TINGLEY	1952-53	TEDDY KELLY	1980-81
CHARLES NASH	1953-54	RICHJARD BONHEYO	1981-82
RALPH NEESAM	1954-55	CLAIRE GODFREY	1982-83
FRED ROSENLIND	1955-57	BARBARA LINCOLN	1983-84
CLYDE HERRING	1957-59	CINDY WRIGHT	1984-86
GENE GREENLEAF	1959-61	MARILYN CASSIDY	1986-87
HOWARD COUPLAND	1961-63	JULIAN SINGLETON	1987-88
JOSEPH COHEN	1963-65	SHARON GURRY	1988-89
BEATRICE STAMPER	1965-66	JANET HAMMOND	1989-90
ARLO STOVER	1966-67	LARRY BERKE	1990-91
MARYELLEN LENTZ	1967-68	GAYLE WIKINS	1991-93
RUTH FAGOT	1968-70	PAM RODGERS	1993-94
JOHN DANENHOWER	1970-71	EMORY MARSH	1994-97
LAVERNE HELBERG	1971-73	NANCY EDDY	1997-98
JOHN PERRY	1973-75	LISA MATOVICH	1998-1999
JAMES LYNOS	1975-76	NANCY EDDY	1998-1999
JEANETTE DAVITON	1976-78	RAUL MEJORADO	1999-2000

Legislative Aides Day

On December 1, 1983, CSD hosted the first *Legislative Aides Day*. Legislative aides to assemblymen and senators representing the districts in Northern California were invited to CSD to meet students, staff, and parents.

Legislative Aides Day is one of the most exciting innovations organized by the Outreach and Training Department. The key of the *Legislative Aides Day* is to introduce aides to the educational program of the California School for the Deaf. Aides then may relay to their offices the optimal picture of how deaf children are educated in an appropriate environment at CSD.

Originally, the *Legislative Aides Day* was held annually, but now it is held every few years. Usually, the day begins with a meeting with the superintendent's cabinet members and other staff. Then, legislative aides are given a tour of the campus. The FEAST prepares a luncheon for aides, some students, parents, and staff. It is followed by short talks by parents and students expressing their experiences and feelings regarding CSD. Often, aides meet with the Community Advisory Council (CAC) for further discussion and questions.

The comments aides have made about the school are centered around the impressive parental involvement, high aspirations of students, good vocational training, and positive energy of the staff. One at the third annual event commened, *"There is no high school in the state that has a program like this one for deaf children."*

Hopefully, legislative aides go back to their respective offices with a clearer understanding of CSD and various programs as well as the concerns that staff and parents have about the impact of pertinent legislation on CSD children.

Plant Operations Crew composed of engineers, carpenters, painters, electricians, janitors and groundskeepers under Barrett Smith, Chief of Plant Operations.

By combining the hands of carpenter Ronnie Davenport and the School-to-Career students of Ron Rhodes' (far right) class. A playhouse was constructed for the children of the Early Childhood Education Department. Jan Epitacio holds the large wooden scissors during the ribbon-cutting ceremony.

Chapter Five

Third Relocation

The Shock of the CSD Status

In the summer of 1972 this writer read *Future Shock* by Alvin Toffler, concluding that millions of people would find it increasingly difficult to deal with rapid technological and social change in the twentieth century. Shortly afterwards, the California School for the Deaf community faced a serious threat of closing or moving the school elsewhere during the school year of 1972-73. Reading *Future Shock* helped one absorb the shock of the CSD status in one stride.

In the middle of July, 1972, a serious problem faced the Department of Education and CSD. As a result of a survey by the State Fire Marshall and the Office of Architecture and Construction, some of the facilities at both the California School for the Deaf and the California School for the Blind in Berkeley were ordered closed until repairs and modifications could be completed to bring the buildings up to the minimum standards of the Building Code.

Norton and Runde Halls, dormitories for elementary students, on the left, closed due to fire and earthquake hazards. Elementary students transferred to Birck Hall and other buildings.

Preceding spread: Aerial view of the Fremont school in 1998.

This was an immediate crisis since CSD could not open the school for the 1972-73 school year without safe facilities as required by the State Fire Marshall. It was determined that two buildings would have to remain closed during the continuing emergency due to the cost and time required to bring them up to code. The buildings closed were Norton Hall (elementary girls dormitory) and Runde Hall (elementary boys dormitory). Immediate action was taken to open Caldwell Hall (elementary classroom building) by September 11, 1972. Students in the closed dormitories moved to other dormitories. These conditions were rather inconvenient, but every way was sought to keep the programs going at CSD without any major interruption. As Dr. Wilson Riles, Superintendent of Public Instruction, said in his reassuring message to the staff and parents, "these conditions will cause some inconvenience but will not seriously impair academic programs or extra-curricular activities. . ."

Caldwell Hall opened after extensive repairs, including rooms painted with fire retardant paint, installment of a fire sprinkler system and fire resistive doors, and transoms sealed. With the California School for the Deaf – Riverside maintenance crew's help, Caldwell Hall opened for the school year of 1972-73. At the entrance of the auditorium (right), were the impressive doors with the windows decorated with metal figures of The Fox and Grapes from Aesop's Fables (below). The door grilles were taken from the auditorium doors and are now imbedded in the doors of the Little Theater at the Fremont school.

To Move or Not to Move

Before plans to recondition Caldwell Hall were started, temporary sites were actually looked at to determine if it was feasible to move all or a part of the school while repairs were being done. Hasty visits were made to facilities at Ukiah, Yountville, San Jose, Paso Robles, Los Gatos, Mountain View, and Clayton Valley. It was a great relief to the staff and parents that none of the facilities were acceptable, so the materials for minimum interim repairs had to be ordered on a rush basis. The hard working CSD maintenance staff received a boost from the painters from the California School for the Deaf, Riverside.

Agreements had to be reached with the State Fire Marshall and the Department of Finance in order to use the condemned facilities. As a result a special memorandum of understanding was drawn up. This agreement permitted CSD to open on September 11 and to operate on a three-year interim basis, with the understanding that minimum corrections were to be made. A schedule of priorities was agreed upon to satisfy the condition of minimum corrections.

Priority No. 1, to be completed by October 1, 1972, called for work on Caldwell Hall. One-hour fire retardant paint was applied to all acoustic tile and to wainscoting. Transoms were sealed off with one-hour wall construction. Doors were replaced with 20 minute labeled doors. Approved "Exit" signs were put up. Battery operated floodlights were placed over exit ways. A fire sprinkler system was installed in storage areas. D'Estrella Assembly Hall was closed for plays, but meetings could be held under strict restrictions after the stage curtains were removed. The balcony was sealed by closure of the entrances. Priority No.2, to be completed by January 1, 1973, called for a number of corrections in the five dormitories that continued to be used. Priority No. 3, to be completed by April 15, 1973, dealt with items in the Stevenson Secondary

Building, the Junior and Senior High Schools. The gasoline dispensing unit was closed, and corrections were made in the dining room area, the kitchen, and Tilden Vocational School. Long and steady hours of work had been put in by the maintenance staff. School had opened and everyone looked forward to a good school year as though nothing unusual had interfered. Many thanks were expressed for the efforts of Superintendent Hugo Schunhoff and the concerned Division of Special Education.

The Kitchen Started the Catch 22

The school's food service facility was constructed in 1931. By 1968, the 37 years of use and gradual obsolescence had created a condition which strongly demanded securing funds for extensive renovation. A request was made, denied, and repeated in the following years. These requests resulted in discussions at high levels which culminated in an appropriation by the 1971 Legislature for a feasibility study of the rehabilitation of both the California School for the Deaf and the California School for the Blind. The thrust was a study of all of the physical needs of both schools located on the Berkeley site. That was the point which placed CSD in a situation of dilemma.

This kitchen was the place which placed CSD in a dilemma. Hence, the crisis led to the mandate for the third relocation of CSD.

Apparently, the mandate for the third relocation of the California School for the Deaf was the direct result of a unique series of restrictions and

circumstances. As Superintendent Schunhoff put it, "With a bit of jest and yet with the truth taken totally out of context, we say it all began in our kitchen. In the total context, it all began with the passage of a series of bills by State legislature, which in its wisdom was cognizant of the need for greater safety for school children."

Hayward Fault: the final blow

The option of rehabilitation of existing structures received its final blow almost before the report was completed. Senate Bill No. 689, 1972 Legislature, had become a law. It mandated that "No school building shall be constructed or situated on the trace of an active geological fault." Geological maps indicated that two parallel tracings of the Hayward Fault pass through the school grounds, one tracing passing directly under three of the dormitories and the other tracing passing under or near the gymnasium and the swimming pool, and along the edge of fill dirt of the athletic field. This mandated the third relocation.

The appropriation bill passed by the 1973 Legislature provided funds for purchase of a new site for the California School for the Deaf and the California School for the Blind, one site for the two schools. The appropriation bill also provided funds for preliminary planning. The Department of General Services was given the task of locating and eventually purchasing a site which would be suitable both to the Department of Education and the Department of Finance. Focus was on the East Bay area including Napa, Concord, Walnut Creek, Danville, Pleasant Hill, and other parts of the Mt. Diablo area. The Fremont area was also being considered.

Dr. Barry Griffing, Assistant State Superintendent of Public Instruction for Special Education. "Dr. Barry Griffing, one of our staff, has the scars to prove his commitment and dedication. His tenacity helped us all keep our pledge to this project," quoted by Dr. Wilson Riles, State Superintendent of Public Instruction on June 1, 1977.

Searching for an Appropriate Site for the Third Relocation

Before the site searching venture, the school community and the deaf community were strongly against the concept of the third relocation. Several "town meetings" were called and concerned discussions took place in favor of renovation and rehabilitation of the Berkeley school. Eventually, it was realized that since Senate Bill 689 had become law, the protest would accomplish nothing. The California School for the Deaf would become extinct if the school community and the deaf community would not cooperate with the Department of Education for the third relocation. So High School Principal Dean Swaim and Adjustment Teacher Kenneth Norton were asked by Dr. Barry Griffing, Assistant State Superintendent of Public Instruction for Special Education, to "represent the deaf community" and help evaluate existing state sites in the Sacramento area, Davis, Fairfield, Napa, Oakville, and Vacaville with the state officials. After numerous trips to those sites, all agreed that those places were unsuitable. At the end of the search, in January 1974, the Board of Public Works approved the further study of three prospective sites for relocation. One site was in Fremont, the second one was partly in Newark and partly in Fremont near Ardenwood Farms, and the third one was in Pleasant Hill. The intensive study of the Fremont site and the Newark/Fremont site was in progress in the early months of 1974.

Sequences of Events Leading to the Future CSD

During the next seven months there were lengthy public hearings before the Ways and Means Committee and the Senate Finance Committee regarding the future of CSD. At the request of the Legislature, a number of public meetings included representatives of local school districts, county superintendents, parents, and interested people. Dr. Barry Griffing, Dr. Hugo Schunhoff, several staff members, and parents were heavily involved in the hearings in defending the existence of CSD in northern California. At one point, separate sites for the deaf school and the blind school were brought up and argued. The Department of Finance blocked the separate site proposal.

Finally, in January 1975, negotiations were completed for the purchase of 91 acres in the heart of Fremont as the future site for the schools for the deaf and the blind, including units for the multi-handicapped. Negotiations were made with the Mormon Church to persuade them to sell the cauliflower patch site to the State. Pressure from the City of Fremont and members of the Assembly

This cauliflower farm bounded by Stevenson Boulevard was purchased from the Church of Jesus Christ of Latter-Day Saints at about $35,000 per acre in 1975. Staff Development Supervisor Ralph Neesam, left, Superintendent Dr. Hugo Schunhoff and Business Manager Robert Watrous reviewing the map of the site.

assisted in winning approval for the sale of the site to the State. The land was bounded by Stevenson Boulevard (no connection to Superintendent Dr. Elwood Stevenson).

> *"The need to relocate these special schools became evident two years ago when the state office of architecture and construction determined that the existing facilities did not meet state earthquake construction standards and that the site in the Berkeley hills was potentially dangerous because of its proximity to the Hayward Fault," Riles said. Planning for the new facilities was to begin immediately under the direction of John Worsley, state architect. They were designed as residential schools for 150 blind pupils and 500 deaf pupils, Riles said. The School for the Blind was approximately 115,000 square feet and the School for the Deaf was approximately 435,000 square feet. Construction costs were expected to total $20 million. Both schools were expected to be ready for occupancy in the fall of 1978. "These new schools will reflect the most modern design of residential schools for the handicapped," Riles said. "They will represent a commitment to quality educational opportunity for the deaf and blind children in California."*

NEWS RELEASE

FROM CALIFORNIA STATE DEPARTMENT OF EDUCATION

On Thursday, January 23, 1975, the California State Department of Education announced the California School for the Deaf and the California School for the Blind would be moved from their current sites in Berkeley to a new site in Fremont. Dr. Wilson Riles, Superintendent of Public Instruction, said the new site in Fremont, which covered 91 acres, was located in the civic center area. Purchase price for the land was $3,116,100.

Dr. Wilson Riles, State Superintendent of Public Instruction, 1971-1983, being interviewed by a local newscaster. Riles supported the relocation of CSD thoroughly.

This special assembly met in the CSD auditorium proved the desire of the staff and students to move CSD to Fremont. It overcame the resistance of the relocation movement.

> ***"The California School for the Deaf and Blind made outstanding contributions to the life and cultural history of Berkeley, and will be missed."***
>
> Lynn Laird
> &
> Stephaine Manning
> Writers for
> *Exactly Opposite The Golden Gate*

Controversial Issues Continue

While the new school was being planned and built, there were a number of on-going controversies about the trace of the Hayward fault and the validity of the exigency of the school relocation. The following serious issues emerged between 1975 and 1980.

1. The Daily California learned after a long investigation that state officials had no valid proof of such an active fault trace when they made their decision to move the schools in 1973.

2. Dorothy Radbruch-Hall, who worked for the U.S. Geological Survey, emphasized that two traces she drew through the schools' sites were inferred traces indicated by dotted lines, and not confirmed traces, which would have been shown by solid lines. The study concluded that the trace drawn by Radbruch-Hall underneath the school buildings, while possibly the location of an active fault 10,000 to 12,000 years ago, was therefore considered inactive under the state law in regard to earthquake hazards.

3. A group of neighbors living near CSD and CSB requested that the state Legislature investigate the schools' move to Fremont. It was apparent that the neighbors had realized that the University of California was active in efforts to secure the school campuses and possible problems that might be caused by a large number of UC students living on the campuses.

4. Opponents of the decision to move the schools were concerned that deaf students in Fremont would be harmed by

the loss of special educational, cultural, vocational, medical, and transportation facilities. They argued that the new site was in a less developed part of the San Francisco Bay area.

5. As a result of the discovery of the "inactive fault" the City of Berkeley Council Committee on the site recommended support for Assemblyman Tom Bates' call for reconsideration of the state's plan to move the schools to Fremont. Bates sent a telegram to Governor Jerry Brown requesting an emergency meeting of state officials to review the decision to relocate the schools.

> ***"The new site was less picturesque than the Berkeley school, but it has 'good access to cultural, vocational, transportation, and medical facilities. The new facilities are also larger and better designed to meet the needs of deaf and blind students.'"***
>
> Dr. Henry Klopping

The officials in the State Department of Education insisted that the plans were past the point of no return and the predication was that the construction was moving ahead. Dr. Griffing stated the error in fault mapping would not prevent the opening of the school facilities in Fremont in September, 1980, which were almost completed constructed.

When Dr. Henry Klopping became the superintendent of the California School for the Deaf in 1975, he was immediately involved in the planning of the relocation of the school. Intensely studying the blueprints of the new school, he readily took charge of the planning process.

He said the new site was less picturesque than the Berkeley school, but that it had "good access to cultural, vocational, transportation, and medical facilities. The new facilities are better designed to meet the needs of deaf and blind students."

After some years at Fremont, Dr. Klopping's statements have proved true. By now Fremont is far better in every respect than Berkeley.

PROGRAM FOR A NEW CAMPUS

In 1973, after the third relocation of CSD was definitely confirmed, the members of the staff were busy doing rough sketches of facilities they desired for the new campus. The result of their efforts was two massive documents titled Program for Construction, California School for the Deaf, serving Northern California, Volumes 1 and 2. These documents provided some general descriptions of the major components of the school, but they were not professional in perspective.

Architects of Ernest J. Kump Associates and Educational Planners of Tadlock Associates Inc. designed a book titled Program for a New Campus, offering new directions to meet the needs of future deaf children within an educational village. It was the result of months of work during the years of 1974-75 with CSD staff, interviews and visits at other nationally recognized

CSD
STREET SIGNS

There are two street signs located on a corner of the CSD campus, *Gallaudet Drive* and *Stevenson Boulevard.*

Gallaudet is named after Thomas Hopkins Gallaudet who pioneered the first permanent work for the Deaf in America and founded the first school for the deaf - the American School for the Deaf in Hartford, Connecticut in 1817.

Stevenson is named for Jack Stevenson who was the first Mayor of Fremont from 1956 to 1958 and again from 1960 to 1964. Some wishful deaf people thought that Stevenson Boulevard was coincidentally named after Dr. Elwood Stevenson who was Superintendent of CSD for 32 years.

schools for the deaf, and intensive study of the literature of the education of the deaf and the lives of deaf people. Members of the Bay Area deaf community and parents of students at CSD lent their support to making the project a success. In addition, the Vocational Advisory Committee of CSD met with faculty and planning staff to determine new directions for the school's career training program.

Under the direction of Dr. Henry Klopping, Superintendent of CSD, and his predecessor Dr. Hugo Schunhoff, a staff planning team was organized and worked directly with the staff of architects and educational planners during the project and completed the book, Program for a New Campus. The key purpose of a new campus was to provide, in a warm and congenial environment, the special learning and living programs that would enable the deaf to function successfully in society.

The Campus Concept

In the early stage of developing the campus concept, it was decided that the major focus would be a "commons," functioning not unlike that of a traditional village. Just off the commons (at present, the open space near the amphitheater is where students meet and socialize after lunch hour and before going to classes) are found the most intensely active social and service buildings such as the auditorium, food services, gymnasium, and as conceived in the planning — the educational center (library and media center).

The diagram on the next page shows the commons in the middle of the campus. Note that it includes the residence of the superintendent and a site for health services. Sadly, these proposed buildings were eliminated from the final construction planning by the state financial analyst. Ironically, in the years of 1895-1898, Dr. Warring Wilkinson, Principal, emphasized to the state legislators the need for a hospital which he had requested in every one of his reports over the years. To this day, the state has not heeded our real need for comprehensive health services. Why? At present, the health services facilities, shared by both deaf and blind students, are housed in a dormitory building on the campus of the school for the blind. However in 1999 the state allocated funds to design a new health service building and the new building should be ready in 2003.

Since the state discontinued the practice of building residences for state officials on state property, the loss of the structure was one of the biggest disappointments in the construction planning. But on the other hand, CSD was fortunate to keep most of the building plans intact. For example, the state analyst reluctantly permitted two courts in the gymnasium due to Dr.

DESIGN OF THE COMPONENTS

"The Campus Concept"

A major focus for the campus could be a commons functioning not unlike that of a traditional village. Off of this commons could be found the most intensely active social and service functions such as food services, auditorium, gymnasium, and–as it is conceived in this program–most certainly the educational center.

The staff was pleased to acknowledge that the architects of Kump Associates had grasped the concept of a new school to meet deaf students' needs. They considered CSD a school and not a substitute for the world off campus, but as a living laboratory for life skills, which would fill a need for the deaf student as great as the need to read. Kump Associates, under the guidance of Dr. Klopping and the heads of departments, created a presentation of a campus concept where the functions were distinct elements in an educational village rather than simply elements in an institution.

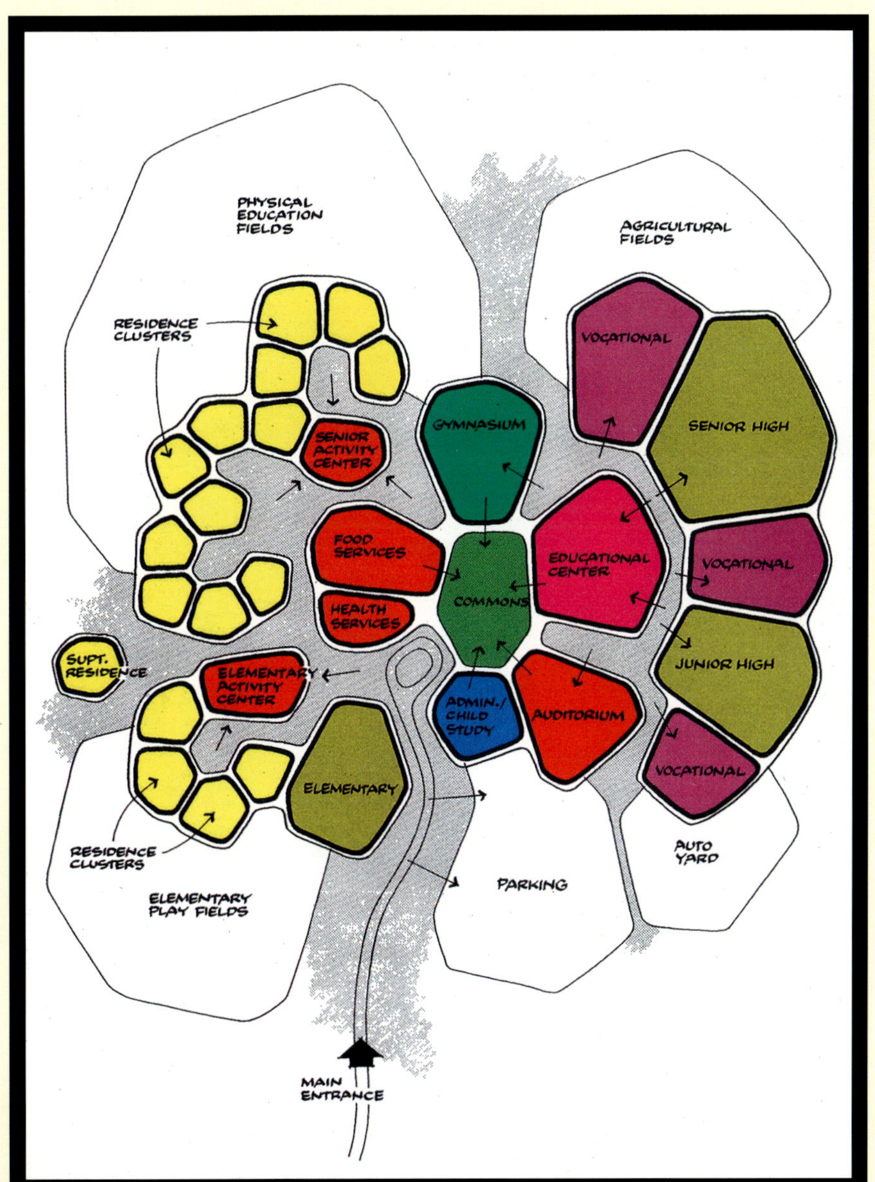

The Little Theater is the center of some of school activities. It has a tiered seating system so audiences always appreciate unobstructed views of programs on the stage.

Klopping's persistent efforts. After all, the gymnasium provides a center for the comprehensive physical education and athletic programs, both curricular and extracurricular. The three main objectives of the program are: 1) to develop optimum physical fitness, 2) to teach and develop the basic skills of team and individual sports, and 3) to develop proper attitudes toward competition and cooperative team participation.

In addition to facilities for physical education, interscholastic and intramural competition, the gymnasium has provided a major meeting area which will seat the entire school for assemblies and performances. Also, the gymnasium includes a refreshment and concession area; storage for equipment and supplies; lockers and showers for students, staff, and visiting teams; office space for instructors and coaches.

The other facility off the commons is the 350-seat Little Theater, which has been the most impressive facility in Fremont. The Little Theater has been especially popular for school and community plays and, also, it has served as a school assembly area enabling students, staff, parents, and others to gather for lectures, large group meetings, movies, storytelling, and community meetings, among other uses. One of the great features of the Little Theater is a tiered seating system so audiences always have unobstructed views of presentations on the stage. Also, the seating areas are accessible for wheelchairs and other essential equipment.

The dining building is the place where students and staff members enjoy associating and communicating with others in four pleasant dining rooms. Banquets and special events of various organizations are also held.

The food preparation and serving area has been one of the important facilities off the commons. The four dining rooms are pleasant places for students as well as staff to meet and communicate with others outside the classroom environment. Three meals a day are served for 400 resident students and the midday food service for approximately 120 day students. The table shapes and sizes vary to enhance a homelike and less institutional appearance. On the walls hang huge framed pictures of graduates of the last five years. Pictures prior to five years ago are stored in the museum and archives.

One of the four facilities surrounding the commons is the hub of the school and campus. The Educational Center, providing students and staff full library services, curriculum materials, development and production services, television and other visual instructional aid services, and special learning resources such as deaf studies, speech therapy, and reading skills resources. In addition to this, the Center houses the captioned film depository, the school museum, and the office and conference room for the director of instruction.

Construction of the New Fremont School

June 1, 1977, was one of the most memorable days in the CSD history. A number of state officials, the school staff, the entire student body, Fremont city officials, interested citizens, and the deaf community witnessed the groundbreaking ceremonies at the California School for the Deaf and the California School for the Blind near the Civic Center site. The ceremonies were held on Wednesday, June 1, 1977, at ten a.m., with Wilson Riles, State Superintendent of Public Instruction, as the keynote speaker. The spectators watched the groundbreaking formalities at the cauliflower field and a dirt road that later was paved and named Gallaudet Drive, the new address of the school.

Chief Deputy Superintendent Donald McKindley served as master of ceremonies and introduced public officials: Gene Rhodes, Mayor of Fremont; Frank Carrol, President, Fremont Chamber of Commerce; Al Bianco, for State Assemblyman Allister McAllister; Alfred Alquist, State Senator (San Jose); Wilson Riles, Superintendent of Public Instruction.

FREMONT'S SLOGAN:

"Fremont- City With a Mission"

> ***"What we have here will be the finest facility of its kind. California will be in the forefront of meeting the national mandate that every handicapped child is provided a public education which is appropriate to its individual needs."***
>
> ---
>
> Dr. Wilson Riles
>
> 

Keynote Speech

Wilson Riles elucidated the efforts to reach the reality of securing the new schools, "What we are seeing today is proof that when we say 'Quality education for all children in California' we mean it."

"It has taken us five years to get to this day. When the decision was made that new facilities would be built for CSD and CSB, what followed was mountains of red tape and seemingly endless bureaucratic procedures. But the commitment to meeting the special needs of blind and deaf children prevailed.

What we have here will be the finest facility of its kind. California will be in the forefront of meeting the national mandate that every handicapped child is provided a public education which is appropriate to their individual needs.

In addition to the quality instruction that children will receive here, they will learn in a pleasing physical environment. These schools will be an important part of the California Special Education Master Plan, reform of special education to meet the education needs of all individuals with exceptional needs.

The people of Fremont are to be congratulated for their cooperation in the selection of this site. I know there are many people to be thanked for their commitment and dedication to this project but I think it's appropriate for me to recognize the efforts of one person in particular, Dr. Barry Griffing, one of

Amid the students, Dr. Wilson Riles, Diane Alejo, President of the student body organization, and Dr. Henry Klopping broke the ground with gold-plated shovels for CSD.

our staff, has the scars to prove his commitment and dedication. His tenacity through thick and thin helped us all keep our pledge to this project.

All of the people who have worked so diligently to make these schools a reality can be proud of what has been accomplished in the best interests of deaf and blind children."

Steps in Construction of the New CSD

Dale Sprankle, an architect representing Kump Architects, Inc., based at Palo Alto, was selected to do the drawings of the CSD plans. Kump Architects, Inc. was well known for school designs. Dr. Klopping had spent a good amount of time at the Kump office to oversee the drawings. At times a department head accompanied Dr. Klopping to Palo Alto to review the plans and often suggested better and more appropriate designs to meet the needs of deaf children.

The skeletons of the vocational building, at left, and the high school building.

By December 1977, the construction was well underway. The athletic field was developed in an early stage. Sewer lines, water lines and underground utilities were in and completed. Unfortunately, heavy rains delayed the building of the residence cottages and mud and healthy weeds covered the campus. Although the light poles and gutters surrounding the school had been installed, entry to the campus was almost impossible, due to still unpaved roads. The contractors, Dickman Construction Company, were waiting for the area to dry and allow machinery to proceed with the work. The state was still in the process of bidding for constructing the academic building in April 1977.

The buildings of media, elementary school, little theater and cottages near the completion while the buildings of dining and gymnasium were not started yet.

By December 1978, the construction of cottages was underway, a vast network of housing for resident students. It was decided that siding for the buildings would be in cedar in lieu of redwood, due to budgetary restrictions at the state level. Under a separate contract, Williams and Burroughs, general contractors, were ready to begin the foundations for the academic, gymnasium,

administration and all other areas except the residential area. The projected opening of the school would be in the fall of 1980.

In January 1980, Robert Watrous, Business Manager at CSD for 17 years, undertook a new and critical assignment. He coordinated the move of the school from Berkeley to Fremont. The new task he assumed was a demanding responsibility, since he not only handled the 1.25 million dollars worth of new furniture and equipment purchased for the Fremont school, but he was also in charge of moving the existing teaching and other materials, furniture and equipment which were in good condition. Watrous coordinated the moving arrangements with the Bekins Company utilizing twelve huge vans shuttling back and forth between Berkeley and Fremont for two summer months. He assisted in employees' claims for moving expenses. A large number of the staff members followed the wave by moving to Fremont or nearby vicinities. Some faculty members remained where they had lived for several years before retiring. Upon the completion of the moving assignment, Bob Watrous officially retired in the fall of 1980.

Business Manager Robert Watrous retired in 1980 after serving as moving coordinator.

New Fremont School 1980

"Growing Pains"

On Wednesday, September 3, 1980, Dr. Klopping heartily welcomed back the CSD staff to the new Fremont school for the 1980-1981 school year. He commented on and was highly pleased by the fact that a tremendous effort had been made by the entire staff in order to receive students for their most significant school year. The staff had only ten days to prepare the classrooms and bedrooms before students swarmed onto the campus.

On Monday, September 15, 1980, school officially began its 121st year of educating deaf children. Enrollment on the first day numbered approximately 420 resident students and 135 day students. It was the football team and the girls volleyball teams who were the first students to reside in the cottages as the football members started early fall practice on August 26 under coach Gene Duve and assistant coach Gil Lentz. The boys practiced twice daily at Hopkins Jr. High School near the CSD campus. They played their first game of the season in Emeryville against Emery High School on September 12. The girls' volleyball members began practice on September 8 under coach Bob Ellis and assistant coaches, Ken Pedersen and Kathleen Cantrell.

The cottages surrounded with the tall weeds in the rear part of the campus were completed long before the other buildings.

All the buildings with the exception of the kitchen and the gymnasium were serviceable for the students as well as the staff at the beginning of the school year. For several weeks the California School for the Blind's kitchen and cafeteria were "borrowed" to cook and feed the CSD students. The football players had to use their own lockers in the cottages to store their practice uniforms. The smelly gear could at times hardly be tolerated. Yet, it was recalled that the students did not complain at all about the inconveniences. They were so excited about the new experience and everything new. They were very proud to be part of the new school development.

New Concept of Cottages

Overgrown weeds crept over the grounds among the cottages and other school buildings as the landscape work began later that year. The concept of the new living quarters for resident students is completely different from that of the dormitory setting in Berkeley. Each of the seventeen cottages for twenty-four students is divided into mini-cottage units.

Seventeen cottages with the privacy of a home-like atmosphere, completely different from that of the dormitory setting in the Berkeley school.

In each unit eight students enjoy the privacy of a home-like atmosphere. There are four bedrooms, each furnishing space for two students. Two bedrooms have an adjacent bathroom. There is a study area in an alcove for four students in a section of a large living room. In the center of each cottage there is a counseling room and bathroom. Adjacent to these rooms is a kitchenette and a utility room. The cottage concept has been a good method to facilitate personal development for various types of deaf children. Seniors have a different setting. Their quarters are an apartment complex so that they have the learning experience that stresses independent living skills.

During the first two months of the school year the sprinkler system crew laid PVC pipes with sprinkler heads in the grounds of the campus. At times when the system was tested, a number of students on the way to classes got soaked among the fountains. They had to get excuse slips from the residence counselors for being late to classes after returning to their cottages for dry clothes.

Complex School

During the first several weeks of the academic program, students as well as teachers groped through the complex classrooms and laboratories that were so unfamiliar to them. The fun lasted for a while before they solved the puzzle of the maze. That was true everywhere at that time. Even the parking areas were so complex that often new drivers became confused as to how to get out of the parking area, causing some laughs. It took most of the parents as well as visitors a year to become familiar with the geography of the new campus.

Going through the phase of "growing pains" at the new school, the staff and the students ran into a series of obstacles due to the situation of "newness." The operation of the new facilities was untried, unfamiliar, unventured, and unaccustomed. Even a simple communication between two departments broke down. One Sunday evening in the fall, some high school students, who stayed on the campus for a special occasion on that day, found the dining room closed and no souls in the kitchens to prepare supper for them. This put the cottage counselors in turmoil. Soon the superintendent solved the problem by ordering more than a hundred McDonald hamburgers, fries, and milk shakes. The kids were happy with the unexpected treat. Unfortunately, the only person who had to suffer this event was Roberta Alexander. She drove her own car to deliver the goodies four times. For the next four weeks she had to suffer with her car reeking of McDonalds!

"American Sign Language (ASL) 'the natural language' of the deaf can be seen in Fremont more, perhaps, than any other place in the country, if not the world."

Richard Mendugno
Argus correspondent

Fremont, a New Site for CSD

Geographicial Ideal

Is Fremont an ideal place for the new school after existing in San Francisco and Berkeley? A definite answer will eventually surface after a number of years. In 1975, when a site was purchased for the California School for the Deaf and the California School for the Blind, many people protested that Fremont was too rural, lacked culture, was deficient in vocational and medical facilities, and had poor access to special education needs for these schools. The site was once a cabbage field and was considered to be in a quite isolated area.

Fortunately, there was a group of people who anticipated that Fremont would be a good location for the schools. Their determination and persistence culminated in the purchase of the Fremont land. What was Fremont like in the 1980s? The new campus faced acres of colorful gladiolus flowers along Gallaudet Drive. Fremont was considered a mid-sized town with light traffic. Few Fremont citizens knew sign language. In fact, often deaf drivers got away with traffic citations since police officers were not familiar with deaf people and

Different angle (opposite page) of the aerial view of the CSD campus. Mission Boulevard, at left, extending toward Mission Peak. On the foothill, right, are Ohlone College and Mission San Jose district.

Before Berkeley and Oakland, there was Mission San Jose, the seed of Western culture in Alameda County.

let them go. There were few restaurants to frequent with friends. Medical facilities were diminutive but adequate. On the bright side, the site is near the end of the BART line, the beautiful Central Park and Lake Elizabeth, Mission Valley shopping center, the HUB and Ohlone College in the Mission San Jose District. Fremont is proud of being the home of Old Mission San Jose, the 14th of California's 21 missions. In 1997, Fremont celebrated the 200th anniversary of Old Mission church. Before Berkeley, there was Mission San Jose, the seed of Western culture in Alameda County.

Booming City

Now, some years after 1980, the city of Fremont itself has boomed. Fremont is home to nearly 200,000 people and covers 94 square miles. It is ten miles long and the fourth largest city in the Bay Area. It is a remarkably beautiful city, from majestic Mission Peak and the Spanish-era Mission San Jose in the east, to serene Coyote Hills and its recreated Ohlone village built on an ancient shell mound in the west, and from bucolic Niles Canyon in the north to the misty ghost town of Drawbridge on the bay in the south. Fremont is home to the nation's largest urban wildlife refuge, spanning 20,000 acres. At Ardenwood Historical Farm, one can see rural life re-created as it was 100 years ago. Fremont has good weather, good schools, good housing, and a good traffic system.

Prior to 1940, there were five towns: Centerville, Niles, Irvington, Mission San Jose, and Warm Springs, within the area where the city of Fremont became chartered in 1945. These five towns merged into districts. Silicon Valley, home base for much of the nation's high tech research and industry, has crept into Fremont's southern tip. The industries in that area have offered great vocational training for CSD students. The author of this book has watched Fremont and its people for almost 20 years, and that has been a most remarkable change. Fremont has been a magnet for a diverse population, so much so that about 130 languages and dialects are spoken in the homes of Fremont school-children. Of course, American sign language (ASL) is one of these languages.

Mission San Jose, one of five districts, celebrating the 200th anniversary of Old Mission church, the 14th of California's 21 missions.

"Martha's Vineyard Island"

It is significant to note that sign language classes given by CSD and Ohlone College have been very popular. Nowadays deaf people feel comfortable going to places in Fremont such as banks, grocery stores, hospitals, restaurants, department stores, and many firms where tellers, clerks, nurses, waiters, service people and others break barriers, knowing how to communicate in sign language. How time has changed! People used to sneer at deaf people for using sign language. Nowadays, in contrast, people apologize to deaf people for not being capable of communicating with them in sign language. Yet, deaf people have become more wary of their private conversations in public places lest there might be some patrons there who are able to read sign language.

Definitely, Fremont has become a community of "Martha's Vineyard Island" on the west coast. What in common do Fremont and Martha's Vineyard have? In the nineteenth century, Chilmark community's bilingualism in Martha's Vineyard Island, Massachusetts, extended into every facet of daily life. Sign Language formed an integral part of all communicative events, due to the Island

"We are building the kind of city that we dreamed of. It is a great place."

Gus Morrison
Mayor of Fremont
1998

Fremont, the All-American City.

having a large deaf population. Plenty of unusual experiences occurred in Chilmark. From *The California News*, January, 1919, *The Baltimore American* (1919) reported:

> **One hearing family of summer visitors was in need of potatoes. They carried a potato to a farm to show what they wanted. The deaf farmer's wife went into the house, got a telescope and signaled to a neighbor at another farmhouse on a far-off hillside for potatoes. Very soon that neighbor appeared carrying a telescope and a bushel of potatoes.**

A telescope was an important instrument for sign language communication at a distance far beyond the range of the human voice in Chilmark at that time. As for today in Fremont, a TTY (teletypewriter) device is a necessity for deaf people for communication at a distance as well as communication with hearing people. Technology has made a big advance in the deaf world.

Sign language has been utilized widely and freely in Fremont as described above. Hence, Fremont could be compared with Chilmark, a town in Martha's Vineyard Island.

On June 7, 1997, the National Civic League named Fremont an All-America City, one of ten cities in the United States. The winner was chosen based upon the level and quality of community participation in addressing civic problems and challenges. The competition was held in Kansas City.

For the second time in recent years, Fremont has been named one of the country's most "kid-friendly" cities in a survey on the best places to raise children. The Bay Area's fourth-largest city placed 16th among 219 cities with populations of more than 100,000 in the survey by Zero Population Growth in Washington, D. C. In 1999, Fremont was named the number one city, of the nation's largest cities, for rasing children.

CSD staff and students are very much a part of Fremont. They have blended into the mold of community life such as in sports, art festivals, politics, religion, career education, and many others. Clearly, Fremont is an ideal place for the California School for the Deaf.

Fremont logo.

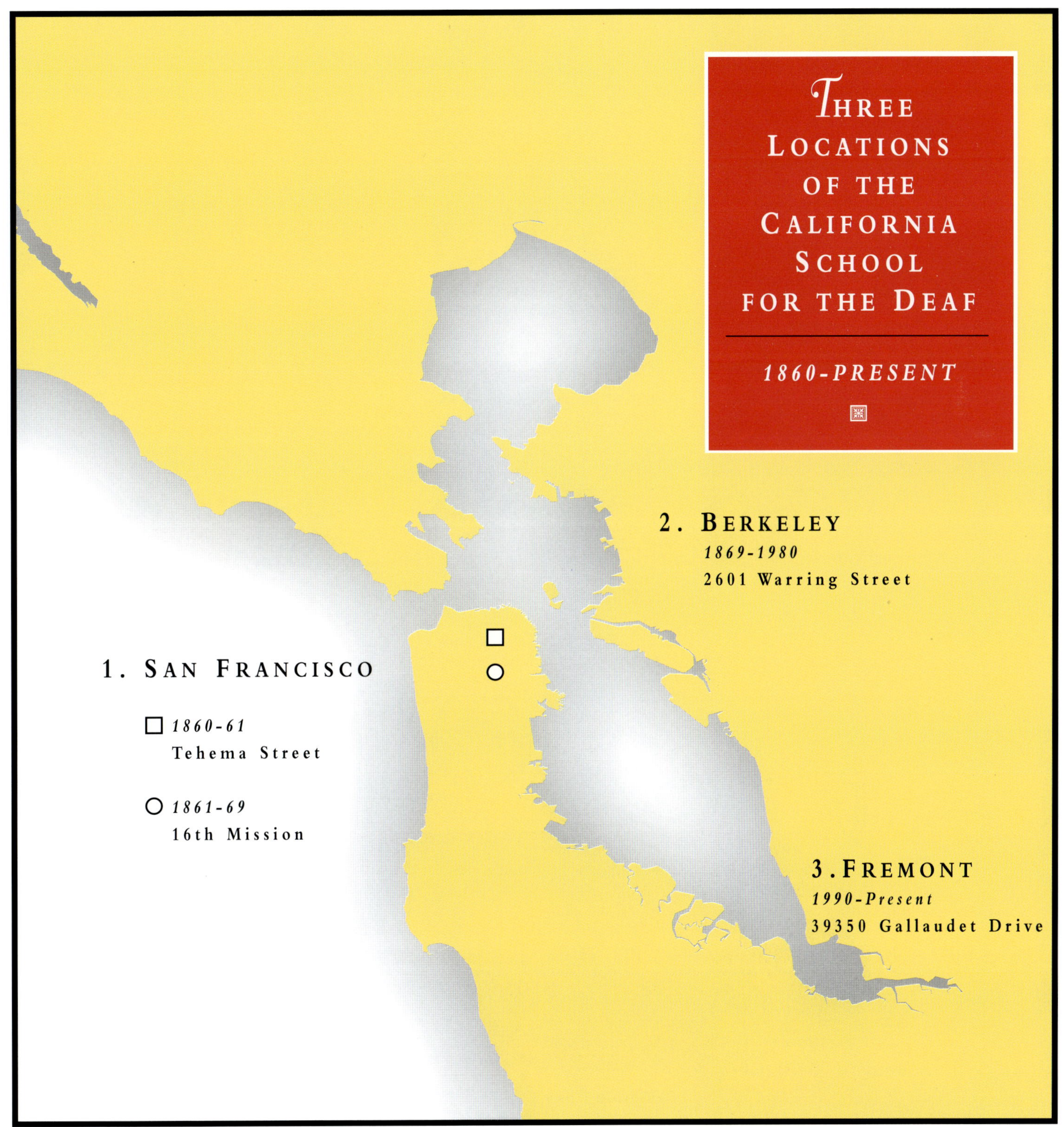
Three
Locations
of the
California
School
for the Deaf
1860-Present
2. Berkeley
1869-1980
2601 Warring Street
1. San Francisco
1860-61
Tehema Street
1861-69
16th Mission
3. Fremont
1990-Present
39350 Gallaudet Drive

THE
LIFORNIA
NEWS
MARCH 1944

alifornia News
MAY, 1953

CALIFORNIA SCHOOL FOR THE DEAF
BERKELEY
1860
CENTENNIAL
1960
MAY 1, 1960

THE CALIFORNIA NEWS
1910
1951

THE CALIFORNIA
NEWS
F
A
A

THE CALIFORNIA NEWS
Senior
Number
JUNE
1952

The
California
News

The
California
News

The California News

THE
CALIFOR
NEWS

THE
CALIFOR
NEWS

THE
CALIFOR
NEWS

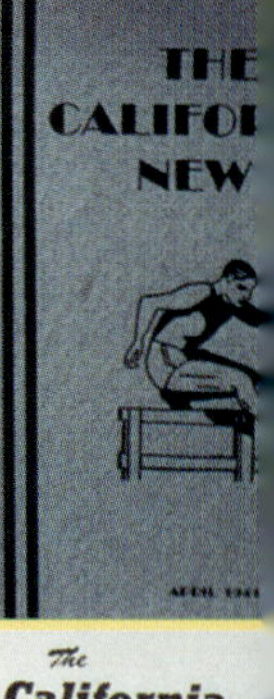
THE
CALIFOR
NEW

The
California
News
1954

The
Californ
News
November
1962

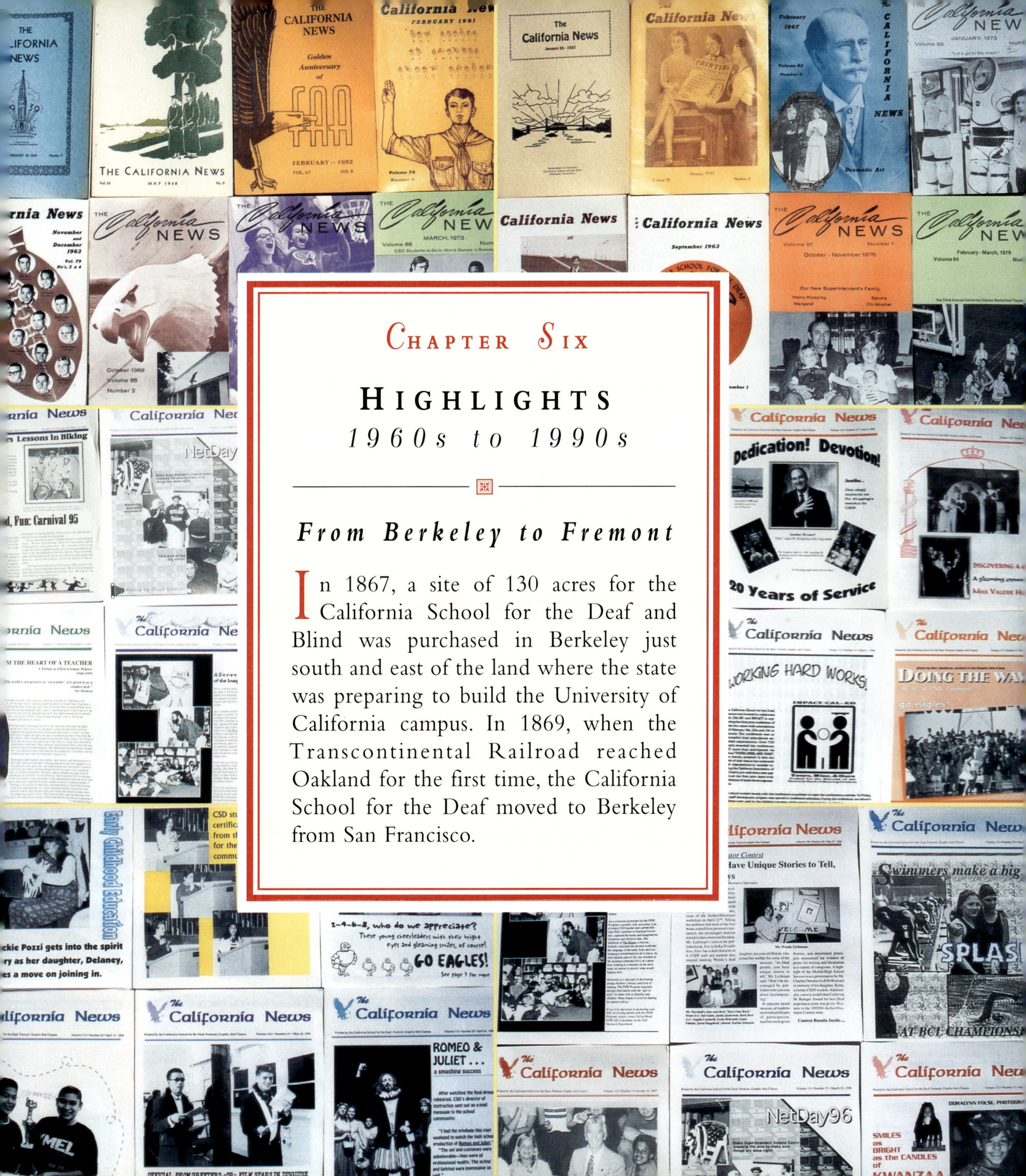

Chapter Six

HIGHLIGHTS
1960s to 1990s

From Berkeley to Fremont

In 1867, a site of 130 acres for the California School for the Deaf and Blind was purchased in Berkeley just south and east of the land where the state was preparing to build the University of California campus. In 1869, when the Transcontinental Railroad reached Oakland for the first time, the California School for the Deaf moved to Berkeley from San Francisco.

The College of California (the University of California) purchased land at the eastern part of the Berkeley community in 1864, but it still held classes in Oakland.

Rear of the school building looking westward toward Berkeley and Golden Gate. Photograph was taken in April 1874 by Edward Muybridge. The University of California, the state's second institution, was started a few years after CSD opened in 1860. It can be seen at the right. The land was purchased in 1864 while the College of California (the University of California) classes were held in Oakland. One thousand eucalyptus trees imported from Australia were planted on the slope at the back of the CSD school buildings. These trees seemed native to the area.

In 1870, the eastern part of Berkeley around the CSD campus was a farming and ranch community, but industrial growth started in the western portion of the community named Ocean View. In 1872, the first horse-drawn trolley on Telegraph Avenue began service. The students as well as the staff members had to trek between the campus and Telegraph Avenue. The records of the school affairs in that year indicate that the staff members and students hired a horse-drawn carriage to haul them between those points. At that time the surrounding area was sparsely populated. On the CSD campus, from one of the school buildings, fields of tall golden grain could be seen in all directions. At Bancroft Way and Telegraph Avenue there were a few homes and a hotel which had a small store and restaurant.

Some years after 1869, the town became a residential community. The University of California (The College of California) moved from Oakland to Berkeley and opened on September 25, 1873. In 1876, a steam train started to run along Shattuck Avenue. Only 16 years later, electric street cars were built in Berkeley to replace horse-cars and steam trains.

Preceding spread:
Covers of the California News, *copies from 1895 to the present.*

University Express trolley drawn by a horse on Telegraph Avenue in 1888. Doubtlessly, CSD students riding in this trolley to Oakland back and forth to the school. The students as well as the staff members had to trek between the campus and Telegraph Avenue. The records of the school affairs in that year indicated that the staff members and students hired a horse-drawn carriage to haul them between those points. The surrounding area was sparsely populated. At Bancroft Way and Telehraph Avenue, there were a few homes which had a small store and restaurant.

ACT OF INCORPORATION

In April of 1878, the Governor of California (William Irwin) signed the Act of Incorporation; and Berkeley became a city, combining the two very different communities of Ocean View and Berkeley. The big change transformed Berkeley from a town to a city that was a viable commuter suburb of San Francisco and Oakland. That year a new building, a brick Romanesque style, was constructed and ready for 200 deaf and blind students. The building was a one story Educational Building.

After the San Francisco Earthquake and Fire of 1906, Berkeley's population doubled within one year. In every direction new houses sprang up and new residents kept coming.

During the years of CSD in Berkeley, CSD had a few opportunities to become involved in the affairs of the city of Berkeley. The Boy Scouts, World War II defense training, and athletic competition were among a few activities that Berkeley was involved in with CSD.

New buildings, brick Romanesque style, for 200 deaf and blind students circa 1885. In 1878, Berkeley became a city, combining the two communities of Ocean View and Berkeley.

The drug store, J. T. Scow Pharmacy, on the corner of College Avenue and Derby Street, three blocks from the CSD campus. Students frequented the drug store in the 1940s. Electric trolley cars running on College Avenue from Oakland to Albany. From the 30s to the 50s, the Key System rail lines (the size of the train was as big as the Bay Area Rapid Transit (BART) helped by providing the residents near CSD with cheap, fast transportation from the Claremont Hotel area or Shattuck Avenue to downtown Oakland and San Francisco. The Key System was taken over by buses in the 50s.

BLUE PASS FOR MOVIES

During the 1940s and 1950s, College Avenue, Telegraph Avenue and Shattuck Avenue were students' favorite places to browse or shop. Going to the United Artist theater on Shattuck Avenue was popular for CSD students, especially since they paid only ten cents with a blue pass granted by the theater for double features. However, the school rules required that girls and boys take turns on alternate Saturdays and Sundays separately. With no captions in those days, naturally students tended to reconstruct the plot and tell their own imaginative versions to each other in the dormitories.

CSD IN THE 1960s:
Leadership

ERUPTION OF RIOTS

During the most radical period in the 1960s, CSD was only a few blocks away from the University of California, Berkeley (UCB), campus known for the Free Speech Movement (FSM) and the once-elegant Telegraph Avenue which was now erupting with flower children in funky clothes imbibing illegal substances. At first, the young people appeared to be idealistic and enthusiastic and many did not know what they were fighting for. They were disillusioned. A large group of policemen arrived with automatic rifles, but no one thought the policemen would use the butts of rifles and tear gas on rioters. Many were injured; many were arrested.

Such a scene created a clear and present danger that alarmed the CSD staff, counselors and parents and they restrained the students from going to town. The students felt deprived of their freedom to stroll on Telegraph Avenue or on the UC campus. On the other side of the nation, there was the massive antiwar and civil rights protest. In short, America was in turmoil.

By 1960, Berkeley was no longer a model city. The middle class, which paid high taxes and demanded relatively few services, had fled to the suburbs, replaced by people who were poorer and in great need of health, housing, recreation, schooling and other city services. Berkeley became a city of diverse neighborhoods. In 1964, anti-war and anti-establishment forces erupted suddenly on the University campus with the Free Speech movement, a conflict so massive and emotionally fraught that it was covered in the world press. In a way the CSD campus was strangely affected. How? The author approached

High School Principal Gilbert Delgado and asked if he could be excused from that afternoon preparation period for he suddenly had a bad case of a cold. He was excused, but when he drove out of the Caldecott tunnel toward Concord, "the chills" were gone. Later it was found that police helicopters had dropped tear gas over the riot area. The westward winds blew it away and it landed on the CSD campus. Some faculty members and students were caught in the attack. That was one of several unpleasant memorable experiences in the 1960s. Another one found the letters CSD on the hill above the campus were painted green and spelled "LSD." Naturally, the Foothills Athletic Association boys immediately responded by painting the letters back in orange!

Sweeping panorma of the Berkeley campus (front) and the University of California (upper right) sided by Memorial Stadium.

The 1960s CSD students, members of the Junior National Association of the Deaf, carried out some projects during the school year of 1966-67. Officers at first row: GaryHemphill, Sergeant-at-arms; Hohn Nickelson, Stamp Collector; Brenda Underwood, Secretary; Librarian Caroline Burnes, Sponsor; James Halseth, President; Claire Clancey, Treasurer; George Pehlgrim, Project Committee; Mary Beserra, Stamp Collector; Gail Gisler, Sergeant-at-arms.

Harold Ramger, Chemistry teacher (1951-1968). Active member of the California Association of the Deaf. Husband of Catherine Marshall Ramger, author of 100 Year History of CSD.

CSD Leaders

In one of history's ironies, in spite of the national crisis, CSD sustained a great image of leadership in education, sports, interpreting and national organizations for the deaf.

As the era of Dr. Elwood Stevenson was concluded, CSD Berkeley opened its new year on September 8, 1960, with a new superintendent, Dr. Hugo F. Schunhoff. He had achieved national recognition in the area of education when he was elected president of the Conference of Executives of American Schools for the Deaf at its 35th meeting in Washington, D. C.

The final phase of construction on the Berkeley campus was completed. A new wing was added to the Advanced Education Building and it opened for service in 1960. Thirteen classrooms and a memorial library housing a museum occupied the wing.

Among the nation's great deaf leaders in the sixties was Byron B. Burnes, a keen intellect, and president of the National Association of the Deaf for six terms from 1946 to 1964 and editor of The Silent Worker for 18 years. He was a master teacher. Ralph Neesam, CSD high school principal, gained recognition as one of the few national great interpreters. He was elected as president of the National Registry of Interpreters for the Deaf (RID). Leo Jacobs, a mathematics teacher, emerged as secretary of Gallaudet College Alumni Association (GCAA) for two terms and later as president of GCAA in the

1970s. Harold Ramger, a chemistry teacher, was a very active member of the California Association of the Deaf and secretary, vice-president, and president of that organization. Ralph Jordan, a CSD teacher, was a founder and an executive director of the East Bay Counseling and Referral Agency for the Deaf (EBCRAD) in 1961 and he initiated the idea of evening deaf adult class programs that led to the establishment of Ohlone College for the deaf program. Emil Ladner, a social studies teacher, was elected president of the International Catholic Deaf Association (ICDA) at its annual convention in Buffalo in July, 1963.

Of the CSD staff members, Helen Myers, popular teacher of English and Reading in the CSD High School Department, was elected President of California Association of Teachers of Deaf and Hard of Hearing Children (CATDHHC). Being very active in that organization, she was best remembered as chairperson of the state convention held in Berkeley in 1963. February 23, 1963 was the big night. The banquet was held by Gallaudet College Alumni Association (Northern California Chapter) to honor the birthday of Dr. Edward Miner Gallaudet, founder of Gallaudet University and Dr. Irving S. Fusfeld. Dr. Fusfeld was loved and respected locally, nationally, and worldwide. At that time, he was approaching retirement after six years as psychologist at CSD. A number of speeches paid tribute to Dr. Fusfeld's forty years at Gallaudet as teacher, dean, and vice-president.

Gilbert Delgado's resignation at the close of the 1963-64 school year was CSD's big loss. He had been Supervising Teacher in the High School Department since 1958. He became Assistant Director of Captioned Films for the Deaf, in the United States Office of Education, Washington, D. C. Delgado was an efficient and popular member of the staff. He was an enthusiastic participant in all school affairs. He was Superintendent of the New Mexico School for the Deaf when he retired in 1994.

CSD alumni played a big part in one of the most memorable conventions of the National Association of the Deaf (NAD) in San Francisco in 1966. The grand old Palace Hotel was the headquarters of the convention. Also, a number of alumni were involved in an unusual variety show with a distinctive San Francisco flavor called the "Barbary Coast" presented at the Palace Hotel and directed by Eric Malzkuhn, a H.S. teacher. Heading the committee was Julian Singleton, a 1952 graduate of CSD.

The sports program of CSD developed prowess and attained much glory during the years of the 60s. Two national champions and three league champions in football were featured. A number of players were elected All Americans in football, basketball, wrestling, and track among all schools for the deaf. Wrestling was established in 1964 and coached by Dean Swaim, a junior high school teacher and Donald Bullock, a vocational instructor.

Ralph Jordan, Junior High mathematics teacher (1951-1982). Founder and Executive Director of East Bay Counseling and Referral Agency for the Deaf *(now* Deaf Counseling, Advocacy and Referral Agency (DCARA).

"We believe that the Deaf can meet the world on equal terms."

Dr. Irving Fusfeld
Coronet April, 1950

Dr. Irving S. Fusfeld, loved and respected locally, nationally and worldwide.

Gilbert Delgado, popular supervising teacher of High School Department, 1958-1964.

In 1968, Ken Norton, a HS teacher and coach, established the first Tryouts for the World Games for the Deaf at CSD and the University of California athletic facilities. The top deaf athletes met on August 9 and 10 for tryouts in five different sports to represent the United States at the World Games for the Deaf in Belgrade, Yugoslavia, in 1969. This was the first time deaf athletes in the United States competed with one another in order to make the U.S. team. A large number of CSD athletes participated and won many medallions at the 1965 World Games for the Deaf at Washington, D. C., and the 1969 World Games for the Deaf.

At the 1965 International Games for the Deaf, standing on the victory stand, CSD's Ken Pedersen (right), only 17 years old, won a bronze medal in broad jump. Albert Couthen (middle), USA, first place; Alexi Suprunov, USSR, second place. CSD-Berkeley was highly proud of its own five top athletes who achieved the most impressive historic marks at IGD at the University of Maryland, June 27 to July 3, 1965. James Davis, Donald Lyons, Ronald Gough, Ken Pedersen, Walter Rothrock and Richard Baraona were the big five "Olympians." Additional information on them is in Chapter 8.

The enormous success of the 1969 Convention of American Instructors of the Deaf hosted by CSD was proudly scripted in history. The participants enjoyed interesting programs, discussions, exhibits, inspiring addresses, and fellowship arranged by the hard work of the CSD staff.

At the opening of the school year of 1968-69, CSD was shocked by the untimely death of Harold Ramger, a science teacher, and his two daughters, due to carbon monoxide fumes which permeated the Ramgers' living quarters from the garage, where they had forgotten to turn off the ignition of their automobile. Catherine "Cato" Ramger regained consciousness on the second day and recovered. She retired soon afterwards.

Edith Una Stevenson, daughter of the well-known deaf educator, Dr. J. Schuyler Long. Stevenson was always a warm friend and champion of the deaf.

Edith Una Stevenson, the wife of the former superintendent, Dr. Elwood Stevenson, passed away on October 30, 1969, at the age of 76. Fluent and graceful in sign language, she was one of the few hearing people who participated socially in the deaf community. She taught at CSD for twelve years and her former students swelled the ranks of her admirers, who came from every walk of life.

During the school year of 1969-1970, a new program was started that was not ordinarily found in CSD's curriculum. Five students took geometry and world history courses part-time at Albany High School. They were: Lynn Denman, Steve Longo, Edward Corey, Gregory Singleton and Philip Taylor, along with a resource teacher, Page Barber. This experimental program was expected to answer questions, such as how well deaf or hard of hearing students could be educated in a public educational center, where they were pretty much removed from their usual way of life and education at CSD.

BARRY L. GRIFFING APPOINTED

Assistant Division Chief

At the beginning of the 1970s, Barry L. Griffing, who served CSD in the capacity of Dean of Students from 1963 to 1965, was appointed Assistant Chief of the Division of Special Education of the State of California. The DSE had responsibility for five residential schools in California and for three bureaus which deal with special education programs in the California public schools. Griffing was the son of W. Theodore "Ted" and Wendell Griffing, well-known deaf educators of the deaf in Oklahoma.

CSD IN THE 1970s: *Uncertainties and Triumphs*

CRISIS AT CSD

The 1970s saw a phase of uncertainties as well as triumphs for CSD. It dealt with unpredictable events that threatened grave situations for the CSD programs, but they were adroitly converted into successes. The main reason for the triumphs was that they were deftly handled by Dr. Hugo Schunhoff, Dr. Henry Klopping, Dr. Barry Griffing, the CSD staff, the parents, the deaf Community, and the California Department of Education.

The pendulum of the1970's had swung drastically and reversed the images of UCB and CSD. UCB which had experienced major destruction resulting from the 1960s riots, now rose into a "Phoenix." In contrast, the peaceful CSD now experienced an obstacle, a threat to its tradition from the Legislature in Sacramento. Due to the threat of an earthquake and economic pressures from organized lobbies, the California Department of Education was now

The 1970s CSD students, sitting in the "LS" form in front of the Berkeley auditorium, were officers and advisers of Theophilus d'Estrella Literary Society. First row, left to right: Diane Alejo, Secretary; Mike Daviton, Vice President; Laura Lyons, President; Jay Salisbury, Boys' Assistant Treasurer; Nancy Rojas, Sergeant-at-arms; Betsy Ford, Adviser. Second row: Debbie Earnest, Girls' Treasurer; Envie Bogan, Sergeant-at-arms, Mary Herrold, Adviser. Third row: Ralph Singleton, Boys' Treasurer; David Peterson, Adviser. Fourth row: Filipele Leomiti, Sergeant-at-arms; Michaele Call, Adviser; Victor Hutchins, Adviser.

considering closing the CSD campus in Berkeley and moving it. It sent a disturbing wave to the CSD staff, parents, and the deaf community as a threat to the education of the young deaf children. The concept of closing CSD was unthinkable and it aroused interested people into taking action to retain CSD in Berkeley. It was the beginning of a twilight struggle for the CSD staff and the deaf community to fight for the status of CSD.

Nevertheless, with the tremendous support of the CSD staff and the deaf community, Dr. Hugo Schunhoff ably maneuvered CSD through the years of 1972 to 1975 to a victory. Instead of closing down, CSD survived and as a result, the Legislature signed a bill for CSD to move to a new site in Fremont by 1978. Dr. Schunhoff, the deaf citizens, several CSD staff members and the California Department of Education were the four great factors in the final process of the transition plan.

Finally, negotiations were completed for the purchase of 91 acres in the heart of Fremont as the future site for CSD and CSB, including units for the multi-handicapped. The land was bounded by Stevenson Boulevard, Walnut Avenue, Overacker Avenue, and a road yet to be built (Gallaudet Drive). It was purchased from the Church of Jesus Christ of Latter-Day Saints at $35,000 per acre. The actual price for public sale was $45,000 per acre.

SWEET DREAMS

During the periods of the 1970s, Telegraph Avenue and Shattuck Avenue were no longer good places for the students to shop or browse. Unlike the rest of Berkeley, Elmwood area near CSD held its small-town charm with a number

of small shops including an old-fashioned donut shop. Sweet Dreams on College Avenue was one of the favorite spots for students who had a craving for sweets and ice cream. Also, it was a choice for award winners from the academic department or residential department.

Vernon and Ruth Birck had the distinction of being the first persons in any residential school for the deaf in the nation to be designated "dean of boys and dean of girls." They joined the CSD staff in 1928, and retired in 1957.

Change of Hands

A change of hands in the office of Assistant Superintendent for Instruction took place in 1971. Myron A. Leenhouts retired after forty years of outstanding services as a distinguished educator of the deaf. During Leenhouts' 27 years at Berkeley, he set a national record for sending a large number of students to college. Jacob S. Arcanin was appointed to fill the vacancy left by Myron Leenhouts. Arcanin was no stranger to CSD, he had formerly been dean of students amongst other positions. Since he was thoroughly familiar with the school and how it operated, he has been a most efficient Assistant Superintendent.

Ken Norton, a teacher in the high school department and CSD's football, basketball, and track coach, was elected to the American Athletic Association of the Deaf (AAAD) Hall of Fame as a coach on April 2, 1971, at St. Louis, Missouri.

In 1972, William Dean Swaim was appointed to the position of High School Principal by Dr. Schunhoff, filling the vacancy left by Ralph Neesam. He entered the new role in CSD upon his return from the Leadership Training Program in the Area of the Deaf at California State University at Northridge. In that year, Ralph Neesam was appointed to the recently established position of Supervisor of Staff Development. Working directly with the superintendent, he directed inservice training in all departments of the school.

Vernon Birck, a CSD retiree for 17 years, passed away on November 15, 1974. He had come to CSD in 1928 with his wife, Ruth, and served as Dean of Boys until his retirement in March, 1957. Mrs. Birck was Dean of Girls until 1957. Mr. Birck was instrumental in establishing the Student Body organization and in selecting its creed, "I Can." His influence had long been felt on the Berkeley campus as he was a "father" to the boys. The students also loved Ruth Birck as their "mother" and her fantastic storytelling sessions.

Speak Out

Until the 1970s, it was not often that deaf people were heard. So, it was Leo Jacobs who had an opportunity to write a book on Deafness, *A Deaf Adult Speaks Out*, in 1974 that broke the silence. Leo's personal life experience contributed to the manuscript and was perfectly relevant.

> *"I conceive of total communication not so much as a method as it is a PHILOSOPHY – a way of thinking which is rational, kind, considerate, and sensitive to the needs of deaf children. In my way of thinking, total communication is any method or a combination of two or more methods of conveying a desired message to a hearing impaired person such that he is able to understand 100 per cent of the message. And, he should also be able to express himself so that his vis-a-vis will understand him 100 per cent. In the latter case, since the person in question is the one who is handicapped, adjustments should be made by the vis-a-vis so that he is able to receive communication 100 per cent from the handicapped person."*
>
> Leo M. Jacobs
> Author of
> *A Deaf Adult Speaks Out*

Vibrant Administrator

In the summer of 1975 appeared a new young, energetic superintendent, Dr. Henry Klopping, with his gorgeous wife, Sandra "Bunny"and a cute three year old daughter, Margaret. Never had there been such youthful spirit of well-being at CSD.The Klopping family brought an inspiring mood to CSD. Starting a new tradition, the Kloppings opened their home on the campus to CSD children for Christmas holidays, graduation class celebrations, and other special events. Also, annually, new parents, APTC, CAC, and other special groups socially gathered at the Klopping residence.

There was a flutter of intense excitement among the CSD staff and the deaf community for this dynamic leader. Dr. Klopping came with a forceful influence, both in thoughts and expression. Instantly, he took up the reins of CSD and expanded various programs such as Continuing and Community Education with Leo M. Jacobs as Coordinator. The CCE program was established in 1975 to serve the needs of the deaf community throughout the San Francisco Bay Area.

Upon the advice from the Legislature, the Special Unit (SU) program was established in 1976. Hence, the first floors of two primary dormitory halls, Norton and Runde Halls, which had been closed since 1972, were reopened after reinforcement repairs.

In addition, Dr. Klopping worked closely with the Department of Finance in Sacramento and the architects in Palo Alto to insure the continuation of the construction program for the new school in Fremont. It was an arduous task. When the legislative analyst was determined to eliminate a superintendent's residence, infirmary, and other possible structures, Dr. Klopping made a logical and most effective defense and saved many facilities .The crux of his argument was that those structures were imperatively needed and that deaf children had the right to them in a residential school.This reflects his advocacy as well as love for deaf children. Mrs. Klopping, a professor at Ohlone College, had shown equal support and love for the school. Under the Klopping guidance, CSD maintained its foremost rank among the schools for the deaf in America.

Kenneth Walters Norton was appointed to be the Dean of Students by Dr. Klopping in November, 1975, after Paul Small, the former Dean of Students, transferred to a new position in the California State Department of Education. Norton's goals were to develop a new program to help children to "learn how to learn by themselves and develop the ability of making their own decisions."Also, he wanted to see every student have a happy student life in the school community.

During 1970s, the term "least restrictive environment" (LRE) had been employed in frequent discussions of both the philosophy and the implementation of the education concept of mainstreaming. This issue had become a blistering controversy and an alarming threat in the deaf community and among the educators of the deaf and the state residential schools. It was of great concern that the interpretation of LRE might create a misleading concept for parents of deaf children.

FIRST ANNUAL CALIFORNIA CLASSIC
On February 19, 1977, the New Mexico School for the Deaf basketball team pulled the upset of the first western states schools for the deaf basketball tournament by defeating Riverside 48 to 45 in the finals to win the first annual California Classic. Added features to the basketball tournament were the wrestling matches and the girls basketball game between the two schools for the deaf in California, Berkeley and Riverside. The Berkeley wrestling team defeated the Riverside team 48 to 13. The girls basketball results: Riverside 30 - Berkeley 28.

Ohlone College, a community college in Fremont. Every year a number of graduates from CSD as well as students from other states and foreign countries are admitted to Ohlone College for further education.

Dr. Wilson Riles (left), Dr. Barry Griffing, Dr. Henry Klopping. Dr. Griffing and Dr. Klopping established the tournament idea called Western States Basketball Tournament first played at CSD. The idea proved a huge success as it has occurred every year since then. The schools for the deaf participating in the tournaments are Arizona, Colorado, Fremont, Idaho, New Mexico, Oregon, Riverside, Utah and Washington.

HEARING AID DATED 1400-1550

A hearing aid used by Costa Rica Indians between the years 1400-1550 A.D. was presented to CSD by Alva G. Stan. This unique but rather crude hearing aid was found in 1860 while the site was being searched for pre-Columbian artifacts. It might have been in a grave site of Costa Rica Indians who were killed during the Christopher Columbus expedition in that area.

The California News
December 1977 / January 1978 issue

Diane Alejo, a senior and President of the student body organization-Junior National Association of the Deaf, had the honor to break the first ground with the gold plated shovel in Fremont representing the students of CSD Berkeley. Dr. Wilson Riles and Dr. Klopping were the others helping with the ground breaking ceremony on June 1, 1977.

After the event, chartered buses took the students and chaperons to the Candlestick stadium to watch a baseball game, which was an annual event, at the invitation of the San Francisco Giants.

As the city of Berkeley was celebrating its 100th birthday in 1978 and the University of California marked its 110th anniversary, CSD was exalted by its 118th anniversary. During the 1870s, there were two villages, Ocean View in the west side of Berkeley and Berkeley itself in the east side where CSD and UC were. It is interesting to note that CSD's first trustee, Frederick Billings, proposed Berkeley be the name for both villages.

In April 1978, the officers of the Stockton Telephone Pioneers donated three No.15 teletypes (TTYs) to CSD as a result of the efforts of C. S. Lamb, parent of CSD students, Sherry and Ann Lamb. TTYs were to become a fixture at CSD and to play a prominent role in giving deaf staff access to communication.

In 1980, CSD moved from Berkeley to Fremont after a long struggle by the University to acquire the 130-acre campus. The school's location in Berkeley had been the site of one of the oldest and most esteemed of the State's institutions. Now the CSD campus is part of the University of California and named Clark Kerr Campus after a former president of the University.

The appearance of No. 15 TTY appears as huge and bulky in contrast to the 1990s small and streamlined TTY machine. It was remembered that No. 15 TTY machine swayed and made uproarious noise when deaf people communicated with friends or relatives.

CSD IN THE 1980s:
Sunrise

"LAND OF OZ"

The decade of 1980 reflected a scene of social, academic, athletic, and political successes of CSD life with the new school in Fremont, a city with open arms to the deaf people. It was a great age. Although most years had sunrises, there were a few sunsets.

On the first day of the Preparation Week, September 3, 1980, the new CSD buildings, without a visible sign, on a barren, treeless landscape resembled new townhouses to a good number of CSD staff members. When they drove until they reached the end of Gallaudet Drive, they immediately realized the "townhouses" were the new CSD campus. Turning back, they entered the campus with a curious mixture of anxiety, hope, and excitement, like penetrating the Land of Oz.

The early 1980s elementary children posing in front of a new cottage at the Fremont school. Some of these students are graduates of Gallaudet University, National Technical Institute for the Deaf or other universities; became all star athletes; are married or teachers. (Front row sitting) Cheyenne Buchan, Amy Green, Julie Cantrell, Dana Clark, Brian Wright, Malaney Rodgers, (front row standing) Fredrick Chinn, Tyrone Kovacs, Michael Bauer, Teresa Maxwell, Erin Thomas, Tara Petrites, Kevin Kovacs, (back row standing) Dana Overgaard, Gary Lundstrom, Jon Kovacs, Ray Maxwell, Dawn Otani, Sudheer Vahn, Rebecca Villegas.

THEY REALIZE THAT THEY CAN NEVER CAN GO HOME (BERKELEY) AGAIN, FOR THINGS WILL LOOK DIFFERENT

Ronald Stern's appointment to serve Fremont's city government was the result of a great deal of interest generated at the KNOW YOUR CITY workshop for Fremont deaf citizens on October 17, 1981. Mayor Mezzetti spoke to the workshop participants and indicated his desire to have deaf citizens in the city government. As Stern's main interest was in recreation, he was most fitting in position of recreation commissioner. Currently, he is Superintendent of the New Mexico School for the Deaf.

The new campus design was not only entirely different from the California Spanish style buildings at Berkeley, but also in a different town, out in the country. To some alumni and CSD staff members, the new school seemed to be so "foreign" that they longed to go back "home" in Berkeley. There was so much nostalgia and sentimentality, but perhaps without a rationale. For illustration, it might be like comparing a beautiful girl with some questionable character. The exteriors of the CSD buildings in Berkeley were indeed beautiful, but the classrooms were small and venerable and the dormitories were antiquated with fragile windows that required constant repairs. On the other hand, the exterior architectural design of CSD buildings in Fremont appears more modern, and includes larger classrooms with better facilities and updated technology. The school, also, afforded the same staff members, the same productive educational programs, goals, and objectives and even the same statue of The Bear Hunt on the campus as in the days back in Berkeley. As the staff and alumni have grown accustomed to the change, the new school flourishes with new spirit and faith for the future.

BOND BETWEEN CSD AND FREMONT

On December 1, 1981, at 8:00 p.m. the Fremont City Council members solemnly assembled in the Council Chamber. A large number of deaf people with an interpreter filled one section. There was much excitement stirring in the air, for it was a special occasion. At 8:10 as the members and the audience rose and cheered, Ronald Stern, a CSD high school teacher, entered and walked down the aisle to the council table. Facing the audience, he smiled and nodded his head acknowledging their support. Mr. Stern was newly appointed to the City Recreation Commission. He spoke briefly with voice and sign language; he deemed the new position as a privilege and an honor to serve on the City Recreation Comission. To many deaf people, it was a rare sight for a deaf person to be participating as a Government official.

At large, the above scene reflected the Fremont citizens' enthusiasm for and recognition of the value to include the deaf people in its community. Through the Know Your City workshop a month before, Mayor Mezzitti had come to know Mr. Stern and was impressed with his leadership, experience and interest in recreation. Hence, an excellent interaction between Fremont City and CSD was established.

NEW EXPERIENCES AT CSD

The years 1981-1985 witnessed the appearance of many students who were identified as the Rubella Bulge. The stress for space at CSD revealed the immediate need for more bunk beds, more classrooms, and more teachers and counselors to serve the rubella deaf children. Through quick action from both

Bernadette Attletweed, recipient of the California Deaf Teacher of the Year, congratulated by her students.

the California Department of Education and the CSD Administrators, the problem came under control.

On Monday, April 25, 1983, an address was delivered by June Newkirk, an Associate Professor from the Department of Special Education at the California State University Northridge (CSUN). Approximately 750 students, members of the faculty, administrators, and counselors, families and friends overflowed the gymnasium. M.s. Newkirk was introduced by her former University of Arizona graduate student, Dr. Klopping. The program consisted mainly of the presentation of the California Deaf Teacher of the Year award to a teacher with a special rapport with her students. When Bernadette Attletweed's name was announced, all eyes turned quickly toward her calm, smiling face. She rose from the seat and walked to the center of the court. (Later, she admitted that when she walked toward the center, she was so nervous and stunned that her hands were in her sweater pocket turning coins. Immediately, she stopped for fear the money would make noise.) The audience stood waving their hands in the air; many others clapped. After receiving the award, she responded graciously. "This award comes as a great honor which I believe each teacher on our staff should receive for their work with the children." She said, "Thank you on behalf of the Teachers of the Deaf." Mrs. Attletweed was given a warm and admiring reception.

The following excerpt is from the formal announcement of the award:

> *"In following the tradition of Laurent Clerc, the first deaf teacher of deaf students, it's very fitting that the seventh California Deaf Teacher of the Year Award goes to an individual who has demonstrated no wavering in her steadfast dedication to teaching. Mrs. Attletweed has an excellent record of teaching deaf students, but her special interest and enthusiasm has been for working with multi-handicapped deaf students...."*

In April 1983, the new redwood sign was installed at the corner of Stevenson Boulevard and Gallaudet Drive to beautify as well as identify the campus site. The other signs also mounted on all the buildings, are of solid redwood and the lettering was etched by a sand-blasting process. These signs are very large to make it easier for people visiting the campus to find the buildings.

The new school is "a monument to determination of parents, deaf people and educators."

Dr. Wilson Riles

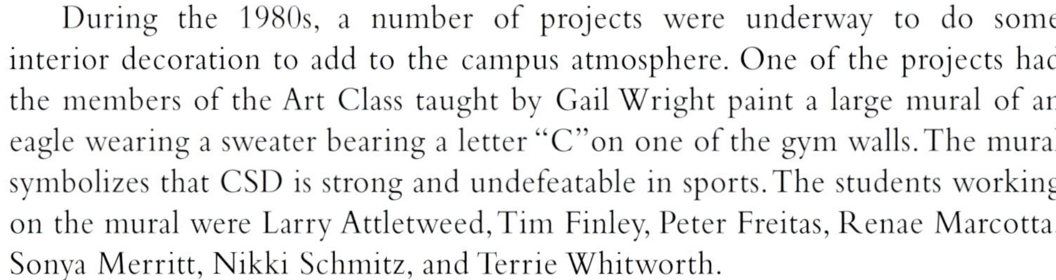

During the 1980s, a number of projects were underway to do some interior decoration to add to the campus atmosphere. One of the projects had the members of the Art Class taught by Gail Wright paint a large mural of an eagle wearing a sweater bearing a letter "C"on one of the gym walls. The mural symbolizes that CSD is strong and undefeatable in sports. The students working on the mural were Larry Attletweed, Tim Finley, Peter Freitas, Renae Marcotta, Sonya Merritt, Nikki Schmitz, and Terrie Whitworth.

The Eagle Mascot became the newest member of the CSD family. It was ready to boost team morale at the California Classic.

Commemorations

Over three thousand visitors attended the Grand Opening of the California School for the Deaf Monday, May 25, 1981. Dr. Wilson Riles, State Senator Alquist, the San Francisco Navy Band, CSD scouts, students, and other guest speakers participated in the afternoon ceremonies. Dr. Riles stressed that the school was an investment for students to become contributing members of society.

The large replica of the mascot of the school which was on the roof of the dining room at Berkeley is now on the roof of the gymnasium. The figure was purchased and presented to CSD by the class of 1969.

Grand Opening of the California School for the Deaf on May 25, 1981.

Traditionally, every year the senior class sneaks off campus for its Senior Class Trip. The goal is to get away without being detected by other students, especially the juniors. That year was unique because they were stranded for three days in the High Sierra. The class left on Monday morning of March 26, 1985, to go to Squaw Valley for two days of skiing and playing in the snow. They planned to return to CSD Tuesday evening. Fortunately, they enjoyed skiing that day, but next day it was snowing heavily and visibility was limited. Deanna Johnson said, "Too much snow! Enough for me!." Leonesa Vitorino said, "Pizza,

Team of the Year of 1985 - the CSD varsity basketball team having the best record among deaf prep schools in the nation. Head coach Ken Pedersen (left), Mike Simmons, Jack Buchanan, Nemo Harreden, Scott O'Donnell, Lance Fabela, Norman Edwards, Rod Pedersen, Fernando Diaz, David Edwards and manager Alan Davary.

again?." Catherine Holsten claimed, "Being selected as Snow Queen is really an honor." Finally Thursday morning the class got on the buses and amid sighs of relief headed back to CSD.

The 1985 CSDF varsity basketball team was chosen as *Team of the Year,* having the best record among deaf prep schools. Art Kruger, sports editor of the *Deaf American*, with a committee of coaches across the nation, made the selection. The team was also champion of the Far West Classic basketball tournament for the third year in a row. The members of the team were Jack Buchanan, Rod Pedersen, Scott O'Donnell, Lance Fabela, Norman Edwards, Nemo Harreden, Fernado Diaz, David Edward, and Mike Simmons. Ken Pedersen was the coach of the team.

The celebration of CSD's 125 Years of Excellence was held at Sunol Country Club on Saturday, November 9, 1985. A highlight of the banquet was the presentation to Bill Honig, State Superintendent of Public Instruction, of a copy of the new book by Mildred Albronda, *The Magic Lantern Man*, a biography of the life of Theophilus Hope d'Estrella. Theophilus d'Estrella, a gifted photographer, was the first male student at CSD, and a member of its first graduating class.

> ***"Don't give up and follow your heart, and you will be successful in whatever you undertake in your life!"***
>
> Marlee Matlin
> Oscar-winning star of
> *Children of a Lesser God*
> in 1997

On March 20, 1986, the Foothills Athletic Association banquet was held at Fremont/Newark Hilton Hotel to honor Dr. Art Kruger, who was sports editor for many deaf papers and magazines during the past fifty years. Also, he was the speaker of the evening. He pointed out the statistics of the schools that had won championships in different sports. His talk was interspersed with fifty years of sports trivia.

On May 11, 1986, Heather Sommerville posed as Lady Liberty for an assembly where CSDF gave a special thank you program to individual students, staff members, and parents who contributed to a fund for the Statue of Liberty restoration. In September 1986, CSDF received a certificate in commemoration of the contribution. The CSDF contributions went to renovations and changes for the convenience of the Deaf. Changes included TDDs installed in the area. In the museum, all audio tapes are transcribed to allow hearing impaired visitors access to research materials.

First place in painting was awarded to Myung Jo Sweeney at the 11th Annual International Creative Arts Festival, which took place at the Center on Deafness in Des Plaines, Illinois, on April 24-26, 1987. As part of her award My Jo was flown to Chicago with Gail Potwin, her art teacher, to attend the festival that included workshops in visual arts, poetry, and performing arts. Academy Award winner, Marlee Matlin, who was one of the judges, was present at the Saturday night banquet to give the award to My Jo. Governor George Deukmejian forwarded a letter of his commendation and deep respect to My Jo.

Marlee Matlin, winner of an Academy Best Actress Award for her performance in *Children of a Lesser God*, paid a visit to CSDF on Monday, June 1, 1987. At an assembly in the Little Theater, she answered many questions asked by the students dealing with her experience and training to become an actress.

Assistant Superintendent Jacob Arcanin worked diligently with the North Coast Section of the California Interscholastic Federation (CIF) to strengthen its rules and programs to benefit high school students of California. Thomas E. Byrnes, Commissioner of Athletics for CIF, made an expressive statement about an appreciation of the expertise provided by Jacob "Jake" Arcanin and his high degree of commitment to the youth of California. Dr. Klopping and the CSDF family were truly proud of Mr. Arcanin, one of the key players in accomplishing this goal.

Betterment

On Sunday, August 16, 1987, the Southern Pacific railroad tracks across Mission Boulevard near CSDF were closed for fourteen hours as engineering construction crews cut through the railroad embankment. The crews then

This tunnel under the railroad embankment as viewed looking north on Mission Boulevard toward the school. After seven years CSD urged for a pedestrian walkway under the Union Pacific railroad tracks that run across Mission Boulevard. The railway overpass was built in 1921. Finally in 1987, 72 feet of concrete pipe was installed so that CSD students and other pedestrians could walk to the Mission Valley shopping center safely through the tunnel.

installed 72 feet of concrete pipe, eleven feet in diameter, to set up a pedestrian tunnel under the tracks. Now students have easy and safe access to the Mission Valley Shopping Center. It took seven years of diligent effort by the city of Fremont to secure the necessary funding and Southern Pacific's approval, since the rail traffic would have to be halted. The crews had fourteen hours to remove the tracks, install the tunnel, and replace the tracks. This job was accomplished with only minutes to spare!

In a memorable moment on March 6, 1988, the Gallaudet University students sent forth a message of protest around the world that a hearing candidate, Elizabeth Zinser, with no knowledge of deafness or sign language, had been selected as the new president of Gallaudet University. They not only demanded that person be removed from the office, but also proclaimed that it was time to choose a deaf person as president of the University.

On March 6, 1988, a message of protest sent around the world that it was timely to choose a deaf person as president of Gallaudet University. The signs saying "Deaf Prez NOW."

"CSDF has enabled me to go out in the real world and do things like being on television and interviewing you, Mrs. Bush."

Michelle Lennert
'89 graduate

More than 500 demonstrators consisting of the CSD students, staff, and Bay Area deaf citizens leapt into the national support for the crusade of the Gallaudet Protest March. On March 8, they marched with signs saying "Deaf Prez NOW" and "Zinser OUT" along Gallaudet Drive, Walnut Avenue, Center Drive, and Stevenson Boulevard, before returning to the CSDF campus. This march as part of the national movement resulted in a decisive victory for the deaf president force. Dr. Irving King Jordan, a deaf man, became the seventh president of Gallaudet University.

Mrs. George Bush visited CSDF October 14, 1988, on a campaign swing of the San Francisco Bay Area on behalf of her husband, the Republican presidential candidate. CSDF senior Michelle Lennert interviewed Mrs. Bush via a closed-circuit television broadcast to the students. Mrs. Bush assured Lennert that she supported residential schools such as CSDF and would tell her husband that she saw "an extraordinary school."

Oliver Sacks, well-known neurologist and author, who was assigned to review a book on deaf history, became intrigued by American Sign Language. He visited the school on October 2, 1989. He described to a crowded assembly his growing awareness and appreciation of deafness as a culture and not a handicap. His new book was *Seeing Voices: A Journey Into the World of the Deaf.*

Barbara Bush posing amid the CSD students and a staff member while visiting the school on October 14, 1988. Bush was lobbied by school administrators and students who were against federal rules that emphasize placing deaf students in public schools with hearing children.

"I'll tell (my husband) I saw an extraordinary school."

Barbara Bush
Wife of President George Bush

CSD in the 1990s:
New Challenges

Through Constant Revision

CSD in the 1990s presents a clear message that if you want to get ahead, you must work hard and only then will you excel. Instead of being contented with the existing education program and routine school life, CSD has strived to change, improve, and prosper through constant revision, addition, and experimentation. What makes CSD stand out is its willingness to face challenges.

At the end of the school year of 1989-1990, two administrative positions were left vacant by Marianne DeLuca, Director of Instruction, and Kenneth Norton, Dean of Students. After decades of service, both decided it was time to enter new ventures for their retirement period. "I hired both of these people in these positions," Dr. Klopping said. "To lose both of them at the same time is a very difficult thing to happen." DeLuca and Norton built loyal staffs and devoted the better part of their adult lives to the school.

Marianne DeLuca, director of instruction, and Ken Norton, dean of students, both traveling in retirement. DeLuca enjoys her new lifestyle, having two homes, one in Arizona and one in Utah. She keeps busy with volunteer activities in Arizona and joins her husband Bill, in snow activities in Utah. Norton discovered his retirement a full-time job. After his ten-year project, the erection of the Bell tower, he undertook the writing for this book, The Eagle Soars to Enlightenment. *Taking him more than three years to complete the book, he plans to "re-retire" after the completition of the book project.*

The statements herewith by Laura Kurtzman were excerpted from the San Jose Mercury News. *"DeLuca was the consummate administrator-soft-spoken, professional, a prolific memo writer. Norton was the archetypical coach figure. He was warm, compassionate, and free with his emotions. He ate lunch with the students, he took them on outdoor adventures and coached them in sports."*

DeLuca came to the Berkeley school in 1957 and taught for many years. In 1981, she became director of instruction, heading a staff that consisted of about 110 people. She oversaw the development of a comprehensive curriculum for kindergarten through 12th grades that emphasized students' reading skills and became a model for schools throughout the country.

In his 29 years at the school, Norton also developed his own programs, starting more or less from scratch. He expanded the athletic, Scouting, and outdoor programs and developed others to enhance and monitor the students' social lives.

Two former employees immediately filled the two vacant positions. Ronald Stern became the new Director of Instruction after spending a year at Gallaudet University as director of athletics. Michael Finneran also returned to the school to become Dean of Student Life after a year's stint as Superintendent of the Mississippi School for the Deaf

With their new ventures, Stern and Finneran faced challenges.

The entrance of the campus was dressed up with a new cosmetic look in June 1990. It was a beautiful marquee sign which was made possible by the Fremont Police Association's annual golf tournament fund-raising event and cash donations in memory of George Laramie, father of Celia May Baldwin. The class of 1990's gift to the school was a box of letters and numbers needed for the sign. Now there are always exciting messages to read as people enter the school campus daily.

The members of CSDF's proud "Iron Girls" *team. Left to right: Carol Bella, Heidi Vincent, Melody Tsai, Dyan Kovacs, Head Coach Robert Ellis, Nevenka Solunac, Margarita Limon, J. J. Huang, and Manager ShaShonie Reins.*

Iron Girls

As a rule, a girls' volley ball team consists of twelve players, six playing on the court and six substitutes. During the 1991 season, the CSD team had only seven players but they determined to challenge this obstacle course. The team nicknamed "The Iron Girls" astonishingly overcame the obstacle with a school record of twenty wins and five losses. In addition, the team won national championships among deaf preps in the nation. Nevenka Solunac, a senior with four years of varsity experience, received first team All-American honors along with Bay Counties League first team honors.

On June 28, 1991, the name of The California News was recognized. The most coveted school-for-the-deaf newsletter honor, Little Paper Family Award, was bestowed upon CSD's The California News by the Gallaudet University Alumni Association for Excellence in the Special Category: Newsletter. It has successfully surpassed all the Little Paper Family Award criteria owing to the work so well performed by the graphic arts classes.

CSD staff and students were shocked by the tragedy affecting three staff members, Sue Loggins and Chris and Carol Argentos, whose homes were destroyed in the firestorm in the Oakland/Berkeley hills on October 20, 1991. Sue Loggins' husband Phil perished in the blaze. The fund, the CSD family Fire Fund, was established immediately. On October 22 and November 18, the Career Education/Vocational Department set up a fund-raiser at Pizza Depot, a Fremont pizza parlor. The staff, students and friends came together to give their time and energy, and to work for a worthy cause. All proceeds were donated to these fire victims. CSDF Assessment Center staff member Sue Loggins, and high school teacher Carol Argentos and her husband Chris, a retired Business Education teacher, sent heartwarming letters of gratitude to the CSD family.

An unusual item, a five-foot-long wooden scissors, created by woodworking students under the guidance of Robert Morrison, was presented to the city of Fremont on November 19, 1991. This beautiful piece of work was very impressive and well crafted and has been used for ribbon-cutting ceremonies of city affairs. Fremont Mayor Bill Ball expressed high praise for the talented students.

This Eagle instilling fighting spirits in CSD athletes.

This beautiful piece of work was given to the city of Fremont from the CSD woodworking students. Left: Mayor Bill Ball, Robert Morrison, Sonny Tate, Samuel Holden, Zulius Lansing, Jose Talavera, Manuelito Vallente, Marcus Jaboneta, and Robert Brodoski.

Challenge Ropes Course

Education has been truly a challenge, both mentally and physically. On October 6, 1992, thirty-two middle school students and eight teachers encountered hair-raising mental and physical challenges at the Challenge Sonoma Adventure Ropes Course in Sonoma, California. An assortment of cables, logs, platforms, and ropes for activities and challenges offered opportunities to develop self-confidence, trust and team building.

The participants tested their agility, coordination, and nerves in order to climb ladders and balance on high tension rope bridges. In the hardest challenge of the day, only Amy Jenkins and Karina Pedersen succeeded. But all students attained an increase in personal confidence and an awareness of one's agility.

A chance to achieve work experience in the community, develop independence, and take steps toward a successful transition to life after graduation was offered to twenty-two high school students by the Hire Learning program. The students were placed in many interesting jobs in the Tri-City area (Fremont, Newark and Union City) during the school year 1992-93. The positive note indicated that the students readily accepted new challenges. Woodwork Furniture, Home Depot, Pac Tel Pagers, Erik's DeliCafe, and Paul's Pet Grooming, among others, offered students stimulating opportunities.

There was no better opportunity for employers from forty different companies and service agencies than at an annual Job Fair for Deaf Youth and Adults to learn of ways of working better with deaf employees, prompting better attitude among hearing and deaf employees, and accommodating hearing and deaf employees in the working environment.

At the Job Fair on April 20, 1993, a good number of qualified deaf people came looking for prospective jobs and proved what they could offer even with limited communication with hearing employers and employees. The results of the Fair was that many employers became enthusiastic about inviting deaf applicants for formal interviews.

The Welcome Back Dance on September 6, 1993, was livened by a juggling demonstration. Neil Stammer, owner of the juggling store at Pier 39 in San Francisco, was brought to the Dance by senior Stanley Liu. Exhibiting a number of different juggling tricks, Stammer performed an incredible act, juggling glowing balls in the dark senior activity center. He put students' hands on his arms and threw balls into the air. These students' faces lit up when, for the first time in their lives, they were juggling!

Middle school students involved in the Challenge Sonoma Adventure Ropes Courses.

Leadership Role

CSDF's future will be clearer and brighter as it has a set of goals which will chart its course for the next several years. The credit for the successful report given by the Visiting Committee was due to CSD's accreditation effort. On

March 27, 28, and 29, 1995, the Visiting Committee representing the Western Association of Schools and Colleges (WASC) and the Conference of Educational Administration Serving the Deaf (CEASD) met with students, staff, and parents who participated in the Self-Study process initiated in October, 1994. The conclusive report was read to the audience on the 29th. Several of the Committee's commendations were for the Bilingual/Bicultural approach to education, the commitment for the classified staff to the school and its program, and to the California State Department of Education for supporting CSD's leadership role.

In December 1995, Ellen Gorman Winters, the High School Principal, retired after 30 years of dedicated service to the students and staff at CSD–B/F. During her tenure, she taught elementary and high school students, and served as the Head of the English Department.

On September 3, 1996, the new CSD brochure was unveiled for the faculty and staff during the opening assembly for the 1996-1997 school year. The first official copy was presented to Dr. Klopping by David West, Director of Outreach and Training Center.

Lam Research Corporation, the second largest employer in Fremont, pledged its support to the Agendas Program and to the notion that the partnership between Lam Research Corporation and CSD continues. The Agendas Program is a new system which permits students to utilize a planning notebook replete with ideas to help students organize their activities at school, at home, and in the community. Also, the Corporation presented an autographed Jerry Rice football jersey to CSD.

Ellen Gorman Winters. Retired after 30 years of dedicated service to CSD. She was a classroom teacher through and through. She started as an elementary teacher at the Lexington School for the Deaf in New York in 1962 and then taught at CSD Berkeley in 1966. When she moved to the high school department in 1975, English was her concentration. Thereafter, her skills and contributitions were such that she was seen by teachers, administrators, professionals, students and parents as an authority in English instruction and curriculum issues. Even when she left the classroom to become Assistant High School Principal in 1988 and then the High School Principal in 1992, she consistently advocated strongly for classroom teachers.

Outstanding CSD Graduates

1996 was an exceptional year for CSD to be proud of its graduates who attended Gallaudet University and the National Technical Institute for the Deaf. The annual Gallaudet Awards Day that year honored six CSD graduates with a total of seven awards. Two 1996 graduates and a 1998 graduate were awarded the Academic Merit Scholarship from NTID.

1992 graduate *Dyan Sue Kovacs*, who played volleyball, softball, basketball, and was on the track team at CSD, was awarded the Female Athlete of the Year Award at Gallaudet University.

Jonathan Lenno Lamberton, a 1994 graduate, was honored with the College Bowl Team Award. Lamberton, as he was affectionately known here at CSD, played football and baseball, in addition to belonging to Jr. NAD, SBG, and FAA.

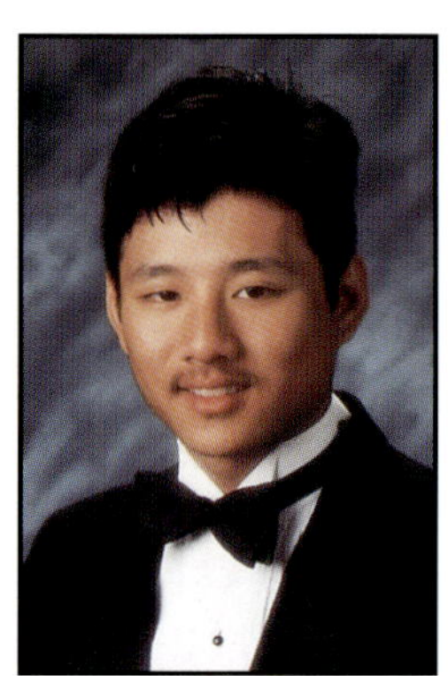

From left to right.

Dyan Sue Kovacs

Jonathan Lamberton

Carrie Sue Nichols

Francis Joseph Tsai, Jr.

Sean Matthew Virnig

Kristen Weiner

Carrie Sue Nichols, a 1994 graduate, was the recipient of two awards that year. She received the Lillian Gourley Rakow Creative Writing Award and the Phi Kappa Zeta Scholarship Award. During her life at CSD, she was very active in all school organizations.

Francis Joseph Tsai, Jr., who graduated in 1994, was awarded the Kappa Gamma International Scholarship Award. While attending CSD, Tsai was a four-year member of SBG, FAA, and Jr. NAD. Also, he participated in football, basketball, and baseball.

Sean Matthew Virnig, a 1992 graduate, received the Phi Alpha Pi Honorary Society Award. Virnig was involved with SBG and Jr. NAD. In 1992, he was president of the '92 class and Jr. NAD. Virnig was voted "Best Leader" in 1992, along with Melody Tsai as "Most Likely to Succeed" along with Carol Bella.

Kristen Weiner, '91, was honored with one of the most important awards, the Leonard M. Elstad Award. (Dr. Leonard Elstad was president of Gallaudet College 1945-1969.) Kristen had a great love for poetry, drama, and the arts.

Althea Boyer and *Laura Willey* were awarded $1,000 Merit Scholarships from the National Technical Institute for the Deaf in Rochester, New York. Each demonstrated exemplary academic achievement by accumulating a high grade point average. They attended NTID.

Hard work and plenty of studying paid off for a '98 graduate, Cham Dee, who received the Academic Merit Award of $10,000 for his efforts from NTID. Dee receives $2,500 per year provided he maintains a 3.0 grade average while attending college. His plans are to study computer software engineering and business marketing at NTID.

In recognition of Deaf Awareness Week, three CSD students, *Dave Jessup, Lidia Lindahl*, and *Erika Geiger*, signed the National Anthem at the Oakland Coliseum for the Athletics' game. It was part of a fundraising activity sponsored by HIP magazine. At noon on September 14, a group of eighty people showed

National Anthem signers at the A's stadium. Left: Dave Jessup, Lidia Lindahl, Erika Geiger.

up for the fund-raiser. The day was started with a "baseball" style lunch—hot dogs, hamburgers and potato chips—held in a special banquet room towards the rear of A's stadium. After lunch, the group took their seats high in the first deck, between first base and right field. They looked up and saw "California School for the Deaf" on the scoreboard. Then, the stadium announcer named the students from CSD who would be signing the National Anthem.

Could CSD keep up with the fast pace of the computer world? Being on the edge of the Silicon Valley, it is natural for CSD to be exposed to the world of technology. The first computer was installed at CSD, Berkeley, in 1973. The laboratory for "Computer Assisted Learning Lab," has been a great aid in motivating the students. In the lab, students naturally bend over the computers with expressions of sheer delight. They could communicate with their fingers with other deaf students as well as develop basic skills. Eventually, they will learn desktop publishing, word processing, spreadsheets, and web publishing.

The instructor, Charles Farr, with many years of experience in the business world, has worked hard to keep his classes on the cutting edge. Each Business Education student has a Pentium computer to work on. The classes developed their own web page — WWW.CSDF.K12.CA.US.

The Mayor of Fremont, Vice Mayor and City Council recognized CSD students for their volunteer efforts over the holidays by presenting them with a certificate. High School Teacher Gene Harris' service learning class joined a Bay

CSD students developing their own web page. CSD's student produced website provides information including academics, student life, sports and The California News *available at http://www.csdf.k12.ca.us. Patricia Medina, '99 and Larwan Berke,'01, are part of the team that created this website of 2000 under the guidance of teacher Charles Farr.*

Area group called the Service Learning Youth Committee in providing a turkey dinner and special program for the Berkeley Emergency Food and Housing Project in memory of Dr. Martin Luther King. The students worked in the kitchen cooking dinner and in the dining room serving the homeless people.

At the City Council meeting, five Service Learning students, under the guidance of Teacher Gene Harris, elaborated their experience of participating in the worthy cause. Two of the five students are quoted:

> *"Hi. My name is Suzanne Torres. I am a freshman. I appreciated working with all different kinds of people–helping them by giving my time. I didn't mind the work. I just wanted to open my heart to other people. Seeing my friends helping to change the world yesterday made my heart feel connected. I was inspired by doing our service work in Berkeley with the homeless people. They helped to open our hearts and increase our understanding. Really, they are the same as everyone else. If everyone can believe in themselves, they can do anything."*

> *"Hi. I'm Allison Marsh. I'm a freshman. I want to express to you how I feel about helping people through volunteering. I feel it helps people to understand what deaf people can do to improve the homeless situation. It helps to let them know we do care. I just want to help people — not just for us, but for the people themselves. Thank you."*

March 18, 1998 is the tenth anniversary of "PAH," the civil rights movement in which Gallaudet University students made a demand that the president of Gallaudet University be a deaf person. On the evening of March 18, 1998, at the Deaf Community Center (DCC) in San Leandro, not only a number of Gallaudet University graduates/ alumni were at the gathering, but a good number of CSD students with potential leadership ability. Nine students were involved in the Deafywood Square game that gave them an opportunity to demonstrate their knowledge of the history of "PAH" and "Deaf President Now" (DPN) issues. Instead of their actual names, the participants were called by the names of the famed 1988 people such as Dr. I King Jordan, Greg Hlibok, Jerry Covell, Bridgetta Bourne, Tim Rarus, Gary Olsen, Dr. Elizabeth Zinser and others. Dan Langholtz, a counselor at the Deaf Center in San Francisco, was host and he entertained both the audience and the participants with acumen. When he questioned the students about the history of DPN, they mimed their responses and answered the questions with the same vigor and mannerisms as their DPN characters. True enough, their gestures and emotions were no less than what had occurred in 1988.

Champions

Coaches Val Herbold and Doralynn Folse and their girls' soccer team had a phenomenal year with a perfect record, 14 wins and 0 losses. For the first time in the CSD history, the Eaglettes won the Fremont Youth Soccer League championship in the Under 10 Years Old division. The coaches said the team's success came from five years of practicing together and everyone's commitment to do their best.

Four CSD students won the competition against academic stars throughout the country for the second annual Deaf High School Academic Super Bowl championship at Gallaudet University on April 24, 1998. The championship

Eaglettes Champions. Front row, L to R: Shanna Grossinger, Becca Eyrond, Mallory Malzkuhn, Zuelika Prader, Monica Foletta. Back row: Coach Valerie Herbold, Tenaya Herbold, Lisa Jarashow, Leala Holcomb, Blair Rasmus, Coach Doralynn Folse.

Academic Super Bowl Champions. Left: Melissa Malzkuhn, Jesse Saunders, coach Gary Olsen, Jerry Pua, and Sho Stern.

team members were Sho Stern, Jerry Pua, Jesse Saunders and Melissa Malzkuhn. The students defeated the other teams by answering questions on the U.S. and world history, language and literature, science, technology, geography, fine arts, mathematics, current events, deaf studies, sports and music. They were coached by Gary Olsen, explaining, "After passing the screening test that fall, the young team practiced at least three times a week at 7 in the morning and after school hours. They also competed in practice matches against CSD teachers. They worked a tremendous amount of time. From there, they went on and won the Knowledge Bowl. They were fabulous. We are very proud of them."

The event was telecast via satellite from Gallaudet University to 181 sites including CSD's Little Theater and Ohlone College. The students and faculty watched the live telecast with spirit of support "which equaled the enthusiasm of Times Square on New Year's Eve" as stated by a student in the Little Theater.

Each member of the championship team, including their coach, received an engraved brass bowl and a personal compliment and handshake from Dr. Klopping for their accomplishments.

Academic Championship Bowls sponsored by Gallaudet University, (from left to right) 1998 Academic Bowl Champion, 1999 Academic Bowl Champion and 1999 Academic Bowl West Regional Champion.

May 20, 1998's ninth annual vocational competition displayed students' projects. Three very special visitors came for a tour of the vocational program: Delaine Eastin, the State Superintendent of Public Instruction; Dr. Ron Kadish, Director of the State Special Schools; and Ann Draper, Director of Economic Development from the City of Fremont. A number of employers who hired students throughout the school year also went on the tour.

Delaine Eastin sent a letter after her visit saying, *"It is always such an uplifting experience for me to visit with so many dedicated teachers and gifted students. I thoroughly enjoyed visiting all the classrooms and talking about your school-to-career program. Observing what the students are doing is absolutely fascinating."*

The high school leaders of the Junior National Association of the Deaf from the schools for the deaf in the nation attended the convention at CSD, July 24-29, to absorb some tips on leadership abilities from a number of workshops. Several of CSD's teachers and counselors worked with high school leadership students on their committees to host the convention.

A Western-Style Testimonial dinner was held to honor Dr. Frank Turk, one of the few people who has dedicated most of his life to the Jr. NAD. He felt honored that the hard work he and many of his colleagues put forth has paid off.

Svenna Pedersen and Ben Jarashaow were the Mistress and Master of Ceremonies at the banquet and pageant. Impressively, CSD participants captured victories at the grand event: Mr. Congeniality - Adam Jarashow; Miss Talent - Jenamarie Daviton-Sciandra; Mr. Jr. NAD - Adam Jarashow; Miss Jr. NAD - Jenamarie Daviton-Sciandra.

A big favor was asked by the City of Fremont to have CSD's cabinet shop build eight huge storage units for project blueprints retained at the city office. Woodworking teacher Bob Morrison and his students undertook the challenge to build the storage units, five feet and nine inches high and sixteen feet long. The outcome of the project was remarkable and attractive. The cabinet was delivered to the city in the spring of 1999.

Mayor Gus Morrison and his staff were impressed with CSD students' craftsmanship. The City of Fremont invited Bob Morrison and his builders for a tour of the Development Center and refreshments. Each of fourteen students and Morrison received a certificate of appreciation for their effort.

Alabama's Kathleen Peavy, left; Fremont's Adam Jarashow–Mr. Jr. NAD and Jenamarie Daviton-Sciandra–Miss. Jr. NAD; and Florida's Rachel Abenchuchan.

Blueprint storage units built for the City of Fremont by the CSD woodworking students. Top, left to right: Maria Damian, Emil Cornish, Adam Tuttle, TianaJohnson-Coleman. Bottom: Robert Morrison, instructor, Antonia Nunz, A Xiong, Robert Shaw, Jeremy Adams, Xue Lee, Jake Clements, and Luis Salas.

Mayor Gus Morrison, right, beaming about more convenient storage of the city's blueprints with Robert Morrison, CSD's cabinetmaking instructor.

The CSD Academic Bowl team successfully defended the National Deaf High School Academic Bowl title, on April 26, at Gallaudet University's Kellogg Conference Center. It was a hard-fought battle as the level of competition among the other teams was greater that year. The members of the elite team were Adam Jarashow, Jane Jonas, Melissa Malzkuhn, Megan Malzkuhn and Brendan Stern. Jack Lamerton was the all-star team coach who helped the team perform better in the area of literature and language arts.

Celia May Baldwin was appointed to be the Dean of Student Life at CSD in September 1999, after Michael Finneran moved to Vermont to be the Director of the Academic and Residence programs at the Austine School for the Deaf.

Two CSD parents, Mike and Jeanne Glads, encouraged CSD to apply for a $10,000 grant from the US Bank, since the Donald N. Parodi Memorial Charitable Trust's board offered to match up to $25,000 if someone would donate money to CSD for computer equipment. The Glads knew US Bank Vice President Leland Ong who, after talking to his boss, suggested that the Parodi Trust apply for a grant from the bank. US Bank agreed to donate $10,000 to the school to match the Parodi Trust's offer, giving the school a grand total of $20,000 for new computers!

The 1999 Academic Bowl Champions. Left: Adam Jarashaw, '01; Melissa Malzkuhn, '99; Brendan Stern, '01; Jack Lamberton, coach; Jane Jonas, '01; Megan Malzkuhn, '01.

$10,000 donation from USBank to CSD students, plus $10,000 from the Parodi Memorial Charitable Trust for computers.

Marion Kuntze

Marlon Kuntze, '71, is the first culturally deaf person to work for a doctorate from Stanford university. He has played an active role in promoting new insights on how deaf children may acquire literacy skills. The focus of his dissertation is on the idea of building literacy through ASL and on the acquisition of English as a second language through reading.

Kuntze was a high school English teacher from 1982 to 1990 before ha assumed a dual position as bilingual/bicultural program coordinator and an ASL specialist. By 1994, he felt the need to go back to school to investigate various questions related to how deaf children may best learn English and what role ASL may play in support learning English skills. He chose to enroll in the language, literacy and culture program in the School of Education at Stanford. He hopes to become active in research and college teaching after completing his training at Stanford.

Kuntze anticipates he will gradaute with a Ph.D. in December 2000.

NAD
JUNIOR
FOOTHILLS ATHLETIC ASSOCIATION
EST. 1901
California School for the Deaf

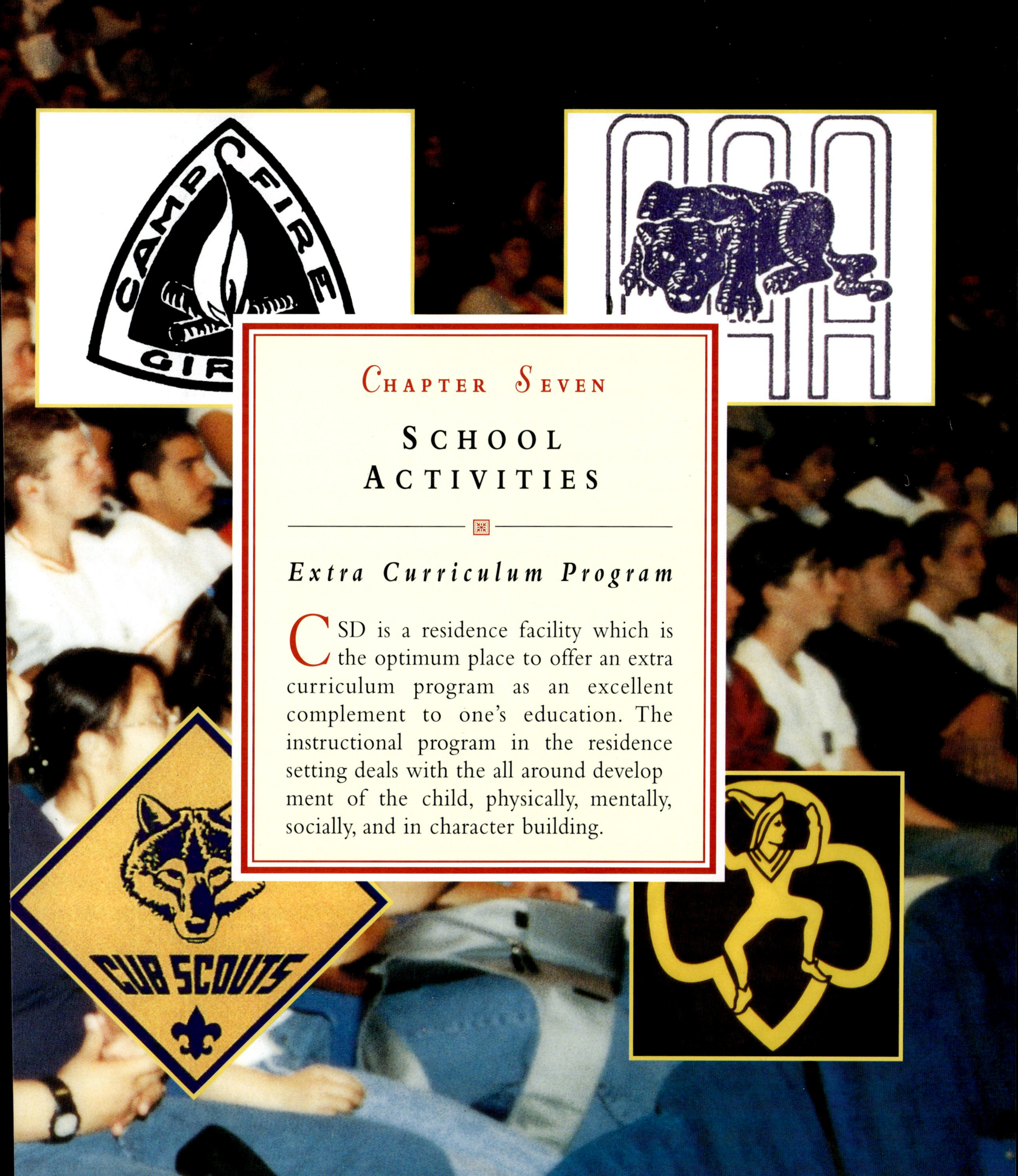

Chapter Seven

School Activities

Extra Curriculum Program

CSD is a residence facility which is the optimum place to offer an extra curriculum program as an excellent complement to one's education. The instructional program in the residence setting deals with the all around develop ment of the child, physically, mentally, socially, and in character building.

One of the CSD's education goals is to maintain the classic school activities program for students of all ages. CSD's extra-curriculum activities produce well-rounded students capable of developing and sustaining social skills into adult life.

FOOTHILLS ATHLETIC ASSOCIATION

Dr. Winfield Runde, founder of the Foothills Athletic Association. The organization was established on September 30, 1901.

A significant moment on September 30, 1901, in the old Bartlett Hall, saw the birth of the Foothills Athletic Association when the boys held a meeting and organized an athletic association, under the direction of a counselor, Dr. Winfield Runde. Dr. Runde, CSD graduate, '96, returned to the Berkeley School after he graduated from Gallaudet College in 1901. The association was formed under the rules used by the Gallaudet College Athletic Association and named the Foothills after the hills by which CSD was situated.

The Foothills Athletic Association (FAA) became inactive due to the absence of Runde, who moved to the North Dakota School for the Deaf to teach. However, the sports teams used the name of the Foothills in the athletic competition.

During its infancy, 1901 to 1910, there were no banquets. The first Foothills Athletic Association banquet, honoring athletes, took place in May, 1911, when Runde returned to CSD as a boys' supervisor. Since then, there has been an annual banquet and dance. In 1929, for the first time, FAA had its banquet and dance outside of the school at the Veterans' Memorial building in Berkeley.

FAA members in 1920. The eagle figuration was made by the students in art class.

Preceding spread: Logos of the students' school organizations

Annually, at the banquet and dance affair, FAA celebrates and honors CSD athletes for their athletics and successful seasons. This picture was taken on February 22, 1940 at the Berkeley school auditorium.

"C" letter award.

Annual Homecoming Event. Karina Pedersen, Senior Princess (left), Sylvia Zarate, Queen, Zachary Johnson and Jason Lamberton.

Girls Athletic Association

During the month of October, 1928, the girls also decided to become involved in athletics. They organized their own Girls Athletic Association (GAA) under the guidance of their physical education instructor, Miss Kathryn Miller, and the aid of their dean of girls, Mrs. Ruth K. Birck. In 1932, FAA's 30th anniversary banquet was held in the refectory (old dining room) and the party took place in Durham Hall with the older girls. GAA had its annual banquet and dance in December while FAA had its in the spring. GAA's mascot was a panther.

Joining of Two Associations

For the first time, in the school year of 1977-78, the FAA and GAA combined into a co-ed organization, due to the requirement of Title IX on sex discrimination. The members agreed to retain the title of FAA for their new organization. The nickname "Foothills" undoubtedly originated because of the hills behind the school. The new school campus in Fremont is still situated by hills.

The purpose of the Foothills Athletic Association is to promote athletic activities for the students of the California School for the Deaf, to foster good will, school spirit, scholarship, good citizenship, sportsmanship, and to uphold the good name of the school. It is also to provide its members valuable experience in carrying out business meetings in an efficient manner and with correct parliamentary procedure, and to afford experience in the management of financial matters and effective business transactions, which is attained by operating a snack bar in the Secondary Activity Center.

The snack bar has been operated by the students since the 1930s. The profits help finance the costs of "C" letter-awards, Most Valuable Athlete awards, the annual banquet, Homecoming events, snow-fun trips and Deaf World Games participants.

Traditionally, the FAA members sign at every meeting the quotation:

"When the One Great Scorer comes to mark against your name, He writes not that you won or lost; but how you played the game."

How You Played the Game.
by
Grantland Rice
well-known sportswriter and poet.

The FAA awards "C" letters to outstanding varsity players and a trophy to the most valuable player in each sport.

The official colors are orange and black with the Eagle as its mascot. The color orange was selected by the members in circa 1886 after the poppy, the state flower, which flourished over the hills above the CSD campus. In those days, a number of eagles soared and perched above the hills by the CSD campus for many years. So the FAA mascot has been the Eagle ever since.

In 2001 FAA will celebrate its 100th Anniversary!

Chairperson of the Board

Dr. Winfield Runde	**1901 to 1902 & 1910 - 1938**
Sheldon McArtor	**1938 to 1953**
Leo Jacobs	**1953 to 1977**
Kenneth Norton	**1977 to 1983**
Dean Swaim	**1983 to 1987**
Daniel Lynch	**1987 to 1992**
Gilmer Lentz	**1992 to 2000**
Mark Bella	**2000 to present**

Junior National Association of the Deaf

Jr. NAD Means Involvement

The concept of the Junior National Association of the Deaf was introduced at the convention of the National Association of the Deaf (NAD) in Dallas, Texas, on July 6, 1960. Caroline Burnes, wife of then NAD President Byron Burnes and one of the authors of A History of the California School for the Deaf, 1860-1960, moved that the Executive Board of NAD take positive steps toward the organization of a Junior NAD within the schools for the deaf. It was passed unanimously. Thus was the Jr. NAD born.

During the year following the convention, Jr. NAD chapters were organized in thirteen schools. Caroline Burnes had the honor of sponsoring the chapter at CSD–Berkeley, a post she held until she retired in 1969. During the early years, the success of the chapters was due largely to the helpful efforts of the first two national leaders, Mervin Garretson and his successors Viola McDowell and Don G. Pettingill.

Caroline Burnes, librarian at the Berkeley school, an instrument for initiating the junior national Association of the deaf in 1960.

Goals of Junior NAD

The goals of Jr. NAD at the time NAD founded were:

1. *To develop potential leaders*
2. *To make the deaf youth aware of the State and National organizations of the deaf*
3. *To acquaint the deaf youth with the leaders of today*
4. *To make the deaf youth more social, civic, and philanthropic minded.*

In the late 60s, the activities of the Jr. NAD grew by leaps and bounds in its regional and national conventions, workshops, and summer camps.

The letters of Jr. NAD formed by the students and sponsors at the quadrangle at the Berkeley campus in 1972.

The Junior NAD logo is a seal on a red, white, and blue shield. These colors represented the American flag and symbolized the Junior NAD chapters all over the nation. The emblem has three stars and signifies the three objectives of the Junior NAD: **developing scholarship, citizenship, and leadership qualities.**

A dramatic increase in Jr. NAD Chapters came with the appointment of Frank R. Turk to the national directorship in 1966. The Jr. NAD headquarters were at the Gallaudet College campus. With many leaders at different schools, many more chapters were added and are still active.

Highlights of the CSD Jr. NAD Chapter

On April 15-19, 1977, the Junior NAD 6th Biennial Youth Conference was held at CSD–Berkeley. Attending were the cream of the crop from the Western States Schools for the Deaf. After a number of fine workshops, tours and entertainment, the participants, who had to leave for home, uttered "We dread leaving the most wonderful workshop of our lives. It really provided us a lot experience."

U Sung Chung and Anne Marie Baer attended the Western Leadership Conference for the Deaf at Great Falls, Montana March 12-17, 1981. Anne Baer won two first place awards for mime, titled The Bottle, and poetry in ASL, and a dance titled "They Say I am Deaf."

The Fremont Chapter hosted the national conference March 25-30, 1988. It was the first time that the Chapter had ever sponsored the national gathering of the youth counterpart of NAD. The convention was very timely since less than two weeks before it started Gallaudet had chosen its first deaf president after a week of student protests and national media attention.

Bull session in one of the crisis situations amid the student representatives from the schools for the deaf in the nation. They are the leaders of the future. On the right, Dr. Frank Turk conducting the workshop.

The Junior NAD Western States Regional Conference was held from April 2 to 5, 1991 at CSD–F. The theme for the conference was: "Joining, Delegating, and Teamwork Produce Leaders of Tomorrow." Solving a variety of crisis situations was everyone's favorite part of the conference.

The Fremont Chapter hosted the Junior NAD's 16th biennial national convention from July 24 to 29, 1998. The theme was "Preparing for the 21st Century - Deaf Youth's Perspective." These five days were filled with workshops, meetings, and entertainment.

Participants from 33 states attended. On Friday, July 24, there was a testimonial dinner to honor Dr. Frank Turk for his 35 years of service with the Jr. NAD. Tuesday night was the final banquet and the Jr. NAD pageant. The winners were both from CSD: Mr. Jr. NAD was Adam Jarashow, who performed a joke/skit, and Miss Jr. NAD was Jenamarie Daviton-Sciandra, who performed an ASL poem. The workshop had a tremendous impact on preparing the youngsters for the future. They participated in the problem solving approach program known as Situations, Options, Disadvantages, Advantages and Solutions (SODAS). Then they participated in a mock political activity at the Civic Center discussing "Gun Control." The other activity was "Crisis Management;"students were given various tasks. The students had to do research and then go about creating practical strategies and solutions for the various challenges. The whole program was geared towards helping the youngsters be better prepared for dealing with issues and concerns of the coming century.

Junior NAD Motto:

Promoting the Tomorrow of all the Deaf by working with the Deaf Youth of Today

Junior NAD Creed:

We believe:

That **Junior** NAD Program is the outstanding textbook helper of the school;

That **Ultimate** educational goals are attainable through motivation;

That **National** competition and recognition promote maximum excellence;

That **Initiative** is the best vehicle for realization of maximum potential;

That **Opportunities** for total development are greater in group situations;

And the **Resourcefulness** and enthusiasm make a more complete deaf person.

Junior NAD Slogan:

Joining Nourishes Adult Development

Jr. Eagle Organization

Little Brother of the Foothills Athletic Association

One of the programs maintained by the Middle School Residential Department (former Jr. high) is the Jr. Eagle organization. Originally, it was the Pee Wee National Association of the Deaf started at the new Fremont school in 1980. Later, the residential staff and students passed a resolution changing the organization's title to Jr. Eagle, which was more befitting its goals. The structure of the Jr. Eagle organization is similar to that of the Foothills Athletic Association (FAA). The purpose of the program is two-fold: to provide training and experience to prepare students for involvement in the more advanced organizations in the high school; and to gain experience in operating a snack bar and participating in sports activities before becoming members of FAA. Terry Sasser and Raul Brown were the first sponsors of the Pee Wee NAD.

Logo of the Middle School's proud Junior Eagle Organization.

Annual Jr. Eagles' Royalty Court Party in 1987, King Scott Eldridge, (left) Queen Becky Luftig, Prince Juan Hernandez, Princess Nevenka Solunac, Kristine Cantrell, Prince Gary Lundstrom.

JR. EAGLE SOARING

In 1983, Carla Pereira, Middle School counselor, became a head sponsor and her leadership abilities placed the organization into the center of the Middle School activities. The module, which was used for the media center in the Berkeley school and moved from Berkeley to Fremont campus, was modified into the Middle School Activity Center, where the snack bar operations and parties are held.

Twice a year, a Leadership Workshop was implemented for intensive week-end training. This endeavor has been effective, for many of the student leaders of this organization in the '80s and early '90s performed above average during their high school days and they went on to complete four years of college.

Annually, Jr. Eagle holds an award banquet to recognize the Middle School athletes and the Jr. Eagle officers, including the most valuable player and most improved player in each sport. The colors of the Jr. Eagle are orange and black. The motto is "Use your talent to make the Eagle fly." Joe MacDougall, Cindy Davenport, Marsha Helmuth, Shirley Dart, and several other counselors were instrumental at keeping the organization in an excellent status. It happens that this writer, who initiated the implementation of the Jr. Eagle when he was Dean of Students, is everlastingly proud of it.

CSD BOY SCOUTS OF AMERICA TROOP 11

INSTILLATION OF PRIDE

CSD has harbored Boy Scouts of America Troop 11, one of the most popular and well–established school organizations, since October 1916. It was reported that it was Carol S. Land, the boys' supervisor, who wished to found a Boy Scouts troop but was not eligible as he was four months short of the permitted age. Land ('15) was still a young man and, also, a good all-around athlete. He took some courses at the University of California–Berkeley in physical culture, in preparation for training the boys in his charge.

University of California–Berkeley Professor Robert Sproul assisted in establishing the Boy Scouts and allowed Land to run the program until he officially became Scoutmaster. He was the youngest Scoutmaster in the United States. The CSD Boy Scouts Troop 11 was formed only six years after Boy Scouts of America was incorporated on February 8, 1910. Troop number 11 was incorporated into the CSD Boy Scouts in 1916.

Scoutmaster Land's first assignment was to attend a scoutmaster's class in Oakland to learn first aid bandaging instructed by Dr. Mead of the University of California. Then Land taught both the Boy Scouts and the Camp Fire Girls the principles of first aid bandaging.

In 1916, Carol Land, CSD's first Scoutmaster and the youngest Scoutmaster in the United States. He got back to Scouting as the Assistant Scoutmaster of Placerville's Troop 67 of hearing boys from 1932 to 1939.

Early Days

In February, 1917, there were sixteen boys in the troop and it was divided into Bear Patrol and Lion Patrol. They started a candy stand, "Boy Scouts Candy Shoppe," to raise funds for the purchase of the troop flag, signal flags, badges, honor medals, etc. A number of camping trips over night were made to Mt. Diablo, Mt. Tamalpais, Wild Cat Creek and other nearby places. In November, 1917, the Boy Scouts began to build a cabin made entirely of dead logs or branches. No lumber from a sawmill was used. The site of the cabin was in the eucalyptus grove above the campus.

By March, 1918, the CSD Boy Scouts received recognition as one of the best troops in the state. On many occasions, they gave exhibitions in drilling and signaling. Edwin Wilson, a 17-year old student, became the first deaf "Eagle" Boy Scout among the schools for the deaf in the nation in May, 1921. In May, 1934, Horace Carlson, '35, father of Gloria Romeo, a secretary at CSD, was the fourth "Eagle" Boy Scout. Carlson attended the National Jamboree at Washington, D. C., with all expenses paid by Troop 11's sponsor, the 20-30 Club.

State Governors Applauded Troop 11

The new governor of California, Goodwin Knight, and the highest ranking prisoner of the Korean War, General William Dean, met six Troop11 scouts and Scoutmaster Ralph Neesam at a United Crusade rally on October 13, 1953, and expressed a great deal of admiration for the boys and the school.

In 1918, the CSD Boy Scouts received recognition as one of the best troops in the state of California. Troop11, the co-called "Deaf Troop" under Land's direction won top national honors in signalling.

The 1938 Troop 11 under the guidance of Scoutmaster Vernon Wall, Edward Scouten and Emil Ladner posing in front of the Boy Scout cabin on the foothill of the Berkeley campus. With Troop 11, Eagle Scouts, Arlie Taylor and Dale Smith.

Frequently at special events all over California in the 1950s and 1960s, Scoutmaster Ralph Neesam led Troop 11 members in the Pledge of Allegiance, the National Anthem or the Lord's Prayer.

In December 1969, two scouts from Troop 11, Brian Rasmus and Jack Jackerson, were invited with Ralph Neesam to recite the Lord's Prayer as the invocation to a banquet in Goodman Hall at Jack London Square in Oakland where Governor and Mrs. Ronald Reagan were guests. Governor Reagan was impressed and Mrs. Reagan outwardly showed emotion. After the invocation, both came forward to shake hands with the scouts and congratulated them on the fine presentation.

Ralph Neesam, Scoutmaster of Troop 11 for thirteen years from 1951 to 1964, awarded the "Silver Antelope."

Ralph Neesam Won "Silver Antelope"

Ralph Neesam, Scoutmaster of Troop 11 for thirteen years from 1951 to 1964, was awarded the *Silver Antelope*, which, next to the *Silver Buffalo*, is the highest honor given by the Boy Scouts of America. He directed the activities which were sponsored by the Berkeley Elks, BPOE 1002 and during that time he developed Troop 11 into one of the best known Scout organizations in the Far West. His boys were repeatedly called upon for demonstrations at banquets of national and district organizations, including the National Kiwanis convention, PTA meetings and United Crusade rallies. Their investiture ceremonies were on Television on numerous occasions. They received numerous Camporee awards.

Other Highlights

Angela Watson was the first female staff member chosen to be assistant scoutmaster in the CSD 's Boy Scout history. Scoutmaster Marvin Thompson, who won the President's award in recognition of his goal attainment in the 1971 commitment to Boy Power from the Mt. Diablo Council of Boy Scouts of America, appointed Watson to take care of 16 tenderfoot boys after 18 years as a girls' counselor.

George Wong, Troop11 adviser, was awarded the 1973 *Silver Beaver* for his distinguished service to the Boys Scouts from 1967 to 1995. In the Mt. Diablo Council, he was adviser of Explorer Post 26, A Neighborhood Commissioner, District Camping Chairman, and member of the Order of the Arrow. Wong was a true "Light unfer the Bushel," quietly going about the task of making Scouting happen in the lives of the boys. He was a Supervising Instructional Counselor when he retired in 1995.

In 1977, Troop 11 went camping into the Klamath National Forest by the Klamath River for rafting, fishing, riding horses and swimming for earning badges.

After the School moved to Fremont, the title of Troop 11 was preserved but it is now part of the new council, San Francisco Bay Area Council. Troop 11 continued to go camping to various sites such as the High Sierras for skiing,

From 1944 to 1998, under Scoutmaster Mark Nelson and Committee Chairperson Brian Rasmus, Troop11 undertook many outdoor activities, such as canoeing, skiing, hiking, camping, and snowboarding.

Emil Cornish, senior patrol leader, 1997-98, became a member of the Order of the Arrow.

Cook's Camp in the Russian River area for canoeing and camping, camporees, and the Point Reyes National Seahorse Park for hiking and camping. In March, 1997, Troop 11 and CSD's Girl Scouts Troop 717 went hiking together in the foothills behind the old CSD campus in Berkeley.

On May 1, 1997, Troop 11 celebrated their 80th anniversary at a dinner and Court of Honor program prepared by Scoutmaster Mark Nelson. Former Scoutmaster Ralph Neesam was a guest speaker. 174 awards including advancement and merit badges were awarded to 40 scouts.

In October 1997, Troop 11 took a camping trip to Camp Lindbad in Boulder Creek, California, for a weekend. They were challenged in survival situations. A fake incident took place as it looked like a boy fell into a creek and "broke" his leg. The other scouts thought it was real and doing a "drill," they carried him back to camp on a stretcher made by the scouts. After they learned the injury was not real, they were told that they had a beneficial learning experience.

CSD Eagle Scouts from 1921 to 2000

1921	**Edwin Wilson**	**1952**	**Donald Chan**
1922	**Henry Bull**	**1973**	**Brian Rasmus**
1922	**Ray Tabb**	**1980**	**Mark Nelson**
1934	**Horace Carlson**	**1986**	**Joel Barish**
1940	**Dale Smith**	**1986**	**Mark Bella**
1950	**Tony Munoz**	**1993**	**Steven Edwards**
1951	**Ronald Hirano**	**2000**	**Adam Tuttle**

Troop 11 Scoutmasters from 1916 to 2000

1916 to 24	**Carol Land**	**1951 to 64**	**Ralph Neesam**
1924 to 25	**Edwin Wilson**	**1964 to 68**	**Hubert Summers**
1925 to 28	**Freeman Rice**	**1968 to 70**	**Kenneth Clemens**
1928	**L. M. Cowman**	**1970 to 72**	**Marvin Thompson**
1928 to 29	**Freeman Rice**	**1972 to 77**	**Raymond Rasmus**
1929 to 32	**Alfred B. Skogen**	**1977 to 78**	**Michael Cardinale**
1932 to 33	**Roy G. Parks**	**1978 to 79**	**Robert Westerhaus**
1933 to 37	**Stanley Estabrook**	**1979 to 82**	**Steven R. Orman**
1937 to 39	**Vernon T. Wall**	**1982 to 84**	**Michael Cardinale**
1939 to 40	**George W. Smith**	**1984 to 90**	**Terry Sasser**
1940 to 41	**Francis C. Gyle**	**1990 to 92**	**Steven R. Orman**
1941 to 42	**Vernon T. Wall**	**1992 to 94**	**Bryan Zinza**
1942 to 46	**Vernon S. Birck**	**1994 to 98**	**Mark S. Nelson**
1946 to 51	**Irvan L. Woodruff**	**1998 to 00**	**Rex Barlow**

Cub Scout, Pack 11 under Den Leader Linda Onishi during the 1980s and early 1990s. Their meetings were held in Cottage 18 on Monday afternoons.

Cub Scouts

Instillation of Self-Image

On Open House Day, February 22, 1966, a charter was granted by the National Headquarters of the Boy Scouts of America to establish a cub scouting program for CSD students, from 8 to 11 years old. The pack was made possible by the sponsorship of the Elks Lodge #1002 of Berkeley, the same organization sponsoring the CSD Boy Scout since 1943. The first CSD pack was under Den Leader John Danenhower.

Cub Scouting has implemented many activities into both the school and residential life. In 1992, for the first time, under Den Leader Linda Onishi, Supervising Instruction Counselor of the elementary department, Cub Scout Pack II participated in the "Scouting for Food" project which involved over four million scouts nationwide. Over 150 canned and packaged foods collected by the cub were given to the families who lost their homes in the Oakland Hills fire.

In 1994, Pack II was highly involved with the Cub Scout Pinewood Derby with 25 scouts participating in the race. A number of scouts' parents, Cub Scout Leader Susan Cherry, Charlie Holmes and Debbie Schugg helped build a huge race track for three cars to race at one time. This activity has been undertaken every since then.

Camp Fire Logo.
The Camp Fire Girls was founded at CSD in 1916, only 6 years after the national Camp Fire was founded in 1910 by Dr. Luther Gulick and his wife as a program for girls similar to the Boy Scouts program he had helped to develop.

Campfire Girls / Girl Scouts

Instillation of Self-Esteem

Camp Fire Girls was established at CSD in 1916, under the direction of Alice Metcalf, academic teacher, and Anna Lindstrom, matron of Durham Hall. The first 23 girls were members with an interest in an organization that offered a love of outdoor life much needed by the girls of that time. It freed them from being confined to indoor tasks.

Camp Fire Girls was a means of organizing a girl's daily home life. It showed that romance, beauty and adventure were to be found everywhere and in wholesome ways; that the daily drudgery could contribute to the beauty of living. It provided healthy and interesting group activities. It was designed to promote a happy social life.

The organization of the Camp Fire Girls corresponded to the Boy Scout movement. The symbol of the campfire was "fire," and the members greeted each other by its sign, which was taken from the sign language of the early American Indians. At "the council fire," the girls wore ceremonial gowns and bead-bands and sat around the campfire.

Camp Fire Girls Activities

CSD Camp Fire Girls received recognition throughout California and in other states. The San Francisco and Oakland papers gave accounts of Camp Fire Girls (CFG) and printed pictures of the girls, time and again. On May 5, 1917,

CSD Camp Fire Girls posed looking like "proud Indians" in the redwood grove on the Berkeley campus in 1918 under the leadership and founder Anna Lindstrom (wearing a long beaded necklace).

Camp Fire Girls during the school year of 1955-56:

A PE YA – (Miss Gifford and Miss Matulich) Janice Sperring, President; Patty Burnette, Vice President; Shirley Begrin, Secretary & Treasurer.

TA WAN KI – (Mrs. Tennis) Donna Walker, President; Astrid Amann, Secretary; Elaine Voegele, Treasurer.

E HA WEE – (Mrs. Philips) Barbara Wilcox, President; Donna Brooks, Vice President; Jeanne Raub, Secretary; Ianthe Richardson, Treasurer.

PIT I HA – (Mrs. Sorensen) Marilyn Cook, President; Clara Jo Canady, Vice President; Joyce Ann Harvey, Secretary.

the girls participated in the big May Day festival at Trestle Glen east of Oakland when CFG took part in a pageant depicting early California, and the period of Indian supremacy. On March 15, 1918, one hundred and fifty CFG from Oakland, Alameda, and Berkeley assembled in the CSD gym to honor the 6th birthday of CF work in the United States. The two groups of CSD girls, dressed in white and carrying red and blue ribbons, gave a most impressive and charming patriotic drill.

In 1937, Mrs. Edward Tillinghast, Guardian, and CFG sewed for the Needle Work Guild. Each member of the group made two baby garments, which were exhibited at the Needle Work Guild tea. Later the garments were given to the poor of Berkeley. In 1939, Troops of CFG from all over the United States congregated at a meeting at Treasure Island. The maidens of CSD troop displayed their exhibits at the World's Fair under the new guardianship of Gladys Gifford and Margaret Hembrook.

World War II curtailed CSD's activities, which also affected the activities of CFG.

Ann Tennis' Outstanding Accomplishments

For twenty-two years, from 1948 to 1970, Clara Ann Tennis served invaluably as the Camp Fire Girls leader. In 1957, she took over as CFG coordinator and continued being a leader of one of four or five groups with the assistance of five to seven teachers. At a banquet at the Claremont Hotel in January 1969, the Codornices Council of Camp Fire Girls, who presented her with a pendant indicative of the Twenty Year Leadership Honor, honored Ann Tennis. Also, she gave 27 years of her life to the teaching of English and social-studies to CSD students.

In 1955, five members of CSD Camp Fire Girls attained the "Torch Bearer" (the highest) rank in Social Leadership. They are shown here with their leader, Clara Ann Tennis, and two hearing girls from Berkeley High School who achieved the award with them. The CSD girls, back row, left to right: Alison Wood, Arlene Shults, Alice Berumen. The hearing girls are the first two in the front row. with CSD girls Margaret Spohr and Nancy Ikeda.

Tennis stated, "One of the highlights of my almost 25 years of working with CF happened in 1959 when five of our girls were awarded "Torch Bearer," the highest rank in Social Leadership. Those girls were: Alison Wood, Arlene Shults, Alice Berumen, Margaret Spohr and Nancy Ikeda."

Camp Fire Girls had many wonderful weekend outings to Yosemite Valley, the Pacific Grove area, and Sonora, staying at cabins. Borrowing the camping equipment from Troop11, CFG started "real" camping trips.

Conversion to Girl Scouts

In 1970, the responsibility for Camp Fire Girls was transferred from academic teachers to dormitory counselors. The CFG program lasted until 1975 when it was converted to the Girl Scout program. In 1977, Girl Scout Troop 2865 had their first campout at Lake Tahoe to play in the snow. Later at the Fremont school, the Brownies adopted Troop 2865.

The Girl Scout program was not so active during the late '70s, but it maintained productive years after the school moved to Fremont. Junior Girl Scout Troop 2882 of the elementary residential department participated in numerous activities through the '90s. From 1980 to 1988, the program was under the leadership of Barbara White. Joyce Lynch took over Troop 2882 consisting of about 25 girls. She ably ran the popular troop program until she retired in 1998.

Here is sample of some of activities CSD Girl Scouts Troop 2882 and Troop 717 (Middle Residential Department) have been doing every year.

- **They invite patrols of hearing Scouts from nearby schools to CSD. They enjoy their association with hearing peers playing games and learning some basic sign language.**
- **They sign Christmas carols at deaf senior citizens' homes.**
- **They make and sell scarves and goodies during Open House. Each year different special crafts such as necklaces and wooden Christmas trees are made for fund raising purposes.**
- **They go camping and on nature hikes to work on outdoor badges several times each year.**
- **Once every month the members' mothers come to a cottage to help them with scout activities to earn badges. They make necklaces, scout vests, pinwheels and sweatshirt designs. They look forward to an annual Award Night for the scouts to receive their badges.**

During Open House Girl Scouts selling homemade goodies and handcrafts for fund raising purposes. The proceeds culminating in a camping trip to Slide Ranch. (Left to right) Carmen Reyes, Erin Ross, Erin's mother, Lacia Baldwin Ashley Chase, Leader Joyce Lynch, Tara Bautista.

Brownie Troop 2865, 1995-96. Front row, left to right: Brianne Catron, Shanna Grossinger, Leila Hanaumi. Second row, L to R: Lisa Jarashow, Rebecca Eyrond, Mallory Malzkuhn, Zuelika Prader, Paige Holderman, Clara Baldwin. Back row, L to R: Karlee Ruiz, Amanda Sortwell, Angela Cassinelli, Vita Vongsikco, Christy Eddy Kristy Fry, Troop Leader Lisa Goetz.

- **They collected and brought canned foods to a homeless shelter.**
- **They prepared homemade goodies and candy cane candles to sell for fundraising.**

In 1999, the Girl scouts were busy at work, selling 1,459 boxes of cookies under the leaders, cottage counselors Becky Jo Baker and Saxon Turner. For the year of 1999-2000, Lisa Goetz was promoted to Girls Scout Troop Leader.

Brownies Troop 2865

Several years after CSD moved to Fremont, Brownies scouts Troop 2865 became active for first to third grade girls. They enjoy the outdoors, hiking, playing games, and learning about nature. At times, they go camping as far as Yosemite National Park. The Brownie program is summarized in the three Brownie B's: Be Discoverers; Be Ready Helpers; Be Friend-Makers. The

Brownies make cards and write letters to penpals from another troop. They have opportunity to meet their pen pals later that year. Every year in May the Brownies have a Court of Awards for badge merits earned in six different categories: environment, education, peace, food and nutrition, health and culture, and heritage. At different times, residential counselors Teresa Ventura, Sharon Allen, Pam Rogers and Lisa Goetz were troop leaders. Goetz has been active leader since 1989. In 1999, Kristen Malm became Brownies Leader.

Girl Scout Calendar

The San Francisco Bay Girl Scout Council every year produces 10 inch by 13-inch wall and pocket calendars featuring color pictures of Girl Scouts from throughout the State, for marketing purpose. For the 1991 calendar, the SFBGS Council selected Junior Troop 2882 for the front cover and Brownie Troop 2865 on the Back. CSD was filled with pride by this distinctive honor. This is one of the highlights in the CSD Girl Scouts' history-possibly once in the lifetime.

Junior Girl Scouts of CSD. (Front row, left to right) Kimberly Eck, Raven Woodward, Natalie Fleet, Valerie Johnson, and Maria Damian express their thanks with smiles and sign language.

Portrayal of CSD Spring Plays

Drama is as natural as breathing for deaf students. It is an essential part of their lives. The power of visual communication, the mime, the movement, the emotions, and sign language electrify deaf students like the painting of two fingertips touching each other as shown on the ceiling of the Sistine Chapel in the Vatican at Rome. To be accomplished, they would need training, since drama compels responsibilities, discipline and clear understanding. Once a deaf student develops this, he is self-contented.

Long ago, Theophilus d'Estrella must have grasped this concept and the value of drama for the deaf students and deaf people alike. One of the first school productions, *The Taming of the Shrew*, was presented in 1905. Both teachers and students participated as actors. Theophilus d'Estrella, a deaf teacher, was both director and actor. He founded a literary society named De l'Epee Literary Society. Later it was renamed after d'Estrella in honor of his drama work. Starting around 1890, drama appeared in the chapel in the Educational

Brownie Girl Scouts of CSD. (Opposite page, front row, left to right) Susanne Arrona, Heather Cassinelli, Paloma McClelland, Cinbrella Saunders, Priscilla Saunders, Sarah Parker, Jeana Williams, Gina Pasini, and Renee Vairora recite the Girl Scout Promise in American Sign Language.

Theophilus d'Estrella is credited with establishing the Literary Society that eventually inspired the idea of annual full-length stage plays.

The Chapel at the Berkeley school was where students and faculty assembled for a storytelling hour, ethics talks, Literary Society programs and silent movies.

> ***Storytelling was enjoyed by the older CSD students on Sunday evening in the old Chapel Hall in the 1940s and 1950s. The storytelling lasted one hour, 7 to 8. Different men teachers gave stories three Sunday evenings each month. Many good stories were told, but the general consensus among the students was that Sheldon McArtor was the top storyteller. Now and then in old days, he told thrilling stories of Monsieur Blackshirt, a mysterious avenger of the oppressed in France, much like Zorro of old California. Chapel Hall shook with the students stomping their feet every time Mc Artor could not finish the story in an hour and he regretfully spelled " To be continued" on his fingers.***
>
> Ken Shaffer
> CSD, '46

Building. The Gothic architectural chapel had beautiful stained windows, a small but adequate stage without curtains and 616 fixed folding "opera" seats which were governed by strict rules. As for seat arrangement, facing the stage the left side was only for girls and the right for boys. In the dark during plays or movies, students were constantly supervised by dormitory counselors or the dean. No hand holding was permitted! (The rule is no longer in effect.) The first Junior Class plays in the1940s were presented in the chapel and were transferred to the new auditorium in the 1950s.

1960 to 1980

Inside the front doors decorated with an Aesop fable ornate wrought-iron grille, the Primary Auditorium exhibited Mission California style architectural features with high ceilings, gilded pillars on the sides, and high wood-paneled walls. The focal point of the room was a stage with navy blue velvet curtains at the rear entrance.This theater was one of the deaf students' most cherished heritage. Rows of folding chairs were arranged so that the audience could see the action on the stage or on other occasions the seats would be removed to allow space for students to dance under the crepe paper decorations with music from a record player.

On the night of April 22, 1961, as the Primary Auditorium lights dimmed, a hush fell on the audience. The blue velvet curtains opened to reveal an uncomplicated living room scene of *The Journey's End.* This Spring play was sponsored by the Theophilus d' Estrella Literary Society and directed by a deaf faculty member, Sheldon Mc Artor, who was also a natural-born storyteller and one of the great acting teachers of his time. With his dramatic flair, he could make a story come alive and take students on a voyage to explore the imaginative world. The effects were immediate and stunning. Sheldon McArtor instilled his crafts in his students for their Literary Society presentation and spring plays.

Sheldon McArtor directed several full length plays at the San Francisco Club for the Deaf. He recognized that the Deaf alumni were particularly interested in full length plays that explore the richness of sign language and dramatic vision in its works or dialogue.Sheldon brought that philosophy to CSD in Berkeley. He initiated the annual full length play in the spring of 1944 with the play *Strange Doings in a Castle.*

Not only did McArtor enhance deaf students' love for storytelling and acting culture, they were also mesmerized and inspired in the following years by energetic, intelligent deaf faculty members such as Leo M. Jacobs, Emil S. Ladner, Bernard Bragg and Eric Malzkuhn. Those masters deserve immense credit for keeping the art of storytelling and acting alive for the deaf students

The front view of the Primary Auditorium (left) with the decor of gold gilt and velvet curtains on the stage. Once a month chairs were removed to allow space for dancing. (Above)The rear side of the auditorium with a balcony.

during the dark age of vocal communication such as radio, movies, and television (no captions at that time). Their artistic venture and interpersonal communication with the deaf students (or actors) made the theater experience a rare one.

Two distinguished deaf educators, Leo M. Jacobs and Emil S. Ladner, worked as high school teachers of mathematics and social studies and were active in deaf community affairs and offices on the local, national and international levels throughout their teaching careers. Their credentials also included writings for *The Silent Worker* and *The California News* and directing spring plays with equal flair. Leo Jacobs directed *One Mad Night* (1948), a comedy *Charley's Aunt* (1953), a play based upon the novel by Jules Verne: *Around the World in Eighty Days* (1958) and a mystery:*The Desperate Hours* (1963). Ladner's directing credits included *The Junior Prom* (1949), *Little Women* (1954), *Too Many Detectives* (1959) and a fantasy-drama: *The Man from Andromeda* (1964).

Bernard Bragg, an accomplished deaf actor, writer, director, and lecturer, has an extraordinary gift of eloquence and a splendid power of rich and

Original design poster by Sarah Shemaria, a CSD student in 1948.

The Sunday Chapel Talks! What wonderful opportunities for the student to learn important ideas and values! People like Emil Ladner, Bernard Bragg, Hal Ramger, Erwin Marshall come to mind. I will never forget Erwin Marshall's simple demonstration of habit formation, using a ball of string. He got two students to participate in the demonstration, one wrapping string around the other's arms and body. He showed how increased wraps of string were difficult to break, as increased repetitions of actions formed habits which were difficult to break. A simple but effective example of habit formation.

Jacob Arcanin
Retired Assistant Superintendent

imaginative use of American Sign Language. During his fifteen years at CSD in Berkeley as an instructor of English and science, two of his highlights were *A Christmas Carol* (1960) and *The Stingy Pawnbroker* (1964). In his first year, he was assistant director of *Little Women* which was a smash hit. Simultaneously, he created a weekly one-man television program for KQED in San Francisco called *The Quiet Man*. His directing credits for the Spring plays included a melodrama: *The Cat and the Canary* and a biographical drama of Helen Keller as a child: *The Guiding Hand* (1960). His last play was a drama in pantomime: *Escape* (1965). In 1967, he departed to become a founder, professional actor, and instructor with the National Theatre of the Deaf. Since then, through theaters, television, lectures, and guest appearances all over the world, Bragg has reached the most distinguished point of his career. Years later, he returned to CSD in Fremont for a guest appearance and as an acting workshop instructor. Dr. Bragg pointed out, "I am a theater person and when I speak of drama, I look at it from a theater standpoint. But in my work with deaf adolescents, I found myself involved creatively in constant experiment and innovation with the language for theater use. Also, I have come to realize that creative drama cannot be narrowly confined to theater activities. It starts, in a group, with the adolescent's awareness of who he is, where he comes from, and what is unique about himself."

Entering CSD in Berkeley in 1968 as an instructor of science, his wit and love of drama soon made Eric Malzkhun popular and prominent. His knack of

A comedy "Charley's Aunt" *directed by Leo Jacobs in 1953.*

transforming signs into stunning visual pictures induced both Deaf actors and audiences to view the theatrical sign language differently with much delight and often in awe. He directed *Two for Love* (1968), *My Sister Eileen* (1969), a musical drama: *South Pacific* (1970), *Arsenic and Old Lace* (1971) and *Little Women* (1972). Because of his life long love for drama, theater experience and his contribution to the National Theater of the Deaf (NTD), Malzkuhn can sit back knowing that his teachings of drama successfully influenced a number of students. Dr. Malzkuhn stated, "Thinking hard, I really can think of only three people who I may have influenced enough to make the world of entertainment their careers, in a way. Two would be Rita Corey, who was Bloody Mary in my South Pacific and her brother, Ed, also acted for me in that show. Also, there was Ella Lentz, who is still knocking them dead with her poetry signing. She was Nellie Forbush in that play."

Malzkuhn emphasized that *South Pacific* was the first attempt, in a school for the deaf, to stage a Broadway musical. Instead of having an orchestra, the play used the Broadway sound track for the songs, and a couple of interpreters for the voice overs. It was interesting that there was a budget of only $85 for this play.

It is of special pride to CSD that the theater at Model Secondary School for the Deaf (MSSD) in Washington, D. C., on October 7, 1994, was named after Eric Malzkuhn: *THEATRE MALZ*.

Among women as directors of Spring plays were Kathleen Philips, Myrle Sweet, Marianne DeLuca, Michele Tiano, and Betsy Ford who made fantastic contributions. However, the one who directed the largest number of plays was Ann Dexheimer. Her total number was seven from 1977 to 1985. She stated that over the years she saw incredible personal growth in the students, many of whom participated in plays all four years of their high school years. The first year's production faced tough challenges; a major accident for a lead role, measles for another, and one suspended! It was a learning experience for all of them but the following year, with *More Than Meets the Eye*, the students began to act as a team. Dexheimer said, "For the last performance in Berkeley we added something new, taking the show on the road. We took the *Drunkard*, a comedy/melodrama, to Sacramento and Stockton, hosted by the local parents of deaf children. Lee Basham, a volunteer, single-handedly developed sets that could be easily taken apart and transported. When he was unable to volunteer the next year, we were no longer able to 'hit the road' so our traveling theater came to an end."

The era of the Literary Society's Spring play at the Berkeley school ended with *The Drunkard* (1980), directed by Ann Dexheimer. Coincidentally, or not, the title was a metaphor of the problem CSD had with the pressure for the school to move out of Berkeley. The play swept the audience with a smile.

Director Bernard Bragg (middle) discusses character relationship during the polishing period of "The Guiding Hand" *dress rehearsal with Elizabeth Canady (left) and Jo Anne Flowers.*

The Theophilus d'Estrella Literary Society

presents

"MY SISTER EILEEN"

Directed by Eric Malzkuhn

Saturday, May 3, 1969—8 p.m.

d'Estrella Auditorium

Program for "My Sister Eileen" *play directed bt Eric Malzkuhn in 1969. Prior to 1960, a prompter either sat below the stage or stood behind the wing curtain to feed lines to actors who forgot them. Since 1960 prompters are no longer necessary as deaf actors are trained to ad lib on their own.*

I would like to mention that in addition to Lee Basham, there were others who worked behind the scenes to contribute to the success of our plays. Betty Hahn, former math teacher at the Berkeley school, was an incredible seamstress. She would show me a design for a costume on Monday, and by the next day it would be done. When she retired, Jeanne Loustalot did a superb job sewing costumes for our plays in Fremont. Even though **"The Wizard of Oz"** *played to standing room only crowds, it was* **"Any Number Can Die"** *that will always be my favorite.*

Ann Dexheimer

1981 to 1990

In 1981, when the play production moved to the new Little Theater at CSD in Fremont, the young actors found the new stage to be a more free-flowing space and equipped with a dressing room, a costume room and a better lighting system. What delighted them was the discovery of the Aesop Fables grilles which had been transferred from the Primary Auditorium in Berkeley to the front doors of the Little Theater. When the people assembled in this theater for a play performance and seated themselves on cushioned seats, they found the theatrical surrounding to be gratifying and the stage more visible due to the tiered seating structure. They would chat amiably with one another until the house light dimmed. *Sight Unseen*, directed by Ann Dexheimer, was the first play at CSD in Fremont.

In 1987, at the CSD Little Theater, Julianne Fjeld directed *Sign Me Alice* which was written by Gilbert Eastman, a deaf professor of the drama department at Gallaudet University. The reason for her selection of this play was that "...he (Eastman) is a humanitarian and a communicator and *Sign Me Alice* is among very few plays that present the deaf point of view." Once again, she was invited the following year to direct *The Miracle Worker* (1988). For the third time at the request of CSD, Juliana returned with a disturbing concern about the Holocaust issue and decided to direct *Into Hiding* (1989) which turned out to be a memorable one.

A scene of the "Miracle Worker" *where Brenda Barrett instructed Anna Counter to sign WATER. At right, John Cassidy (left), Michelle Boren, Sophia Castillo.*

The poster for *Into Hiding* showed the painting of Anne Frank done by Morris Broderson, a well known Deaf artist. Broderson personally knew one of the characters in this play by the name of Meips Gies, a Dutch lady who helped hide the Frank family and other Jewish friends.

Interestingly, during the *Into Hiding* rehearsals, there arose a Gallaudet University protest. The issues of the Holocaust, the Gallaudet University protest, the rehearsals and the homework were certainly a great learning experience for the young actors.

The "Miracle Worker" *cast and production staff. Julianna Fjeld at the second upper stairs directed the play in 1988.*

"The Wild Minds"
play was developed from the creative writing and theater project in 1991 under Bob Hiltermann, producer and director.

Actors wrote and acted out their dialogues based on their experiences.

1991 TO 2000

Two English classes, one high school and one middle school, wrote the script for 1991's Spring Play, *The Wild Minds*. Bob Hiltermann, who was a screen writer, appeared in the movies *Children of a Lesser God*, and the made-for-TV movie, *Bridge to Silence*, directed the Creative Writing and Theater Projects, a four week program designed to develop the writing, language and theater skills of the students. Middle school teacher Karen Lucania was the assistant director.

Hiltermann pointed out, "This experience of writing, directing and acting has given the students a total involvement of theater development." Out of this came a *The Wild Minds* production, fifteen scenes written, directed and performed by the high and middle school students. He added, "The production is a wide array of styles ranging from adventure, comedy, romance, horror, and fantasy. Each of the stories is an individual expression of the thoughts, concerns, and fantasies of our youth." Examples of the scenes were *The Murder of Mona Lisa, PAH, Who's to Blame,* and *The Bear Hunt.*

Charles N. Katz directed two plays: *The Hunchback of St. Jaques* (1993) and the charming *Anne of Green Gables* (1994) before leaving for his doctoral study at the University of Texas. He pointed out that: "It is a habit of mine to adapt most of my theater productions to the Deaf frame of mind so let's imagine Anne herself deaf."

Sara Stallard, left, Louise Stern and Jon Lamberton in "Anne of Green Gables."

Charles J. Jones, a director, a choreographer, a drummer, a comedian, and a NTD actor, came to CSD directly from Hands Across Communications, Inc. as both actor and executive director in Los Angeles, to direct *A Funny Thing Happened on the Way to the Forum* (1995). In addition to this, he also conducted various acting workshops for the students during the week and performed a one man show during one weekend. He also flew to perform a one man show in other states. In spite of his heavy schedule, Jones held the audience in his heart in that he would communicate with them at the beginning, the middle (intermission) and the end of his plays. For example, before the beginning of *The Cat and The Canary* (1996) Jones teased his audience with ".. Enough of my thoughts (on this play), let's sit back and enjoy! But wait a minute, remember to hold onto each other, it's a suspense time!"and slipped quickly behind the blue curtains. The audience roared with laughter until they heard or felt eerie music. His last play, *Aladdin and the Wonderful Lamp* (1997) was a magic time and a colorful work of storytelling. The audience went home with a light heart.

Julianna Fjeld's ultimate return to CSD was a blessing when the school sorely needed a director for the 1998 production. Out of the blue she appeared on the campus and quickly took over the reins of the *Romeo and Juliet* production with ease. With the skillful scenic designer and builder, Bob Morrison, woodwork instructor, and a cast of thirty-two actors, the production of *Romeo and Juliet* unfolded into a thing of beauty and magically swept over the audience. Observing a work of Shakespeare turn from a classroom text class into a visually colorful production on a stage stimulates the imagination and creativity of the young actors and students. This precisely followed Fjeld's goal and it was achieved. *Romeo and Juliet* was considered as one of Fjeld's praiseworthy accomplishments by the audience.

Fjeld delivered another successful production, *Little Women* in April, 1999. She advanced the time frame from the 19th century to the 20th century and portrayed a version of a typical Deaf family. The tide of audience and performers was still high for Fjeld and her work.

Since Spring Play not only inspires, but also teaches, drama is considered part of the educational process for students. According to the custom of the theater, when a play ends, the audience waves their hands high in the air. Here is special applause for Theophilus d'Estrella.

L.M. Montgomery's
Anne of Green Gables
dramatized by Joseph Robinette
performed by the students of the California School for the Deaf, Fremont
directed by Charles N. Katz

Thursday, March 31, 1994 at 7:00 p.m.
Friday, April 1, 1994 at 7:30 p.m.
Saturday, April 2, 1994 at 1:30 p.m.
Saturday, April 2, 1994 at 7:30 p.m.

at the Little Theater
California School for the Deaf
39350 Gallaudet Drive
Fremont, CA 94538

General Admission
$5.00
Students
$3.00

for information,
call Outreach at (510) 794-3707
(Voice and TTY)

Performed in American Sign Language with voice-over via headphones

Director Charles Jones (right) suggests a comic effect in mime for a jester, Jerry Pua. In the background, from left to right: Tina Johnson, Jesse Saunders, Ramadon Furgan, Michael Davis, Brian Morrison.

Fair ladies in dancing act, (from left to right) Shohannah Stern, Kamilah Dyer, Lanetta Williams, Sheila De La, Shanna Winesburg.

Shoshannah Stern in the balcony scene of "Romeo and Juliet."

Jay Baldridge as Romeo.

Holiday Plays

Not only does the CSD school provide the Spring Plays, but also many other plays during the school year. The purpose of these plays is to celebrate particular events, such as the Christmas holiday, Abraham Lincoln's Birthday, George Washington's Birthday, Veteran's Day, Gallaudet Day, Laurent Clerc, "PAH" Day and Miss Beauty Pageant. It is not possible to mention every performance since 1960 but to highlight several memorable plays.

The Nutcracker by the Elementary Students

Aside from the Spring Play, there has been an annual Christmas innovative program where every three or four years the elementary students express the season through song, poetry, stories and skits with costumes and props. It is first developed in various classrooms and gradually transferred to the stage for a dress rehearsal before its final performance in the Little Theater. One of the most beloved Christmas tableaux was *The Nutcracker*. Its popularity brought it back in 1976 and 1988. The latter was directed by Laureen Newman Feldhorn.The performances in 1992 and 1996 were directed by Ed Copra. *The Nutcracker* is expected to be continued in subsequent years.

Circa 1890 Washington's Day program.
"I Cannot Tell a Lie."

Who best draws response from the deaf student?

The trained deaf person.

This is as it should be. Isn't this one of our primary objectives — to have skilled deaf teachers in vital positions of leadership among deaf teenagers? The world requires not only the fullest possible communication, but the fullest possible identification of the student with his guide, as he/she awakens to his/her own potential and develops confidence and self-esteem.

Dr. Bernard Bragg
Former CSD teacher

The Nutcracker.

Highlights Given by the Middle School Students

One of the most favorite plays performed by the Middle School students has been *The Stingy Pawnbroker*. In 1964, it was directed by Bernard Bragg, who composed the play with a combination of ideas gleaned from Charlie Chaplin's silent film, Charles Dickens' A Christmas Carol, and Marcel Marceau's pantomime. That play was brought back by popular demand in the following year, 1965. Bragg's interpretation of that play was majestically and soulfully expressive, bringing the play to an encore.

In 1991, *The Stingy Pawnbroker* adapted by Celia May Baldwin was once again performed. It was one of three parts of A Winter Trilogy. The other two

parts, *The Gift* and *Santa Claus and His Reindeer Tap Dance*, were directed by Chuck Baird, well known actor from the National Theater of the Deaf and an artist-in-residence at CSDF that year. The plays were not only enjoyed by the school students and staff members, but also many hearing and deaf students from various schools in Fremont and San Jose.

In 1995, following the modern leaning on the national bestseller book, *Chicken Soup for the Souls*, the Middle School students gave its premiere of *Chicken Soup*, directed by Karen Luttage and Debbie Golos. The young deaf actors wrote and acted out their individual life experiences. The art and craft classes designed their own props and set. The play became a hit.

> ***"The Winter Program was awesome! It helped us learn to memorize because if we have tests, we may or may not be ready to memorize something. It helped me to get along with others in the play. It helped people to gain experience acting."***
>
> Sarah Parker
> 1996 Middle School Student

High School Level

Due to heavy athletic activities in the fall, the High School Department has only presented Christmas plays on occasion. Spring plays have been the focus of high school students.

One of the finest high school Christmas plays should not go unmentioned. It was a somewhat unusual play taking place in December 1968. Eric Malzkuhn was cut from quite a different cloth as he demonstrated in his original one-act comedy-drama. *The Flying Zarillas* which flashed the lives of a circus family on Christmas Eve with humor and colors. The masterful comedy-drama writer and director developed and revealed the characters and plot very artistically. The audience raved over the play so it was shown again in February, 1969. It was rare to bring a wealth of expressiveness to a stage play. Adding much to the glitter were the sequined costumes which were designed by Elizabeth Hahn, a HS teacher. Colorful posters of by-gone circus days and authentic props borrowed from the Salvation Army added a realistic touch.

The Flying Zarillas, *1968-1969. Written by a staff member, Eric Malzkuhn, who also directed, the play was one-act comedy-drama revolving around complications in the lives of a circus family. (Photo at left, left to right) Ray Ponciano, Claire Clancey, Helen Hachiya, and David Ash. (Photo at right, left to right) Gregory Benson and David Ash.*

> ***"I couldn't believe that I won - I thought all the girls competing were great! It was a rich experience. I encourage other girls to join the 3rd pageant in 1985."***
>
> Jane Hammons
> 1983 Miss CSD

CSD Beauty Pageant

On March 26, 1981, the first beauty pageant to select Miss California School for the Deaf was sponsored by the combination of two student organizations, the Junior National Association of the Deaf and the Student Body Government. Debbie Saavedra, a senior from San Jose, California, was chosen by a panel of judges as the first Miss California School for the Deaf, Fremont. Staff members from the academic department and the residence department have helped to make this a successful and colorful pageant.

The winner represented CSD at the Miss California Association of the Deaf Pageant at Universal City, California, during the California Association of the Deaf (CAD) convention on September 3-5, 1981.

This CSD event inaugurated the tradition to coincide the beauty pageant with the CAD convention every two years. Miss CSD will compete for the Miss Deaf California Title during the California Association of the Deaf Convention. The winner from there will compete at the National Association of the Deaf Convention in the following year. The categories of competition are usually the Pre-stage Private Interview, Beach Wear, Talent Show, Evening Gown, and Public Stage Interview.

The winners of the CSD beauty pageant since 1981:

1981 Debbie Saavedra

1983 Jane Hammons

1985 Barbara Hemstreet

1987 Ivanetta Ikeda

1989 Tara Petris

1991 Krissten Weiner

1993 Adele Ann Eberwein

1995 Darla Thompson

1997 Valerie Hottle

1999 Bonnie Morrison

> ***"When I was growing up, I had a natural confidence in myself. Then, acting the role of Schaherazade in this year's Spring Play helped me to develop the confidence and poise I needed for the stage."***
>
> Valerie Hottle
> 1997 Miss CSD

Debbie Saavedra, CSD's first Beauty Pageant winner in 1981.

Student Leadership Conference at Asilomar

The California School for the Deaf, Berkeley, held its first Student Leadership Conference at Asilomar in Pacific Grove October 12 to 14, 1973. Jacob Arcanin, Assistant Superintendent, initiated the concept of the conference. The aim of the conference was to develop student leadership skills and enhance school atmosphere. The goals of the Leadership Conference were to discuss qualities of leadership and to identify activities in which leadership might be exerted on the campus. The participants are usually presidents of the student organizations and potential leaders of the future. Every year several staff members accompany the young leaders to the rustic state operated park with buildings for meetings and workshops. As for accommodations, Hill Top, the rustic building with 14 multiple-bed rooms with a fireplace in the lobby, offers a cozy and comfortable atmosphere. The food served in the big dining room is usually appreciated.

Situated on the tip of the Monterey Peninsula overlooking the Pacific Ocean, Asilomar State Beach and Conference Grounds is a unit of the California State Park System. The name of Asilomar was derived from the

Thirty-nine CSD students and six staff members took part in a two-day Student leadership Conference at Asilomar on the Monterey Peninsula, California, October 3-4, 1984.

STUDENT LEADERSHIP CONFERENCE is a place where potential student leaders are groomed.

The annual Asilomar Student Leadership Conference takes place in October. Thanks to the support and worthy endeavors from the school and the Association of Parents, Teachers, and Counselors (APTC). The funds cover the accommodations and meals for about 30 students and five staff members.

They usually spend more than 12 solid hours at work, learning about each other, setting goals for school organizations, reinforcing student leadership skills, and learning more about the importance of student involvement in school activities. Above all:

WHAT CAN THEY DO FOR THE SCHOOL?

Spanish words, *Asilo*, meaning retreat, and *mar*, meaning sea. Asilomar is a perfect site for retreat purposes and offers a tranquil atmosphere. Many students have blossomed into fine leaders since attending the Conference.

The participants usually leave the school Monday morning for Asilomar and are ready for registration before lunch. In the afternoon session, the staff members or students start with talks about the goals of the conference and then resume with workshops. In the evening after the workshops around nine, stories, jokes, skits, and ghost stories are shared among the students as well as the staff before the blazing fireplace. The traditional snack such as roasted marshmallows with chocolate squares on graham crackers is served.

The following morning focuses on a brain storm discussion and the students usually come up with a number of positive ideas that would be offered to the school. In the early afternoon after lunch, their treat for hard work is usually to play at the beach.

The topics that have been covered at Asilomar:

Reorganization of the Student Government

Contemplation of parliamentary procedures

Development of the student handbook

Implementation of the Judicial Board

Discussion of positive communication among students

Implementation of peer counseling

Instillation of more mature behavior among students

Improvement of consistency of information between staff and students

Maintenance of communicating, sharing, and treating Special Unit students with proper etiquette and due respect

Development of decision-making skills

Role of peer leaders and acknowledgment of responsibilities

Improvement of leadership skills and passing them on to others

Establishment of goals and objectives of student organizations such as FAA, SBG, Cottage Councils, Senior class and Junior class, Jr. NAD, and other clubs

The following student report from a conference at Asilomar on October 16 and 17, 1989,mentions typical activities at Asilomar:

> **The purpose of the conference was to improve leadership skills and pass them on to others who did not attend Asilomar. We also worked together to try to improve CSDF. When we arrived, we started working right away! We were introduced by each other to "break the ice," and then separated into three groups called Real Genius, Tippy, and Dream Masters. We were very competitive to earn points because we all wanted to win a prize. We listened to many lectures and explanations about leadership, and each group had some "leader's vocabulary" to explain. We tried our best to explain the qualities of leadership as winners would get bonus points.**

CSD students and staff members including a public defender of Monterey and Kurt Norton, an investigator for the Bay Area public defender office, discussing the Judicial System to increase awareness of laws and court system. It occurred in 1987 at Asilomar. Counselors, Terry Sasser (left) and Holly Benedict Duve, (sitting at right) conducting the "bull session" with the student participants.

After registration, the three groups were put into different rooms to work on "crises." The crises were, for example, if you are dean of students, and a problem shows up then another, and another. That is the same principle — it happens all the time in the real world, so the sponsors wanted to train us for it.

The sponsors, Ken Norton, Steve Orman, Joe MacDougall, Terry Sasser, Debbie Call, and Carlene Pedersen, aimed to see if the groups could divide responsibilities for each crisis that showed up. The students had only four hours to deal with all crises, and they developed many creative and solvable ideas which were quite impressive to the staff.

"Asilomar,
thy lessons learned
well within
thy dear gates,
Will ever keep us
strong and true
out where the world
awaits."

Asilomar
scrapbook

A good night's sleep was spent after brownies, cake, and hot cocoa were served. The morning session focused on tips and training on how to operate meetings of classes, Student Body Government, Foothills Athletic Association, and the Judicial Board. After lunch they were off to the beach for diversion. Naturally they had so much fun and were reluctant to leave for the school.

After a few years lapse due to a financial crisis, another leadership conference was held on May 16, 17, 18, 1997. The location was shifted to a more rugged camp site, Pema Osel Ling in the Santa Cruz mountains, instead of at Asilomar. It was an upscale conference center.

CSDF Students Attend Leadership Retreat

The school staff members assumed primary responsibility for organizing a Leadership Conference at the Pema Osel Ling Buddhist Camp. One of the purposes of the Leadership Conference was to provide selected students an opportunity to be exposed to a variety of basic leadership and self-awareness topics, and experiences that would enable them to obtain a better understanding of themselves as leaders and team players.

The conference began with a welcome from Dr. Klopping, a review of the conference program and a motivational speech by CSDF teacher Ethan Bernstein.

"Every year at the Conference no work is unimportant at Asilomar."

Ken Norton
Former Dean of Students

1) *Why Do We Have Students Organizations?*, by Gary Olsen
2) *A presentation by the middle school principal,* by Celia May Baldwin
3) *Information on Leadership Styles,* by Bridgetta Bourne-Firl, Community Education Coordinator with the Outreach Division
4) *Discussion of Styles,* by Michael Finneran, Dean of Student Life
5) *Respect for Self and Others,* by Ronald Stern, Director of Instruction
6) *Project Management*, by Diana Herron-Rhodes
7) *Personality Styles*, by Cheryl Boyd, Outreach Specialist
8) *Responsibility*, by Jacob Arcanin, Assistant Superintendent
9) *Good Communication,* by Patricia Moore, Principal of Vocational Department, and Bill Ash, from the Vocation Program

Many staff members referred to the conference as a great experience for the students and the staff. It was an event that will be long remembered by all.

Bing Crosby / AT&T Golf Tournament

"Look what we got from the Golf Tourney," the students exclaimed after returning to the school on January 29, 1967. They had autographs by Jack Nicklaus, Arnold Palmer, Johnny Miller, matinee idol Robert Goulet, SF 49er Joe Montana, actor Clint Eastwood, actor George Scott, actor Robert Wagner, Bing Crosby, Bing's wife, Kathleen, and many, many other celebrities.

Students of CSD being invited as special guests to the Bing Crosby/ AT&T Pro-Am Golf Tournament at Pebble Beach became an annual event commencing in 1967. Charles Benson, parent of Gregory, a 1969 graduate of CSD Berkeley, was instrumental in beginning the CSD tradition of inviting seniors to the Golf Tournament. Benson was an executive for the phone company and at one time the Mayor of Del Rey Oaks, a community near Monterey. For a number of years students and several staff members were

The main event for the trip to Monterey was watching the professional golfers playing with amateur partners all day at three famous golf courses. Usually the students split up and wandered around the courses watching the golfers make bogies, pars, birdies, and sometimes eagles. At one time after playing the tenth hole, Jack Lemmon asked his caddy if he had missed seeing any students from CSD. So the caddy made some requests around and finally the CSD students were grouped at the eighteenth hole waiting to greet Jack Lemmon. Then Jack happily signed autographs for each of the students.

In 1985, Jack Nicklaus amid the CSD students. (Left) Kevin Hendrix, Leonesa Vitorino, Olaf Attletweed. (Bottom) Coleen Mahan.

President Gerald Ford centered in the group of the fans, CSD students and staff members. On that day in 1976, President Ford just ended his presidential term and flew to Monterey in time for the Bing Crosby Pro-Am Golf Tournament.

invited to stay in the barracks of the Presidio of Monterey, known as the Defensive Language Institute, and "bunk in" with young men in various branches of the military who were learning a foreign language. Benson would arrange for some celebrities, such as actor George Scott, pro golfer Jack Nicklaus, actor Efram Zimbalist Jr., and others, to visit with the students in the evening.

January 1973, the Edward Ray Thornberg Memorial was established as a means of honoring this outstanding citizen of Del Rey Oaks. It was presented each year to a CSD boy who had shown outstanding scholarship and athletic ability. The first winner was David Herdich and the 1974 winner was Harold Stuart. Gilmer Lentz the winner for 1975. In 1976, the girls were invited to attend the golf tournament for the first time. Then the stay at the Presidio of Monterey was discontinued. Since then the seniors spend one day roaming the golf courses every year.

A number of CSD graduates who experienced the trip to the Pro-Am Golf Tournament have taken up recreational golf during adult life. Many of them have participated in the golf tournaments arranged by the deaf communities in the nation. A former CSD student named Cranberry has become a professional golfer.

On March 22, 1994, CSD lost a friend and advocate of the deaf when Charles Benson passed away. Irwin Marshall, former principal of the middle school for many years, collaborated with Charlie when he first brought forth the idea. Marshall said, "Charlie was an individual with class; he had a dignity that drew people to him. He will be missed so much." Ken Norton, former dean of students recalled visiting Benson's home and remembers him as a sincere and kindhearted man. He said, "Charlie is far away now but his heart is always at CSD."

Mayor Benson's wife Faye has kept the tradition alive. She makes all the preparations so that CSD students can continue to het involved in the event. Every year she contacts AT&T volunteer Dick Searle to secure tickets and program booklets, the Elks Lodge to make lunches, and the Del Rey Oaks Police Department to meet students and staff, and bring them their lunches.

For 21 seniors, February 1, 1996, at the AT&T Golf Tournament was the perfect day. The next three days of the tournament were washed out and the tournament was canceled.

Class of 1996 was lucky enough to meet golf greats like Jack Nicklaus, Arnold Palmer, Phil Mickelson, and celebrities like Clint Eastwood, Huey Lewis, Andy Garcia and many others.

On February 3, 2000 a group of nineteen seniors, three retirees, three staff members, and *The California News* editor were present at the tournament. The students had their choice among three courses-Poppy Hills, Spyglass Hill, and Pebble Beach. Naturally, almost all of them took Poppy Hills so that they could watch Tiger Woods playing golf.

Over thirty years, the tradition of CSD students attending the tournamnet continues.

Charles Benson first brought forth the idea of inviting CSD students to the Pro/Am Gold Tournament annually.

60

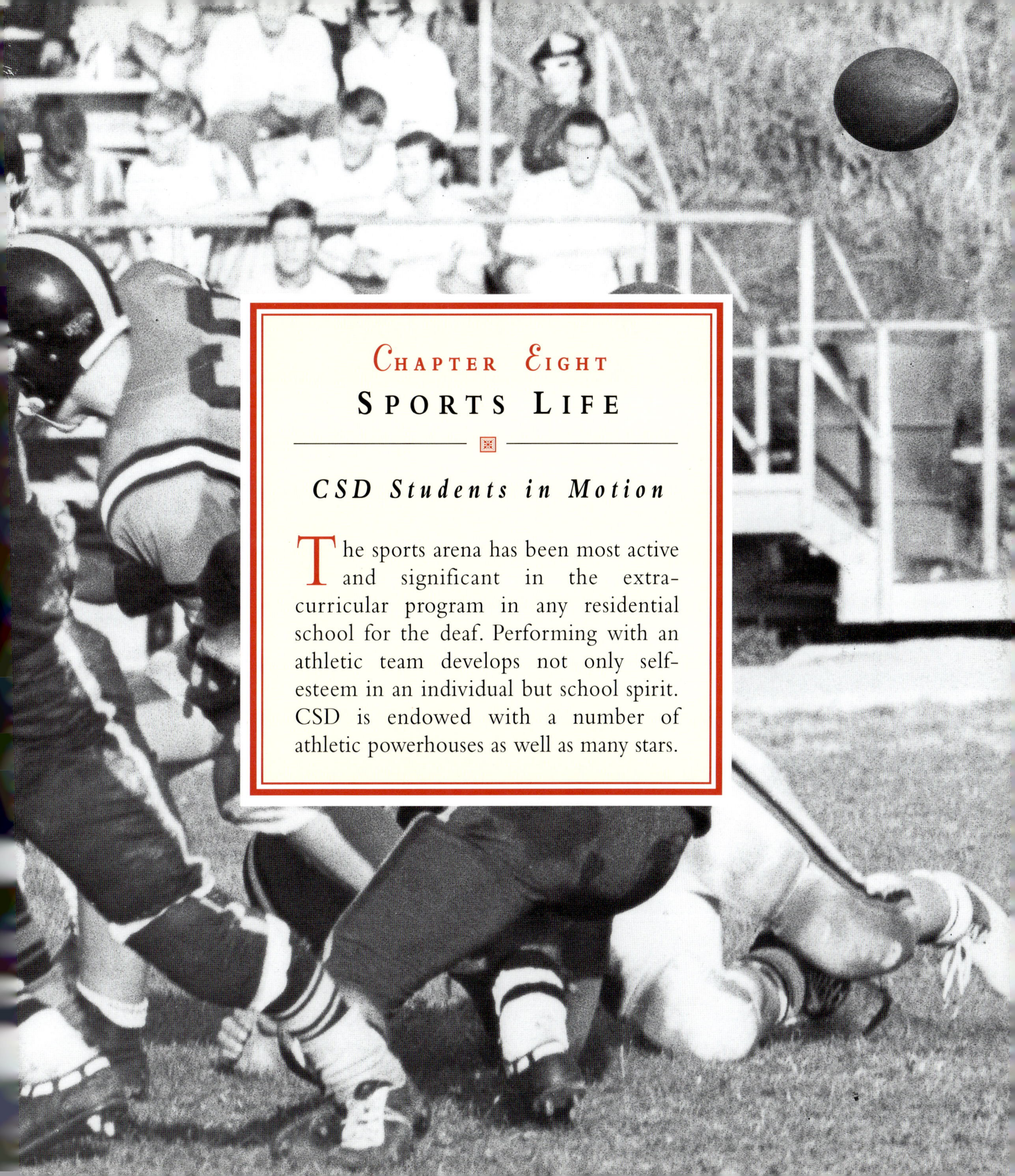

Chapter Eight
Sports Life

CSD Students in Motion

The sports arena has been most active and significant in the extra-curricular program in any residential school for the deaf. Performing with an athletic team develops not only self-esteem in an individual but school spirit. CSD is endowed with a number of athletic powerhouses as well as many stars.

One of the popular exhibits at the library-museum is the revolving cases featuring the historical photographs of the sports teams.

Baseball was the only sport the boys played for many years until football commenced. The baseball seasons lasted from fall to spring, sometimes for more than 60 games.

The CSD athletic competition program has evolved into one of the most important activities for the students. There are explosions at times. The games often become an emotional spectacle. This has been so since CSD's first sport, baseball, was played in 1866 in the San Francisco school.

Photographs of different sports teams are preserved in the revolving cases in the school library for public review, including the first formal picture of the baseball team in 1879.

Sports Explosion

The 1960s saw not only the new reins at the helm of the administration and the athletic program, but also the beginning of a new "Golden Age" of sports. This was especially noteworthy for football, basketball, wrestling, volleyball, and cross country. The stars of the sixties were of a different culture, with modern techniques offering them exposure never dreamed of in earlier generations. There were more of them vying for the affection of a wider audience. For many years, prior to the 1960s, the competition in sports was rather mediocre although CSD had several fine football seasons, great baseball teams in the 1900s, and great track seasons in the 1930s. After 1961 the "sports explosion" began.

In the 1960s, the CSD athletes' performance was more sophisticated; athletes were smarter and more aggressive in their games. Publicity for CSD sports, especially football and basketball, widened after 1961, following their winning streaks.

The drive for more teams has played a part in many areas, including the Civil Rights movement (Title IX). With more girl's sports available, girls showed a dramatic advance in being able to participate in strenuous sports like any boy.

A brief account of each of the sports played by CSD students is documented in the following pages.

Preceding pages:
WHERE IS THE BALL?
The football game was played between CSD and Lick-Wilmerding of San Francisco in 1965. CSD won 27-0.

This 1894 team played with the big name teams in the Bay Area, such as the University of California.

Emeryville - the Oldest Rivaly

CSD was admitted to California Interscholastic Federation, North Coast Section, Division B, (the conference) in spring 1931. Emeryville was one of the members of the conference and is the only school that has remained along with CSD since then. That was when the rivalry between CSD and Emery commenced. It is possible that the rivalry is the oldest in the North Coast Section. The first game played with Emeryville High School was a baseball game in April, 1930. The game resulted in a tie, 7 to 7. CSD made 16 hits while Emeryville had 8 hits. The first football game with Emeryville was played on November 6, 1931. Foothills completely routed Emeryville, 41 to 6.

This photo manifests a typical star baseball player named Joe Beck in 1893.

Baseball

Days of Old

When the school moved to Berkeley from San Francisco in 1869, the interest in baseball flourished even more. By the year of 1892, the Foothills (CSD) team played with the big name teams in the Bay Area such as St. Mary's College, the University of California, Stanford University and the Oakland clubs.

Foothills 14 St. Mary's College 4

Foothills 7 University of California 5

Foothills 8 Stanford University 21

This 1903 team had one of the highest winning seasons, 60 games won and only 7 games lost. They are: (back row) Calude Page, William Baker, Clarence Doone, Dan Sherman and Laban Smith. (middle row) Philip Carroll, Stuart Evans, Coach Winfield Runde, Adolph Hartman and Ray Green. (front row) Albert Clark and Walter Hannorn.

> ***"The first organized effort at athletics amongst the pupils of the California School for the Deaf was the baseball club formed by Henry Frank (a new teacher from New York). This was in 1866, while the school was located in San Francisco."***
>
> *The California News*
> May 1927, Vol.43, No. 9

The Foothills baseball season of 1903 was one of the finest seasons, 60 games won and only 7 games lost. The season started in December 1902, and lasted until June 1903.

UNIQUE OCCURRENCES

It was reported that the University of California baseball team never had nine good players on a team, so the UC team "borrowed" several CSD stars to play on its side to ensure winning some games. The Foothills continued beating the UC Dental College team in 1902 and the strong freshman team of UC in 1914. Carol Land, '15, the school's best pitcher, played with Metropolitan Life Insurance Company of Oakland. His record was 24 men struck out in a nine-inning game. At that time he was a supervisor of older boys at CSD. Also, he was CSD's first scoutmaster.

One of the unique experiences of the Foothills baseball team during the 1910s was a game with the United States Naval Training Station at Yerba Buena Island. In those days there was no Bay Bridge through the Island or Treasure Island. The team and forty friends from the school rode on a train to the San Francisco Bay pier in Oakland to catch a ferryboat. Arriving on the island, the team went on a tour where Uncle Sam made Marines out of the 800 men in training there. As the game progressed, the chance of winning over the Marines

Baseball was discontinued in 1935, and interest in baseball was not rekindled until 1987. Ronald Obray (first person, back row) was the coach with the inspiration to reestablish the CSD baseball team.

was slim because they had the advantage of years and experience. There were numerous fouls that landed in the bay. The balls became soggy and weighty which made hitting impossible. The result of the game was 16 to 5 with the marines at the big end of the horn.

During that season, other than the marines, the team that challenged the Foothills team was the College of Physicians and Surgeons of San Francisco. The Foothills defeated the College twice. They also played with St. Mary's College, Oakland High School, Fremont High School and CSD Alumni team.

The names of the following, possibly the best baseball players pre-1935, are mentioned in *The California News*:

James Harlan (1875)
Stuart Evans (1901)
James Baker (1902)
Adolph Hartmann (1902)
Henry Bonetti (1913)

Baseball was disbanded in 1935 due to a more serious interest in track, which depleted the number of boys needed to play baseball.

This team was named the Deaf Baseball Team of the Year. Manuelito Vallente (left, front row) was named the 1993 Deaf Prep Baseball Player of the Year. Coach Mike Pereira was awarded the Deaf Prep Baseball Coach of the Year honor (right, back row).

Ernesto Gallegos displaying a heroic spirit and courage regardless of a prosthesis.

Rekindling Interest in Baseball

An excellent baseball diamond was constructed at the new Fremont school in 1980 but the reestablishment of baseball did not occur until 1987. The intense interest in playing baseball among the boys prompted the school to resume the sport. Since then, the teams have had some successful seasons.

By the 1989 season, the team improved from a 1-7 record in 1987 to 8-8-1, just a game away from making the Bay Area league playoffs. The 1989 Deaf Baseball Coach of the Year honor went to Ron Obray. Barry Strassler, Sports Editor of National Association of the Deaf Broadcaster, announced it.

In1993, CSD was named the Deaf Baseball Team of the Year. Despite their 7-9-1 records, it was best among the few schools for the deaf fielding baseball teams. This team swamped sister rival CSD-Riverside, 24 to 2 and 26 to 5 in a double header.

Being the most respected hitter in the league, Manuelito Vallente was named the 1993 Deaf Prep Baseball Player of the Year. Coach Mike Pereira was awarded the 1993 Deaf Prep Baseball Coach of the Year honor. Pereira's love for baseball commenced in the first grade and he starred at Moreau High School and Chabot College. He also played with the Yankees' Summer Babe Ruth team.

Ernesto Gallegos, a 1996 pitcher, was in the spotlight when he was chosen by the Oakland Athletics, to throw out the ceremonial first pitch at the Oakland A's game on national television. What made him exceptional was the fact that his left leg was amputated just above his knee to remove a cancerous bone tumor.

ALL-AMERICANS SELECTED BY THE DEAF PUBLICATIONS

1991	1992	1993	1994	1995
Juan Machado	John Dee	Manuelito Vallente	Nate Twitchell	Jesse Conner
Trenton Marsh	Sonny Tate	Chet Virnig	Derrick Jull	Jacob Mills
Sostenes Alvarez	Manuelito Vallente	Lio Saechao	Lio Saechao	Derrick Jull
Tory Watson	Nate Twitchell	Nate Twitchell	Jesse Conner	Doug Keifer
Sal Alvarado	Leo Willey			John Curtis
John Dee	Sly Alvarez			

1996	1997	1998	1999	2000
Jesse Conner	Phaivanh Xayavony	Jonathan Curtis	Marty Peres	Pablo Cobarrubia
John Curtis	John Curtis	Christian Klim	Gian Marcucci	Joey Mignone
Daniel Harnish	Grant Grohman	Chris Beltrami	Pablo Cobarrubia	Jacob Ryan
Chris Beltrami	Daniel Harnish	Jonathon Kramer	Jonathon Kramer	
Ernesto Gallegos				

Girls' Baseball and Softball Teams

From what The California News reports, the first girls' baseball team started as far back as 1903. The team was called "The Parrots." The sport was played on and off for years.

In 1973, CSD formed a girls' softball team in the Berkeley school, which lasted for only two years. Badminton and track took over the spring sports and continued until CSD moved to Fremont. Starting in the spring of 1981, swimming and track became the girls' major sports and continued until 1987. That year a new sport, softball, was formed for the girls, coinciding with the boys' newly formed baseball team which had been "dormant" since 1935. During the first two years, the Girls' softball team demonstrated an improvement in its game strategies. Pat Bernstein, Supervising Instructional Counselor, earned the honor as the1989 Deaf Girls Softball Coach of the Year, taking the team from a 1-9 record in the 1988 season to a 6-4 record in the 1989 season. Her 1990 team won the national championship among the schools for the deaf.

Melessa Lancaster, Argus' *Athlete of the Week, a terrific player in both batting and pitching.*

In 1994, Kevin Bella took over the coaching assignment of the girls' softball team. The Coach of the Year honor by Silent News was awarded to Bella in his rookie year. He steered his girls to a 7-9 record after going 1-13 a year before. In 1995, the Fremont girls, the only team in the nation to post a winning record, won Team of the Year honors. Kevin, who starred in baseball as a CSD student and two years at Gallaudet University, has brought the benefit of his successes to the softball program.

In May 1998, Melessa Lancaster won the Argus, Athlete of the Week for her outstanding execution as a pitcher as well as a hitter. Her feats helped CSD beat

The 1990 team won the national championship among the schools for the deaf. Pat Bernstein earned the honor as the 1989 Deaf Girls Softball Coach of the Year (right, back row).

the Texas school twice, the Model Secondary School for the Deaf twice and split with the Riverside school in the spring extravaganza, and West Coast softball tournament at the Fremont school. Hence, the CSD team was considered the best of the three teams at the spring competition.

Silent News named the CSD 1998 girls softball team the TEAM of the YEAR among the schools for the deaf in the nation.

ALL-AMERICANS SELECTED BY THE NATIONAL DEAF MAGAZINES

1994

Jessica Hinman
Amy Jenkins

1995

Jessica Hinman
Sonja Varney
Clare Cassidy

1996

RimeCornish
AliciaStraub
Melessa Lancaster
Barbara Smith
Stacie Young
Barbara Smith
Elena Tobola
Nicole Simms

1997

Melessa Lancaster
Barbara Smith
Nicole Sims
Stacie Young

1998

Melissa Lancaster
Barbara Smith
Elena Tobola
Nicole Sims
Melissa Malzkuhn

1999

Sarah Parker
Melissa Malzkuhn
Nicole Sims
Nicole Lanning

2000

Erin Cohen
Valerie Hom
Sarah Parker

The 1995 Team of the Year (above). The Coach of the Year (right) was awarded to Kevin Bella.

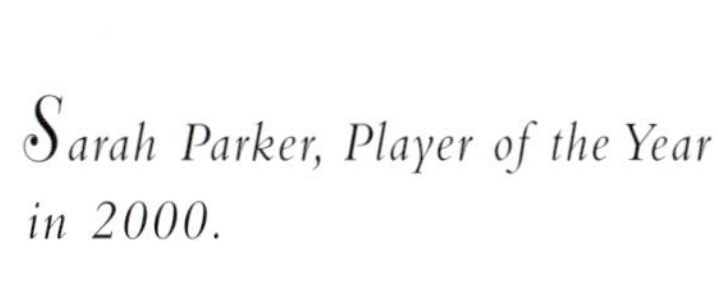

Sarah Parker, Player of the Year in 2000.

Football

Origin of Football: Rugby

The Foothills boys initially became interested in rugby and had the first training session in March 1885, when the popularity of rugby was recognized at the high school and college levels.

In 1886, the first school colors, BLACK and ORANGE, were selected for rugby "suits:" black jerseys with orange bands, orange stockings and black caps. From time to time, between 1887 and 1911, rugby (football) at CSD was disbanded and reorganized, depending on the interest of boys. The real reason for this uncertainty was that in that era football evolved from soccer and rugby, with the rules constantly changing and creating confusion.

It developed slowly as a student activity due to the higher interest in baseball. Pure American football competition at CSD started circa 1890 when tackling below the waist was legalized. The 1902 team was one of the greatest teams, with two outstanding players, Stuart Evans and James Baker, coached by James Howson. The 1908 team played five games and won all as the forward pass was legalized even though the football was a fatter and rounder ball. In

In 1974 CSD's Gerald Bragg's spectacular 93-yard touchdown gallop on the first play from scrimmage against the CSD-Riverside team. Quarterback Gil Lentz aroused the Eagle rooters in the fourth period when he intercepted a Cub pass at the Eagle four-yard line. He then engineered a 96 yards, 18-play touchdown drive with 2:20 to go, plunging one yard to pull out a 14 to 12 win.

The 1902 team was one of the greatest teams of CSD, with two outstanding players, Stuart Evans and James Baker (above), coached by James Howson.

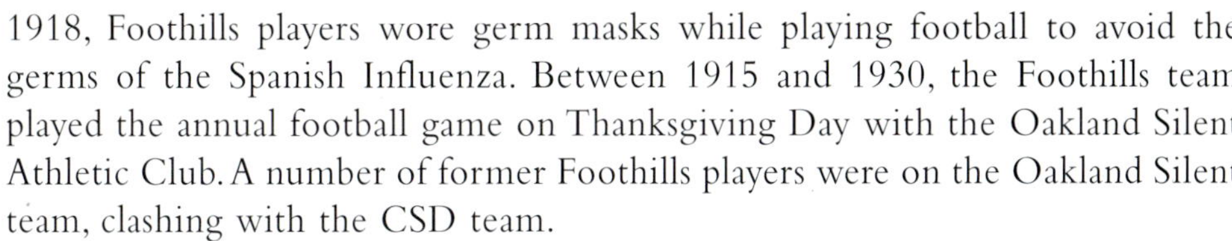

1918, Foothills players wore germ masks while playing football to avoid the germs of the Spanish Influenza. Between 1915 and 1930, the Foothills team played the annual football game on Thanksgiving Day with the Oakland Silent Athletic Club. A number of former Foothills players were on the Oakland Silent team, clashing with the CSD team.

Most Illustrious Moments in Football

1940 **-** The 1940 team was recognized as National Champions for the first time in the school's history. Louis Byouk coached the team with three All-American players.

1962 - The Eagles reveled in their finest season in history with a 6-1 record and shared a two-way tie for the Bay Counties League championship. Coach Dave Fraley was the first to give most of the credit to his assistant, Ken Norton.

1963 - CSD trounced St. Vincent's, 28 to 6, ending the season undefeated in the Bay Counties League and won the undisputed championship of the league. James Davis, All-American player, won the "TV Prep Player of the Week" award for his outstanding performances at the San Rafael Military Academy game.

The 1940 team — National Champions. Among the twenty-eight schools for the Deaf with football teams, CSD was rated "Number 1 Team in the Country" by Art Kruger in the New York Journal of the Deaf. *Angelo Skropeta, guard, and Lloyd Escobar, halfback, were placed on Kruger's All-Scholastic Deaf Team.*

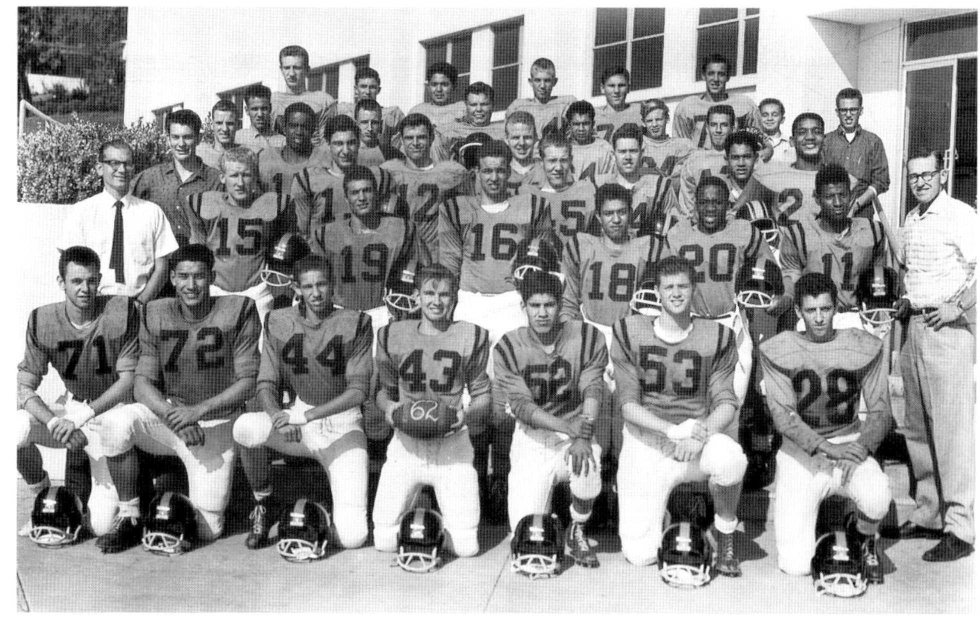

The 1962 team — First League Champions in CSD history.

Richard Zanon was selected the Prep of the Week by the *Berkeley Gazette*, and also the Team Player of the Week by the *San Francisco Chronicle* for his dazzling efforts, both passing and running, in the Menlo High game. Art Kruger of the *Silent Worker* selected Zanon the Player of the Year, the highest honor among the deaf prep footballers.

The CSD team won the league championship in 1963.

The 1963-68 and 1972-73 coaching staff, Dean Swaim and Ken Norton.

Co-Champions among the schools for the deaf in the nation in 1966.

Don Lyons (below left) maneuvered an amazing high-jump to catch a pass in one of the 1963 football games.

Along with the National Champions, Coach Kenneth Norton was selected as Coach of the Year. He was credited with installing a new system which built the championship team. Since he came to Berkeley in 1961 the teams had won 14 games, lost five and tied one. Dean Swaim joined the coaching staff as defensive coordinator.

1966 - CSD and the Kentucky School for the Deaf were named Co-Champions among the schools for the deaf in the nation. Both schools enjoyed the season's records of six victories against two defeats. All-around athlete,

Passing was CSD's bread and butter that season due to Eagle quarterback Pedro Landeros' exceptional air attacks. Louis Casinelli, 6'3" was one of 5'9" Landeros, favorite target.

A solid 1968 team brought CSD their first crown since 1964.

Ken Pedersen, was honored with the Maggini Award, symbolic of supremacy on Berkeley's prep athletic fields as the *Gazette* "Prep-of-the-Week." Also, he was named Back of the Year by the *Silent Worker*. Ray Ponciano and Larry Apolinar were the other outstanding leaders in the defensive unit. East Bay prep writers voted Ray Ponciano, popular Eagle linebacker, "Sportsman of the Week." Coach Norton said, "A 5'6", 155 pounder, Ponciano has been the team's sparkplug, calling defensive signals and just doing a great all around job for us. He plays with all his heart."

1967 - The 1967 edition of the Junior Varsity football team clinched the Bay Counties Athletic League championship with a 2-0-1 record, competing against Menlo School, San Rafael Military Academy, and St. Vincent's of Petaluma. The neophyte gridders, coached by Dan Lynch, had a fine 6-1-1 report card for the season's efforts.

Eastbay members of the All-Bay Counties League varsity football team were Eiichi Takayama, Wilyman Cano, Louis Casinielli and Pedro Landeros. Halfback Roy Rodriquez won the *Weekly Berkeley Gazette*-"Maggini Chevrolet Award" for his four-touchdown explosion against Lick Wilmerding in a 53-7 Eagle win.

1968 - The Eagles team surprised the preseason critics by winning the Bay Counties League championship. A solid team combined with several league upsets brought CSD their first crown since 1964. Wilyman Cano, R. Rodriquez, Johnny Modica, Tim Brill, Stanley Groman, and Bruce Aribas were picked all-league players with Dennis Yanke and John Sandoval getting honorable mention. Cano was named Prep of the Week in the *Weekly Berkeley Gazette*-Maggini Chevrolet poll.

The 1974 team — Northwestern League Champions. Mark Pena (front row, left) James Cano, Filipele Leomiti, Mervin Telles, Joe Sortwell, David Daviton, Ralph Nieves, Marty Carroll, Alvin Spain. Coach Kennneth Norton (second row) Superintendent Hugo Schunhoff, Michael Johnston, Steven kirk, Sheldon Basiste, Gerald Bragg, Gilbert Lentz, Stanley Baker, John Webber, Larry Byrd, Jay Salisbury, manager Paul Eyrond. Manager David Alejo, (third row) Chapman Hom, Raymond Lopez, Kenneth Van Gorder, Fred Martinez, Donald Shelton, Enos Gomes, Rickey Lindsey, Brett Kuntze, assistant superintendent Jacob Arcanin, athletic director David Fraley (assistant coach Dave Peterson not in picture.)

1971 - Kenneth Norton was elected to the American Athletic Association of the Deaf Hall of Fame as a coach. He was formally inducted at a luncheon at the annual AAAD basketball tournament in St. Louis, Missouri, on April 2, 1971. Norton was an athletic coach at both the Oklahoma and Berkeley schools for 19 years, retiring in 1969. (He returned to football, coaching from 1972 to 1975.)

1973 - Sheldon Batiste, John Webber and Criss Brown were named to the 1973-1974 season's Prep All-American Football Yearbook list compiled by Coach and Athlete Magazine. The Yearbook published at Atlanta, Georgia, paid tribute to the high school football program and recognized superb athletic success in the high school arena.

1974 - "It was CSD's finest hour. With all the fanfare of a typical Big Game, CSD and Riverside lived up to the history-making billing as the first Northern California game matching the state's only two deaf high school teams." -Dave LeVecchio *Oakland Tribune* Sports Writer

For the record, CSD won 14 -12 to climax its best season since 1968 with a 6-3 record. CSD came back in the later stage of the game against Emeryville and won the Northwestern League championship. Gilmer Lentz Jr., quarterback, and Ralph Nieves, tackle, were recognized in the 1974-75 Prep All-America Football Yearbook in recognition of outstanding athletic achievement and sportsmanship in the high school football arena.

In 1978 Dale Lugo led the team in rushing for a 1,000 yard record.

Undefeated champions (right) of the Northwestern League and first round in the playoffs

Tim Siaki was named to the Deaf All-America team twice (1981 and 1982). The 235-pound fullback gained 553 yards rushing in 1982 but he enjoyed playing nose guard on defense.

1978 - Under the reins of Coach Don Bullock and Assistant Coach Dean Swaim, after having gone undefeated in the Northwestern Football League, for the first time CSD entered a play-off game for the California North Coast Section Class B Championship. All-American Dale Lugo led the team in rushing for a 1,000 yard record.

1981 - Jason Ingraham and Tim Siaki, major powerhouse in CSD's 6-3 season,were named both ways to the All-Bay Six League football team. Ingraham, a junior, was picked as a linebacker and tight end. Siaki, the only sophomore, made the elite team as a lineman and a fullback. Leslie Firl, a quarterback, Shawn Jones, a tackle, and U. Sung Chung, a linebacker, were also selected to the all-league team.

1982 - Junior Varsity team won co-champion of the Bay Six J.V. League, coached by Jovette McCallon and Michael Teague.

1985 - The Eagles compiled a 6-2 record, including a 22-20 upset of Bay Six League champion,Valley Christian, under the reins of Coach Gene Duve. The team was selected the National Deaf High School football champion by a national deaf magazine, *The Deaf American*. Norman Edwards, Defensive and Offensive Player of the Year named by *The Deaf American*, was the first deaf prep to participate in the annual Alameda and Contra Costa Counties All Stars Classic. His Alameda County team won the game.

1987 - Michelle Lennert made a big impact on the CSD's football history due to the fact Lennert was a female! Playing for the junior varsity, she overcame odds and made the team as a starting offensive tackle and as an occasional defensive tackle. She earned second team honors on the Bay 6 League All-Junior Varsity Team.

National Deaf High School Football Champion in 1985.

1989 - Kevin Wallace became the school's all time career rushing leader with 2,001 yards, he rushed for 911 that year. *Oakland Tribune* again picked him the player of the year of the school league for two consecutive years, 1988 and 1989.

1991 - With an impressive record and winning the Bay Six League championship, the Eagles entered the first round of the North Coast Section playoffs for the second time in the school history. "Quicksilver" Justin Buckhold was named the Athlete of the Week by the *San Jose Mercury News*. Quarterback Sonny Tate was picked by the *Fremont Argus* as the Prep Athlete of the Week. In the "Air Lentz" initiative, developed by Coach Gilmer Lentz Jr., Tate set a new record of the single season passing yardage with 1,441 yards.

Bay Six League Champions and the second playoffs participation in 1991.

Phaivanh Xayavong, a dedicated, tough player.

1992 - After starting 0-4, the team won 4 in the last of 5 games and qualified for the North Coast Section playoffs for the second year in a row, losing to Upper Lake in the first round. Sonny Tate became the school's all time career passer with 3,001 yards. For the first time in the Big Game series, CSD grabbed the lead over CSD-Riverside, 10-9 with a convincing 49-0 victory on the road.

1997 - Phaivanh Xayavong of Porterville, California, eclipsed the school's season rushing record with 1,369 yards. Helped by strong blocking, he set two school rushing records in CSD's memorable 41-0 win over St. Elizabeth. He was selected as league most valuable player in offense.

LEAGUE CHAMPIONS

1962 - *Bay Counties League* (5-1) Co-Champion
1963 - *Bay Counties League* (5-0)
1968 - *Bay Counties League* (5-1)
1974 - *Northwestern League* (5-1)
1978 - *Northwestern League* (5-0)
1991 - *Bay Football League Class B* (5-1)

The Berkeley school football field is believed to be one of the most impressive with the splendid panoramic view of the San Francisco Bay Area.

NATIONAL CHAMPIONS AMONG THE SCHOOLS FOR THE DEAF

1940 *Silent Worker* (5-3)
1963 *Silent Worker* (5-1-1)
1966 *Silent Worker* (Co-Champion) (6-2)
1985 *Deaf American* (6-2)
1963 *Player of the Year* - Richard "Ricky" Zanon
1963 *Coach of the Year* - Ken Norton
1966 *Back of the Year* - Ken Pedersen
1971 *AAAD Coach Hall of Fame* - Ken Norton
1985 *Player of the Year* - Norman Edwards
1994 *Player of the Year* - Kalani Ledbetter
1997 *Player of the Year* - Phaivanah Xayavong

Quarterback Richard "Ricky" Zanon, (left), led the 1963 National Championship team. Ricky excelled in both passing and running.

Classy Ken Pedersen (right), all-around footballer playing as quarterback, halfback and flanker back.

ALL-AMERICANS SELECTED BY THE NATIONAL DEAF MAGAZINES

1938 Michael Skropeta & Arlie Taylor
1939 Angelo Skropeta
1940 Lloyd Escobar & Angelo Skropeta
1948 Lloyd Hendricks
1950 Epifanio Arce
1951 Daniel Lynch
1955 Jose Gonzales
1962 Anthony Ziviello
1963 James Davis - Donald Lyons - Peter Murello - Richard Zanon
1964 Henry Bella
1965 Danny Chittenden
1966 Larry Apolinar - Ken Pedersen - Ray Ponciano
1967 Wilyman Cano & Pedro Landeros
1968 Wilyman Cano & Stanley Groman
1970 John Sandoval
1971 Tom Marvel
1974 Ralph Nieves
1978 Dale Lugo
1981 Jason Ingraham & Tim Siaki
1982 Jason Ingraham & Tim Siaki
1985 Jerry Bonheyo - Norman Edwards - Robert Garcia
1987 Mark Bella
1988 Kevin Bella & Kevin Wallace
1989 Troy Watson
1990 Troy Watson

Arlie Taylor (above), "Fearless" right tackle.

Lloyd Escobar (right), halfback smasher.

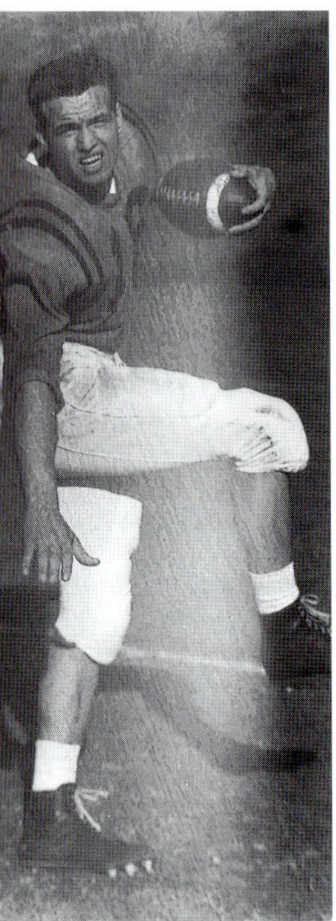

Daniel Lynch, (above) fullback, linebacker and team motivator.

Anthony Ziviello (left) "Mr. Football," fullback and blocker.

Peter Murello, fullback and tackler, "Steamroller."

1991 Justin Buckhold - Sonny Tate - Phil Tooch - Leo Willey
1992 Sonny Tate & Chet Virnig
1993 Jon Lamberton & Joseph Serrato
1994 Reg Hansen - Kalani Ledbetter - Lio Saechao
1995 Jesse Conner & Duc Nguyen
1996 Ricardo Gomez & Michael Davis
1997 Phaivanh Xayavong & Brian Morrison
1998 Jonathion Kramer & Gian Marcucci
1999 Pablo Cobarrubia & Mark Crawford

The record of the Big Game series with the California School for the Deaf-Riverside

	Berkeley	Riverside
1972	6	20
1974	14	12
1976	12	39
1977	0	30
1978	6	12
1979	0	14
	Fremont	Riverside
1980	14	32
1981	20	0
1982	32	6
1983	26	13
1984	28	0
1985	57	6
1986	20	22
1987	18	7
1988	18	20
1989	38	12
1990	12	20
1991	25	8
1992	49	0
1993	23	6
1994	28	0
1995	55	0
1996	46	12
1997	52	14
1998	12	7
1999	56	0

Henry Bella (left), three-year veteran, impenetrable guard.

Wilyman Cano, (middle), great workhorse halfback.

Kalani Ledbetter, (right) "Deaf Barry Sanders." Unstoppable, unbelievable.

Phaivanh Xayavong (left), the man with the quickest feet.

Justin Buckhold (middle), slickest receiver.

Sonny Tate (right), CSD's Golden Arm.

Gil Lentz (below), Mentor of the Eagles' teams, 1979 to current.

"Eagles" marked at the endzone of the CSD football field (left) for an annual Big Game with the Riverside school.

Cross Country

First Meet in History

"How come CSD decided to start a cross country program this year?" The question was asked of Dean of Students Kenneth Norton. He explained, "Football and volleyball are the major sports for our students during the fall season but some students are not interested in participating. It was timely to set up cross country. Because it is not a contact sport, it has appeal as a co-ed sport, and it has high student interest. Cross country was implemented in the fall of 1976 and it has rapidly become a popular sport. Andy Smith, who was one of the high school boys' counselors, eagerly volunteered to coach the first Cross Country team in our school's history."

The 1977 Cross Country team becoming a popular co-ed sport under coach Ron Cleary.

For the first training session the participants ran at Woodminister in Oakland's San Joaquin Miller Park. The first members were Fred Adock, Doug Chase, Dan Johnson, Graham Koetz, Quinn Mosbarger, Don Perridon, Mark Reeke, Roland Weaver, Lisa Yee, and John Cardenas, manager. Cross Country has very few rules. It appears to be just RUN and RUN for between 2 and 3 miles. Five runners are required to comprise a team. If there are less than five runners, they have to compete individually in lieu of a team.

Cross Country has helped to develop a long distance runner for spring track team and perhaps for the United States Deaf Olympic team. Also, it has added to the school,s excitement along with other fall sports. The first meet in history occurred on September 30, 1976 with University High School from San Francisco. All of CSD team finished the race with Graham Koetz coming in a strong second behind the University High victor. Ron Cleary, a counselor, joined the coaching staff the following year.

The first female harrier, Tamara Gaudet making an outstanding effort by placing 41st out of 102 competitors in the North Coast championship.

Series of Jim Koetz's Winning Harriers

Joining the CSD faculty in 1978 as a teacher in the Special Unit Department, James "Jim" Koetz readily took charge of the Cross Country program. His Cross Country coaching career for nineteen years was rewarded with high achievement. His coaching techniques were remarkable and unique for he brought the best out of each Cross Country runner.

During the years of rebuilding the program, with his great rapport with the students, Koetz enticed some students to become interested in Cross Country. This sport could be exhausting and required a great deal of stamina. Nevertheless, Koetz motivated the boys to RUN, RUN, and RUN to reach the caliber of the Cross Country teams.

Cross Country's Awesome Streaks

By the year of 1981, Koetz's team started to develop a winning spurt. The first CSD female runner, Tamara Gaudet made an excellent showing by placing 41st out of 102 competitors in the North Coast Section (NCS) championship. She was placed second in the Bay Area Counties League by one second. Eventually, she became Koetz's assistant coach. Anne-Marie Baer and Reyna Soto were the other girls who gave fierce competition.

The 1987 team of Koetz and Assistant Coach Vaughn Hallada was chosen No.1 in the nation among the schools for the Deaf. Koetz won the honors as Coach of the Year. These honors were the first in the CSD's cross country history. Unsurprisingly, since then Koetz has been credited with nine national championships and more than twenty-five All American harriers that brought great honors to the Fremont school.

The 1987 CC team was No. 1 in the nation among the schools for the Deaf. Jim Koetz won the honors as Coach of the Year.

A plaque presented to Jim Koetz

Jim Koetz(left), conferring with a coach of Head Royce School of Oakland.

In late 1998, CSD was saddened by the news that Koetz was dying of brain cancer. At the Bay Counties league CC championship at Golden Gate Park in San Francisco, a plaque was presented to Jim Koetz in recognition and appreciation of 19 years of dedication and service to the BCL and the sport of cross country by the BCL schools and coaches. On February 17, 1999, a memorial service for Jim Koetz was held at the CSD gym, which was the most fitting place where he left his impressive vestige.

HIGHLIGHTS IN CROSS-COUNTRY

1986 - Lynn Barlow, CSD's premiere cross country runner, was selected as the girl harrier of the Year by the National Association of the Deaf *Broadcaster* news publication. Also she, the only runner on the girls cross-country team, was named Prep of the Week by the Fremont Argus.

1989 - CSD claimed its third straight mythical national boys CC championship. The team flew to Washington, D. C. to take on Model, Maryland and Louisiana in an all-deaf meet, handily beating its opposition. Merrill Samuels picked up his second straight Deaf Boys Harrier of the Year honor. At the State CIF Cross Country Meet, Samuels, fourth CSD athlete participating in the State CIF Meet of all sports, placed 45th out of 142 runners.

He was the first CSD cross country harrier entering the state meet.

1992 - CSD hosted the 6th annual National Deaf Cross Country championship on October 10 at Garin Park, Hayward, California. The schools for the Deaf, Arizona, Maryland, Model Secondary School, South Carolina, and Ohio, were participants. CSD harriers captured their third straight Deaf Athletic Federation of the United States (DAFUS) prep CC championship.

1995 - Jason Hardy competed in the State CIF Cross Country Meet and finished 29th of 147. He was the Cross Country Runner of the Year and CSD's second athlete.

1996 - Jose Gutierrez successfully defended his title at the 10th annual DAFUS CC Championship. He won Harrier of the Year honors. Gutierrez placed third in the North Coast Section and competed in the State CIF Cross Country Finals. He earned a State Championship certificate and CSD's third athlete in the State CC Meet.

Hardy runner Jason Hardy, participating in the CIF State Cross Country Meet. He was the second athlete racing in the State Meet.

11th Annual Deaf Prep National Champs, CSD Cross Country in 1996.

The 1998 team with Brice Pruyn, right, first CSD harrier receiving a medal at the State CIF Cross Country Meet.

CSD's harriers running beneath the famous San Francisco misty fog in the Golden Gate Park in the NCS Meet in 1998.

As it seems, CSD always produced winning runners under Jim. His specialty was making many winners out of those who were neither interested nor rugged enough to play football, and thus bringing CSD up to many league and national deaf championships. For that, he would be easily qualified as one of the most elite coaches in the deaf nation.

Compiled by
Donald Ingraham

1998 - Brice Pruyn, made history for CSD as the first Eagle to receive a medal at the State CIF Cross Country Meet in which he finished the race in 9th place with the time of 16:52. Out of 109 runners who competed in the State Meet, only ten of them received a medal. Not far behind Pruyn, Arturo Lopez ended the race in 12th place.

Pruyn is the fourth athlete in the State CC Finals.

NATIONAL CHAMPIONS AMONG THE SCHOOLS FOR THE DEAF SELECTED BY *SILENT NEWS*

1987 1988 1989 1990 1991 1992 1994 1995 1996

ALL-AMERICAN CROSS COUNTRY FIRST TEAM SELECTED BY THE NATIONAL DEAF PUBLICATIONS

1986 Lynn Barlow
1987 Merrill Samuels
1989 Merrill Samuels & Jose Garcia
1990 Aldo Serrano - Kris Hatch - Robert De La Cruz
1991 Jason Hardy - Aldo Serrano - Cornelio Vera
1992 Aldo Serrano - Ferris Myers - Cornelio Vera -Felix Gonzales
1993 Jose Gutierrez
1994 Jason Hardy & Jose Gutierrez
1995 Jose Gutierrez - Brice Pruyn - Corey Thompson
1996 Arturo Lopez - Brice Pruyn - Grant Grohmann
1997 Arturo Lopez - Brice Pruyn - Grant Grohmann
1998 Brice Pruyn & Arturo Lopez

Girls' Volleyball

Early Stage of Enthusiasm

The new sport, volleyball, was introduced to the girls' athletics program in 1927 under the direction of Mariette Beattie, a new physical education director from the University of California. That year's sports consisted mainly of basketball, baseball (softball), swimming, and volley ball. The girls had only an hour to practice due to the fact that they had many class sessions in the afternoon. At the time they had not formed a regular team to challenge outside teams and volleyball was considered a recreational activity.

Volleyball was part of the "Play Day" program in which members of the Girls Athletic Association participated in 1946.

In 1946, volleyball was again initiated into the girls' after school activities, when the Girls Athletic Association was invited to join Richmond, El Cerrito, Berkeley, and Albany high schools in having "Play Day" five times that year, three times in the spring and two times in the fall. Play Day was the day on which they all got together at one of these schools to play all kinds of sports, such as volleyball, basketball, softball and swimming. After the activities, refreshments were served. Their first Play Day was in 1946. About one hundred girls were involved. Each girl was given a tag to show what games she was to play and where they were played. Apparently, enthusiasm in the girls' sports was rekindled after the lull during World War II.

Further Competitive Sport

In October, 1950, the girls' volleyball team commenced play with Emeryville High School and won five straight games out of nine. The members of the Girls Athletic Association continued to be involved in the Play Day activities for about twelve years. Their interest in sports had increased considerably, especially when volleyball became a popular fall sport. The CSD girls' volleyball competition was with Anna Head, El Cerrito, Concordia, Harry Ellis High Schools, and the Riverside school.

In 1958 CSD's GAA volley ball team beat the Riverside school in the first annual game.

The first annual volleyball game between CSD's Girls Athletic Association team (GAA) and the Riverside school team occurred on January 25, 1958, at the Berkeley school gymnasium. GAA won the competition, two out of three games, 15-13, 12-15 and 15-12. The following year, the games were held at the University of California-Riverside gymnasium. The Riverside school beat GAA in both varsity and junior varsity games. After a long series of defeats, CSD finally had its first victory over the Riverside school in 1978.

MOST IMPORTANT EVENTS HAPPENED THESE SEASONS

1978 - After a lengthy drought of 19 years and the series of defeats by the Riverside volley ball team, the 1978 Berkeley team under the reins of Robert Ellis finally broke the string by beating the Cubs, 2-1.

1979 - The CSD team rode on the Amtrak train to Washington State to play volley ball with the Washington school. CSD defeated them by the scores of 15-7 and 15-9.

The Junior varsity team clinched the Eastern Bay Counties League championship. The coaches were Robert Ellis and Ken Pedersen.

The 1979 Girls' Junior Varsity volleyball team won the Eastern Bay Counties League championships. Dako Tiku (left front row), Anita Vandercourt, Ladena Evans, Klesha Chapman, manager Marjorie Charles. Coach Ken Pedersen (left), Becky Bonheyo, Coreen Farquar, LuAnn Knutsen, Katie Keller, assistant coach Bob Ellis.

1988 - The Eagles posted an 11-3 overall record that year. They earned a spot in the league playoffs by making the 8-3 record in the Bay Area Conference. The main reason for this fine season was the 5-foot-3 senior, Quilla Mosley, known as "lighting quick." Coach Robert Ellis stated "Mosley will do anything to keep the ball from touching the floor." Mosley was selected as one of The Argus Preps of the Week.

Robert Ellis was honored as Coach of the Year by a national deaf publication.

1990 - CSD captured the national championship among the schools for the deaf and achieved the best season in the school history with 20 wins and 5 losses. They also set a new school record for a winning streak of 18 games. The Fremont Argus and San Jose Mercury News tapped Dyan Kovacs for Prep Player of the Week during the height of the team's winning streak. This incredible team with only 7 players managed to go through the season without any serious injury, illness or academic problems. Coach Bob Ellis was extremely proud and called this special team "Iron Girls." These girls were Dyan Kovacs, Nevenka

Solunac, Carol Bella, Melody Tsai, Jian Huang, Heidi Vincent, and Margaret Limon. CSD will always remember this team as one of the all-time greatest teams in CSD's sports history.

1994 - Coach JoDee Dike's team won first place in the Division Two of the Bay Counties League by beating Head Royce, one of the top teams in East Bay. CSD was placed third (14-3) among the schools for the deaf. Nora Yates won the honors as Player of the Year and Catherine Cassidy was selected an All-American player by *The Silent News*.

Eastern Bay Counties League Championships in 1994. Heather Lewis (front row left), Amy Jenkins, Theresa Contreras, Beth Langley, Louise Stern. Coach Karen Gilbert (back row left), Sonja Varney, Jessica Hinman, Catherine Cassidy, Clare Cassidy, Karina Pedersen, Nora Yates, Coach JoDee Dike.

1996 - The Eagles dug themselves out of an upset game with the Riverside team and it turned out to be one of the greatest comebacks in the school's history. Riverside led with the first two games in its bag. At this point, it was inconceivable that CSD girls could win three straight games to capture a win. They did it! In the fifth game, CSD got in a bad fix by trailing 7 points (0-7), CSD slithered back and took the victory home (15-11). Naturally, the Eagles and CSD's spectators went wild on the court.

Senior Karina Pedersen earned the All-American honors among the schools for the deaf. The credit for the successful season went to Coach JoDee Dike.

CSD's Pride: *Two Stars at Gallaudet University*

CSD's former great VB players, senior Dyan Kovacs and junior Karen Gilbert were selected to the American Volleyball Coaches Association All-Region Team. Kovacs was previously named Capitol Athletic Conference Player of the Year for leading Gallaudet to a 41-4 regular season record and the CAC championship in 1995.

It was the second time each was named to the AVCA All-Region Team. Kovacs received the honor in 1994 and Gilbert was named in 1992. CSD is proud of its alumni, who continue to excel in athletics and academics.

League Champions

1994 - Eastern Bay Counties League

National Champions among the schools for the deaf

1990 - *Silent Worker* (20-5)

Player of the Year

1988 - Quilla Mosley
1989 - Karen Gilbert
1994 - Nora Yates

All-Americans Selected by the National Deaf Publications

1988 - Quilla Mosley
1989 - Karen Gilbert & Alicia Flores
1990 - Nevenka Solunac
1991 - Dyan Kovacs
1994 - Yates & Catherine Cassidy
1996 - Karina Pedersen

Dyan Kovacs (bottom left).

Karen Gilbert (bottom middle).

Karen Gilbert in action.

Basketball

New Indoor Sport in 1900s

Basketball is one of the few games of strictly American origin which can be pinpointed to a day in 1891 when Dr. James Naismith fixed a peach basket atop a pole. Then, to a balcony. Hence, the game of basketball was born using a soccer ball. Soon basketball grew in popularity in the country but it reached CSD slowly. The main problem was that a gymnasium was not yet built on the CSD campus in the 1900s. Still the roots of basketball grew in playgrounds, school yards, in driveways and backyards.

"The Atalanta"

An interesting historical point about the first girls basketball team in 1902. The team was named the "Atalanta." According to Greek mythology, Atalanta is a beautiful, swift-footed maiden. They won a number of games!

In 1902, the game of basketball was all the rage among the girls of Durham Hall when it was officially organized. The girls attempted to learn the new strategies and practiced every Saturday afternoon. As the years passed, they played only a few games every year. In 1908, the girls were elated when Principal Warring Wilkinson announced that the surface of the outside court would be reconditioned. The cost of the improvement was $250.00. The girls' team was called the "Atalanta," winning the first game of that year, 14 to 6 against the Franklin school in Oakland.

The following is the Atalanta's record in 1908-09.

October 16	**Atalanta 14**	**Franklin 6**
November 11	**Atalanta 6**	**McKinley 8**
November 18	**Atalanta 14**	**McKinley 7**
November 26	**Atalanta 15**	**Ex-pupils 11**
March 12	**Atalanta 12**	**Whitter 2**
March 19	**Atalanta 16**	**Whitter 6**
March 20	**Atalanta 18**	**McKinley 11**
March 27	**Atalanta 23**	**Whitter 2**

Establishment of Boys' Basketball

In December 1908, captain for the boys' basketball team was elected at the Foothills Athletic Association meeting. Edward Brodrick was the captain of the basketball team and Mr. Bartlett was the coach. However, the basketball team was officially organized in 1909 and lost all four games. Both basketball and baseball games were played in the same season. In 1910, the record improved, winning two out of three. Nevertheless, the boys indicated that they desired to keep up their interest in basketball as it had become recognized as one of the best indoor school sports and was coming into existence in schools all over the nation. The team continued practicing and playing outdoors!

CSD's first Basketball team formed in 1916. Oscar Guire (standing left) Paul Denton, Morse Dodge, Clarence Modisett, Earl Poole. Vincent Gemignani (kneeling), Harry Scwarzlose and Crom Boam.

The boys' enthusiasm in basketball was accelerated when construction of a new gymnasium commenced in 1915. It was ready for games on January 12, 1916. G. H. Briggs, a graduate of the University of California and a member of the champion basketball team of 1906-07-08 volunteered to train the CSD basketball team that year. The season lasted until the end of April despite the fact that the opponents were mostly "six-foot-ers" and it was hard for CSD players to attain their level. The opponents were Oakland Technical High School and Berkeley High School freshmen.

The girls' team played against a Y.W.C.A. team in Berkeley. The game was won by CSD, 21 to 18 in 1917. Not many schools had girls teams at that time. Each year they scheduled too few games which discouraged their interest.

By the year of 1920, boys' basketball continued to be of high interest among the boys while baseball was almost half dead. Girls' basketball became inactive due to lack of interest. In the1940s, girls' basketball returned as an active sport when the Girls Athletic Association participated in the Play Day activities with the schools nearby.

Girls' competition now generates as much anticipation as the boys' event. Their spirit in sports is a spectacular new occurrence that has happened in just the last seventeen years.

Southern Alameda County Athletic League Champs in 1938. Roy Miller (front row left), William Harris, Michael Skopeta, Glen Kearney, Theobaldo Ruffa, coach Louis Byouk. Angelo Skropeta (back row), Jorma Ranta, Henry Bernard, Charles Pruitt, Dale Smith, Roy Frazier, Joseph Posposil.

Highlights of CSD's Basketball Programs After 1935

1935 - James Lazzarini, guard, was CSD's first All-American basketball player, chosen by New York Deaf-mutes' Journal All-American Deaf Board of Basketball. He was adept in shooting with both hands at the same time as well as playmaking.

1938 - Michael Skropeta, center, and Theobaldo Ruffa, guard, were selected to *Silent Worker* All-American Basketball team. They were the reasons for helping CSD win the first ever Southern Alameda County Athletic League championship. Coach Louis Byouk called Skropeta "The Deaf Hank Luisetti," after the famed all-time Stanford great.

1946 - Led by Captain Evelyn Thornborrow, the Girls Athletic Association "A" Panthers crushed Berkeley High School, 29 to 14 on the CSD court. Supported by the team's excellent teamwork, Thornborrow scored 14 points while Helen Arbuthnot placed second with 10 points. Beverly Cotton scored the remaining 5 points. The Panthers team played only four games.

1956 - On January 28, the CSD gymnasium was packed with eager spectators watching the first game in the history of the schools between the Berkeley team and the newly formed Riverside team. CSDB 47 - CSDR 27.

1964 - Don Lyons, 6' 4" center, was the nation's top deaf prep cager of the 1963-64 campaign. Also, he was the most publicized high school player in Northern California. His records are as follows: Most career points (2,072 in four years), most points in a single season (918), and most points in a single game (69). His coach Dave Fraley said, "Don was murder under the boards and gave us rebound control." Lyons was Northern California highest scoring player for two consecutive years and was picked as Northern California high school all-star FIRST team. Lyons was named the top athlete and achieved a place in the American Athletic Association of the Deaf (AAAD) Hall of Fame for his outstanding athletic performances for CSD in football, basketball and track. His basketball jersey (#14) was retired with many marvelous and memorable deeds by Don Lyons to the CSD gym display case.

The B (junior varsity) team, under Coach Ken Norton, finished second in the race, just behind Emery (12-2). Jim Koetz, Ken Pedersen and Ray Ponciano were the stars of the B team.

Don Lyons having a fabulous basketball career at the Berkeley school.

1966 - The varsity team had an exceptional year, 19 - 6 with great support from the aces of Dan Chittenden, Louis Cassinelli, Jim Koetz and Ken Pedersen. They defeated Riverside in a Big Game, 60 to 58.

The 1966 basketball team held to be one of the CSD's finest team with the record of 19 to 6. Ken Pedersen (front row left), Karl Reed, Dan Chittenden, Louis Cassinelli, Jim Koetz. Manager Jim Halseth (middle row left), Ray Ponciano, John Nickelson, Tom Ahern, Hal Foster (back row left), Bill Whitlock, Vernon Jones, coach David Fraley.

1969 - The Sportrayers Club of Las Vegas, composed of sportswriters and sportscasters, presented awards to outstanding individuals at the Silver Club fight program. Don Lyons, member of the University of Nevada-Las Vegas basketball team, was selected Athlete of the Year.

John Sandoval, CSD's No. 1 all-time scorer with 2242 points in 95 games.

Becky Bonheyo, one of the CSD's finest all-around athletes, boosting the victory in the 1983 California Classic.

1970 - John Sandoval, the finest cager CSD had in a number of years, received a slew of post-season awards, testifying to his pre-eminence among the elite of cagedom in the Bay Area. His fine play also won him Prep of the Week from the Berkeley Gazette and Bay Counties League Player of the Year from the San Francisco Examiner. Sandoval, captain and guard, broke a school record for career points and became CSD's No. 1 all-time scorer with 2242 points in 95 games. His coach Gene Harris said of Sandoval in comparison with CSD's all-time cager Don Lyons, "Johnny has the same ability but doesn't have the size Don had, but he has great driving ability. John also has a beautiful outside shot."

1974 - The first traditional basketball competition between the girls' teams, the Berkeley and Riverside schools was played at Riverside. CSDR out-played CSDB, 38 to 14.

1977 - The first regional high school basketball tournament for the deaf in the western United States was hosted by CSD. It was an annual event rotating between Berkeley and Riverside and was thus named the "California Classic." Daniel Lynch, Director of Student Activities, chaired the three-day affair. Eight schools: Arizona, Berkeley, Colorado, New Mexico, Oregon, Riverside, Utah and Washington, participated in the Classic Tournament. The New Mexico School for the Deaf team pulled the upset of the first Western States Basketball Tournament by defeating Riverside, 48 to 45.

Added features to the "California Classic" were the wrestling matches and the girls basketball game between Berkeley and Riverside. Wrestling results: Berkeley 48 Riverside 13. Girls Basketball results: Riverside 30 Berkeley 28.

Dr. Wilson Riles, Superintendent of Public Instruction, honored CSD by presenting the awards at the tournament.

1983 - CSD Fremont came out on top in both divisions! For the first time in the history of CSD, one school won both the boys and girls championships at the California Classic. All-Tournament players, Elena Gee and La Dena Evans led the girls team to first place. All-Tournament cagers, Mark King and Ken Thigpen, directed the boys team to the championship game. Mark King was the Most Valuable Player of the California Classic and was named the nation's Deaf Prep Player of the Year. Ed Leighton retired after seven years of coaching the Eagles.

1984 - CSD varsity boys captured the Far West Basketball Championship for the second straight year, held at the Oregon School for the Deaf in Salem. The girls finished in sixth place.

1985 - The boys varsity team was chosen as TEAM OF THE YEAR, having the best record among deaf prep schools (19-10). This team was the

FIRST NATIONAL prep championship that CSD had received in the school history. The team was also champion of the Far West Classic basketball tournament for the third year in a row.

1986 - CSD's 36 to 23 victory over College Prep awarded the Eagles (10-1) the championship of the Bay Area Conference. It was the second time in the school's history it had captured a league basketball title. The first title occurred in 1938. Coach Ken Pedersen stated the score was low due to College Prep's (9-2) traditional attempt to hold on to the ball. The team's press on the Eagles team failed by All-American Rod Pedersen's able dribbling control. Ken Pedersen, Rod Pedersen's uncle, emphasized "That was the key to the game. Rod broke right through their press."

This team entered the State North Coast Section playoffs for the first time in the CSD history. It lost to Lower Lake High School in the first round but this team had the best season, 22-8, in the CSD history.

The 1986 team won the conference championship. Only the second time in the school's history it had captured a league title. Scorekeeper Bill Dye (left), Mike Simmons, Dennis Sweigart, Paul Wood, Nemo Harreden, Norman Edwards, Scott O'Donnell, Rod Pedersen, Mike Moss, Darrell Harrison, Norman Lieu, Manager Mike Denning. Head Coach Ken Pedersen (sitting).

The 1986 girls basketball team had an exciting year, especially beating the Riverside team by two points and winning first place in the Western States Basketball Classic. Manager Debbie Trapani (front row left), Dionne Agriss, Jodi Oritz, Susan Schluter, Trudy Evans, Diana Trammell, (back row), Jamie Farquar, the Eagle mascot, Sonya Merritt, Sally Garza, Angela Vogler, (Coach Daryl Wetzel not in picture).

Also All-American Norman Edwards and Scott O'Donnell were the reasons for promoting the finest season. This team won their fourth consecutive championship at the 10th annual Western States Basketball Classic at Riverside. Rod Pedersen and Norman Edwards were selected to the first team All-Star Tournament. Rod Pedersen won this honor for the fourth time.

The girls' team once again captured its second championship at the Western States Basketball Classic. The girls fought hard to overcome Riverside, a very strong team, 53-51, after Riverside led by eleven points at half time in the final game. Jamie Farquar, Diana Trammell and Trudy Evans were named to the All-Stars team.

1989 - The Boys team established a national record by winning its seventh consecutive championship title in the Western States Classic in Vancouver, Washington. Six-foot-6 freshman center, Nicky O'Donnell scored 14 points and dominated the boards with 18 rebounds.

CSD's Eagle emblem on the court floor.

1990 - Alicia Flores scored 20 points and teammate Karen Gilbert added 19 points as CSD at Fremont rolled to a 60-29 championship victory over the Idaho school. Idaho could not find a way to stop the outside shooting of Flores. The Redskins were frustrated for not solving the riddle of Gilbert who used her height advantage and quickness to score underneath.

The CSD boys team lost a heartbreaking game in overtime to Oregon, 49-48. It ended Fremont's seven-year reign.

1993 - Before Ken Pedersen announced his retirement from coaching sports, his basketball team won the Western States Classic championship in Gooding, Idaho, for the eighth time in his eleven-year varsity basketball coaching career. Sonny Tate and Tim Varney starred in that game. For the climax of his career, he was honored by being selected Coach of the Year.

Clare Cassidy, sophomore center, played so well in the consolation championship of the WSBC, as she poured in 40 points for the CSD girls team, she set a school record. For her performance, Cassidy was named The Argus Prep of the Week.

1995 - The CSD girls team achieved one of the most successful seasons. The record was the best ever in the school history, 16-8. They won the championship at the King's Academy Christmas Tournament in which the hearing teams participated, for the first time in the school history. Nona Yates was honored as the most-hustle player in the tournament. In that year, a heartbreaking game was experienced when the CSD team lost in a thrilling championship game in overtime, 42 to 41, to the Idaho School for the Deaf in the WSBC. Twin sisters, Clare and Catherine Cassidy and Nona Yates were the standouts in the tournament.

2000 - The excerpts from Dr. Henry Klopping's account of the CSD's ascendancy in the 2000 Western States Basketball Classic tournament at the Oregon School for the Deaf are as follows. The CSD boys' team played a thrilling game. It appeared with one minute thirty-eight seconds left in the game that they would lose the championship game because they were behind by 6 points and two of the first stringers were fouled out. Coach Chris Hamilton "pulled a rabbit out of the hat" in winning his "Cinderella victory." The CSD team played an outstanding game. In that minute and thirty-eight seconds, they scored 15 points and won the game by nine points! Klopping emphasized that he doubted anyone could think of a game in WSBC history where a team came back that strongly in such a short time. Also, the CSD girls' team and cheerleading did the outstanding performances during the Classic.

Vernon Birck, Dean of Boys (1928-57) and writer for the **California News** ***about the athletic activities, mentioned that CSD was proud of its record in athletics. Although not always on the winning side, they had always done their best, never quitting, no matter how badly beaten they might be.***

Brendan Stern making a basket on the way to win the 2000 WSBC title.

Michael Skropeta (left), the main reason for league championships.

Rodneyn Pedersen (right), a methodical player.

LEAGUE CHAMPIONS (BOYS)

1938 Southern Alameda County Athletic League (4 - 2)
1986 Bay Area Conference (10 - 1)

WESTERN STATES BASKETBALL CLASSIC CHAMPIONSHIP (BOYS)

1981, 1983-1989, 1993, 1994, 1995, 2000
Fremont won 12 of the 23 boys, WSBC titles from 1981 to 2000.

WSBC CHAMPIONSHIP (GIRLS)

1981, 1986, 1990, 1991, 1998

NATIONAL CHAMPIONS AMONG THE SCHOOLS FOR THE DEAF (BOYS)

1985 *Deaf American* (19 - 10)
1993 Coach of the Year - Ken Pedersen

BOYS' ALL-AMERICANS FIRST TEAM SELECTED BY THE NATIONAL DEAF MAGAZINES

1935 James Lazzarini
1938 Michael Skropeta & Theobaldo Ruffa
1960 Salvadore Flores
1963 Donald Lyons
1964 Donald Lyons
1966 Dan Chittenden
1967 Louis Cassinelli & Ken Pedersen
1968 Louis Cassinelli
1970 John Sandoval
1981 Adam Celaya
1983 Mark King
1984 Lance Fabela & Rodney Pedersen
1985 Norman Edwards, Lance Fabela & Rodney Pedersen
1986 Norman Edwards & Rodney Pedersen
1987 Scott O'Donnell
1993 Sonny Tate
1995 Anthony O'Donnell

GIRLS' ALL-AMERICANS FIRST TEAM

1982 Becky Bonheyo
1990 Alicia Flores, Karen Gilbert & Dyan Kovacs
1991 Dyan Kovacs
1992 Dyan Kovacs
1994 Clare Cassidy
1995 Clare Cassidy & Norma Yates

"SILENT FIVE ERA"

In 1940, because of the age limit, a number of high school boys were not permitted to participate in regular conference games. So, a new team called "Silent Five" was formed. The Silent Five found its schedule quite busy, playing with such as young people associations, business clubs, fraternity clubs, and other adult teams. However, the survival of the Silent Five was off and on, depending on the availability of material.

Erwin Marshall, junior high teacher, had the privilege of coaching the Silent Five from 1948 to 1958. He reminisced about his 1951 team defeating the Los Angeles Club for the Deaf team that had won championships in national tournaments and in the Far West competition every year for many years.

One of Erwin Marshall's most memorable companies, the 1952 Silent Five basketball team. Kenneth Snider, front row, left, Donald McCune, coach Erwin Marshall, Daniel Lynch, manager Lawrence Alexander. Epifanio Arce, back row, left, Robert Sewell, Julian Singleton, Jovette McCallon, Joe Maxwell, George Ramponi.

Wrestling

New Sport in 1964

One of the most ancient and universal athletic contests is wrestling in which two persons attempt to throw each other to the ground. The walls of many ancient tombs on the Nile show scenes of wrestling and depict virtually all of the holds and falls known today. The popularity of wrestling in its various forms continues throughout the world today.

It was noted that a number of the high school boys, especially footballers who did not participate in the basketball program, tended to wrestle playfully when football season was over. These boys became restless and inclined to horseplay in the dormitory during the winter season. Thus, this led CSD to make a decision, forming a new sport, wrestling, during the school year of 1963-64.

Coincidentally, William Dean Swaim, who was a wrestling champion at Gallaudet College during the years of 1950-53 and started wrestling programs at the Wisconsin School for the Deaf, and the Iowa School for the Deaf, started his teaching tenure at CSD that year. He took over the implementation of the wrestling program from scratch.

CSD's first wrestling squad in 1965 under coach Dean Swaim.

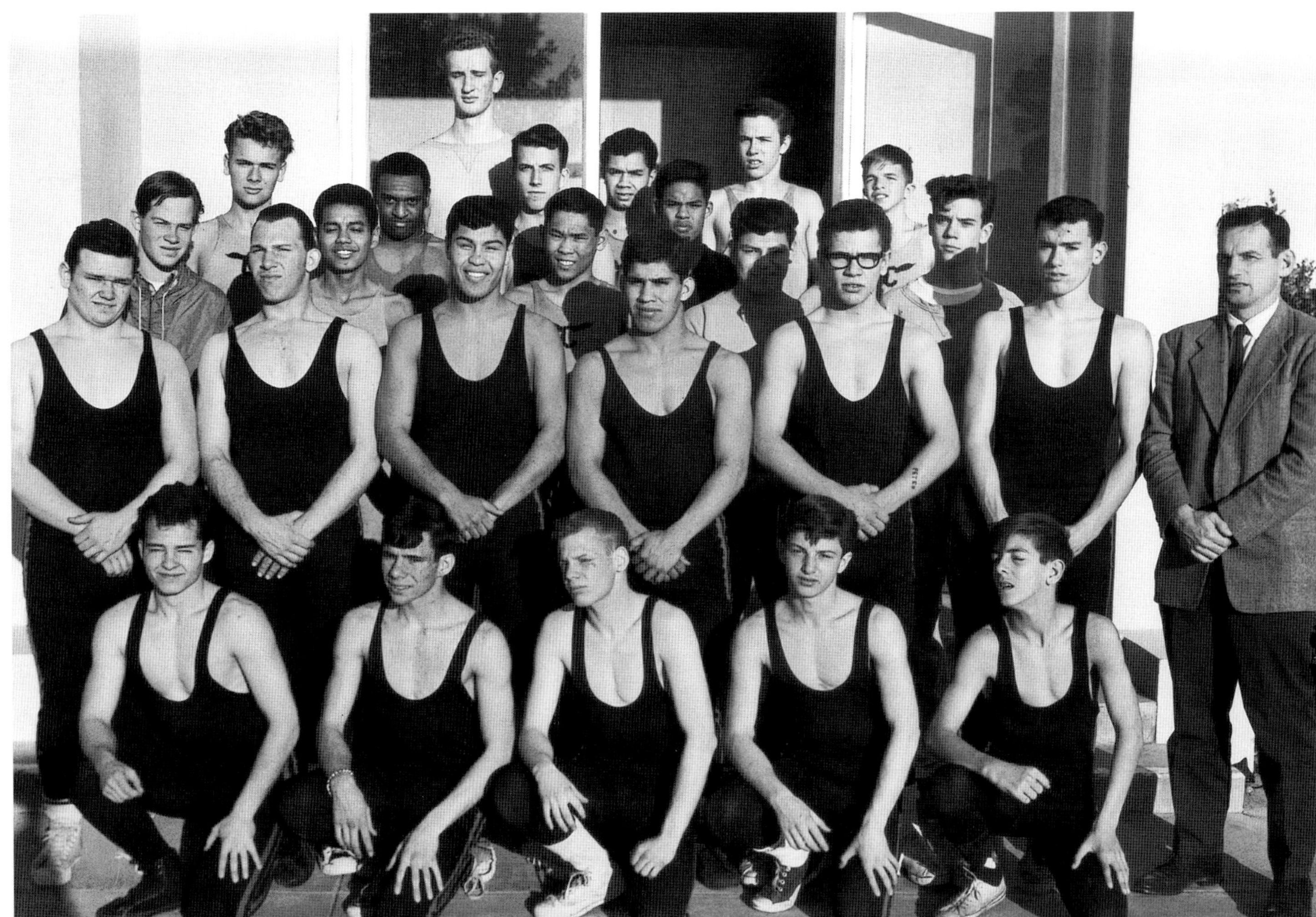

Immediately, he whipped the team into shape and managed to have matches with several high schools. In 1965, Henry Bella was the first CSD wrestler who advanced to North Coast Section, capping one win and one loss.

CSD's first team in history was fielded as follows:

95 lb. - Richard Joiner
103 lb. - David Ford
112 lb. - Philip Haley
120 lb. - Anthony Tenorio, Steven Aquino & Michael Hill
127 lb. - Steve Grainer, Arthur Hermosillo & Jeryl Chase
133 lb. - Winfred Ho, Sylvester Varela, Vincente Pinuela, Douglas Hale, Walter Rothrock & D. Herbold
138 lb. - Peter Johnson & Troy Williams
145 lb. - Henry Bella, Ronald Cohen & Larry Apolinar
165 lb. - Steve McCullough & Maxwell Williams
180 lb. - David Powell & Michael Hagerty
Heavyweight - Donald Edmonds, Barry Nimtz & Dale Dahl
Manager - Daniel Ulrich

During the school year of 1965-66, Donald Bullock, a new member of the CSD staff, joined Dean Swaim as an assistant coach. Prior to this, he was a stellar wrestler at Gallaudet College and a wrestler coach at the Indiana School for the Deaf and the West Virginia School for the Deaf. They were overwhelmed by the high interest shown by the number (47) of boys who turned out for wrestling. The result was that the team won the Bay Counties League (BCL) title for the time in the CSD history with Bob Pinuela, Douglas Hale, Albert Jacobs, Charles Willey and Larry Apolinar's impressive performances.

The 1966 team won the Bay Counties League title for the first time in the CSD history. CSD wrestling teams continued winning titles for the next five straight years.

Highlights of CSD's Wrestling Contention

1967 - Seven CSD champions: John Lynch, Richard Joiner, Tony Tenorio, Ron Gough, Donald Rogers, Larry Apolinar and Dennis Ellis, clinched the second BCL championships.

1967 - Again, the grapplers handily won their third straight league crown. Nine CSD grapplers became champions: Wesley Feria, Pete Corveleyn, Ron Gough, Donald Rogers, Charles Willey, Terry Breckner, Gary Govi and Tom Brill.

1969 - For the fourth time the Foothills grapplers defeated their league rivals to nail BCL league championship with seven champions: Wesley Feria, Dave Price, Walter Price, Charles Willey, Eddie Hauschildt, John Modica and Terry Sasser. The fund-raising drive sent Ronald Gough and Wesley Feria to the 11th World Games for the Deaf in Belgrade, Yugoslavia, August 10-16. They made a good show in wrestling against the tough competitors of Europe.

In 1969 one of the most admirable wrestling teams, capturing the fourth league title and sending two grapplers to the 11th World Games for the Deaf.

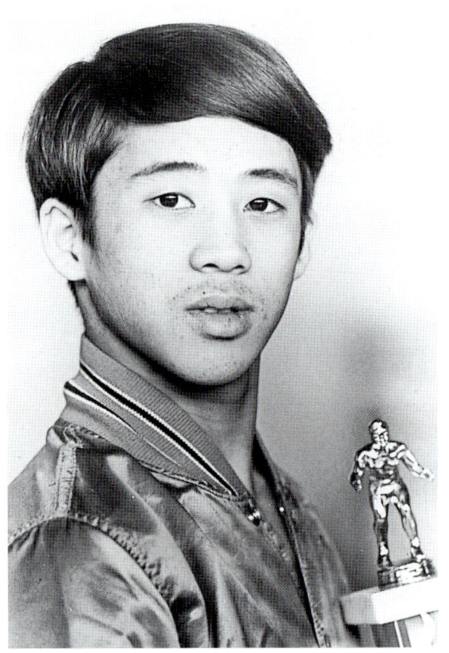

In 1970 Wesley Feria, the first CSD grappler to reach the highest level of wrestling competition in the North Coast Section Championship.

1970 - Wesley Feria advanced to the North Coast Section meet along with Clarence Gerling, David Herdrich, Jesse Macias and Joseph Aribas. In the finals, Feria pinned Nakazsota of Ygnacio Valley High School to clinch the championship of the North Coast Section. He was the first CSD grappler to reach the highest level of wrestling competition.

1972 - The team chalked up a record with nine wins and only one loss and got honorable mention in the Bay Area High School Wrestling Poll reported in the Oakland Tribune. David Herdrich won the Prep of the Week award in the East Bay. At the North Coast Division 2 wrestling tournament in Del Valle High School, competing against much large schools, CSD proudly ranked only seventh out of more than 35 schools. At 148-pound class, David Herdrich took second place which reached the highest level in the CSD's wrestling history. Clarence Gerling, heavyweight, was placed fifth in the North Coast Division 2 competition. Final East Bay wrestling poll listed CSD as one of the top ten, placed ninth. This honor is the highest in the CSD's wrestling history. Donald Bullock became head coach when Dean Swaim departed due to a new assignment as HS principal. David Peterson joined as assistant coach.

David Herdrich considered by coaches CSD's most outstanding grappler, undefeated in the 1972 season with 10-0 mark including 8 pins.

1973 - CSD proudly sent David Herdrich and Harold Stuart with Coach Dean Swaim to the XII World Games for the Deaf held in Malmo, Sweden, July 21 to 28. Former CSD wrestler, Ron Gough, went along with them. David Herdrich won a bronze medal (third place) in Greco-Roman wrestling. Harold Stuart made an impressive showing in freestyle wrestling. During the wrestling season Herdrich became the first CSD wrestler qualifying at the State Wrestling Championship. Clarence Gerling, heavyweight, was named Prep of the Week for his undefeated dual meets, advancing to the Sectionals. He established a gleaming 33-8 record during his four-year reign at CSD.

Harold Stuart making an outstanding record in 1974,especially qualified entrant at the State Wrestling Championships.

1974 - Harold Stuart clinched the championship with an overpowering pin over his Arroyo High counterpart in the finals. He became the second CSD wrestler to win the North Coast Section championship and, also, he was the second boy who advanced to the State Wrestling Tournament. At the award ceremonies, Stuart received a standing ovation for being named the outstanding middle weight wrestler.

1977 - Becoming football coach, Donald Bullock was obliged to retire from the wrestling circle. Jovette McCallon took over the reins. An added feature to the first Western State School Basketball Tournament was the wrestling matches with CSD˜Riverside. The Eagles defeated Riverside Cubs, 48 to 13.

The record against Riverside was four wins and one loss since 1972.

Clarence Gerling winning all dual meet matches in two years, 1972-73.

1979 - The outstanding wrestlers, U-Sung Chung, Don Baer, Juan Zamarripa and Tom Blair, carried the load for the team and was placed third out of eight teams in the Bay Counties League- North Section League. They defeated the Riverside team, 58 to 12.

1982 - 1983 - The most impressive records were made by Leslie Firl and Juan Diaz who posted a 7-1 record each. Andrew Rodriquez posted a 12-1 record and third place in North Coast Section qualifying tournament.

With the 1986 team under coach Mike Teague, Robert Garcia, middle row (second row, fourth from left) one of the CSD's finest wrestlers, ending his career with 73 victories. Scorekeeper Dana O'Reily (front row left), Donald Nolan, Brian Meagher, Jerry Bonheyo, Randy Stevens, manager Rima Ortega. Neil Dutra (second row), statistican Juile Orr, Roger Miller, Robert Garcia, scorekeeper Ayleen Tupfer, scorekeeper Trevor Ingram. Manager Joe Shetley (third row), Coach Michael Teague, Tim Fischer, Rick Jordan.

1984 - Sophomore Robert Garcia led the Eagles with a 28-2 record and a second place finish in the Mission Valley Athletic League tournament (MVAL). He was named Prep of the Week by the Argus newspaper.

1986 - Robert Garcia proved himself to be one of CSD's finest wrestlers, ending his wrestling career with 73 victories, a handful of tournament championships and a 21-6 season record. He won the MVAL championship at American High School, wrestling at one hundred ninety-four pounds.

1990 - CSD grapplers demonstrated their individual superiority over rival sister school, CSD-Riverside, by coming out victorious in 9 out of 11 total matches in a dual meet. Due to lack of full participation by the Fremont students, the eagles were unable to overcome a 30-point deficit in forfeits.

1991 - Under Coach Steve Holt, Phil Tooch became the first CSD wrestler to qualify for the North Coast Section tournament in 17 years. Tooch took third place in the 145-pound class, edging out his opponent 2-1 in the consolation finals in the Hayward Area Athletic League championships. Robert Delacruz got the alternate position to NCS at 130 pounds, losing a close battle in the final minute. Delacruz was 1990's most valuable player for CSD.

1999 - The Eagles team, for the first time in history, participated in the Eastern States for the Deaf Athletic Association Open Invitational Wrestling Tournament. Headed by coaches Michael Estrada and Kyle Emard, Brice Pruyn achieved second place. Tim Lopez and Laben Hur landed first place in the tournament which brought an opportunity to make lasting friendships among the grapplers from the different schools for the deaf in the East.

"CSD-Berkeley always had a coterie of fleet sprinters. It is true that they practiced rigorously under Coach Roy Parks, but I like to think that their best daily practice was to run to Moss Hall (boys' dormitory) for showers".

Eric Malzkuhn
Coach Roy Parks' shot putter

WRESTLING LEAGUE CHAMPIONS

1966	**Bay Counties League**
1967	**Bay Counties League**
1968	**Bay Counties League**
1969	**Bay Counties League**
1970	**Bay Counties League**
1974	**Bay Counties League**

Track and Field

Oldest Form of Organized Sport

Primitive man gradually refined his skills of running, jumping and throwing - until, in ancient times about 1500 B. C., the first known competitive prize was awarded. The sport of track and field plodded through the ages in evolutionary leisure until it exploded in the 20th century with an era of fantastic and incredible feats of swiftness, strength and endurance.

CSD's first successful track season under coach Roy Parks in 1934. Shot putter state champion Joe Hill, fourth from right.

Track and Field Adopted at CSD

As the interest in baseball began to diminish due to the lack of winning streaks in the 1930s, track and field was formed in 1931 under coaches Roy Parks, an academic teacher, and Louis Byouk, a boys counselor.

That year CSD was admitted with some reluctance to California Interscholastic Federation (CIF), North Coast Section 2, Division B. One of the reasons for this attitude was a lack of understanding of deafness. Ironically, according to a letter in The California News, May 1931, it was Washington Union High School in Centerville (now a district of Fremont) that gave full support for CSD's admission to CIF. The letter was sent by Mr. Hodges, principal of Washington Union High School to Vernon Birck, director of athletics of CSD. In 1934, the CSD track team won the first track championship of Southern Alameda County Athletic League (SACAL) held in Centerville. Livermore, Centerville and CSD were involved in the track competition.

Flourshing Successes in Track

The very first victories in the CSD track's history were a mile relay (Shigeo Nakamura, Lyle McIntyre, Gene Sullivan and Paul Cope) and 440 yards run (Paul Cope, 55 seconds flat) at the conference track meet on April 30, 1932 at Hayward.

The interest in track heightened after the CSD team won the first track championship of SACAL. Hence, the era of baseball was put to an end because of the inability of CSD to defray traveling expenses for two spring sports. CSD won the championship of SACAL every year from 1934 to 1938. From 1934 to 1936, Joe Hill was CSD's most consistent first place winner in the shot put, occasionally coming out second in broad jump, discus, or 220 yard hurdles. The shot put was his specialty. His best record was 54 feet 9 inches. Today his CSD record stands unchallenged for 64 years. Roy Parks departed CSD in 1938 and eventually became superintendent of the Arkansas School for the Deaf. Louis Byouk took over coaching track and continued until 1948. CSD continued to win track league championships from 1934 to 1948 with an interruption during World War II from 1942 to 1945.

The 1939 team (facing page), one of the CSD's finest group of talented tracksters. Assistant manager Issac Hutcheson (front row left), Jorma Ranta, Michael Corson, Frances Price, Lawrence Shoemaker, Harold Castro, Dale Smith, Melvin Davis. Arlie Taylor (second row), Stanley Vranesh, Donald Nowdesha, Charles Pruitt, Angelo Skropeta, Walter Kirby, Henry Hauschildt, Roy Miller. Manager Frank Sladek (third row), Luther Norred, James McKee, Edward Koshelnik, LeRoy Pate, Frank Paniagua, Allen Goldsmith, Charles Dana, Robert Grinde. Mike Bianchi (fourth row), David Logan, Donald Peabody, Dominic d'Innocenti, Larry Simpson, John Leon, Robert Stanley, Thomas Martin, Coach Louis Byouk.

CSD BOYS TRACK RECORD FROM 1931 TO 1939

Events	Record	Champion	Year	Site
100-yd dash	10.01	Horace Carlson	1935	Centerville
220-yd dash	22.0	Frank Davis	1936	Livermore
440-yd run	54.2	Lawrence Quijada	1938	Piedmont
880-yd run	2:03.7	Edward Silva	1938	Davis
Mile run	4:42.2	Harold Castro	1939	Brentwood
120-yd high hurdles	18.0	Joe Hill	1936	Livermore
220-yd low hurdles	25.8	Glen Kearney	1938	Davis
Broad jump	21' 6"	Ross Scott	1938	St. Helena
High jump	5' 9"	Jorma Ranta	1939	Brentwood
Pole vault	11' 7"	Roger Specht	1938	St. Helena
Shot put	54' 9"	Joe Hill	1936	C.I.F., Gridley
Discus	130' 9"	Joe Hill	1936	Livermore
Relay	1:34.3	Glen Kearney Roy Miller Lawrence Quijada Larry Shoemaker	1938	St. Helena

Ken Pedersen (left), the second CSD trackster in the CIF State Meet in 1966 and shattering the world's record, tops in the world of deaf thin-clads.

EXCEPTIONAL TRACK YEAR

1936 - Joe Hill was the first CSD athlete to participate in the CIF State Meet and won first place in the shot put, 54' 91/2" against the entire top high school competitors of California.

1952 - For the first time, CSD's girls had an official track meet under coach Willie Dreyer who was a national Olympic champion. The events included the discus, shot put, 25 yard dash for 10-12 years old, 50 yard dash, 100 yard dash, 220 yard hurdles and relays. Fifty-five girls went out for the first practice.

1964 - As captain of the track team, James Davis ran the 100-yard dash in 19.4 in a 65-48 win over Menlo School. At the St. Helena Relays, he helped win the 880-yard relay in 1:36.1 with Don Lyons, John Ternullo and Larry Apolinar. In Benicia, Davis set a new school record of 10 seconds flat in the 100-yard dash and 22 seconds flat in the 220-yard. Davis was selected by The Silent Worker as the 1965 Athlete of the Year after winning three gold medals at the 10th International Games for the Deaf in Washington, D. C.

1966 - Ken Pedersen flashed to break the world and American records of the 880-yard run in 1:54.6 and he emerged the first deaf prepster to break the 2-minute barrier. He shattered the world's record held by a Russian who won the Xth Olympics with 1:55.1. Just before the trials in the State Meet sponsored by CIF, Pedersen developed a cold so, unfortunately, he came out sixth in the trials but his time was a superb 1:54.6. He was only the second CSD trackster who competed in the CIF State Meet. He won the DEAF PREP TRACKSTER OF 1966. His coach Ken Norton called Pedersen, "the finest competitor in track he has ever coached."

National Champions in 1967.

1981 - The boys and girls track teams won first place honors at the Bay Area Conference track and field championship on May 13 at the College of San Mateo, Rohnert Park, California. The star tricksters, Ann Baer and Bruce Price, were each multiple winners. Baer set records in winning the 800 and the 1600 Meter events. Price won the 300 low hurdle and the 110 high hurdles. Both were also on the relay teams winning the mile relay.

The 1981 girls track team winning first place honors at the Bay Area Conference track and field championship at the College of San Mateo. Also, the boys team won first place at the Conference.

1985 - As a sophomore, Lynn Barlow was a Deaf All-American in four track events: 800, 1,600 and 3,200 Meter runs and part of 1,600 Meter relay team. She had the fastest times among deaf runners among the schools for the deaf in the nation.

CSD's many trophies displayed in the trophy case at the gymnasium.

1986 - Ken Pedersen and Jim Koetz's girls track team glided to the National Deaf Track championship including six first places in all the track and field events. Lynn Barlow won the national 800, 1600 and 3,200 meter runs, earning herself the prestigious 1986 Trackster of the Year Award. Ken Pedersen won the Coach of the Year honors for the success of the track season.

Norman Edwards became the third CSD athlete in the school's history, participating in the CIF State Meet in the triple jump. Edwards jumped 45' 31/2" which was an exceptional jump by deaf standards but could not overcome the top ten in the meet.

1990 - After establishing meet records in the 100, 200 and 400 meter dashes at the North Coast Section and the Meet of Champions, Merrill Samuels advanced to the CIF State Meet at Cerritos College in Norwalk, California, on

CSD BOYS TRACK RECORD FROM 1940 TO 2000

Event	Record	Champion	Year	Site
100-yard dash	9.8	Ron Wood	1960	Drake Relays San Anselmo
100-meter dash	10.68	Merrill Samuels	1990	Meet of Champs U.C. Edwards Sta.
220-yd dash	22.3	Gary Tyhurst	1955	St. Helena H.S.
200-m dash	21.82	Merrill Samuels	1990	State Meet Cerritos College
400-m dash	47.7	Merrill Samuels	1990	State Meet Cerritos College
880-yd run (longer than 800-m)	1:54.6	Ken Pedersen	1966	State Meet U.C. Edwards Sta.
1600-m run	4:39.0	Brice Pruyn	1999	NCS, Mendocino Jr. College, Ukiah
3200-m run	10:09.6	Brice Pruyn	1999	Meet of Champs Chabot College
110-m high hurdle	15.5	Don Lyons	1964	
180-yd low hurdle	19.9	John Tingley	1955	
300-m inter. hurdle	39.6	Bruce Price	1980	NCS, Laney Col.
400-m relay	43.6	Anthony Cass Merrill Samuels Darrell Harrison Justin Toca	1987	NCS, Santa Rosa Junior College
800-yd relay	1:31.5	Harold Foster Arthur Hermosillo Ken Pedersen Larry Apolinar	1966	BCL U.C. Edwards Sta.
1600-yd relay	3:31.5	Jeff Hinds Jerry Hause Roy Rodriquez Ken Pedersen	1967	BCL U.C. Edwards Sta.
Dist. med. relay	11:52.3	Ken Pedersen Jerry Roundy James Koetz Jesse Rios	1964	Drake Relays, San Anselmo
3200-m relay	8:23.1	George St. Clair Daniel Rosenthal Pat Smith Rod Pedersen	1984	CSD Invitational
400-yd hurdle relay	1:01.4	Oscar Bibb Ken Pedersen Don Lyons John Ternullo	1964	Drake Relays, San Anselmo
High jump	6'3"	Harold Foster	1966	BCL U.C.Edwards Sta.
Long jump	21'10"	Bruce Price	1981	Valley Christian Inv., Los Gatos,CA

Triple jump	45'3"	Norman Edwards	1986	State Meet, Cerritos College
Pole vault	12'6"	Justin Coleman	1988	Meet of Champs U.C. Edwards Sta.
Shot put	54'9"	Joe Hill	1936	CIF Meet Gridley, CA
Discus	157'8"	Tim Siaki	1984	Meet of Champs U.C. Edwards Sta.

CSD GIRLS TRACK RECORD FROM 1940 TO 2000

Event	Record	Champion	Year	Site
100-m dash	12.2	Julie Green	1983	Meet of Champs U.C. Edwards Sta.
	12.2	Melissa Green	1984	Meet of Champs U.C. Edwards Sta.
200-m dash	26.3	Quilla Moseley	1987	Meet of Champs U.C.Edwards Sta.
400-m dash	60.8	Gabriella Ramirez	1991	BCL, CSD
800-m run	2:30.7	Rebecca Bonheyo	1981	NCS, Sonoma State University
1600-m run	5:50.0	Lynn Barlow	1987	Santa Rosa Junior College
3200-m run	12:12.0	Tamera Gaudet	1984	Meet of Champs U.C. Edwards Sta.
100-m low hurdle	16.8	Debbie Saavedra	1981	NCS, Sonoma State University
300-m low hurdle	51.0	Rebecca Bonheyo	1981	NCS, Sonoma State University
400-m relay	52.0	Florence Chin	1984	Meet of Champs U.C. Edwards Sta.
		Melissa Green		
		Pamela Timms		
		Julie Green		
800-m relay	1:54.1	Ayanna Durio	1986	Valley Christian Invitational
		Quilla Moseley		
		June Nasukiewicz		
		Pamela Timms		
1600-m relay	4:21.6	Deanna Brown	1981	NCS, Sonoma State University
		Asa Lodge		
		Rebecca Bonheyo		
		Julie Green		
3200-m relay	10:42.0	Lisa Goetz	1981	CSD Relays
		Tamera Gaudet		
		Ann Baer		
		Rebecca Bonheyo		
Sprint relay	2:03.6	Klesha Chapman	1981	CSD Relays
		Asa Lodge		
		Julie green		
		Rebecca Bonheyo		
Dist. med. relay	14:39.2	Rebecca Bonheyo	1981	CSD Relays
		Coreen Farquar		
		Tamera Gaudet		
		Ann Baer		

Event	Record	Champion	Year	Site
400-m hurdle relay	1:17.8	Reyna Soto Tamera Gaudet Rebecca Bonheyo Debbie Saavedra	1981	CSD Relays
High jump	5' 2"	Karen Gilbert	1988	Meet of Champs U.C. Edwards Sta.
Long jump	16' 2"	Asa Lodge	1981	Valley Christian
Triple jump	30' 7"	Karen Gilbert	1988	NCS, Sonoma State University
Shot put	33' 8"	Debbie McCutcheon	1982	CSD/Calistoga Meet
Discus	98' 5"	Sally Garza	1986	NCS, Sonoma State Univ.

Ron Wood, holds the 100-yard dash record, 9.8 since 1960. Undoubtedly, his record lasts a lifetime because of all runs measured in meters starting in 1980.

June 1 and 2, bringing together the best high school athletes from northern and southern California. Samuels ran a 48.28 for third place in his trials which qualified him for the finals. Competing against the best in the state, he finished fifth with a time of 48.13. Samuels became CSD's fourth athlete running in the CIF State Meet.

The girls team carried away nearly all of the first place honors in the Bay Area Conference track meet at the CSD field. Karen Gilbert took first in the triple jump and high jump; Zully Maldonado won both the shot put and discus; Ursula Richardson captured first place in the 100 meter; LaShawn Witt won first in the 200 meter; Melody Tsai took first in the 110 low hurdles; Dyan Kovacs captured first in the 300 low hurdles; and the 1600 meter relay made up of Karen Gilbert, Lisa Orellano, Heather Ainsley and LaShawn Witt took first place honors.

LEAGUE CHAMPIONS AND NATIONAL TITLES AMONG THE SCHOOLS FOR THE DEAF

CSD track squads set many records during the years from 1934 to 1995 in the league meets. In 1955, CSD won for the first time in a newly-formed Bay Counties League and continued winning championships in BCL successively from 1962 to 1968, from 1973 to 1978, and from 1986 to 1995. Also, CSD won in 1981, 1983 and 1984.

The Silent Worker picked the 1955, 1960, 1965 and 1967 CSD track teams as TEAM OF THE YEAR.

The girls track team won the Bay Counties League every year from 1980 to 1993 with the exceptions of 1982, 1985 and 1989.

Deaf American selected the 1986 and 1987 teams as TEAM OF THE YEAR.

Outstanding track stars of 1986-1990:

Lynn Barlow (right in near photo), tenacious runner in the 3,200 run and 400 relay.

Quilla Mosley, (below left) fleet sprinter in 100 yard dash, 200 yard dash and 400 relay.

Norman Edwards, (far left) all-around athlete, the third CSD athlete participating in the CIF State Track Meet.

Merrill Samuels (left), potent sprinter, CSD's fourth athlete running in the CIF State Track Meet.

Swimming

Most Natural Sport

Swimming is known as the most natural sport. To swim, you do not need a bat, net or goal post; all it requires is a body of water and you. It does not take very much to enjoy the sport, either. Swimming and diving as sports have been around for thousands of years.

Yet, starting only in 1916, CSD students first splashed in the school pool in the new gymnasium. Prior to construction of the gymnasium, they swam in ponds, creeks, beaches and ocean only during summer when they were home for vacation. Initially, having fun in the school pool was the sole purpose. As the years passed, swimming changed rapidly as it turned into a serious, competitive sport.

In 1916 the new inside pool in the gymnasium building became the most used among the students. Boys and girls took turns enjoying the aquatic sport.

CIRCA 1927 - Every Thursday evening the boys went swimming at the CSD pool. The water was heated and filtered all the time. Sometimes the boys had friendly races, just for fun. That year the boys had a contest with the hearing boys from San Francisco. The opponents won, 11 points to 8 1/2 points but they learned that it was not proper to laugh at the deaf.

During the late 1920s and 1930s, the entire school took part in the annual picnic and track events from 9:30 A. M. to 4:30 P.M. The staff members conducted the races under a system of checking off points won in the games. Games played were: coat relay race, potato relay, sack relay, jockey relay, backward relay, clothes basket relay, hand to hand relay. Wherever possible boys and girls played on teams half and half. The climax of the day came with aquatic sports. Both showed their skills in fancy diving and speed.

Swimming did not occupy a prominent role during the years of 1940 to 1962 because of the interruptions of World War II and the razing of the old brick building and construction of the new Spanish-style buildings.

In 1962 a new outside pool was built above the vocational building.

1962 - A new swimming pool was completed at the south end of the new gymnasium and was in constant use by CSD students. On October 26, the pool was formally opened with a ribbon-cutting ceremony in which state and school officials and students participated. Honorable Don Mulford, State Assemblyman, 18th District, was part of the program, delivering greetings from the State Legislature. At the closing of the ceremony, a swim meet was held between the School for the Deaf and the School for the Blind.

1972 - Randy Roberts, '73, took the Red Cross course at St. Marys College in Moraga with the help of Vic Hutchins, CSD high school teacher, who served as Roberts' interpreter. Out of 49 in the class, Roberts was one of the 15 who passed. Next he earned his Handicapped Instructor's certificate. Soon he became the first deaf instructor with the Concord Department of Leisure Services. As a volunteer, he taught handicapped children including the very hard of hearing, deaf dysphasic and aphasic how to swim.

National Championship banners.

1976-1980 - The swimming teams were informally organized during these years before CSD moved to Fremont from Berkeley.

1980 - An attractive outdoor Junior-Olympic-size pool including an area for diving was built at the new Fremont school. It has been utilized for the physical education program as well as competitive sports.

1994 - This team was one of the best CSD has ever had. With help and guidance from the new coaching staff, head coach Jacqie Mosqueria and assistant Mike Deming, the boys and girls teams improved their swim techniques and learned league rules. Both boys and girls teams defeated CSD Riverside in the first ever CSD vs. CSD-Riverside swim meet.

This 1994 swim team was considered one of the best CSD had ever.

1995 - In the junior varsity level, the team's best achievement was that Amy Jenkins, Natalie Fleet, Sheila DeLao and Susana Stern won a first place medal for the 200 medley relay at the Bay Counties League. The boys team's

record was five wins and four losses. Both of CSD boys and girls teams defeated the Riverside teams.

1996 - One of the best CSD's girls swimming teams broke eleven team records in the junior varsity level. The five CSD girls, Shella DeLao, Julie Dolezal, Jenamarie Davition-Sciandra, Natalie Fleet and Shoshannah Stern participated in the Bay Counties League Championship Meet at Spieker Aquatics Center At the University of California^Berkeley on May 18. Stern came in first place in the 50-yard breaststroke and might be the first CSD swimmer to get a first place medal in an individual event. Daviton-Sciandra was awarded two individual 3rd place honors in the 100-yard freestyle and 200-yard freestyle.

The swimming program still survives in spite of the other popular spring sports: softball, baseball and track. Every year at the Bay Counties League the CSD swimmers display exciting competition and continue defeating the Riverside team in the annual meet.

The 1996 girls team making an impressive achievement by breaking eleven team records. Manager Dustin Knott (front row left), Julie Dolezal, Heather Montero, Jenamarie Daviton-Sciandra, Jilian Havandjian, manager Jeremy Peterson. Coach Erika Domatti, Kim Bogel, Heather Lewis, Lauren Miller, Courtney Rushing, Sho Stern, Coach Jacquie Mosqueira.

CSD Record of Boys Varsity Swimming

Event	Swimmer	Time	Year
200 medley relay	Dean Krohn Brian Morrison Darrell Ritter Kenyon Cahill	2:21.07	1995
200 freestyle	Kenyon Cahill	2:38.40	1994
200 individual medley	Kenyon Cahill	2:52.17	1995
50 freestyle	Dean Krohn	26.94	1995
100 butterfly	Dean Krohn	1:26.62	1995
100 freestyle	Dean Krohn	1:05.07	1995
200 free relay	Kenyon Cahill Brian Morrison Darrell Ritter Dean Krohn	1:56.60	1995
500 freestyle	Kenyon Cahill	7:14.97	1995
100 backstroke	Benjamin Lewis	1:19.83	1999
100 breaststroke	Jose Aldana	1:33.45	1994
400 free relay	Andy Gurry Dean Krohn Kenyon Cahill Jose Aldana	4:50.31	1994

CSD Record of Girls Varsity Swimming

Event	Swimmer	Time	Year
200 medley relay	Jenamarie Daviton Sho Stern Heather Montero Heather Lewis	2:21.05	1997
200 freestyle	Heather Montero	2:27.84	1999
200 individual medley	Gina Pasini	2:41.68	1999
50 freestyle	Heather Lewis	30.87	1997
100 butterfly	Gina Pasini	1:11.41	1999
100 freestyle	Heather Montero	1:09.44	1999
200 free relay	Gina Pasini Rene Vairora Gloria Farr Heather Montero	2:12.87	1999
500 freestyle	Heather Montero	6:51.64	1997
100 backstroke	Esther Swanson	1:25.31	1995
100 breaststroke	Sho Stern	1:24.58	1997
400 free relay	Jenamarie Daviton Sho Stern Heather Montero Heather Lewis	5:12.92	1997

Cheerleading

Let's Go! Let's Fight! Let's Win!

It is unknown exactly when the first cheerleading squad was formed at CSD. However, it was believed to have occurred in the 1940s. It might have started with only two girls, Theresa Connors (Burstein) and Eleanor Elmassian (Nuernberger) in 1945. At that time it was realized that football and basketball games needed some encouragement, cheerleaders led the crowd with cheers—to great effect. Up to the present time, they were usually dressed in colorful orange and black uniforms and using props such as pom-poms. Within the last 20 years CSD cheerleading has developed into a very complex art. The girls have athletic skills to perform gymnastic routines, different jumps, partner lifts and stunts.

The CSD cheerleaders in 1957 boosting the Rooters that was noted the best in one of the Bay Counties League football games. Marla Gille, left, Donna Voegele, Janice Sperring, Gregg Brooks, Judith Crabb, Julie Hensley, Lee Ann Crabb, James Walter, kneeling.

Almost every year since 1982, CSD has sent its cheerleading squad to summer training camps. They learn new techniques for cheers and stunts, share spirit-raising ideas and earn awards for their achievements. CSD has participated in cheerleading competition, doing flips, leaps, jumps and other acrobatic steps. Usually female students dominate cheerleading activities. Once in a while one or two male students join the cheerleading squad.

Flavor Added to the Game

1957 - The CSD rooters were named the best in the Bay Counties League during the football games with the help from six girls and two boys of the cheerleading squad.

The 1965 Football Pompon Girls. Judy McIntyre, front row, left, Carlene Canady, Claire Clancey, Nancy Harmon. Judy Porter, back row, left, Brenda Underwood, Connie Contreras, Kathy Haas.

1986 - At Riverside the CSD cheerleaders were in high spirits as they led the fans in support of the Eagles during the five games played at WSBC. The attention to details and hours of practice put in by Barbara Hemstreet (captain), Julie Gobel, Deanna Johnson, Cindy Chadd, Cathy Clarkson and Jennifer Nasukiewicz paid off as they won the first place award. This was the first year they put their routine to music, dancing to the hit song "We Built This City" by the Starship, trained under coach Carlene Pedersen.

1994 - CSD sent its cheerleaders, Sara Stallard, Cheyenne Buchan, Yessiea Martinez, Jolene Mahoney and Alethea Boyer to the WSBC at Tucson, Arizona with coach Becca Johnson. In the competition, they performed almost flawlessly and won its second championship at WSBC. Martinez was named to the first team.

Also, the "B" cheerleaders gave a chant to the Middle School students for a pep rally before the Middle School boys' last basketball game of the season. In the fall, along with a new coach, Glenna Wurm, the cheerleaders got a new look, new style and a new name "CSD Spirit Squad." The new look, style and name raised the skill level and professionalism of the CSD Squad to match the local public schools. While attending the United Spirit Association Summer Camp at the University of California-Santa Cruz, the squad won a superior rating and took home several blue ribbons. The squad was also awarded top honors by receiving "the Spirit Stick" which exemplified high spirit all week long, and the Unity Award. The Award was voted by all other attending school squads. Squad members: Jolene Mahoney, Alethea Boyer, Susana Stern, Natalie Fleet and Julie Dolezal.

1995 - At CSD the WSBC cheerleading contest took place and the participating schools all gave dazzling performances. The contest was in three categories: a required cheer mastered by the United Spirit Association, the school cheer and a dance routine. CSD's cheerleading team won the third championship honors under coach Glenna Wurm.

The CSD Spirit Squad traveled each year to the Boonville Classic Tournament. During the Classic, the cheerleading squads competed for the championship award. Each squad was judged on its game performance. The judges looked for appropriate game cheers that matched the situation on the court, spirit led by the squad throughout the games, and superior skills demonstrated during each quarter break and half time performance. CSD came out on top as the Classic cheerleading champions. Squad members: Sylvia Zara, Susana Stern, Natalie Fleet, Svenna Pedersen, Heather Montero. Coach Glenna Wrum.

1997 - The Eagles cheerleaders soared to an impressive high when they demonstrated their flair before a crowd of 1,000 fans at the Big Game between Fremont and Riverside. The members were Svenna Pedersen, Heather Montero, Erica Parker, Kristin Richter, Bekah Mandel and Shoshannah Stern. The coach was Tamara Taves.

1998 - For the first time, the Eagles cheerleaders participated in a dance competition sponsored by United Cheerleaders Association of Northern California Regional. The CSD team was placed 9th place out of the numerous high school cheerleaders teams from all over the Northern and Central California involved in this dance competition. It was an impressive achievement. The members of this team were Heather Montero, Svenna Pedersen, Bekah Mandel, Shoshannah Stern, Kristen Richter and coach Tamara Taves.

1999 - During the summer, CSD's spirit squad attended a camp named United Spirit Association (USA) for a week in Santa Cruz, California, with about 40 cheerleading teams from other high schools. At the end of the week, USA committee voted on the best for unity and good character. CSD won! As a result, the CSD cheerleading squad was invited to cheer during the National

The 1994 Spirit Squad. Natalie Fleet, left, Svenna Pedersen, Susana Stern. Phung Ha, top.

Football League Pro Bowl in Honolulu, Hawaii. In addition, the squad was the only school at the camp to win the Superior Plaque, the Unity Plaque and the Spirit Stick.

This squad was the first Deaf cheerleading group ever to cheer at the Pro Bowl! Since the trip cost them $10,000, all of the cheerleaders, seven girls and two boys, worked at the Shoreline Amphitheater until they earned enough money to go.

The Eagles Spirit Squad joined a group of 300 high school cheerleaders on the Aloha Stadium field. They performed their cheer during half time. The members claimed, "What an experience!" They were Tina Johnson, Gloria Farr, Tara Holcomb, Bekah Mandel, Svenna Pedersen, Renee Varirora, Ben Lewis, Michael Davis, Raechelle Wolfert and coach Tamara Taves.

The challenge to today's cheerleaders lies in enticing those around them to take pride in developing that individual spirit.

CHEERLEADERS CHAMPION AT THE WESTERN STATES BASKETBALL TOURNAMENT

1986, 1994, 1995

This cheerleading squad earned a golden opportunity to cheer at the Pro Bowl in Honolulu, Hawaii in February 1999. They were the first Deaf cheerleading squad to ever cheer at the Pro Bowl. They deserved the special honor for they won the unity award and a superior rating for their "home cheer" at Camp USA. Benjamin Lewis (left), Gloria Farr, Bekah Mandel, Rachelle Wolfert, Svenna Pedersen, Renee Vairora, Tiana Johnson, Tara Holcomb, Michael Davis.

CALIFORNIA SCHOOL FOR THE DEAF
HALL OF FAME

Sponsored by CSD Alumni Association

In 1995, the establishment of the CSD Sports Hall of Fame was undertaken by Donald Ingraham. The first introduction of the Hall of Fame, Ingraham's lifelong dream, occurred at the 1995 CSD Alumni Reunion. The committee, composing of Bob Ellis, Ed Leighton, Kenneth Norton, Ken Pedersen, Eugene Rianda, Dean Swaim and Dr. Henry Klopping, helped Ingraham initiate this worthy endeavor to honor the former athletes and coaches who brought glories to CSD.

THE FIRST 1995 CSD HALL OF FAME INDUCTEES

Carol Land, Baseball Pitcher (1912-15)
Louis Byouk, Coach (1928-48)
James Lazzarini, Basketball Player (1933-35)
Joe Hill, Shotputter (1934-36)
Theobaldo Ruffa, Basketball Player (1935-38)
Michael Skropeta, Football & Basketball Player (1936-39)
Kenneth Norton, Coach (1961-68; 1972-75)
Donald Lyons, Basketball Player (1961-64)
James Davis, All Sports Player (1962-64)
Ken Pedersen, All Sports Player (1963-67)
John Sandoval, Basketball Player (1968-71)

Donald Ingraham, CSD Hall of Fame Chairperson, 1995 - 2000.

THE SECOND 2000 CSD HALL OF FAME INDUCTEES

At the 2000 CSD Alumni Reunion, new inductees were announced. Three new categories are added to CSD Sports Hall of Fame: ARTS, COMMUNITY, EDUCATION.

ARTS	COMMUNITY	EDUCATION	SPORTS
Theophilus d'Estrella	George Attletweed	Byron B. Burnes	Donald Bullock
Douglas Tilden	John Galvan	Roberet Davila	Lloyd Escobar
Granville Redmond	Harry Jacobs	Emil Ladner	Frank Sladek
Joseph Velez	Leo Jacobs	Ralph Neesam	Dean Swaim
	Terence O'Rourke	Winfield Runde	
	Julian Singleton	Elwood Stevenson	

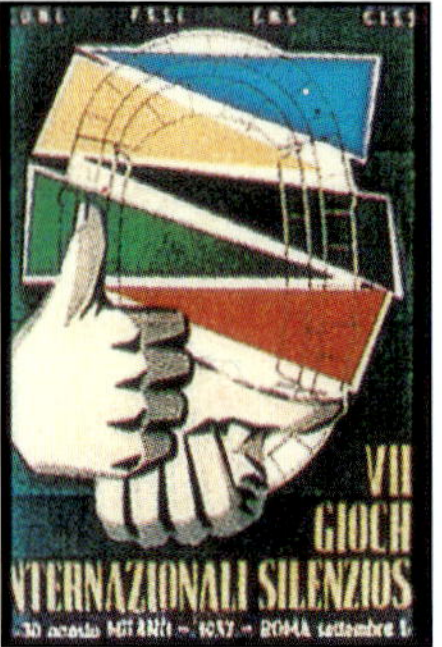

1957

1965

1969

1973

1977

1985

Deaf World Games

"Deaf Olympics"

There is a world athletic association for the deaf, known in French as the *Comite' International des Sports des Sourds* (CISS). In English, it is the International Committee of Sports for the Deaf, founded in 1924 in Paris, France, to carry out international games. The by-laws and constitution of CISS are patterned after the hearing world's International Olympic Committee. Nearly all of the countries in the world that have sports clubs for the deaf that are affiliated with CISS. Hence, CISS is an organization looking after the interest of sports of the deaf of all nations. The result of it was the birth of the Deaf World Games.

The Deaf World Games (DWG), also known as "deaf olympics" occur every four years at pre-selected sites all over the world. Usually several thousands of deaf athletes participate in intense and high-class competition. Three medallions are awarded to competitors in each event, gold to first place, silver to second place and bronze to third place. Approximately, 15 different sports are included in the games.

American participation began in 1935 when S. Robey Burns, a coach at the Illinois School for the Deaf, brought two athletes to the International Games for the Deaf in London. The name of the Games was later changed to the World Games for the Deaf. In 1999, it was renamed the Deaf World Games.

Sites of the Deaf World Summer Games

1924 - Paris, France
1928 - Amsterdam, Netherlands
1931 - Nuremberg, Germany
1935 - London, England
1939 - Stockholm, Sweden
1949 - Copenhagen, Denmark
1953 - Brussels, Belgium
1957 - Milan, Italy
1961 - Helsinki, Finland
1965 - Washington, D.C., U.S.A.
1969 - Belgrade, Yugoslavia
1973 - Malmo, Sweden
1977 - Bucharest, Romania
1981 - Cologne, West Germany
1985 - Los Angeles, United States
1989 - Christchurch, New Zealand
1993 - Sofia, Bulgaria
1997 - Copenhagen, Denmark
2001 - Rome, Italy
2005 - Melbourne, Australia

In 1957, the United States involvement reached an all time high with 40 athletes participating. That year the American Athletic Association of the Deaf (AAAD) took over organizing the United States' team. In 1965, the Summer

Games under the sponsorship of AAAD was held in Washington, D. C. These were the first games run by Deaf Americans. The second conducted by Deaf Americans was held in Los Angeles in 1985.

ROSTER AND RESULTS OF CSD PARTICIPANTS IN THE GAMES

1957 - For the first time, CSD products, one student, five recent graduates and a Gallaudet College junior took part in the 8th International Games for the Deaf in Milan, Italy, August 25-30. All six CSD tracksters except Joseph Maxwell were standouts on the 1955 Berkeley school squad which swept the national title in track and field.

Joseph Maxwell, '57 - Silver medal in high jump (1.77m). His jump was a feat because he was sick all the way on the trip to Milan, lost weight, and missed many practice sessions.

Kenneth Decker, '57 - Bronze in pole vault (3.30 m).

Reno Coletti, '57 - Fifth place in high jump (1.70 m)

John Tingley, '57 - Participated in 400 meter hurdle.

Tom Rosenlind, '58 - Participated in 1500 m run and 5000 m run. His father, president of the Parent-Teachers Association of CSD, worked hard to raise the money for his son Kenneth Decker for their travel expenses.

Jose Gonzales, '57 - Participated in 800m run.

Gary Tyhurst, - Unfortunately, Tyhurst got a pulled muscle in pre-games training which kept him out of the two sprint events. He would have been the favorite at Milan, if not for his injury. He won the 100 and 220-yard titles in the mythical meet among the schools for the deaf in the nation in 1955.

Joseph Maxwell, CSD's first silver medallist in the 1957 International Games.

1961 - CSD's Olympic hopefuls were two students, one recent graduate and three former students at Gallaudet College. The Ninth International Games for the Deaf was held in Helsinki, Finland, August 6-10. No medals were won.

George Lowe, '64 - Fourth place in high jump (1.75 m).

Sal Flores, '61 - Seventh place in pole vault (3.30 m).

Ron Wood, '63 - Due to a serious injury to his leg before the games, he did not participate in any running events.

Caroline Skedsmo, '57 - Sixth place in 80 meter hurdle (14:6), New USA Record and ninth place in shot put (9.28 m).

Margaret Spohr, '56 - sixth place in javelin (25.68 m).

Michael White, '60 - Participated in swimming, 400 m free style and 1500 m free style, but eliminated in the trials.

Susan Pier, - Participated in swimming, 100 m backstroke, but eliminated in the trials.

1961

James Davis, 1965 WGD Conqueror. Winner of Gold medals from flashing on this track at the right.

1965 - CSD-Berkeley was highly honored that its own five top athletes achieved the most impressive historic marks at the 10th International Games for the Deaf, held at the University of Maryland, June 27 to July 3.

James Davis, '65 - Three gold medals in 100, 200 meter dashes and sprint relay team. He set world records in 100 and 200 meter dashes. His trip was financed by the U.S. Navy crew of U.S.S. Ranger. During two weeks of training at Gallaudet College, he usually placed second or third in the trials. Yet during the Games Davis exploded and surprised everybody by edging out his teammates. He was clocked at 10:08, winning first place. Also, Davis swept everything in the 200 meter dash, establishing a new world record, 22 seconds flat. Again he helped the U.S. relay team win first place in the 4x100-meter relay (42.7), New World Record. He is the possessor of three gold Olympic style medals!

James Davis was named the World Athlete of the Year, shared with Viatcheslav Skomarokhov of Kiev, Russia, by the American Athletic Association of the Deaf. He received his award in Boston on March 31, 1966.

Donald Lyons, '65 - Three silver in 400 meter hurdle run, 110 meter hurdle race, and relay team. The 400-meter hurdle run was one of the most strenuous events in which he raced against the Russian star, Viatcheslav Skomarokhov, who was a member of the Soviet's Olympic team at the Tokyo and Mexico City Olympics. Lyons ran on the 4x400-meter relay and placed second. He owns three silver medals.

Ken Pedersen, '67 - Bronze in broad jump (21-3). Winning the bronze medal was a noteworthy feat for a 17-year old. Pedersen won fourth place in the 800 meter run during the trials. The fact that only three Americans qualified for the Games did not deter Pedersen. He requested placement with the broad jump team. The coaches denied his first plea, since three Americans had already been selected. But he was finally granted a try-out and of course he made the broad jump team and in the finals, the bronze medal for third place went to him.

Walter Rothrock, '67 - Gold and bronze in rifle shooting. Rothrock, a well disciplined rifle shooter trained by his expert father, was sponsored by the Optimist Club of San Leandro. He beat veteran shooters from Italy, Sweden and other lands in the 300-meter free rifle competition. In the 50 meter small bore prone he won third place.

Richard Baraona, '65 - Participant in cycling. He was sponsored by a bicycle club, was the best cyclist among the Americans. Since most of the foreign contenders were veterans of Olympic competition and over 25 years of age, Baraona was only 16 years of age and still impressively placed 5th in the 35 kilometer individual chronometer, and 8th in the 1,000 meter sprint on the road.

1968 - The first National World Games for the Deaf Trials at Berkeley, California, August 9-10, proved the most satisfactory method of choosing representatives for the U.S. WGD Squad. The Berkeley Classic, as the Trials were called, was a series of competitions designed to help select the U.S. squad for next WGD and crowned champions in track and field, swimming, tennis, wrestling, table tennis, and volleyball. 325 deaf athletes participated in the Berkeley Classic. Deepest appreciation went to the following committee members for their endless hours of unselfish time in making possible the dream of the first National WGD Trials: Eric Malzkuhn, Donald Renzulli, Angela Watson, Leo Jacobs, Dean Swaim, General Chairman Ken Norton, John Galvan, Walter Thompson, Roger Munoz, Dave Fraley, Dan Lynch, Don Bullock, Mary Lou Shistar, George Shistar and Tom Berg, Track Head Coach and Technical Advisor.

Panting after the strenuous 400-meter hurdle run against the Russian ace, Don Lyons won silver medal. Still, he was the best American hurdler. This run placed second in the 10th International Games for the Deaf in Washington, D.C. in 1965.

1969 - CSD took great pride in sending six students and former students to the 11th World Games for the Deaf at Belgrade, Yugoslavia, August 9-16. Thirty-six nations were involved in the games. This was a far cry from the first assemblage in Paris in 1924, in which only six nations participated.

Harold Foster, '67 - Silver medal in high jump (6' 2 3/4"). Silver in 4x100 m relay (42.3) New American Record. Silver in 4x400 m relay (3:17.6) New American Record. Fourth in 200 m dash (22.3).

Ken Pedersen, '67 - Silver in 4x100 m relay (42.3) New American Record. Silver in 4x400 m relay (3:17.6) New American Record. Bronze in 400 m run (49.2) New American Record.

Cheryl Pierce, '65 - Member of the US volleyball team that was placed third. A new sport, volleyball, was introduced in WGD that year.

Ron Gough, '68 - Sixth place in Greco-Roman wrestling. Fifth place in freestyle wrestling.

Wesley Feria, '71 - Sixth place in Greco-Roman wrestling.

Richard Baraona, '65 - Silver in cycling, 35 kilometer time trial. Sixth place in 105 kilometer road race.

Walter Rothrock, '67 - Bronze in 300-meter free rifle shooting. Fourth place in team three positions of shooting. Sixth place in individual kneeling shooting. Participated in four other shooting events.

Ken Norton, '45 - Track sprint and relay coach.

1973 - Eight CSD graduates and a senior played a big part of the history made during the XII WGD at Malmo, Sweden, July 21-28.

Harold Foster, '67 - Gold medal in high jump, 201 c. (6' 7 1/8"), New World Record, breaking the old record set by a Russian in 1965.

Don Lyons, '65 - Gold with the US basketball team.

Sharp Shooter Walter Rothrock, American team's pride.

Richard Baraona, only 16, the US's best cyclist.

Tom Berg (left), USA track team head coach (assistant Dean of Student Affairs at Gallaudet University); Ken Norton, assistant track coach; Art Kruger, team director (sports writer); preparing the participants into shape at the training grounds in the Fanwood School for the Deaf in New York before departing for Belgrade, Yugoslavia.

Ken Pedersen, for a second time participated in the Deaf Olympics. Two silver medal winners in relays.

David Herdrich and Harold Stuart, (bottom left) scare to European and Middle East wrestlers.

Group of CSD participants. Walter Rothrock (left) Wesley Feria, Harold Foster, Ken Norton, Cheryl Pierce, Ron Gough, Ken Pedersen and Richard Baraona.

Gold medal winner in 1993 and 1997, cyclist Paul Wood.

Richard Baraona, '65 - Two silver in cycling.

David Herdrich, '73 - Bronze in Greco-Roman wrestling.

David Thompson, '69 - Bronze in pole vault.

Ronald Gough, '68 and Harold Stuart, '74 - Participants in freestyle wrestling.

Dean Swaim, '48 - Assistant coach in wrestling.

Ken Norton, '45 - Track sprint and relay coach.

1985 - Fremont Staff played a big part in the XV WGD at Los Angeles, July 10 to 20. The following are: *Track Commissioners:* Ken Norton, Emory Marsh, Mel Pedersen, Vaughn Hallada, Dane Norton, *Interpreter*; *Badminton Commissioners:* Dean Swaim, Donald Bullock; *Handball Commissioners:* Ron Stern, Gene Duve; *Volleyball Commissioners:* Bob Ellis, Ken Pedersen, Kathy Cantrell; *Water Polo Commissioner:* Scott Kramer; *Track Coach:* Jim Koetz; *Basketball Statistician:* Dr. Henry Klopping; *"Village" Newspaper Reporter and Helpers:* Bunny, Margaret, Chris, and Kimi Klopping.

Charles Holmes - Fifth place in men's volleyball.

1989 - Graduates of CSD accomplished in capturing gold, silver, and bronze medals at the XVI WGD in New Zealand in January.

Jon Schmitz, '89 - Two gold medals in cycling. Bronze in another cycling race.

Paul Wood, '87 - Silver in cycling sprint race. Bronze in road race.

Rod Pedersen, '86 - Silver with the US basketball team.

Mike Bauer, '89 - Silver in freestyle wrestling.

Norman Edwards, '86, Jason Ingraham, '83, Scott O,Donnell, '87 - Bronze with the US handball team.

Other CSD participants: Jude Castaneda, '89 in Greco-Roman wrestling; Justin Coleman, '88 in pole vault; Richard Machado, '81 in cycling; Daniel Rosenthal, '87 in the marathon; Walter Rothrock, '67 in sharpshooting; Merrill Samuels, '90 in track; Charles Holmes - Fourth place in men's volley ball. Ron Stern - Director of Team Development. Jack Lamberton - Logistics Officer.

1993 - American cycling hopes hinged on the performances of elite cyclists, Paul Wood and Jon Schmitz at the XVII WGD in Sofia, Bulgaria.

Paul Wood, '87 - Gold medal in 1000m sprint in cycling. Silver in 35km time trials in cycling. Fourth place in 50km individual point. Fifteenth in 100km road race.

Jon Schmitz, '89 - Silver medal in 1000m sprint. Seventh in 100 km road race.

Scott O'Donnell, '87, Norman Edwards, '86 - Seventh place with the US handball team.

JoDee Dike - Gold medal in womens' basketball.

Charles Homes - Silver medal in men's volleyball and honored as a Flag Bearer leading the American athletes in the opening ceremony.

Alex Ash, '84, Member of the U.S. cycling team.

Ron Stern - Director of Team Development.

Jack Lamberton - Logistics Officer.

1997 - Paul Wood, '87 - Gold in 1000 m match sprint. Silver in 100 km road race in the World Championship in Lille, France. Honored as AAAD Athlete of the Year.

1997 - Paul Wood, '87 - Gold in 100 km road race. Gold in 50 km point race. Silver in 1000 m sprint race.

JoDee Dike - Bronze medal in women's team bowling.

Charles Holmes - Fourth place in men's volleyball.

Ron Stern - Director of Team Development.

Jack Lamberton - Team Director

Earl Ruffa, '41, skiing down a mountain slope in Portillo, Chile, South America on August 31, 1959. (Note the outline of the top of the mountain in this photograph is similar to the profile of this skier.)

DEAF WORLD WINTER GAMES

Quite a few skiers from CSD participated in the Deaf World Winter Games which were first run in Seefeld, Austria in 1949. In 1967, the Sixth International Winter Games was held at Berchtesgaden, Germany where Earl Ruffa, the first CSD product was on the United States team. At age 45, the oldest on the team, he raced in the giant slalom, one of 47 competitors. He was 30th with a time of 2:18.6. Ruffa built a chalet at Donner Ski Ranch where he still lives.

In 1979, the CSD graduate and student who raced in the Winter Games in Meribel, France, were Leslie Romak, '76 and Douglas Dickinson, '81. At the skiing tryouts in Keystone, Colorado, in 1978, Romak finished first in the women's giant slalom and slalom downhill. Dickinson, only 16 years old, placed fourth in the men's giant slalom and downhill.

In 1983, Dickinson ventured in the Italian Winter Games, racing in the giant slalom and super giant slalom. As assistant coach and technician, he continued being a member of the USA skiing team in Banff, Canada, 1991, Yllas, Finland, 1995, and Davos, Switzerland, 1999.

Douglas Dickinson racing down the slope in the Winter Games in France in 1979.

Motivated and inspirited elementary basketball team of 1998. Front row, left: Weston Arthurs, Mark Grossinger, Sal Guido, Tim Miller. Austyn Randle. Middle row: Edgar Abrica, Justin Jackerson, Zac West, Shawn Smith, Judio Amador, Wesley Singleton. Back row: Coach Charles Holmes, Sam Phillips, Alfie Parker, Carlton Williams, Chase Whitten, Adrian DeHoyos, Luis Ledezma, Assistant Coach Nino Ecarma.

ELEMENTARY SPORTS ACTIVITIES

Both elementary girls and boys participate daily in an after school exercise and physical fitness program. Team sports include soccer, basketball and softball. Sports competition with public schools have sprouted dramatically since the school moved to Fremont.

The following account is one of the most exciting elementary sports events. In 1998, the CSD's Eaglettes, girls soccer team, glided to the Fremont Youth Soccer League's Championship in the Under 10 Years Old Division with a 14-0 record. Undefeated in the league, the Eaglettes fell only one victory short of winning the regional championship. This team was considered the CSD's best soccer team in the school's history. The coaches, Valerie Herbold and Doralynn Folse, who are also teachers at CSD, considered the team's success came from years of working together and everyone's commitment to do their best.

Most of the time, cottage counselors take up coaching duties during the after school activities.

Middle School Sports Activities

The students of the Middle School are customarily eagerly involved in sports activities in order to be better prepared for the high school sports programs. The boys' sports are flag football, basketball, wrestling and softball. Girls are involved in soccer, volleyball, basketball and cheerleading. The Middle School residential department implemented more sports programs after CSD moved to Fremont. The Fremont School District welcomed CSD's participation in the district's after school sports program. Middle School is the best time to entice new enrollees to play sports and become aware of all the opportunities out there.

The 1900-2000 CSD Wrestling Team: (back row) Amandeep Girn, manager, Colin Hermann, manager, Timothy Gough, coach, Mal Grossinger, head coach, Cindy Ramirez, manager Jvita Figueroa, manager. (Middle row) Sean Ryan, Ern Williams, Sam Phillips, Jared Luke, Wyatt Baldwin, Eric Jimdra, Alfie Merino, Davey DeHoyos, Justn Jackerson, Eddie Riddle. (Front row) Nikolas Bryant, Sal Guido, Shawn Smith, Weston Arthurs, Egar Abrica, Luis Guerrero, Kenneth McPherson, Julio Amador, Zac West, Mark Grossinger Nick Comegna, Austyn Randle.

Young Wrestling Squad Makes CSD History

The Popularity of wrestling continues as an after school activity in the middle school. The 1999-2000 squad of 24 wrestlers emerged as the best team in CSD history. Under coaches, Mal Grossinger and Tim Gough, the team won the championship title in the Mendenhall Tournament in which they competed against 17 much larger schools.

In May 2000, at the end of the season, eight of CSD's middle school wrestlers made their way to the State Wrestling Championships for Kids in Fresno. The tournament was an awesome experience for these young grapplers at the 15,000 seat arena. The coaches stated that many coaches with other experienced teams were impressed by the excellent job the CSD grapplers did in the tournament, considering it was CSD's first entry at the state level.

Tenaya Herbold was the only girl on the team, occasionally beating some of the boys during practices. During competitions, Herbold competed only against other girls. She beat every girl except one in the matches.

Weston Arthurs and Shawn Smith remained undefeated throughout the season before the state championship. 

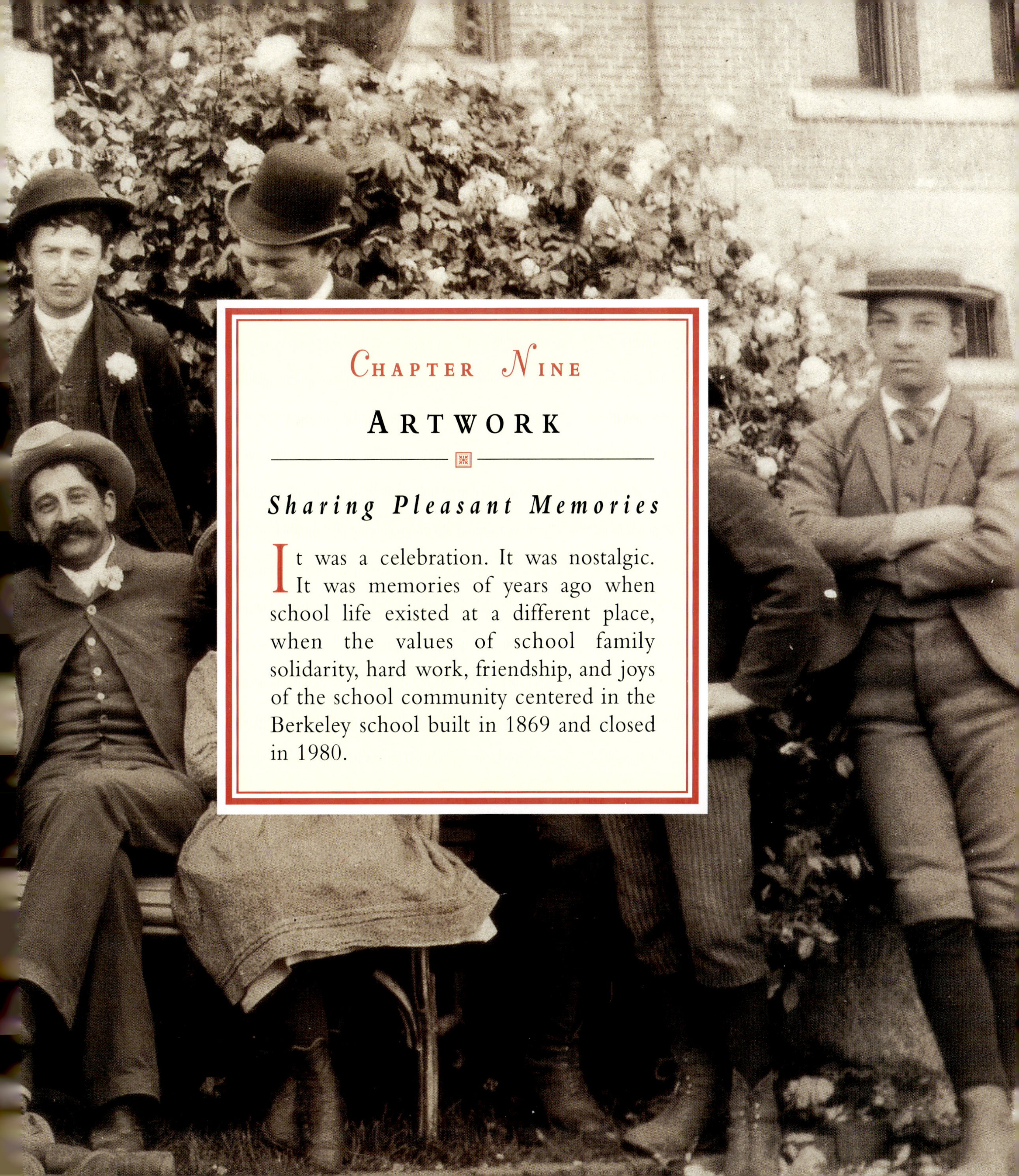

Chapter Nine

Artwork

Sharing Pleasant Memories

It was a celebration. It was nostalgic. It was memories of years ago when school life existed at a different place, when the values of school family solidarity, hard work, friendship, and joys of the school community centered in the Berkeley school built in 1869 and closed in 1980.

Like cherished memorabilia are the CSD treasured pieces that cling tenaciously to the past. They belong more to the past of the Berkeley school than the present, preserved in time like fossils. Yet, surprisingly, all the works of art from the Berkeley school have harmonized well with the settings on the Fremont campus where they have been installed.

On a 1980 summer day, the statue was lifted flawlessly from the Berkeley campus before a few surprised witnesses as it was thought the statue was anchored to the base.

At the new home, The Bear Hunt *being embedded securely in front of the CSD entrance before a big crowd of students and staff members.*

Preceding spread: Our noteworthy figure—Theophilus d'Estrella. Young student of CSD in San Francisco (insets left to right). A member of the Sierra Club. A popular teacher at the Berkeley School. Elder faculty member. Amidst his students (spread).

The Bear Hunt Statue

On December 5, 1980, one happy occasion was a big crowd of students and staff members watching The Bear Hunt statue being installed in the cavity filled with cement. The cheers from the gathering testified that the famous statue was saved and brought cherished memories from the old campus to the new campus. Since CSD was in the process of moving to Fremont, the University of California had tried every avenue to retain the statue at the Berkeley campus, for the "bears" of the statue would fit with the University's mascot, *Golden Bear*. It was also reported that some students of either Stanford University or the University of California in the 1950s contemplated the possibility of lifting and snatching the statue. At that time, the Indian symbol was the mascot of Stanford University. So, the statue would be a piece of cake for the Indians.

CSD outsmarted them by acting fast. Immediately after the school closed for the summer in 1980, a truck with a tall crane came in and within minutes the crane effortlessly lifted the statue. It was quite a surprise to a few witnesses that the statue was not attached to a platform at all. It could be picked up with ease if anyone would dare to do it. Now the statue is secured safely at the Fremont School. The statue area is a public plaza where students are dropped off or picked up by parents and individuals meet before attending activities on the campus.

The Bear Hunt by Douglas Tilden, one of America's noted works of art, had been situated in front of the old Educational Building from 1895 to 1950. It was then moved to a small plaza between the administration building and the residence hall for intermediate boys in 1951. Douglas Tilden, the deaf sculptor, was a graduate of the Berkeley School, in the Class of 1879. He studied at the University of California and was an instructor for a while at CSD, Berkeley, before leaving to study sculpture in Paris. *The Bear Hunt* is among a number of Tilden's works, mostly in San Francisco. A book, *Douglas Tilden: The Man and his Legacy*, by Mildred Albronda, is recommended.

THE NATIONAL GAME

The Art Exhibit of Foreign Masters opened in San Francisco's Shreve Art Rooms on February 28, 1891. Amongst the pieces of art loaned for this exhibition, such as Rembrandt, Monet, Delacroix and others, the only work by an American artist in the display was Douglas Tilden's *Baseball Player* statue or *The National Game,* as it was originally named. The *Baseball Player* was the principal attraction and well received in the display. William E. Brown of the Southern Pacific Railroad purchased the statue for $1,700 and donated it to San Francisco for Golden Gate Park. The unveiling ceremony occurred on July 8, 1891. The statue in bronze and over life-size still stands in the park by John F. Kennedy Drive.

In 1999, the new pedestal for the *Baseball Player* was enhanced by the San Francisco Public Works. The base looks appealing as shown in the picture (left). Among the artifacts, mementos, paintings and documents in the CSD museum, a bronze statuette, 21 1/2" tall (left), is proudly displayed. Possession of the statuette was made possible by the donations from the Donald Parodi Memorial Charitable Trust and the Friends of CSD.

The art deco bird bath situated outside in the quadrangle by the side of the auditorium in the Berkeley school is well remembered by the students from 1932 to 1980. Now it is resting in the front of the Little Theater.

MEMENTOS AT THE LITTLE THEATER

At the entrance of the Little Theater at the Fremont School, the windows in the tall doors are decorated with metal figures of the fox and grapes from Aesop's Fables. They were created for the school auditorium in1932 by artists from the Work Projects Administration. The theme of the fox and grapes was based on one of the twenty-one classic books adapted by the other WPA workers. Naturally, the preservation of the theater door grilles has thrilled the alumni who had admired them at the Berkeley School.

The art deco bird bath situated outside in the quadrangle by the side of the auditorium in the Berkeley School is well remembered by the children of the 1930s - 1970s. During recess time or after class hours, they took pleasure in playing around and even climbing over the bird bath. Now it is resting in front of the Little Theater and it keeps reminding the alumni of their happy childhood.

In 1994, for the first time, portraits of all superintendents (called principals in the old times) were assembled and now are hanging on the wooden panel walls in the lobby of the Little Theater. Most of these 20 x 24 photographs were enlarged from small photographs and printed in black and white. In contrast, following the current technology, the photograph of Dr. Henry Klopping appears in color.

Mementos in the Library Atrium

The spirit of *Rip Van Winkle* by Washington Irving can touch one's heart whenever the dwarf-like, odd-looking personage bowling at ninepins, is visited in the atrium of the CSD library. With the dwarf is a bowling ball built by WPA workers in the 1930s. They were situated at the stairway of the elementary boys' dormitory, Runde Hall, in the Berkeley School. Another object with the dwarf in the atrium is an elephant created from *The Jungle Book* by Rudyard Kipling. At CSD Berkeley, elementary boys often climbed over and "rode" on the elephant and fantasized of being Toomai on Elephant Kala Nag. The theme of these objects emerged from the adapted classic books.

Part of the elephant was damaged during the move to Fremont. Fortunately, the employees of the CSD maintenance department were capable enough to reconstruct the damaged elephant and preserve its memories.

The spirit of Rip Van Winkle is carried on from the Berkeley school to the Fremont school.

Photographs and Other Objects

The photographs of CSD graduates, formerly displayed in the Berkeley dining room, are stored in the Archives. The last five years of framed graduate pictures hang in the Fremont dining room. The most recent one is exchanged every year for the oldest, then that goes to the Archives.

The above works of art are only a few among hundreds of others so that it is not possible to enumerate them all in this book. Visitors are always welcome at the museum and the archives. To the people of CSD, these objects are a living link to the past - a time machine- creating a lasting memory.

The only other memento we wished we could take from Berkeley was the football field below the hill with the "CSD" letters on it. From the football field was the world's best panoramic view of the city of San Francisco, the Bay Area, and two famed bridges which could be gazed at breathlessly beneath the blazing sunset.

The "Old-timer's Gallery" in the library exhibits the long view of the Berkeley campus (left) and the revolving cases of the photographs of the athletic teams from 1889 to 2000 (middle).

The CSD Historical Museum and Archives

Circa 1910, Charles Perry (left) and Theophilus d'Estrella were the "curators" of the museum on the third floor of the Educational Building. Numerous items from the other countries were presented to CSD in gratitude of their officials' visit.

After one hundred forty years, CSD has grown rich in history and overflowed with unique events. CSD sensed a need to treasure and to house historical documents and artifacts by creating a Historical Museum and Archives, for they deserve recognition and vigilant scrutiny.

The original museum was developed as a result of Theophilus d'Estrella's keen interest in collecting artifacts and documents. The museum was neglected after he died in 1929 and collected dust until the demolition of the educational building. The historical objects were then packed and stored in the basement of the new administration building in 1950.

The CSD Historical Museum opened in the basement of the new wing attached to the high school building in 1960 with a few displays of artifacts among the piles of unopened boxes, waiting for its dream of a new historical museum to transform it into a reality. Such a scene aroused curiosity among students and visitors to inquire about the history of CSD.

Was Tilden actually deaf? Who was Wilkinson? So many questions begged to be answered. These boxes were a link to the past. They needed to be opened to satisfy those questions. How could one go about setting up a museum? It seemed to be such a huge task that the project had been postponed. Moving to Fremont halted the progress of the museum in Berkeley.

After years of lying dormant, the concept of a historical museum in Fremont was renewed by a group of volunteers in 1993 under the guidance of resourceful Ralph Neesam, retiree from the CSD staff. After an extensive renovation for two years, the "new" CSD Historical Museum reopened for public view. The transformation was magnificent. The reaction of visitors to the museum during the Alumni Reunion in July 1995, proved the museum renovation project to be a great success.

The CSD Historical Museum merges a museum room with an archives room to preserve artifacts, documents, photographs and other cultural objects dating from 1860 to the present in five units of a mobile storage system and ten file cabinets.

Under Ralph Neesam's leadership and directorship, the CSD museum at the Fremont school was reorganized with a group of volunteers.

The Douglas Tilden Gallery in the Foyer

At the entrance of the museum, in a small white foyer, the two walls exhibit silver framed black and white photographs of incredible sculptures by Douglas Tilden, better known as *The Nineteenth Century Sculptor*, and "the father of sculpture on the Pacific Coast" in his time. Among the photographs, a mask of a *Medusa* stands out on a threshold; it is a 1994 white plaster copy from the mold of an 1894 original. Below the *Medusa's* head is a colored photograph of the Stone House in Oakland, 1894, showing six *Medusa* heads on the portico above the front entrance. On one of the walls, a group of photographs depicts many monumental sculptures presently scattered throughout the city of San Francisco. Those sculptures are masterpieces that CSD would love to have in its possession. The only Tilden sculpture CSD has in its possession is the Bear Hunt statue located at the entrance of CSD campus which is the pride of the deaf community.

In 1912 Tilden created frames of *Twelve Stages of Man* for the water fountain at Lakeside Park in Oakland, California. One original frame of the fourth stage of two males in a stance position came into Dr. Byron B. Burnes' possession which he later generously donated to the CSDF Museum. It can be seen currently on the commode in the foyer under the black and white photographs.

This is the fourth stage of Twelve Stages of Man *frames created by Douglas Tilden.*

The Historic Museum

The historic room gives an impression of entering a baroque-like atmosphere, rich with massive Neo-Gothic mahogany bookcases (built in 1891 by the deaf students, talented cabinetmakers) on the north, east and south sides of the room. A large-scale artwork dominates the space on the east side; it is an oil painting of a haunting winter morning scene titled *Matin d' Hiver* (1896), painted by Granville Seymour Redmond, a well known deaf impressionist artist. This painting was exhibited at a Paris salon during Redmond's four years in Paris. Above two other Redmond paintings is a charming photograph of twenty-seven-year-old Redmond. An interesting note is that Douglas Tilden was one of his teachers and that they were roommates in Paris in 1893-94 pursuing their careers. In the center of that wall is a tall slender bookcase filled with Theophilus Hope d'Estrella's collection of philosophy, anatomy, and literature such as Don Quixote and Guy de Maupassant volumes. They reflect

The entrance of the CSD historical museum in the library.

Granville Redmond's oil painting (bottom) of a haunting winter morning scene titled Matin d'Hiver.

Theophilus d'Estrella often walked long distances along California's rolling hills with the heavy camera equipment to capture the ideal settings or the ideal mood. The photographs were his work.

him as a voracious reader. The next section demonstrated his other talents in sketching, sculpture and photography. Several black and white photographs show his art class in 1887 where students considered him a strict teacher, a young male student (father of Ken and Earl Norton and also a good friend of d'Estrella) sitting at the bottom of the steps with an Irish setter dog and puppies, and a group of girls in long dresses and hats sitting and standing on a hill overlooking the city of Berkeley. In those days when the cameras were bulky and heavy and the films were larger than nowadays, d'Estrella often walked long distances along California's rolling hills with the heavy equipment to capture the ideal settings or the ideal mood. At his request, the female deaf students pulled up their long dresses to climb up the hills and pose for the camera at the top overlooking the campus below. Apparently, their reward was listening to his stories, for he was a great storyteller and a popular conversationalist. Above those photographs is a large oil painting of d'Estrella attired in a smock, slightly bent with age and in a pensive mood.

One of the CSD Museum's most precious artifacts is d'Estrella's lantern projector that was saved from a fire that destroyed his five cameras and over two thousand negatives.

In front of the huge bookcase on the north side, a large desk is situated near the center of the room. It is where Patricia "Suzie" (Marshburn) Jacobs, '63, works as the museum coordinator, always quick to respond to a request by a visitor or CSD Museum and Archives volunteer. She pounds information and data into her computer at the west side and at times she pauses to look up at the collection of Granville Redmond's forty paintings, attached to the wall with earthquake proof bolts. They are certainly one man's passion.

"Deaf people are extremely interested in their past."

Ralph Neesam
a retired staff member

These impressive Neo-Gothic cabinets were created by the CSD students of 1891 for the library..

Nowadays the cabinets store the valuable books, periodicals, copies of The California News *and numerous records.*

An elephant from the stairway of Runde Hall in the Berekeley school (top) is now situated in the atrium of the CSD library (above).

The silence is often interrupted by a sudden appearance of several volunteers entering from the Archives to check the records of *The California News* for the specific names or dates for the old photographs. Helen Barber, a dedicated volunteer, compiled the records and photographs related to the three giant artists, Tilden, Redmond, and d'Estrella. Ray Rasmus was a big help with the upholstery work on the historic chairs and the framework on many of Redmond's paintings. The other volunteers, Donald Ingraham, Eugene Rianda, and Ken Norton, labored in collecting the CSD sport team photographs which have been placed in revolving cases. Helen Chism focused on selecting the most highlighted statements from Dr. Elwood Stevenson's correspondence files. Audree Norton concentrated on organizing the records, programs, and photographs of the CSD's annual spring plays and holidays plays that are now filed orderly in three draws of a file cabinet in the Archives.

Bernadette Attletweed often opened the doors of the Neo-Gothic cabinets on the south side and returned the old record of the students dating back to1860. Next to this record book is a small white bust of *Abbe de l'Eppee* and a first edition of the *Abbe De L'Eppee and Other Early Teachers of the Deaf* with a printed price of seventy-five cents on its cover. These are two prized possessions. The third object is an achievement award of a green marble plaque inscribed Laurent Clerc Award emblem that was awarded to Dr. Burnes in 1981 by Gallaudet University for outstanding social contribution by a deaf person in the interests of deaf people. The award is a fitting tribute to Dr. Byron B. Burnes. Above those artifacts are European books on deafness in French and German languages. Ralph Neesam and Ken Norton were the "advisers" to the volunteers and assigned them to specific tasks which were often tedious. Sorting through hundreds of old photographs without names or dates, trying to solve the undocumented mystery, and putting the delicate things in safe places could be frustrating and time consuming. Once an accurate name or date was discovered, the volunteer would smile with delight. These volunteers are the key people for preserving the priceless history of CSD. The other volunteers who came to the museum doing various assignments from time to time were Elmarie Barlow, David Fraley, Lester Rudy, Joyce Ingraham, Robert Schmidt, James McKee, Lee Ann Poynor, Roger Munoz, Carola Rasmus and Janet Pratt.

The historic museum has impressive cases that have exhibited an ancient hearing aid, correspondence between Dr. Wilkinson and Dr. Edward Miner Gallaudet, President of Gallaudet University, and many other interesting items. Several Redmond paintings, Tilden's sculpture pieces and some artifacts are displayed around the campus for public view. Most permanent collections were donated by the alumni, staff, and families of deceased alumni.

An odd object must be mentioned to complete the description of the museum. It is a five hundred year old hearing aid donated in 1978 by Alva G. Starr, retired principal of the Oakland school system. He made several trips to Costa Rica on digging expeditions, searching for pre-Columbian artifacts. The aid was used by Indians when Christopher Columbus discovered America.

Suzie Jacobs, museum coordinator, does the voluminous work to assemble the photographs, valuable documents, artifacts, publications, and books in the secure places in the museum and archives. She also coordinates the assignments among the volunteers. In this picture, Suzie Jacobs moves manually the mobile storage system that saves up huge space for storage purposes.

The Archives

The entrance gallery at the left leads to the Archives, where rows of ten metal file cabinets and five units of mobile storage system cabinets are organized. The cabinets provide optimal storage facilities for documents, photographs, artifacts and others objects. The mobile storage system is one of the main attractions. It often raises visitors' eyebrows with delight when the cabinets move swiftly and flawlessly at the mere command of one finger on its knob.

At one side of the room stands a row of file cabinets where the lives of most deaf students, staff, and administrators are chronicled alphabetically. Only Tilden, d'Estrella and Redmond each has his own file cabinet drawer.

One large map drawer is reserved for oversized photographs and posters. One drawer shows the *Proclamations of Deaf Awareness* dated from 1976 to 1999 along with yellowed newspaper articles and blueprints of both CSD schools in Berkeley and Fremont.

Nearby a light fixture in the shape of crescent moon appears suspended from the ceiling. It used to hang in the stairway of Runde Hall for elementary girls in Berkeley. Below the moon is a green wooden cabinet. Julian Singleton remembers that many pieces of furniture at CSD in Berkeley were painted green, apparently a favorite color during the 1930s.

All the objects, letters, papers, books, documents, and maps of school history have been inventoried by the volunteers since 1993.

Perhaps the heart of the CSD Historical Museum and the Archives is a living history told by volunteers and visitors who grew up at CSD in Berkeley. Their stories reveal the achievements, hilarious days, mischievous and heart-breaking experiences with joy, appreciation and pride in the CSD history.

The hammer inside the upper part of the tower hit the bell six times (six o'clock) in a quivering effect that prompted the students to roar in delight at the unveiling ceremony.

Historical Bell Rings Again....

On the evening of May 3, 1994, at the unveiling ceremony, the Bell Tower was alive with CSD students swarming around its base with their hands on the sides and eyes peering upward. The hammer inside the upper part of the tower hit the gong six times in a quivering effect that prompted the students to roar in delight.

Before the unveiling ceremony, a dedication banquet was held for the Bell Tower donors who contributed $250 and up to the project. A dramatic moment occurred when Chairperson Ken Norton asked the hearing people to wave their white napkins to let the deaf donors know when the Bell Tower hammer struck. The door was left open to allow the echo of the chimes enter the room. At six, the hearing people stopped eating and signaled with their napkins in the air. In accordance, the deaf people synchronized in waving their napkins. It was to herald the existence of the Bell Tower. After the dinner they all joined the crowd on the slope of the amphitheater below the Bell Tower to celebrate the special event, the dedication program regarding the success of "reactivating the Bell."

In 1980 the CSD staff collected a few valuable items in the Berkeley school, such as the Strauss bell from the tower, the Bear Hunt statue, decorative door grilles, the chandeliers and some concrete statuettes from the campus and delivered them to the new school in Fremont. Soon afterwards, the bell was placed in the museum by the library.

Inquiring about the bell idling away its time in the museum, the citizens of the Deaf community discussed with the school staff the options of the new tower to house the historic bell. This exciting idea promoted the California Alumni Association to establish a committee consisting of George Attletweed, Larry Pratt, Julian Singleton, and Dr. Henry Klopping, adviser, with Ken Norton as chairperson. The first step was to contact Harry Jacobs, Jr., an architect and a former president of California Council, the American Institute of Architects, who in turn started the idea of having students from the six accredited universities of architecture in California to help with the design. Several of the requirements for a diagram was to design a tower to house the bell and to include a clock on each of four sides with some regard to aesthetic effect and, above all, visual effect. In addition, the tower was to be designed to harmonize with the CSD environment. Ninety-five candidates applied, and their diagrams entered a contest that was to be judged by a panel of architects and representatives of CSD at the Asilomar Grounds at Pacific Grove. Ken Norton said, "I admired those young architects' enthusiasm and creativity that put the judges in a difficult position in selecting the first, second, and third prizes." One design by Janith Johnson, a graduate student in architecture at Cal Poly Ponoma, won the first place as "the architectonic perfection of the new tower." The design allowed the bell to move down and up every hour like an elevator. This is visual perfection for the deaf students. Everyone admired the original design but it was sadly realized that such a design would be at great expense. It appeared necessary for the bell to remain immobile and for a hammer to be substituted to hit the side of the bell.

The bell rested in the CSD library during the Alumni Reunion in 1986 to inspire a fund raising project to house the bell. It was built in Baltimore, Maryland, in 1889.

The diagrams of towers were part of ninety-five diagrams designed by young architects from the accredited universities of architecture in California to house the CSD bell. The diagrams in the contest were judged by a panel of architects and representatives of CSD at the Asilomar Grounds in Pacific Grove, California.

Success of the Fund Raising Campaign

At the California Alumni Association convention in San Jose in 1986, Norton proposed the project construction following the basic principle of Johnson's architecture with a formal fundraising drive. It was unanimously agreed as it was a worthy cause. For the first fundraising event, the result was a huge surprise to the members who contributed cash as well as pledges. The fundraising amount reached as high as $20,000 in a single night, which probably has never happened before among deaf citizens. The fundraising success was a reflection of fantastic enthusiasm. It proved that the idea of a tower construction was fully supported by the alumni and friends.

In 1890, a bell was placed in the tower on the Educational Building on the Berkeley campus. It was said that the symbol of the bell was meaningful. . . perhaps a meaningful gesture from the philanthropist's sincere interest in the Deaf children.

Why is the bell so special? A donation of $5,000 was presented to CSD by the Louis Strauss family which is related to Levi Strauss, the founder of the company in San Francisco. Then a bell was secured through the fund in 1890 and was placed in the tower on the Educational Building on the Berkeley campus. It was said that the symbol of the bell was meaningful. . . perhaps a meaningful gesture from the philanthropist's sincere interest in the Deaf children. A dormitory was named after Strauss during that time. So Ken Norton marched off to Levi Strauss's office in San Francisco and had a meeting with Myra Chow, manager of community affairs. Eventually after maintaining communication through letters and telephone calls, Levi Strauss Company agreed to donate $10,000 to the Bell Tower project. In addition, the committee campaigned for fundraising donations through letters to the CSD alumni and friends, with an explanation that the donors, names would be engraved on plaques on the lower side of the Bell Tower.

> ***" For years at Berkeley, the works of the bell were invisible, but now they are visible in Fremont."***
>
> Harry Jacobs, Jr.
>
> 1995

The Design and Construction Plans for the Tower

A representative of Schulmerich Carillons, Inc., Dick Lemington, noticed some articles on the Bell Tower project in the *San Jose Mercury News* and the *Argus* and quickly contacted Norton with a proposal that the Schulmerich Company in Sellerville, Pennsylvania construct the Bell Tower. After a number of negotiations, Norton discovered that the Schulmerich Company's design would not meet the California Building codes which was imperative for earthquake safety. Designing and Engineering Systems (DES) of Fremont was the most logical choice for the design blueprint job. After the office of State Architect approved the DES designs, Beals Martine Company of Milpitas was selected through bidding to undertake the construction of the foundation.

This bell was not visible at the Berkeley school as it was placed inside the tower. The bell is now visible at the Fremont school

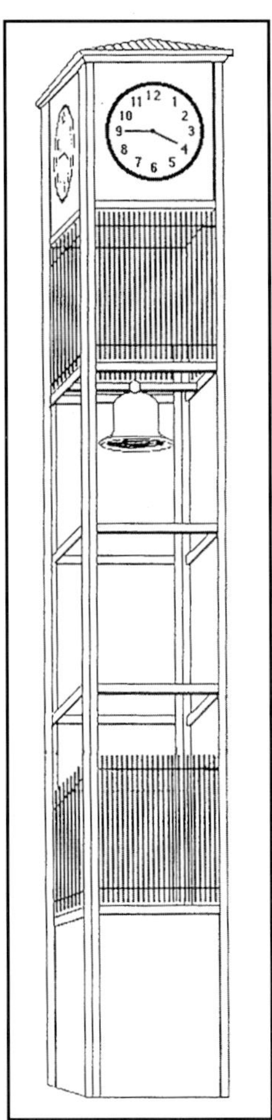

The Bell Tower project had become so huge that it demanded that more people be involved. At that point, it was sad to acknowledge that George Attletweed, better known as "ATTY," beloved by the Deaf community, had passed away and his wife Bernadette Attletweed, was asked to take his place on the committee. Joyanne Burdett and Gilmer Lentz joined the committee. The committee with the guidance of Dr. Henry Klopping often met to help make final decisions on the tower structure and solve numerous problematic issues. Barrett Smith, chief of CSD plant operations, who worked closely with Norton for the last two years of the project, was an effective instrument as liaison between the five different firms that were part of the tower construction.

Ground Breaking Ceremony

On the cool afternoon of May 15, 1992, a throng consisting of CSD staff, students and supporters stood on the sidewalk by the library to witness the groundbreaking ceremony. Dr. Klopping was eloquent in praising "the spirit of the deaf community and their effort in bringing the Bell Tower project into reality." Norton heralded the ceremony as "a big step forward toward our goal." The exciting moment came when the committees took turns in ramming the "gold" shovel into the dirt. The audience cheered, clapping and waving their hands up in the air.

Accumulatuing Cost

Due to the California Building code, Schulmerich's design was not accepted, thus the new design to meet the code caused the cost to increase. The reason for this was that the new code required that steel columns be thicker, with stronger reinforcement, and a special welding for the construction of such a tower. The total increase was $26,000.

The original committee was formed in 1986. Left to right: Larry Pratt, Julian Singleton, Ken Norton, Chairperson, George Attletweed. Dr Henry Klopping was the advisor of the committee. Later Berna Attletweed, Joyanne Burdett and Gil Lentz joined the committee.

Schulmerich finally got the green light to construct the tower and clock mechanism in Campbellsville, Kentucky. Another additional cost of $13,000 went to the inspection of the construction process of the tower in Kentucky. The Consolidated Testing Company in Pleasanton, California, sent a state licensed inspector to supervise the assembling of the tower for three weeks.

Arrival and Erection of the Tower

On the morning of December 3, 1993, at 8:00 AM, the brown steel tower lying on the bed of a truck arrived at the campus entrance. People flocked and filled the sides of the route where the Tower on the truck bed proceeded slowly in silence, passing the Bear Hunt statue. Near the site the crew men assembled the four clocks and the Bell inside the upper part of the Tower. The crane lifted and moved the tower with its swinging arm over to the top of the hill. The Tower squatted on the concrete table in a slow ascent, complete with roof and the bolts secured. Finally, the Tower arrived and was erected with pride. All of a sudden, the process was completed at 4:00 PM. It became a new landmark because of its historical significance.

> ***" We see four moons up in the sky. Sometimes we see five moons!"***
>
> A student
> 1994

On the morning of December 3, 1993, the crane lifted and moved the Tower with its swinging arm over to the top of the hill. The Tower squatted on the concrete slab in a slow ascent and the bolts secured. Finally, the Tower arrived and was erected with pride.

The Granite Marker and the Bronze Plaques

On the morning of the dedication day of the Bell Tower, May 3, 1994, the granite rock with the bronze plaque was erected at the foot of the slope from the Tower. The inscription on the plaque epitomized the account of the historical Bell and the dedication of the Tower as following:

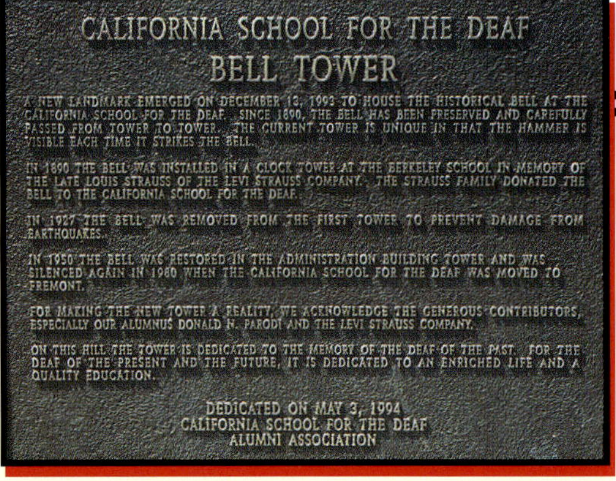

California School for the Deaf
Bell Tower

A new landmark emerged on December 13, 1993 to house the historical Bell at the California School for the Deaf. Since 1890, the Bell has been preserved and carefully passed from tower to tower. The current tower is unique in that the hammer is visible each time it strikes the Bell.

In 1890 the Bell was installed in a clock tower at the Berkeley School in memory of the late Louis Strauss of the Levi Strauss Company. The Strauss family donated the Bell to the California School for the Deaf.

In 1927 the Bell was removed from the first tower to prevent damage from earthquakes.

In 1950 the Bell was restored in the administration building tower and was silenced again in 1980 when the California School for the Deaf moved to Fremont.

For making the new Tower a reality, we acknowledge the generous contributors, especially our alumnus Donald N. Parodi and the Levi Strauss Company.

On this hill the Tower is dedicated to the memory of the Deaf of the Past. For the Deaf of the Present and the Future, it is dedicated to an enriched life and a quality education.

DEDICATED ON MAY 3, 1994
CALIFORNIA SCHOOL FOR THE DEAF
ALUMNI ASSOCIATION

Donald N. Parodi

It is Donald N. Parodi who donated the lion's share to make the 45-foot tower possible. His contribution was 50% of the total contributions from all other sources. In remembrance of Don Parodi, his portrait now hangs by the entrance of the CSD museum. In addition, it is to recognize Don Parodi's great love of the school and his most generous contribution to the Donald N. Parodi Memorial Charitable Trust.

Unveiling Ceremony of the Plaque

On July 1, 1995, a great crowd attending the CSD Alumni Reunion, June 30 through July 3, witnessed the very inspiring unveiling ceremony of the plaque with the names of the Bell Tower Project Fund donors of $250 or more.

The second plaque of donors, who made contributions later, was added during an Alumni Day picnic on July 19, 1997.

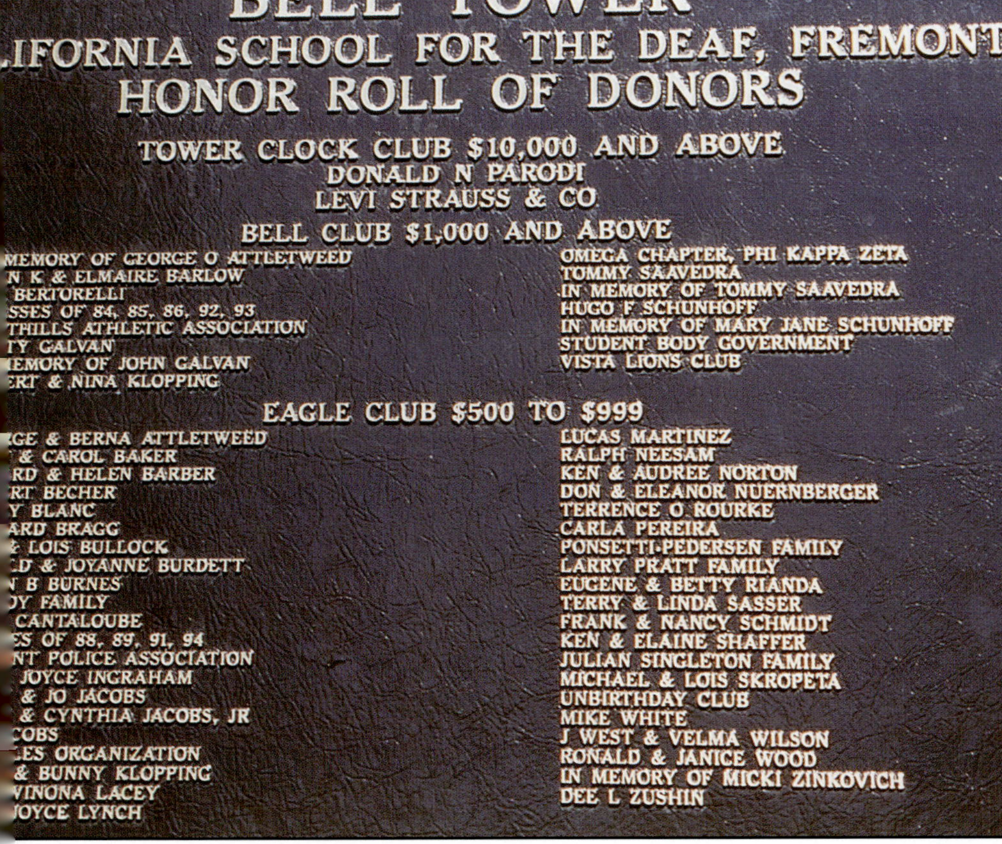

This is part of the plaque listing the donors who contributed money to the Bell Tower project that made the construction of the tower possible. Below is the entire plaque at the base of the tower.

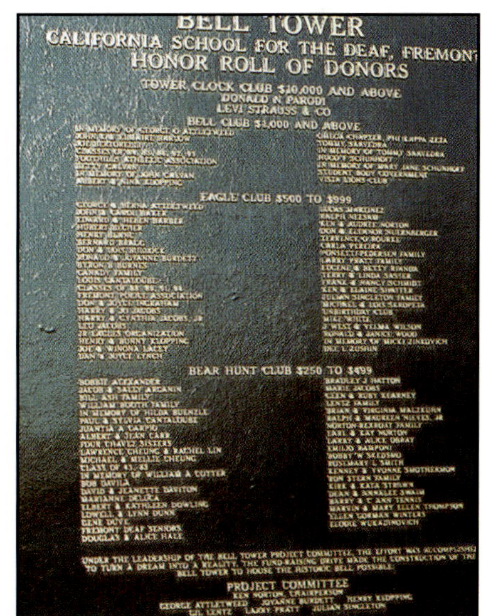

The electromagnetic hammer is assembled with the old bell (1890) at the Bell Tower at the Fremont school. This device is designed to ring the old cast Bell by electromechanically striking the Bell at the sound bow, on the outside wall of the Bell casting. The vibrations of the Bell striking can be felt explicitly by holding hands on the base walls. CSD students have enjoyed the feelings of the strikings!

Evolution of the Alumni Association

In June 1873, once the first students, Theophilus d'Estrella and Charles Smith, graduated from the California School for the Deaf, the CSD Alumni originated. Although the alumni had flourished, the alumni association was not organized until the 1940s. For several years between 1930 and 1938, the annual alumni picnic on the Fourth of July was hosted by CSD in Berkeley.

According to the October 28, 1905 issue of *The California News*, on October 22, 1905, nine deaf people met in the studio of Douglas Tilden, '79, discussing the possibility of the organization of the alumni association. Those present were Mr. and Mrs. Douglas Tilden, '94, Mr. and Mrs. James Howson (Bessie Hinman, '04), Miss Florence Alexander, '97, Mr. Doney Goodrich, '92, Mr. Edward Lohmeyer, '91, Mr. Connelly and Mr. Theophilus d'Estrella, '73. Douglas Tilden pointed out in the meeting that they could not expect to see their ultimate goal for the association immediately after its organization. He emphasized every beginning had its difficulties and it would take time and patience for an organization to develop. Tilden was elected chairman. Apparently, their dream did not become a reality. It was believed that the same group's interest was diverted to the California Association of the Deaf and the San Francisco Division, No. 53, National Fraternal Society of the Deaf (NFSD). At that time, both organizations were considered essential to the welfare of deaf people. The California Association of the Deaf was established in December 1906. The San Francisco Division No. 53, NFSD, was installed on May 7, 1915. The Berkeley Division No. 79, NFSD was established in 1920. As these organizations offered deaf members an exciting social life, the enthusiasm for starting the alumni association dwindled. *The California News* was the only source to keep abreast with the lives of alumni, where alumni editors, usually staff members, had a wide acquaintance and correspondence with former students. In 1930, *The Alumni News* was broadened and published articles of interest pertaining to CSD graduates. In 1983, the Alumni Association's *The Alumni Eagle* newsletter took over and has been a consequential link with the alumni.

California School for the Deaf Alumni Association. Strong leadership is necessary for the successful life of the Alumni Association.

The most recent officers of the Alumni Association, 1995-2000: (Left to right) Mary Ellen Lentz, Secretary, Joyanne Burdett, Executive Director, Don Ingraham, Treasurer, Candi Daviton, President, Joyce Ingraham, Vice President and Editor of The Alumni Eagle.

Formation of the First Alumni Association

During the Thirteenth Biennial Convention of the California Association of the Deaf held in Santa Cruz, California, August 29-September 1, 1941, the Constitution and By-laws of the CSD Alumni Association were adopted as stated in *The California News*, January 1942. Hence, it is fitting to say the Alumni Association was formally founded in 1941. The first elected officers of the Alumni Association were as follows: Edwin Wilson, '22, president; Lester Naftaly, '31, vice-president; Robert Miller, '33, secretary; James West Wilson, '20, treasurer and Mrs. Bessie (Hinman) Howson, '04, Emil Ladner, '30, and Sheldon McArtor, '19 were members of the board of directors.

It was thought that due to World War II, the Alumni Association had not engaged in any particular action till 1960. On May 29, 1960, the alumni spirit became animated at a dinner in Jack London Hall, Oakland, California, to honor Dr. and Mrs Elwood Stevenson on the former's retirement from the superintendency of the school after thirty-two years. Hundreds of alumni got together to show their appreciation of his service as the head of CSD. At the dinner, the oldest alumna, member of the 1896 class, was represented by Mrs. Isabella Tripp in her vigorous eighties.

In 1990, the Alumni Association commenced the tradition that an association reunion be held every five years at the California School for the Deaf, Fremont, or some other place. The alumni cherish an opportunity of acquainting with their classmates and friends at reunions. Business meetings, a banquet, Hall of Fame awards, museum visitation, and a picnic are included during the three-day reunion.

Alumni Reunions

The Alumni Association then passed into "hibernation" until 1976. On Saturday, October 2, 1976, over 400 of the CSD alumni convened at the Fresno Sheraton Inn at a banquet to commemorate the first official alumni reunion. Dr. Hugo Schunhoff and Dr. Henry Klopping were guest speakers. Dr. Schunhoff highlighted his 15-year administration. Dr. Klopping covered the hassle to get the new school in Fremont started. Elsie (Paxton) O'Connor, '42 (then Vincent) spearheaded the notion of realizing the first alumni reunion.

Second Reunion

Over one thousand alumni were present at the CSD Berkeley reunion, June 30-July 2, 1978. Former students were housed in the dormitories and they reminisced about their school days while occupying the same room and some of the same beds of years gone by. Charles Pale of the Class of 1910 was the oldest alumnus at the gathering. The highlights of the reunion were a banquet at Goodman Hall in Oakland, a visit to the CSD museum, a general assembly where future plans and a report on the Fremont site were discussed and a tour to the Fremont campus.

Fred Buenzle, '25, one of the oldest alumni attending all of the Alumni Reunions. He was employed as a printer for many years in San Francisco.

Third Reunion

About 500 alumni attended the third Reunion at CSD, Fremont, August 10-14, 1983. In the general meeting, the strong support proved the need of the alumni association to be a permanent organization with an officer slate elected from a local area. The agreement was unanimous with a new president, Leo Marcus Jacobs, '33. This association, after many years of ups and downs, was once again firmly established upon a strong foundation. In addition to the inspiring aura of the meeting, it was agreed to publish *The Alumni Eagle* newsletter three times a year. The editor was Joyanne (Rasmus) Burdett, '65 and Roy Holcomb was co-editor for a brief period.

Fourth Reunion

The Fourth Reunion was held in the Fremont/Newark Hilton Hotel August 1-3, 1986. About 500 alumni attended. President Leo Jacobs and the Reunion Committee Chairperson Norbert Enos, '65 presided. The highlight of this Reunion was the kick-off to the Bell Tower fund-raising campaign.

Fifth Reunion

President Reno Coletti, '57 presided over the fifth Reunion with a "Wild West" theme at the Holiday Inn in Fresno, California, in the summer of 1990. Most participants wore cowboy attire, which highlighted the week-end event. A young, vibrant alumna, Joyanne K. (Rasmus) Burdett, '65 was selected president and continued as editor of the newsletter.

At the 1995 reunion banquet, Ralph Nieves disguised as Charlie Chaplin in a skit. The reason for a "Charlie Chaplin" theme was that his first films he made were in Niles.

Sixth Reunion

On June 30-July 3, 1995, the sixth reunion at the Fremont/Newark Hilton with a "Charlie Chaplin" theme was presided over by adept President Joyanne (Rasmus) Burdett and Committee Chairperson Lynn (Mason) Dunn, '76. Everyone stated the 1995 Alumni Reunion was the best ever in history with a record-breaking attendance of 732 people. Every event of the reunion was sold

Sixth Reunion at the California School for the Deaf, June 30-July3, 1995.

out. The oldest CSD alumnus was J. West Wilson, '20, of Los Angeles, along with three generations of his family. The highlights of the reunion were the new Sports Hall of Fame founded by Donald Ingraham, '50, a fabulous banquet with "Charlie Chaplin" skits, and the election of Candi Marie Daviton, '79 as president for the term 1995-2000. Joyanne (Rasmus) Burdett became executive director.

SEVENTH REUNION

On June 30-July 2, 2000, the seventh Alumni Reunion was an exciting millennium affair at the CSD Fremont campus. One of the special events was the tour at former CSD in Berkeley. It was really no "return" to the Berkeley school for most of the alumni. Only the exterior of the buildings remained somewhat the same, except for the tower at the administration building. After the tour, could the alumni formally say "Goodbye" to the Berkeley school?

A number of the alumni and former staff members were inducted into the CSD Hall of Fame: Arts, Community, Education and Sports. The tour in the Historical Museum in the library was greatly appreciated by the reunion visitors especially the impressive famed Baseball statuette, a 21 1/2-inch replica of the famous Baseball Player statue located in the Golden Park in San Francisco.

Approximately 450 people enjoyed the well-planned programs at the 140 years old school reunion.

THE ALUMNI EAGLE

As explained above, *The Alumni Eagle* newsletter was first published after the third reunion. The lapse of the publication occurred between 1986 and 1991. Since 1991, the newsletter has become more popular and well-received among the alumni as well as friends. After two issues Joyce (Harvey) Ingraham, '61 who did the layout chores of the newsletter became editor/layout editor. Joyanne (Rasmus) Burdett continues being associate editor. Bernadette (Gallagher) Attletweed is proofreader and editing consultant. It is commented that the editing staff does a fantastic job in upgrading the quality of the newsletter which features many interesting and exciting articles about the alumni and other issues. *The Alumni Eagle's* regular contributor, Kenneth Shaffer, '46 has inspired many wonderful memories from the Berkeley school. Frank Sladek, '41 has contributed his interesting articles on "Did you know..." and, also, presented alumni plaque made by himself to the Alumni Association.

"Oue heritage grows and grows from all the information in these newsletters!"

Joyanne Burdett
Executive Director

CSD ALMA MATER

Hail to thee, Our Alma Mater
Hail to CSD
Hearts and hands say California,
Eagles proud we are.

Inspired by our Bear Hunt Statue
and Bell Tower,
Standing brave and strong.
Proud to claim you, Alma Mater,
Raise your name in song.

Here we learned, made true friends,
And friends we'll always be.
School of mine in days of youth.
Live on memory.

Whatever comes in future years,
We pledge devotion true
Through smiles and tears,
dear CSD
We'll stay a part of you.

Special Tribute to
Eugene Rianda

WHAT have members of the Alumni of CSD accomplished in their adult lives? Not so surprising, each individual has his/her own unique way in accomplishing his/her dreams and goals successfully. Features of their accomplishments have been disclosed widely in the publications of various magazines, newspapers of small and big towns and newsletters in the nation. In this pictorial book, Eugene Rianda, '46 CSD graduate, has for the first time attempted to bring together a collection of articles and photos of the Alumni achievements. It may provide a clear picture of what a number of Alumni have done during the years of 1860 to 1998.

His great interest and skill in collecting such memorabilia led him to accumulate a volume of interesting clippings, articles, and photos of the Alumni. Over several years the collection has grown. It was decided it was too good to be put aside or filed in the archives, so with the sponsorship of the Alumni Association, the collection was transformed into a form of a "book" called a scrapbook.

The Alumni Association takes pride in Eugene Rianda's accomplishment, which is a worthy endeavor.

Ken Norton, '45

Special Tribute to
HELEN CORA (ARBUTHNOT) BARBER

HELEN Barber, '47, concluded a ten-year research project by donating her completed work of two huge and important binders to the California School for the Deaf and its Alumni Association. The incredible gifts are: A 699-page binder containing an alphabetical register of 5,943 students who have attended CSD San Francisco/Berkeley/Fremont from 1860 to 1993 with pertinent information including dates of entry and departure, and names of spouses. Another binder contains yearly Senior Class lists in chronological order plus the class motto, class flower and class colors. It was a paramount task, but Barber, on her own, decided to take on the project as she felt it was needed for the school and the alumni. Upon her retirement, she came to CSD frequently to gather names and facts. She had to type and retype for ten years! Now these are valuable documents. This project is a never-ending endeavor that needs to be maintained with the admission of every new student. Thanks to Helen for laying the foundation.

Ralph Neesam
Former CSD Staff Member & Director of CSD Museum

Chapter Ten

Golden People of CSD

A Collection of Outstanding CSD People

The saga of CSD people is legendary. There are heroes and idols who inspired deaf students in special ways. Chapter Ten identifies some distinguished teachers and honored alumni with events and pictures that make each era so unique. Also, there is a collection of several CSD products at work with stories that reflect the past 140 years of deaf workers.

"If you want to know about deafness or deaf culture, ask deaf people themselves."

Dr. Byron Burnes

Dr. Byron Benton Burnes
A Man for All Seasons

Proficient orator.

Dr. Byron Benton Burnes is one of the 20th century deaf giants who defended the deaf citizens' rights. By different accounts, he is defined as "BBB," "unassuming genius," "a gentleman," "scholar," "gentle but gritty," and "master teacher." He has reshaped the education and the politics of the deaf world. What made such a man work with the California School for the Deaf, Berkeley, as mathematics teacher for 28 years from 1941 to 1969 and the National Association for the Deaf (NAD) as secretary/treasurer for nine years and NAD president for eighteen years from 1946 to 1964 but his labor of love and exceptional dedication to the deaf.

After the second attempt in fourteen years, Dr. Elwood Stevenson, superintendent of the California School for the Deaf in Berkeley, finally convinced Byron Burnes to move to Berkeley to teach in 1941. Being Lincolnesque, he had the ability to convey his thoughts and teachings so lucidly to his students. Burnes was much admired by both the students and staff members alike. Among his contributions were his long term editorship of *The California News*; his many literary contributions on professional subjects, and perhaps greatest of all, his instructional contribution to the multitude of students, who by his genius, qualified for higher education, and in many cases, gained fame in their careers. In 1955 Gallaudet awarded Burnes an honorary doctor of letters degree and in 1981 he received the Gallaudet University Alumni Association Laurent Clerc award and the University named one of the buildings on its Northwest campus for him.

NAD Devotee

Dr. Burnes devoted most of his free time to the endeavor of the National Association of the Deaf. In 1947, Burnes was at his desk in the den on the second floor of his home in Oakland five times a week from seven in the

Preceding spread: Signing for "Success" by Benjamin Jarashow, CSD '99. Taken by Mike Peterson, CSD '79.

evening to one in the morning, to answer a daily stack of letters from deaf leaders and educators on an Adler manual typewriter. At one time, he typed sixteen letters one evening! Afterward, he shifted his attention to the *Silent Worker* (SW) as the editor. His task was to review articles from various deaf and hearing writers, to collect photographs and to write an editorial column based on an inspiration from readings and discussions with deaf people.

Burnes and his energetic and very supportive wife, Caroline, often entertained their friends at their lovely home. He frequented the local deaf clubs and attended state and international conferences, where he spoke articulately on the deaf's rights among other issues. Through these contacts, Dr. Burnes sensed the pulse of the community with keen interest and love for his fellowmen and portrayed them in the *Silent Worker*. As a result, the number of subscriptions increased more than 66 percent and the magazine was heralded by the deaf Americans.

Establishment of NAD Home Office

To improve and strengthen the organization, Burnes advocated a NAD home office. He argued that "it was time for the association to stop trying to function with its office in the president's kitchen." Through a successful fund raising campaign, a new home office was set up on the corner of Shattuck Avenue and Dwight Way in 1952. Burnes with his Adler typewriter moved in and remained for the next twelve years.

Deeply concerned about the issues of inadequate education, injustice in court, lack of motorist' rights, false and inadequate advertising and public relations about deafness, Dr. Burnes had inspired other organizations for the deaf and deaf leaders to persuade congressional committees, state legislatures and other agencies to alter unconstitutional laws through skillful pressure and influence. He was an eloquent spokesman for the deaf people and their rights. Burnes emphasized he was one of the spokes in a wheel and was always concerned about these issues, especially improving the public image of deaf people. Jack R. Gannon, Author, *Deaf Heritage*, pointed out, "Dr. Byron B. Burnes is a man who possesses a broad, deep knowledge of our Deaf American history. As a former editor, he has a sharp editorial eye. He made a significant contribution to *Deaf Heritage*. I benefited greatly from his assistance, input and wisdom while writing the book."

Background of BBB

Dr. Burnes was born April 13, 1904, in Batavia, Iowa. When he was three years of age, the family moved to Fruitdale, Alabama. It was his mother, a school teacher and then post mistress, who introduced Burnes to the virtues of life. He became deaf from a complication of chicken pox and influenza at the age of 15.

Special Friend of Bill White

A good friend of Burnes, Bill White of Sacramento, California, recalled his days with Burnes, "I first met BBB in 1941 when I was 20, and I'm sure I needed him more than he needed me. Our social and vocational experiences couldn't have been more different. He was in his 15th year as a teacher; I had been deaf for only a few years, and was in my second year as an Oakland shipyard worker. Obviously, I needed an introduction to a lifestyle different than the one I knew, and I couldn't have found a better mentor than BBB. He exposed me to the adult world of deafness, its aggravating social problems, and the leading players in it. These people seemed to beat a pathway to his door, and they tolerated me because of who he was."

> *"Dr. BBB was an educator, a writer and editor and a strong, articulate, national leader. He never lost sight of his convictions or what he believed best for deaf people. He gave un-selfishly more than a century of his life to the service of his deaf fellow men without thought of reward. We Americans owe this southern gentleman an immense amount of gratitude."*
>
> 
>
> Dr. Jack R. Gannon
> Author, *Deaf Heritage*

Burnes attended the Alabama School for the Deaf. Eventually, he enrolled at Gallaudet College with the aspiration to be a sportswriter with a newspaper. As a Gallaudet student, he did a whirl at sportswriting, covering Bison games and rushing the stories to Washington newspapers. Might Burnes be one of the famed sportswriters if he had not altered the course of his career? Most fortunately for the deaf world, he turned out to be an educator and a leader to make the world a better place for deaf people. After graduation in 1926 with a bachelor degree, he taught one year at the Colorado School for the Deaf and eight years at the South Dakota School for the Deaf in Sioux Falls, South Dakota. He was assigned to teach mathematics to classes preparing for college by Superintendent Edward S. Tillinghast. Then he obtained a bachelor of arts in mathematics from Augustana College in Sioux Falls. After eight years, Burnes transferred to the Minnesota State School for the Deaf, where he taught and was editor of *The Companion*, the school's monthly publication, for six years. During the summers he studied at the University of Chicago, where he earned a masters in education in 1939.

In 1949 Dr. Burnes married Caroline Hyman, a librarian and a deaf leader in her own right. Caroline Burnes was co-author of the *History of CSD, 1860 to 1960* and instrumental in establishing a Junior NAD branch at CSD. It was her motion at a convention of the NAD that led to establishment of the national Junior NAD. She had two daughters and passed away on February 27, 1975.

Burnes had to leave his teaching position in Berkeley for an eye treatment in January 1969. After surgery, Dr. Burnes thought it would be fun to dabble in retirement. It would provide more time for playing golf.

He enjoyed going to Oakland Athletics games. All things have worked well for BBB. Dr. Burnes, at the age of 95, passed away on August 25, 1999, peacefully in his sleep, at his home in Martinez after a brief illness .

"What would the California School for the Deaf have been like without Ralph Neesam during the years of 1947 - 1983."

RALPH NEESAM
DEDICATED SERVICE TO THE DEAF

Because of Ralph Neesam, CSD's Boy Scout Troop 11 developed into one of the best known troops in the country through its demonstrations at conventions and banquets for Kiwanis, Lions, Rotary, United Crusade, Red Cross and numerous other organizations. Neesam directed many creative activities for Troop11, which also entered floats in local parades and came out with award ribbons. In 1959, Neesam was awarded the Silver Antelope Award, the highest scouting award in Region XII (Western States). The award was presented for noteworthy service of exceptional character to youth. Ralph Neesam was born to famous deaf parents in Delavan, Wisconsin. He participated in Delavan High School athletics while his father coached three major sports at the Wisconsin School for the Deaf. Neesam graduated from the University of Wisconsin just in time to serve in the army during World War II. In 1947, he received his master's degree at Gallaudet College and was appointed a teacher at CSD, Berkeley. Soon afterward he became scoutmaster of the school's Troop 11.

Because of Ralph Neesam, the Registry of Interpreters for the Deaf (RID) became a meaningful organization, changing from a voluntary interpreting service to a profession. He was involved in establishing criteria and classifications for interpreters, setting up evaluation procedures and interpreting training. Neesam became 2nd President of RID and continued on the board for a number of years. He won a RID Distinguished Service Award.

The subjects of history and civics were the most favorite classes among Ralph Neesam's students. He formulated the subjects into animated scenes with his dramatic flair in sign language. With his great experience as a classroom teacher, he was appointed principal of the high school department in 1965. With no secretary available, he was yet able to handle all correspondence, the

"Ralph Neesam is a walking encyclopedia of CSD - with a goal to make it the best school for the deaf children."

Dr. Henry Klopping
CSD Superintendent

One of his numerous skills was to illustrate the class subjects into animated scenes with his dramatic flair in sign language.

attendance of all students, and sub as a teacher whenever necessary. Added to his workload, he became editor of The California News and continued the position for ten years. Another promotion came in 1972 when Neesam became the school's first Supervisor of Staff Development. With his encouragement, the teachers received training to keep abreast of new educational developments. Also, he set up ASL classes for staff members to attain higher communication skills in order to receive $50 a month bi-lingual pay increases.

Due to Ralph Neesam's hard work, excellent public relations with the city of Fremont were developed when the school moved to Fremont. As director of the Outreach and Training Division, he arranged for the training of the entire city police department in the basics of sign language. Added to his long list of interests, he took a keen interest in art. He taught sign language to many museum docents in San Francisco and Oakland. Today the deaf enjoy guided tours in their own language. Neesam also gathered several of the Granville Redmond paintings and placed them in the CSD museum.

Under Ralph Neesam's leadership and directorship, the CSD museum was reorganized. He recruited a group of volunteers, retirees and friends, to help with the museum inventory and proper storage of precious historical articles and papers. Ralph has incessantly flowed with astute ideas as to how the articles should be displayed decorously. Hence, the museum is now appreciated by the visits of alumni, staff members, students, and friends.

On May 12, 1984, there was no other place so fitting for him as the grand dining room of the old CSD in Berkeley where a huge crowd celebrated and honored Ralph Neesam's memorable years with CSD as well as the deaf community. As for his retirement years, he has enjoyed going to some Athletics' baseball games with his good friends, bowling every week, basking under the sun in the south during the cold days, and doing some creative work at the museum. In November, 1997, he was a proud guest at the dedication of the new gymnasium at the Wisconsin School named after his father, Frederick Neesam, who taught at the school for 60 years and coached for 41 years.

One of My Favorite Memories at CSD

During my sophomore year, our energetic history teacher, Mr. Ralph Neesam, was scribbling some information on the blackboard. At that moment, I grabbed the opportunity to discuss plans for a coming school dance with my classmate next to me. Alas! I was too slow and got caught. Immediately, I visualized what the consequences would be, but I was wrong. Mr. Neesam simply came up to me and before I knew it, we were dancing! I, of course, was dumbfounded. Later back at my seat, I paid attention during the rest of the class. What an exemplary teacher he was! Ever since that incident, I find myself using his unique, gentle manner of discipline occasionally. *Thank you, Mr. Neesam!* JOYANNE K. (RASMUS) BURDETT Class of 1965

"John Galvan loved to give ten minute classroom talks to the students about all facets of life in the deaf world."

Julian Singleton
Retired CSD teacher

John Galvan
A Master Teacher

Before one of many legislative committee hearings, John Galvan explained the complexities of placing blind children and deaf children in the same school. At times, he ironically joked about this topic and brought loud laugher from the legislators. Galvan enjoyed his role of being a lobbyist who often succeeded in getting sensible messages across to the legislators. In some ways, his endeavors led to what is now the Fremont School. When the school was in the design phase and the legislative analyst was recommending major cuts in the program and pushing for the blind and deaf to share common buildings, Galvan was ready to do battle with Goliath-and Johnny won. One of the hearings ended up with a top aide to a state senator laughing so hard at what Johnny said, that he was literally "knocked down" by Johnny's comments and the top aide went away with his tail between his legs.

Galvan's parents moved to Hawaii all the way from Zahara, Spain where they were born. They, with a group of immigrants, worked on a plantation. In 1919, Galvan was born in Waialua, Hawaii. When he was six years old, on route to California by ship, he contacted spinal meningitis which caused his deafness. The Galvan family and friends were appalled by his mother's determination to send him to an "institution." However, he enrolled at CSD in 1926.

Upon his graduation at CSD, he went to Gallaudet College in 1938. He became a printing instructor in the Kansas and Minnesota schools for the deaf before returning to CSDB in the fall of 1949. He produced numerous skilled journeymen in the printing trade and prepared students for the fast changes in the world of work. He printed many nationally recognized books including *History of the California School for the Deaf, Berkeley, 1860 - 1960, The World*

Betty and John Galvan.
John Galvan produced many skilled journeymen in the printing trade and prepared students for the fast changes in the world of work. He printed many nationally recognized books and newsletters.

Joe Hill, even though he later became a prize-fighter and pro wrestler, did not like to get hurt. When he was on the football team, Coach Louis Byouk told him to rush the line, and he refused. So Byouk had John Galvan do it. Galvan was 100 pounds lighter, but fearless!

Games for the Deaf Tryout Program, The Deaf at Work, and *The Magic Lantern Man*, a book about Theophilus d'Estrella. He was noted for his creativity in all jobs.

Julian Singleton who worked with him in the printing shop for 36 years, first as teacher and student, then as co-workers, explained, "Galvan loved to give 10 minute classroom speeches to the students about all facets of life in the deaf world. His students wouldn't let him stop talking. They both loved and benefited from him."

In 1981, Galvan retired from CSD, and the following year his wife Betty joined him in retirement after teaching for twelve years at CSD. In 1985, the news of John Galvan's death saddened us all. He is survived by his wife and their three children, Dennis, Judy and Greg. Dennis is an assistant professor at Gallaudet University. Judy is a computer engineer at Edwards Air Force Base in Southern California. Greg is a graphics artist, living near Boston.

Deaf people, and parents of deaf children and CSD have been the recipients of the fruits of John Galvan's labor. Galvan was a master teacher. Also, he was very active in the deaf community. He was a steadfast and unswerving member of the California Association of the Deaf for a number of years. Galvan was President of the California Association of the Deaf at a time when critical issues for the deaf occurred. He was one of the advocates to secure free TDD's for the deaf and fought to establish an office with the Department of Social Services specifically to address the needs of the deaf.

Whenever he was asked to do something to benefit anyone, especially deaf people, John was more than willing to do it. In our lives there are significant people who touch and enrich us. John Galvan was such a person. He was a friend to all of us - no matter how young or old, no matter what our station in life.

"Leo was a man of words. He was one of the most articulate men that I have met and he was articulate whether he was speaking (signing) or writing."

Dr. Henry Klopping
CSD Superintendent

Leo M. Jacobs
A Deaf Adult Spoke Out

In 1974, Leo M. Jacobs spoke up on how deaf people felt about deafness and its implications by writing a book, *A Deaf Adult Speaks Out* which was released by Gallaudet College Press. He was the first deaf person to voice his concerns regarding the common and genuine problems deaf people face in the hearing world. The book in some ways has conveyed insight into the real sensitivities of a deaf person. What made him speak out? Jacobs was educated at the California School for the Deaf-Berkeley, and entered Gallaudet College at the age of fifteen. He received his B.A. degree at the age of nineteen, an age when a good many students enter college. Jacobs earned his Master of Arts degree at San Francisco State College (now California State University-San Francisco) in 1957. There were three others from CSD with him: Caroline Burnes, Catherine ("Cato") Ramger and Harold Ramger. For more than forty years, before writing the book, Jacobs had represented the deaf society. So he was the perfect person to draw from his own life experience since he was intimately exposed to a large segment of the adult population.

Leo Jacobs cherished and enjoyed the social life immensely especially among his deaf friends. He was rarely noted to miss any of the important or special events his friends provided in town where Jacobs resided. Being jovial and joking among his colleagues and friends was typical of him.

Powrie V. Doctor Chair

When Jacobs was selected to be the first recipient of the Powrie V. Doctor Chair at Gallaudet College, it was the opportune time to publish the book. This book is still on sale at any book store. Dr. Gilbert L. Delgado, who at that time was dean of the Graduate School at Gallaudet College, explained about the author of *A Deaf Adult Speaks Out*, "When Jacobs was chosen from a group of well-qualified applicants to be the first Professor of the Powrie V. Doctor Chair, the winning phrase was: 'Leo is a deaf person—head to toe.' At the end of the

Leader of the Deaf Community

"Contrary to the popular image of state institutions, a state school for the deaf holds a very positive image in students who attend them. They are homes away from homes. They are in their own community where communication is free and easy. In a state school the extra curricular program is usually well planned and they usually have a choice of participating in various activities including regular sports as full-fledged members. They usually have many adult deaf models to follow. This encourages a high self-esteem which will help provide a very productive and enjoyable life."

Leo Jacobs

The Leo Jacobs Family. Lisa, Leo, Dorothy, Sheila.

book, the positive tone about the deaf world during the 70s is expressed through the growth of post-secondary educational programs, the expansion of continuing deaf adult education, the toleration of the concept of total communication, the success of the National Theater of the Deaf, and the expansion of the media services and captioned films.

51 Years as Student, Counselor, Teacher & Coordinator

The son of deaf parents, Jacobs was, himself, deaf from birth. His older brother, Harry, was also deaf. Their parents were the products of the California School for the Deaf Berkeley. Jacobs enrolled at CSD on August 27, 1923, and graduated on June 1, 1933. He entered Gallaudet College and after graduating in 1938 returned to CSD as a boys' counselor. In 1947, he became a teacher in the high school department. Most of his teaching years, he taught mathematics. In 1975, he became Coordinator of Community and Continuing Education, the position he held until 1979 when he retired after spending 51 years as a student, counselor, teacher, and coordinator.

Leo Jacobs had been a leader of the deaf community during his teaching-days and has continued during his retirement days. Jacobs was elected president of the Gallaudet College Alumni Association at its 28th triennial Reunion, held June 21-23, 1973, in Indianapolis, Indiana. He was an active member of GCAA for 23 years, secretary in 1963-67 and board member for a number of years.

Well Known for His Quick Wit

One day in 1983, a hearing teenager driving a car bumped Jacobs' car at an intersection. Soon Fremont policeman and paramedics reached the accident scene. In the course of checking on Jacobs' injuries, one of the paramedics asked Jacobs if he had any kind of allergy. He responded, "Yes, I am allergic to teenagers." The policeman and paramedics immediately burst into laughter. Jacobs has been known for his wit. Being jovial and joking among his colleagues and friends was typical of him.

Jacobs was married to the former Dorothy Morrison, a Gallaudet graduate, Class of '55. She was a teacher of deaf children in Oakland before she passed away in 1978. Jacobs had two daughters: Sheila, a marriage, family, and child counselor; and Lisa, a consultant in the Washington, D. C. area.

Jacobs passed away on the Christmas Eve in 1998 and was brought back to California where he was buried with his wife Dorothy. On January 10, 1999, a beautiful memorial service was held at the CSD Little Theater which was an appropriate place in honor of Leo Jacobs.

"Myron's twenty-seven years at Berkeley, California, set a national record for sending a large number of well-qualified students to college."

The California News
1971 Senior Number

Myron A. Leenhouts

From Principal to Assistant Superintendent for Instruction 1944 - 1971

In the commencement address on June 13, 1971, Myron A. Leenhouts proclaimed to the Class of 1971, "My retirement is also a form of graduation. It required 27 years for me to do it, whereas you have done it in 12 or 13." Being jovial and joking with his colleagues as well as students was typical of him.

Leenhouts retired after forty years of outstanding service as a distinguished educator of the deaf. A native New Yorker, he received his early education in Rochester, New York. He was awarded his Bachelor of Arts degree from Hope College, Holland, Michigan, and his Master of Arts degree from Gallaudet College.

Before coming to CSD-Berkeley, to accept the position of principal of the Advanced (high school) Department in 1944, in place of Marshall Hester, who became superintendent of the New Mexico School for the Deaf, Leenhouts was a teacher and then principal at the Rochester School for the Deaf. He was also a coach and counselor at that school. While there, he married Mildred King, a member of the teaching staff. Their daughters, Linda and Judy, followed the family tradition and both became teachers of the deaf. It is interesting to note that Mildred King was one of five sisters who grew up in Sulphur, Oklahoma, near the School for the Deaf, and all five sisters decided to become teachers of the deaf

In 1961, when the title, *Principal*, was modified, Leenhouts was assigned the working title of Assistant Superintendent for Instruction. He assumed that role until he retired in 1971. The vacancy was filled by Jacob S. Arcanin, coming

Twenty-seven years of outstanding service as Principal and Assistant Superintendent.

from the National Technical Institute for the Deaf in Rochester, New York, where he was a counseling specialist.

Leenhouts' professional writings and affiliations were numerous. During his twenty-seven years at Berkeley, he set a national record for sending large numbers of well qualified students to college. He was also instrumental in the various phases of curriculum development. He was recognized for establishing one of the first programs involving parents in the education of deaf children in the United States.

After retirement he continued to be involved by reading books on tape to the blind, teaching sign language, and by serving on the scholarship committee. He passed away February 18, 1993, in Florida.

"You have labored hard in all you have done and you have touched the lives of many people throughout the state and our country."

Dr. Henry Klopping
CSD Superintendent

Jacob S. Arcanin
Assistant Supertindent, 1971 - 1999

A Man with a Vision

In 1968, two aspiring young men met for the first time in Tucson, Arizona. They turned out to be friends for their analogous philosophy and dreams for the education of the deaf. Little did they know that they would be teamed as Superintendent Henry Klopping and Assistant Superintendent Jacob Arcanin seven years later. From then into the year 2000, they have continued being a team operating the California School for the Deaf-Fremont.

A young native Californian, Jacob Arcanin, who was quite familiar with the CSDB staff members as well as having friends in the Bay Area, was appointed to fill the vacancy left by Myron Leenhouts, who retired in 1971 after forty years as a distinguished educator of the deaf. Jacob Arcanin, known as "Jake," was no stranger to the CSDB environment and operations, as he was a dormitory counselor for two years. Before working at CSD, he received his BA in Philosophy from the University of San Francisco in 1959.After graduation, he married Sally Hurley. In 1961, he received the Zellerbach Scholarship to pursue his education at San Francisco State College to secure training in teaching the deaf. Following this, he became a classroom teacher in the Junior High School Department. Three years later, he was moved into the position of Dean of Students. After two and a half years in that position, he participated in the National Leadership Training Program in the Area of the Deaf at San Fernando Valley State College (now California State University-Northridge) where he received his Master's in educational administration.

In the fall of 1968, Arcanin became a counseling specialist at the new National Technical Institute for the Deaf in Rochester, New York. In that position, he was actively involved in guidance and counseling, curriculum development, and teaching. His title was that of assistant professor. His duties also required him to travel throughout parts of the United States, giving informative talks on the academic programs offered at N.T.I.D.

" I remember the wonderful pageants directed by Ralph Neesam celebrating special historical days. The involvement of so many staff and students, the "grand scale" of the pageants, and the unselfish dedication displayed by Ralph are wonderful memories, indeed."

Jacob Arcanin
Assistant Superintendent,
1972-1999

HOMECOMING FOR JACOB ARCANIN

CSDB was very pleased to welcome Arcanin back to the CSDB team in his new role. He brought his family, his wife Sally and two daughters, Katie and Kellie. They settled in a cozy fairytale type house in Rockridge District, Oakland.

Jacob and Sally Arcanin amid their large family brood, including two sets of twin grandchildren.

An educational leader, an outstanding mediator and masterful communicator.

> ***"I am pleased to share with all of you the information that Jake Arcanin received a very important award at the CAL-ED/IMPACT Convention in San Jose, March 1998. Jake received the Special Recognition Award for his many years of exemplary service to education of the Deaf. I know that everyone at CSD knows the tremendous value he has been and continues to be in the lives of Deaf children and CSD. He richly deserves the recognition that he received."***
>
> Dr. Henry Klopping

Arcanin's move to CSD marked a homecoming for him. Since then, his influence related to education has continued and many of his educational visions have been fulfilled. He was the spearhead of the retreat for the annual Student Leadership Conference.

In 1982, Arcanin relinquished the responsibility of the instruction to Marianne DeLuca, who became Director of Instruction. As Assistant Superintendent, working closely with Superintendent Klopping, Arcanin has assumed responsibility for admission, implementation and coordination of I D E A compliance, liaison with local school districts and Special Education Local Program Agencies, California Interscholastic Federation-Interscholastic Athletic Governance, accreditation process, Liaison with professional and constituting groups such as IMPACT, LIDAC, CAL-AD and various State Department Committees and Task Forces.

Proficient Communicator

Arcanin is considered an educational leader, an outstanding mediator and masterful communicator. He is admired for his diplomatic skills, his agility at thinking, counseling skills and his perseverance in the pursuit of peace. An impressive letter from Thomas E. Byrnes, Commissioner of Athletics for the California Interscholastic Federation (CIF) was sent to Dr. Klopping. Byrnes commented on Arcanin's effort in administering and working toward the goals of developing a comprehensive program for Interscholastic Athletics. Byrnes stated:

> *"It is the opinion of this office (CIF) that Arcanin has been one of the key players in accomplishing this goal through his participation on the State CIF Federated Council. Without the voluntary efforts of such educators like Arcanin, the work of the CIF would grind to a halt. It was only through dedication and the giving of time and energy that CIF is able to offer quality interscholastic programs to high school students of California."*

Not only with the CSD community or the athletic program has he been active but, also, with the Catholic deaf community.

"Emil was on various committees bringing to fruition many projects. He usually rose to leadership in each organization he joined."

The California News
January 1971

Emil S. Ladner

Man of Many Interests

The Silicon Valley in Santa Clara County is where Emil S. Ladner as a young boy romped among the fruit orchards. Having a liking for fruit, he consumed and shared a lot of fruit with his schoolmates. He even continued sharing fruit with his pupils at the California School for the Deaf-Berkeley when he was a teacher. Ladner was deafened at the age of four from scarlet fever. His mother died when he was nine and he was raised by his father with much help from both sets of grandparents. It was said Ladner developed his devilish sense of humor as a youth as evidenced by his childhood nickname "Pancho Villa." He commenced his education at the old St. Joseph's School for the Deaf in Oakland, California. He enrolled in the California School for the Deaf to complete his high school education and graduated in 1930. He matriculated at Gallaudet College, graduating in 1935.

His leadership qualities emerged during his days at Gallaudet. He was elected Class President four times and selected Valedictorian of the Class of 1935. He helped organize his class gift to the College of a flagpole which still stands proudly in the front of Chapel Hall. He was active in the literary life of the campus, serving as Editor-in-Chief of the *Buff and Blue* during his senior year. He also was active in athletics, playing basketball, track, and football, where he earned the nickname "Loco" in his prep year, 1930.

After Ladner graduated from Gallaudet College, he became a teacher at the California School for the Deaf-Berkeley and spent his entire years of teaching in social science. At first, he had classes of elementary children. (Incidentally, the author was one of the children in 1937 and he remembered Ladner passing prunes among his pupils.) Since Gallaudet did not offer an accredited degree, he decided to earn an additional Bachelor's degree at the University of California-Berkeley. In lieu of attending class, he studied only from the books

Not only an excellent consumer education teacher, Emil Ladner was a sports fan and frequently was found talking with students as well as staff members about the latest sports news-triumphs and defeats.

With wife Mary, Ladner enjoyed his robst life for 54 years.

with his professors' permission. He completed his B.A. in Education with excellent grades in 1948. He taught history, geography, and consumer education in the high school department. Ladner developed a sound course of study on consumer education, which was widely used.

Dedicated Worker for CSD

During his teaching career, Ladner was actively involved with the literary society (LS) work. Every month on Sunday evening at the literary society meeting he was there to offer his help with running the program in addition to meeting with students whenever necessary. He did his best to follow the tradition of the LS established by Theophilus d'Estrella. He also imparted his deep interest in chess. Ladner was editor of the chess section in *The Deaf American* and president of the chess club for many years. Photography was another of his favorite hobbies. Hundreds of 4x5 negatives stored in the CSD archives are Ladner's work. He was always on hand taking pictures of groups at the school. Again, he carried out d'Estrella's love for photography. He was a sports fan and frequently was found talking with students as well as staff members about the latest sports news-triumphs and defeats.

Tireless Leader in the Deaf Community

However much time Ladner spent at the school, his activities were not limited to his responsibilities and interests on the premises. He was a member of many outside organizations of and for deaf people. He was on committees that produced many fruitful projects. Ladner had an ability to rise to leadership in each organization he joined. His record of offices included the presidency of the California Association of the Deaf, of Division No.79, National Fraternal Society of the Deaf, International Catholic Deaf Association, and the Council of Organizations Serving the Deaf. Also, he was a director of the Convention of American Instructors of the Deaf and a treasurer of the East Bay Counseling and Referral Agency of the Deaf (now Deaf Counseling, Advocacy and Referral Agency). He served on the Board of the East Bay Club of the Deaf for over twenty years, as a Director of the Conference of American Instructors of the Deaf, on the Board of the Center for Independent Living in Berkeley, and the Board of Self-Help in San Francisco that trained and placed deaf clients.

Retired After 36 Years of Teaching

Emil Ladner was married to the former Mary Blackinton for 54 years. They have four grown children, Suzanne, Richard and David (twins), and Jennifer. Suzanne and David are teachers of the deaf. Richard is a professor at the University of Washington. Jennifer is a registered nurse. Mary Ladner retired from CSD in June 1970, after 20 years of teaching. When Ladner retired from CSD on January 1, 1971, after a teaching career of thirty-six years, he participated in the Leadership Training Program for the Deaf at San Fernando Valley State College, Northridge (now California State University-Northridge).

After he received his M. A. degree, Ladner became executive director of the Council of Organizations Serving the Deaf headquarters in Boston for several years before Federal support was terminated. Then he returned home to Berkeley and enjoyed his retirement days with Mary. He was an avid golfer and participated regularly in golf tournaments with deaf golfers. Ladner founded the Northern California Golf Association of the Deaf and the Far West Golf Association of the Deaf in 1970 and he was the first member of the FWGAD Hall of Fame. He, with Mary, joined the Walnut Creek Deaf Seniors activities every Wednesday before he passed on in 1992.

"Lil was a pioneer advocate of Adult Education during Dr. Ray Jones' tenure at San Fernandino Valley College / California State University-Northridge."

Marjoriebell Holcomb
Educator, writer, administrator

Lillian Hahn Skinner

Guidelight in the Deaf Community and Sports

With a twinkle in her eyes, her uncanny mind, wit, fluency in American sign Language and love of bridge, Skinner is known as a person with great aplomb and expertise in the areas of sports and civic service administration.

Skinner was the first deaf woman elected to chair the American Athletic Association of the Deaf (AAAD) National Basketball Tournament in Los Angeles in 1964. As one of the early women in an administrative role, she matched male resistance with perseverance and quiet demeanor. The results of the successful AAAD and other national organization events earned her much respect. In 1985, Skinner was inducted into the AAAD Hall of Fame as the first

"I have known Lil ever since we were pre-teens, when she enrolled at CSD and we became classmates and rivals. She was not only academically gifted but also talented in many other ways. After she graduated from Gallaudet College, she served the deaf community, both professionally and socially. She was on numerous committees nationally and locally in the Los Angeles area. Her leadership ability was in heavy demand, and with her at the helm, conferences and social events were sure to succeed. Now she can look back at her achievements with great satisfaction, knowing that the deaf community is much better off through her efforts."

Leo Jacobs

deaf woman in the Leadership and Sportswriter category. She also served on the NAD Board for eight years. It is a tribute to her power as an administrator.

Skinner uses the same energy in her home state of California. She was president of the California Association of the Deaf for two years, the Hollywood Club and Los Angeles Club for the Deaf. She served five terms as secretary and subsequently as a two-term president of the Farwest Athletic Association of the Deaf (FAAD). Her success brought her recognition in the FAAD Hall of Fame.

In 1977, Lillian Skinner, one of two deaf members, was appointed to the reorganized fifteen member Rehabilitation Advisory Committee of the State Department of Rehabilitation. The purpose of this department was to listen to voices of direct consumers and providers of rehabilitation services, and to give input to improve services for the disabled.

Advocacy for the Deaf Community

Among her accomplishments, Skinner has been recognized for her civic work and services. As an advocate for deaf elders, she served as the first chairperson on the Board of California Home for Aged Deaf, where she also chairs a task force. In addition, she has been on the Board of Greater Los Angeles Council on Deafness (GLAD) and is presently on Boards of Self-Actualization Institute of Deaf, Center of Communicative Development, and California Home for the Deaf.

Skinner has provided drama in sports, the deaf community, and the education field. She has both a commitment to change and the skills to make things happen. What lies in her personality and background?

Lil's Background

Born of Korean parents in Manteca, California, Skinner became deaf at the age of 10 from spinal meningitis after a week in a coma. In 1929 she enrolled at the California School for the Deaf Berkeley. Skinner graduated as class valedictorian in 1934.

After graduating from Gallaudet College with a degree in liberal arts in 1939, she returned to Los Angeles, California, and met two influential men. One was Tom Elliot, a legend in the deaf community, mostly noted for his leadership and sports activities. Elliot became her mentor and taught her how to handle the responsibilities, to confront challenges and to seek solutions for organizations. The second man, Bob Skinner, a basketball player for the Los Angeles Club for the Deaf and later the Hollywood Silent Recreation Club team, she met at Lockheed Aircraft and married him. He provided her strong support and encouragement for her leadership. Her leadership skills developed rapidly as she became active in various local events and was elected to offices in both civic and sports organizations. In 1994, Skinner was awarded a plaque and a sculpture for the Governor's Hall of Fame for People with Disabilities by the Department of Rehabilitation. She earned a masters in guidance at California State University-Northridge in 1966. She taught at the Maryland School for the Deaf for two years, thirteen years at Arroya Elementary School in Simi Valley and worked for five years as a guidance counselor at CSUN.

Bob Skinner worked as a Senior Programmer Analyst. Bob and Lillian have three daughters. One is a registered nurse, the second a physical therapist and the third a teacher in special education with an administrative credential. She is vice principal at an elementary program.

Skinner retired at the peak of her career and achievements. She was very active playing bridge. She passed away during the summer of 2000.

As one of the early women in an administrative role, she matched male resistance with perseverance and quiet demeanor.

"The Parsons family lived in the style of the Swiss Family Robinson for six and half years in Vairao, Tahiti. They dwelled in a thatched house."

Hester Hester

Hester "Polly" Parsons

Authoress, Audacious Adventurer and World Traveler

In 1975, two books, *Humorous Illustrated Idioms and Their Origins* and *Easy Illustrated Idioms and Proverbs for the Deaf*, were developed and written by Hester Parsons, who was known as an insatiable seasoned world traveler and an authoress of four books and many articles about deaf grassroots. The books were

When Polly Parsons was fifteen years old, she survived the lifestyle of the Swiss Family Robinson in Vairao, Tahiti. With her family, she dwelled in a niao, *a thatched house with bamboo floors, with rather primitive living conditions.*

dedicated to her beloved mother, who taught Hesterx the wonders and spice of language when living in Tahiti. (Since there are two Parsons in this chapter, the first name is mentioned instead.) The books brought positive comments from deaf adults, foreigners and younger students, who understood idioms. The illustrations were drawn by Hester's husband, Koni Battad from Kauai, using his own imagination and ideas to depict the clear meaning of the idioms.

In January 1969, Hester moved to Hawaii to study at the University of Hawaii and get credits for her M. A. in special education. She started the first Adult Basic Education program and became a program instructor at Kaimuki Community school for three years. She also taught part time at the Diamond Head School for the Deaf at Honolulu, Hawaii.

In 1973, Hester moved to Los Angeles where she earned an M. A. degree in Special Education at California State University-Northridge. With success and experience as a para-professional coordinator for deaf adults with needs for Basic Education, she started and taught the first Special Education Program at Los Angeles Technical Trade College for five years. In 1981, she moved to her birthplace, El Cajon. For the third time, Hester started a special education program and taught at San Diego City College for eight years before retiring in January 1989.

Formal Family Education

Hester and her identical twin sister, Frances (15 minutes younger), were born in a small village near San Diego in 1923. Discovering the twins to be deaf at the age of four, etiology was attributed to either premature birth, possible undulant fever at infancy or whooping cough at three and a half years of age. After rounds of oralism, public schools and speech reading in San Diego, the twins were enrolled at the California School for the Deaf-Berkeley at the age of nine. Three years later in 1935, being unsatisfied with the girls, educational progress and troubled by the 1930s depression, the parents decided to move to Tahiti, "a paradise of the Pacific."

The Parsons family lived in the style of the Swiss Family Robinson for six and half years in Vairao, Tahiti. They dwelled in a *niao*, a thatched house with bamboo floors. Settling in the new environment, with rather primitive living conditions (no running hot water, kerosene lamps, an outdoor "stove" made of rocks mixed with cement and an iron grill on top), their mother, a certified teacher and principal, was determined to educate the twins personally while their father was a "cowboy," overseeing land for Princess Terei, the last line of Pomare royalty, raising pigs,making *copra* from coconuts and growing beans to sell. Mother developed "lessons" called *Step-O-Gram*, drawings with statements.

She cleverly devised this step-o-gram to maintain the twins' interest in world history from the birth of the universe through Egyptian history, Medieval times, weaving in Shakespeare's novels, and the Pilgrims to the present time. The twins were quite knowledgeable about world history, literature, geography and many other subjects. Nearing the end of six and half years in peaceful Tahiti, their mother felt that the twins were well enough educated to go on to Gallaudet College.

Three books were written by Hester Parsons. Part of Hester Hester book was written by her mother telling about Parsons family's Polynesian life in Tahiti.

Return to the States

Just before the family departed from the island in a two-masted schooner, *Benicia*, a hurricane leveled the family's palm and bamboo woven niao house. On the voyage to Hawaii, they again were caught in a fierce storm. Fortunately, Captain Lou Chataigner skillfully maneuvered the *Benicia* through the storm, escaping from sinking and finally reaching Honolulu with some damage. After a week of being repaired, it sailed on rough seas for two weeks and reached San Francisco on March 6, 1941 with their adventurous story blazed on the front page of San Francisco newspapers - nine months before the Pearl Harbor attack.

Back in California, after attending CSD for a year, Hester was admitted to Gallaudet College. Her success was fully credited to her mother's zealous teachings. In 1947, she graduated from Gallaudet College with a B.S. degree and returned to California where she was married to Charles Bennett. They had twin daughters, Bonnie Sue and Donna Lou, and another daughter, Allyne Beth.

Polly's Lone Saga Around the World

After 12 years of marriage, Hester got a divorce and supported the three girls for five years. Then she was the first deaf woman to travel alone around the world for one year - 1966-67. It took a lot of courage to travel with the locals on old trains, old ricky buses, horse-drawn carts, camels, and freighters. She encountered several dangerous experiences, poverty and hardships. At the end of her one year long saga, she came home, went to Gallaudet for two years where she majored in Library Studies and then in 1969, moved to Hawaii where she completed two books, *Road Girl* and *Hester Hester*. Her mother originally wrote the first part of *Hester Hester* telling about the Parsons family's Polynesian life in Tahiti.

Presently, she lives in West Hills, California with her daughter, Donna Lou Bennett, after living in Utah for eight years with Allyne and her family. As for her travels, she crossed the Equator, International Datelines, Artic Circle and rounded cape Horn and the southern-most tip of New Zealand. Also, fortunately, she witnessed the "Midnight Sun," the sun shining 24 hours throughout the day and night in the Arctic, and a total solar eclipse on August 11, 1999.

"My goal was to make sure that the state of California would have good laws for all children — able or disabled."

George Attletweed

George Attletweed

First Deaf Person on State Advisory Commission

George Attletweed was well known for his knack for blending his sense of humor with serious talk that easily melted people's hearts.

George Attletweed was the first deaf person to be appointed to the Advisory Commission on Special Education by Governor George Deukmejian. His appointment indicated a heightened level of awareness about special education and the needs of all children in special education programs. The commission advised the State Board of Education, the Department of Education, the Legislature, and the Governor on the unmet needs of handicapped children in the state. California has about 365,000 children who are designated as handicapped. Approximately 6,000 of these children between the ages of three and twenty are in hearing impaired programs. Attletweed was Chairperson (1987-88) and Vice-chairperson (1989-90) on the Commission. It was said that his sense of humor could sparkle and brighten up many a dreary meeting at the commission. He had much understanding and compassion in his wise leadership.

Formal Education

Attletweed, a 1947 graduate of CSDB, earned a bachelor,s degree in 1966 and master's degree in 1974 from San Francisco State University, where he majored in English. He was a teacher for six years in the San Jose Unified School District, working with hearing impaired children before becoming the first chairperson of the Ohlone College Hearing-Impaired Program, a position he held for four years. He was an adviser and counselor at Ohlone College, primarily serving the large population of deaf students when he passed on in

1991. He is survived by his wife, Bernadette, and a daughter, Kathleen Strawn, a son, Olaf Lawrence Attletweed, and four grandchildren, George Thomas Strawn, Alicia Mae Strawn, Lauren Ashley Attletweed, and Olaf L. Attletweed, Jr.

George and his devoted wife Berna.

Great Communicator

One of George Attletweed's specialties was to give speeches and lead discussions for parents of deaf children, audiences at formal banquets, panels of professionals, and critical hearings. His great knack was to blend his sense of humor with serious talk that easily melted people's hearts. Below is an excerpt from his appearance as guest speaker at the 1984 graduation banquet.

> *. . . . "At first, I did not want to be the guest speaker. I believed that there were others who richly deserved the honor of standing here before you and offering you words/signs that will inspire you. Looking around, I am glad to be your guest speaker. Why? Because many memories came back to me while I looked over the names of the seniors. Many of you I know on a personal level, and I remember your parents from different times in different places. So it is good to be here. We should look at the love—yes, deep and true love—that your parents had and still have for you. This love brought all of you to this school.". . . .*

One of the highlights of his life was an award for his outstanding efforts of upgrading the communication gaps between the hearing and deaf communities presented by a special organization named Deaf Services Network at Upper Fort Mason in San Francisco on May 13, 1983. Attletweed received special awards for his achievements from: The California Legislature Assembly Resolution, Alameda County Bar Association's Liberty Bell Award, and the Deaf Counseling and Referring Agency.

Attletweed served as President of DEAF Media and co-host of "Silent Perspectives," a weekly program about deafness aired over KCSM (Channel 14). For a number of years he was co-producer and editor of Dial-A-News (DAN) a weekly newspaper service for Deaf over the phone lines by usage of TTY.

Attletweed will always be remembered not only by the people of Ohlone College and CSD, but the deaf community as well for his many contributions in effort and time toward the leadership in deaf education, and advocacy for all special needs of children in California.

"Bernard Bragg, Prince of Deaf Players. His influence on many of the finest Deaf actors, storytellers, mimes, and poets today is immeasurable."

Robert Panara
Emeritus Professor
National Technology Institute
for the Deaf

Bernard Nathan Bragg

The Man with the Golden Hands

Bernard Bragg experienced a sensational and eventful life while teaching at CSD-Berkeley for fifteen years. CSD rarely employed inexperienced college graduates but Bragg made a breakthrough, beginning his teaching career right after graduation from Gallaudet College in 1952. As an English teacher and a drama instructor and director, he encouraged young deaf students to create themselves independently and creatively in both academic and theater. He earned a Masters in Education and a minor in Drama from San Francisco State University. Bragg was a valued Junior High School teacher before the idea of helping establish the National Theatre of the Deaf lured him into this new venture as actor/administrator/signmaster in 1967.

Born in Brooklyn, New York, of a pioneer actor-father, Wolf Bragg, Bernard Bragg had imbibed from his father the art of masterful signing from early childhood. Wolf Bragg may not have been an ideal father, but in his time he had no peer as a master signer who passed on his talent and artistry to his impressionable son. Not only that, but Bernard Bragg was blessed with an angel of a mother. They also helped tremendously that, while attending the New York School for the Deaf, known as Fanwood school, in White Plains, he came upon another great influence in his life and career, teacher Robert Panara. With Panara's help he developed his love and enthusiasm for literature through dramatic signing. Although Bragg was already a skilled mime and signer, he was enthralled and stimulated by the colorful, exciting and creative way Panara acted out in Sign quotations, poems and favorite passages from literature. Sign Language could be a rich, inspiring, and powerful medium. The combined influence of those two giants of Deaf Theater, his father and Panara, provided the nourishing rich soil for the growth of Bragg's own unique talent and artistry to unprecedented new heights. His "golden hands" can express the entire gamut of feelings and ideas, like Beethoven's piano. Panara called Bragg "Prince of Deaf players." His influence on many of the finest Deaf actors, storytellers, mimes, and poets today is immeasurable.

Blooming into a Professional Performer

During Bragg's years in Berkeley, he gained recognition nationally as a mime and actor, flourishing a talent which became a life-long career. In 1956, he met Marcel Marceau, the noted French mime, in San Francisco. Marceau invited him to study under him in Paris that summer. Soon after, Bragg's performances in the San Francisco and Los Angeles night clubs were the talk of the cities for he captivated all who saw him. As the pace of his life accelerated, he became a successful and popular entertainer. He was well known as "The Quiet Man," a half-hour children's program aired once a week on KQED television in San Francisco, where he acted out Aesop's fables and fairy tales in mime and afterwards nationwide under the overall title "What's New?" for four years. He recreated "A Christmas Carol," told on TV without words, in which he played all the parts himself. Bragg originated and used his Visual Vernacular technique to "switch from one character to another with lightning speed within an imaginary film frame, using long-shots, close-ups, slow motion, zooming, high and low angles and crosscuts." He also did the same thing with Shakespeare's "Hamlet."

Call to the Theater

Teaching and communicating with the audience in a classroom holds the same proficiency with the audience as from the stage of the world. Bragg felt compelled to follow the call to the theater, henceforth he has been practically each year traveling to Europe to perform, direct plays, and appear on television there. Naturally enough, he was asked to become one of the founders of the National Theater of the Deaf in Chester, Connecticut. His contributions to the rise of that first professional theater of the deaf are invaluable. He also became the subject of a biography by Helen Powers, *Signs of Silence*, published in 1972. In the same year, Bragg was hired as a technical production consultant for a television movie, *And Your Name Is Jonah*, and as a coach for Jeff Bravin, starring in the title role. Because this film portrayed genuine deaf culture, it was heralded as a huge success.

After ten years with NTD, Bragg toured for six months as the American goodwill ambassador to deaf and hearing people in 25 countries, performing one-man shows and giving workshops and lectures. During the winter of 1973, he spent six weeks in Russia as an artist-in-residence with the Moscow Theater of Mimicry and Gesture.

In the entertainment section on June 20, 1958, the Los Angeles Times featured Bernard Bragg as "Brilliant Young Mime who is, without qualification, magnificent."

Two of the world's most famous mimes, Marcel Marceau and Bernard Bragg. They became close friends as they met from time to time all over the world.

Bragg was a visiting professor and artist-in-residence at Gallaudet University for fifteen years before he retired. In Fall 1995, he worked with the leading German Theater of the Deaf on a new play, "On the Eve of the Golden Wedding Anniversary." In 1996, he embarked on cross country tours of his one-man show in Germany and Japan, doing book-signing for his autobiography, which has been translated into Japanese. In 1988, Gallaudet awarded Bragg an honorary doctorate of letters degree. Also, in 1975, he was the recipient of the International Medal Award from the World Federation of the Deaf for his continued leadership in promoting theater by the deaf. He continues to write, lecture, conduct workshops, perform in mime in every corner of the world. He co-wrote three books: *Tales from a Club* (with Gene Bergman), *Meeting Halfway in American Sign Language* (with Jack Olson) and *Lessons in Laughter* (with Gene Bergman). Once in a while, Bragg returns to his beloved school in Fremont, giving one-man shows or conducting workshops.

Never Ending

Ultimately, Bragg landed in Los Angeles by purchasing a three-bedroom house, called "BB's White House" by his friends, in the Hollywood Hills. Since living in this area, he periodically performs and consults at the Deaf West Theater. Also, he teaches a drama class at California State University-Northridge. He wrote, directed and produced two-well received plays "To Whom It May Concern" and "Laugh Properly, Please." His influence and contribution continue to flourish in this country and abroad. On October 9, 1998, he has established in concordance with Gallaudet University a $1-million endowment for the "Bernard Bragg Chair: Deaf People in the Theater Arts." In1999, he directed the German version of the former play with the Towering Company of the Leading German Deaf Theater. He plans to conduct a workshop at Deaf Way in Washington, D. C. in 2002. Bragg has established a meaningful connection between himself and the world. What makes the man go on and on is best explained by Taras Denis. This is an excerpt from a poem—*Bernard Bragg: A Tribute.*

Certainly never ever, in the sense
That you chose, alone and in the face
Of improbability—or perhaps, impropriety—
to lift yourself unto a stage
and wherewith those same hands of gold
proclaim to the eyes of the world:
look, I can, why not, we can!

Taras Denis, Deaf Theater Critic and Former Fanwood School Administrator

"Mary Ellen vitalized many deaf senior citizens' lives and installed hope. Her workshop became so popular that she was invited to set up workshops elsewhere."

Ken Norton
Author of
The Eagle Soars to Enlightenment

Mary Ellen Lentz

Woman of Unquenchable Vitality

Mary Ellen Lentz at 76 years of age sparkles with unquenchable vitality and it has earned her national recognition among deaf communities, especially for her advocacy for aerobic exercise for all ages. She not only participates in marathons and long walks, but also creates aerobic workshops and provides consultation. Wherever she goes, she changes people's attitude toward themselves and others.

In 1997, Lentz was invited to speak to a class at Ohlone College on the issue of senior citizens. For a dramatic effect, Lentz attired herself in ragged clothes and thick glasses and appeared in a wheelchair. After her speech and a question and answer session, she departed. When the instructor asked the students of their impression of the speaker, they discussed her poor sight, feeble physical appearance, and dementia. Shortly, Lentz reappeared in an aerobic outfit and a smile and commanded the students to get up and follow her aerobic techniques. In ten minutes the students were exhausted, but Lentz's energy remained high. The class instructor revealed that Lentz, the aerobic instructor, was the same person in the wheelchair. He explained that the reason for this act was to eradicate their negative myth of elders and to promote a better understanding of senior citizens. Lentz spoke of her experience as an aerobic instructor and her firm belief in maintaining good health through aerobic exercises, strength training, and walking. When she finished, there was a moment of silence. The class rose and applauded as she left.

ASL as Third Language

Born in Watsonville, California, Lentz was deafened by a freak accident from shock at sixteen months of age when she accidentally lost her balance and her forearms landed and were stuck to the side of a very hot cooking wood stove. A neighbor rushed in and poured wine over her hands to release them. After medical treatment at a hospital, she became deaf.

Lentz first learned European sign gestures from her immigrant Yugoslavian grandmother and later American Indian sign language at a reservation close to her home in Banning, California. When Lentz enrolled at CSD in Berkeley, she acquired American Sign Language as a third language. Her background of different sign languages did not only provide a means of communication, but also a belief that an external sign language should harmonize with physical appearance as a whole being. This led to her interest in aerobics years later. She graduated as a class valedictorian in 1943.

Married to Gilmer Lentz from North Carolina, they raised two children, Ella Mae and Gil. Gil is a CSD head football and assistant track coach and works as a Middle School counselor. Also, he is a golf instructor for the deaf at the San Jose Municipal Golf Course.

While running a child care at her home, she managed to secure a certificate in water safety instruction. She taught water safety to children, adults and veterans who had lost limbs.

Mary Ellen Lentz bubbles with unquenchable vitality which earns her national recognition among deaf communities, especially for her advocacy for aerobic exercises for all ages.

High Demand as Aerobic Instructor

In 1970, aerobic techniques intrigued and inspired Lentz to take a number of courses at the University of California-Berkeley, Chabot College, Laney College, Merritt College, and Ohlone College. Glenda Smith, an aerobics instructor at Ohlone College, was so impressed with Lentz's skills that she encouraged her to become a certified instructor in aerobics. In 1988, Lentz received an instructor's certificate. From then on, she provided workshops and retreats both locally and nationally for senior conferences, deaf women's organizations and schools.

High Sierra Country hearing people sweat after fitness exercises in Mary Ellen Lentz's class.

At the Senior Citizen Conference in Phoenix in April 1997, Lentz was asked to set up an aerobic workshop, one of many workshops. On the second day her class overflowed with deaf citizens who had heard through the grapevine about her workshop. By the third day, the enrollment was out of control. People discussed Lentz in the lobby, in the restaurant and even at other meetings. In the lobby, Lentz was surrounded by admirers. Lentz provided advice and encouraged positive attitudes on self-image. Before meeting Lentz, many deaf senior citizens felt discouraged by their advanced age and the concept of aerobic exercise that was limited only to hearing young people. She now vitalized their lives and installed hope. Her workshop became so popular that she was invited to set up workshops elsewhere.

Lentz taught aerobics to the students of all educational departments at CSD in Fremont. She got the students moving with warm-ups and aerobic exercises. She even took them outside and taught them the correct way to walk. She stressed to the students that building strong muscles supported their bones and cautioned them about overdoing sports activities, missing warm-ups and good nutrition.

Mary Ellen and Gilmer Lentz used to live in a cabin in Pioneer, California, where she continued volunteering to teach aerobics three times a week to high country people. Currently, they live in Hayward, continuing to lead active lives.

*"In **Arsenic and Old Lace**, in 1942, Eric Malzkuhn wore the precious "lucky" shoes that Boris Karloff first wore as the monster in **Frankenstein**, in 1930."*

Ken Norton

Eric Malzkuhn, Jr.

Masterful Creator of the Jabberwocky (in Sign)

Every time the audience poured out of theaters where Eric Malzkuhn, Jr. gesticulated "Jabberwocky," it began to fathom the meaning of Lewis Carroll's

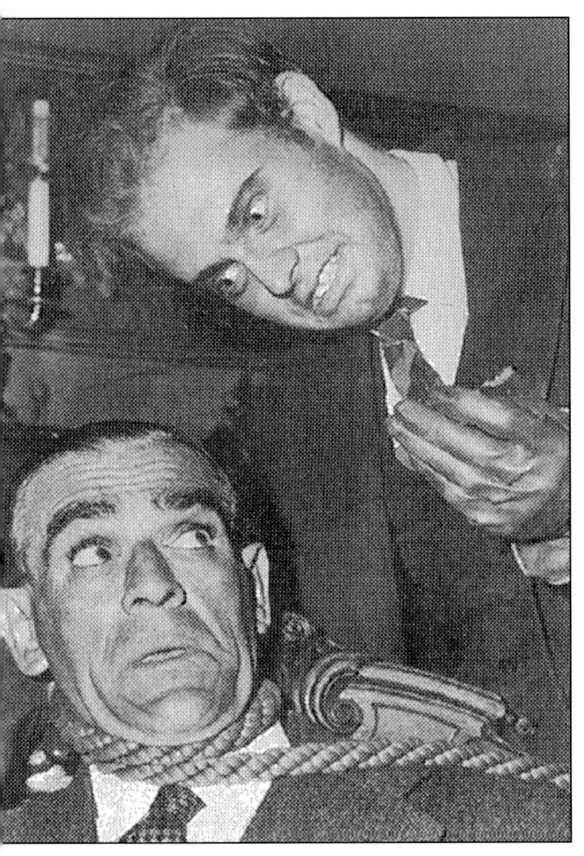

Eric Malzkuhn, upper, "threatening" Boris Karloff who was a well known actor in "Arsenic and Old Lace."

famous poem, a staple of *Alice In Wonderland: Through the Looking Glass.* Comprehending this poem is quite onerous but once watching Malzkuhn translate the poem with his sprightly antics, the meaning of "Jabberwocky" becomes crystal clear. No one had captured the imaginative impact of this classic before Malzkuhn did it with his insouciant translation into ASL. Under Malzkuhn's guidance, Joe Velez, '56 CSD graduate, delivered this version of "Jabberwocky" on the National Theater of the Deaf tours in 1968 and 1969. His energetic gyrations and rubber-faced expressions also made him famous.

In 1942, as a student very active in the Gallaudet College drama club, Malzkuhn spearheaded the effort to obtain the rights to bring the Gallaudet Drama Club troupe to Broadway while the original production was still running. This was a Broadway first. "Arsenic and Old Lace" took over the stage of the Fulton (now Helen Hayes) Theater on Sunday, May 2, which was an off night for the regular cast. Malzkuhn played Boris Karloff's role as the villain Jonathan Brewster, and received rave reviews (as did the whole production). Karloff took time out from his daily stints as Jonathan to coach Malzkuhn for three days prior to the opening of the sign language version of 'Arsenic.' On opening night, Karloff did the make-up on Malzkuhn and lent him the use of his star dressing room, his valet, costume (a fine suit that had seen better days) and the precious "lucky" shoes that Karloff first wore when he strode into the macabre consciousness of the whole world as the Monster in "Frankenstein" in 1930.

Malz

Malzkuhn, a well known signmaster, actor, theater buff, writer, teacher, storyteller, and retired member of the faculty of the Model Secondary School for the Deaf at Gallaudet University, has often been asked to speak at various programs throughout the world. When he was a preparatory student at Gallaudet, the upperclassmen dubbed him "Malz" (because they deigned to wrestle with the spelling of his last name) and this is how he prefers to be known. He participated in his school band in the Burlingame area before he became deaf at the age of ten. Becoming deaf was a difficult experience for him but after entering the Berkeley school, he became involved in writing sports for *The California News*. He subsequently became Sports Editor/Columnist and Associate/Literary Editor of the Buff and Blue at Gallaudet, as well as a staff sports writer for his hometown daily every summer during his college years and sportswriter for an industrial newsletter and occasional writer for almost every Deaf publication. While at Gallaudet he also coined the name "Blue Bisons," managed the famous "Five Iron Men," hurled the shot and the discus for the track team and first translated "The Jabberwocky."

In 1938, graduating from CSD, Malzkuhn gave an oral valedictory address at the commencement. Edwin Preston delivered this in sign. He received a Bachelor of Arts degree in English and Biology in 1943 from Gallaudet College. Later he studied at Eastern Michigan College, the University of Michigan, and the General Motors Institute of Technology. At this time he taught at the Michigan School for the Deaf in Flint for four years, then working as a Field Agent with the Department of Vocational Rehabilitation, based in Detroit. After being hit with polio in the epidemic of 1953, he moved his family away from snow and ice, back home to San Mateo, California, where he worked as a printer.

Returned to His Love of Teaching

In 1967, Malzkuhn returned to his Alma Mater at CSD-Berkeley, as a teacher of English, science and drama. Working with students in the Literary Society plays and running the Photography Club were some of his happiest days. In 1968, he was asked to join the National Theater of the Deaf as one of the teachers/adapters for the NTD productions. His style in signs was used in a number of plays as well as "The Jabberwocky," and his influence continues. He has also written nine plays, most of which have been presented in the deaf community.

It was CSD's big loss when Malzkuhn accepted a teaching position at the Model Secondary School for the Deaf in 1973. He made his name at MSSD for directing numerous successful plays. After he retired from 17 years of teaching there, he was awarded an honorary degree, Doctor of Fine Arts, by Gallaudet in 1993. At the 25th anniversary of MSSD, Malzkuhn had the honor of seeing the theater being named after him: changed from *The Auditorium* to **Theatre Malz**.

Golden Opportunity Knocked

While teaching at the Michigan school, Malzkuhn met one of his students, Mary, who became his wife after she left the school. They have been married for 55 years. She used to work in a candle firm in Burlingame, California, a town next to San Mateo. Upon moving to Washington, D. C., she seized the golden opportunity to continue her higher education by attending Gallaudet University. Although an older student, she became popular among the young ones and even went through probation with the others selected to join a sorority, Phi Kappa Zeta. She then earned a Masters degree in Deaf Education from Gallaudet University and a Doctorate in Government and Politics from the University of Maryland. As a full time professor of the Government Department at Gallaudet, she teaches courses in American government, the U.S. Constitution, and civil rights and liberties. She is an advocate for human rights,

"When I first entered CSD I was placed in Moss Hall with the "Big Boys" because I was in the 8th grade. Not then able to sign, I got into some ludicrous situations. The first week I was at CSD was miserable, kids all teasing me or ignoring me. One evening Joe Hill, a huge student, approached me and asked me to help with his English homework. I did that and next time Joe Hill saw a kid abusing me, he picked him up by his belt and said: "Finish!" So I was left in peace until Hill left CSD, but by that time I was big enough to take care of myself."

Eric Malzkuhn

deaf rights and a better education system for deaf children. Mary Malzkuhn has been involved in international deaf history as well, serving as editor of the journal for this group. Mary has traveled the world, speaking on human rights and deaf rights and the rights of women. In 1991, she was selected Gallaudet Faculty member of the Year, and President I. King Jordan recognized her as mother of the DPN (Deaf President Now).

For the summer and holidays, Mary and Malz frequently come to Fremont to visit with their children and grandchildren, including: Brian (CSD '68) and his wife Ginny (CSD '69), their three children, Matthew, Melissa and Megan. Brian teaches at Ohlone College and Ginny is an Academic Counselor at CSD. Also living in Fremont and hosting parents from time to time are Max (Brian's younger brother) who is in the computing field, and his wife, Sylvia, (teacher in CSD preschool), their children, Mallory and Clay. Eric (Brian's older brother) lives in Maryland. He is a teacher at a technical school for seamen.

Eric and Mary Malzkuhn amid their family brood. Clay, front row left; Max, Mallory, Sylvia, Eric, and Mary. Melissa, back row left, Matthew, Megan, Brian, Ginny and Eric III.

"Senators on both sides of the aisle found Robert Davila a very charming individual and put aside their partisan differences."

Philip Link
Education Department's
Executive Administrator

Robert Davila

First Berkeley Product Earning Doctoral Degree

In 1989, a singular event occurred at the highest levels of the United States Government. Dr. Robert Davila, a 1948 graduate of CSD, became the highest ranking deaf official in the Government when he was nominated by President George Bush and confirmed by the Senate as Assistant Secretary for the Office of Special Education and Rehabilitation Services (OSERS) of the United States Department of Education. That milestone was one of many in a fascinating journey by a deaf man who began his academic career as a young child at the California School for the Deaf-Berkeley.

Bob Davila was born in San Diego, California, and raised in Carlsbad, a hearing child in a family that spoke only Spanish. When he became deaf from spinal meningitis at the age of eight, he enrolled at the CSD-Berkeley. English was the language of learning, and Davila quickly learned both American Sign Language and English. It was a tall order for a Spanish speaking, totally deaf child, but Davila, a quick learner, mastered both languages. In the 1940s, all the students who made the honor roll were treated to the movies. Davila saw more movies than any other student did because he hit the honor roll every time. Upon graduation from CSDB, he attended Gallaudet College and flourished as a sports editor of the college newspaper, a volunteer with a Boy Scout troop, a leader in Gallaudet's governing council and captain of the track and cross-country teams. In 1953, Davila received his bachelor's degree in education.

Upon graduation from Gallaudet, Davila married Donna Ekstrom, a deaf sign language teacher he met on the beach at Santa Monica, and joined the faculty at the New York School for the Deaf in White Plains, New York. For fourteen years, Davila taught several generations of deaf students, and he and Donna raised two hearing sons, Brian and Brent.

Davila felt he had to continue the pursuit of opportunity for further education. He aspired to become an administrator, but the obstacles were formidable-he realized that in the entire nation,s schools for the deaf, only two administrators were deaf. Aware that his ticket to a brighter future lay in advancing his own education, Davila enrolled in Hunter College in New York City and received a Master of Science degree in special education in 1963. He then became a Fellow in the Education Technology for Educators of the Deaf at Syracuse University and received his Ph.D. in educational technology in 1972. He has the distinction of being the first deaf man to earn an advanced degree from Syracuse University. He is CSD's pride for being the first CSD graduate to earn the highest degree.

Pursuit of Further Education

Over his long and distinguished career, Bob Davila has never lost sight of his role in the long struggle for minority rights. He pointed out, "Deaf people have the right to succeed - and to fail - like anyone else. That is a very important part of the empowerment movement in the deaf community. It comes down to this: You've got to accept me for what I am - my language, culture, habits, and opinions. If you can't accept me on that basis, then don't accept me, period. It has to be all the way through or not at all."

Stuart Low
Staff Writer
Rochester Democrat and *Chronicle*
November 24, 1996

Promotions at Gallaudet

Davila returned to Gallaudet College in 1972, first as a teacher in the department of education and two years later, he became director of the Kendall Demonstration Elementary School. He steadily moved up Gallaudet's ranks. In 1978, Davila became vice president of Gallaudet's Pre-college Programs. He served in this position until 1989. In the latter role, Davila regularly made pitches to Congress to beef up Gallaudet's federal funding. In June 1975, the Convention of American Instructors of the Deaf elected Davila as its president, the first time a deaf person had ever been chosen for the position in the organization's 125-year history. Later he also became the first deaf person elected President of the Conference of Educational Administrators Serving the Deaf and the Council on Education of the Deaf.

Assistant Secretary of OSERS

In Bob Davila's four years as Assistant Secretary of OSERS, he helped boost funds for teachers of the deaf and expanded programs for deaf children and sign language interpreters. He also pumped new money into deaf community theaters and film captioning for hard of hearing viewers. Notwithstanding the fractious nature of many disability rights groups in and out of Washington, D. C., Davila was able to forge a consensus in the Congress. As Philip Link, the Education Department's executive administrator recalled, "Senators on both sides of the aisle found him a very charming individual and put aside their partisan differences."

Upon the change of administration in Washington in 1992, Davila resigned to become Headmaster of the New York School for the Deaf in White Plains, his old stomping grounds as a young teacher fresh out of Gallaudet. During his tenure at Fanwood, he upgraded the standards of the educational programs and revitalized its faculty.

Robert Davila frequently finds himself roaming and communicating with students and staff members on the NTID campus.

HELM AT THE NATIONAL INSTITUTE FOR THE DEAF Dr. Davila continued the pursuit of opportunity for advancement in the professional field. The National Technical Institute for the Deaf (NTID) made a significant step in its 30-year history by appointing Dr. Davila as the Institute's first deaf leader. As vice president for one of the seven colleges of Rochester Institute of Technology, Davila has become a visible proponent for the 1,100 deaf students of NTID. Due to Davila's advocacy, the RIT community is more understanding and sensitive to everyone's communication needs. Students have greeted him with great warmth. "It's an inspiration to me, because we need to 'grow' deaf leaders across the country," said Eric Hamlow, a 22-year-old student from Stockton, California, who coincidentally graduated from the California School for the Deaf at Fremont.

Robert Davila and his wife, Donna, now live in Pittsford, a charming suburb ten miles from the RIT campus. Both their children, Brian and Brent, are now grown and married with their own children. The two sons became civil engineers in Maryland and live there with their families. The Davila legacy continues.

The California School for the Deaf is exceedingly proud of its graduate, Dr. Robert Davila, who has risen to the top of his profession and diligently pursues excellence in educational programs for the deaf students.

Robert and Donna Davila embracing their sons and daughter-in-laws.

"Considering Beijing the noisiest country, a traveler asked me if the loud noises bothered me. I drily replied, "No, I didn't hear the Dragon roar.'"

Frances Parsons
Author of
No, I Didn't Hear the Dragon Roar

Frances "Peggie" Parsons

International Goodwill Ambassador

A lecturer for twenty years, Associate Professor Frances M. Parsons was coordinator of international history collections at Gallaudet University Learning Center for the years 1989 to 1993. However, she had worked at the University since 1968. She continued her globe trotting, visiting ministries of education, and presenting countless lectures to educators, parents, and government officials. As a result, she has been to practically every corner of the world except the Antarctic. Frances activated a deaf Peace Corps (PC) program in the Philippines and was the first PC participant - traveler/consultant in Asia, islands in the Pacific and Africa. She is an expert in working with foreign deaf and hearing teachers and parents, and no stranger to their modes of living, thinking and communicating.

Frances and her twin sister, Hester "Polly," were born prematurely in 1923, to hearing parents, a teacher and a cowboy rancher in El Cajon near San Diego, California. Frances was near death lying in a cigar box, but her father's constant nursing and Frances' determination to live saved her life.

Tahiti Bound

Learning the twins were deaf when they were five years old, their parents sent them to several oral schools before enrolling them at the California School for the Deaf-Berkeley. Much later Frances realizes how lucky she was to attend CSD, that did not segregate the profoundly deaf, using only manual communication, from the hard of hearing who were to use only oral methods. The "combined system" was emphasized at that time.

The depression during 1935 gave her and the Parsons family no choice but to move to Tahiti, where she spent six lonely early teen years in paradise. She devoted her free time to writing and reading books. Her diary was later published as *Sound of the Stars*. Only a few months before the bombing of Pearl Harbor, she and her family escaped from Tahiti on board a tiny two-masted schooner, the *Benicia*. The escape was very dangerous because of the Japanese submarines infesting the Pacific. Toward Hawaii, the ship was caught in a fierce storm that almost wrecked the *Benicia*. Due to Captain Lou Chataigner's skills, the ship safely entered the harbor of Honolulu. From there, they resumed their voyage to San Francisco, arriving after one month and a half of sailing.

Two books and deaf periodicials written by Frances Parsons. She believed that successful deaf individuals have all succeeded for the same single reason: "Guts."

Total Communication Endeavor

Returning to CSD facilitated Frances' admission to Gallaudet College. After her freshman year at Gallaudet, her marriage and raising two hearing daughters prevented her from continuing her college education. At the age of 40, she was determined to uproot her life in San Diego and complete her college education at Gallaudet.

Frances earned a B.A. degree in history of art at Gallaudet College and a M.A. degree and A.B.D.in the same field at the University of Maryland. She was known to be the first grandmother ever to graduate from Gallaudet. She said, "Never too late." After a stint as a teacher of English at the Maryland School for the Deaf, she was an Assistant Professor and then Associate Professor of History of Art for twenty years, and then coordinator of international history collections at Gallaudet. Frances' endeavors had taken her around the world eight times, heralding total communication to fight oralism. Some years later, she revisited the oral schools and she was astounded to see how deaf children's sign language helped with better communication and faster learning. She was pleased with the positive results.

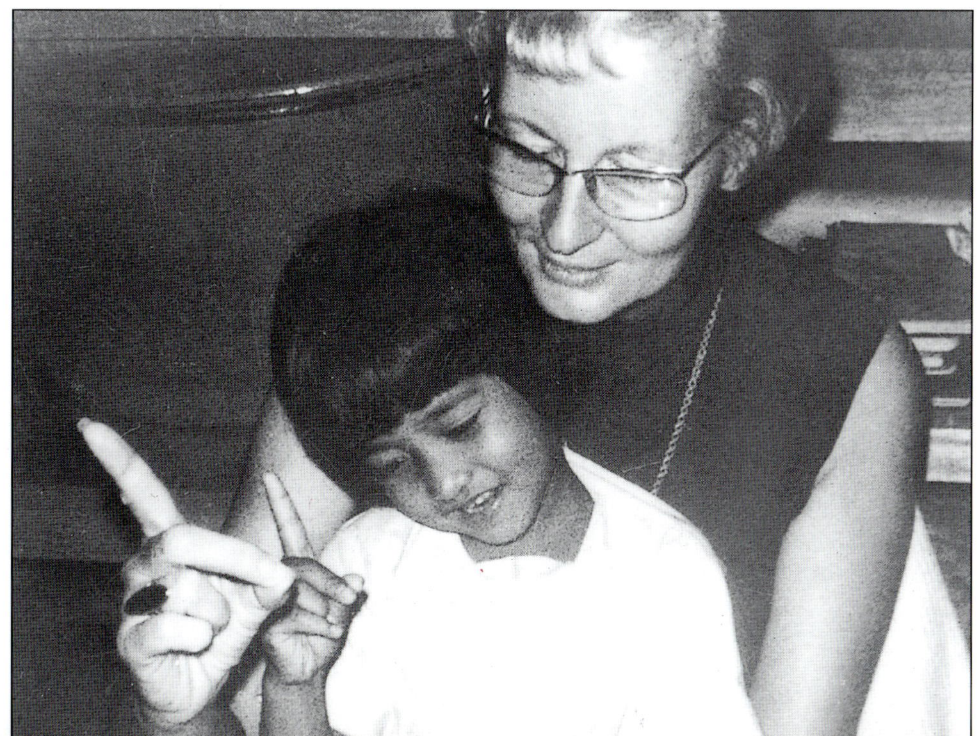

Francis Parsons teaching fingerspelling to the deaf children at the Missionary School for the Deaf in the Philippines. Her interest and insight into the anthropology, customs and language of international countries originated from her early teens on the island of Tahiti.

> ***"As an adult, Frances Parsons toured Europe eight times. She traveled through parts of Africa, India, Southeast Asia, Russia, and South America before making her solo journey from Hong Kong to Kathmandu - through the heartland of China."***
>
> 
>
> Frances Parsons
> 1988

Apparently, her interest and insight into the anthropology, customs and language of international countries emanated from her early teens on the island of Tahiti. During her travels in a number of countries, such as the Philippines, Iran, India, Malaysia, the Far East, Australia, Africa, Russia, Europe and South America, Frances experienced several harrowing situations that threatened her life.

Frances emphasized, "I believe in following the customs of the countries that I visit. In one country, I slept on the floor, even with giant cockroaches crawling out of the wall and getting in my hair." "When in Rome, do as the Romans do," she counseled.

She was the author of *I Didn't Hear the Dragon Roar* and deaf periodicals about successful deaf individuals. She believed that they have all succeeded for the same single reason: "Guts." After retiring from Gallaudet, she continued traveling in the United States and Canada with Rubette, her pet mini-pinscher, as well as going solo overseas.

Most Recent Travels

Frances recalled one harrowing experience in traveling in Siberia with a forged Russian passbook that contained a Russian name which was arranged by Igor Abramov, then President of Moscow Society of Deaf. He invited her to give lectures at schools, factories, clubs and organizations of deaf. She was accompanied by Victor Palenny, a Russian travel agent. On one train stop "a conductor and a police inspector gestured to me to show my passbook. I indicated my deafness and he scribbled in Russian that petrified me. In a split second, Victor with ashen face, hastily explained my poor eyesight and that he had to read for me. They looked at us oddly because I had my journal on my lap. Russian women are not supposed to write journals. They relentingly left. What a close call!"

When the King of Thailand declared a new law that English be implemented in every school, concerned Thai educators of the deaf in Chiang Mai invited Frances to come and to teach them English and English signs. Frances described the experience as "a challenge crash course in 3 1/2 weeks." She managed to complete T. J. O'Rourke's ABC Basic Course in Manual Communication to the first group of 20. Under her supervision, they, in turn, conducted the seminar of 60 teachers, including 12 deaf adults, in the second group. Lastly, some of the teacher-students and 8 deaf adults instructed 40 students of Chiang Mai School. The last two days were spent in teaching 18 teachers on English signs at Dusit School in Bangkok. Notwithstanding the hectic, exhausting assignment, Frances had accomplished her mission.

"Wrestling is known to be one of the oldest sports, dating back to 3,000B.C. Nevertheless, wrestling at Gallaudet College was a 'new sport' which fascinated Swaim."

Ken Norton

Dean Swaim

Novel Wrestling Hold: His Achieved Career

When Dean Swaim retired from the California School for the Deaf in 1988, he reminisced that becoming the first deaf high school principal in California was his proudest accomplishment. His wrestling coaching career with the CSD wrestling powerhouses and teaching career were labors of love, ranking up there with the principalship. Swaim was vocational principal when he left CSD with his wife, Anna Lee, who was a junior high mathematics teacher. They built a new country home in Markleeville, near Lake Tahoe, where they have enjoyed their retirement years.

Introduction to Grappler's World

At the age of one, Swaim was stricken with spinal meningitis that caused his deafness. Born and raised in a small farm town, Winton, California, he enrolled in the California School for the Deaf-Berkeley in 1936 and was admitted to Gallaudet College in 1948. Wrestling has been known to be one of the oldest sports, dating back to 3,000 B.C during the Egyptian Empire. Nevertheless, wrestling at Gallaudet was a "new sport" which fascinated Swaim. His closest friend, Donald Bullock, raved about wrestling, as he was a year ahead of Swaim. So, Swaim joined the wrestling team and during their glorious days in the world of wrestling, they both relished their many victorious matches under the helm of Coach Thompson Clayton. What made this even more special about Swaim and Bullock was that it was rare for any college to land two great grapplers who had never been on a wrestling mat before. Swaim vanquished more than 90 per cent of his college opponents, losing only one or two matches every year in the 145 pounds class during the years of 1948 to 1953. He and Bullock won

Gallaudet College President Leonard Elstad, left, DonBullock, Dean Swaim, Coach Tom Clayton, kneeling. Dean Swaim and Don Bullock savored their success in wrestling contests in 1951.

second place in the Mason Dixon Wrestling Conference tournaments for four years. One of Swaim's most exciting moments was winning the Washington, D. C. Amateur Athletic University (DCAAU) wrestling crown in 1951. He closed his career in wrestling and football when he graduated in 1953. In 1996, Swaim and Bullock were inducted into the Gallaudet University Hall of Fame in wrestling. Along with four other Hall of Famers from the same team, Swaim and Bullock helped putting Gallaudet College on the map. Gallaudet,s wrestling team got the nation's attention, as they steamrolled bigger Eastern colleges or universities, such as University of Maryland, University ofVirginia, City College of New York.

Teaching and Coaching in Five Schools

After graduation from Gallaudet College, Swaim not only started his teaching career at the Iowa School for the Deaf, but he implemented a wrestling program and tutored green grapplers with his rich knowledge of holding maneuvers. In 1956, he moved to the West Virginia School for the Deaf to become mathematics teacher, football, basketball and track coach, and scoutmaster. Wrestling did not exist there due to a small enrollment. In 1958, Swaim and Donald Bullock teamed in athletics; Swaim was an assistant coach and Bullock as head coach at WVSD that won the national deaf high school football championship. In 1959, Swaim transferred to the Maryland School for the Deaf to teach mathematics in the high school department, and become athletic director and basketball coach. In 1962, Dr. Huff of the Wisconsin School for the Deaf lured Swaim from Maryland to become junior high mathematics teacher. Back in to the wrestling business, he started a new wrestling program at Wisconsin.

Return to Alma Mater

After only a few months in Wisconsin, Dr. Schunhoff brought Swaim back to his alma mater to teach mathematics and initiate the wrestling program at the Berkeley school in 1963. His wrestling teams won league championships for seven straight years from 1966 to 1972 and he sent several boys to the California State Championship Tournaments. Don Bullock was his assistant coach, but Swaim stated, "Bullock is more than just an assistant, a real coach on the same level as I am." Bullock had mutual feelings about Swaim ever since he was assistant football coach with head coach Bullock at the West Virginia School. From 1963 to 1968, Swaim was assistant coach with Ken Norton as head coach; they relished winning seasons in football. They won three league championships and two national championships among the schools for the deaf. They also accompanied six Olympians from CSD to Malmo, Sweden, where the World

Games for the Deaf were held. Swaim and Norton, respectively, coached the U.S. wrestling team and the U.S. track team.

Dean and Anna Lee Swaim enjoy living in the high Sierra country during their retirement years.

New Venture in Education and Community Services

In 1972, returning to CSD from a Leadership Training Program in the area of the Deaf at California State University-Northridge, Dean Swaim became principal of the high school department. Later he transferred to the vocational department as principal. Swaim also found time to be active in community activities. He was President of the Vista Lions Club for several years and also served as President of the Deaf Counseling and Referral Agency Board from 1972 to 1978.

Swaim was appointed by Governor George Deukmejian to the Governor's Committee on Employment of the Handicapped, focusing on training and transition from school to work. Also, he was on the Vocational Advisory Committee. He was a member of the Fremont Chamber of Commerce from 1983 to 1988. He was awarded an Award of Merit from Conference of Educational Administrators Serving the Deaf for significant contributions as a teacher and role model for deaf youth in the academic and vocational programs at CSD.

Since his retirement in 1988, he has enjoyed flyfishing, golfing, bowling, and traveling with Anna Lee in the Sierra Nevada. In addition, both have been active in the deaf communities in Nevada and Northern California, covering various organizations such as Reno Silent Club, Nevada Association of the Deaf, Sierra Tahoe Golf Club, and Northern California Angling and camping Club. Dean Swain is secretary of the Nevada Association of the Deaf. Also, he is on a committee that is working to establish a state bureau for the Deaf and Hard of Hearing in Nevada.

They have three grown children, Debra, Cheryl and Billy. Debra is a manager of IBM's financial division in San Jose. Cheryl is an office administrator of a law firm in Seattle. Receiving a degree in commerical refrigeration from Phoenix Technical institute, Billy secured permanent employment as a commerical refrigeration installer in Phoenix.

"Terrence was a strong advocate for the deaf people. He took on the task of consultant in the field of sign language education in its advent."

Ken Norton

TERRENCE JAMES O'ROURKE

TRAILBLAZER IN AREAS OF POLITICS AND SOCIAL ACTIVITIES FOR DEAF CITIZENS

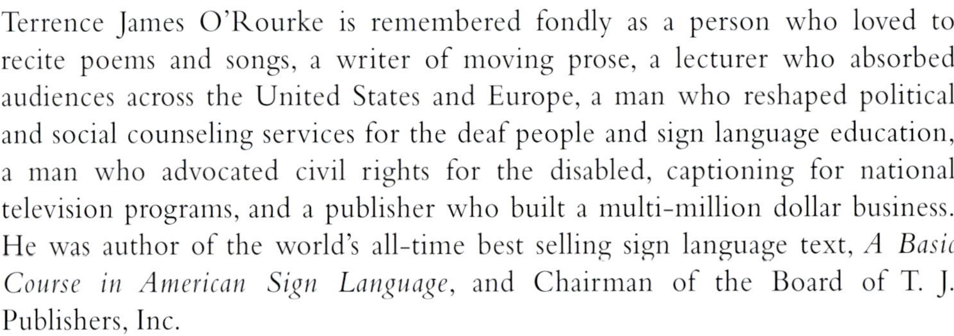

After being a classroom teacher for more than ten years, Terrence O'Rourke plunged into the world of publishing as well as being an advocate for the deaf people. He was author of the world's all-time best selling sign language text, A Basic Course in American Sign Language.

Terrence James O'Rourke is remembered fondly as a person who loved to recite poems and songs, a writer of moving prose, a lecturer who absorbed audiences across the United States and Europe, a man who reshaped political and social counseling services for the deaf people and sign language education, a man who advocated civil rights for the disabled, captioning for national television programs, and a publisher who built a multi-million dollar business. He was author of the world's all-time best selling sign language text, *A Basic Course in American Sign Language*, and Chairman of the Board of T. J. Publishers, Inc.

On January 10, 1992, O'Rourke died of heart failure at his home in Silver Springs, Maryland, "just short of his 60th birthday," according to Mervin Garreston, Professor and Vice President, and a colleague of O'Rourke at Gallaudet College. Garreston recalled his first contact with young student O'Rourke (better known as Terry or TJ) when he came to Gallaudet to teach summer school. Garreston enjoyed telling the story of "Terry greeted me by signing and fingerspelling from memory, word for word, a number of my own poems! My amazement turned to wonder at finding someone so like myself in love of songs (at least the words to songs) and a familiarity with classical, renaissance and 19th century poetry."

Besides these talents, O'Rourke was also a proficient writer, an imaginative one with a heart of sentiments. Among his many works in prose, most notably were *The Hand of Fate* (printed in Silent Muse), *The Feel*, and *There Is No Place Like Home*, but most of his work dealt with advocacy for sign language education and civil rights for the disabled. They earned him international recognition.

O'Rourke was born on April 17, 1933, in Bellingham, Washington. In 1943 spinal meningitis deafened him overnight and left him distraught because "music and medicine were," according to Ann Fortson (in *The Deaf American*, July 1971 issue), "his two great loves" and he was already accomplished on four different musical instruments. At the time of Terry's deafness there was very little counseling available to a deaf person and his family, but fortunately, the O'Rourkes were advised immediately to enroll Terry at the California School for the Deaf in Berkeley, where he encountered many adjustment problems and found no one to help him through the traumatic period.

Since life consists, to a large degree, of changing environmental situations, the young Terry used his active imagination that allowed him to assimilate the school regulations and school life in the new CSD environment as well as to cope with the older boys. When the older boys encircled looking down on O'Rourke, he was quick with words that were unfamiliar to them and eventually earned their respect and friendship. An ironic twist, this resulting experience was useful for his advocacy and career in years later.

O'Rourke graduated from CSD-Berkeley in 1948. He went on to Gallaudet College, where he received a degree. His academic career included teaching, coaching, and journalism at the North Dakota and North Carolina schools for the deaf, subsequently at Gallaudet College in the English Department from 1960 to 1968 and consulting at numerous institutions, including Western Maryland College.

It is remarkable how he accomplished the following career and advocacy. He was the national director of the Communication Skills Program of the NAD in 1968, a post he held until 1978. He served as both vice president and president of the American Coalition of Citizens with Disabilities, where in 1977 he helped organize a ten-city take over of the national/regional headquarters building of HEW. In 1982, O'Rourke was the first Deaf person to underwrite captioning for an entire television program, The Perry Como Christmas Special. The following year he founded the Caption Club, a voluntary organization that supported the efforts of the National Captioning Institute (NCI).

He received numerous awards for his lifelong defense of civil rights for the deaf and people with disabilities, from the National Association of the Deaf, Registry of Interpreters for the Deaf, NCI, the Texas Association of the Deaf and others.

David Pierce, Vice President of production for KALEIDOSCOPE, America's Disability Channel, developed a television mini-documentary: "Portrait of a Deaf Irish American: Terrence James O'Rourke," a 1992 documentary which tells the life of TJ as author, public servant and civil rights activist who led the way for sweeping political and social change for deaf people in America.

"Terry O'Rourke, more than anyone during his generation, deserves credit for founding the profession of interpreting for the deaf. His work on behalf of the National Association of the Deaf and later as an entrepreneur, to promote expansion of interpreter training opportunities and programs, assemble and distribute curriculum materials and encourage the writing and publication of books on sign language and interpreting created new career paths for many deserving hearing persons while concurrently expanding access for deaf Americans."

"It has always been a measure of personal pleasure and pride to have shared a major part of my life with Terry. He was an outstanding person and his untimely demise has left a lonesome place against the sky."

Dr. Robert Davila
A classmate of
Terry O'Rourke at both CSD
and Gallaudet College

"Not only a tireless advocate in the Deaf community, Julian always finds time to take on a new task for any worthy cause."

Ken Norton

JULIAN SINGLETON
MAN WITH LEADERSHIP ABILITIES

Julian "Buddy" Singleton is one of the most significant deaf leaders in the San Francisco Bay Area as well as a strong advocate for the deaf community.

Standing tall and poised on a stage, presiding over a meeting with total confidence, you will often find in the Deaf community Julian Singleton. His leadership, his perseverance in the pursuit of harmony among the Deaf, his diplomatic skills, and his keen thinking are the elements that reinforce the people's trust in him. Being a retired CSD teacher and senior citizen, Singleton has devoted most of his free time in the pursuit of a project — the senior citizen housing complex. Currently, he is president of the Bay Area Coalition of Deaf Citizens, which is the newest organization to meet the Deaf citizens' needs.

BACKGROUND
Born to deaf parents, Singleton grew up in Los Angeles with two hearing sisters, who are now doing interpreting services. He enrolled at the California School for the Deaf-Berkeley in 1942 and graduated in 1952. After attending Gallaudet College for three years, Singleton married his childhood sweetheart, Bernice Hoare, '54. They raised three children: Paul, a program analyst at the Pentagon, Washington, D. C.; Ralph, supervisor of microwave vacuum tube specialty at the Communication and Power Company in Palo Alto; Jenny, a professor at the University of Illinois.

CHANGE OF CAREER
After working at the Oakland Tribune as a printer for twelve years, Singleton decided his heart was set to work directly with deaf children. He landed a position as a printing instructor at the Oregon School for the Deaf. In 1975, his dream came into reality, as he returned to his Alma Mater as Graphic Arts teacher and worked with his former teacher, John Galvan.

Promptly, he plunged himself into becoming involved with numerous activities in the school community as well as the deaf community. He has a long history of interests in the welfare of the Deaf. Here is a list of several of numerous endeavors in which Singleton participated.

- **California Association of the Deaf, Vice-president and President**
- **Northwestern Athletic Association, Vice-president and President**
- **Telecommunications for the Deaf, Inc., Board Member**
- **National Captioning Institute, Inc., Consumer Advisory Board**
- **DEAF Senior Housing Project, Board Member**
- **Northern California Flying Hands RV Camping Club, Treasurer**
- **DCARA Board of Directors**

Below is a list of a few of many awards Singleton received for his achievements.

- **Northwest Athletic Association Hall of Fame recipient in the area of leadership**
- **California State Department of Education Sustained Superior Achievement Award**
- **California Deaf Teacher of the Year in 1985**
- **Phi Kappa Zeta Dorothy M. Jacobs Memorial Community Award recipient**
- **Deaf Counseling and Referral Agency Harold Ramger Award**

Julian Singleton's staunch supporter is his wife Bernice in every project Julian undertakes.

Founder of Camp Taloali

In 1973, while teaching at the Oregon School, Singleton and Royal Teets, Oregon School alumnus, were approached by a cousin of Royal Teets who inquired as to what kind of service would be best for a site of 48 acres. Singleton quickly suggested a camp for deaf youth. The process of gaining the site followed. Singleton and Teets are befitting co-founders of Camp Taloali for the Deaf in Stayton, Oregon. With enormous help from the Oregon National Guard in clearing the grounds, the Elks Club for building material, and the deaf community for building labor, Camp Taloali became one of the nation's preferred camps for youth. Eventually, the size of the establishment grew to 111 acres and the site is used annually for the deaf adult festival known as Timberfest. A trail is named after Singleton on Camp Taloali grounds.

Bernice Singleton, a Supporter

Bernice Singleton, who was an elementary counselor for 18 years at CSD, is a staunch supporter of her husband's endeavors. Bernice herself has performed many community activities. Both of them enjoy five grandchildren whenever they are not busy with community work. Both in their enthusiastic and constructive manner have contributed much to what is now BACDSC. Buddy Singleton said in simple words, "I like to do good deeds for the Deaf community."

"Nothing is impossible for our 'everything' leader whose nickname is Buddy. A busy man like Buddy always finds time for friends. Too bad that we have only one Julian 'Buddy' Singleton. He should be cloned"

Daniel Lynch
A'53, Retired CSD Teacher

"For Julianne Fjeld, the odyssey took ten years of battling with the Hollywood studios to film the Greenberg story, **In This Sign** *(changed to* **Love is Never Silent***)."*

Ken Norton

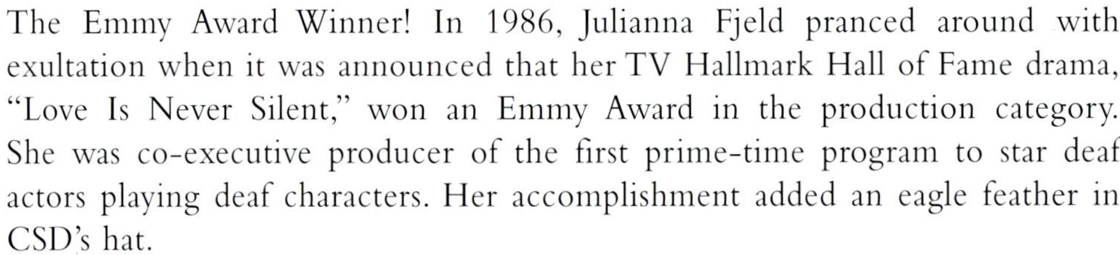

Julianna Fjeld

First Deaf TV Prime-Time Executive Producer

Julianne Fjeld's diligent persistence succeeded in bringing fame to a TV movie, "Love is Never Silent," an Emmy winner.

The Emmy Award Winner! In 1986, Julianna Fjeld pranced around with exultation when it was announced that her TV Hallmark Hall of Fame drama, "Love Is Never Silent," won an Emmy Award in the production category. She was co-executive producer of the first prime-time program to star deaf actors playing deaf characters. Her accomplishment added an eagle feather in CSD's hat.

Born deaf of hearing parents, Fjeld aspired to be an actress through her meeting with Spencer Tracy at John Tracy Clinic in Los Angeles. Fjeld described her experience of "meeting a man with white hair." "He would perform magic and entertain the deaf children. I liked his gentleness, his ability to communicate, although I was not aware that he was a famous movie star until four years later when my parents took me to a movie, 'The Mountain', starring the magician, Spencer Tracy. He became my idol. I decided I wanted to be an actress." This inspiration of becoming an actress remained with Fjeld in the years ahead.

Because her father was an Army colonel, requiring the family to move from base to base in different locations, Fjeld as "an Army brat" attended six different schools. She was educated first at John Tracy Clinic, subsequently at the Kansas School for the Deaf, Percy M. Hughes (mainstreaming school for the handicapped), the Kendall School for the Deaf, then back to the Kansas School and finally CSD-Berkeley in 1964. She was "delighted to find the communication and the culture with students and teachers ideal. They made all the difference. I was also involved in different school plays." She graduated from CSD-Berkeley in 1966 and enrolled at Gallaudet College the following fall.

After performing roles in several theatrical college productions, Fjeld graduated with a degree in English Language and Literature from Gallaudet University in 1970. (In 1988 one of her classmates, I. King Jordan became the first deaf president of Gallaudet.) Fjeld joined the National Theatre of the Deaf, where she toured with the company nationwide and abroad for five years.

After leaving NTD, she went to Paris, France, for a brief period to guide a visual workshop with deaf adults and became one of the team players of the International Visual Theatre. It was a worthwhile experience, but in the back of her head there was a persistent dream to televise Joanne Greenberg's novel *In This Sign*. She had read the book when she was a senior at Gallaudet University. In search for a screen writer, she returned to Los Angeles in 1977. For a living, she worked at the Mark Taper Theater on DATE (Deaf Audience Theatre Experience) as a consultant off and on for fourteen years. She was also involved in one of the visual workshops that developed a method for both hearing and deaf actors to harmonize with each other for an upcoming new play titled "Children of A Lesser God (COAL)." She served as a consultant to the first production of "COAL" at Mark Taper Theatre and later during the final six months of its two-year Tony Award-winning Broadway run in New York City, she had an opportunity to perform in the lead role of Sarah whenever Phyllis Frelich needed a break. The *In This Sign* dream quickly put her back on track.

After changing screenwriters several times, Fjeld found Darlene Craviotto to be the ideal person and the one who introduced her to Marion Rees, the producer of "quality." Rees and Fjeld teamed as co-producers to film the Greenberg story for television. The title of *In This Sign* was changed to "Love is Never Silent." The task was paramount. For Fjeld, the odyssey took ten years of battling with the Hollywood studios to film the Greenberg story. It took some time for both producers to find a studio that would agree to hire only deaf actors to portray deaf characters. The NBC studio and the Hallmark Hall of Fame company agreed to film the story on the producers' terms. "Love is Never Silent" was heralded as an award winner.

Fjeld was hired as a co-Artistic Director of the National Theater of the Deaf in 1990 for one and half years. In 1993 her mother died, which was very traumatic for her. She moved back west. In 1998 she moved to the San Francisco Bay Area and then she was hired to direct "Romeo and Juliet" at CSD-F. She also appeared in a "Lower Depths" play for Studio American Conservatory Theater (ACT) in San Francisco with hearing actors and two other deaf actresses.

In television, Fjeld's acting credits include the films of "Johnny Belinda," "Hear No Evil," and appearances in "Dallas," "Seasame Street" and "Captain Kangaroo," which earned that show its first Emmy award. She also appeared in

"Life with Julianna has been a treasure chest of riches. Over the past thirty-three years, I have had the pleasure of seeing her grow as a theatre professional . . . . from the first time when I laughed my head off as she played an Old Maid and embarrassed the heck out of some Jr. NAD conventioneers. . . . to her never-to-be-forgotten performances as leading lady in "The Glass Menagerie" and "A Streetcar Named Desire." Our friendship has been such a wonderful source of support as we each have traveled over the mountains and down through the valleys of our lives."

Dr. Don Bangs
Scriptwriter and director of plays

"A Child's Christmas in Wales" on BBC and CBS with the NTD cast. She performed in the feature film "Golden Girl" and was the subject of an award-winning documentary about her life: "Julianna: A Portrait."

As for other stage work, she also portrayed the Spirit of Christmas Present in "A Christmas Carol" at Mark Taper Forum theater and was one of the stars in an award-winning production of "Trojan Women" at the Los Angeles Actor's Studio.

Fjeld has returned to CSD on three occasions to serve as a drama consultant to the academic departments and to direct the annual school play. *Into Hiding*, *Romero and Juliet*, and *Little Women* are dramatic productions for which she brought acclamation to her student performers at CSD.

In person, Fjeld radiates serenity and a sense of humor. Her perseverance, creativity and talents have made her popular wherever she goes.

"When Ella Mae Lentz signs her poems, she inspires us and makes us feelproud of our language and culture."

Ken Mikos

One of three authors of *Signing Naturally*

Ella Mae Lentz

A Woman with a Mission to Launch the True Meaning of ASL

As a student in June 1971, Ella Mae Lentz became an honor student and class valedictorian like her mother, Mary Ellen Lentz, depicted on pages 367-69, and was a budding poet. When she enrolled at Gallaudet College the following fall, her potential was challenged by the Drama Department to expand her acting skills and to recognize the American Sign Language as a language with its own grammatical system. It became clear to Lentz that American Sign Language need no longer be a compensation for English language in poetry, storytelling and drama. ASL is a true language. To analyze the structure became her all consuming interest, which proved to be useful in her future work. She embraced such challenges the way she thrives on her personality. At Gallaudet College, she won a poetry competition and was awarded a Kappa Gamma Poetry Award and the best actress category for her leading role in *The Lion in Winter*. She graduated with a bachelor's degree in English and Drama in 1979.

Moving Venture

Following her graduation from Gallaudet College, she worked in various ASL research laboratories including Northeastern University in Boston with Dr. Harlan Lane and Salk Institute with Dr. Ursula Bellugi before working for the National Association of the Deaf (NAD) in the Communication Skills Program as coordinator of an ASL teacher training project under the director, Dr. S. Melvin Carter, Jr. While there, she had the opportunity to perform the role as Sarah Norman for the production of *Children of a Lesser God* at the Milwaukee Repertory Theatre.

Returning to California, she taught at Ohlone College in Fremont as a part-time and later a full-time instructor in various subjects but later focusing specifically on ASL and Interpreter Preparation. Eventually, she transferred to Vista College in Berkeley, continuing her career in teaching ASL.

The extraordinary approach used to film Ella Lentz's poems create a rich dialogue between cinematic language and Sign Language poetry never seen before.

Signing Naturally Tools

After some time she sensed that hearing students were being "unnatural" with their learning of ASL and that something was missing. Her inquisitive, logical way of looking at ASL has improved her technique for teaching ASL to the students. Her success has inspired students to master their skills. This led her to incorporate with Ken Mikos (former CSD teacher) and Cheri Smith (daughter of Larry and Rose Shoemaker, CSD '40). They developed the best selling *Signing Naturally* textbook, workbook, and educational videotapes that examine the phenomena of ASL as the one unifying language. Various schools and universities, both nationally and abroad, frequently use these *Signing Naturally* tools. In addition, they invite Lentz to set up workshops and to lecture. The person the viewers see is a joyful, dynamic person on the platform just as on and off the stage. Ella Mae Lentz provided the same techniques to workshops in Japan, France, Canada, and Italy. As a result, *Signing Naturally* has been adapted into an Italian textbook. She has given thousands of hours to the pages of textbooks on ASL and thinks nothing of working long hours.

Her other love is the theater, as is the theater for her. One of the remarkable professional stage play theaters is San Jose Symphony Theatre in San Jose. The theater itself is gorgeous, but what makes it even more beneficial for deaf audiences is two professional theatre interpreters, Charlottee Toothman and Joe

> ***"I am fortunate to have been a friend of Ella's... working with her on the 'Signing Naturally' Books, I have come to see how very perceptive and instrumental she has been in exploring and understanding ASL so that we can better teach the language and share our culture with other people. Not only is Ella a strong advocate of ASL and Deaf culture, she is also a wonderfully expressive poet - when she signs her poems, she inspires us and makes us feel proud of our language and culture."***
>
> 
>
> Ken Mikos
> One of three authors of
> *Signing Naturally*

Quinn. They are top flight interpeters with a flair and a vivid imagination for ASL in an eloquent way. Ella Mae Lentz has been consulting theater interpreters on their translation choices. As a result, the deaf audience experience a complete enjoyment of ASL interpreting stage production.

A Well-Known Deaf Poet and Her *Treasure*

As a poet and an entrepreneur, Lentz used her flair to launch an unusual videotape product: *The Treasure*, written and performed by herself. She is one of the partners of the In Motion Company along with Cheri Smith and Kenneth Mikos that produced *The Treasure*, a collection of Lentz's original poems, and a description of ASL techniques for each poem. They are marked by sentiment, humor, flashing rhetoric of a deaf child's identity, philosophical acuteness, grasp of human nature, and natural charm. One person pointed out that "there wasn't a dry eye in the audience." Lentz's interpretation of her own poems brings grace to ASL. Yet, she attributed her inspiration and success to her high school teacher, Eric Malzkuhn, to whom she dedicated her "Travels with Malz" poem.

Ella Mae Lentz is a poet, a teacher, a lecturer, an actress, an entrepreneur and "famous ELLA" as acclaimed by some strangers who have seen her videotapes, books or performances. Lentz anticipates the publishing of advanced level of *Signing Naturally.* She also is contemplating writing a book and perhaps a return to the theater. As a nature of her character, she serves a call to challenge whatever comes her way.

CSD Products at Work

CSD has produced thousands of productive workers as well as solid, taxpaying citizens. They buy their own houses, attend church, and join clubs and benevolent societies. To list all of them is not possible but here below are several selected at random to give an example of what they did or are currently doing.

Teacher / Coach - *Frank Sladek*

The Arizona State Schools for the Deaf and Blind, Board of Directors, dedicated the Frank Sladek Gymnasium on May 15, 1993, and presented a certificate in recognition and heartfelt appreciation to Frank Sladek for outstanding service to the Arizona State Schools for the Deaf and Blind in Tucson, Arizona. His services covered his role as a coach for 31 years, a teacher for 34 years and a lifetime of service to the deaf and hearing community.

Sladek graduated from CSD-Berkeley, in 1941 and from Gallaudet College in 1946. He played right end on the 1940 football team that won the National Chapionship among the schools for the Deaf.

Sladek not only excelled in his personal athletic success, but he produced the greatest gift of all by sharing his athletic talents with young people through 31 years as a head coach in major sports. He volunteered his time to serve in the following positions: 12 years as basketball coach, 30 years as track coach, and 8 years as football coach. He guided the ASDB "Sentinels" to four state class "C" titles and 13 division titles in track, the conference co-champion for six-man football in 1952, and the conference championship and Southern Arizona District Consolation Championship in basketball. He was named Deaf American Basketball Coach of the Year in 1952.

Sladek has been inducted into three Sport Halls of Fame: Farwest Athletic Association, American Athletic Association of the Deaf, and Pima County Sports Community. His philosophy of education that reflected his career is "active involvement among the students" as a teaching prerequisite.

Artist - *Morris Broderson*

World class painter, born deaf in Los Angeles, California, November 4, 1928, Morris Broderson was educated at the California School for the Deaf-Berkeley, and schools in the Los Angeles area. His talent for art was first recognized in his adolescence and he began serious study at the age of 14 under Francis de Erdely at the Pasadena Museum and the University of Southern California. In Broderson's mid-thirties, he became a famed artist when his creative energy burst into a unique style in his paintings. Broderson was one of the first deaf artists to incorporate the manual alphabet into some of his paintings.

Broderson's paintings celebrate the simple joys of life and clearly reflect his characteristic concern for people and nature. Robert Barrett, Chief Curator of Fresno Art Museum, said, "His paintings are richly textural. Layers of patterns, forms and meaning crowd the format and press to the foreground of the picture plane. By juxtaposing diverse objects from a variety of periods and cultures, he creates a melange of symbols that point to the interconnectedness of the sacred and profane." Broderson is an artist of national repute, and his works are in major museum collections throughout the United States. In addition, a number of his paintings are owned by celebrities. He already has over forty one-man shows to his credit.

Baker - *Michael Skropeta*

Michael Skropeta entered CSD-Berkeley in 1931. During his high school years, he developed a great interest in baking under the guidance of a dedicated teacher, William Wilcoxson, who had a direct influence on Skropeta's career.

At the age of 20 with only 26 dollars to his name, Skropeta set out on his own and landed his first job as an apprentice baker at the White Cross Bakery in Oakland. He pocketed only 17 dollars for six days' work. Soon he was promoted to journeyman baker, skipping three years of apprenticeship.

By the age of 33, after being employed at several bakeries in the San Francisco Bay Area, Skropeta located a bakery in Lafayette and leased the building. He started up a family business with his three children. The landlord was so impressed with Skropeta's prompt lease payments that he sold him the building, which he named the Cake Box. Soon it became a well known and popular bakery in the community.

Skropeta and his wife, school sweetheart, Lois Kersch, who is a business accountant, with their children enjoy the success of all those many years of hard work. They have traveled the world and still kept their eyes on the trade's newest ideas and techniques.

Computer Engineer - *Timothy Wata*

Timothy Wata is employed with Lockheed Martin, the most respected electronics and missiles company, as a senior engineer in Orlando, Florida. For 23 years as a staff engineer, Wata has worked directly with many engineers to develop various computer programs. His current responsibility is to assist the computer facility system manager to control computer machines at the branch laboratory, for system management and programming consultations.

Wata graduated from CSD in 1972 and from Gallaudet College in 1977. In spite of a lack of knowledge in engineering, he was nevertheless hired by Martin Marietta because of his impressive interview and resume. At his new job, he succeeded overcoming communication obstacles. Eventually, Wata's employer and fellow workers learned sign language in order to carry on conversations at the work location. Apparently, the employers and workers value Wata's contribution to work.

Cartographic Draftsman / Writer - *Kenneth Shaffer*

At about age 5, Kenneth Shaffer developed a great love for trains after frequently watching the trains running through Corcoran, California, where his grandfather worked as a telegrapher. He was deafened at age 3 1/2 after an attack of spinal meningitis. In 1935, his parents moved to San Francisco to be near their parents, relatives and Shaffer, starting his schooling at CSD-Berkeley in 1932.

As a senior in 1946, Shaffer participated in a writing contest in Berkeley under the auspices of the Berkeley Elks Club and was awarded the top prize of $300 to help with extended studies at Gallaudet College. (This was the same Elks Club that has sponsored CSD's Boy Scout Troop 11 in its scouting program for many years).

Upon graduation from Gallaudet, Shaffer secured a position as a cartographic draftsman with the United States Geographical Survey (USGS) in Arlington, Virginia, and Menlo Park, California, producing color maps of the Atlantic and Pacific Regions. On the sideline, he is a proficient writer. He has been a feature columnist for the *Dee Cee Eyes*, a monthly newsletter of the deaf community in the Metro D. C. area, after he retired from the USGS in 1986 following 35 years of service.

Shaffer has continued his interest in trains by boarding many excursions, both steam and diesel. His wife, Elaine, and their children, Lance and Karen and Karen's family enjoy tagging along on the rides. Shaffer has contributed entertaining stories about his train ride experiences to magazines, including *The Alumni Eagle*.

Team Leader - *Ralph Nieves, Jr.*

Ralph Nieves, Jr., '75 CSD graduate, was a Team Leader of the hood assembly in the body shop for nine years at New United Motor Manufacturing Inc. (NUMMI) in Fremont, where they assemble Toyota Corolla, Chevrolet Prizm and Tacoma pickups. He supervised twelve hearing workers in that department, solving or adjusting problems that arise from the assembly line. His supervisor commended Ralph for his hard work and dedication and called him a remarkable troubleshooter. Ralph has been employed by NUMMI for fifteen years. During his football days, he was captain of the team, which reflected his leadership ability. Ralph has made NUMMI history by becoming the first ever Deaf forklift driver.

Clinical Technologist - *Colleen Daviton*

In 1998, Colleen Daviton, '73 graduate, was recognized as a recipient of the National Technical Institute for the Deaf's Distinguished Alumni Award. The award is presented annually to outstanding deaf or hard of hearing alumni who are successful and highly commendable in a chosen field of study or career, contribute to the betterment of the Deaf community and promote spirit among NTID alumni.

Daviton, "Collie" known by her friends, received her AAS in Medical Laboratory Technology from NTID in 1977. Then she earned her Bachelor of Science in Biology in 1983. She is currently working as a clinical technologist at University of Rochester - Medical Center, Strong Memorial Hospital where she performs with surgical tissues in preparation for microscopic slide examination. She also works with autopsy sectioning and research projects. She received a certification in Histopathology from American Society of Clinical Pathology.

Beyond her professional accomplishments, she has been a tenacious advocate for the Deaf Community, volunteering her time locally with Deaf Women of Rochester. She was involved with Deaf Women United serving on the national board and in 1997 as chairperson, hosted the 6th biennial national conference.

A transplanted Californian, Daviton has lived in Rochester, New York, since her college days, is the oldest daughter of deaf parents, David and Jeanette (Davis). They graduated from CSD-Berkeley in 1948 and 1952 respectively. All her deaf siblings: David, Michael and Candi also attended the Berkeley school and graduated in 1975, 1977, and 1979 respectively. As the third generation in her family being educated in the same school, her niece, Jenamarie, graduated in 1999.

Cabinet Maker - *Eugene Rianda*

Eugene Rianda, '46 CSD graduate, retired in December,1990 from Lockheed Space and Missiles Company in Sunnyvale, California, where he worked as a mock-up and tooling bench mechanic for 30 years. Spaceships are not made of wood but Rianda did operate various power machines that functioned on wood only. Following precise blueprints, he cut patterns that served as a guide for metal parts to be made for spaceships. He received 17 commendations for his workmanship. His experience in woodworking was acquired at CSD, where he was trained in the cabinet shop. As a carpenter he worked in Alaska for two years. His wife Betty, former student of CSD, worked at Lockheed, too, as a verifier for 27 years and retired in August, 1990.

During his retirement years, for his love of CSD, Rianda faithfully volunteers reorganizing the CSD museum on Tuesdays. He was the one who developed a scrapbook called *Memories of CSD Alumni* consisting of a collection of articles and photos of Alumni achievements. Not surprisingly, the scrapbooks were sold out, for the alumni cherished the good old days at CSD.

Director of Blind Services - *Robert L. Miller*

Robert L. Miller, '33 CSD graduate, was presented the prestige award, the Alice Cogswell Award for valuable services to the deaf-blind people from the Gallaudet University Alumni Association in 1996. He was the first Director of the Deaf-Blind Services at the Lighthouse for the Blind in San Francisco. When Miller discovered that the deaf-blind clientele had no regular activities or employment, he turned them into productive factory workers who were capable of manufacturing salable items for such companies as Pan American Airways and the Christian Brothers Wine Company.

Insurance companies agreed to provide coverage for deaf-blind factory workers after Miller convinced companies that deaf-blind were able to use power tools safely and skillfully.

After retiring from a 40-year career of service at the Lighthouse, Miller and his supportive wife, Sally, enjoyed living in Hawaii for some years. Presently, they live in Santa Rosa near their children.

Architectural Draftsman - *Ronald M. Hirano*

Ronald M. Hirano, CSD Eagle Scout and a '52 graduate, who is now retired, worked as an architectural draftsman for several companies in the San Francisco Bay Area for the past 37 years. He used to teach drafting and designing at Southwest Collegiate Institute for the Deaf at Big Spring, Texas, before he returned to California. Presently, he conducts an income tax service named The Tax Signs serving deaf and hearing clients.

Hirano is busily involved with the Bay Area Coalition of Deaf Senior Citizens and Deaf Seniors of America. He used to be an alpine guide/leader for backpacking and mountaineering trips in the Sierra. Presently, he lives in San Francisco with his wife, Catherine Farkas, a graduate of the day deaf class of Lincoln High School in Milwaukee, Wisconsin.

Visual Merchandiser - *Cary Barlow*

Cary Barlow works as visual merchandiser at an exclusive department store, Neiman Marcus in the Stanford Shopping Center in Palo Alto, California. Whenever you shop there, throughout the store, the eye will be in contact with his high fashion displays. He has a great flair for creating fashionable displays in store windows and showcases.

After graduating in 1980 from CSD, he headed for New York City where he enrolled at the Fashion Institute of Technology and received an A.A. degree in apparel design. He worked on Seventh Avenue in the garment district. Then he went on to do window displays at the men's stores at Bloomingdale's and Heralds Square Macy's. The toughest assignment he had ever experienced was to complete 24 windows every week at Macy's in New York City. Yet, he recommends that deaf people enter the career of visual merchanding. He states it is such an exciting venture.

Worker with Many Skills - *Charles Corey*

Charles Corey, known as "A Man of Many Talents," was employed at the Oakland Tribune newspaper company from 1960 to 1988. He was with the San Francisco Examiner newspaper company as a mailer, the Jensen Company in Emeryville as a welder that manufactured warplane parts during World War II, and the Hughes Company in Los Angeles producing eight titanium engine mounts for the huge all-wood flying boat known as "Spruce Goose" before landing a permanent job with the Tribune. Corey assumed the lead in the inserting machine department at the Tribune. He was credited with the invention of several devices that facilitated the function of the machines.

In 1967, as one of the founding members of the newly established National Theater of the Deaf, Corey and the cast traveled in the United States and

Europe for three years. After retiring, Corey and his wife, Florita, who was a professional Flamenco dancer performing in the United States and Spain, moved to Rancho Cordova near Sacramento.

Almost all of his life, Corey has been fascinated with aviation. Presently, he works on a second Spad fighter renovating project. As for a hobby, he builds and flies free flight model airplanes, and does mechanical repairs for many satisfied customers. Also, an excellent artist, he designed the cover of the book, *The Deaf at Work*, published in 1967.

Senior Computer Analyst - *Steve Longo*

At the Lawrence Livermore National Laboratory, University of California in Livermore, California, Steve Longo is a Senior Computer Associate. His major responsibilities are to analyze and correct system failures, to evaluate, recommend, and install/upgrade software and hardware on Windows NT networked with UNIX platforms, in addition to being available as a resource to the Hot Line and other consulting team members. He assumes a long list of functions daily at the Laboratory.

Longo got involved in computers as early as 1970 when he first hacked into the Stanford computer system from one of those clunky computer terminals at CSDB. The new security safeguard still did not stop him at all.

Perhaps, that is how Longo became a Computer Safeguard Security Officer who made sure there is no illegal activity and network configuration. In 1999, he was promoted to position of Systems Administrator who provides advanced systems administration of NT workstations and servers in a multi-tasked, highly demanded, team-oriented environment. His special assignments also include consulting with system administrators for future expansion in the area of software, hardware, and network. Additional assignments include macros for automation and event report on NT server, developing coursework materials for hands on training to NT administrators and consultants, and developing custom applications for consumers in Access, Visual Basic, Visual FoxPro, or Visual C++.

Longo is well known in the San Francisco Bay Area as a computer wizard. He is under heavy demand in doing favors for his friends to repair computers or install new programs. For relaxation, he enjoys creating multimedia projects with his wife who is a CODA (child of a deaf adult).

THE NORTON FAMILY

Granddaughter Tessa, front, left, Ken, Audree, Grandson Travis. Gary, husband of Nikki, Daughter Nikki, Brother Earl, Son Kurt.

Staunch family support was the motive to boost the author's persistence in writing the book. Because this is the history of our beloved CSD, the author feels compelled to salute not only those who urged and encouraged the writing of this book but also those who nurtured and impacted the life about which it has been written. As time goes on, the author realizes how blessed he has been with his cherished family and so many fine friends. He would like to extend his boundless gratitude to those who shared their stories and suggestions. He hopes the virtue of the book is considered a catalyst toward historical synthesis.

CSD's illustrious past and dynamic present portend a vital future. Indeed, CSDers want to see their school march into the 21st Century as it did into the 20th - *proud, opportunistic and productive*. May the rich history of our past serve as the inspiration for the future.

Acknowledgements

My treasured wife *Audree Lauraine Norton* not only encouraged me to write but critically observed the draft documents, and greatly contributed to my happiness and well being while the work was going on.

Innumerable acknowledgments are due to *Dr. Henry Klopping* for suggesting that I organize my research material into writing a book, and for editing the entire documents. His genuine interest in the rich history of the school and how much of that history had been passed down to the present day, is immeasurably appreciated.

Hearty gratitude goes to my admired friend, *Patricia Gillilan Symons*, for offering continuing valuable suggestions and support throughout the project.

Tremendous appreciation is awarded to *Dr. Byron Benton Burnes* and to his step-daughter, *Mary Jane Higuera*, who diligently proofread every word of my documents. Dr. Burnes was my enchanting high school teacher for two years and is befittingly considered my life-time teacher.

Special appreciation goes to *Robert "Robb" Pawlak* our book designer. Not only a creative freelance designer, Robb has become my sincere friend. He has spent many hours making the computer layouts with me, a rewarding and fun-filled experience. Without the ingenious enlightenment of Robert Pawlak, the book would not be complete.

Many personal thanks belong to *Patricia Jacobs, '63, Eugene Rianda, '46, Joyanne Burdett, '65, Donald Ingraham, '50, Patricia LaBrie, Bill Ash, '60, Jack Lamberton, Ken Pedersen, '67* and *Eliseo Diaz, '85,* for special assignments in congregating valuable information and priceless photographs needed for this book.

In addition, I wish to express my gratitude and appreciation to the many kind people listed below who assisted me in obtaining information during the past three years. *Deborah Guthmann, Jacob Arcanin, Roberta Alexander, Ron Stern, Ralph Neesam, Leo Jacobs, Celia May Baldwin, Jack Gannon, Pat Moore, David West, Hedy Stern, Meta Metal, Eric Malzkuhn, Kenneth Shaffer, Joyce Ingraham, Leslie Kramer, Mike Finneran, Mark Nelson, Carla Periera, Dee Kennedy, Helen Barber, Les Rudy, Gil Lentz, Gene Duve, Ron Rhodes, Joyce Lynch, Lisa Goetz, Charles Holmes, Eugene LaCosse, Vikki King, Steve Orman, Bonnie Loeffler, Rick Herbold, Charles Farr, Bob Morrison, Laura Peterson, Glenna Wurm, Jacqie Mosqueira, Peter Rivest, Gordon Craig, Bev Stevenson, Kevin Bella, Debbie Ayres, Barrett Smith, Jim Long, Ron Davenport, Doralynnn Folsee, Gail Wright, Gloria Romeo, Bernard Bragg, Eric Malzkuhn, Dean Swain, Don Bullock, Bob Ellis, Craig Salonen, Ann Moxley, Charles Holmes, Derek Johnson and Ronald Burdett.*

Copyright Acknowledgements:

The California News, 1885 to 2000
California School for the Deaf

California School for the Deaf
Museum and Archives

Stanford University Museum of Art
Stanford University
Stanford, California 94305

San Jose Mercury News
Tom Van Dyke, Photographer
310 University Avenue #200
Palo Alto, California 94301

Oakland Museum of California
1000 Oak Street
Oakland, California 94709

The Imagery Group
Commercial Photographic Laboratory
28302J Industrial Blvd.
Hayward, CA 94545

Ohlone College
College Relations
Fremont, CA 94539

Memories of the California School for the Deaf-Berkeley/Fremont Alumni, 1995, Eugene Rianda

University of California. The Library
Berkeley, CA 94720

Courtesy of the Bancroft Library
University of California, Berkeley

Dawn Bradley, Editor
National Association of the Deaf
814 Thayer Avenue
Silver Spring, MD 20910

Douglas Tilden, The Man and His Legacy
1994, Mildred Albronda

Granville Redmond
1989, The Oakland Museum

The Magic Lantern Man
1985, Mildred Albronda

San Francisco Bay Girl Scout Council
P.O. Box 2249
Oakland, CA 94621

The Argus of Fremont
Aric Crabb, photographer

Berkeley, California, the Story of the Evolution of a Hamlet into a City of Culture and Commerce, 1933,
William Warren Ferrier

Goeff Geiger
American Protective Services, Inc.
P.O. Box 6757
Oakland, CA 94603

The Tired Boxer, 1892,
Fine Arts Museums of San Francisco,
Gift of Alice Vincilione
and Mary L. Tiscornia

Students 1860-2000

1860
Benjamin, Brazilliar
Clanton, Samuel S.
D'Rutte. Theophilus H.
(d'Estrella), Theophilus
Hope
Doran, Bridget
Downey, Emma
Giddings, Henry R.
Hegler, Manuel S.
Kramer, Henry
Markham, Columbia
Mead, Kate
O'Farrell, Garrett
Sandercock, Thomas
Sherk, Jenny
Wertheimer, Susan
Wright, Mary E.

1861
Davis, Samuel
Dickson, Henry A.
Gayon, Marcelin
McKail, Mary
Phillips, William M.
Rogers, Mary A.
Shirley, Evadne
Slater, George

1862
Ballard, Byron
Coates, Mary A.
Devoe, Henry
Harlan, James C.
Musgrove, James R.
Wilts, Mary L.

1863
Bassett, James
Bassett, Jane A.
Bentley, John W.
Griswold, Carrie
Holding, John A.
Hull, Frank
Lindsay, John
Quelet, Susanna
Smith, Charles

1864
Blish, Preston
Jesus, Juam
May, Anna
McKail, James Jr.
Murphy, Preston
Willsie, Joseph T.

1865
Badger, Harriet T.
Colby, Edwin
Krantz, Louis
LaRue, John H.
McTigue, Augusta
Shattuck, Frank B.

1866
Aronsohn, Caroline
Butler, Millard F.
Hard, Amy B.
Ide, Lemuel H. C.
May, America
Nichols, Henry
Tilden, Douglas
Uhl, Anna M.
Wilson, Joseph

1867
Gilbert, Hippolite
Hill, Elbridge B.
Hill, Marlow S.
King, Eliza
Nolan, Mary
O'Brien, James P.
Robinson, John W.
Santa Cruz, Jose
Theobald, Catherine
Wright, Albert R.

1868
Aronsohn, Martin
Bateman, Wilbur
Street, Catherine
Thomas, Anthony R.

1869
Brown, Harriet L.
Coultner, Dora N.
Craig, William C.
Kerby, Mary
Lucas, Maggie
Nealon, Mary
Roesler, Annie K.
Sandercock, Cathy
Warren, Annie
Willitts, Joshua M.

1870
Aronson, Moses
Ayers, Dora
Boothe, Meta M.
Carrillo, Merihildo
Cronin, Edmond
Cronin, Ellen
Grady, Theodore
Hoke, Harmon A.
McCabe, James H.
McClure, Wm. C.
Ritchie, Lewis D.
Stoke, Harmon A.

1871
Cummins, Alva C.
Derrick, Francisco
Doe, Alonzo C.
McComb, Elizabeth
Moesser, George
Selig, Kossuth

1872
Budd, Charlotte
Mast, Herman
Oldham, William G.
Prout, Fanny E.
Ross, Nellie

1873
Best, William C.
Gard, Peter
Goss, Nancy J.
Lynch, William H.
McCormick, Francis
Redman, William W.
Rosenbaum, Nathan
Schreiner, Henry
Taber, Henry W.
Wallace, Gertrude J.
Winslow, William H.
Wood, Benjamin M.

1874
Feehan, James T.
Ford, Catherine
Gautier, Paul L.
Hawkins, Sallie E.
Jones, Sophia A.
Madigann, Emma J.
Sievers, Charles
Sullivan, Torrence W.

1875
Awbrey, Eliza B.
Bailey, Sarah J.
Bartels, Laura A.
Black, Joseph F.
Bradley, Arrenia I.
Christeen, Frederick
Christianson, Lewis
Crosby, George L.
Darling, Sarah F. J.
Demaree, Louis F.
Hannah, Andrew M.
Henning, Emma F.
Lambert, Norman
Munson, Mary E.
Shoaf, George A.

1876
Aldersley, Lyell
Botta, Orelia
Bradley, Catherine
Dickerson, Benjamin
Foland, Katie M.
Funkenstein, Leon
Gilbert, Angele
Harding, Robert L.
Holman, Willis G.
Lander, James
Lewis, Josephine
Palmer, Louis A.
Reichsrath, Charles
Rahmstorff, George
Schlamm, Solomon

1877
Cohn, Max
Coulter, Charles B.
deWolf, Joseph
Rhorer, Joel N.
Schleweck, Simon
Smith, Ellsworth
Stewart, Francis F.
Wright, Honorah C.

1878
Buckling, George F.
Butler, Louis L.
Collischonn, Frederick
Connelly, John Jr.
Cushman, Ira D.
Decker, Delia
deFrees, Mary A.
DeGouy, Margueritte
Dobner, Harry
Doran, Theresa
Durkee, Mary L.
Egan, William B.
Emry, Frances E.
Funkenstein, Pauline
Gee, William E.
Harding, Joseph G.
Kuffel, Wilma E.
Lewis, Beverly
O'Brien, Daniel
Olivas, Dolores
Peralta, Mary
Poyser, Harry
Price, Edmund M.
Raymond, Harry L.
Saltenberger, George
Schietz, Mathilda
Schilling, William
Sieferman, Emilie
Sieferman, Louisa
Sisterna, Juanita
Williams, Leo C.
Wood, Edgar

1879
Billings, Charles W.
Dinsmore, Bruce
Ewing, William
Goodrich, Doney H.
Gross, Charles A.
Halloran, Maggie
Kiddell, May G.
Lohmeyer, Edward
McLaughlin, Sophie
McMillam, Charles
McQuillan, Charles
O'Rourke, James P.
Porter, Fannie W.
Redmond, Granville
Thorpe, Charlotte C.

1880
Cator, Azro A.
Eades, Ida
Gassagne, Adela
Hatton, Jr., John S.
Horrick, Lizzie
Johnson, James H.
Johnson, Lucy M.
Lake, Frank D.
Muth, Elizabeth
Selig, Isadore
Vallejo, Camile

1881
Ankener, Frances L.
Bassett, John
Cole, Elizabeth D.
Gerstle, Fredrica E.
Heckman, Friedrich
Howell, Marcia C.
Kaiser, George H.
Ledden, Gertrude M.
Lipsett, Robert A.
Maury, Laura
McCarty, Wm. E.
Miller, Joseph
Sanguinetti, Antonio
Scranton, Edward
Wardlow, Helen L.

1882
Cohn, Celia
Dugan, Edward
Isert, Gustav
Leonard, Hattie E.
Shaw, James
Stewart, James H.
Tripp, Wm. H.
Weidmuller, Charles
Wells, Sarah Z.

1883
Cleveland, May
Coder, Sherman B.
Cotter, William
Crawford, Caroline J.
Dilke, John T.
Gande, Mabel A.
Gordon, Rosa
Hadlock, Hathron
Hatch, Adeline
Hatch, Joseph
Jacob, Isadore H.
Kavanaugh, William
Mucha, Rosa
O'Malley, John M.
Reynolds, Emma
Reynolds, Robert B.
Schroder, George
Watson, Fred W.

1884
Campbell, Marie N.
Craddock, Rosa
Daggett. Mary E.
Dobner, Ethel
Dugan, Mary E.
Miller, Charles F.
Laughlin, Joseph
Norton, Frances A.
Pomber, Juan M.
Strobel, Frederick G.
Taber, Hal
Welch, Nellie
Westfall, Dora A.
Williams, Halleck

1885
Balaam, Lewis
Bean, David M.
Burgess, Rybert J.
Cromley, Caroline B.
DiVecchio, Ida
Hennessy, Isabella
Howson, James W.
Love, Dugald M.
Lynch, Irene
Nordyke, Isaac F.
Presley, Patty B.
Rafetto, Frank
Sievers, Henry

1886
Bacigalupi, Fred L.
Cole, Jay
Gale, William S.
Garrido, Francisco
Hinman, Mabel A.
Hoffman, Edward
Horn, Sigmond
Jones, Edith May
Koch, Charles G.
Lewis, James
Lindstrom, Anna M.
McLeod, Jane
Morse, Elmer R.
Murphy, Maggie
Petersen, Rasmine C.
Wiley, Thomas

1887
Cohn, Benjamin
Daggett, James W.
DeMartini, Andrew
Donoho, William K.
Downes, Mary
Guenessi, Victor
Hawver, George E.
Jackson, Louis B.
Lehmann, Conrad
Lorensen, Emma D.
Martinez, Natividad
McGrath, Margaret
Norton, Mayhew
Pearson, Willia
Peralta, Corina
Peralta, Maria A.
Presley, Hiram L.
Saunders, James I.
Stiles, Franklin A.
Taber, Oscar D.

1888
Adair, Mary J.
Alexander, Florence
Brown, George W.
Cretzer, Eliza
Fritz, George H.
Hartman, Edwin P.
Hinman, Gage J.
Jackson, Estella P.
Keesing, Barnet
Kinevan, Patrick C.
King, Chauncey
McPeake, Thomas
Murphy, Joseph
O'Toole, Maggie T.

Phelps, Fannie M.
Regli, A. Josephine
Reichert, Mabel I.
Rowe, Mathilda D.
Stewart, Alva
Veary, Edward
Walters, Frank J.

1889
Anderson, Adolf
Boyer, Lillie D.
Casey, Cora B.
Chandler, Margaret
Hughes, William
Isert, Herman H.
Latutcho, John
Lester, Walter M.
Mensor, Fred
Munch, Anthony J. B.
Page, John
Reeves, Clair
Robles, Louisa
Robles, William
Runde, Winfield S.
Taylor, Nellie
Williams, Leister

1890
Ashworth, Jessie
Beck, Joseph
Brimmer, Lenore
Carpenter, Ernest J.
Curtiss, Fred W.
Finch, Ethel E.
Gande, Ida L.
Genung, Margaret
Gould, Louise F.
Gould, Maude H.
Green, Ray
Haley, James F.
Hatch, Josephine
Hopper, Lenney
Jacobs, Monroe
Lamey, Lydia
Larner, Theresa C.
Liddle, Bertrand L.
Locicieto, John
Miller, Clara S.
Parlour, John G.
Rhodes, Rodney F.
Silva, Charles
Stafford, Monterville
Summers, Jessie
Sweetman, John

1891
Beck, Jacob
Bemis, Samuel R.
Carroll, Philip
Devendorf, Ethel E.
Draeger, William
Dutra, Jose
Hannan, Walter
Hartmann, Adolph C.
Hinman, Bessie M.
Hunt, Thomas
Johnson, Martin F.
Keesing, Elizabeth
Kern, Lilly
Logan, Ebert J.
Lucy, Mary
Page, Marl A.
Scott, Elfred
Shepley, Hellena G.
Suber, Lottie L.
Tickner, Gerald R.

1892
Baccus, Celine
Beall, Robert V.
Brannan, Nicholas
Cardano, Louis
deClercq, Arthur
deClercq, Rene
Depew, Roscoe D.
Galloup, Margarita E.
Griggs, Vester A.
Hays, Clara I.
Knuckey, John
Lipsett, Isaac R.
Mier, Rapheal N.
Moldenhauer, Emma
Moore, John V.
Norton, Ernest E.
Slocum, Elsie
Stacks, Nancy F.
Wilson, Jennie P.

1893
Anderson, Ella M.
Bernstein, Benjamin
Bradley, George
Cavalli, Julius
Curran, William
Doane, Clarence H.
Gleason, Thomas
Guenther, Alice
Jones, Susie A.
Keesing, Grace
Matchette, Mary
Morris, Manuel F.
Page, Claude A.
Smith, Leban P.
Stoltz, Raymond E.
Wood, Golden C.

1894
Akers, Lester
Bradley, Lizzie
Cox, Ollie G.
Craze, William R.
Haagensen, Agnes
Hall, Raymond V.
Holcomb, Hugo A.
Jones, Henrietta M.
Kerr, Joseph V.
Luddy, Mabel I.
McDonald, Isabella
Parks, Lulu
Robles, Daniel
Robles, Francisca
Sherman, Daniel K.
Sherman, Wm. T.
Skaine, Alice
Songey, Ernest E.
Wolf, Abey

1895
Baker, James W.
Baldwin, Edward
Bullock, Bertha
Carr, Constance E.
Clark, Albert G.
Davis, George
DuBois, Charles
Evans, Stuart
Fletcher, Clayton
Gabrielli, Guiseppi
Gavin, Ethel G.
Gianbruno, Giuseppi
Hart, William I.
Hopkins, Amy R.
Ikin, May F.
Johnson, William J.
Lawton, Wm. C.
McLean, Maggie
Matauda, Mary
Matheis, Melville J.
Moynahan, John
Niel, Henry H.
Phelps, Minnie A.
Phelps, William C.
Reece, May
Russell, Charles
Souther, Vannum C.
Tillman, Leslie
Walsh, Lily
Walters, Annie

1896
Blanco, Robert
Bodwell, Raymond
Buker, Raymond
Cambria, Manuel
Camisa, Louisa
Christianson, George
Elmer, Leslie
Franck, Henry
Golden, Algie M.
Grose, William
Hawvichorst, Robert
Holcomb, Lydia A.
Holcomb, Mabel
Johnson, Myrtle B.
Krambeck, Herman
McGruder, Lizzie
Newman, William
Phelps, George E.
Roncalli, Angela
Roncalli, Lizzie
Sherman, Abraham L.
Sink, Genevieve
Small, Ward
Thompson, Lois M.
Valdez, Jose E.
Wharton, Valley
Wilson, May E.

1897
Allen, Wirt H.
Billings, Caro
Binzer, William
Fowler, Bret H.
Gilmore, Edward S.
Hoffmann, Ma\rtha
Pale, Charles J.
Phillips, Charles B.
Pickering, Gladys
Stacks, Sarah E.

1898
Alviso, Rita
Barthe, John
Beck, Marcus W.
Bryan, Hattie
Bunyard, Hattie I.
Cordano, Louis'
Cowles, Inez I.
Ericson, Elma
Freel, Ida B.
Hare, Irene M.
Jessen, Louise E.
Knarston, Helen I.
Knarston, James I.
Konz, Gerty
McPherson, Marybel
Nagiller, Ida
Patheal, Monroe
Pierce, Leslie L.
Terrell, Stella
Timm, Walter
Waters, Ava K.

1899
Beaver, Bertha M.
Case, Viola
deLarge, Irene
Douglass, Mattie A.
Fine, Erle B.
Hill, Robert V.
Hogan, Myrtle
Kohrumel, Willie
Lopez, Clemons
McKenna, Mamie
Mitchell, Wildey
Musladine, Peter
Rossi, Umberto
Schilling, Henry
Schroyer, Laurel
Sherman, John F.
Sturtevant, George H.
Sullivan, Charles D.
Turner, Lorene
Watson, George H.
Woodruff, Albert

1900
Abbott, Ashbell
Baldwin, Eleanor
Barwise, William
Bonzani, Charles
Campbell, Frederick
Cartwright, Leonard
Cloer, Gracie
Conrad, Alvin D.
Conrad, Goldie
Cota, Maria Del Carmen
Dick, Arthur C.
Dougall, Sidney L. P.
Kett, Robert J.
Larimer, Mildred E.
McCarthy, Sandie
Otis, Charles
Reeves, Eunice
Stephens, William W.
Thomas, Walter
Walker, William

1901
Beal, Elsie
Brieger, Elizabeth
Brooks, Lloyd W.
Burrell, Fred
Curtiss, Almon H.
Curtiss, Oscar A.
deGrosellier, Albert
Ghiorsi, Maria
Hoffman, Virginia
Keeley, Alfred C.
Keeley, Joe G.
Keeley, Kate
Kenny, Anna
Millar, Irene
Noll, Martha
Phillips, May
Shattuck, Phoebe J.
Shea, Lillian
Smith, Arthur L.

1902
Bonzani, Pauline
Brodrick, Amy I.
Brodrick, Edward W.
Cook, Mae B.
Cordero, Augustine
Crouch, Oma A.
Delmas, Carolina
Dunsmuir, Dora L.
Fitgerald, Golda M.
Freitas, Annie
Gregory, Elva
Hall, Grace E.
Hytti, Hjalmar
Martinez, Ida
Ross, Leslie F.
Shiminowsky, Dora
Smith, Lionel
Spencer, Albert L.
Whitworh, George
Winters, Elbie L.

1903
Bonar, James
Comacho, Anna
Cruz, hortense
Dwyer, Jolly V.
Glidden, Don
Hawks, Alexander H.
Jensen, William
McNeilly, Harold A.
Marketta, Pearl
Matson, George
Rose, Alexander
Simpson, Mollie L.
Simpson, Norah L.
Stubbs, Gertrude T.
Taylor, Charles F.
Wilder, Herman

1904
Baertschieger, Anna
Beebe, Arthur
Cohn, Anna
Cohn, Ida
Dutton, Olive
Egan, Edna G.
Forbes, Ramona
Harrison, Carmelita
Issoglio, Arthur
Kibby, Norman
Poole, Earl
Risher, Mary F.
Ryden, Edward G.
Taylor, Helen
Tyhurst, Wm. A.
Wimber, John W.

1905
Baars, Charlotte
Burton, Lee R.
Cohn, Millie
Crawford, John B.
Garcia, Josefa
Gardner, Charles R.
Guerrero, Rebecca
Hansen, Meta M.
Land, Bruce W.
Lytle, Ruth
McNeil, Charles A.
Montgomery, Gladys
Montgomery, Joycie
Neber, Carl C.
Overton, Georgia L.
Peixotto, Antonio
Peters, Maggie
Phillips, George C.
Roy, Ella R.
Schiff, Lena
Sherman, Lafayette
Smith, Alice E.
Sturm, Hattie
Thom Wohrden, Edna
Walker, Myrtle E.
Weber, Carl D.
White, Albert A.
Wood, George

1906
Arnold, Lillian
Beck, Hyrum
Bilby, M. Estella
Cowden, Violet
Cox, Agnes J.
Croll, Martin M.
Gemignani, Vincent
Guire, Oscar D.
Harde, Freda
Heitshusen, John
Johnson, Mary A.
Johnson, Harold
Kaiser, Augusta
Kaiser, Dietrich
Lee, Lillie
McLaughlin, Charles
Marshall, Ruth E.
Mathews, Charles
Nelson, Carl
Nelson, Edith M.
Nutting, George L.
Schneck, Georgie
Smith, Alexander

Stevens, William
Thomas, Rhea
Thurman, Merle E.
Walker, Carrie E.
Wilsey, Silas
Zilk, Harry

1907
Becker, Mary
Cademartori, David
Castro, Milletino
Connick, Platt H.
Cundiff, Beulah
Davidson, Melvin C.
Ferguson, Harold
Fonseca, William
Francis, George E.
Fries, Ethel V.
Hickson, Ernest S.
Moynahan, Anna
Mutch, Viola E.
Nash, Mary E.
Purbeck, Ernest M.
Sangmaster, Nome O.
Stewart, Ernest
Tanzman, Helen
Thorn, Milton
Vaio, Charles
Wile, Edward
Wills, Edward
Yung, Ah

1908
Behl, Joseph
Bonetti, Henry
Bonetti, Oliver
Brinkley, Ray
Comerford, William
Dodge, Morse
Dunnigan, Florence
Dwyer, Loren
Grider, Edna D.
Jones, Verdi
Lund, Libby R.
Majourau, Victor
Marlatt, Thomas
Mortorano, Michele
Moore, George C.
Heil, Grace
O'Brien, Meredith
Reilly, Mary E.
Sanchez, Reginaldo
Schmidt, Frida
Schneider, Milton
Schwarzlose, Harry
Stauts, Edith L.
Valiant, Walter
Walker, Ethel
Yeghoian, Joseph N.
Zoanni, Maria

1909
Adams, Charles V.
Alvarado, Jose
Bizzini, Nellie
Bizzini, Pierina
Bloss, Mildred
Cardoza, Clara
Cardoza, Joseph
Cardoza, Minnie
Clark, Thomas B.
Claver, LaMont
Copp, Ralph W.
Crane, Jessye M.
Fries, George
Hooper, Edith M.
Jatta, Arthur J.
Johnston, Frederick
Judge, John
Lee, Oscar
Losano, Jose G.
McGowan, Genevieve
Millet, Raymond H.
Neubauer, Martha
Richards, Elsie
Richeson, Audrey E.
Sheehan, Mamie
Stokes, Frank H.
Trathen, Hazel
Watts, William
Williamson, Nellie A.
Wilson, Harry P.
Wilson, James West
Wood, Bernice

1910
Barthe, Peter M.
Blakesley, Alta E.
Boam, Crom F.
Burkhart, Hazel G.
Ciancimino, Alfred
Coleman, Thelma M.
Dowling, Elbert
Eisner, Charlotte
Fleek, Ralph
Goodale, Brady
Goodale, Buster
Jenkins, John P.
Johnson, Clara G.
Kaafman, Ernest
Kohlberg, Phillipine
Koopman, Earnest
Land, Carol
Mees, Beulah G.
Modisett, Clarence
Money, Beulah
Moran, Canuto
Ratto, Stephen
Smith, Mabel F.
Stinsky, Agnes
Waddell, Donald
Waddell, Paul B.
Wampler, William
Williams, Horace
Wilson, Joseph E.

1911
Becher, Otto
Blanc, Henry
Childress, Gertrude
Crites, Harold L.
DeWitt, Fenner J.
Glougie, Clarence D.
Houser, Emma M.
Kearns, Mary E.
Kuhn, Frederick E.
Martin, Blanche
Melrose, Roland A.
Melton, Forest S.
Miguel, Isabel
Norman, John
Rolls, Laurence W.
Scaramella, Selina
Walker, Beatrice
Wampler, Thelma
Willis, H. Clinton
Wilson, Arthur C.

1912
Adams, Blanche
Allison, Anna
Allison, Mae
Anderson, Esther
Ashby, Corinne
Atkinson, Agnes
Bean, Leo R.
Benedict, Clinton M.
Benedict, Edwin G.
Bradley, Mabel O.
Canon, Harriet
Corbett, Margaret
Covell, Harry
Denton, Paul
Elliott, Katie
Engelskirchen, Mary
Flanagan, Francis
Fritch, Helen
Haworth, Olive E.
Henbest, Don
Hitesman, Cora H.
Johnson, Harry
Jones, Earl R.
Kelly, Roy A.
Meeker, Florence
Mepham, Robert
Park, Helen
Peterson, Lewis
Pittman, Ruth
Poolinelli, Silvo
Price, Isabelle D.
Ramirez, Antonio
Ramirez, Maria C.
Ramirez, August
Richatoff, Mike
Schmidt, Mathilda
Seitz, Augustine
Simpson, Harold
Steinman, May V.
Tabb, Ray
Tricomo, Mary
Wallk, John

1913
Armstrong, Don
Brower, Lucille
Bull, Henry G.
Childers, Wm. I.
Clawges, Alice C.
Cocoran, Edward
Day, Clifford
Denning, Harvey M.
Donnelly, Ralph H.
Dowling, Lillian
Duncan, Harry
Eisner, Amelia
Ellis, Alfred J.
Garofalo, Mary
Gilbert, Mabel I.
Granum, Olga
Hanna, Mark
Harrigan, George
Harris, Arthur
Kellogg, Milo M.
McGinness, John C.
Martinez, Lucas
Moldrup, Helen B.
Pollinelli, Silva
Reich, Abraham
Sundeen, Florence
Thompson, Elijah
Velasco, Doris

1914
Bertoni, Joseph
Billa, John C.
Blanke, William W.
Boyer, Leonard
Campi, Lorenzo
Carel, Dell
Crispi, Clara
DeWitt, Ethel
Enos, Maurice
Enos, Rose
Farrar, George F.
Felizardo, Paula
Fultz, Floyd
Granum, Ole
Harreden, Mildred
Harum, Wilson
Hemmings, Dorothy
Indart, Emily
Jacaville, Ernest
Jacobs, Harry M.
Kearns, Carvel
Lagoria, Stephen
Lambdin, Almeda
Larimer, Gracie
Lozensky, Mixal
Mangan, Aloysisous
Matson, Arthur
Miller, Joseph
Pastori, Lena
Patheal, William T.
Poindexter, John
Reich, Ada
Recih, Libby
Rooney, Floyd J.
Seay, Annie May
Vargas, Elvira
Velena, Peter M.
Wearne, William
Williamson, Clyde

1915
Ames, Robert
Biscay, Jennie
Bray, Dorothy H.
Brown, Evelyn
Catlin, George
Cano, Dorothy E.
Cardinez, Roy
Coats, Edward
Crockford, Mansell
Damiano, Tony
Fletcher, Myrtle M.
Hansen, Charlie O.
McGowan, Eleanor
Nigero, Rocco
Negri, Thomas
Sarrat, Arthur
Scott, Ethel
Service, Alexander
Toombs, Charles C.
Valena, Peter
Woods, Benjamin C.

1916
Adcock, Edwin J.
Artensio, Lincoln
Backlund, Hilda
Bertolone, Ercole
Coleman, Margaret
Devencenzi, Joseph
Ehrich, Leah
Enos, Mamie
Gibellini, Jennie
Greer, Fred A.
Harreden, Donald
Helmuth, Marjorie
Henry, Elizabeth
Jensen, Wilbur
Jura, James
Lechuga, Helen
Losano, Frank
Marshall, Eleanor
McArtor, Sheldon E.
Moore, Corbett
Preston, Beatrice
Preston, Kathleen
Pugsley, Raymond
Pulliam, Joe
Ratner, Morris
Russell, Dixie
Reusser, Edward
Smith, Mary L.
Stumpf, Anna
Tarver, Russell E.
Williams, Violet

1917
Barnes, Thelma H.
Blackburn, Georgia
Blackburn, Stella M.
Blois, Alice M.
Brown, Florence
Buenzle, Frederick
Clark, May E.
Connolly, Mary
Enright, John
Gilbert, William S.
Harmola, Edward
Hunt, Vina M.
Keesee, Hershel
La Dico, Josephine
Mabrier, Edith
Mathew, Ethel L.
Nickerson, Charles F.
O'Malley, Everett W.
Pankey, Denver H.
Patrick, Edwin
Rhodes, Harriet A.
Roberts, Jesse
Sammerano, Thomas
Smith, Ruth
Stead, Mildred
Sullivan, Eugene

1918
Broadway, Thelma
Brown, Harvey
Bush, Violet M.
Cano, William H.
Contreras, Adelaida
Contreras, Irineo
Crow, Leland S.
Derr, Ruby W.
Enos, Tony G.
Fox, Marjorie L.
Frisbey, Mark E.
Goldwater, Kaufman
Gries, Fred
Hovland, Lloyd
Ingraham, Bonnie D.
Jeffers, Mary E.
Jones, Elmer
Jones, Laura
Loorz, Iva P.
McCall, Neola
McCoy, Mary J.
Marsh, Meryl
Massey, Joe R.
Miller, Henry
Mordine, Isador
Nakamura, Shigeo
Nieto, Sepriano
Nunez, Adelina
Oliver, Madge
Ortiz, Edward
Ott, Thelma
Pirovich, Ernest
Sandercock, Stover
Smith, Lois
Sowell, Minnie
Stuck, Marcus W.
Sullivan, Bettina F.
Williams, Ethel M.
Young, Anthony M.

1919
Aiello, Peter
Anderson, Claude
Anderson, Jenkins
Anderson, Mattie
Berryessa, Alexander
Brown, Edward
Brownstein, James
Carlson, Horace E.
Chisholm, Dudley E.
Coulter, Doris E.
Cromie, Charles H.
Deasee, Michael J.
Doolittle, Russell
Gonzales, Secilio
Haritonoff, Vera
Haynie, Agnes V.
Hecker, Antone
Hecker, Leonard
Inman, Everett A.

Laswell, Gladys
Littlefield, Marie
McCormick, Ferris L.
McIntyre, Lyle K.
Martin, Eduardo
Muller, Edwin J.
Pestana, Manuel
Phillips, Susie M.
Pope, Rose W.
Procaccio, Maria
Rose, Herbert
Sandoval, Rosa
Santos, Pedro
Stasneck, Agnes V.
Thomson, Sarah
Ukai, Kikue

1920

Adams, James
Barnard, Velma M.
Bryant, Charles C.
Borsoff, Alexis
Brock, Rickey O.
Budech, Sophie
Burke, Philip
Campbell, Robert
Costigan, Dorothy V.
Cowan, Frederick R.
Dentici, Frank
Engel, Herbert
Heaton, Audrey
Krug, Walter J.
McKean, Guy
Mermontz, Tillo
Miller, Thelma L.
Newman, Tillie
Olvera, Robert W.
Ponsetti, Dominick
Ponsetti, Teresa
Rosenthal, Solomon
Ruggeri, Louis
Santos, Joe F.
Stewart, Arthur
Upchurch, Egbert L.
Vance, Fern D.
Vance, Floyd
Vega, Patrick
Weisbrod, Iva
Whitsett, Florence E.

1921

Affonso, Henry A.
Berry, Edward
Bonvecchio, Eda
Chambers, Edward E.
Costigan, Henry E.
Crissy, Yvonne
Dominick, Tony
Ghera, Jennie
Grenfell, Frederick
Hall, Lois V.
Harvey, Alvin F.
Harvey, Leona
Hilgendorf, Otto
Hill, Stuart
Holland, Ruth
Howard, Jeanette
Lawrence, Freda
Lewis, Raymond M.
Losano, Consuelo
Loustalot, Alice
Loustalot, Sr., George
McCray, Wallace M.
McKee, Jesse R.
McKee, William W.
Matson, Edward
Miller, Eugene
Moran, John J.
Nielson, Emma
Owen, Valrie V.
Quadro, Mildred
Ragsdale, Howard
Richard, Howard
Schroeder, Clara
Senteno, Patrosinio
Slaughter, Gladys
Smith, Walter
Tavluian, Yervant
Thompson, Wm. E.
Volland, Edward
Wilson, Milton A.

1922

Aho, Lillian W.
Bella, Mary L.
Berkowitz, Elizabeth
Bettencourt, Frank
Blackman, Thelma
Boettcher, William
Bruno, Jennie
Cola, Alfred
Crabtree, Helen M.
Crabtree, Opal V.
Cronin, Daniel
DePauli, Arturo
Duncan, Bradley
Duncan, Clay
Edwards, Vera M.
Fay, Marguerite
Glans, Albin D.
Hammerlund, Walter
Hewlett, Melvin
Klopfstein, Elizabeth
Michardi, Alfred
Orlando, Genevieve
Phillips, Madeline
Quayle, Raymond
Rico, John
Schwaderer, Mary D.
Scribner, Herbert
Smith, Mayzel
Smolensky, David
Thomas, Ray M.
Thornton, Thelma
Tingen, Alice J.
Varni, Mary
Walling, Rowena E.
Washburn, James L.
Welch, Eugene

1923

Bettencourt, Mamie
Bock, Albert H.
Chrismer, Theodore
Cuengco, Bernardo
Davis, Norman L.
Garner, Duen
Ginno, Nancy E.
Glover, James P.
Jacobs, Leo M.
Leavitt, Beulah K.
Lewis, Wilbur V.
Lookadoo, George F.
Naftaly, Lester
Ornelas, Frances
Pale, Henry S.
Petruzzi, Carmelita
Priola, John
Rose, John W.
Rosenblatt, Dina
Ruffa, Emma
Rutledge, Marvin
Schiro, Demetrio
Silvestri, Pat
Slonicker, Seward L.
Varella, Belen

1924

Baker, Franklin W.
Bardfeld, Ernest
Basso, Lawrence
Botta, Evelyn
Brown, Florence M.
Bruner, Jesse L.
Date, Masako
Degliantoni, Florence
Dunlap, Harriet S.
Ewart, James E.
Ferrara, Filomena
Fong, Rosie
Francis, Esmeralda
Goodson, Louie
Goodson, Scott
Groat, Velma E.
Hopkins, Pauline
Jones, Lois R.
McGraw, Dorothy L.
McMeen, Opal
Meeks, Alson T.
Munoz, Consuela
Musso, Jake R.
Owens, Mary E.
Pospisil, Joseph F.
Preston, Edwin
Reicheneker, Howard
Robinson, Earl
Ruffa, Theobaldo
Terry, James W.
Thomas, Etta M.
Thomas, Marceil
Tyrrell, Lillian L.
Varella, Eleanor
Watson, Estella
Weaver, John M.
Winkler, Lila
Winkler, Lora

1925

Anderson, Edgar R.
Arnold, Gwendelyn
Chaves, George A.
Cochrane, Robert E.
Coyner, Stephen L.
Cushing, Lucille
Del Colletti, Lena
Dietering, Pearl
Drake, James R.
Edwards, Jessie
Hill, Hazel
Iacono, John
Kanihin, Nicholas
Lee, Sang Quong
Manard, Thea L.
Margaroli, Henry R.
Melle, Albert
Paniagua, Antoinette
Pewitt, Lois E.
Rogers, Jadie F.
Schmidt, Loretta E.
Schneider, Pauline
Silva, Edward M.
Silveira, Raymond
Slayter, Homer
Sones, Frances S.
Specht, Roger N.
Sutherland, Dorothy
Turturici, Salvatore
Winkler, Willa V.

1926

Azzarella, Anna
Bettencourt, Elzira
Both, William E.
Brown, Robert A.
Callens, George
Cook, June
Cowdrey, Grace
Crowder, Giffin I.
Donnel, Harold
Donnel, Marie
Evans, Sharpie
Flanery, Claudie
Frazier, Roy R.
Galvan, Jr., John
Garcia, Manuel
Gross, Hugo J.
Grose, Vera
Guerra, Johanna
Hutcheson, Issac C.
Ikoma, Shezuka
James, Irene L.
Kearney, Glen D.
Lazzarini, James
MacNider, William
Matteucci, Alfred
Menichetti, Lena M.
Moen, Glen C.
Moxley, Earl E.
Oto, Mamoru
Pursell, Donald L.
Quijada, Lawrence
Smith, Gerald L.
Smith, Hazel D.
Wright, Percy

1927

Ballestero, Lewis E.
Beale, Clarence E.
Boulbard, C. Pansy
Cannizzaro, Peter
Cardoza, Elsie
Donnel, Dorothy M.
Doss, Dillon
Forbes, Carol
Fulmer, Curtis R.
Garbutt, Robert E.
George, Goldie M.
Ghilarducci, G.
Giorgis, Peter
Long, Katherine M.
Malone, James M.
Manuel, Edward
Miller, Christine G.
Miller, Robert L.
Miller, Robert M.
Negri, Rose
Nix, Lillie J.
O'Branovich, Anton
Owen, Johnnie H.
Patrick, Chester H.
Pickersgill, George
Pico, Eva
Powell, Hubert
Prohoroff, Stella
Ruffa, Earl
Shoemaker, Lawrence
Silveira, Lawrence
Taylor, Arlie R.
Trask, Roberta E.
Vaughn, Juanita R.
Walker, Johnnie M.
Warner, Martha E.
Watson, William H.
Yamamoto, Tadashi

1928

Anderson, Eleanor M.
Bagby, Jack W.
Bagby, Richard A.
Benedict, Jr., Clinton
Bibb, Henry S.
Bird, Horace Gordon
Boomer, Sarah E.
Burkert, Elaine
Campos, Annie F.
Cole, Warren B.
Cope, Patricia A.
Cope, Paul A.
Courrejou, Elie
Davis, Merle
Hill, Joe T.
Holt, Francis W.
Huey, Carlo
Katona, Frank
Kellogg, Sarah J.
Kirby, Walter J.
Ladner, Emil S.
Lichtenberg, Otto
Macomber, Roy C.
Morendaerde, Alice
Matteri, Guido
Mendoza, Jesusa
Morgan, Clarence A.
Owen, Howard R.
Price, Gladys L.
Price, Lawrence F.
Pruitt, Charles E.
Quijada, Rosalie
Reed, Irene L.
Robbins, Charles W.
Russell, Lesa A.
Sasaki, Toshiro
Sturm, Bonetta
Tenuta, Virginia
Tormey, William H.
Welch, George
Young, Hazel
Zignego, Michel J.

1929

Bovendaerde, Alice
Butero, Josephine
Canas, George
Collins, William R.
Corey, Charles
Corral, Pilar
Costigan, LaRae
Davis, Woodrow A.
Escobar, Lloyd M.
Gerhardt, Herbert J.
Gilbert, Lucille
Goldsmith, Lorena
Gonzales, Guadelupe
Hahn, Lillian
Hammett, Edna M.
Heron, Robert B.
Hoy, Rosie
Hudson, Joe
Johnson, David W.
Jones, Elsie L.
Kirby, Lily E.
Koshelnik, Edward
McFarland, Nitia E.
Martin, John
Mayda, Teddy
Monteleone, Vivian
Moore, George R.
Nicholson, Lenora E.
Pate, John LeRoy
Ranta, Jorma J.
Salido, Frank
Sheehan, Arthur
Streaser, Patricia D.
Taylor, Betty M.
White, Robert
Wight, Leda E.
Williams, Vernon S.

1930

Alden, Thomas P.
Attwell, James E.
Azevedo, Frank S.
Azevedo, Lucy S.
Berg, Elodie
Bianchi, Mike
Bigcraft, June D.
Cowell, Faye
Cracolice, Frances
Dana, Charles J.
Donnel, James C.
Elliott, Thomas O.
Florio, Clara C.
Gardner, Jimmie R.
Gilley, James B.
Goddard, James F.
Goebel, Geraldine H.
Grasso, Delmas
Hickey, George S.

Ingebretsen, Thomas
Ingraham, Albert H.
Jacobson, Daisy M.
Jiminez, Jose D.
Jones, Virginia
Koerner, Clarabel M.
Laughon, Virginia E.
Laybourn, Lloyd H.
Laybourn, Lynn S.
Lenz, Elizabeth
Luna, Esperanza
Luna, Maria J.
Lydiatt, Laura J.
McClendon, Idamae
McClendon, W. L.
Martin, Thomas
Meister, Charlotte
Paxton, Elsie V.
Shrimpton, James W.
Smith, Arthur G.
Ward, Velma A.
Willey, Leo E.
Willey, Mary E.
Wilson, Geraldine

1931
Aldersley, Marilyn
Anguelo, Cepriano
Askew, Clarence D.
Avila, Madeline
Bernard, Henry A.
Bourk, Kathryn
Button, Eugene M.
Charles, Melvin A.
Clingenpeel, Robert
Cordova, Isabel
Corson, Michael
Curtin, William J.
Depew Ruth E.
Dunn, Bessie M.
Estep, Violet
Fiscus, Frank J.
Fisher, Ila A.
Giovanetti, Mary
Green, Carrie M.
Green, Leila F.
Hanson, Clifford W.
Harris, Audrey M.
Hildreth, Richard H.
Hubert, William
Jobe, Martin L.
Lange, Barbara
Leichel, Anita S. H.
Leichel, Pauline E.
Lima, Joe
Lowrence, Raymond
Luna, Frank
McBurney, Lucille
McKee, James H.
Marshall, Catherine
Miller, Ada R.
Miller, Roy C.
Mederios, Donald
Najarian, Haig
Nash, Newton
Nelson, Lawrence H.
Nitta, Roy
Norton, Kenneth W.
Nowdesha, Donald E.
Ostoich, Maryellen
Owen, Richard R.
Parsons, Frances M.
Parsons, Hester W.
Rianda, Eugene M.
Rodriquez, Frank
Rodriquez, Jesse
Rothschild, Rita
Scott, Beatrice
Shelby, Pearl
Simpson, Lawrence J.
Skropeta, Angelo
Skropeta, Michael
Smith, Bruce L.
Smith, Hazel L.
Smith, Helen V.
Smith, Winona R.
Stewart, Sherwin A.
Walker, Billy J.
Ward, Ruthalee G.
Watso, Aleck L.
Watts, Owen
Wilson, Patricia J.
Wingett, Bernice E.
York, Jr., Elmer T.

1932
Ansberry, Ramona
Bentley, James E.
Biavaschi, Aida
Bollman, Georgia M.
Brother, Alvin R.
Brown, Melvin I.
Broyles, Ernest R.
Christensen, Dorothy
Davis, Norman L.
D'Innocenti, Dominic
Droge, Helen
Fail, John
Fanning, John M.
Fowler, William
Gregorieff, Boris
Harrington, Clifford
Herold, Alfred A.
Houck, Glenn E.
Jones, Lois L.
Jones, Thelma T.
Jordan, Evelyn C.
Knightsen, Evelyn L.
Lopez, William
Lovell, Evelyn I.
Miller, Helen E.
Opperman, Joseph T.
Perry, Frances C.
Powell, David
Powers, Wallace E.
Ruiz, Juan
Ruiz, Matilda
Shaffer, Kenneth V.
Shelton, Selma S.
Simpson, Olive C.
Smales, Betty J.
Smalley, Martha
Smith, Mary E.
Stafford, James
Thornton, Wilda O.
Whitehead, Willard
Wilson, Alexander J.
Wood, Carolyn S.

1933
Arbuthnot, Helen C.
Armenta, David
Bell, Miriam A.
Cardoza, Bernice I.
Cayous, Gloria
Chester, Charlotte E.
Christl, Beatrice M.
Cisneros, Manuel
Colby, Jess L.
Dabbs, Robert E.
Engel, Margaret F.
Furno, Ernest J.
Graham, Helen J.
Griggs, Patricia R.
Gunnar, Robert K.
Henry, Beatrice L.
Hill, Kenneth
Hoare, Ailene C.
Holman, Leon
Inga, Sylvestro
Ingvaldsen, Wilma
Johnson, Virgil J.
Keohane, Francis
Klein, Anita
Le Bre, Rosanna
Leon, John
MacCartney, Jean
McKindley, Willa A.
Madrid, Carmen
Mains, Kathryn M.
Miller, Edward W.
Miller, John A.
Millspaugh, Gloria
Millspaugh, Orlin J.
Monahan, Dell N.
Morris, Anna M.
Murillo, Antonio
Nemir, Jamil
O'Connor, Charles G.
Owen, Vilma M.
Paxton, Clyde D.
Pruitt, Opal
Rasmussen, Marjorie
Redmond, Edward G.
Reed, Joy J.
Scott, Slagle R.
Simon, Arthur R.
Smith, Earl R.
Staznitti, Pietrino
Steelman, Dorothy D.
Stilwagen, George W.
Stutzman, Marjorie
Thornborrow, Evelyn
Van Nepes, Manuel
Van Nepes, Thomas
Wallace, Jr., Grady
Warnberg, Gustaf W.
Whitcher, Lloyd J.
Whitley, Lucy A.

1934
Alvis, Vivian M.
Andrews, Eva
Arbuckle, Phyllis
Barkley, James E.
Becher, Hubert A.
Beckwith, Irma R.
Brodersen, Morris G.
Calderaz, Ignacio
Cano, Stephen
Castro, Harold
Contreras, Maria
Davis, Frank M.
DeLa Cruz, Victor W.
Diamond, Sanford N.
Dimick, William M.
Dunn, William J.
Dupuy, Dorothy J.
Edwards, Jack T.
Elmassian, Eleanor S.
Elmore, Henry
Enos, Henry
Fromm, Greta M.
Fitzjarrold, Betty M.
Fitzjarrold, Billy T.
Fitzjarrold, Wilma Z.
Harris, William G.
Hauschildt, Jr., Henry
Jacobi, Olga M.
Johnson, Berwick B.
Jones, Alvin W.
Jones Sr., Neil
Kenyon, Dorothy A.
Kerr, Fredricka J.
King, William H.
Lawson, Charles E.
Logan, David S.
Lucido, Frank
McDaniel, Jacqueline
Malzkuhn, Eric F.
Metzner, Yvonne
Moore, Georgia M.
Norred, Jr., Luther
Orona, Apolonio
Parra, Abolino
Patrick, Jack
Ramirez, Virginia
Raridan, Rosemary L.
Rodriquez, Rudolph
Sanders, Jeanie
Sanford, Ceilon
Schubkegel, Elsie
Scott, Stanley D.
Sheld, Lulu M.
Sladek, Frank E.
Sladek, Mary A.
Snyder, Joe
Torgerson, Elberta
Torgerson, Marjory
Varnes, Charles T.
Wagner, Christine
Wilson, Beverly E.

1935
Bareno, Berta
Boyer, Wilma L.
Buffington, Grace L.
Cody, Bobbie F.
Cotton, Beverly
Crites, Tonnie G.
Davis, Allan V.
Depew, Verna M.
Evans, Marilyn
Feeley, Marion
Filippone, Frank
Fleeman, Betty B.
Gomez, Tomas
Hooker, Irene G.
Howell, Nancy R.
Inman, William J.
Kubotsu, Teruko
Luna, Mercedes
McIntosh, Constance
McNairn, Mary E.
Monahan, Donald
Nuckles, Glen T.
Peabody, Donald J.
Pierce, Harley N.
Ramponi, Emilio
Roach, Carlie A.
Skeahan, Edna A.
Takacs, Joan B.
Takagi, Hanna T.
Takagi, Ruth T.
Tranchina, John M.
Williams, Sara A.

1936
Aguire, Manuel
Atkins, Ronald A.
Bennett, Mabel G.
Besso, Virginia K.
Blackmon, B. Pauline
Boccio, Pauline M.
Buck, David E.
Cikoch, Teresa R.
Cohen, June
Collins, Robert F.
Cronic, Dorothy M.
Curtis, Helen M.
Duggins, Betty M.
Duggins, James A.
Dunbar, Louie A.
Dutra, John M.
Fryer, Harvey S.
Fryer, Robert L.
Fryer, Ruby V.
Funk, Chris A.
Gates, Dick
Goldsmith, Allen
Grinde, Robert L.
Grose, Willie J.
Harado, Tamao
Hernandez, Jventine
Hosford, Elsie
Ingraham, Donald E.
Johnson, Jr., Henry
Jones, Chloe A.
Jones, Lawrence
Kitchen, Patricia A.
Lind, Martha
Lund, Rex L.
McEdward, Betty J.
Mares, Mary E.
Mead, Gerald M.
Moreno, John
Moriconi, Mary J.
Noland, Jacqueline L.
Putica, Milan
Raimonde, Joseph V.
Rosenwirth, Nettie
Rosenwirth, Shirley
Scott, Nanna L.
Shiratsuki, Satoru
Smith, Dale
Sommerville, Robert
Swaim, Wm. Dean
Teague, Irma I.
Thrush, Jack W.
Vallery, Russell C.
VanNess, Lyell U.
Wass, Robert
White, Billy R.

1937
Alcaroz, Gilbert
Ames, John
Bautista, Emilia
Bullock, Donald M.
Castle, Alvin E.
Cisneros, Augustine
Daviton, John David
Dear, Jack H.
Del Bono, Albert
Delgado, Eva
Dickerson, Beatrice J.
Digesti, Gino
Effman, Earl A.
Engstrom, Catherine
Fay, Sue A.
Gilliam, Orban E.
Gomes, Grace R.
Hale, Elbert
Ikeda, Annabelle Y.
Ikeda, Rosie K.
Inga, Frances
LaBelle, George
Leon, Geraldine
Lloyd, Ernest L.
McDowell, JoAnn
Montgomery, Glenn
Nichols, Wilfred
Paniagua, Frank
Pesguera, Albert
Pesguera, Arthur
Rees, Arthur W.
Rodriguez, Ofelia
Ross, Norman A.
Shemaria, Sarah
Simmons, Cleo L.
Stanely, Charles R.
Taylor, Marion E.
Velez, Joseph
Vranesh, Stanely
Wood, Eula L.

1938
Arce, Epifanio
Attletweed, George
Bloise, Eugene
Bond, Cherie J.
Burton, Junior C.
Castro, Roberta
Chavez, Guadalupe
Cox, Ceasar L.
Craig, Martha A.
Cruz, Antonia
Davis, Jeanette D.

Davis, Max E.
Downing, Richard O.
Elder, Denise L.
Esparza, Helen N.
Fisher, Geraldine M.
Freeman, William
Goding, Ella F.
Gomez, Dimas
Gregory, Philip A.
Halloran, Patricia J.
Hartmann, Betty M.
Henderson, Roberta
Hendricks, Lloyd W.
Hirano, Ronald M.
Hottinger, Anna G.
Johnson, George R.
Johnson, Gerald M.
Laible, Patricia C.
Locke, Jack T.
Loewen, Sevylla G.
Long, Darrell G.
Long, Wanda M.
Longoria, David
Lucas, Barbara J.
Miller, Paul L.
Momii, Kazuko
Moore, Billy Joe
Nordlund, Elmarie
Olinger, Robert Lee
Ortiz, Antonia
Perry, Donald W.
Phelps, Edrice E.
Pickering, Charlotte
Quintanilla, Esther
Ramey, Madeline
Raridan, James R.
Richards, Betty J.
Romero, Jose
Russell, Mary G.
Schmidt, Albert C.
Schmidt, Frank J.
Smith, Frank A.
Smith, Jacqueline M.
terHorst, Mary H.
Tottino, Neo
Villar, Virginia
Wade, Geneva M.
Wells, Jr., Everett L.
Williams, Roberta T.
Wright, Robert E.

1939

Alexander, Lawrence
Arnold, Clair C.
Avilla, Mary F.
Barton, James F.
Bertorelli, Joe
Bo, Janice M.
Brown, Bettie R.
Chick, Robert
Cody, Harold R.
Davenport, Alice M.
Davenport, Troy E.
Dickinson, Donald
Doyle, Douglas
Druilard, Sybil A.
Ferguson, Alliene O.
Fitzgerald, Barbara L.
Hay, Levina D.
Ikeda, Ernest Y.
Jason, Benny
Johnson, Barbara J.
Landucci, Fortunato D.
Lee, Corrine
Lee, Myron
Lien, Raymond E.
Lynch, Daniel J.
McCune, Donald G.
Maxwell, Joseph R.
Moreno, Eleanor
Munoz, Esther
Munoz, Mary
Nelson, Phyllis A.
Nichols, Marie
Otterbeck, Maurice
Pesqueira, George
Robinson, Ann R.
Rovetti, Flora
Shanks, Doris E.
Sill, Frank C.
Smith, Roberta J.
Taylor, James W.
Teixeria, Duard L.
Vargas, Lorraine R.
Wharton, Robert

1940

Becher, Dalrene L.
Berrios, Jr., Jose R.
Boggs, Norma L.
Carriere, Mildred R.
Collins, Richard L.
Collins, Kay J.
Combs, Robert D.
Coronado, Jessie
Dakan, Granville H.
Fode, Fern H.
Glavey, Donald L.
Gotori, Junior Toru
Harmon, Jeannette
Hoare, Bernice M.
Jones, Warren G.
Karns, Jr., Omer H.
Kersch, Lois J.
King, Robert L.
Kren, Julie A.
Lara, Virginia
Larson, Alice J.
Longoria, Nicholas
McCaslin, Barbara R.
McConnell, Frederick
Moniz, Charles
Munoz, Antonio
Ramarez, Fred
Rios, Pedro
Smothermon, Kenney
Smothers, Warren
Toste, Franklin W.
Toste, Joseph D.
Villanueva, Marie
Yaws, Odessa M.

1941

Ball, Paula L.
Binder, John E.
Brown, Thomas A.
Casner, Albert D.
Chan, Dong Fong
Corrao, Antonio
Cowan, Mollie A.
De Berry, Lemuel A.
DeMers, James D.
Earhart, Lorene A.
Fernandes, Genvea F.
Garcia, Ronald
Grijalva, Lillian
Hamilton, Charles
Hardy, Max L.
Higby, James R.
Howell, Lou Ella
Hulen, Harolene J.
Kawahisa, Yoshiko
Kirkpatrick, Richard
Klingensmith, Stanely
Munoz, Roger
Neep, Marlene
Nordlund, Irene A.
O'Brien, Lynn A.
Petersen, Katherine
Piland, Nancy J.
Post, Sr., Jerry R.
Ramponi, Goerge
Ross, Helen L.
Shaw, Marie E.
Spencer, Melvin L.
Taylor, Jacqueline R.
Taylor, Joseph H.
Timmons, Robert F.
Villalovos, Richard
Wood, Carolyn M.

1942

Alvarez, Maria E.
Avilla, Richard A.
Berumen, Alice
Betancur, Jose
Bettencourt, Richard
Bishop, Mildred L.
Braden, Charles F.
Braden, Lou K.
Bratton, Wanda Jo
Brewster, Robert F.
Brown, Carla J.
Brown, Jacqueline E.
Bruno, Sam B.
Burke, Alice C.
Carson, Geraldine
Cisco, Grace L.
Connors, Theresa B.
Cordero, Stanley L.
Cowdrey, Carroll B.
Culver, Robert G.
Dailey, Nancy J.
Davenport, Dorman
Eggman, Shirley
Evans, Larry G.
Folkner, Clovie M.
Forbush, Ronald
Garavalia, Shirley R.
Green, Howard J.
Grow, Stanley G.
Harbert, Jr., Melvin
Harreden, Arthur W.
Heard, Alvin G.
Henderson, Bonnie J.
Herring, Thomas J.
Hill, Donald L.
Ingold, Claudine S.
Innocencio, Ruby
Jackson, Donald
Jastremsky, Walter E.
Jola, LaRue
Jones, Janelle G.
King, Douglas L.
Leoz, Theresa C.
McCallon, Jack D.
McCallon, Jovette H.
McCallon, Joyce M.
McClure, Vivian C.
Martin, Diane C.
Matteson, Joanne L.
Nash, Charles R.
Palmer, Jr., Howard
Pascoe, William I.
Poss, Bert E.
Rohn, LaRue E.
Ross, Joyce R.
Sedgwick, Sandra L.
Sickinger, Jacob, J.
Singleton, Julian S.
Sloan, Dorothy
Snider, Kenneth J.
Spohr, Margaret D.
Spohr, Marilyn E.
Toste, Melvin L.
Wermuth, Philip J.
Whitt, Prentis
Wildmon, Windall
Wilson, Vivian I.
Wing, Donald L.

1943

Allison, Maxine L.
Arnswald, Robert L.
Belliveau, Kathleen
Blackwell, William J.
Blake, Samuel
Brixey, Martha U.
Brown, Violet E.
Chavez, Victoria
Danhouser, Edward
Dellinger, Dolores G.
Duncan, Marilyn A.
Ellis, Archie R.
Emens, Lorraine R.
Emmer, Frank L.
Fryer, Shirley M.
Gelling, Ernst
Henderson, John E.
Hollingsworth, Philip
Holmes, Roland F.
Hopps, Doris I.
Katz, Beverly N.
Keener, Mary I.
Laffoon, Stanely C.
Lee, Robert
Legner, Jackie C.
Lihner, Betty J.
Locke, Kenneth E.
McIntosh, Raymond
Marquez, Olivia
Marshall, Leonard A.
Mulder, Marvin
Nesvig, Wallace L.
Nicholson, Wayne A.
O'Rourke, Terrence
Reno, Harry C.
Selva, Eugenia
Shafer, James L.
Shults, Arlene F.
Smith, Alvin
Smith, Gordon A.
Smith, Oliver L.
Switzer, Harold
Tyhurst, Gary
Unruh, Adena
Wells, Edwin L.
Wells, Robert M.
White, Thelma J.
Wood, Alison M.

1944

Adkins, Leslie C.
Allen, Wanda F.
Ames, Marie R.
Bell, Alta F.
Burback, Deanna L.
Burroughs, Bruce K.
Bush, Joan J.
Canady, Dovie H. C.
Chadwick, Ronald L.
Cook, Kenneth E.
Cotten, Dolores D.
Davila, Robert R.
Encinas, Margaret
Fisher, Thomas G.
Ford, Patricia L.
Frederick, Donald J.
Gentry, Wanda F.
Gonzales, Edna Jo
Haas, Billie J.
Harreden, Mildred E.
Hart, Rosella
King, Betty J.
King, William E.
Larsen, Jean G.
Lee, Jacklyn R.
Lewis, Thomas J.
Lunsford, Jeanette J.
Meltzer, Elaine C.
Mertz, Renola A.
Millard, Marcia C.
Nordman, George L.
Patterson, Juanita S.
Patton, Cleo
Quintanilla, Juan C.
Ramos, Lillian S.
Rapp, James L.
Rienkenberg, Alan R.
Rush, Carol L.
Russell, Dale G.
Scharff, Thomas L.
Schwartz, Melvin E.
Sewell, Jack B.
Sewell, Robert R.
Smith, Herbert
Sniffen, Ruth E.
South, Jerry R.
Standley, Glen P.
Stephens, Betty Jo
Sterling, Robert M.
Stratton, David E.
Strom, Donald F.
Thomas, Beulah F.
Tidwell, Lonnie L.
Tory Betty J.
Tovar, Gilbert
Troon, Donna J.
Turner, Donna R.
Vicencio, Marvin L.
Victoria, Armida
Weaver, Betty L.
Willey, Joan P.
Woods, John E.
Young, Phyllis L.

1945

Bender, David C.
Boughton, Ronald L.
Bounds, Lottie M.
Bray, Mary E.
Burnette, Patricia L.
Calmels, Arthur E.
Canady, Mary P.
Cato, Richard A.
Coletti, Reno P.
Cox, Roger
Cuevas, Richard
Diaz, Luis
Dobbins, Judith
Douglas, Charlotte R.
Elliott, Pauline M.
Fitch, Jayne M.
Gannon, Jack R.
Gonzales, Lois M.
Gonzales, Nicholas
Gonzales, Vidal
Hamilton, Charles E.
Hedge, Donna D.
Jones, Patty S.
Kahnert, Gerald T.
Kinney, Alice L.
Kizziar, Donald
Lewis, Draga
Mow, Shanny
Norick, Gloria A.
Ogles, Jr., Oscar R.
Payne, John E.
Reece, Caroline S.
Roberts, Lily C.
Sauvageau, Roland
Scribner, Robert W.
Simpson, William R.
Spence, Molly J.
Thompson, Betty J.
Weatherby, Dwayne
Wicks, Phyllis J.
Willis, Jr., George
Zimmerman, Joan M.

1946

Arrellanes, Maria
Asin, Jerry
Begrin, Shirley Y.
Bird, Barbara A.
Blake, Gene R.
Blankenship, Myrna
Burge, Owida J.

Cale, Richard L.
Cantaloube, Louis
Cantaloube, Paul
Chandler, John W.
Chavez, Dolores J.
Chavez, Esther
Chavez, Lucille
Chavez, Mary J.
Chavez, Verona A.
Clark, Matt Ben
Cunningham, Jerry L.
Dowling, Janet C.
Dutcher, Dorothea
Ellison, Sr., Michael
Fontenot, James A.
Fragoza, Hilda
Franklin, James W.
Fry, Roger N.
Fujii, Amy
Garcia, Rosa
Gentry, Michael W.
Griggs, Robert E.
Harpel, Frank L.
Hawkey, Patricia M.
Hensley, Julie F.
Herstedt, Gene R.
Hooper, Lois B.
Hull, Joan J.
Hyre, Frederick L.
Jones, Betty Jo
Jones, Douglas E.
Jones, James E.
Keith, Virginia A.
Lichnovsky, Elsie E.
Lundeen, Julia A.
Marsh, Jean M.
Mendoza, Ernest
Miyashiro, Tsuruko
Murer, Rena M.
Oguin, Ethelene
Onate, Martha I.
Parodi , Donald N.
Paulsen, Martha M.
Peacock, Kenneth R.
Peters, Milton T.
Phillips, Theodore P.
Rowe, Thomas B.
Salisbury, Jack W.
Shelby, Delores
Skedsmo, Caroline P.
Sokolis, Linda L.
Sterling, Callie J.
Wood, Dean A.
Woodson, Willie L.

1947

Armstrong, Esther M.
Baker, Judith L
Barnes, Henry C.
Barton, Bruce A.
Beck, Charlene L.
Booth, William J.
Calhoun, Henry W.
Danderson, Rae A.
Dante, Gillbert A.
Davis, Emma L.
Fleming, Marjorie L.
Garcia, Victor R.
Garrison, Jerry W.
Gottschalk, Ernest
Greenberg, Leonard
Hale, Marjory D.
Heryford, Doris A.
Horn, Karen L.
Lugo, Orlando L.
Manuel, James L.
Martinez, Mary N.
Marvene, Michael
McCaskey, Phyllis M.
Miller, Gary A.
Mosley, Maurice C.
Pandula, Lou
Pylant, Royce E.
Raine, Gloria E.
Richardson, Ianthe E.
Ritchie, Dougles M.
Roby, Margaret E.
Rockenbaugh, James
Rodriguez, Frank E.
Rodriguez, John
Sanchez, Rosie D.
Sigman, Robert E.
Smith, Chris B.
Smith, Mary A.
Sosa, Jessica
Spoonemore, Helen
Thomas, Barbara A.
Tingley, Jr., John D.
Turner, Constance R.
Turner, Judith A.
Tuttle, Bonnie L.
Walter, James L.
Wilcox, Barbara L.

1948

Bibb, Arthur R.
Black, Connie M.
Botello, Albert
Boynton, Marion E.
Brothers, Glenda A.
Brown, Clifford I.
Brown, Edith I.
Burch, Donna R.
Butts, Charlie E.
Carrancho, Louis R.
Day, Donald R.
Donaldson, Patricia
Ferini, Robert A.
Flowers, Jo Anne
Gille, Marla J.
Green, Betty L.
Green, Delphine
Halbert, Russell R.
Hannah, Ronnie H.
Herkelrath, Karl W.
Hout, Gary L.
Kevil, Lorellie L.
Lamb, Michael E.
Lockwood, Barbara J.
Lowell, John W.
McCabe, William R.
McClish, Bryan L.
McGahey, Sandra F.
McMichael, Berniece
McNew, Gerald B.
Morales, Gloria J.
Murray, Tana L.
Pedersen, Melvin D.
Pezas, Panayiota
Phillips, Larry G.
Philpott, Deloris J.
Radford, Jr., Tommy
Radisch, Maresa D.
Read, Jack C.
Reinhart, Kenneth R.
Reynolds, Bruce L.
Robertson, Phillip
Settlemoir, James C.
Stevenson, Diane E.
Stull, Dave E.
Thompson, Diane E.
Titsworth, Bonnie G.
Triplett, Howard C.
Triplett, Mary E.
Walker, Donna E.
West, Karen L.
Williams, Robert O.
Wilson, Raymond F.

1949

Ash, William D.
Attwell, Robert L.
Banks, Roger S.
Bennett, Evelyn B.
Blackstone, Connie
Canady, Elizabeth R.
Cano, Judy R.
Cavazas, Jose
Chance, Thomas A.
Cisneros, Norma J.
Cummings, James A.
Cummins, Robert D.
Cunningham, Fredrica
Downing, Mildred E.
Elliott, Neilius L.
Enos, Shirley M.
Faber, Carolyn J.
Fonseca, Rene J.
Franich, Beverly L.
Freeman, James J.
Gamache, Beverly A.
Garbini, Connie M.
Gibb, Dean E.
Goodgame, Vivian
Goodman, Nolen G.
Griggs, Bobbie J.
Herring, Robert R.
Hildreth, Stanley D.
Hill, Shirley A.
Jacobs, Evelyn M.
Jones, Steven D.
Josephs, Susan
Karch, Darren D.
Katemopoulos, M.
Larson, Donna J.
Lentz, Richard J.
Long, Jackie B.
Mackey, Larry D.
Marcus, Johnny L.
Mendoza, Genevieve
Mora, Nicholas
Nelms, Lulu M.
Nelson, Joan D.
Nelson, Richard N.
O'Neil, Patrick G.
Phares, Shirley H.
Saling, Patricia A.
Sandel, Kenneth W.
Sawyer, Robert A.
Shemaria, Abraham
Simpson, James H.
Sims, Julia R.
Skedsmo, Bobby W.
Smith, Doyle H.
Sperring, Janice L.
Spicer, Jerry T.
Starnes, Nancy J.
Stewart, Beverly J.
Whitbey, James W.
Wilkinson, James A.
Wilson, Beverly B.
Wood, Ronald E.
Wyatt, Patricia R.

1950

Acuna, Mercedes
Alberto, Myra
Anderson, Elmer E.
Ball, Clarence E.
Beaty, Donald L.
Behmer, Junior Paul
Blumenstock, Frances
Brooks, Gloria
Callahan, Nancy D.
Comer, Michael L.
Davis, Kenneth
D'Errico, Judith K.
Downs, Maureen A.
Duggins, Frances B.
Flores, Salvadore
Gamache, Yvonne M.
Gathercole, Marjorie
Golden, Daniel L.
Grimes, Delane
Harvey, Joyce A.
Hauschildt, Mary L.
Herman, Carole
Hoffman, James D.
Ikeda, Samuel T.
James, Ava L.
James, Jacqueline
Jensen, Robert E.
Johnson, Sonny A.
Lambdin, Patricia
Livermore, James L.
Lopez, Gloria J.
McGuire, Lana
McIntyre, Patricia L.
Mangum, George W.
Marshall, Gary A.
Martin, Daniel J.
Missildine, Charles
Nyquist, Marlene R.
Oaks, Gay Nell
Parsons, Robert L.
Pearson, Billie
Pugh, David L.
Quick, Ronnie J.
Sevall, Glenn W.
Smith, Orville E.
Smith, Stanley F.
Stermolle, Joyce E.
Terrett, Jr., John E.
Todd, Susan E.
Wann, Vickie D.
Williams, Betty B.
Zimmerman, Edwin

1951

Arnold, Robert L.
Ashley, Elizabeth F.
Ambler, Joy A.
Ames, Diana R.
Askew, Vonny R.
Baker, Johnny L.
Baker, Joseph R.
Balla, George C.
Belliveau, Kathleen
Bibb, Oscar D.
Bledsoe, Gloris M.
Blicharz, Carl G.
Braga, Mary M.
Brennan, Robert D.
Burr, Ronald B.
Bush, Larry T.
Canady, Clara Jo
Clay, Joyce E.
Coleman, Harry A.
Comaskey, Michael
Courtright, Paula D.
Davidson, Jerry R.
Decker, Kenneth R.
Elam, Avis M.
Elkins, Cecil K.
Embring, Anna M.
Enos, Norbert A.
Erickson, Laura J.
Evans, Jr., Ben
Finch, Donna E.
Fleming, James T.
Garcia, Rachel
Garner, Kenneth H.
Glidewell, Kenneth
Goodwin, Robert D.
Guibor, Janice L.
Hagerty, Michael M.
Hamilton, Sarah
Harris, Eunice F.
Haskins, Dorothy J.
Hernandez, Maria
Hill, Michael C.
Howell, Barbara A.
Hubbs, Judith D.
Johnson, Dottie P.
Jones, Dennis M.
Lindberg, Carol L.
Long, Jackie E.
Lyons, Donald C.
Madrid, Richard T.
Mahoney, Patricia K.
Marshburn, Patricia
Martin, Donald P.
Monroe, Joyce L.
Monteverde, Patricia
Mueller, Bobby G.
Murphy, John T.
Norrberg, Inga
Northcutt, Michael L.
Nunez, Rudolfo
Olivas, Josette A.
Pedersen, Ethel R.
Pellissier, Barbara J.
Pickard, Richard J.
Pierini, Lena
Porter, Dennis M.
Prijoles, JoAnn
Pusateri, Josephine
Quartermus, Lillian
Raffaelli, Jeanette
Ramirez, Roselie
Reading, John A.
Riley, Donna A.
Rosenlind, Thomas E.
Roundy, Jerry W.
Rudkin, Connie A.
Sargent, Ella A.
Scolaro, Jr., Frank G.
Smith, Dwayne D.
Smith, Martha R.
Stamps, Wendell T.
Stempczynski, Ronald
Staudenmayer, Judith
Swain, Dorothy M.
Ternullo, Domenic J.
Thexton, Romer
Toops, Robert K.
Toste, Anthony
Trainos, Freddie W.
Turley, Rosa M.
Vasquez, Carl M.
Vaughan, Chester L.
Windfeldt, Paul E.
Young, Linda L.
Zaragoza, Robert
Ziviello, John A.

1952

Adams, Elizabeth M.
Alvarez, Maria O.
Arias, Augustine P.
Arroyo, Francisca
Austin, Kenneth W.
Boccio, Margharita
Boles, Wilma S.
Byrd, Patricia A.
Calzada, Suzanne
Cameron, Francince
Carlsen, Patricia M.
Champion, Monte E.
Chan, Dong Lum
Cisneros, David R.
DePosta, Jimmy R.
Durrett, Barbara S.
Fallin, Virginia L.
Figureida, Donna K.
Fletcher, Peggy K.
Fontaine, Patricia L.
Franklin, Joel A.
Freeman, Carolyn S.
Gamino, Theresa
Garrett, Mary E.
Glougie, Gaile J.
Gonzales, Frederick
Gonzales, Jose
Griefnow, Leon E.
Gutierrez, Connie L.
Haddock, Frances L.
Halseth, James A.

Harper, Steven L.
Henderson, Louise A.
Hermosillo, Arthur Y.
Hopkins, Judy A.
Howard, Patricia J.
Huskins, Joyce L.
Johnson, Jr., Leonard
Johnsen, Nettie A.
Johnson, Robert D.
King, Richard F.
Krumme, Karen K.
Lamberton, Jack C.
Lifton, Theodore G.
Lockhart, Richard
McKean, Gary E.
McKenna, Kathleen
Mallon, Johnita S.
Marquis, Rae E.
Melton, Shirley R.
Mendez, Dora
Morrill, Sandra J.
Moy, Terry
Myers, Jonathan S.
Nimitz, Jr., Barry
Norwood, Jr., Roy W.
Pedersen, Vera S.
Perez, Gloria D.
Perez, Linda F.
Phanton, Robert J.
Plein, Harold R.
Poochigian, Janvarjan
Poochigian, Nazaret
Preston, Mary D.
Rael, Gilbert
Reynoso, Marilyn
Riggs, Barbara L.
Riodan, Michael J.
Sargent, Alice R.
Scates, Thomas H.
Slavin, Paula J.
Smith, Jimmy L.
Snyder, Warren G.
Stacy, Stephen T.
Stephens, Jack E.
Stillwell, William L.
Stuparich, Elissa M.
Tanfield, Ronald W.
Telles, Mary A.
Thompson, James E.
Thompson, Lois G.
Toney, Mary J.
Viduya, Ronald L.
Walters, Sam S.
Wells, Janice L.
Wheeler, Phyllis A.
Wilcox, John C.
Wiley, Denis G.
Willey, Brenda J.
Williams, Billy C.
Womboldt, Robert P.

1953
Aquino, Steven W.
Arroyo, Francisco Jr.
Bailon, Belia C.
Barber, Wayne R.
Baroana, Richard
Basque, Russell
Besheers, Reuben R.
Blanco, Reginaldo L.
Brooks, Gregg M.
Bryant, Alice F.
Bryant, Donna R.
Bumgarner, Kerry W.
Coffey, Nancy I.
Cook, Marilyn I.
Corazza, Harold L.
Cox, Michael
DeLaRosa, Ernest N.
Dominguez, Betty J.
Dominguez, Cecelia
Eaglin, Jr., Charles
Elkins, Kathryn S.
Farrell, Frances K.
Flores, Esther
Furtado, Allen J.
Gibbons, Patricia D.
Givan, John H.
Green, Joe C.
Hilburn, Robert L.
Hill, Judd James
Johansen, Michael
Johnson, Peter J.
Kawelmacher, Daniel
Kennett, Thomas R.
Klein, Joan C.
Lafferty, Sharon K.
Large, Cecil E.
Lowe, George E.
Lowe, John R.
Lowrey, Barbara A.
McClain, Dorothy F.
McNealey, Thomas P.
Medley, Forest R.
Olson, Anita Jo
Pacheco, Anastacio
Pedersen, Kenneth C.
Pehlgrim, George M.
Philbrick, Gary
Pierce, Cheryl J.
Raschein, Kathleen
Raschein, Kevin E.
Reynard, Edith M.
Rothrock, Walter T.
Ruf, Barbara P.
Russell, Robert C.
Schwab, Janice C.
Shewmaker, Janice L.
Shoemaker, Nina J.
Smith, Christine
Stahl, Clifford R.
Taylor, Jerry B.
Ulloa, Norma E.
Utley, Glenda C.
VanZandt, Patricia R.
Voegele, Donna A.
Voegele, Elaine J.
Weeks, Don B.
Whaley, Jay A.
Wilson, Jr., Henry H.

1954
Aldridge, Wanda K.
Barnett, Barbara L.
Bisiaux, Jr., Robert
Braden, James E.
Bradshaw, Shirley J.
Brooks, Donna D.
Buehler, Donald F.
Burgess, Rosella M.
Butcher, Kenneth D.
Canady, Carlene
Canady, John C.
Carns, Jerry L.
Cass, William H.
Chittenden, Danny E.
Clark, Joyce A.
Contreras, Connie
Cosgrove, Christine
Coupland, Daniel
Dahl, Dale M.
Daniels, Richarld A.
Daw, Leslie J.
Downs, Sarah
Edmonds, Donald R.
Foster, Gloria G.
Fowler, Douglas E.
Frank, David M.
Friedman, Lenore A.
Galindo, Evelyn A.
Graves, Darlene A.
Herring, Lois A.
Higgins, Heather M.
Howe, Clinton W.
Huff, Sherrie A.
Hulsey, Richard E.
Hunt, Linda M.
Jandle, Cynthia L.
Jandle, Ramona F.
Joffrion, Jr., Harold J.
Johnston, William R.
Landyshev, Eugene
Leavitt, Patricia L.
Lee, Jr., William O.
Leo, William
Leon, Yvonne A.
Logan, Karen
Lopez, Joeann C.
Lynch, John C.
Maestas, Glenn W.
Malcolm, Don D.
Metzner, Floyd J.
Morin, Daniel R.
Nelson, Larry C.
Nickelson, John
Ocariza, Sharon
Ortega, Gilbert
Pacheco, Shirley A.
Palm, Michael L.
Parker, Linda J.
Ponciano, Raymond J.
Powell, David E.
Pratt, Jerry A.
Pratt, Larry A.
Reed, Karl W.
Rios, Jesus L.
Rodrigues, Diane M.
Rogers, Donald R.
Schafer, Eugene W.
Sims, Daniel
Spring, Dennis L.
Texeria, Jr., John
Tusing, John L.
Ulrich, Daniel S.
Walker, Sandra D.
West, Judy M.

1955
Aldrich, Robert K.
Amann, Astrid A.
Amann, Franklyn A.
Amann, Paula C.
Ash, David A.
Baker, Louis W.
Beyer, Jeffrey
Blicharz, Paul
Bosworth, Linda K.
Bray, Elizabeth A.
Bridges, Dennis M.
Brown, Raul E.
Bush, Gerald D.
Canady, Joseph W.
Castillo, Margarita
Chan, Yim
Charlton, Joseph
Christie, Annabelle
Dahl, Pearl A.
Elliott, Pamela
Elliott, Marilyn
Evans, Esther E.
Frausto, Robert M.
Garr, Ellen R. M.
Geist, Donna R.
Greenleaf, Joe G.
Griffis, Carol J.
Hale, Sherdeene
Haley, Philip R.
Hardisty, Karen A.
Harmon, Donald E.
Harreden, Shirley J.
Harris, Donald E.
Harris, John
Ho, Winfred
Hochderffer, Randy
Kantor, Cynthia
Koetz, James R. G.
Lamkin, Delilah I.
Landeros, Pedro G.
Laymon, Harriet
Lieurance, Alice J.
Maxwell, Michael
McIntyre, Judy A.
Miller, Donald L.
Mitchell, Margaret A.
Morrison, Jerrold S.
Newman, Blaine M.
Peckham, Stephen
Plautz, David D.
Pruitt, Darlene R.
Ramirez, Christine
Raub, Jeanne E.
Reed, Michael H.
Ribeiro, Verna T.
Richardson, Robert E.
Rodgers, John
Rodriguez, Angela
Ross, Xaverie M.
Roth, Sharon M.
Sarza, Teresita D.
Sherman, Margaret L.
Shewmaker, Roy W.
Smith, Joseph R.
Smith, Lauren
Stamper,. Kristine M.
Stamper, Thomas
Stephenson, Kirk D.
Swacker, Janis M.
Thompson, Ivan K.
Tufts, Carol S.
Varela, Alice
Varela, Sylvester N.
Whitlock, William

1956
Aldrich, Vivian
Anderson, Ethel
Avila, Rebecca M. R.
Bergstrom, Dorothy
Beserra, Mary
Bonaldi, Richard
Burton, Jr., Gerald
Cannon, Sherry
Cannuli, Susan J.
Carroll, Robert J.
Carter, Monroe E.
Charlton, Judith A.
Clark, Donna L.
Cluck, Jackie A.
Crabb, Judith E.
Crabb, Laura B.
Crabb, LeeAnn
Cross, James O.
Dehart, Merle G.
Dettman, Zoe A.
Dille, Judith M.
Dunn, Loretta C.
Hartjen, Mary B.
Hauschildt, Henry E.
Hernandez, Jerry
Hickerson, Elmo C.
Holm, Richard A.
Jaech, Timothy A.
Jiminez, Robert
Johnston, Lola M.
Jones, Darlene C.
Kirby, Naomi R.
Laxague, Michel P.
Loughmiller, Joan D.
McBaine, Ronald
McCabe, Richard A.
Meyer, Patrick J.
Miller, Janet
Mitchell, Charles H.
Mitchell, Terreen F.
Monson, Judith M.
Mosher, Linda V.
Moyer, Linda A.
Murray, Barbara A.
Pereira, Carla V.
Persons, Bonnie J.
Price, Jr., Lawrence
Roberts, Kathleen R.
Ross, Gwendolyn M.
Ruggiero, Paul A.
Sasser, Terry W.
Searcy, Lorena C.
Searcy, Richard L.
Searcy, Roy W.
Sedano, Ralph
Shramek, Rodney J.
Smith III, Franklin
Snider, Christina M.
Soto, Alice A.
Soto, Irene M.
Starkes, Frank C.
Stillford, Randall E.
Thorpe, Carol A.
Underwood, Brenda
Wells, Kenneth D.
Whaley, Sharon E.
White, Michael D.
Williams, Doris J.
Wilson, Gregory L.
Wilson, John A.
Woods, Cathy L.

1957
Abuan, Juan B.
Apolinar, Larry V.
Biell, Randall B.
Blakley, Maralee J.
Brooksher, Kathy S.
Caloroso, Anthony
Canady, David E.
Cass, Ernest D.
Chambers, Bruce M.
Chavira, Aurora
Cohen, Ronald A.
Cota, Shirley A.
Folsom, Kenneth R.
Foster, Harold J.
Gritts, Jennifer
Groninger, Susan K.
Harreden, Lois J.
Harvey, William L
Hearty, David A.
Heath, Billy R.
Holderman, Mary A.
Hom, Chuck
Howe, Jr., William
Howell, Karen G.
Krauss, Virginia L.
Lantheaume, William
Leomiti, Filipele
Linder, Carolyn J.
Malzkuhn, Brian L.
Marmolejo, Sylvia A.
McBride, Morris W.
McCoy, David W.
McCullough, Stephen
Mitchell, Kent T.
Montjano, Daniel
Moreno, Trindad
Murello, Peter T.
O'Donnell, Richard
O'Shea, Joseph L.
Pedersen, Diana T.
Pickus, Barbara A.
Ponciano, Heloise I.
Price, David L.
Prock, Glenelle
Ramey, Robert L.
Reed, Karen L.
Ross, James H.
Roselle, Sandra L.
Silva, Mary A.
Slawson, Hershell R.
Squires, Allen W.

Stout, Billie L.
Suniga, Robert
Telles, Elisa
Tenorio, Anthony G.
Timberlake, Linda L.
Vierra, Ronald L.
Young, Voncella D.

1958

Berkebile, Joe
Briggs, Lorena
Burton, Frances A.
Cardoza, Dennis
Carter, Karen
Christy, Teri
Cochran, William
Daniels, Luther
Davis, Helen
Davis, James A.
Dowler, Elizabeth
Driggers, Carol
Dunn, Lowell
Ford, Larry
Fulton, Suzanne
Garcia, Linda M.
Garcia, Phillip
Godwin, Christine
Gomez, Rocky
Hernandez, Juanita L.
Holliday, Diane
Holliman, Marilyn
Ingle, Paula
Ingle, Randy Jo
Joiner, Richard
Jones, Karen
Kutscher, Kathleen
Kutscher, Keith
Kutscher, Rosemary
Larkin, Daniel
Lingra, David
McKinney, Andre
Marquez, Enrique
Marvel, Everete
Maxwell, Betty
Maxwell, Shirley
Modica, Johnny
Moore, Dian
Morgan, Lynn
Moseley, Lewis
Parr, Jr., James
Porter, Judy
Robinson, Patricia L.
Salgueiro, Kenneth
Scoggins, Gary
Smith, Patrick
Stein, Gary
Stoddard, Juanita
Thompson, David
Trowbridge, David
Weiner, Karen
Weiner, Virginia
Willey, Edward
Woldridge, Louis

1959

Aghabalian, Gary
Alexander, Frank
Baker, Dwain H.
Bella, Enrique
Bench, Daniel
Bettes, Katherine
Black, Carol A.
Blair, Pamela
Campbell, Helen
Chrisman, Carol
Clancey, Claire
Cordero, August
Corey, Rita
Correa, David
Cummins, James
Davenport, Beatrice
Dugan, Teresa
Farnsworth, Wendell
Fleming, Rita M.
Gerling, Clarence
Gisser, Robert
Gottstein, Jayna
Gray, Carol
Gray, Gordon W.
Haas, Kathryn
Hammons, James
Hart, Debra
Hemphill, Gary
Herdrich, David
Hinds, Karen
Hinds, Karlin K.
Hinds, Donald
Johnson, James
Johnston, Lois A.
Jones, Barbara
Lampe, John
Kuntze, Marlon
Landis, Mary A.
Leininger, Lani
Lentz, Ella Mae
Loustalot, Jr., George
Macias, Jesse
Matthews, Richard
Marvel, Tommy
McCombs, James
Monteiro, Nancy
Mouroux., William
Norris, David
Pasisz, Michael
Paulsen, Kathy
Pehlgrim, Carol
Perry, James
Pinuela, Jr., Vinente
Prieto, Jesse
Rasmus, Joyanne K.
Rasmus, Judith A.
Roehrick, Gordon
Rosas, Maria
Smith, Henson D.
Stone, Letitia
Stover, Coleen
Temple, Roney D.
Toth, Alice
Waterhouse, Dennis
Wegener, Timothy
Worthen, Beatrice
Yanke, Dennis
Zanon, Richard P.

1960

Anaya, Christopher
Aribas, Joseph
Barnhart, Johnny
Bowman, Sandra
Brokenleg, Lesley
Cano, Leroy
Cano, Wilyman
Chapman, Carl
Chase, Jeryl
Corey, Patricia
Danielson, Gregory
Davenport, Patricia
Davidson, Gregory
Daviton, Colleen
Dickinson, Wade
Evans, Allen
Evans, Alvin
Fagot, Wayne
Freitas, Jane
Gallaway, David
Gianola, Lonita
Herbold, David
Hochholter, Beverly
Johns, Robert
Joiner, Dennis
Keslar, Lynda
Leathers, Ritchie
Leonard, Vontrece
Lessard, Christopher
Makepeace, Arthur
McLaughlin, Judith
Murrell, Dorothy
Musci, Susan
Poh, Sally
Re, Terry
Roeback, Christian
Ross, Dennis
Schnell, Raymond
Schwarzman, Lonita
Spruell, Sharon
Stewart, James
Stover, Barbara
Tanner, Kim
Tullis, Janice
Wata, Timothy
White, Sylvia
Willits, David

1961

Adamson, Delores
Ames, Vivian
Astesana, Katherine
Baca, Jeri
Barron, Donald
Behr, Randy
Benson, Eddie
Berman, David
Bleasdale, Stanley
Brown, Wanda
Burger, Thomas
Burroughs, Gloria
Campbell, Deborah
Cano, James
Chase, Robert
Coppedge, Elvin
Corveleyn, Petrus
daSilva, Deborah
daSilva, Robert
DeFonseka, Tyrone
Eberwein, John
Ellis, Vicki
Eyrond, Paul
Ford, David
Gibson, James
Gilfillan, Ronald
Groman, Stanley
Harrenden, Stanley
Harris, Melinda
Hasey, Jr., Forrest
Hicks, Terry
Holfinger, Jr., John
Huey, John
Issac, Paul
Jacobs, Albert
Jewel, Linda
Jones, Vernon
Klaman, Ronald
Klaman, Richard
Koetz, Deborah
Kuntze, Francine
Long, Craig
Lyles, Lonnie
Martinez, Genevieve
Moore, Martha
Pugh, Claude
Ramirez, Kenneth
Ranson, Ronald
Rasmus, Brian
Reaves, Lawrence
Robinson, Kenneth
Smith, Mary
Speck, Jennifer
Sugg, Edward
Sulisky, Betty
Sulisky, Patricia
Tague, Teresa
Thomas, Steven
Troutman, Manual
Vaughn, Harold
Warren, Laurie

1962

Akins, Judith
Alejo, David
Baldwin, Pamela
Batman, Diane
Beecher, David
Benson, Gregory
Blanco, Jr., Santos
Breckner, Glennda
Breckner, Terry
Byrd, Larry
Camacho, Candelaria
Campos, Guadalupe
Carroll, Marty
Clark, Patricia
Contreras, Aurora
Davis, Clarence
Daviton, David
Ellis, Dennis
Estes, Maria
Foust, Jr., Robert
Francis, Johanna
Fulwider, David
Harmon, Nancy
Hildreth, John
Hix, Debra
Hopkins, Bobby
Hunt, Yvonne
Keyser, Nikki
King, Kirby
Lentz, Jr., Gilmer
Lopez, Laura
MacDonald, Cheryl
Makaiwi, Robert
Manker, Debra
Maxwell, William
McDonald, Harrison
Mendoza, Jose
Morgan, Lynn
Myhre, Bonita
Nash, Rebecca
Navarro, Maria
Nunley, Marvin
Nunley, Steven
Oliveras, Anna
Otto, Marvin
Petersen, Claudette
Pinto, Elizabeth
Ramirez, Maria
Richardson, Troy
Riggs, Evelyn
Rushing, Sandra
Salcido, Rita
Salyer, Donald
Schaeffer, Cynthia
Silva, Maria
Smith, Linda
Smith, Roxane
Spain, Alvin
Takayama, Eiichi
Telles, Mervin
Williamson, Lucy
Wong, Jr., George
Zamarripa, Andres
Zamarripa, Andria

1963

Aghabalian, Karen
Aragon, Lexie
Aragon, Phillip
Arterberry, Zannet
Berbs, Vincent
Berry, Russel
Burnett, Robert
Candelas, Ruby
Celli, Alfred
Chan, Hing
Charles, Beverly
Charles, Jr., Melvyn
Davenport, Troy
Daviton, Michael
DeHerrera, William
Ellison, Jr., Michael
Flanagan, Cynthia
Fleck, Betty
Gillespie, Peggy
Gisler, Gail
Gough, Ronald
Govi, Gary
Grainer, Steven
Guel, Carmen
Hachiya, Helen
Hale, Douglas
Harris, Graeme
Hauschildt, Harry
Hazelwood, Tracy
Hyre, Darrell
Johnson, Brent
Keoppel, Carol
Kolos, Richard
Kuntze, Brett
Love, Colleen
Marvel, Chester
Mason, Madelynn
Miers, Allison
Miers, Tamara
Munoz, Victoria
Price, Walter
Ramos, Felipe
Rodriguez, Roy
Rouse, Adolfo
Sanchez, Maria
Schmidt, Barbara
Shelton, Sim
Singleton, Paul
Street, Carol
Street, Patricia
Sullivan, Deborah
Toalson, Charles
Tom, Linda
Valdez, Gloria
Verburg, Georgjana
Vidales, Luis
Voice, Susan
Waters, Tommy
Willey, Charles
Williams, Maxwell
Williams, Troy
Wiseman, James
Woo, John
Young, Keith
Yourdon, Keith
Yourdon, Sherie

1964

Ahern, Thomas
Alejo, Diane
Ault, Judy
Barnes, Nace
Bartunek, Debra
Batiste, Sheldon
Beem, Karen
Bettencourt, Louis
Blanco, Daniel
Brill, Timothy
Camaliza, Jeanette
Carlson, Barbara
Cartledge, James
Cassinelli, Luigi
Cessna, Brenda
Clary, William
Dameron, Lance
Dean, Rayline
Dickinson, Lydia
Enos, Kathleen
Evans, Rhondlyn
Field, Julianna
Fischer, Kathleen
Gardner, Robert
Glass, Matthew
Goessling, Sharon
Gonzales, Mario

Gosnell, Toni
Gregg, John
Hall, John
Hashida, Darren
Hilton, Cherie
Hines, Charlotte
Hopkins, Billy
Howard, Lois
Jackerson, Jack
Jackerson, Jaime
Jasey, Christina
Johnson, Thomas
Johnston, Gloria
Jung, Patricia
Katsanos, Dean
Kelley, Seth
Lane, Sheila
Lehner, Paul
Lessard, Paul
Lopez, Jesse
Lowe, Jesse
Loza, Stella
Manker, Teri
Massa, Harold
Matta, Verna
McMahan, Janice
Miles, Theodore
Miller, Theodore
Montgomery, LaRue
Morris, Kathleen
Morrow, Penelope
Muth, Gabriele
Myers, George
Nelson, Rex
Pena, Mark
Peterson, Mark
Prevost, Carlotta
Przybyla, Sandra
Quigley, Steven
Rabbitt, Eileen
Revander, Duane
Reyes, Jr., Ruben
Roberts, Mary
Robertson, Andrew
Rodriguez, Joel
Rojas, Nancy
Simonet, Stanley
Singleton, Gregory
Singleton, Ralph
Smith, Sherry
Sproul, Terry
Stecker, Linda
Stuart, Harold
Teachout, Jerry
Throop, Keith
Ward, Judy
Williams, Don
Williamson, Diane
Wroten, Jennifer
Yuen, Sui

1965

Adcock, Fred
Aguinaldo, Darrell
Alvarado, John
Amado, Ceceila
Andrews, Chris
Aponte, Lydia
Bailey, Diana
Baker, Stanley
Bogan, Envie
Bonnetti, Richard
Bravo, Mary
Brugge, Sharon
Burrows, Bonnie
Campos, Michael
Cheeseman, Delmar
Conrad, Jr., Willis
Corsello, Trina
Cyr, Jerry
Dean, Reginald
Dickerson, James
Dolorfo, Marilou
Fancher, LuAnn
Feria, Elizabeth
Feria, Wesley
Fischer, Cathleen
Fortenberry, C.
Fuentas, Linda
Gage, William
Granberry, Doren
Gray, Lloyd
Guevara, Rose
Havens, Vicki
Hill, Randall
Howard, Rodney
James, Douglas
Jones, Charley
Karsh, Scott
Kidd, Cynthia
King, Bobbi
Kirk, Pamela
Koetz, Graham
LaCount, Robert
Loshakoff, Roland
Martin, Patricia
Mask, Dennis
McAlister, Mark
Moore, Marilyn
Motta, Judith
Moulyn, Richard
Mundt, Mary
Nichols, Sally
O'Conner, Charlotte
Ogles, Bella
Ordaz, Jose
Pratt, Linda
Propp, George
Rangel, Linda
Reis, Deborah
Rivera, Adelia
Rivera, Armando
Rivera, Pablo
Sanchez, Corina
Sandoval, John
Sexton, Marilyn
Smith, Dennis
Sutherland, Michael
Swearinger, Debra
Thomas III, Merritt
Torres, Stephanie
Tripp, Colleen
Virgen, Helen
Wasson, Loretta
Weiss, Thomas
Wilms, Debora
Zamarripa, Eva

1966

Ackernecht, L.
Aguilar, Hector
Aguilar, Martha
Alvarez, Bibiana
Amundsen, Pamela
Arias, Josalina
Balestrieri, Thomas
Barnard, Patricia
Belemecich, Leslie
Boudreau, Susan
Burnett, Jerold
Byers, Shana
Crawford, Stephen
Dean, Mary
Denman, Lynn
Diaz, Cynthia
Ellison, Elmer
Gaines, Katherine
Garcia, Debra
Garrad, Theresa
Hammons, Valgene
Hause, Jerry
Hernandez, Juan
Hubbard, Cynthia
Ivory, Chester
Jiminez, Ramona
Keeling, Donald
Klein, Robin
Kurtz, Donna
Letterman, Larry
Lewis, Shelton
Lira, Johnny
Luckert, Larry
Madewell, Donna
Martin, Johnny
Martinez, Frederick
May, Larry
May, Lonnie
Mc Ghee, Charles
Martinez, Frederick
Metzger, Robert
Moffatt, Kristian
Moralli, Deborah
Nash, Charles
Navarro, Jose
Owens, Marianne
Pier, Michael
Powell, Gary
Powell, Kara
Rivas, Eve
Scott, Lawrence
Smith, Rose
Spencer, Glen
Taff, Penny
Van Burkleo, Sylvia
Velasquez, Rebecca
Villasenor, Steven
Weigart, Ronald
Williams, Rickey
Wills, Nancy
Winston, Gwen
Wyant, Cary

1967

Adams, Donald
Adams, James
Allen, Bobby
Back, Eric
Barlow, Rex
Barrett, Richard
Barriga, Guadalupe
Bartlow, Kenneth
Bayle, Daniel
Beebe, Janice
Bettencourt, Michael
Blanco, Maria
Boles, Barry
Brinkmeyer, Carol
Brooke, Linda
Campos, Martha
Cannady, Maxine
Castorena, Jose
Caudill, Bobby
Coulbourn, Deborah
Dahlman, Maria
DeBeck, Robert
DeNava, John
Dickinson, Douglas
Dobbs, Sarah
Duncan, Danny
Echavarria, Sylvia
Felthauser, Joy
Fitzpatrick, Ronald
Garrad, David
Hancock, Richard
Helberg, Lenore
Hoffman, Linda
Hughes, David
Infante, Jr., Blas
Infante, Jose
Jiminez, Jorge
Johnson, Buddy
Johnston, Vickey
Korn, George
Lacey, Lawrence
Learn, Richard
Leeks, Yvonne
Lindsey, Rickey
Lowrey, David
Mason, Forrest
McClain, Suzette
McLaughlin, Charles
Miller, Nancy
Mora, Russell
Morales, Johnnie
Morales, Herlinda
Morales, Virginia
Myers, Michael
Nash, Russell
Ogles, Lisa
Policicchio, Elaine
Poynor, Polly
Reed, Donald
Reid, Tamma
Roberts, Randy
Rose, Ricardo
Seid, Judy
Simonetta, Gary
Tagholm, Jefferey
Taylor, Phillip
Tollner, Steven
Van Gorder, Kenneth
Whitney, Dennis
Wright, Denise
Zamarripa, Juan

1968

Alarcon, Julian
Augustine, Ronald
Autry, Grady
Biggins, Robert
Boswell, Laura
Bradford, Pattie
Buchan, Alan
Burnham, Doreen
Carrera, Maria
Chamberlain, Stephen
Chase, Douglas
Chen, Pom
Condrey, Anthony
Cooper, Steven
Corey, Edward
Davenport, Connie
Davenport, Ronnie
Davidson, Terry
Duffield, Paul
Estrada, Dora
Finch, Allen
Flores, Jr., John
Fraga, Sue
Ganfield, Sandra
Harbert, Janet
Harrison, Phyllis
Hilbert, Pamela
Holt, Mary
Hopkins, Patrick
Jayne, Stephen
Leeds, Clinton
Longo, Stephen
Parrish, Allyson
Parsons, Michael
Poynor, Priscilla
Prout, Steven
Rabago, Mildred
Rios, Janie
Schuck, John
Silbernagel, Danielle
Silveira, Esauro
Smith, Linda
Stubblefield, David
Taber, Timothy
Tyson, Roger
Vega, Bablina
West, Kathleen
Wheeler, Logan
White, Steffine
Williams, Kenneth

1969

Alexander, Thomas
Andrews, Michael
Baggett, Sharon
Barnachea, Antonio
Bradshaw, Eldon
Bragg, Gerald
Carter, Deborah
Charles, Marjorie
Chock, Kevin
Deu, Ina
Epps, Gary
Farazian, Lila
Forsyth, Robert
Fulwider, Kenneth
Gonzales, Aly
Goodwin, Steven
Giusti, Craig
Hansen, Russell
Harris, Jr., Nathaniel
Hatch, Kenneth
Johnson, Daniel
Kirk, Stephen
Lessard, Wendy
Lopez, Raymond
Mattison, Steffine
Moore, Darren
Moore, William
Mort, Joseph
Nash, Deborah
Nieves, Ralph
Olivarez, Mary
Olivarez, Robert
Ortiz, Elizabeth
Parker, Glen
Peel, Scott
Piffero, Sharon
Pratt, Donald
Pratt, Judy
Prudholm, Duaine
Ragar, Timothy
Rodgers, David
Rodgers, Janet
Root, Nancy
Schmidt, Barbara
Shelton, Donald
Shields III, Albert
Smith, Lorraine
Smith, Wesley
Stidham, Elaine
Swenson, Randy
Turner, Jerry
Twinn, Carol
Valenzuela, Gloria
Yee, Lisa

1970

Acosta, Felix
Alcorn, Todd
Amundsen, Sandra
Andry, April
Attletweed, Kathleen
Behr, Russell
Brigham, Patricia
Brown, Sharon
Buckmaster, James
Bunce, Jeffrey
Chee, Stanley
Christiansen, Vesta
Davis, Cynthia
Elizarraraz, Elizeo
Ellis, Edward
Enriquez, Stephanie
Fatke, Raymond
Foust, Julie
Fresquez, Louise
Garman, LeRoy
Gomez, Michael
Goodwin, Judith
Hart, Gayle
Hilliard, Pamela
Hiramoto, Julie
Hogston, Karen
Hom, Chapman

Ingraham, Jason
Jamison, Matthew
Jones, Robert
Kennedy, John
Kirton, Marcel
Littlejohn, Duane
Lyons, Laura
Mah, Su-Young
Malbreau, Patricia
Maulding, Jerold
McDonald, William
Mullen, Paul
Nichols, Cynthia
Ordaz, Marta
Parker, Louis
Pedersen, Charles
Peralta, Ruth
Riley, Patricia
Rodriquez, Irene
Russo, Regina
Ruzicka, Lee
Saavedra, Thomas
Sastini, Johnny
Schaefer, Robert
Schmidt, Michael
Sermeno, Anthonio
Sierra, Susanne
Sortwell, Joseph
Speck, Sharon
Stone, Cheryl
Vivas, Ernest
Vogt, Jr., Earl
Watkins, Johnny
Watt, Brant
Watt, Cherie
West, Jeannie
Wong, Shui
Wright, Malcolm
Yarbrough, Dean
Yee, Joan
Yun, Matthew

1971

Ayres, Martin
Baer, Carolyn
Baer, Donald
Barnett, William
Berg, Noreen
Berry, Wildea
Blair, Timothy
Brown, Criss
Bucher, Mark
Caldwell, Diann
Cullen, Allison
Daviton, Candi
Dunlap, Deborah
Fernandez, Emiliano
Hetman, Mark
Higgs, Dorene
Huffman, Dina
Jackson, Gerald
Jacobs, Lisa
Jenkins, Deborah
Johnson, Douglas
Johnson, Eugene
Llorens, Wanda
Loftin, Dwain
Marquette, Christine
Martinez, Tina
Matherly, David
McWilliams, Deborah
Mock, Julia
Nakatani, Catherine
Nelson, Mark
Newport, Vicki
Osuna, Maria
Pendley, Wade
Peterson, Michael
Plubell, Robert
Poynor, Paul
Pratt, Susan
Quinn, Paula
Real, Colleen
Renke, Mark
Riggs, Kimberly
Robinson, Carlis
Russo, Michael
Salisbury, James
Seiden, Matthew
Spiers, Robert
Swearengin, Deanna
Swinger, Dina
Thomas, Vicki
Treumer, Karen
Wang, Chung
Wilson, Jennifer
Woods, Susan

1972

Barlow, Ricardo
Barnett, Jr., John
Bell, Alfredo
Belotz, Judith
Busby, Teresa
Ceja, Jose
Chan, Kenneth
Corey, Earl
Cunningham, Donald
Dynes, Leshun
Fong, Sunny
Garrett, Rebecca
Goguen, Mark
Guido, James
Gutierrez, Steven
Louis, J. Scott
Murray, David
Netherton, Timothy
Pennington, Marcia
Rodgers, Theresa
Sanders, David
Watson, Jr., Gerald
Wedin, Robert
Yuen, Leung

1973

Armstrong, Steven
Barbour, Steve
Bartram, James
Booth, Stanley
Burgess, Drema
Chan, Mei Chi
Chapman, Klesha
Cole, Carolyn
Delgado, Susan
DuMond, Michael
Earnest, Debra
Fernandes, Vicki
Flores, Maria
Frazier, Nancy
Gomes, Enos
Goode, Donald
Graves, Danny
Harper, Jimmy
Harthun, Judy
Hendrix, Kevin
Henslin, Kathy
Horn, Robert
Idica, Helen
Iturbide, Steven
Jacques, Armando
Johnson, Michael
Jones, Debra
Jones, Norman
Jones, Peter
Kennedy, Rodney
Koehn, Robin
Krueger, John
Lind, Brent
Lind, Brian
Meadows, Kenneth
Milliken, Timothy
Morin, Diana
Perez, Gregario
Peterson, David
Poe, Nicholas
Quinn, Patricia
Reza, Armando
Santos, James
Schulte, Ricann
Soriano, Timothy
Spear, Alan
Szpakowski, Nemo
Vasquez, Eliel
Walker, William
Wash, Lorenzo
Webber, Essex
Wilcox, Jr., George

1974

Ashley, Jeffrey
Bartlett, Katherine
Belser, Kerry
Bettencourt, Kathy
Border, Douglas
Brooks, Katherine
Browning, Penny
Busby, Paula
Canada, Sandra
Clark, Charlotte
Colangelo II, Pete
Cordero, Anthony
Dockery, Daniel
Fields, Linda
Flamer, Jr., Floyd
Haggerty, Cornell
Harvey, Mark
Hegge, Evelyn
Howard, Joseph
Johnson, Daniel
Jones, Jeffrey
Jones, Jr., Webster
Lamb, Ann
Lamb, Sherry
Lamp, Terry
Lee, Gary
Lemer, Paula
Lew, Robert
Lewis, Robert
Martin, Cynthia
Martinez, Alexander
Mayes, Mona
Morgan, Doris
Mosbarger, Quinn
Pierson, Heidi
Randolph, Diana
Rathert, Joseph
Resch, David
Stecker, Janice
Torchia, Ronald
Tully, Matthew
Vandenburgh, Gerald
Vosbury, Therese
Wood, Paul
Wyatt, Stephanie

1975

Abson, Tessie
Angeli, Denise
Arnold, Margaret
Barlow, Cary
Bizicki, Christopher
Campbell, Ruth
Cardenas, John
Cervantes, Melodye
Christy, Shelly
Clark, Jeffrey
Cole, Richard
Cordova, Jesse
Crews, Robert
Crow, Russell
Curtin, Deborah
Dawson, Kevin
De Angelis, Mary
Dodd, James
Edwards, David
Estacio, Guadalupe
Evans, LaDena
Felicianio, Carmen
Fogle, Rickey
Foreman, Celeste
From, James
Garcia, Estella
Garfield, Karen
Gilleland, Timothy
Gosselin, JoAnn
Gray, Brenda
Herger, Franklin
Hickerson, Timothy
Jeung, Connie
Johnson, Aarion
King, Christie
Knutsen, LuAnn
Lewis, Paul
Lucero, Victoria
Martinez, Brian
McKnight, Tessie
Merino, Johnny
Montgomery, Debbie
Morgan, Jr., Jesse
Mott, Mildred
Pean, Christopher
Pena, Alex
Perkins, Larry
Perridon, Donald
Perry, Elizabeth
Pershe, Mark
Plummer, Wilma
Price, Bruce A.
Quinonez, Jamie
Raby, William
Rames, Geraldine
Reaves, Darrel
Rivera, Rhonda
Robinson, Aladrian
Romak, Leslie
Romano, Vincent
Row, Billie
Rutter, Ronald
Santos, Noe
Schwedhelm, Wendy
St. Louis, Shirley
Stacy, Ronald
Thigpen, Kenneth
Voreck, Denny
Walz, Catrina
Weaver, David
White, Craig
Wilson, Willette
Zeigler, Bonnie

1976

Albericci, Gae
Allen, Scott
Arellanes, Daniel
Attletweed, Olaf
Bailey, Robert
Baldwin, Theodore
Bennett, David
Bennett, Nancy
Borden, James
Brewer, Bruce
Brown, Deanne
Carrillo, Timothy
Chacon, Robert
Chagoya, Jerry
Chung, Sung Won
Crowell, Elizabeth
Davis, Michelle
DeSantis, John
Douglas, Darleen
Duran, Seymour
Egbert, Suzanne
Engleford, Bradley
Enos, Bert
Evans, Trudy
Fields, Eugina
Fontanilla, Edmund
Gaitan, Jr., Domingo
Galyean, Kathy
Gaudet, Tamera
Gee, Calvin
Gonzalez, Rene
Gorton, Adrienne
Hartman, Robin
Hefner, Eric
Hiner, Kitty
Hopkins, Lisa
Howe, Andrea
Huddleston, Joyce
Johnson, Derek
Katsura, Winston
Keegan, James
Kellogg, Sally
Klinger, Joel
Lagrimas, Stephanie
Lauraya, Dennis
Lucas, Bryan
Martin, Corey
Mau, Karl
McConnell, Charles
McCullough, Candy
McCullough, Stephen
McGee, Felecia
Mecham, Philip
Mitchell, Toni
Moreno, Mario
Muscacchia, Paul
Muscadine, Joanne
Nelson, Brandi
Pacheco, Jose
Parreira, Anthony
Pedersen, Rodney
Peters, Jon
Petersen, Terry
Peterson, Sandra
Prader, Brian
Ramos, Dawn
Ramos, Joe
Redeker, Darrell
Rivera, Eloise
Robinson, Debra
Rosenthal, Daniel
Ryan, Inga
SanMiguel, Rudy
Schwieger, Lisa
Silvania, Kerry
Simonalle, Frank
Sims, Deborah
Smith, Danien
Smith, Laurel
Smith, Tyrone
Sontag, Thomas
Stack, Lloyd
Steel, Candy
Symmes, Richard
Tallmon, Stuart
Todd, Delia
Toste, Sarah
Trosin, Renee
Valdivieso, Gabriell
Vier, Tammy
Wares, Antonio
Weber, Ron
Wiley, Ivan
Williams, Linda
Williams, Virgil
Wood, Mark
Woodard, Kevin
Wroten, Christopher
Young, Elly
Zemach, Rachel

1977

Agnew, Laura
Akin, Corina
Avilla, Lori
Banks, Theresa
Bates, Rhonda

Bauer, Julie
Bautista, Rex
Bouma, Todd
Bracco, Deborah
Brewer, Annette
Brooks, David
Bryant, Barbara
Caigoy, Emilinda
Calica, Barry
Carlino, Michael
Carmichael, Kirsten
Carson, Mauricio
Cass, Anthony
Caulkins, Wendy
Chapman, Gary
Chavez, Terri
Chung, U Sung
Clark, Timothy
Cunningham, Donnell
Daniels, Curtis
Danti, Laura
Davis, Cynthia
Dawson, Erwin
Delgado, Ronda
Diaz, Armando
Diaz, Juan
Divine, John
Dorris, David
Drake, Todd
Durio, Ayanna
Easley, Delyte
Estrella, Alex
Estrella, Jamie M.
Farquar, Coreen
Fernandez, Rafael
Field, JoAnn
Filson, Cheryl
Firl, Leslie
Friedman, Rachel
Garnett, Suzanne
Glenn, David
Gobel, Julie
Godfrey, Stephen
Gosselin, Christine
Green, Julie
Green, Maurice
Hagmann, Melody
Hammond, Jane
Hammond, Linda
Harper, Ruth
Harris, Tina
Hartman, Merlin
Heaton, Leslie
Hernandez, Mark
Higgins, Tessa
Higgs, Diane
Hirt, Lawrence
Hughes, Craig
Ikeda, Ivanette
Ikeda, Jonathan
Ikeda, Stuart
Johnson, Jeannie
Kadin, Stacey
Kawahira, Diane
Kessler, Noah
Klein, Jeffrey
Koons, Clinton
Laa, Sarah
Ladewig, John
Lander, Jack
Laughlin, Brian
Leano, Janet
Lee, Gregory
Lincoln, Jerry
Lodge, Asa
Lopez, Alfred
Louie, Andrea
Lugo, Alicia
Machado, Richard
Mancill, Larry
Mancill, Jr., Emmett
Marquez, Carlotta
Marquez, Damian
McAllister, Jarvis
McDaniel, Karen
McFarland, Steve
McGregor, Lilianne
Mendoza, Francisco
Mesa, Esther
Montes, Lidia
Montoya, Steven
Moore, Douglas
Nixon, Robert
Norton, Thomas
O'Donnell, Scott
Parker, John
Peterson, Cal
Piver, Kenna
Pocci, Igor
Quigley, Shelley
Reyes, Gloria
Reihm, Anthony
Rios, Lawrence
Rogers, Scott
Saunders, Cynan
Senning, Herbert
Shulte, Timothy
Silva, Jr., Joseph
Sloan, Juan
Stanton, Daniel
Stecker, Nancy
Sweetwood, Edward
Sweigart, Dennis
Thompson, Robert
Torres, Jr., George
VanderCourt, Anita
Vasquez, Ada
Verrett, Kerwin
Ward, Terri
Wertz, David
Wheadon, Sheila
Whitney, Mark
Witt, Roger
Wright, Kecia
Young, Michael

1978

Alexander, Scott
Alvarez, Vincent
Arceneaux, Stacy
Bailey, Samantha
Barnes, Charlette
Bean, David
Bible, Desiree
Blackmore, Mike
Blance, LeDe
Brantley, Kenneth
Brown, Angela
Burke, Joseph
Cameron, Christine
Cantergiani, Amy
Cantrell, Kristine
Carpenter, Virginia
Casel, Jamal
Chalenor, Aaron
Cobb, Angela
Daniels, Genelle
DePalma, Rabi
Dillion, Ronald
Dingel, Nathan
Doan, Sonovan
Don-Pedro, Anne
Douglas, Robert
Drake, Janet
Eads, Julian
Estrada, Ricardo
Farbes, Derrick
Farbes, Vanessa
Finley, Tim
Garza, Sally
Gee, Elena
Godinez, Amelia
Gonzales, Aqustin
Gonzales, Carmen
Gray, Sophia
Halcomb, Roxanna
Harakal, Brian
Harmon, Denis
Harris, Abigail
Herring, Jean
Holderby, Rhonda
Houston, Eli
Hyde, Eric
Jackson, Lisa
Jarvis, Tommy
Jennings, Rida
Jones, Michael
Jones, Robin
Kaestner, Wendy
Kellar, Katherine
Kelly, Patrick
Kem, Jack
Kent, Margie
Kido, Shari
Kimsey, James
Kindrick, Matthew
King, Lisa
Lengjel, Christopher
Lorello, Tommy
Lowe, Sabrina
Lugo, Adam
Lugo, Dale
Lynn, Michael
Mahan, Coleen
Marin, Arnold
Marshall, Jeff
Martin, Tim
Matthews, Sarah
McCracken, Matthew
Melton, Selena
Moberg, Daren
Moon, Jeffrey
Moore, Garrett
Moser, James
Mullins, Christina
Myers, Kristina
Nasukiewicz, S.
Neeley, Amy
Nelson, Petrina
Nolan, Donald
Nole, Robin
Ogo, Jude
Olson, Sonjie
Orcutt, Jerry
Patterson, Janel
Pease, Richard
Perkins, Timothy
Pratt, Tom
Quenga, Henry
Quinn, Sean
Relei, Brian
Rodriquez, Julian
Romano, Nicholas
Russell, Donald
Samuels, Merrill
Sanchez, Chris
Santos, Jesse
Schmidt, Deron
Schulter, Susan
Schwab, Theresa
Scotton, John
Serna, Chris
Smith, Garrett
Smith, Elbert
Smith, Michael
Smith, Laura
Soto, Reyna
Spehar, Howard
Starek, Richard
Stevenson, Sheri
Stotler, Robin
Svanda, Paula
Takken, Mallory
Theriot, Terrylene
Theriot, Terry
Torres, Lillian
Trammel, Diana
Warmsley, Renee
Wesley, Kalonji
Wiley, Ivan

1979

Agraviador, Craig
Ainsley, Jennifer
Ainsley, Heather
Aleshire, Todd
Almajed, Mishari
Alvarado, Jose
Austin, Swanhilda
Bardsley, Janet
Barrett, Daniel
Barrett, Brenda
Batterson, Debbie
Bella, Carol
Bella, Kevin
Bella, Mark
Bonheyo, Becky
Bonheyo, Jerome
Brumley, Brent
Callejas, Michael
Campbell, Cynthia
Celaya, Adam
Chadd, Cynthia
Chadd, Wendy
Chung, Julia
Cloud, Jeff
Collins, James
Cortes, Lucia
Crisler, John
Davarpajooh, Alan
Diaz, Fernando
Douglas, Eric
Duckworth, Jessie
Dyck, Aganeta
Farquar, Jamie
Fishbein, Rosemary
Flores, Monica
Foster, Carol
Francis, Monique
Freisen, Mike
Gamaza, Gary
Gomes, Renie
Gosselin, Heidi
Hack, Pei
Hansen, Richard
Harmon, Denis
Harris, Machial
Harvey, Glenora
Heffernan, Autumn
Hewling, Wade
Howe, Clinton
Jimenez, Liandro
Jones, Grace
Jones, Rhonda
Jones, Tina
Keener, Cynthia
Leon, Danny
Lewis, Steven
Lieu, Norman
Limpin, Stanley
Lopes, Filomena
Marsh, Shannon
Marsh, Trenton
Martinez, Abel
Matlock, Debbie
McCoy, Melissa
McIntyre, Cliff
McKenzie, James
Medina, Robert
Mendes, Harvey
Merino, Alfredo
Miller, Pam
Miller, Roger
Moeckel, Neva
Morriese, Arthur
Mumford, Tracey
Nasukiewicz, Jennifer
O'Reilly, Dana
Palaia, Christopher
Parker, Theron
Pelfanio, Christopher
Phillips, Kevin
Ramirez, Elizabeth
Ramirez, Manuel
Ramos, Michael
Reins, Shonie
Richau, Catherine
Ritchie, Taren
Rodgers, Donna
Rotert, Julie
Rothrock, Seena
Salazar, Juan
Sandoval, Donald
Saunders, JoJo
Saunders, Jonas
Scott, Michelle
Sewell, Traci
Siaki, Tim
Simon, Robert
Smith, Eric
Soto, Jesus
Souza, Patricia
Stickler, David
Stine, Nancy
Stogdell, Tamera
Thompson, Jeri
Torres, Victor
Trapani, Debra
Turnage, Scott
Wertz, Stormy
Whitworth, Traci
Will, Adam
Willey, Leo
Williams, Tanya
Wines, Debbie
Winston, Charles
Witt, LaShawn
Wyman, Tom
Zapata, Juan

1980

Adams, Cynthia
Aguilar, Dora
Alfredo, Merino
Allen, Robert
Anderson , John
Anthone, Geraldine
Anthone, Julia
Apple, Tuesday
Ash, Alex
Armstrong, Terry
Arnold, Rhonda
Baer, Anne Marie
Barish, Jed
Barish, Joel
Barrows, Scott
Basso, Frances
Behunin, Jason
Boren, Leroy
Boren, Michelle
Boswell, Julie
Bravin, Debbie
Bravin, Jeffrey
Bravin, Seth
Camacho, Frances
Cantrell, David
Cantrell, Julie
Carney, Mark
Carrasco, Mark
Cass, Anthony
Cass, Christine
Coffelt, Kenneth
Cornish, Richard
Davison, Kelli
DeBartolo, Anthony
Dehaesus, Mark
Delapina, Rachelle
Devine, Eric

Dominquez, Tim
Durham, Tommy
Dykes, Andre
Evans, Jay
Fabela, Lance
Ferguson, Bridgett
Finney, Laura
Flores, David
Flores, Felix
Flores, Henry
Ford, Antoinette
Fraire, Julian
Freitas, Peter
Fylstra, Nathan
Gobel, Julie
Goetz, Lisa
Gomez, Gilbert
Gonzales, Carlos
Gonzalez, Jr., Abdon
Guevera, Michael
Halverson, Craig
Henry, Darius
Hofstede, Mark
Howland, Matthew
Horn, Nicholas
Ingram, Trevor
Jackson, Scotty
Jiminez, Nancy
Jiminez, Ramon
Johnson, Sheila
King, Mark
Kissinger, Donna
laMarsna, Reeca
Lander, Jack
Lee, Chi
Lee, Kin
Lehmann, Jay
Lehmann, John
Lindeman, Elizabeth
Little, Kevin
Lopez, Beatriz
Lyles, Kevin
Martin, Cedric
Martin, James
Martinson, Eric
Mathews, Sarah
McClutcheon, Debora
McDaniel, Darin
McDonald, Wendy
Meagher, Brian
Melendez, Carlos
Menjivar, Jeannette
Merritt, Sonya
Mestaz, Frank
Mouilee, Jeanne
Norsworthy, Timothy
O'Donnell, Nicholas
O'Donnell, Robert
Olafson, Erin
Olafson, Rina
Olson, Troy
Omila, Jesus
Ortiz, Benjamin
Osburn, Mark
Pappas, Karen
Perry, Daniel
Pfahl, Rogann
Phillips, Damon
Pickard, Violet
Reece, Janna
Renda, Anthony
Rock, Christopher
Rodriquez, Andrew
Romero, Stephanie
Ruano, Nahun
Rudd, David
Salemme, Anthony
Sapida, Christine
Scales, Arthur
Schmitz, Jon
Schmitz, Nicola
Sisk, Terry
Sivella, Keith
Souza, Shelley
Spradley, Lynn
Stevens, Gina
Stevens, Randall
Stout, David
Stracener, Rickey
Sullivan, Ladaynia
Taylor, Larry
Terrazas, Angelica
Texera, Rodney
Thomas, Erin
Tiku, Aselefech
Torres, Stephanie
Trowbridge, Wayne
Tsai, Joseph
Tsai, Melody
Tupfer, Aylleen
Tupfer, Yvonne
Vallente, Mannelio
Vincent, Heidi
Vitorino, Leonesa
Whitworth, Terri
Wilson, Shelly
Winston, Charles
Ziegler, Regina

1981

Afonso, Anthony
Austin, Sheila
Battle, Sherry
Bauer, Michael
Buchan, Cheyenne
Chin, Florence
Chin, Frederick
Cleary, Joyce
Click, Michael
Cobb, Gillia
Cuellar, Robert
Cummins, Colleen
Deming, Mike
Duarte, Kathleen
Dye, William
Easley, Anthony
Edwards, Norman
Felon, John
Fitzpatrick, Clay
Frenna, Rosanna
Galey, Mark
Galicia, Rudy
Garman, Richard
Godoy, Mario
Gray, Jason
Green, Amy
Guerrero, Carlos
Haberman, Mike
Herrera, Joe
Hetherington, J.
Hixson, Sherri
Holsten, Catherine
Jenkins, Kelly
Johnson, Matthew
Kassel, Arianne
Kassel, Renny
Kinney, Clarissa
Knox, James
Kovacs, Dyan
Kovacs, Jonathan
Kovacs, Kevin
LaVau, Milanda
Lundstrom, Gary
Marcotte, Renae
Maxwell, Ray
Maxwell, Teresa
Mello, Lana
Mitchell, Kenneth
Mitchell, Sunshine
Moreno, Juan
Najar, Edward
Nasukiewicz, June
Ortiz, Jody
Ortiz, Robert
Otani, Dawn
Overgaard, Dana
Pacheco, Sofia
Petrites, Tara
Pitzak, Wayne
Ramirez, Raul
Rice, Gregory
Rodgers, Malaney
Rosale, David
Sachez, Maria
Sharp, Benson
Siemens, Lisa
Sivao, Tina
Smith, Melissa
Smith, Peter
Snyder, Kathleen
Stallard, Sara
Stenger, Kristine
Stewart, Duane
Tambornini, Rochelle
Timms, Pamela
Tomko, Paula
Trinh, Hiep
Vhan, Sudheer
Vigil, Dana
Villegas, Rebeca
Vincent, Calvin
Wagenhoffer, Deena
Watkins, Roberto
Winklepleck, David
Wright, Brian

1982

Andrews, Gregory
Barrientos, Jose
Benson, Samantha
Bricker, Aaron
Brown, Tamar
Burciaga, Randy
Canas, Mickey
Carrasco, Isabel
Cass, Scott
Chau, Ton
Cheema, Kiren
Coleman, Justin
Contreras, Regina
Corter, Trisha
Cranfield, Dean
Cully, Kimberly
Dibler, Denise
Dobyns, Teri
Fairbanks, Christian
Flores, Miguel
Fong, Tony
Garcia, Jose
Garfield, Christopher
Green, Clare
Green, Melissa
Hamilton, Laurel
Hamilton, Susan
Harrison, Darrell
Harwood, Jacqueline
Hernandez, Pedro
Hoffman, James
Hwang, Ken
Jaboneta, Marcus
Jepsen, Alisia
Johnson, Darlene
Johnson, Timothy
Jones, Ted
Jordan, Jeff
Jull, Derrick
Kellner, Teresa
Klier, Jason
Lenda, Andrea
Little, Margaret
Lobo, David
Lujau, Joann
Mansfield, Mike
Moore, Deborah
Moore, Mike
Nasukiewicz, Steve
Navarro, Juan
Newcomb, Sharon
Norton, Ronald
O'Donnell, Anthony
O'Donnell, Celeste
Pulidio, Tony
Reppert, Carl
Roberts, Jennifer
Rosetti, Achille
Ryder, Karna
Saelee, Sarn
Salvador, Bennett
Shima, Nicole
Shives, Kimberly
Simon, Marcelle
Smothermon, David
Soriano, Ricky
Sweeney, James
Sweeney, John
Sweeney, Myung
Tafoya, Stephen
Thompson, Darla
Thompson, Karen
Tomlinson, David
Toney, Marcia
Tunnell, Kristine
Viera, Edward
Ward, Craig
White, Dale
White, Sharon
Whitworth, Lawrence
Wright, Rebecca
Younan, Alvin
Young, Patrick
Yusi, Erlinda

1983

Addison, Roland
Agnew, April
Amaro, Lisa
Arce, Danella
Austin, Darrell
Bannister, Melody
Barlow, Lynn
Bayardo, Jesus
Beeson, James
Bero, Katie
Birkholz, Cynthia
Brown, Jarrod
Buchan, Alan
Cantrell, Jennifer
Cardinale, Jeff
Cassidy, Catherine
Cassidy, Clare
Cassidy, John
Chrisos, Paula
Ciaramaglia, Diane
Clark, Yovonya
Claytor, Rachele
Competente, Christina
Crandall, Jennifer
Daprile, Annamarie
DeBono, Rita
Dominguez, Maria
Egan, Victor
Fernandes, Anissa
Fischer, Timothy
Franzke, Sophia
Garcia, Jacquelyn
Ghiotti, Derek
Gonzales, David
Guitierrez, Victor
Gunabe, Christine
Gurley, Rosemarie
Harrell, Karen
Hayden, Duane
Henderson, Kevin
Herin, Robert
Hull, Gene
Irizarry, Luis
Johnson, Karen
Johnson, Zachary
Jones, Maureen
Jordan, Rick
Lara, Maria
Lee, Ken
Malone, Ray
Malzkuhn, Matthew
Martinez, Martin
Mastrocola, Ambriel
Mastrocola, Richard
Mendoza, Rosa
Medina, Aurelia
Miller, Sonja
Molis, Robert
Mosley, Quilla
Navarro, Phil
Norton, David
Odom, Robert
Olguin, Thomas
Orellano, Lisette
Ortega, Rima
Otani, Angela
Pace, Veronica
Parent, Christopher
Pedersen, Karina
Perez, Jose
Powers, Stephen
Reyes, Stacey
Richardson, Tammy
Ritter, Darrell
Romero, Soretta
Saechao, Sou
Santos, Rebecca
Scheelje, Babette
Silveira, Sandra
Simanek, Dorothy
Sommerville, Heather
South, Damien
Spann, Christina
Stern, Louise
Stern, Susana
Sullivan, Ladaynia
Tovar, Abel
Troche, Louis
Troche, Ralph
Valdez, Dominic
Venti, Virginia
Vinciguerra, Yolanda
Vogler, Angela
Wilkins, Roger
Williamson, Lewis
Woo, Patrick
Wymer, Donna

1984

Adams, Keith
Ankrom, Walter
Ballesteros, Walter
Barraza, Mario
Burns, Brian
Bush, Andrea
Cahill, Scott
Christianson, James
Cortez, Marcila
Counter, Anna
Criner, Helen
Daffern, Jeremy
Davis, Jennifer
Dee, John
DeTrinidad, Ernesto
Diaz, Alejandro
Dillard, David
Dixon, Lisa
Edwards, Steven
Fitzpatrick, Dawn
Florentino, Martin
Flores, Alicia
Frias, Alejandro
Fung, Alejandro
Gilbert, Karen
Glad, Michael

Gray, Travis
Guzman, Dina
Guzman, Lucia
Hansen, Kimberly
Hanson, Leo
Harper, Gordon
Harvey, Daniel
Hemstreet, Barbara
Hemstreet, Julie
Hernandez, Juan
Hildreth, Treva
Humfrey, Richard
Hunter, Kimberly
Jackson III, Garland
Johnson, Deanna
Jones, Theophadus
Knight, John
La, Phat
Lansing, Zulius
Lennert, Michelle
Levine, Natalie
Lisenby, Anisa
Llanes, Raul
Lozada, Elizabeth
Mahurin, Byron
Malzkuhn, Melissa
Martinez, Susan
McDowell, Marvin
Medina, Patricia
Mejia, Jose
Musick, Ann
Myers, Robert
Orr, Julie
Ortega, Raelein
Pelaez, Marcos
Pedersen, Svenna
Pham, Hieu
Preston, Christopher
Pua, Jerry
Qualls, Cherie
Quiroga, Jeremy
Ralphs, Richard
Ruiz, Robert
Rushing, Sandra
Salazar, Roy
Sandoval, Manuel
Shetley, Joseph
Simmons, Jr., Michael
Slick, Chond
Sloan, Charles
Smith, Azeria
Sodhi, Dilveer
Som, Peoul
Sorkin, Elizabeth
Srour, Anthony
Suitor, Casper
Sullivan, Maureen
Tanke, Douglas
Tillson, Heather
Toca, Justin
Ton, Sa
Tooch, Philip
Trevino, Catherine
Turner, Dennis
Van Dyken, Lloyd
Varner, Ronald
Vasquez, Miguel
Wagner, Kathleen
Walters, Todd
Wicks, Katherine
Willhite, John
Willingham, Theodore
Willey, Laura

1985

Agriss, Yael D.
Amador, Ronald
Andrade, Imelda
Baello, Dino
Brown, Phillip
Buchan, Mele
Buskirk, James
Cabatingan, John
Castillo, Sophia
Clarkson, Cathy
Constantino, Graciela
Cornish, Rima
Couts, Tasha
Crenshaw, Mildred
Crisler, Michelle
Curry, Nicole
Dorton, Raven
Drier, Chris
Drum, Jamie
Dupure, Tony
Eldridge, Scott
Fain, Danielle
Ferguson, Melissa
Flores, Lilia
Fong, Ryan
Foust, Rodney
Govi, James
Hamlow, Eric
Hammond, Curtis
Hart, Dale
Hatch, Christopher
Helton, Debbie
Herbert, Gina
henderson, Rona
Hernandez, Albert
Housley, Mary
Huerta, Mario
Hur, Laban
Johnston, Bo
Josephson, Corina
Kovacs, Dyan
Kovacs, Jon
Kovacs, Ty
Lara, Graciela
Lattier, Shawn
Law, LaShonda
Lewis, Jesse
Longoria, John
Martin, Robert
McDonald, Jason
McDonnell, Paul
Miller, Landon
Miller, Tara
Moss, Mike
Noia, Jeana
Nordstrom, Eric
Paredes, Anthony
Parker, Mary
Pone, Demetrius
Ratell, Benjamin
Reid, Valerie
Roth, James
Roth, Robert
Rubalcava, Paul
Ryder, Kerry
Sais, Lupe
Saletrero, Tito
Samson, Lee
Sanchez, Carlos
Scarborough IV, D.
Schubin, Stuart
Seeley, Angela
Spotts, Lisa
Stern, Brendan
Swafford, Julie
Swicker, Rayford
Thorton, Sherri
Trammel, Dan
Trzesniewski, Peter
Virgil, Latonya
Wagner, Robert
Wallace, Kevin
Watson, Tory
Webber, Gene
Werley, Robert
West, John
Williams, Dwight
Williams, Leonard
Wiltz, Tonya
Wykle, Heather

1986

Adi, Gilbert
Anderson, Rachel
Apple II, Richard
Arkeder, John
Arrona, Susanne
Asghari, Shekib
Bayarsky, Kyle
Bayarsky, Tyler
Bergin, James
Boyer, Althea
Brewster, Thomas
Bryson, William T.
Chavez, James
Clark, Darci
Collier, Michael-John
Cornish, Emil
Cragen, Rachel
Devaurs, Denice
Dominquez, Raul
Fanning, Mark
Ford, Chanel
Ford, Tommy
Froman, Mathew
Garcia, Anthony
Graef, Benjamin
Harris, Lisa
Hauschildt, Sean
Herbold, Blake
Herbold, Charles
Hethcox, Landon
Holland, Richard
Idiado, Alita
Jacobson, Heather
Jarashow, Adam
Jarashow, Benjamin
Johnson, Christopher
Johnson, Valerie
Jones, Matthew
Kleiwer, Nathan
Lessard, Chris C.
Lessard, Trisha
Liu, Stanley
Lorenzana, Maria
Luftig, Rebecca
Ly, Sela
Malzkuhn, Megan
Marsh, Allison
Melvin, Dennis
Miranda, Francis
Montenegro, Tony
Nelson, David
Nichols, Carrie
Oliver, Robert
Olson, Brandy
Owens, Joel
Pacheco, Kevin
Parker, Erica
Parker, Sarah
Patel, Rasheed
Richardson, Ursula
Rogers, Melani
Simoes, Tony
Singleton, Wesley
Singleton, Zachary
Solunac, Nevenka
Spangler, Lance
Stalker, Daniel
Swanson, Esther
Thevenin, Tiffany
Tinetti, Denise
Twitchell, Nathan
Vaca, Tony
Valencia, Jeanette
Wandersee, Kristine
Wemken, Darci
Williams, Jan
Woodall, Annick

1987

Ackworth, Holly
Alcantar, Isaura
Alvarado, Salvador
Arellano, Mario
Ashlock, Kristine
Beall, Heather
Brock, Aaron
Brooks, Ferris
Burt, Larissa
Camara, Michelle
Campos, LaVonne
Campos-Espinosa, X.
Carpenter, Kelly
Castaneda, Jude
Castillo, Jennifer
Chaney, Dorsey
Cornish, Vina
Davis, Joaquina
Dyda, Michael
Eberwein, Adelle
Eberwein, David
Garner, Chad
Gorgen, Scott
Grim, Shameka
Gurry, Andrew
Hall, Tanya
Him, Phy
Hornick, Solomon
Huang, Jian
Jackson, Louis
Johnson, Karina
Jones, Ian
Kaldani, Charlotte
Kaldani, Jason
Kozicki, Shelley
Lambert, Theresa
LeMaster, Ronnie
Lewis, Tiffany
Limon, Margaret
Linker, Kimberly
Lopez, Bertha
Lucas, Lucrecia
Lutke, Joseph
Ly, Xuyen
Machado, Juan
Machado, Martin
Mahoney, Jolene
Manalastas, Liza
Martin, Christine
Matovich, Megan
McClelland, Paloma
Medina, Cesar
Migone, Joseph
Millburn, Teri
Ojeda, Yadira
Onnalea, Lucrecia
Ove, Ian
Peknik, Daniel
Phillips, Ronnie
Reagan II, Ronald
Sandoval, Esmeralda
Schugg, Oskar
Sciovoletti, John
Silva, Marcos
Smith, Barbara
Smith, Micah
Smith, Roxeann
Stewart, David
Vairora, Renee
Vass, Jr., Roger
Warthan, Rachel
Weiner, Kristen
Wickstrom, Viki
Williams, Ricco

1988

Asuncion, Mario
Barraza, Josue
Bartlett, Desiree
Bate, Aaron
Benson, Keith
Brinlee, Lisa
Brock, Joshua
Brock, Nehemiah
Buchholz, Shawna
Cahill, Kenyon
Chandr, Avinesh
Conner, Jesse
Cortes, Joyce
Costa, Ana
Crisler, Donny
Damian, Maria
Dunwoody, Timothy
Flaucher, Robert
Gador, Joseph
Gayle, Angelina
Glover, Timothy
Gough, Michelle
Gough, Thomas
Gough, Timothy
Hernandez, Andrew
Hoffman, Erica
Holden, Samuel
Hollingshead, Danny
Hughes, Eric
Huster, Kimberly
Jantz, Victoria
Jones, Merry
Jones, Pamela
Keifer, Douglas
Lentz, Ryan
Lerma, Roy
Lo, Long
Lopez, Franceasca
Maes, Michael
Mallari, Jayson
Maung, Donald
McKay, Matthew
Medina, Angelica
Miller, Jessica
Moreland, Anthony
Morillo, Alexander
Mutti, Nick
O'Mullen, Johnathan
Ortiz, Natalie
Pasini, Gina
Petersen, Evelyn
Powell, Artemis
Rasmus, Blair
Roberts, Marcus
Robinson, Chris
Ruys, Tanya
Saunders, Priscilla
Shaw, Aaron
Shively, Godi
Silva, Ana
Silverie, Coreen
Smith, Corbett
Soto, Monica
Stickler, Jonathan
Strickler, Sheila
Tate, Sonny
Teeters, Amy
Thomas, Barry
Thompson, Jonathan
Torres, Joseph
Trammel, Christina
Traylor, Jolie
Vang, Doua
Varney, Sonja
Varney, Timothy
Walker, Natalie
West, Isaac
Wilkins, Erica
Williams, Jeana
Yancey, Robert
Yang, See
Yang, Doua
Young, Stacie

1989

Alarcon, Luis

Alcon, Tisha
Andres, Monel
Barr, Tanya
Brinlee, Tracie
Buckhold, Justin
Bye, Anthony
Cassinelli, Heather
Castillo, Jessica
Chaiyasan, Nuane
Chappell, Brian
Chastain, Casey
Chinn, Hubert
Contreras, Jenny
Craig, Makela
Curtis, Jonathan
Davis II, Ronnie
Dawson, Yeru
Eastman, Tiffany
Eck, Kimberly
Ewert, Thomas
Fraire, Julian
Freeman, Bill
Gaglione, Danielle
Gonzalez, Alvaro
Guido, Salvatore
Hall, Donte
Hammons, Heather
Harnish, Daniel
Harris, Felisha
Herbold, Tenaya
Hicks, Luz
Hill, Aaron
Hinman, Jessica
Jackerson, Jana
Jackson, Matthew
Jarashow, Lisa
Jashini, Bhagwan
Jenkins, Amy
Jindherd, Khalil
Joseph, Lisa
Kalo, Dina
Kassees, Charley
Khan, Urfan
Krohn, Dale
Krohn, Dean
Kwiatkowski, David
Lake, Jowea
Lawrence, Stephanie
Lee, Justin
Lewis, Heather
Lopez, Ariana
Lopez, Karla
Maldonado, Zukeika
Martinez, Adrian
Martinez, Florence
Maynard-Bowers, R.
Mayorquin, Rogelio
McClellan, Shannon
McGee, Linda
McRaney, Angus
Mendoza, Jose
Mills, Myung
Moore, Tosha
Naveed, Farrukh
Nixon, Edward
O'Hara, Timothy
Oliver, Rachel
Olney, Kyle
Padilla, Anthony
Pasco, Mark
Pedersen, Jory
Pinkel, Erik
Pinola, Reyna
Pruyn, Brice
Ramirez, Gabriela
Regan, Keri
Renner, Suzanne
Rodriquez, Jose
Ruiz, Fermin
Rushing, Chevy
Salvador, Jennifer
San Miguel, Rudy
Saunders, Cinbrella
Schoen, Michael
Schutz, Mathilda
Scott, Ryan
Serrano, Aldo
Shaw, Robert
Sheppard, Gregory
Stockert, Amber
Taggart, Joann
Thompson, Orion
Torres, Crispin
Trieu, Serena
Trujillo, Angelica
Uribe, Jonathan
Walker, Jr., William
Wallen, Brian
Williamson, Richard
Zamora, Jr., Jesus

1990

Alvarez, Sostenes
Arp, Vanessa
Awalt, Gregory
Baldridge, Jay
Baldridge, Jeb
Barfield, Tamara
Bautista, Maria
Bibb, Jeffrey
Bowers, Jennifer
Burrows, Danielle
Bustamante, Rita
Callaway, Justin
Camargo, Victoria
Carrasquillo, Lee
Carter, DeVon
Catron, Brianne
Cervantes, Iriana
Christopher, Jamie
Christy, Anita
Clark, Orval
Contreras, Maria
Corkey, Cliona
Dahlman, Trisha
Davis, DeAndre
DeConteras, Emiliano
Dewees, Jamie
Donaldson, Ronald
Dubnick, Bridgett
Duran, Michelle
Edwards, Jr., Charles
Fife, Elayne
Foster, Michael
Gallegos, Jr., Ernesto
Garcia, Moises
Gomez, Ricardo
Gonzalez, Felix
Graniello, Jeffrey
Gray, Jesse
Grossinger, Mark
Grossinger, Shanna
Hammons, Benjamin
Hanaumi, Leila
Harbin, Michelle
Hicks, Joshua
Higginbotham, T.
Hornsby, Julisa
Jackerson, Jeni
Keyes, Jesse
Kwoh, Esther
Lamberton, Jonathan
Levy, Galen
Liedberg, Lawrence
Liu, Steven
Lor, Panhia
Loreman, Charles
Malzkuhn, Mallory
Mao, Lek
Marsh, Gabriel
Martinez, Miguel
Martinez, Robert
Martinez, Yessenia
Martinez, Yessica
Maxwell, Dawn
McAdams, Michael
Metzger, David
Mills, Jacob
Montero, Heather
Myers, Ferris
O'Hara, Molly
Orozco, Sergio
Pardee, Luke
Parker, June
Payne, Michael
Poplin, Jr., Daniel
Rada, Bernie
Reynosa, Gilbert
Rivera, Rosemarie
Rodrigues, Bradley
Ross, Erin
Ruiz, Amy
Rushing, Cyndey
Schmaling, Kimber
Serrato, Joseph
Slaten, Dustin
Sorenson, Jeremy
Steward, Cyquita
Straub, Alicia
Talavera, Jose
Taylor, Andrew
Tritsch, Zachary
Tuttle, Adam
Vang, Pao
Vera, Cornelio
Vazquez, Margarita
Virnig, Sean
White, Kellie
Willey, Sherrie
Xiong, Yang
Yang, Nou
Yang, Pao
Zabbo, Dana

1991

Adams, Jeremy
Aguirre, Christina
Allen-Cowell, R.
Alvarado, Moses
Alvarez, Andrea
Behnke, Lyra
Beshears, Xylophila
Betts, Olaf
Brister, Carl
Burnaugh, Gina
Burns, Edward
Burrell, Zsa
Busenbark, Jackson
Cassinelli, Angela
Chavez, Carlos
Chen, Terry
Chhi, Rita
Claiborne, Rachelle
Coldwell, Rachell
Cross, Tanya
Dominge, Elizabeth
Downey, Denise
Dunmon, Jr., Larry
Duran, Monica
Dyer, Kamilah
East, Korie
Fishburne, David
Garmen, Cedric
Godfrey, Antionette
Gonzales, Eduardo
Gonzalez, Fernando
Halimsaputra, P.
Harding, Alise
Hardy, Jason
Holcomb, Leala
Holcomb, Tara
Huckaby, Eric
Jackerson, Justin
Janssen, Sarah
Johnson, Jeremy
Kellywood, Lavar
Kenney, Jr., N.
Kimball, Richard
Kingsford, Jared
Knott, Dustin
Lamberton, Jason
Langley, Beth
Ledbetter, Kalani
Lerma, Gabriel
Lor, Xeng
Lowe, Ezekiel
Lowe, Hezekiah
Martinez, Aaron
Mercado, Jose
Mora, Amy
Moreno, Jose
Morrison, Bonnie
Morrison, Brian
Muhammad, K.
Musgrave, Tammy
Nunez, Antonio
O'Brien, Jennifer
Owens, Mark
Panighetti, Angela
Patton, Jamieson
Paul, Jory
Perkins, Jim
Pinal, Rosa
Plants, Larry
Porter, Jake
Porter, Kirk
Ramirez, Michelle
Rasmus, Shea
Reynoso, Girlie
Rhoades, Ryan
Robinson, Jacques
Rodriguez, Steve
Rucker, Latasha
Saechao, Lio
Sanchez, Ronald
Sarmiento, Tristan
Schmidt, Janel
Silberberg, Steve
Smith, Stacie
Smith, Travis
Spalding, Zachary
Szpakowski, Otto
Ton, Hung
Ty, Rhina
Virnig, Chester
Williams, Karlee
Wong, Victor
Wright, Jeffrey

1992

Abueg, Roy
Ackerman, Christina
Amable, Khrystyna
Amable, Matthew
Arana, Monica
Arenas, Pablo
Baldwin, Clara
Barnes, Eric
Beltrami, Christopher
Bennett, Kilee
Blaettler, Courtney
Bogle, Kimberly
Bowden II, Herbert
Brown III, Harold
Brown, Nicki
Cannon, Emilie
Cardenas, G.
Castellanos, Edwin
Cohen, Erin
Corey-Dunn, Renca
Cox, Seth
Cross, Jarlene
Daviton-Sciandra, J.
Dee, Chamroen
Driggs, Blake
Fahmie, Liane
Fishbein, Lisa
Frederickson, Jeffrey
Furgan, Ramadon
Giansianti, Terry
Glenn, Baanka
Guido, Anthony
Ha, Phung
Hamilton II, Eric
Hammons, Jeff
Hannula, Sarah
Hansen, Jr., Reg
Harris, Anthony
Jaro, Michael
Jiminez, Beatrice
Kass, Tracy
Khan, Haroon
Khoomsrivong, B.
Kramer, Jonathon
Lanning, Tara
Lee, Raymond
Lopez, Timothy
Maas, Jesse
Mayorquin, Rogelio
McGuire, James
Mendoza, Beatriz
Miller, Timothy
Morgan, Jason
Mounts, Frank
Nava, Ray
Nguyen, Duc
Nielson, Dustin
Nitko, Blake
Nitko, Chad
O'Hara, Ellen
Oliver, Daron
Paratore, Andrew
Pedersen, Cody
Platas, Micaela
Pritchard, Ashley
Quinones, Daniel
Rae, Michelle
Ramirez, Salvador
Reguera, Marcus
Rivas, Antonio
Rivera, Juan
Rodriguez, Rigoberto
Sanchez, Saira
Sarmiento, Bertrand
Shabon, Susan
Smith, David
Syon, Ollie
Taylor, David
Thompson, Corey
Tobola, Elena
Torres, Phillip
Urbina, Chrisian
Vollmar, Scott
Vongsikeo, Vita
Warner, Heather
White, Montrell
Whitten, Chase
Williams, Duronte
Williams, Gretchen
Williams, Jr., Carlton

1993

Apineru, Teuaililo
Arizaga, Eliseo
Bautista, Tara
Bernstein, Amelia
Catron, Ryan
Chan, Arthur
Chan, Norman
Chang, Jennifer
Chase, Ashley
Clements, Jacob
Costa, Aaron
Crane, Devlin
Crump, Troy
Davey, Jessica
Davidson, Brittany
Dean, Brandon

Eyrond, Rebecca
Fortney, David
Garrett, Estela
Gonzalez, Francisco
Guitierrez, Jose
Harrison, Danetta
Henderson, Leeann
Hogaboom, Brian
Holden, Julius
Hom, Jason
Hom, Valerie
Ispas, Michael
Itson, Sarah
Kabasinskas, Irene
Laccay, Paul
Lancaster, Melessa
Lee, Sue
Mancillas, Rosa
Marcucci, Gian
Marrs, Gary
Martin, Stephen
Miller, Lauren
Montalette, Mark
Moreno, Luis
Moua, Xo
Mahinu, Ross
Navarro, Janette
Navarro, Jose
Newton, Heather
Nieva, Monica
Norris, Abram
Perez, Blanca
Pureco, Lina
Ramirez, Taranthony
Rivers, Angela
Rodriguez, Nubia
Romera, Alcira
Ryan, Sean
Saelee, Meuy
Saengthip, Bounsong
Shelton, Damon
Smith, Josiah
Smith, Shawn
Stanfield, Bryan
Superticioso, L.
Tikhonoff, Jonathan
Torres, Jose
Turman, Lance
Williams, Lynnetta
Zarate, Sylvia

1994

Ahmad, Fareez
Ahmadzai, Wagma
Ahmadzai, Waheeda
Aldana, Jose R.
Aleman, Monica
Apple, Richard
Bacarro, Michael
Barker, Ryan
Berry, Twila
Bluhm, Jason
Bye, Aaron
Carpenter, Kevin
Carrasco, Roy
Cheek, Nicholas
Clark, Adam
Cobarrubia, Jr., Juan
Cohen, Marissa
Cummins, Jackson
Davis, Frank
Davis, Ramar
Diaz, Carlos
Diaz, Rocio
Doe, Ann-Marie
Duran, Oletha
Edmond, Khal-vyn
Edwards, Jeremy
Eyrond, Mark
Eyrond, Troy
Featherstone, D.
Flores, Jr., John
Fonesca, Kaylie
Frankel, Tamar
Frazel, Shane
Friel, Samuel
Gage, Zamica
Gallegos, Angela
Gallman, Mark
Garberoglio, C.
Garcia, Jose
Garcia, Mauricio
Garner, Brenda
Geiger, Erika
Goodson, Tony
Grohmann, Grant
Gutierrez, Leticia
Harris, Donny
Hellum, Marissa
Herdon, Tavarie
Hernandez, Taylor
Hildreth, Daniel
Hinks, Amanda
Holcomb, Cary
Hopper, Jeff
Howard, Edward
Johnson-Coleman, T.
Jonas, Jane
Khong, Sim
Lambert, Jesse
Lanning, Nicole
Lay, Talea
Lee, May
Leiker, Bryce
Lopez, Connie
Lynn, Carol
Macias, Karina
Madison, Matthew
Mandel, Bekah
Mazion, Donna
McCurdy, Matthew
McPherson, Kenneth
Mead, Travis
Medina, Norma
Miller, Alexandrina
Morales III, Pablo
Moreland, Carol
Mosquera, Lawrence
Munguio, Emilio
Neil, Robert
Nguyen, Quang
Paterson, Kristen
Perez, Maria
Peterson, Jeremy
Phillips, Andrew
Pompa, Erica
Prader, Zuelika
Quiles, Ramona
Reasol, Ronzian
Retana, Carmen
Risenhoover, Jennifer
Rocha, Daniel
Roche, Ricardo
Ruane, Kelli
Saechao, Sou
Saelee, Lo
Saeliaw, Kaomang
Sanchez, Nicole
Settle, Tawnya
Smith, Dennis
Smith, Everett
Smith, Reka
Strickland, Charity
Taylor, Tonie
Tellez, Patricia
Traina, Edward
Verduzco, Santiago
Vasquez, Jr., Pablo
Walsh, Cheryllynn
Watson, Jerry
Weber, Lee
Welsh, Raymond
Williams, Lanetra
Wise, Jesse
Xayavong, Phaivanh
Yates, Noreen
Zepeda, Jose
Zesati, Sophia

1995

Abordo, Megan
Aguilar, Aracelia
Aguilar, David
Amador, Julio
Apple II, Richard
Barker, Todd
Barlow, Tiffany
Brown, Tenisha
Carabajal, Jason
Cardenas, Jose
Carrin, Joshua
Casillas, Luis
Castillo, Elsie
Chang, Yang
Cherry, Myron
Cheung, Michelle
Clark, Nicole
Copeland, Lacharrie
Cordero, Jullisa
Corona, Maria
Corral, Shurie
Davis, Monica
Dillard, Cameron
Earnest, Robert
Eddy, Christina
Farr, Gloria
Farr, Mark
Farr, Valerie
Floyd, Brittany
Fry, Kristy
Garcia, Marcela
Garcia, Martha
Glenn, Everett
Gonzalez, Paulina
Gottumukala, Varma
Higgins, Thomas
Holderman, Paige
Huck, David
Jones, Jon
Joya, Elia
Ledezma, Luis
Lindahl, Lidia
Lira, Marcos
Marroquin, Carlos
Martinez, Julio
Masalosalo, Etisone
McLarin, Michael
Merino, Dennis
Momakov, Christo
Navarro, Araceli
Nelson Higgins, Thomas
Nusbaum, Aaron
Olafsson, Gunnar
Ortiz, Gabriel
Palamides, Alex
Parris, Justin
Porter, Casey
Quigley, Sheila
Ramos, Edlynne
Richter, Kristin
Roe, Peter
Rose, Richard
Ruiz, Karlee
Saesee, Chan
Salazar, Alejandra
Sampson, Mary
Sanchez, Guadalupe
Sanchez, Jesus
Saunders, Jess
Smith, Clint
Sortwell, Amanda
Spillane, Damien
Stevens, Jesse
Stevenson, Chrishana
Thao, Bao
Vazquez, Rosa
Velasco, Ambrocio
Vo, Dona
Walker, Christian
Weber, Austin
Wolfert, Raechelle
Wynn, Tanya
Xiong, A.

1996

Abrica, Edgar
Acevedo, Salvador
Agustin, Maria
Aiken-Forderer, V.
Alvarado, Valentin
Amaral, Carmen
Anaya, Jorge
Ashford, Irme
Baldwin, Lacie
Bloom, Sinclair
Boissiere, Danny
Castaneda, Daniel
Castellanos, Destiny
Cohen, Erin
Datuin, Charlene M.
Davis, Brett
Davis, Michael
DeSouza, Christopher
Diaz, Allan
Dubler, Rupert
Epitacio, Jan
Esquibel, Desaree
Estrada, Brenda
Ferreira, Krishna
Finley, Lizzie
Foletta, Monica
Forde, Wendy
Fritz, Sarah
Garman, Cedric
Gonzalez-Vera, L.
Gosselin, Lucas
Griffith, Ashley
Griffith, Shayla
Hardin, Jessica
Havandjian, Jillian
Herrmann, Colin
Hottle, Valerie
Howell, Marvin
Jessup, David
Ketchum, Megan
Kim, Dae Joon
Kim, Dae Kin
Kleeber, Heather
Kulwitzky, Caleb
La, Steven
Lenihan, Shane
Lippe, Jennifer
Lopez, Arturo
Marsicano, Denise
Martinez, Ruben
Medugno, Miranda
Mercadal, Danielle
Nix, Joshua
Patron, Beatriz
Patron, Emmanuel
Raffanti, Michael
Ramos, Christina
Reis, Dustin
Reyes, Carmen
Riddle, Edward
Rios Reyes, Ana P.
Rodman, Kurtis
Rodriques, Bradley
Ruano, Brandon
Schabram, Mirja
Simms, Nicole
Slyter, Misty
Smith, Jill
Smitley, William
Smyrniotis, Erica
Stevens, Robert
Swails, Cody
Tansier, Rachel
Vargas, Daysy
Walker, Nigel
Walker, Sacha
Weber, Dalena
Whiting, Damien
Winesburg, Shanna
Yuan, Yao-Li

1997

Aguilar, Alejandra
Aguilar, Andrea
Ahmadzai, Nageena
Arthurs, Weston
Baldwin, Walter
Bautista, Joana
Beamon, Cherie
Belorusets, Y.
Benavente, Shawn
Bolger, Nicholas
Booth, Shaz
Bravo, Alfonso
Brown, Nicholas
Bryant, Nikolas
Call, Brandon
Cantril, Judith
Carmona, Claudia
Carolyn, Dominque
Carranza, Fawn
Cassidy, Kerjsen
Cassidy, Klaudia
Castaneda, Lorenzo
Chang, Jennifer
Cordova, Jose
Costa, Richard
Cram, Jacob
Crawford, Jr., Mark
Cruz, Hilario
Davis, Michael
DeHoyos, Adrian
Dike, Brittany
Farr, Brittany
Feliciano, Andrea
Figueroa, Jovita
Flores, Mark
Ford, Jonathan
Ganancial, Glenmore
Garry, Briana
Gavarrette, Frank
Go, Jake
Greenman, Andrew
Guzman, Mike
Hair-Cooper, DeVon
Helms, Cameron
Hernandez, Isaac
Hursin, Andrew
Hursin, Britnee
Jesso, Jon-Erik
Jimenez, David
Jones, Quientosha
Jones, Shaunda
Jourdan, Kenneth
Kanta, Christine
Klim, Christian
Kray, Jordan
Lai, Pui-Lam
Lipnitsky, Eugene
Lopez, Carlos
Martinez, Fernanda
Martinez, Martha
Miller, Jacques
Miller, Lisa
Minard, Tonishia
Misenas, Jansen
Mostepan, Eugene
Muribus, Michael
Navarro, Jose Luis
Nguyen, Hai
Parker, Alfie
Perez, Martin
Phillips, Samuel

Plancarte, Bertha
Ramirez, Fernando
Randle, Isaiah
Razo, Krystle
Richardson, Rachelle
Saia, Michael
Sanchez, Reyna
Smith, Adam
Smith, Justin
Smith, Rachel
Soto, Joey
Sowders, Jeffrey
Soyland, Shane
Tang, Richard
Tanner, Erica
Tovani, Amber
Vang, Ia
Vang, Mai
Vang, Yer

1998

Aguiniga, Jr., Martin
Ary, Melinda
Baldridge, Merle
Baldwin, Wyatt
Baldwin-Gomez, J.
Ben-Moshe, Ilan
Birdsong, Sarah
Botello, Daysy
Braun, Dan
Brinkley, Alexandria
Cali, Christin
Campos, Albert
Cantrell, Jayme
Castaneda, Priscilla
Clark, Matthew
Chavez, Yovane
Corpuz, Jericho
Davis, Paul
Dike-Pedersen, J.
Duarte, Karylin
Duenas, Cristal
Elmasri, Ali
Ensele, Taryn
Espinoza, Dulce
Figueroa, Irene
Finley, Angel
Gomez, Daniel
Guerrero, Luis
Guzman, Ian
Guzman, Moses
Guzman, Omar
Harris, Cora
Harris, Darnell
Herd, Misty
Hyland, Samantha
Huynh, Ann Thao
Jamison, Charlene
Johnson, Kena
Johnston, Cody
Keels, Derek
Kong, Kou
Long, Jr., Craig
Lopez, Marebel
Martin III, Alfonza
Medina-Arroela, N.
Mejorado, Marissa
Mercado, Tierra
Mertens, Felicia
Miller, Alexandria
Morales, Arthur
Morton, Quintin
Oldham, Erin
Pasini, Gina
Pepper, Lisa
Peralta, Stephen
Pretto, Hubert
Ramirez, Dontae
Reilly, Kathy
Robinson, John
Rodriquez, Veronica
Rubio, Jesus
Ruelas, Esperanza
Ruelas, Jr., Juan
Sabate, Karl Masada
Sabate, Karl Nikolas
Sanchez, Darlene
Santana, Araceli
Shamblin, James
Simas, Trent
Sithida, Phieng
Tafeamalii, Francisco
Tauaefa, Manuuli
Todd, Eugenia
Vasquez, Jr., Pablo
Visser, Zoe
Wafer, Craig
Waterhouse, Laura
Watkins, Jr., Michael
Yuan, Yao-Li
Zuniga, Michael

1999-2000

Arroyo, Erik
Aguirre, Cindy
Ayala, Sandra
Baldoza, Michelle
Bartolome, Gladys
Beamon, Cherie
Bernard, Quintin
Call, Christina
Cano, Erik
Clay, Alexandria
Cobarrubia, Juan
Colvin, Porchia
Comegna, Brittany
Comegna, Nicholas
Cortes, Jed
Cram, Micah
Crespin, Richard
Daley, Heather
Davidson, Brittany
DiPoala, Rebecca
DeLa Cruz, Krystle
Edwards, Jon
Ellithorp, Terrance
Fairbairn, Daniel
Ferrer, Daniel
Floriani, Nicholas
Freeman, Jered
Ganancial, Brian
Gomez, Jr., Vincent
Greenwall, Rochelle
Greer, Kiera
Girn, Amandeep
Guerrero, Luis
Gustaston, Ashlee
Gutierrez, Brendaliz
Hamilton, Leroy
Hamlin, Jonathan
Hayes, Mariko
Hernandez, Elizabeth
Hernandez, Jr., A.
Hilbert, Rachel
Hill, Christina
Hunter, Tonique
Jackson, LiAn
Jacuindes, Lupe
Jenkins, Heather
Jindra, Eric
Jones, William
Kim, Jean
Kim, Nha
Kong, Kou
Korolev, Dmitri
Lee, Liane
Lopez, Jose
Luke, Jared
Mahan, Anastasiya
Maldonaldo, Jasmine
Marshall, Kevin
Martinez, Ruby
Marvel, Jerome
Mata, Miguel
McCullough, Jinkie
McCullough, Raven
McEntire, Jr., Daniel
McMahon, Shari
Meraz, Adolfo
Miller, Sukie
Mogaew, Panuphong
Mulligan, Tommy
Nicolay, Brianna
Norton, Gino
O'Sullivan, Ian
Ortega, Maria
Pearson, Samuel
Pedersen, Jacy
Peralta, Stephen
Pershe, Steve
Prader, Zepsi
Pridgen, Marcus
Poor, Justin
Quinones, Daniel
Ramirez, Cynthia
Ramirez, Dontae
Robinson, Rashid
Rodriguez, Jose
Rodriguez, Veronica
Romero, Victoria
Rothrock, Jerome
Ryan, Jacob
Sandoval, Nivia
Serrano, Oracio
Sims, Darnell
Smith, Roxiann
Spriggs-Cudjo, Gregory
Stockwell, Rachel
Thompson, Carrie
Thompson, Dakota
Thompson, Janelle
Thurman, Romel
Tisnado, Fernando
Tjiang, Meeya
Todd, Eugenia
Tramble, Christopher
Tyner, Aurora
Valle, Manuel
Vallejo, Elsa
Vasquez, Jr., Pablo
Walters, Brian
Webb, Brandon
Wilmoth, Nicole
Xiong, Kou
Zepeda, Jose

CSD graduates on the back cover (left to right).

Mary Kerby, *1877*
William Oldham, *1882*
Larry Shoemaker, *1941*
Eleanor Elmassian, *1945*
Joe Velez, *1950*
Peter Murello, *1965*
Carla Pereira, *1970*
Cheryl Filson, *1980*
Klesha Chapman, *1982*
U Sung Chung, *1983*
Richard Hanson, *1990*

Douglas Tilden
1860-1935

THE BEAR HUNT statue is well known as one of Douglas Tilden's greatest works of sculpture. The photo of the top part of the statue is shown in the front inside cover. Tilden, 1879 CSD graduate, became interested in sculpture while he was a teacher at CSD in 1883. Later he secured training in Paris under the guidance of a deaf sculptor. As years passed, he became a famous sculptor and left a number of his masterpieces in the San Fracisco Bay Area.

Faculty 1860-2000

1860
Crandall, H. B.

1862
Burgess, H.
La Rue, John
Roe, Azel S., Jr.

1864
Cornell, Meribah
Harwood, Eliza

1865
Francis, J. M.
Nunn, Charles
Wilkinson, Warring

1866-67
Frank, Henry
Pratt, Amasa

1867-69
Jeffrey, Joseph
Porte, Peter

1869-71
Paterson, Christian
Zabel, John

1871-73
Fowler, Foland P.
Goodall, George P.

1873-75
Brauner, William
Phillips, William M.

1875-77
d'Estrella, T.
Dochez, L. A.
Smith, Charles T.

1877-79
Pike, E. P.
Stewart, Nettie
Wright, Phebe J.

1879
Caldwell, William A.

1880
Tilden, Douglas A.

1880-82
Carter, Anna B.
Crandall, Kate
Dutch, Mary A.
Garratt, Annie B.
Handy, Carrie E.
Warren, Annie

1882-84
Watson, S. E.
Wilkinson, Mrs. A.B.

1884-86
Carroll, E. R.
Whipple, N. F.

1886-88
Grady, Theodore
Jensen, C.
Moffat, Miss Lizzie
Nourse, Daisy
O'Donnell, Frank
Perry, Charles S.

1892-94
Owen, F. E.

1894-96
Barker, E. H.
Bennet, Cordelia L.
Goode, Cornelia S.
Goode, Harriet C.
Owen, Horace

1896-98
Gompertz, Anita
Orr, Marie P.

1898-1900
Coplin, Ethel A.
McCarthy, A. P.

1900-02
Howson, James W.

1906-08
Harman, Augusta

1908-10
Gabrielli, J.
Keith, Dougles A.
Surber, Margaret

1910-12
Christy, Nettie L.

1912
Milligan, Laurance E.

1912-14
Austin, Alma H.
Baars, Fred W.
Biondi, Alexander
Brown, Etta
Comp, Ruth C.
Cooper, Clara B.
Driggs, Burton Wells
Ervin, Julia (Mrs. Coburn)
Kuhne, Mr.
Metcalf, Alice
Morgan, Florence
Nyquist, Mr.
Runde, Winfield S.
Schroder, George

1914-16
Brown, Marguerite
Dahl, Mabel
Houghton, Dorothy (Mrs. Richardson)
Walker, Hazel

1916-18
Barnes, Mrs. Virginia
Carpenter, Miss Irene
Grandadam, John C.
Land, Carol G.
Minister, Miss Alice
Roth, Mrs. Nell
Sharkey, Miss Stella
Watson, Afton

1918-20
Blaker, Miss Sallie
Briggs, Miss Louise
Dickhaut, Marion
Geddes, James T.
Hallett, Mrs. Mary
(Mrs. Cooper)
Hunt, Mrs. Blanche
Ingle, Mrs. Helen F.
Jenks, W. R. L.
Kinnaird, Miss Angie
Long, Miss Dorothy
McGlynn, Miss Edith
(Mrs. Struck)
(Mrs. Kesert)
Mepham, Robert
Rice, R. R.
Vinson, Marietta

1920-22
McKinley, Frances
Martin, Esther K.
Runde, Mrs. Frances

1922-24
Henderson, Myrtle
Holle, Stanely E.
McCafferty, Margaret
Oliver, Miss Mary
Patterson, Alpha W.
Tiss, Miss Lauretta

1924-26
Beattie, Mariette
Berry, George W.
Collatt, Myrtle
Holzinger, Bessie S.
Jordan, Paul
Lewis, Mrs. Beatrice
Meyrick, Mrs. Ruth
Mooseau, Minnie
Rhodes, Katherine

1926-28
Ainsworth, Dora
Birck, Vernon S.
Cowan, Mrs. Celia
Franck, Henry
Lynndelle, V. S.
Shaw, Miss Dathene
Wilcox, Miss Ida

1928
Allingham, Dora
Stevenson, Elwood A.

1929
Hatfield, Jesse
Helvey, Mrs. Belle
Ingle, Truman L.
Lester, Mrs. Isabel
Wolf, Edna Long

1930
Bruns, Henry
Kelly, Margaret
(Mrs. Jacobberger)
Londergan, Mary
Parks, Roy G.
Robinson, Miss Mary

1931
Brysch, Adelaide
Gifford, Miss Gladys
Gordon, Miss Anne
Hembrook, Margaret
Olsen, Miss Gladys
O'Rourke, Roberta
White, Miss Dorothy

1932
Biedenbach, C.
Hester, Marshall
Hjorth, Ernst Jr.
Stark, Miss Evelyn

1933
Glenn, Miss Margaret
McCarthy, Margie
(Mrs. Watts)

1934
Bruns, Miss Margaret
Fleming, Christine
(Mrs. Stricklin)
Hulick, Miss Helen
(Mrs. Beebe)
Tillinghast, Edward
Vaughn, Miss Juanita

1935
Ladner, Emil
Tillinghast, Adelle
Whitcomb, Cynthia
(Mrs. Ashumun)

1936
Brill, Richard G.
Burgess, Miss E.
Byouk, Louis M.
Chamberlin, W.O.
Fenney, Miss Mary
(Mrs. Pometta)
McArtor, Sheldon
Palmer, Miss Julia
(Mrs. Trenham)
Smith, Miss LeVere

1937
Carl, Miss Faith
Hester, Winifred
Higgins, Calisth
Louargand, Edna
Meyers, Miss Jean
Newland, Elizabeth
Orr, Miss Helen
(Mrs. Russell)
TenBroeck, Catharine

1938
Cummings, Lois
Lapides, Michael
Patterson, Donaldina
(Mrs. Tennis)
Ramsdell, Dorothy
Russell, Lang
McIntosh, Rosemary
Whitsell, Alice
Wilcoxso , Wm. C.

1939
Chapman, Laura
(Mrs. Spurrier)
Kulda, Alice
(Mrs. Johnson)
Marshall, Catherine
(Mrs. Ramger)
Matulich, Miss Grace

1940
Elder, Miss Kay
Harrison, Lloyd A.
Litner, Miss Emily

1941
Black, Natalie
(Mrs. Graves)
Burnes, Byron B.
Mayhew, J. Wesley
McCarthy, Sally
Starcevich, Alberta
(Mrs. Nessler)

1942
Anderson, Miss Inez
Gyle, Mrs. Alice
Wartenberg, Rudolf

1943
Paxson, Miss Grace
Pingree, Mrs. Sabey
Stevenson, Edith
Worth, Miss Barbara

1944
Goetzinger, Cornelius
Gusmano, Barbara
King, Willa Mae
Kowalewski, Felix
Leenhouts, Myron
Prever, Edith
(Mrs. Brody)
Spainhour, Virginia
Stone, Melissa
Wilson Dorothy
(Mrs. Nixon)
Wood, Miss Jane
(Mrs. Wood)
Woodruff, Irvan L.

1945
Goetzinger, Mrs. Rita
Hess, Miss Iris
(Mrs. DePangher)
Hofsteater, Marie
Jack, Miss Hazel
Johnson, Frances
(Mrs. Young)
Lawrence, Dorothy
Leenhouts, Mildred
Mahar, Kathleen
Nyhus, Helen
(Mrs. Smith)
Polley, Walter
Tittsworth, Laura

1946
Bergl, Mrs. Gertrude
Dunning, Francis
Gardner, Miss Jane
Palagi, Irene
(Mrs. McPherson)
Thompson, Damaris
(Mrs. Copperud)

1947
Anderson, Effie
Jacobs, Leo
Marshall, Erwin
Moore, Georgia
Myers, Helen
Peterson, Clara A.
(Mrs. Tennis)
Pruff, Dorothy
Neesam, Ralph

1948
Best, Dorothy
Stone, Mary
(Mrs. Youngs)
Willis, Arthur

1949
Elmassian, Nazalie
Fraley, David
Galvan, John

1950
Baxter, Charles
Burnes, Caroline
Corfield, Barbara
(Mrs. Hersey)
Fraser, Sarah
Gastman, Carl
Gruber, Barbara
Ladner, Mary
Merrell, Marjorie
Newbrough, Betty
Points, Betty
Purcell, Edythe

1951
Buck, Frank
Fitzgerald, Denise
Jordan, Ralph
Kopecky, Dorothy
Loquvam, Marty
Ramger, Harold
Rogers, Barbara
Sellner, Hubert

Sommers, Rosalind
(Mrs. Bradford)

1952
Abcarian, Janet
Boxell, Mary
Bragg, Bernard
DelChiaro, Norma
Emerick, Aletha
Gunderson, Rosella
Hellekson, Ruth
Lewis, Lucy

1953
Aldridge, Velma
Barkes, Alice
Beach, Charlotte
Bulkley, Katherine
(Mrs. Philips)
Getz, Steven B.
Harris, Juanita
Jackson, Eileen
Lindsay, Doreen
Meissen, Shirley
Raffo, Gloria
Robson, Mary

1954
Crossman, Agnes
Noble, E. LeRoy
Simmons, Mary E.

1955
Allen, Dale
Fitzerald, Barbara
Garber, Nettie Mae
Igleheart, Betty
Keeley, Beverly
Maynard, Mary L.
Sorensen, Barbara
Srnka, John

1956
Campbell, Mary
Hamilton, Helen
Leonard, Jean
Williamson, Kathryn

1957
Cronenwett, Sandra
DeLuca, Marianne
Fusfeld, Irving S.
Knudsen, Kathleen
McRoberts, Janet
Nicholson, Sue
Pym, John

1958
Calvert, Rae
Carpenter, Nora
Countryman, Wanda
(Mrs. Miller)
Delgado, Gilbert
Lee, Naomi
Morris, Lena
Reinker, Phyllis
(Mrs. Gaines)
Williams, Fern
Zumbrun, Ann

1959
Attletweed, Berna
Barthen, Jean
Davis, Olen
Leavitt, Gaile
Miller, Nancy
O'Neill, Marlyn
Viole, Carol

1960
Barton, Deanna
Byers, Lois
Curry, Carol
Hamilton, Helen
Lake, Diane
Mazzoil, Judith
Schunhoff, Hugo

1961
Crosby, Carol
Estes, Caroline
Grosse, Margaret
Norton, Kenneth
Raybould, Marilyn
Russel, Lang
Sweet, Myrle
Watrous, Robert

1962
Arcanin, Jacob
Beach, Charlotte
Connors, Theresa
Coupland, Howard
Lawrence, Donna
Malone, Joan
Mayerson, Janet
Meyer, Hannah

1963
Bayba, Sandra
Coleman, Margaret
Roche, Georgia
Summers, Hubert
Swaim, Dean

1964
Ayabe, Dorothy
Day, Mary
Henon, Helen
Herrick, Margaret
Irwin, Vincent
Jacobs-White, Leona
Miller, Wanda
Muzzy, Barbara
Painter, Claire

1965
Bullock, Donald
Davidson, Lynn
Fallon, Judith
Hicks, Susan
Mangan, Kathee
Powell, Michaele
Stelling, Jessica
Tickner, James
Shellgrain, Evelyn

1966
Bachman, John
Burke, Florence
Evans, Patricia
Lewis, Larri
Lynch, Daniel
Ording, Maureen
Small, Paul
Winters, Ellen G.

1967
Ladd, Leslie
Bowen, Carol
Griffin, Sheila
Clemens, Kenneth
Davidsen, Anita
Hahn, Elizabeth
LeBaron, Margaret
Malzkuhn, Jr., Eric
McDermott, Maryann
Wishman, Claudia

1968
Brown, Pamela
Balsukot, Connie
Coakley, Joanne
Hogan, Patricia
Kochendorfer, Joanne
Loeffler, Bonnie
Pollard, Gerald
Schmitt, Robert
Sergurson, Harriett
Wright, Gail

1969
Argentos, Carol
Barber, Eleanor
Barber, Helen Cora
Betz, Beverly
Bringer, Stanton
Capps, Rosemary
Caughrean, Diane
Harris, Graham
Hopfinger, Dorothy
Kleinman, Elsa
Lombard, Mary
Reese, Ronald
Smith, Carroll
Smith, Stanley
Fenix, Janice

1970
Bermelin, Elizabeth
Ford, Elizabeth
Galvan, Betty
Gancheff, Penny
Keller, James
McTigue, Eloise
Mikos, Kenneth
New, Hazel
Nolan, Sam
Pezel, Bonnie
Sakamoto, Susan
Wilson, Marie

1971
Boldizar, Gloria
Burnes, Caroline
Durston, Diana
Gorin, Polly
Jozwicki, Suzanne
Leshgold, Lynn
Lickiss, Marilyn
Peterson, David
Whittom, Merle

1972
Baim, William
Burdett, Joyanne
Clark, Joyce
Davidsen, Anita
Ford, Betsy
George, Richard
Griffin, Sheila
Hackett, Kathleen
Serna, Joanne
Swaim, Anna Lee
Tiano, Michele
Wecht, Susan
Zawolkow, Geoffrey

1973
Copeland, Rebecca
Germany, Jeremiah
Lundmark, Susan
Jacobs, Leo
Ladd, Leslie
Pezel, Bonnie
Von Tickner, Carmen

1974
Dean, Charlene
Finneran, Michael
Hutchins, Victor
Pollock, Christine
Renzulli, Florence

1975
Call, Michaele
Herrold, Mary D.
Klopping, Henry
LaCosse, Brenda
LaCosse, Eugene
Leighton, Edward
Rudy, Les
Singleton, Julian
Wright, Mary

1976
Balfe, Tim
Bradley, Sandra
Carr, Albert
Dexheimer, Ann
Dullaghan, Michael
Feibusch, Marianne
Gatehouse, Lois
Gatehouse, James
Harries, Rhonda
Harris, Lois
Kramer, Judy
Kramer, Scott
Lynch, Onita
Malzkuhn, Brian
Morton, Diane
Morishima, Alice
Minton, Nina
Rivest, Peter
Schmidt, Nancy
Stern, Hedy
Stern, Ron
Warren, Lu
Yalowitz, Rhonda

1977
Beggs, Patrick
Dorrance, Pat
Duve, Gene
Ellis, Robert
Kennedy, Dee
Loggins, Susan
Loustalot, Jeanne
Lunger, Sharon
Pedersen, Kenneth
Porter, Kathy
Schlutt, LaVerne
Sweet, Myrle

1978
Brett-Holmes, Bev
Cantrell, Byron
Cantrell, Kathleen
Downie, Marcia
Goetsch, Betty
Healy, Craig
Herbold, Rick
Kallman, Marilyn
Koetz, James
Michaud, Ted
Moxley, Ann
Rudy, Gaye
Zinza, Leslie

1979
Bonheyo, Richard
Bridges, Christina
Brill, Nancy
Copra, Edward
Feldhorn, Sanders
Herbold, Val
Holcomb, Roy
Koraltan, Lynda
Marsh, Emory
Tibble, Terrence
Thompson, Julie
Viall, Terry
Wait, Mildred

1980
Coughlan, Trisha
Diaz, Barbara
Elliott, David
Fletcher, Lori
Keim, Dave
Lentz, Alyce
Marsh, Jeanne
Rangel, Theresa
Riley, Dawn
Stedt, Joe
Storey, Pat
Vitek, Julie
Wolfram, Linnea

1981
Duge, Scott
Hyatt, Carol
Hobson, Edward
Koch, Susan
Muscadine, Diane
Silver, Helene
Teague, Michael
Willoughby, Vicky

1982
Angeli, Denise
Chambers, Lisa
Cox-Kuntze, Linda
Jew, Valerie
Kuntze, Marlon
Littleford, Barbara
Swaim, Dean

1983
Jordan, Janice
LaCosse, Brenda
Newman-Feldhorn, L.
Rose, Suzanne
Tompkins, Michelle
Tucker, James
Whettle, Marian

1984
Harris, Lois
Newman-Feldhorn, L.
Wilkinson, Debra

1985
Cohen, Jill
Ingraham, Donald
Marsh, Jeanne
O'Neill, Debbie
Parker-Lipshutz, Amy
Rishel, Judy
Schribman, Andra
Stern, Hedy U.
Weakley, Irene

1986
Baldwin, Celia May
Clayton, Carolee
Coughlan, Trisha
Crabiel, Steve
Danko, Mary
Heil, Joseph
Kully, Lisa
Loesener, Jill
May, Marilyn
Mead, Rebecca
McNeill, Joyce
Miles, Mary Lou

Nelson, Michele
Roberts, Anne
Wissman, Karen

1987
Bizer-Hansen, Lisa
Halpern, Debbie
Libby, Bonnie
Moore, Pat
Rogers, Mary

1988
Berke, Larry
Garland, Cynthia
Havard, Joan
Jaeger, Carol
Rasmus, Brian
Wankmuller, K.
Wissman, Karen
Shackelford, Suzanne
Wing-Hayakawa, D.

1989
Bosso, Jr., Ed
Call, David
Johnson, Rebecca
Luttge, Karen
Malzkuhn, Virginia
Miller, Faye
Mosqueira, Jacqie
Peterson, Laura
Silberg, Debbie
Smith-Kyne, Joy
Welt, Nancy

1990
Atchley, Toni
Billings, Jennifer
Cambone, Carol
Carter, Christine
Catron, Dennis
DeLong, Yvonne
Grossinger, Linda
Grossinger, Mal
Heilig, Susan
Mattingly, Wallace

1991
Coakley, Joanne
Cole, Rick
Dike, JoDee
Folse, Doralynn
Gonzalez, Susan
Huff, Cynthia
Jennings, Margaret
Katz, Charles
Lund, Sandra
Marbury, Nathie
Morrison, Barbara
Morrison, Robert
Rhodes, Ronald
Vickers, Sharon
Wood, Sylvia

1992
Call, Brenda
Kraemer, Pamela
Kuerbis, Tracy
Madera, Rose
Nichols, Jeremy
Nitko, Anthony
Teh, Poh Gaik
Trippett, Sharon
Vollmar, Lawrence

1993
Ash, Bill
Baer, Julie
Berger, Cathy
Berke, Wanda
Brodsky, Michelle
Cohen, EJ
Helsel, Jennifer
Labow-Evangelista, C
Lamberton, Jack
Lamberton, Juddie
Newkirk, Jane
Owens, Nelly
Powers, Tamara
Stotts, Janice

1994
Anderson, Kay
Barlow, Scott
Curtis, Vicki
Gaines, Michelle
Golos, Debbie
MacIntyre, Ann
West, Stacy
Whetten, Beverly
Willette, Della

1995
Anderson, Andy
Beveridge, Cassie
Domatti, Erika
Farr, Charles
Podell, Laine
Statler, Theresa
Sully, Lisa

1996
Delgado, Mike
Firl, Leslie
Grossinger, Mal
Haushaun, Lori
Jindra, Sarah
Markham, Lisa
Orton, Janice
Woodbury, Anna

1997
Ayres, Deborah
Baer, Joey
Bichnevicius, Vaiva
Boyd, Cheryl
Cole, Melinda
Harris, Gene
Helmuth, Marsha
Herron-Rhodes, D.
Hettwer, Greg
Holmes, Paul
Kordus, Natasha
Lauer, Francine
Loudenback, Jer L.
Mockus, Kathy
Wood, Gina
Zane, Robin

1998
Albee, Patricia
Brooke, Clark
Bye, Mary
Davin, Anthony
Eberwein, David
Farr, Kat
Froggatt, Michelle
Gonzales, Len
Gurvey, Jennifer
Kirkendall, Lois
Longson, Julie
Neblett, Andrea

1999-2000
Adams, Keith
Alefhi, Andrea
Bourne-Firl, Bridgetta
Cantrell, Jennifer
Degasparis, Laura
Eberwein, Adele
Eilbert, Stacy
Firl, Leslie
Finch, Janice
Giroux, Margaret
Gold, Stacy
Hamilton, Christopher
Helmuth, Marsha
Herbold, Ronald
Hochkeppel, Matt
Holcomb, Kathy
Johnston, Shari
Keen, Laura
Kenny, Veronica
Krause, Kati
McCarthy, Jerry
Novotny, Sarah
Officer, Karen
Radford, Delores
Ribera, Rita
Saline, Sue
Schroder, Elaine
Sloan, Heather
Yoshitake, Cheryl

1937 CSD FACULTY

Three of the 1937 staff members eventually became superintendents of a school for the Deaf. Marshall Hester (front row, left) New Mexico School for the Deaf, Edward Tillinghast (third from left) Arizona School for the Deaf and Roy Parks (fourth from left) Arkansas School for the Deaf.

Granville Redmond
1871-1935

THE picture spread on the back endsheet is one of Granville Redmond's distinctive features of California landscapes. He discovered "gold" in the hills of California's coastal ranges, where endless fields of golden yellow poppies bloomed every spring. Redmond, 1890 CSD graduate, studied art at Academic Julian in Paris. He was well established in Charlie Chaplin's film studio as a scenery painter as well as an actor. Redmond was considered as a transitional figure among California landscape painters of the early twentieth Century.

Residence Staff 1860-2000

Acosta, Robin
Adams, Mark
Aguzin, Michael
Ahern, Beverly
Albers, Caroline
Alexander, Bobbie
Alexander, Charles
Alford, Nellie
Allen, Leola
Allen, Sharon
Allison, Thomas
Alvarez, Sly
Anderson, Donna
Anderson, Kathy
Anderson, Steve
Arcanin, Jacob
Arey, Emily
Arvizu, John
Ash, Alex
Ash, Chris
Ashby, Joyce

Bach, Ellen
Backlund, B.
Baer, Joey
Bagwell, Beth
Bahan, Benjamin
Bailhache, N.
Baker, Becky Jo
Baker, Lee
Bales, Roger
Bangs, Amanda
Barber, Edward
Barensten, Joni
Barlow, Barry
Barlow, Elmarie
Barlow, Lucille
Barnes, Virginia
Bass, LaRee
Batty, Marjorie
Bauserman, Elaine
Bayarsky, Mark
Beasley, Robert
Bella, Kevin
Bella, Mark
Bennett, Laurolyn
Bergman, Eugene
Berke, Douglas
Bernstein, Pat
Berry, Janet
Berry, Marian
Bigelow, Tim
Billings, M.S.
Birck, Ruth
Birck, Vernon
Birmelin, Elizabeth
Bissell, B.
Blackburn, Maxine
Blodgett, Janet
Bogard, Katherine
Bowen, Mildred
Bowles, Carol
Bowman, Martha
Brennan, William
Breslow, Holly
Brewer, Anne
Bricetti, Kathy
Bricker, Eddia
Briley, Kim
Bringer, Stanton
Brocchini, Joyce
Brown, David
Brown, Dot
Brown, Marion
Brown, Martin
Brown, Phillip
Brown, Raul
Browne, Patricia
Browning, Anna
Browning, E.
Bryant, Anna
Buckley, Sue
Bull, Tom
Burjoski, Alan
Burrell, Grace
Busch, Elizabeth
Busch, Lois
Butcher, John
Byouk, Louis

Call, Deborah
Callahan, Lorita
Camarena, Mary
Cameron, Martha
Campbell, Crystal
Campbell, Jesse
Canimet, Helen
Cannon, Debbie
Cantrell, Daisy
Capilla, Shari
Cardinale, Lynette
Cardinale, Michael
Carsey, Edward
Catron, Dennis
Catron, Judy
Cawley-Way, W.
Ceasar, Audrey
Cease, David
Ceci, Michelle
Ceglia, Delia
Cerf, Barbara
Chambers, Lisa
Chann, Henry
Chapman, Klesha
Charles, Alexander
Chase, Hazel
Chase, Jeryl
Chatman, Ida
Cherry, Susan
Chesler, Beatrice
Chessman, Mary
Chesterson, Eliza
Cheung, Michael
Chevallier, Ada
Christensen, Neil
Chin, Fred
Clark, Margaret
Clark, Rhoda
Clarkson, Beatrice
Cleary, Ronald
Cline, Ruth
Cole, Chester
Coleman, Zannet
Collins, Janet
Comaskey, Al
Compston, Susan
Constabileo, Cathy
Cook, Harry
Cook-Morse, K.
Corcoran, Thomas
Corey, Sandra
Cornell, Beatrice
Cornell, Meribah
Cory, Carolyn
Cotter, Una
Courtright, Delores
Cowan, Janessa
Cown, L. Morrell
Craig, Peggy
Creed, Thomas
Crosby McCoy, K.
Cumberland, Debbie
Cunnington, Marie
Cutler, Koli

Dadzie, Emmanuel
Dale, Barbara
Danenhower, John
Daniels, Anita
Daniels, Christy
Daniels, Dianne
Dannis, Elin
Darden, Jr., Linnie
Dare, Dena
Dart, Shirley
Davenport, Cindy
Davidson, Wildey
Davidson, William
Davis, Anthony
Davis, Barbara
Davis, Hazel
Davis, Veronica
Daviton, Candi
Day, Ruth
Dearing, Richard
Deering, Mary
Deisler, George
Delgado, David
DePew, Josephine
DeVere, Carol
Diaz, John
Dickinson, Doug
Diehl, Kathy
Dike, Barbara
Dillard, Dan
DiNapoli, Ann
Disbenett, Indus
Dobson, Jessie
Dominguez, Paul
Donchin, Gwen
Dorsett, James
Dreffs, LeeAnn
Driggs, B. W.
Drolet, Rene
Dubois, Grace
Dunlap, Andy
Dunn, Jeffrey
Dunne, Barry
Dupree, John
Duve, Holly
Dwyer, James

Earl-Southall, Valda
Earlye, Charles
Ebli, Janis
Elhard, Anna
Ellison, Ann
Engstrom, Mary
Epstein, Gerald
Estrade, Michael
Evans, Pamela
Evans, Sarah

Falbo, J.
Falk, Adolf
Farris, Muriel
Faulkner, Judith
Feldman, Stanley
Ferguson, Barbara
Field, Valerie
Finch, Janice
Finneran, Virginia
Fisher, Allan
Fitting, Marion
Fletcher, Douglas
Flores, Sue
Floyd, William
Foster, Harold
Fox, Margaret
Frampton, O.
Frank, Mrs. Henry
Franklin, Lorraine
Frazel, Shane
Freeman, Jesse
Frey, Pearl
Fry, Laurel
Fulcher, Connie
Fullilove, Mary

Gamblin, Gertrude
Garcia, Charles
Garcia, Elizabeth
Garrison, Geraldine
Gibbs, Linda
Gill, Dorothy
Gimble, Lindsay
Girogi, Stan
Glickman, Arthur
Glover, Melody
Goetz, Lisa
Goldwater, Millie
Gomez, F. R.
Goorgian, Helen
Gordon, Jeffri
Gough, Judy
Gough, Ron
Gough, Tim
Gove, Helen
Green, Robert
Griffin, Edward
Griffing, Barry
Grilk, Dorothy
Grissette, Marguerite
Griswold, Julia
Groswird, Shirley
Grubbs, Jennifer
Guggenheim, Laurie
Gunton, Judy
Gustafson, John
Gyle, Francis

Hafey, Caroline
Hagenbach, Dave
Halischak, Norma
Hali, Gregory
Hallada, Carol
Hallada, Vaughn
Hallenberg, Bill
Halseth, Karen
Hansen, Lisa
Harbert, Lucia
Hare, Venie
Harris, Eugene
Harris, Theo
Harris, Therese
Harrison, Ellen
Hart, Carol
Hart, David
Harts, Jacqueline
Harvey, Mark
Hass, Ethel
Hassell, jerry
Hasson, Kaye
Hasty, Patrick
Hause, Lawrence
Hawk, Mary
Hedges, Kristy
Heins, Brian
Helmuth, Marsha
Helvey, Bella
Henderson, Malcolm
Hendrix, Giselle
Hendrix, Kevin
Henry, Helen
Herbig, William
Hernandez, Esther
Hernandez, Jean
Herrick, Helen
Hetzel, Elma
Hickerson, Betty
Hill, Velma
Hilton, Maud
Hobson, Ed
Hoburg, Martha
Hoffman, Mary
Holman, M.\tab
Holmes, Charles
Holmes, Heidi
Holt, Steve
Horan, Lisa
Horve, Eileen
Houston, Ila
Howell, Richard
Howze, Darla
Hughes-Hill, V.
Hullfish, Suzanne
Humphrey, Miriam
Hunt, Frank
Hunter, Phyllis
Hurd, Glenn
Hurych, George
Hutchins, Vic
Hyder, Ruby

Ingraham, H. S.
Iverson, Katharine

Jackson, Robert
Jacobs, Leo
Jacopetti, Kenneth
Jamieson, Marian
Joe, Mamie
Johnson, Derek
Johnson, Joy
Johnson, Mae
Johnson, Mark
Johnson, Pam
Johnson, William
Johnstone, Alicia
Jonsson, Dena

Katayama, David
Kaufman, Clara
Kearns, Aileen
Keefe, Charles
Kekke, Catherine
Kelly, Evelyn
Kennedy, Edward
Kennedy, John
Kidd, Linda

King, Marie
Kirk, Sadie
Kirk, Sarah
Klatt, Nona
Kniveton, Douglas
Koch, Harold
Koch, Margot
Korpi, Donna
Kovacs, Tyrone
Kresge, Susan

LaBarbera, Phil
Lacroix, Kimberly
Lake, Baker
LaLoge, Emily
Lamb, Beatrice
Land, Carol
Lane, Jennifer
Lapides, Michael
Lasner, Nancy
Lastufka, Betty
Latchison, Patrick
Latrash, John
Lavey, Susan
Lawrence, Mrs. T.
Lawrence, Robert
Lazorchik, Frank
Lee, Annie
Lee, Francis
Lee, Fred
Lee, Mary
Leiter, Carol
Lentz, Gil
Lessard, Melissa
Lewis, Ann
Lickiss, Mike
Light, Jerome
Lincoln-Burpee, C.
Lindstrom, Annie
Linstad, Esther
Lipscomb, James
Little, Tim
Littleford, Barbara
Liu, Stanley
Locker, Judith
Loken, Christine
Lopez, Vina
Loustalot, George
Lowe, Huberden
Lowenstein, Alvin
Lozler, R. J.
Lucero, Danny
Luken, Amelia
Lyall, Josephine
Lynch, Joyce
Lynn, Eric

MacDougall, Joe
Mack, Overlin
Mackay, Helena
Majors, Marcia
Mallach, Ruth
Malm, Kristen
Malzkuhn, Virginia
Manley, Helen
Mann, Wolfgang
Marin, Eric
Martin, Marion
Massey, Vivian
Maung, Sonny
May, Bonnie
Mazzela, Carmelia
McCallon, Jovette
McClain, Richard
McCombs, Susan
McCormick, A.
McCoy, Beth
McEntyre, Linda
McKeehan, E.
McKellip, Mrs.
McLaughlin, C.
McNamara, Blanche
McWhorter, Cleo
Meadors, Ruth
Mellinger, A.
Merritt, Monique
Meyer, Florence
Middletown, Bernice
Miller, Miss K.
Miller, Mark
Miller, Marlene
Miller, Walter
Mills, William
Mitchell, Archie
Montgomery, Walter
Moore, Julie
Morganstein, Amy
Morrell, L.
Morris, Jennifer
Morris, Mary
Morrison, Doris
Morse, Kathleen
Moser, Nancy
Moyer, Patricia
Muna, Pete
Munoz, Josephine
Munoz, Roger
Munroe, Alice
Myers, Grant
Myers, Ricardo

Nation, Dorothy
Navarrette, Inez
Neddenreip, K.
Negherbon, Ann
Nelson, Mark
Newton-Caesar, E.
Nicoson, Ellen
Nogosek, Anthony
Nolan, Barie
Norris, Brenda

Oakie, Gladys
Obray, Alice
Obray, Jean
Obray, Ron
O'rquote Donnell, Scott
Oken, Judith
Olney, Martha
Olsen, Harold
Onishi, Linda
Orman, Steve
Orndoff, Linda
Osgood, J.
Ostertag, Kenneth
Ott-Bales, David
Oulman, Gwen
Overholser, Charles
Owens, Frank
Owens, Marianne

Park, Garret
Parks, Terry
Parlier, Catheryn
Paschal, John
Passon, Marc
Patterson, Bev
Patterson, Dona
Patterson, C.
Patterson, Lisa
Paul, Elizabeth
Pedersen, Amy
Pedersen, Carlene
Pedersen, Jamie
Pereira, Carla
Pereira, Isabella
Pereira, Mike
Perez, Avelardo
Perry, Huberdean
Peterson, Geneva
Peterson, Gloria
Peterson, Ora
Phillips, Kip
Phillis, Geneva
Pirrello, John
Pizio, Pat
Povelite, Lavern
Powell, Mary
Pratt, Linda

Presley, Harold
Price, Bruce
Prock, Ruth
Purkiss, Jessie

Quintero, Victor

Ragsdale, Judith
Ramsey, L.
Rasmus, Carola
Rasmus, Raymond
Rath, Arthur
Redden, Nancy
Reed, Gayle
Reed, John
Reeves, Ildiko
Reneau, Ora
Renzulli, Donald
Rhea, David
Ribera, Reyes
Riley, Shirley
Rivers, Raymond
Roberts, Agnes
Roberts, Donald
Roberts, Ida
Roberts, Wylie
Rodgers, Janet
Roelle, June
Rogers, Barbara
Rogers, Melani
Rogers, Pam
Romeo, Gloria
Rose, Mary
Rose, Ricardo
Rose, Suzanne
Ruehle, Jon
Runde, Frances
Runde, Winfield
Russel, Lang
Russell, Diane
Rutter, Ron
Ryosa, Nona
Rytkonen, Helen

Sacharoff, Stanley
Sadowski, Odessa
Samples, Ina
Sanchez, Joseph
Sanchez, Pasquel
Sasser, Terry
Saunders, Jane
Saxton, Charles
Schob, Denise
Schoenberg, Kathy
Schoenberg, Steve
Schugg, Debbie
Schugg, Oskar
Sedano, Ralph
Sellers, Shirley
Sharr, M. E.
Schickler, Cathy
Shook, Carolyn
Shpungina, Mira
Shuman, Suzann
Shumway, Eleanor
Simas, Lisa
Simmons, James
Simpson, Cressida
Singleton, Bernice
Singleton, Michael
Skedsmo, Bob
Skogen, Alfred
Sloan, Mrs.
Small, Paul
Smeeds, Melissa
Smith, Andrew
Smith, Andy
Smith, Archie
Smith, Barrett
Smith, Ella
Smith, Evelyn
Smith, Leotine
Smith, Oveta
Smithey, Ethel
Sohlberg, Evie
Sorensen, Dorothy
Southall, Valda
Spaan, Kathryn
Sparks, Nancy
Spenst, Melanie
Spencer, Glenand
St. Clair, Ivy
Stack, Ernest
Stack, Josephine
Stangle, Shirlee
Stansfield, John
Stansfield, Millie
Stevenson, Bev
Stevenson, Spencer
Stewart, Amanda
Stinnett, Mattie
Stolz, Natalie
Strandtmann, S.
Striker, Judy
Stryker, June
Sundberg, Joyce
Sutherland, Laura
Sutherland, Mike
Suzuki, Michio
Swartz, E.
Sykes, Mrs.

Taber, Nancy
Tao, Chung
Tau, Nora
Taylor, Marjorie
Teeter, Lina
Thexton, Russell
Thigpen, Ken
Thomas, Lorene
Thomas, Shirley
Thompson, E.
Thompson, Marvin
Thompson, Mary E.
Thrapp, Sandra
Thronson, Larry
Thunen, Esther
Tinnin-Bass, LaRee
Tipton, M.
Towers, Terry
Trethaway, Holly
Turner, Adeline
Turner, Byron
Turner, Saxon

VanderCourt, Anita
Vandergrift, Edna
Vassis, Margaret
Vaughn, John
Ventura, Theresa
Ventura, Paul
Vineyard, Christine
Vrooman, Grace

Wade, Jesse
Wagner, Kyle
Wagner, Winifred
Wales, Rae
Wall, Katherine
Wall, Vernon
Wang, Elona
Ward, Joyce
Washburn, Arthur
Washington, Kathryn
Washington, N.
Watson, Angela
Wayne, Kathryne
Webb, Halbert
Weiler, Alfred
Wein, Sue
Wells, Roberta
Westerhaus, Mary
Westerhaus, Robert
White, Barbara
White, Sid
Whyte, Bonnie
Willard, harriet
Williams, Everteen
Willimas, Diana
Williams, Mary
Williams, Mildred
Williams, Willie
Willis, Ellen
Winsor, Any
Wiseman, M. J.
Withrow, Thomas
Wong, George
Wood, Richard
Wright, Gail
Wright, J.

Youman, Judith
Young, Christine
Young, Jean
Youngs, Joseph

Zike, Phillip
Zinza, Bryan

INDEX

BERKELEY CAMPUS

FREMONT CAMPUS